Drug Use, Misuse, and Abuse:
Psychopharmacology in the 21st Century

Drug Use, Misuse, and Abuse:
Psychopharmacology in the 21st Century

Cecile A. Marczinski
Northern Kentucky University

WILEY

Publisher:	Jay O'Callaghan
Editor:	Chris Johnson
Assistant Editor:	Brittany Cheetham
Marketing Manager:	Margaret Barrett
Editorial Assistant:	Kristen Mucci
Photo Editor:	Elizabeth Blomster
Cover Designer:	Kenji Ngieng
Associate Production Manager:	Joyce Poh
Production Editor:	Jolene Ling
Cover Photo Credit:	© Willyam Bradberry/Shutterstock

This book was set by MPS Limited.

Founded in 1807, John Wiley & Sons, Inc. has been a valued source of knowledge and understanding for more than 200 years, helping people around the world meet their needs and fulfill their aspirations. Our company is built on a foundation of principles that include responsibility to the communities we serve and where we live and work. In 2008, we launched a Corporate Citizenship Initiative, a global effort to address the environmental, social, economic, and ethical challenges we face in our business. Among the issues we are addressing are carbon impact, paper specifications and procurement, ethical conduct within our business and among our vendors, and community and charitable support. For more information, please visit our website: www.wiley.com/go/citizenship.

Evaluation copies are provided to qualified academics and professionals for review purposes only, for use in their courses during the next academic year. These copies are licensed and may not be sold or transferred to a third party. Upon completion of the review period, please return the evaluation copy to Wiley. Return instructions and a free of charge return mailing label are available at www.wiley.com/go/returnlabel. If you have chosen to adopt this textbook for use in your course, please accept this book as your complimentary desk copy. Outside of the United States, please contact your local sales representative.

Library of Congress Cataloging-in-Publication Data

Marczinski, Cecile A.
  Drug use, misuse, and abuse : psychopharmacology in the 21st century / Cecile A. Marczinski, Northern Kentucky University. – 1st edition.
    pages cm
    Includes index.
    ISBN 978-1-118-53910-1 (pbk.)
    1. Drugs. 2. Psychopharmacology. 3. Drug abuse. 4. Drugs–Physiological effect. I. Title.
HV5801.M3237 2013
362.29—dc23

2013024347

10 9 8 7 6 5 4 3 2 1

To Chris, Isabella, and Giselle

BRIEF CONTENTS

CONTENTS

13   ANTIDEPRESSANT, ANTIANXIETY, AND MOOD-STABILIZING DRUGS   **351**

PREFACE

My path to psychopharmacology was indirect. As an undergraduate, I did not consider that I might develop a research career studying the effects of combining alcohol and energy drinks. In fact, energy drinks did not exist when I was an undergraduate, which demonstrates that psychopharmacology is a quickly moving and constantly changing field. Given my own indirect path to my chosen career, I sympathize when undergraduate students come to me for guidance about the future. Confusion can result from the many options to pursue and choices to be made. In my experience, students are often unaware of the many of the possible paths that can be taken, especially the many options related to psychopharmacology. For me, a career in psychopharmacology is a joyful one. I absolutely love this topic area within psychology. I love teaching psychopharmacology, writing about psychopharmacology, and conducting research in psychopharmacology. The science in the field of psychopharmacology is still new and growing. The questions that need to be answered are numerous. The implication of knowledge about psychopharmacology on the everyday well-being of so many in society is great. Whether I am teaching in the classroom or mentoring an undergraduate student in my lab, psychopharmacology never ceases to amaze as a field of study with many questions still needing to be answered.

My motivation for writing this book was simple. I saw a need for a psychopharmacology book properly serving today's students and instructors. The existing books seemed old and stale to me. They didn't reflect the dynamic and constantly changing field, and they certainly lacked a little passion for the subject matter. The voice and style of existing books did not resonate with my students. Existing books also did not help instructors prepare student learning outcomes or address assessment. In light of the need to develop scientific literacy and critical thinking in college students, I perceived an opportunity to develop these skills more comprehensively. While many existing textbooks adequately discuss the science of psychopharmacology, they are not written using best practices to increase scientific literacy and critical thinking. That seemed a shame, as psychopharmacology is well suited to developing scientific literacy and critical thinking skills. Moreover, it seems we may have traditionally perceived our undergraduates as less capable of understanding science than they actually are. Especially when the science has to do with drugs, students are willing to make the effort to grasp the material. Just tell a student that a course covers alcohol, nicotine, cocaine, and marijuana, and suddenly the most science-phobic student is ready to listen, learn, and participate.

I wrote this book to address the needs of my students and my fellow instructors. First, I thought about the needs of my students. Whenever I start a psychopharmacology course, initial enthusiasm for the topic is initially high. Some students can sometimes lose interest if the course does not discuss individual drugs early enough or if too much knowledge about basic science is assumed. However, students already having a strong background in science can become bored if not sufficiently challenged. Keeping the needs of various students in mind, this book opens with three background chapters that set the stage for the exciting material on each drug that will come later in the book. The intent is that all students, whether or not they are strong in science, fully comprehend the background material needed to understand psychopharmacology by the end of the third chapter. Starting with the first chapter, original studies are discussed so that even the most prepared student will learn new things about the science of psychopharmacology. Following the introductory three chapters, the student embarks on a journey of discovery about each psychoactive drug. Chapter 4 begins this process with a drug familiar to everyone: caffeine. To best serve the student, various features of each chapter provide the structure that will help develop the necessary knowledge and skills to succeed in this course and beyond. Each chapter contains two quick quizzes, including both multiple-choice and short-answer questions, to help in exam preparation. Each chapter also includes *In the News*, *More about the Science*, and *Myth Busters* features that are designed to develop skills in scientific literacy and critical thinking. In all of these features, the student is challenged to apply recently learned knowledge in novel contexts. Finally, undergraduate students must constantly be thinking about the next step in their lives. What comes next after this course or after college is completed? The *Focus on Careers* feature provides a multitude of avenues by which psychopharmacology can be the launching point for a fun and exciting career. Some of these career options are probably obvious, such as becoming a substance abuse counselor, but other options such as a health care administrator and a political lobbyist are less intuitive, yet incorporate psychopharmacology nonetheless. I tried to include a mix of career options. Some of the careers are suitable for a recent graduate who has completed an undergraduate degree in psychology or related major. Other career options might require additional training or experiences beyond a traditional undergraduate degree. In each chapter, I want all students reading the *Focus on Careers* section to think critically about what their future might look like and how they might work to achieve their goals.

I also wrote this book with the needs of my fellow instructors in mind. Teaching, especially teaching psychopharmacology, is highly rewarding. The material in this textbook is intrinsically fascinating. However, like my fellow instructors, I live in the world of continual emphasis on assessment that often does not rank high on a "things we enjoy doing list." The recent shift in undergraduate education toward more accountability for quality education means that instructors must set clear expectations and write student learning outcomes. This book will help the instructor with these increasingly common challenges. It appears that the American Psychological Association Guidelines for the Undergraduate Major are the most widely adopted guidelines for curriculum goals and suggested learning outcomes for undergraduate psychology majors (APA, 2007). Even if the APA guidelines are not specifically adopted in a department, similar guidelines are often in place. Therefore, this book was written to satisfy APA program guidelines. The APA provides ten goals in its guidelines for the undergraduate psychology major. This textbook alone directly addresses eight of these goals. By providing the information helping the instructor address assessment questions, more time is available for the real focus: teaching psychopharmacology! In addition, there is a trend toward more online course offerings. Psychopharmacology can work well as an online course, but the approach taken to teach online is different from the one used in a traditional classroom. This book provides a structure that, in my experience, is necessary for this online course format. Finally, the features designed to help students should result in better-prepared students. This should help instructors, since it is much more enjoyable for everyone (students and instructors alike) when students come to class having read the assigned material. In this book, I have tried to make the writing compelling and thought-provoking enough that the student will enjoy reading this book and come to class enthused to discuss the material. My goal is to provide a book that helps both the student and the instructor finish the semester thinking that the material was so fascinating and the discussions so thought-provoking that both groups wished that the class did not need to end.

FOR THE STUDENT

Welcome to the wonderful world of psychopharmacology! This topic is fascinating, thought-provoking, and relevant to your life. It is likely the information that you learn in this textbook will be applied to your interactions with family members or friends in the future. You may even decide to pursue a career related to psychopharmacology. Thus, I have written this book to help you learn more about legal and illegal psychoactive drugs. In addition, I will challenge you to develop your scientific literacy and critical thinking skills. These skills, while not especially easy to develop, will serve you well long after this course is complete. My hope is that you will remember this course fondly as you look back on your undergraduate experience. However, to succeed in this course, you must be intentional about achieving success. Below are tips explaining how I wrote this book to help you succeed and how you can best capitalize on the book's features.

How This Textbook Is Organized

The organization of this textbook was planned to help you learn psychopharmacoloogy in the most effective and enjoyable way. The first few chapters (1–3) provide you with the necessary background knowledge to understand the field. These chapters cover all of the basic principles of psychopharmacology and also provide a review of the nervous system. The next set of chapters cover each of the stimulant drugs (caffeine, nicotine, cocaine, and amphetamines) individually (4–7). Next, the sedative drugs (alcohol, opiates, and marijuana) are covered (8–10). Note that the stimulant and sedative drug sections begin with the psychoactive drugs that you are most familiar with (caffeine in the stimulant drug section and alcohol in the sedative drug section). Finally, the hallucinogens, steroids, and psychotherapeutic drugs (antipsychotics, antidepressants, antianxiety, mood stabilizing, and smart drugs) are covered (11–14). In every chapter, potential career options related to psychopharmacology are discussed. I strongly encourage you to consider all of the career possibilities, as there are a multitude of them. It is never too early to consider what you will be doing once you complete your degree. In fact, there are many things that you can do while a student to help you toward your career goals.

Features That Help You Learn

Learning about the field of psychopharmacology can be challenging. There is great demand on your learning and memory skills, as the topic incorporates many scientific concepts. This book contains several features that can help you learn the material more easily. You likely will take tests on the material presented in this book. How can you improve your performance? There are features in this book to help you. At the start of each chapter are learning objectives. Learning objectives are a guide to what you should be getting out of each chapter. Once you have read a chapter, go back to the learning objectives and confirm that you have acquired this important knowledge. If not, you should revisit topics. Each chapter also has two quick quizzes. These quizzes test your knowledge using both multiple-choice and short-answer formats. A growing body of research demonstrates that repeated testing during study improves memory for material, since students directly recruit those same memory processes needed during an actual test (Szpunar, McDermott, & Roediger, 2008). Please take the quick quizzes and then check your answers at the end of each quiz. This feature, in particular, is designed to help you improve test scores.

There are three additional features intended to help you apply your knowledge and develop your critical thinking and scientific literacy skills. *In the News*, *More about the Science*, and *Myth Busters* all utilize in a novel context what you have learned in the core material. The *In the News* feature discusses a recent news story relevant to the chapter material. After the news story, questions help you think about the accuracy of the content in the news story and its relationship to the textbook material. You will increase your critical thinking and scientific literacy skills by using this feature. In the *More about the Science* feature, a detailed description of a recent research study is provided. The purpose of *More about the Science* is to delve deeply into the methodology, results, and conclusions from scientific research. Various chapters will cover animal and human research studies, allowing you to see how the knowledge base in psychopharmacology is gradually being built. *More about the Science* also asks a series of questions that help increase your scientific literacy and critical thinking skills. Finally, *Myth Busters* is a fun feature disputing common misconceptions about psychopharmacology. The myth is described and then the reality (based on the science) is clarified. This feature also should help increase your scientific literacy and critical thinking skills.

Ultimately, the goal of this book is not only to provide a multitude of facts to memorize about psychopharmacology. The goal is to have you, the student, asking new questions and developing thoughts about the scientific approaches that could be used to answer these new questions. As you will see when you read this book, psychopharmacology is a relatively new field and many questions remain. It would make me proud as a textbook author if I helped provide the appropriate foundation that allowed you to answer one of these questions about psychopharmacology!

For the Instructor

If you are like me, you are delighted when assigned to teach psychopharmacology. The material is fascinating, and the field is constantly changing. My vision for this psychopharmacology textbook is to bring a new approach to covering the basic principles and major topics found in a typical psychopharmacology course. This book includes the newest exciting and controversial findings in the study of drug use and abuse. At the core of my approach is a strong emphasis on developing scientific literacy and critical thinking in the student. This textbook covers the major drugs typically discussed in an undergraduate psychopharmacology course, including caffeine, nicotine, cocaine, amphetamines, alcohol, opiates, marijuana, the hallucinogens, antipsychotics, antidepressants, antianxiety medications, and many others. Moreover, the content emphasizes the latest scientific findings in the field, including advances in imaging the living brain. I include information on careers related to psychopharmacology, a feature not found in other books in the field. This book also incorporates a variety of pedagogical features that help students learn, making it appropriate for an instructor of either a lecture-based, online, or hybrid course.

Goals of the Book

This book is designed so that you can spend more of your time teaching and less time searching for recent news articles or research to create or update your lectures. Various features in this book, such as the *Myth Busters*, can be the jumping off points for class discussions. I have included controversial research that will help initiate class discussions including both your best and least-prepared students. This book is written in a conversational style so that all students will find assigned reading enjoyable. Finally, you are probably tasked with preparing student learning outcomes or addressing assessment questions about gains that will be made by students taking your course. The table below gives you the American Psychological Association Guidelines for the Undergraduate Major, the most widely adopted guidelines for curriculum goals and suggested learning outcomes for undergraduate psychology majors (APA, 2007). Even if not specifically adopted in your department, these guidelines may help you address assessment and student learning outcomes. Note that the APA provides ten goals in its guidelines for the undergraduate psychology major. This textbook alone directly addresses eight of these goals. More information about the APA guidelines can be found at the following website: http://www.apa.org/ed/precollege/about/psymajor-guidelines.pdf

APA Learning Goals Integrated in This Textbook	
APA Learning Goal and Description	**How This Textbook Achieves the Goal**
APA Goal 1: Acquire Knowledge Base of Psychology	Major central concepts in psychology (such as the role of classical and operant conditioning in drug effects) are covered in this textbook. Students will thoroughly learn how psychoactive drug use and abuse can

(Continued)

APA Learning Goals Integrated in This Textbook

APA Learning Goal and Description	How This Textbook Achieves the Goal
	alter normal nervous system functioning and brain anatomy. The assessment and appropriate treatment of substance abuse and other mental disorders is covered. Empirical findings, including original research studies, are covered in detail in every chapter of this psychopharmacology textbook. Thus, many key topics that form the core knowledge in psychology can be acquired using this textbook.
APA Goal 2: Understand and Apply Research Methods in Psychology	This textbook describes the major research designs and their application to the study of psychopharmacology. Both human and animal studies are thoroughly discussed. Human studies cover a wide range of research in the field: from surveys to studies of brain imaging to clinical trials that assess new treatments. Animal studies emphasize all levels of analysis, from the acute effects of drugs on neural receptors to changes in the whole brain and observed behavior. Interpretation of findings will be emphasized while also asking the student to think about issues that might impact the interpretation of the results. Unlike other textbooks, extensive detail about the research methodology is provided. As a result, students will clearly see that study results sometimes need a fair amount of interpretation, which alters how we see a drug-related problem and solution. Moreover, our personal biases and societal norms/laws are sometimes counter to available scientific findings. The medical use of marijuana and the necessity of abstinence as part of alcohol dependence treatment are just two examples of why understanding and applying research methods is critical to interpreting knowledge in psychopharmacology.
APA Goal 3: Use Critical Thinking Skills in Psychology	Critical thinking and scientific literacy is developed in the student using various features found in each chapter of this textbook. Each chapter includes recent news media stories (see *In the News*) featuring drugs discussed in that chapter. Students can then think critically about whether media portrayals are an accurate reflection of what is known about the science. Scientific literacy is developed as students consider whether conclusions from scientific research studies are appropriate (see *More about the Science*). Critical thinking is also developed when widely held beliefs about psychoactive drugs are disputed (see *Myth Busters*).
APA Goal 4: Application of Psychology to Personal, Social, and Organizational Issues	Research findings from psychopharmacology will be integrated with questions of personal relevance to students throughout this textbook. This textbook has high social relevance, as psychopharmacology principles are easily applied to organizations such as schools and places of business. Moreover, material on career choices related to psychopharmacology will make explicit how the topic of psychopharmacology is applied in the real world and could be central to one's chosen career.
APA Goal 5: Acquire Values in Psychology Including Ability to Weigh Evidence and Tolerating Ambiguity	In this textbook, students will be asked to weigh the evidence of the risks of drug use and abuse, for each of the drugs studied. Ambiguity is part of this field. Sometimes, scientific evidence guides social policy, but this is not always the case. We are yet uncertain about how best to prevent children from taking their first drink or smoking their first cigarette. The research in psychopharmacology has produced many answers, but there are still many more questions. Tolerance of ambiguity (a key value in psychology) will be emphasized. Moreover, this topic area raises many

APA Learning Goals Integrated in This Textbook

APA Learning Goal and Description	How This Textbook Achieves the Goal
	ethical concerns that can help students develop critical thinking skills about life choices.
APA Goal 8: Recognizing and Respecting the Complexity of Sociocultural and International Diversity	Sociocultural and international diversity are integrated throughout this textbook, which provides this book with an international flavor that exceeds most other books on this topic. Looking to other cultures and countries provides clues about what our country does right and what we do wrong. Countries that are culturally similar to us (such as Canada) and countries culturally dissimilar to us (such as Yemen) can be struggling with similar or different concerns related to psychopharmacology. In addition, ethnic and gender differences in drug effects are discussed throughout this textbook.
APA Goal 9: Personal Development Including Growth in Insight into Own and Others' Behavior and Mental Processes	Many of the topics in this book (such as binge drinking in college students) have personal relevance for the students reading the book. Developing insight about one's own and others' behavior will be a focus of this book. The intent of this textbook is to help the student be a better and more informed family member or friend to an individual who has a drug problem. Statistics indicate that drug and alcohol use and abuse (and mental illness in general) are common in the United States. Developing a better understanding of the complexity of struggles with addiction, including the dramatic changes in brain chemistry that can occur in those struggling with addiction, should help students become more compassionate toward others.
APA Goal 10: Career Planning and Development	Unlike any other psychopharmacology book on the market, this book will cover specific material in each chapter about career choices available to college graduates who have a passion for psychopharmacology. Some students may become researchers in this field and pursue the life of a scientist (anywhere from bench to bedside). Others may have careers in the helping professions (such as a substance abuse counselor, clinical psychologist, social worker, or health educator), facilitating recovery for individuals suffering from substance abuse problems. Others may have careers in law enforcement (police, lawyer, judge) or public policy (political lobbyist) that require knowledge about how drugs impact people and society. Those in business may need to know the specifics of drug testing or how to help employees with substance abuse issues. Multiple career possibilities in the pharmaceutical industry will also be featured. While many upper division classes in psychology have application to future careers, psychopharmacology is one of the most promising areas of psychology related to many career possibilities. This textbook helps make these connections for students by providing the specific steps to enter each career as well as other information such as typical starting salaries.

About the Author

Cecile A. Marczinski, Ph.D., is an associate professor of psychology at Northern Kentucky University. She earned her doctoral degree in psychology from McMaster University (Canada) in 2001. She completed postdoctoral training in psychopharmacology at the University of Kentucky under the mentorship of Dr. Mark Fillmore. Since arriving at Northern Kentucky University, she has received accolades for both her teaching and research. She was the winner of the 2011 Outstanding Junior Faculty Award from the College of Arts & Sciences at Northern Kentucky University. She is a strong advocate for undergraduate research, mentoring many students in her lab and also serving as an elected member of the psychology division for the Council on Undergraduate Research. She is an avid researcher, conducting human psychopharmacology studies examining the acute effects of commonly used psychoactive drugs including alcohol and caffeine. Her recent research, funded by the National Institutes of Health, has examined the combined effects of alcohol and energy drinks. This work has received favorable attention from both the scientific community and the popular press. Her research was cited in recent Food and Drug Administration (FDA) investigations into the safety of caffeinated alcoholic beverages, energy drinks, and other caffeinated foods and beverages. In addition, she appears frequently in print, on radio, and on television discussing her research. Her psychopharmacology research has been covered by various major national and international news networks including ABC, BBC, CBC, CNN, NBC, NPR, *Bloomberg Business Week*, the *New York Times*, the *London Telegraph*, and *Time* magazine. She is also the author of the book *Binge Drinking in Adolescents and College Students*. In her free time, she and her husband enjoy spending time traveling with their two young daughters.

There are various ways to connect with Dr. Marczinski, including the following:

Her website:	http://amedlab.jimdo.com/
Her lab Facebook page:	http://www.facebook.com/amedlab
Her Twitter account:	http://www.twitter.com/DrMarczinski

ACKNOWLEDGMENTS

This book came to fruition thanks to many people who were extremely supportive of this project and personally helpful to me. First, I must really thank my editor, Chris Johnson at John Wiley and Sons, for his unwavering enthusiasm for this project. From our very first conversation, I had complete confidence in his ability to guide and direct the development of this textbook in a way that would best serve both students and instructors. Chris has an innate ability to positively guide an author and provide helpful advice so that a book is not only completed in a timely manner, but also done really well. In addition to my editor, I am also appreciative of the help from the kind and cheerful staff at Wiley. Greg Malandruccolo, Maura Gilligan, Jolene Ling, Kristen Mucci, Elizabeth Blomster, and Rebecca Heider were available to provide advice, answer my questions, and solve problems quickly.

I am also extremely grateful to the many reviewers who carefully reviewed the chapters. This textbook was tremendously improved thanks to the many comments and suggestions of fellow instructors who also love to teach psychopharmacology. The reviewers' excellent feedback certainly helped me write a book that best served the needs of both instructors and students. I am also thankful for the help of my research assistant, Amy Stamates. She found research papers for me, organized images, and did many other tasks that helped bring this book to completion. She always did these tasks quickly and cheerfully. In addition, she kept my lab running smoothly while I was busy writing.

Finally, but most importantly, I would like to thank my family for their unwavering support for this project. My husband Chris had endless energy to help me with this project, whether discussing ideas about how best to present a concept or by taking our children to the park so that I could squeeze in a few extra hours of weekend writing. In addition, my girls, Isabella and Giselle, were always patient with my ambition to complete this project. Even though they are only 6 and 3 years old, they would often ask me, "How is the book coming along?". My debt to my family is great, and I will not be able ever to fully repay it. However, I will at least try to show them how thankful I am, starting with a trip to Disney World.

Cecile A. Marczinski, Ph.D.
Northern Kentucky University
Highland Heights, KY
May 23, 2013

THANK YOU TO THE REVIEWERS

This textbook was tremendously improved by the many cogent comments and helpful suggestions of fellow instructors who reviewed the chapters while this book was being written. The reviewers' excellent feedback certainly helped me write a better psychopharmacology textbook that best served the needs of both students and instructors. Thank you to the following reviewers, who, through their reviews, clearly revealed to me that they have the same passion for teaching psychopharmacology that I do.

Todd Ahern	Quinnipiac University
Jeff Bailey	California State University at Northridge
Joseph Banken	University of Arkansas at Little Rock
Susan Barron	University of Kentucky
Katey Baruth	Post University
Melissa Birkett	Northern Arizona University
Pamela Brouillard	Texas A&M University at Corpus Christi
Jeffrey Calton	California State University at Sacramento
Melloni Cook	University of Memphis
Chris Correia	Auburn University
Donald Daughtry	Texas A&M University at Kingsville
Mark Davis	The University of West Alabama
George DeRoeck	University of Arkansas at Little Rock
Adrian Dunn	University of Hawaii
Perry Fuchs	University of Texas at Arlington
Chad Galuska	College of Charleston
Angela Grippo	Northern Illinois University
Scott Hall	University of Maryland
Chris Jones	College of the Desert
George Ladd	Rhode Island College
Fred Leavitt	California State University at East Bay
David MacQueen	University of South Florida
Paul Merritt	Clemson University
Maryse Nazon	Chicago State University
Margaret Ruddy	The College of New Jersey

Timothy Shearon   The College of Idaho
Jessica Siegel   Sewanee: The University of the South
Susan Snycerski   San Jose State University
Ilsun White   Morehead State University
William Zingrone   Murray State University

INTRODUCTION TO PSYCHOPHARMACOLOGY

Introduction

Humans have been using drugs for thousands of years. Whether involving the consumption of alcohol, the injection of heroin, or simply having a cup of coffee for its caffeine, using drugs allows us to feel pleasure, feel better, do better, or to satisfy curiosity. For some, drug use causes little or no harm. For others, drug use can have serious or devastating effects. When the use of drugs becomes compulsive and out-of-control, there are medical, social, economic, and criminal justice consequences (NIDA, 2010c). Remarkable discoveries about how drugs alter brain activity have revolutionized our understanding of substance use, abuse, and addiction. Despite these scientific advances, we are not yet preventing the harmful consequences of drug abuse and addiction that continue to affect people of all ages in our society. From babies exposed to legal and illegal drugs in the womb to elderly people drinking alcohol and smoking, there is no age group that seems immune to either the appeal of drugs or the problems that arise from drug use.

Scientists study the effects that drugs have on the brain and on behavior to provide solutions for substance abuse and addiction, with the intention of preventing substance abuse and helping people recover from addiction. Notwithstanding this research effort to address the significant problems with drug use, it is also clear that many people try drugs and never develop significant problems. This variability in outcomes makes the study of psychopharmacology incredibly fascinating. Why is it that in your classroom, you can look around and see some people who have struggled with alcohol, cigarettes, marijuana, and addictions to pain medications, yet others have tried these same substances with no long-term consequences? Throughout this book, we will examine these and many other questions in our journey through an introduction to the incredible science of psychopharmacology.

LEARNING OBJECTIVES

Learning objectives can help you organize your studying. Before we begin this chapter on Introduction to Psychopharmacology, keep in mind that by the end of this chapter, you should be able to . . .

1. Define various terms such as pharmacology, psychopharmacology, tolerance, withdrawal, substance use, substance abuse, and addiction.
2. Explain how a variety of pharmacological factors and nonpharmacological factors can contribute to the drug experience for a user.
3. Explain the history of U.S. drug laws and how the current U.S. drug scheduling system works.
4. Apply your knowledge regarding when a determination should be made that drug use is harmful.
5. Evaluate the validity of the claim that hitting rock bottom is necessary before a drug abuser can get help.

What Is Psychopharmacology?

For several thousand years, humans have used various drugs to feel euphoric, alter mood, socialize, be more assertive, and block pain, as well as for a multitude of other reasons. The field of psychopharmacology endeavors to understand how drugs cause these changes and why people are drawn to using drugs. The term *psychopharmacology* comes from the joining of two words that you are probably already familiar with, *psychology* and *pharmacology*. Psychology is a broad field that involves the scientific study of behavior from biological, behavioral, and cognitive perspectives. Pharmacology involves the scientific study of drugs, including the effects of drugs on living systems. As such, **psychopharmacology** refers to the scientific study of the effect of drugs on behavior. Humans are social creatures, so psychopharmacology also incorporates knowledge about how social and environmental factors impact the effects of drugs.

Since psychopharmacology involves the scientific study of the effects of drugs on behavior, we should first clarify what is meant by a drug and which drugs will be emphasized in this textbook. While most people have an intuitive sense about what constitutes a drug, the definition is sometimes misunderstood by the general public. The most widely used definition of **drug** was arrived at by experts at the World Health Organization (WHO). They stated that a drug is "any chemical entity or mixture of entities, other than those required for the maintenance of normal health (like food), the administration of which alters biological function and possibly structure" (WHO, 1981, p. 227). They also defined the term **psychoactive drug** as a drug that alters mood, cognition, and behavior. Cognition refers to mental processes including attention, memory, language, solving problems, and decision making. In this textbook, we will limit our discussion to psychoactive drugs, which are the drugs that strongly impact behavior. For example, a drug that makes a person feel high and leads him or her to seek out more of it results in changes in behavior. By contrast, a drug that only decreases blood pressure or reduces cholesterol is not of interest to psychopharmacology, since ingestion of that type of drug typically causes little change in behavior. It should be noted right up front that psychoactive drugs also tend to be the ones that are abused by some people (to the point of physical or psychological harm to oneself or others).

While the terms "drug" and "psychoactive drug" seem relatively straightforward, the reality of their categorization can be less so. For example, how should we think about nutritional supplements such as vitamins? We need vitamins for the maintenance of normal health. However, some nutritional supplements may alter cognition or improve behavioral performance. Should we consider them drugs, using the WHO definition? Further, we have a tendency to think of drugs as powerful or extremely harmful. However, the definitions for drug and psychoactive drug do not incorporate the concept of harm, which is why some compounds that are drugs are often not considered as such by the general public. As a recent example, the American Beverage Association stated that "caffeine is not a drug" (American Beverage Association, 2011). However, the scientific evidence is clear that caffeine improves mood, speeds reaction times, decreases fatigue, and binds with adenosine receptors in the brain to alter various biological functions. Further, there is no need for caffeine in the maintenance of normal health. Therefore, caffeine clearly fits the definition of a psychoactive drug.

The Drug Experience

When a drug is available, what motivates people to try it? While the answer is complex, there are probably four main reasons why people are initially motivated to take a drug (NIDA, 2010c). The first is to feel good. For almost every psychoactive drug that we will talk about in this book, feelings of pleasure result when the drug is taken for the first time. The feeling of pleasure may range from a mild positive mood state to an extreme sensation of euphoria. For example, people report that they feel "high" after taking cocaine, a stimulant psychoactive drug. They also report feeling powerful and self-confident, in addition to feeling increased energy. The euphoria experienced after using an opiate such as heroin is different in quality. Since heroin is a sedative drug, users report a feeling of relaxation and satisfaction. The second reason that people try a drug is to feel better. If a person is depressed, stressed, or anxious, psychoactive drugs may lessen these aversive feelings. For example, if a college student is prone to social anxiety and is going to a party, he might have a few drinks before the event to lessen anxiety. The third reason that people use drugs is to do better. It is possible to chemically improve athletic or cognitive performance by using various drugs. For example, anabolic steroids, caffeine, amphetamines, and cocaine have been used to enhance performance. Athletes often make the news when steroid use is revealed since their use is an illegal way to enhance athletic performance. The fourth set of reasons for trying a drug involves curiosity and social influences. Use of a new drug can be thrilling, somewhat risky, or part of a social situation. During the adolescent and young adult years, peer influences are particularly strong, contributing to the likelihood that a person will try a drug.

When a person takes a psychoactive drug, they have a drug experience. The drug experience is influenced by a variety of factors, some of which will seem obvious, and others perhaps less so. What is probably obvious is that the chemical action of the drug is part of the drug experience. If a person drinks several alcoholic beverages, it is the alcohol content that contributes to the experience. However, research has also illustrated that the chemistry of the drug is not the entire story. In fact, there are a variety of pharmacological and nonpharmacological factors that contribute to a drug experience.

Pharmacological Factors

Pharmacological factors that contribute to a drug experience include anything related to the drug's biochemical and/or physiological action. There are three main pharmacological factors to consider. First is the chemical structure of a drug and how it acts on the body. For example, the drugs we will discuss in this book look remarkably similar to naturally occurring chemicals in our nervous system called neurotransmitters. When a drug is ingested, it can act like or alter the levels of these naturally occurring chemicals, which contributes to the drug experience. The second factor is how the drug enters the body, which is called the **route of administration**. There are a variety of ways to get a drug into the body, including swallowing, smoking, and injection. The route of administration is particularly important for psychoactive drugs, since the drug experience is a function of activity in the brain. Getting the drug to the brain requires the bloodstream to transport the drug from the point of administration to the brain. Some routes of administration facilitate this journey, such as when a user injects the drug directly into a vein, which affords direct access to the bloodstream. Other paths are relatively slow. When a user swallows a drug, it takes some time for the drug to reach the bloodstream and ultimately the brain. With oral ingestion, the drug travels initially via the digestive system and absorption into the bloodstream occurs when the drug reaches the small intestine in many cases. How quickly the drug reaches the brain has an impact on the drug experience and the route of administration contributes to the speed at which the drug reaches the brain. The third factor is the **drug dose**, the amount of drug ingested. It is perhaps not surprising that the dose of drug can matter a great deal. If the amount of drug is too low, the person may not experience appreciable changes. Likewise, too high a dose can be very problematic, or even fatal, for many of the drugs that we will talk about in this book. In many cases, there is an optimal dose for a person to achieve the desired drug experience.

Nonpharmacological Factors

Nonpharmacological factors that contribute to a drug experience include everything not directly related to the pharmacological action of the drug itself. The important role of nonpharmacological factors in contributing to a drug experience can be surprising for some. Until recently, scientists would often study only the pharmacological factors, thinking that nonpharmacological factors matter very little in a drug experience. However, it is becoming increasingly clear that nonpharmacological factors can be incredibly important (Vogel-Sprott, 1992). There are two main types of nonpharmacological factors. The first are the characteristics of the drug user. These characteristics can range from biological ones, such as the genetic makeup of the individual, to characteristics that are clearly the result of experience. Genetic makeup refers to those biologically inherited differences among people that can alter how a body will react to a drug. For example, some people have a genetic predisposition for addiction to alcohol (alcoholism runs in their family), yet others tend to have aversive responses to alcohol, such as nausea and feeling flushed when drinking, which protects them from becoming addicted to alcohol. Some genetic predispositions to use and abuse substances are specific to one type of drug (alcohol or nicotine), while others are more general predispositions increasing the likelihood of substance use and abuse. Some personality traits that have an inherited component making a person want to seek out risks and try drugs for the thrill. In addition to genetics, other biological characteristics such as gender and age also impact the drug experience.

Learned characteristics of the drug user also impact the drug experience. As a person goes through life, the individual acquires knowledge, attitudes, thoughts, and expectations about a drug. This learning can occur from personal experience or from watching others (observational learning). For example, little children have very specific expectations about alcohol. If you ask an 8-year old child what happens to people when they drink alcohol, a typical response might contain some sort of statement like 'alcohol makes them act silly' (Hipwell et al., 2005). Expectations also come from direct personal experience. College students drink coffee or soft drinks because they know from past experience that consumption of these beverages may help them stay up late to study or work on a paper.

Biological and learned characteristics of the drug user can combine to contribute to a drug experience. Drug **tolerance** occurs when a regular user of a drug finds that a certain dose becomes less effective over time, with the person having to use higher doses to achieve the same effect. There is a biological element to this change, as the body becomes adept at handling the drug, with the brain becoming less sensitive to the effects and the body moving faster to metabolize the drug. There is a learned aspect as well, as the person adapts to cues in the environment predicting drug administration. Regular consumers of alcoholic beverages may learn that a certain amount of alcohol makes them unsteady on their feet. As such, they learn that they should walk more slowly and perhaps a bit closer to a wall in case they feel imbalanced. Tolerance will be discussed in great detail in Chapter 3 because its development is so central to understanding psychopharmacology.

In addition to biological and learned characteristics contributing to a drug experience, there is also the role of the setting. People take drugs in different places such as at home, in hotels, and at bars. The immediate physical environment influences a drug experience. For example, LSD is a hallucinogenic drug that makes you hallucinate or 'see' things not actually present. Users report that the drug experience can be unpleasant or downright frightening in dark environments. The same drug dose may result in more favorable outcomes for the user in a well-lit environment. Likewise, the presence of other people can influence a drug experience. The environment can also be part of learning. Cues in the environment can prompt the body to prepare for the arrival of a drug dose. Environmental cues can be specific to a drug (a needle) or they can be sights, smells, and sounds associated with a person's home. It should be noted that the environment also encompasses laws pertaining to drug use. Laws can differ by location, both within and between countries. Knowing that you are breaking or not breaking a law can be part of the drug experience. We will discuss current U.S. drug laws at the end of this chapter.

The powerful role that nonpharmacological learned factors have on the drug experience is illustrated by two pieces of evidence. First, when people ingest a placebo, they sometimes report a strong 'drug' experience, even though a **placebo** is a chemically inactive substance (Cami, Guerra, Ugena, Segura, & de la Torre, 1991; Fillmore, Carscadden, & Vogel-Sprott, 1998). In psychopharmacology research, a placebo is designed to be very similar to the active substance. For example, a placebo for alcohol should be a beverage that looks like alcohol, smells like alcohol, and tastes like alcohol, without actually containing alcohol. In many studies, it has been shown that when people think that they have received a drug, they behave like they have had the drug. A strong belief that one has consumed a drug can sometimes be enough to produce an effect. If you think that alcohol makes you more talkative and you consume a drink that you think is alcohol, you may get more talkative after consuming the beverage even though you consumed a placebo. A second illustration of a nonpharmacological learned factor is the role that the environment plays in drug overdose deaths (Siegel, Hinson, Krank, & McCully, 1982). When drug users accidentally die from overdosing, the user frequently used the typical dose of drug in a novel environment. For example, a heroin user may inject a dose of the drug in his or her apartment on a regular basis without a risk of an overdose. However, the same dose may be lethal when administered in a hotel. Learned cues in the familiar apartment provide information to the brain to get ready for the dose and counteract some of its effects. When these cues are absent, the body does not attempt to compensate for the drug coming on board and the user unfortunately overdoses.

Given that the drug experience can be altered by a variety of pharmacological and non-pharmacological factors, scientists from many different backgrounds are involved in understanding what causes people to use and abuse psychoactive drugs. Understanding substance use, abuse, and addiction requires research at multiple levels of analysis, ranging from what is happening at the synapse of a neuron to the greater role of society. As such, psychopharmacology as a field of study is very broad in scope, and it incorporates both interdisciplinary and translational research. **Interdisciplinary research** is the combination of two or more traditionally defined academic disciplines, and it can be extremely beneficial to solving the issues of concern for this field. For example, it is common for psychologists who study psychopharmacology to spend time talking to colleagues in neuroscience, medicine, biology, chemistry, sociology, social work, anthropology, and nursing, among other professions. Since drug addiction is a complex problem, the answers are also complex. **Translational research** is also applied to the field of psychopharmacology. Translational research attempts to translate basic research findings into clinical practice. Translational research is also called bench-to-beside research, a descriptive term emphasizing that the findings of a biochemist sitting at a lab bench should ultimately help the person suffering from drug addiction in a bed at a drug rehabilitation facility. Translational research also often involves taking learning from animal studies and applying it to humans. In this book, we will cover all kinds of research in psychopharmacology, so that substance use, abuse, and addiction can be better understood. A course in psychopharmacology is a terrific means to get a strong foundation in science and scientific thinking, particularly since so many disparate approaches are needed to understand this complex problem. It should be noted that both interdisciplinary and translational research are lofty goals in psychopharmacology, since it is not always easy for a biochemist to talk to a therapist treating a patient. However, people who work in various capacities in the field of psychopharmacology do ultimately want to help the person suffering from an addiction. While not every scientist in psychopharmacology incorporates interdisciplinary and translational research, many do. Ultimately, any research that helps the person suffering from addiction, or prevents an addiction from occurring in the first place, should benefit society as a whole.

In the News:

Garcia, Angela (2012, April 15). Heroin vaccine won't "cure" what ails addicts. *Los Angeles Times.*

When news broke about a vaccine that could be used to treat heroin addiction, headlines proclaimed that heroin addiction might become a thing of the past. The vaccine would prevent heroin taken into the body from reaching the brain. If the heroin would not reach the brain, the user would no longer feel any pleasure from the drug. Consequently, the user should eventually stop taking the drug. This would be no small achievement considering that the addiction to opiates (heroin, morphine, or other opiate pain medications) is notoriously difficult to treat, perhaps the worst addiction to overcome. With an estimated 1 million heroin addicts in the United States alone, there is great appeal in the idea of just going to the doctor's office, getting a vaccination, and no longer having a devastating problem. While not approved for humans, the vaccine thus far has been shown to be effective in mice. However, not all news stories were universally enthusiastic about the possibility of a heroin vaccine for human use. One article written in the *Los Angeles Times* took quite a different tone. The author of the article, Dr. Angela Garcia, is an anthropologist from Stanford University who studies drug addiction in rural New Mexico. Though academics rarely write news articles for the general public, Dr. Garcia's background as a medical journalist may have prompted this article. In the story, she emphasized that the most effective anti-addiction vaccine will not solve the underlying factors that make people prone to using drugs of abuse, including heroin. These factors include poverty, violence, and lack of opportunity. She noted that while an effective vaccine may no longer prompt a mouse to self-administer the drug for pleasure, the mouse does not have the option to turn to another pleasure-producing substance. Humans obviously do not live in a sterile laboratory environment. While a vaccine for humans could potentially block the pleasure from heroin, other forms of pleasure-seeking, including the use of other drugs, might nevertheless occur. Dr. Garcia noted that in many cases, drug use is an attempt to relieve suffering. In her work with poor Hispanic families in rural New Mexico, which has the highest per capita heroin-related deaths in the United States, these people suffer from a disproportionate burden of addiction, depression, and incarceration. She has observed that there is an intertwined history of heroin use, poverty, and colonial history in the area where she works. While a vaccine might eliminate the pleasure of taking heroin, it cannot eliminate poverty and social problems that motivate people to seek out drugs.

Use This News Article to Test and Apply Your Knowledge:

1. A variety of reasons for using drugs are mentioned in this article. We just finished a section discussing the pharmacological and nonpharmacological factors that contribute to drug use and addiction. In this story, what were examples of each of these factors?
2. This article emphasizes that the problem of heroin addiction is complex and requires the expertise of different types of scientists. We discussed that research in psychopharmacology is often interdisciplinary and translational in focus. How could these ideas be applied to this article?

Answers

1. For pharmacological factors, the role that the drug itself plays is mentioned, with heroin increasing the feeling of pleasure. If a vaccine were given, this pleasure would be eliminated when the drug can no longer reach the brain, which is the site of action for all drugs of abuse. Nonpharmacological factors included poverty, violence, and depression. These factors are not related to the drug's action itself, but they contribute to the response a person might feel when taking the drug initially and also contribute to subsequent addiction.
2. The article mentions that while a vaccine might be effective in mice, the effectiveness of a vaccine in humans may depend on access to other drugs to reduce depression or increase pleasure. This emphasizes that translational research would need to incorporated to determine whether a vaccine that is effective in mice would also work in humans. Moreover, the article mentioned that heroin addiction in rural New Mexico probably has several contributing factors. As such, interdisciplinary research would be

helpful in understanding why there are such high rates of heroin addiction and overdose deaths in this region of the country. Psychologists, anthropologists, sociologists, and economists among others could bring their varying perspectives on how depression, poverty, and cultural history are contributing to and maintaining addictions.

What Do You Think about This News Story?

This article highlights the complexity of addiction to psychoactive drugs. What do you think of the idea of a vaccine to help with drug addiction? Do you think that a vaccine could help people overcome the circumstances, such as poverty, that contributed to the addiction problem? Keep your answers in mind as we delve further into the large amount of alcohol and drug use that occurs in the United States and around the world.

Use of Alcohol and Drugs

In the United States

Abuse and addiction to alcohol, nicotine, and illegal substances cost Americans half a trillion dollars a year, when the combined medical, economic, criminal, and social impact is considered (NIDA, 2010c). This incredible amount of money arises from a variety of sources, including medical care for substance abuse treatment, law enforcement costs to deal with drug-related crime, to foster care required for a child whose parents are unable to care for the child because of addiction. Moreover, the costs are not just in dollars, but also in lives. More than 100,000 Americans die each year with the abuse of illicit drugs and alcohol as contributing factors, while tobacco is associated with an estimated 440,000 deaths annually (NIDA, 2010c). In the United States, many people are using alcohol and drugs, and some of this use leads to significant problems for the user and society in general. To make legal, tax, educational, and health policy decisions, the federal government goes to great expense to conduct national surveys to obtain understanding of who is using which drugs. In epidemiology, scientists gather two types of information regarding alcohol and drug use: prevalence and incidence.

Prevalence refers to the total number of cases in the population at a given time. Prevalence data is used to estimate how common an activity is, such as reporting how many Americans drank alcohol in the past year. By contrast, **incidence** refers to the number of new cases in a population in a given time. Incidence data, such as reporting how many Americans tried methamphetamine for the first time in the past year, is helpful in revealing how a problem might be changing. Epidemiologists would say that both prevalence and incidence data are helpful in planning how tax dollars should be spent to address health concerns facing a community. Moreover, gathering prevalence and incidence data can be useful in helping a country make plans, since the data can reveal if a particular drug use problem is escalating or declining over time.

National Household Survey

One national survey conducted annually by the Office of Applied Studies in the Substance Abuse and Mental Health Services Administration (SAMHSA) gives an idea about drug usage rates in the United States. It is called the *National Household Survey* because it includes people living in the general civilian population (i.e., living in households). Therefore, some people are excluded from these annual surveys, including those serving in the military, individuals in long-term institutions, and prisoners. These annual surveys provide valuable information about the use of alcohol, tobacco, and illicit (i.e., illegal) drugs in the U.S. population for people aged 12 years and older. To gather this data, the government conducts face-to-face interviews with approximately 67,500 people each year. Participants are selected from each of the 50 U.S. states and the District of Columbia. Can you imagine the logistics and cost involved in doing this kind of research annually? The data below were collected for the 2010 survey. Only the main findings are reported here. Further information is freely available on the Internet if you are interested in looking at it in further detail (SAMHSA, 2011a).

First, we will examine the findings from the 2010 survey for the legal psychoactive drugs: alcohol and nicotine. Note that in this survey, the researchers do not ask about caffeine, even though it is a psychoactive drug. This decision stems from the fact that caffeine causes little concern for society. We will first discuss alcohol. The researchers found that slightly more than half of Americans reported that they were current drinkers of alcohol (52%), with current drinking defined as having had an alcoholic beverage within the past 30 days. Recall that this survey is conducted with participants 12 years and older, so this rate of current alcohol use does include underage drinkers. The survey data suggests that approximately 131 million people in the United States have consumed an alcoholic beverage in the past month. For reference, the 2010 U.S. Census counted 308,745,538 people living in the United States. Making an estimate of the overall use of alcohol is possible since participants were carefully selected to be representative of the U.S. population as a whole. Just like results of a political poll can be used to predict the outcome of an election (if participants are representative of the overall population of voters), the overall use of drugs in the general population can be established based on the findings from this survey. While the findings from the 2010 survey are reported here, it is remarkable that use rates are largely consistent from year to year, even though different people are surveyed every year. This consistency is evidence that the estimates for the overall use of various drugs is largely accurate.

The survey also asks about how much alcohol is consumed and how often. The researchers found that nearly one-quarter (23%) of respondents reported binge drinking, which was defined as having five or more drinks in a row on at least one day in the past 30 days. In addition, 7% reported heavy drinking, which was defined as binge drinking on at least five days in the past 30 days. Thus, approximately 17 million people in the United States are drinking very heavily, putting their brains and livers at risk for serious problems, which we will see in Chapter 8, the alcohol chapter of this book. Given that the consumption of alcohol is illegal for persons under the age of 21 in the United States, it is also interesting that the survey data suggested that there are an estimated 10 million underage drinkers nationwide. Finally, the survey asked about driving under influence. Approximately 11% of the sample of all survey respondents reported driving under the influence in the past year. The highest rate of impaired driving was for ages 21 to 25, where the rates of driving under the influence was 23% (nearly 1 in 4 people for this age group!).

What about tobacco? The survey asked about their past month's use of any tobacco product, including cigarettes, cigars, and chewing tobacco. Approximately 27% of the sample reported current tobacco use, which translates to about 70 million people in the United States. Most of this tobacco use is cigarettes, as 23% of the sample reported smoking at least one cigarette in the past month.

What about illicit (illegal) drug use, including marijuana/hashish, cocaine (including crack), heroin, hallucinogens, inhalants, or prescription-type psychotherapeutics used nonmedically? For clarification, use of a legitimate prescription, such as oxycontin for pain, would not be included. If an individual reported the use of oxycontin and did not need the drug for a medical reason (the drug was diverted from its original intent), such use would be classified as illicit drug use. The survey results indicated that approximately 9% of respondents used an illicit drug in the past month. This translates to approximately 23 million Americans using an illicit drug in the past month. You might wonder how the researchers were able to acquire this information, since people may be wary of admitting to illicit drug use due to criminal ramifications or impacts to employment status. In fact, this survey always collects anonymous data (names or other identifiable information are not recorded with survey responses) and thus there are no criminal implications of admitting to illicit drug use on this survey.

As for which illicit drug is used most commonly, marijuana leads use with 17 million current users. Examining only the data from the current illicit drug users, it was estimated that marijuana was used by 77%, and marijuana was also the only drug used by more than 60%. The second most commonly used illicit drug after marijuana was the nonmedical use of psychotherapeutic drugs, estimated at 7 million U.S. users. These drugs include pain relievers, tranquilizers, stimulants, and sedatives that were originally prescribed for a real medical condition and then used recreationally. An example might be a college student who buys a friend's stimulant medication (originally prescribed for attention deficit/hyperactivity disorder) to help with studying for exams.

The National Household Survey data also provides us with interesting demographic information about who is using which drugs. A consistent observation in these surveys is that there are particular characteristics highly associated with alcohol and drug use differences. For legal and illegal psychoactive drugs, there are a few important demographic predictors. The first is age, with the greatest use in the late teenage years and early 20s. The second is gender, with men using more drugs than women. Third is ethnicity or racial differences, with Whites consuming the most alcohol, followed by Hispanics, Blacks, and Asians consuming the least. For illicit drugs, a slightly different pattern is observed: Blacks use the most illicit drugs, followed by Whites, then Hispanics, and finally Asians consume the least. Employment status also is associated with legal and illegal drug use, with unemployed people using the most.

To better understand these demographic differences, it is helpful to look at findings from the 2010 survey results, particularly for illicit drug use. Approximately 23% of 18–20-year-olds reported using illicit drugs, with the second highest rate (21%) among 21–25-year-olds. Rates of illicit drug use increased during the teenage years, peaked in the late teens and early young adulthood, and then declined after that. Among people aged 65 or older, the rate of illicit drug use dropped to a low of 1%. For gender, the overall rate of current illicit drug use was much higher in males (11%) than females (7%). Males were much more likely than females to be current users of marijuana, cocaine, hallucinogens, as well as to be nonmedical users of psychotherapeutic drugs.

What about illicit drugs people tried for the first time in the past year? The pattern of results is similar to what is found with illicit drug users overall. Figure 1-1 illustrates the first specific drug associated with illicit drug use among past year initiates. Of the 3 million Americans who took an illegal drug for the first time in the past year, the majority (62%) did so with marijuana, with the nonmedical use of pain relievers a distant second (17%).

Finally, the survey provided information about who went to treatment or considered treatment for substance abuse in the past year. Figure 1-2 illustrates the substance for which most recent treatment was received. By a wide margin, most people go to treatment for problems with alcohol. Interestingly, many people who need treatment did not receive it. The reasons for lack of

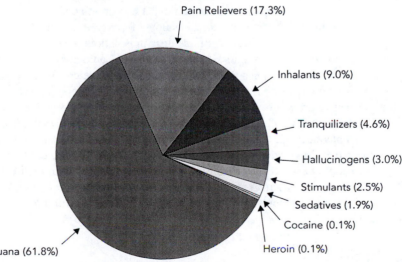

Pain Relievers (17.3%)

Inhalants (9.0%)

Tranquilizers (4.6%)

Hallucinogens (3.0%)

Stimulants (2.5%)

Sedatives (1.9%)

Cocaine (0.1%)

Heroin (0.1%)

Marijuana (61.8%)

3.0 Million Initiates of Illicit Drugs

FIGURE 1-1
The first specific drug associated with initiation of illicit drug use among past year illicit drug initiates aged 12 or older when surveyed in 2010 (SAMHSA, 2011a).

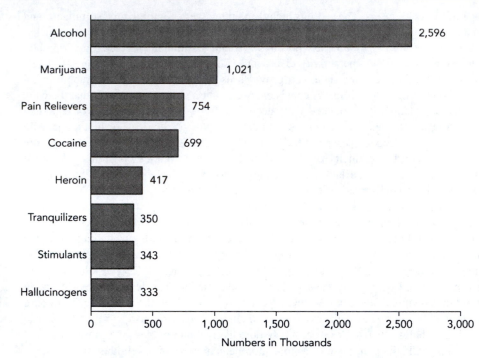

FIGURE 1-2
The substances for which most recent treatment was received in the past year among persons aged 12 or older in 2010 (SAMHSA, 2011a).

treatment are reported in Figure 1-3. The first major reason was lack of health coverage, with the second being not ready to stop using.

In summary, it is fair to generalize that a large number of people in the United States are current users of a variety of legal and illegal psychoactive drugs. Unsurprisingly, the use of legal psychoactive drugs (alcohol and nicotine) is far more common than the use of illegal drugs, with approximately 52% of individuals being past month alcohol users and 27% being past month tobacco users, as opposed to 9% being past month illicit drug users. However, even current illicit drug use rates are high, particularly among demographic groups such as adolescents and young people. One final important observation from these survey results is that drugs are frequently used in combination. For example, an individual who reports current use of marijuana will often report current use of alcohol and tobacco. This phenomenon is called **polydrug use**, because the individual is using two or more psychoactive drugs to achieve a certain effect.

Polydrug use can add additional complexity to the study of psychopharmacology. Most research in psychopharmacology involves the study of one drug in isolation; the effect of a single drug can be complicated enough to understand! However, increasing amounts of research has been devoted to understanding what happens when two or more drugs are consumed together, since that is what is often happening in the real world. In the subsequent chapters of this book, we will examine each psychoactive drug in isolation, while some of the exciting research examining the combined effects of drugs will also be introduced where applicable. For example, it is particularly dangerous to mix alcohol with tranquilizers. Unfortunately, many accidental overdoses have occurred when these two drugs were combined (Buckley, Dawson, Whyte, & O'Connell, 1995). Likewise, young people have become enamored with mixing alcohol with high-caffeine energy drinks. This practice can lead users to misattribute how intoxicated they really are, leading to high rates of impaired driving, accidents, and injuries in users (Marczinski, Fillmore, Henges, Ramsey, & Young, 2012).

Around the World

Alcohol and drug use is common in the U.S. population. Is the same true in other countries around the world? This question is somewhat difficult to answer, in part because there are so many

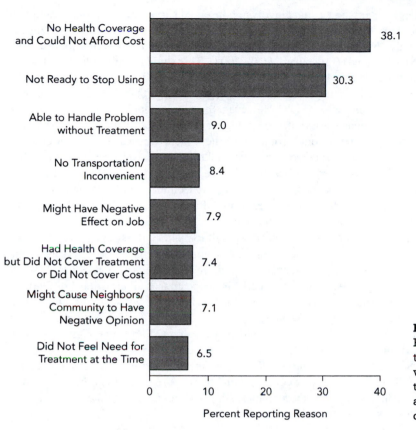

FIGURE 1-3
Reasons for not receiving substance use treatment among persons aged 12 or older who needed and made an effort to get treatment but did not receive treatment and felt they needed treatment: 2007–2010 combined (SAMHSA, 2011a).

different ways to approach it. For example, face-to-face surveys may be conducted in some countries, whereas other countries may rely on Internet surveys. Moreover, there are a multitude of ways to frame questions regarding drug and alcohol use. To make international comparisons meaningful, the same question needs to be asked in each location. One cannot easily compare responses regarding lifetime use in one country with past-month use in another. Despite these challenges, international comparisons of alcohol and drug use have been undertaken. Vega et al. (2002) surveyed lifetime use (prevalence) and age of first use (onset) for alcohol, marijuana, and other drugs in cities located in six countries (United States, Canada, Mexico, Brazil, Germany, and the Netherlands). The researchers surveyed over 27,000 individuals who were between the ages of 14 and 54 years. They asked respondents about lifetime alcohol use, which they defined as consuming an alcoholic beverage at least 12 times in one's lifetime. The researchers also asked about lifetime drug use, which they defined as using an illicit drug at least five times in one's lifetime. Note that these definitions are different than those used in the SAMHSA surveys mentioned earlier. Despite these methodological differences, three findings from this data appeared to be similar to the SAMHSA results. First, men use more alcohol and drugs than women. Second, marijuana is the most commonly used illicit drug. Third, the use of other illicit drugs occurs at a much lower rate than marijuana. Despite many similarities, there were interesting country differences. For example, alcohol use was highest in the Netherlands and lowest in Mexico. Alcohol use was also high in Canada and the United States, which ranked second and third after the Netherlands. Marijuana use was also quite variable. Marijuana was used at a rate of 29% in the United States versus a low rate of 2% in Mexico. Despite differences in lifetime use, the age of first use was similar across the various locations.

Another recent larger international study involved household surveys in a combined sample of over 85,000 people carried out in 17 countries (United States, Mexico, Columbia, Belgium, France, Germany, Italy, Netherlands, Spain, Ukraine, Israel, Lebanon, Nigeria, South Africa, Japan, China, and New Zealand) (Degenhardt et al., 2008). This study examined lifetime use and age of initiation of tobacco, alcohol, marijuana, and cocaine. Similar demographic patterns were observed as found in the earlier study, with males using more drugs than females, and younger people using more drugs than older people. However, the researchers found interesting international differences in marijuana use, with much higher rates in the United States and New Zealand (both at 42%) compared to other countries. Where there were differences in drug use across countries, the researchers wondered if international differences were related to local drug laws (such as whether laws were strict or lenient). The researchers did not observe any strong relationship between illicit drug use rates and drug policy. Countries with stringent user-level illegal drug policies did not appear to have lower levels of use than countries with liberal ones. We will discuss U.S. drug laws at the end of this chapter.

In sum, while international comparisons can be difficult to make, it does appear that there may be more similarities in use rates than differences. For example, the consistent observations that men use more than women and that younger people use more illicit drugs than older people seems to be consistent across geographies. However, there also appears to be international differences, which suggests that culture matters. In future chapters in this book, we will examine international data on use rates for individual drugs, since there are often a variety of factors leading to different use rates. However, one additional mention should be made regarding economics. In general, international comparisons have noted that high-income countries have substantially higher rates of illicit drug use than low-income countries. When low-income and middle-income countries have higher rates of illicit drug use, those countries tend to be close to an illicit drug production area (Degenhardt & Hall, 2012). Beyond economics, simply having access to the drug is a factor when considering drug use rates.

QUICK QUIZ 1-1

1. Dr. Jones is a physician who treats patients suffering from addiction to alcohol. Dr. Vasquez is a sociologist who studies the role that society plays in why some children succumb to alcohol addiction. Drs. Jones and Vasquez meet at a conference to discuss how they might collaborate on a research idea. Their research could be considered:
   a. Translational
   b. Interdisciplinary
   c. Interactive
   d. Independent

2. Sarah is in a study where she is given a beverage that the researcher says is alcohol. After drinking the beverage, she feels more talkative and sociable. However, the researcher did not actually give Sarah a beverage containing alcohol. The beverage Sarah received is a called a
   a. Dose
   b. Setting
   c. Placebo
   d. Psychoactive drug

3. Route of administration is a _____ factor in the drug experience.

   a. Pharmacological
   b. Nonpharmacological
   c. Mediating
   d. Psychoactive

4. Based on the SAMHSA data from the National Household Survey, which illicit drugs are most commonly used?
   a. Marijuana and cocaine
   b. Marijuana and diverted prescription drugs
   c. Heroin and cocaine
   d. Methamphetamine and cocaine

5. You read in the newspaper that marijuana use is more common in Europe than in the United States. In support of this statement, the author notes that 35% of Europeans have tried marijuana in their lifetime, whereas 5% of Americans have tried marijuana for the first time in the past year. What is problematic about this comparison?

6. Vaccination may be a potential treatment for drug addiction. What is one positive and one negative aspect of this approach to treatment?

ANSWERS TO QUICK QUIZ 1-1:

1. b. – interdisciplinary
2. c. – placebo
3. a. – pharmacological
4. b. – marijuana and diverted prescription drugs
5. The problem with this comparison is that the author is not looking at the same type of data. The European data is prevalence data (reflecting lifetime use of marijuana). The U.S. data is incidence data (since it reflects first time users of the drug). Moreover, it is probably too vague to compare all European countries combined to the United States for marijuana use rates, as European countries will differ in economics, culture, and drug availability, among other factors.

6. Vaccination for drug treatment may be a favorable approach, since it prevents the user from experiencing the high that the drug typically would give. Thus, the user will decrease use of that drug over time, which should help treat the addiction. However, vaccination does not help with the psychological and societal factors that contribute to addiction. If the user lives in poverty, has no job skills or job prospects, and is depressed, the vaccine alone will not address these problems for the user, who may seek out another drug instead.

Defining Substance Use, Abuse, and Addiction

When Is Drug Use Harmful?

Earlier in this chapter, we discussed the main reasons people try psychoactive drugs including to feel good, to feel better, to do better, curiosity, and peer influences. The question of course is, if the use of a psychoactive drug makes us feel good, what is the problem? For many people, there is no problem. The data on the widespread use of psychoactive drugs in the United States and worldwide reveals that many people use alcohol and drugs without concern. However, a subset of individuals develops problems that can range from mildly disconcerting to devastating, including death. These problems stem from the fact that the short-term pleasure following use of a drug occurs because the drug alters chemical levels in the brain. These chemicals, called neurotransmitters, are always in a delicate balance. When this delicate balance is disrupted on a regular basis (as when substance use becomes habitual), the body adapts and changes to accommodate to this new "normal." For example, if a drug elevates the levels of the neurotransmitter dopamine in the brain, the body will produce less of its own dopamine in order to keep dopamine at a desired target. Over time, if drug use continues and escalates, the user will need more drug to elevate dopamine levels and the body will produce less and less of its own naturally occurring dopamine. The user will find that pleasurable activities in life become less pleasurable, and drug use becomes necessary for the user simply to feel normal. These subjective feelings arise because of the adjusted new balance in neurotransmitters in the brain. Unfortunately, there is no medical test to determine when substance use has gone from a pleasurable activity to abuse and addiction. In an ideal future, it would be possible to assess neurotransmitter activity via a medical test. However, we currently must rely on behavioral observations and the self-report of the user and family members or friends to assess when seeking and taking drugs is causing problems. Sometimes an interaction with the criminal justice system (an arrest for drug possession or impaired driving) is a clear symptom that something is not right and drug use is becoming harmful.

If this approach of relying on behavior and self-reported symptoms in identifying drug abuse and drug addiction seems unscientific, consider the diagnostic procedures for other psychological conditions, such as depression, anxiety, or schizophrenia. For many psychological disorders, we rely on observations of behavior and on self-report of symptoms to determine diagnoses. If a person is suspected of suffering from depression, we diagnose this by asking about the person's feelings, changes in appetite, or difficulty sleeping. We may observe that they look tired and deflated. A family member may report that the person is not eating well, is sleeping poorly, or is crying a lot. These symptoms help a psychologist or physician determine that a diagnosis of major depression is probably appropriate. Of course, the determination of an appropriate diagnosis also requires that other possibilities be ruled out. As we will see, the same approach for assessing symptoms is also used for diagnosis of substance abuse and addiction. Further, diagnoses do more than merely put a label on a problem. They allow clinicians and scientists to communicate better with one another about the same problem, since each knows the diagnostic criteria and what specific cluster of symptoms is being discussed. If a physician diagnoses a problem in a patient as alcohol dependence in a routine office visit, this information can be easily conveyed to the substance abuse counselor to whom the patient is subsequently referred. Diagnoses help with communication among specialists.

Using the Diagnostic and Statistical Manual (DSM-IV-TR)

In the United States, the diagnostic system used to classify mental diseases is called the *Diagnostic and Statistical Manual* (DSM), with the current version called the DSM-IV-TR, published in the year 2000. This diagnostic system is a set of definitions about various mental illnesses. The American Psychiatric Association (APA) created the diagnostic system in the early 1950s, and various revisions over time have been made as knowledge about mental disorders has improved. A **diagnosis** is a name given to a cluster of symptoms. For alcohol and drug use, the DSM-IV-TR specifies criteria for both substance abuse and substance dependence (see Table 1-1). The table illustrates that substance abuse is a less concerning diagnosis than substance dependence. The physical manifestations of being addicted to a drug (such as feeling sick from withdrawal symptoms if the person suddenly stops using the drug) are only present with the substance dependence criteria. It should also be noted that the DSM-IV-TR approach requires that only one (or more) of the four possible symptoms must be present for a diagnosis of substance abuse, whereas three (or more) of the seven possible symptoms must be present for a diagnosis of substance dependence. This difference highlights that substance dependence is a more severe problem than substance abuse.

Two additional things should be mentioned regarding these criteria. First, the term *substance* is not specific in these criteria. Any psychoactive drug that is covered in this book could be used instead of the term *substance*, including both legal and illegal drugs. For diagnostic purposes, the approach is the same regardless of whether the person is having difficulties with alcohol or cocaine. Second, a person should only be diagnosed with substance abuse or substance dependence, but not both, for the same drug, since the problem is either less or more severe for a particular drug. However, a person could have both diagnoses for two separate substances. For

Table 1-1   DSM-IV-TR Criteria for Substance Abuse and Substance Dependence.

a. **Substance Abuse**

    1 (or more) of the following in a 12-month period:

  1. Substance use resulting in a failure to fulfill work, school, or home obligations

  2. Use in physically hazardous situations

  3. Substance-related legal problems

  4. Persistent social/interpersonal problems from use

b. **Substance Dependence**

    3 (or more) of the following in a 12-month period:

  1. Tolerance

  2. Withdrawal

  3. Escalating use

  4. Unsuccessful in cutting down use

  5. Time is spent in substance-related activities

  6. Other activities reduced because of substance use

  7. Use despite physical or psychological problems

Source: Adapted from American Psychiatric Association. (2000). *Diagnostic and Statistical Manual of Mental Disorders: DSM-IV-TR*. Washington, DC: Author. For full criteria and exact wording, please see this document.

example, a person could have a significant drinking problem and fit the criteria for substance dependence for alcohol. The same person might also have driven an automobile while using marijuana and fit the criteria for substance abuse for marijuana.

You may have noticed that the diagnostic criteria for substance abuse and substance dependence do not actually contain the word *addiction*. However, the term *addiction* is often used in psychopharmacology and should be explained, since it is implied by the DSM-IV-TR criteria. **Addiction** has traditionally been defined as compulsive drug use. If one is strongly involved with using a drug, getting an adequate supply of it, and having a strong tendency to resume use of it after stopping for a period, we would say that addiction is present. The notion of addiction, while not specifically mentioned in the diagnostic criteria, is reflected in criteria 3, 4, 5, and 6 under the DSM-IV-TR diagnosis for substance dependence. Criteria 3 through 6 all reflect the compulsive nature of drug use. Particularly, drug addiction changes a person's focus in life to being all about the drug. The person wants to use the drug, get more of the drug, avoid situations that don't involve the drug, can't stop using the drug, and can't even reduce the use of the drug for any length of time. This loss of control is what distinguishes addiction from a voluntary decision to take a drug. In the past, it was thought that people who were addicted to drugs simply lacked willpower and motivation to control their problem. However, brain imaging studies from drug-addicted individuals show distinct physical changes in areas of the brain that are critical to making good decisions and having control over behavior. It is thought that these changes alter the way the brain works, explaining why the behaviors of people who are addicted to drugs are especially compulsive and destructive (NIDA, 2010c). This is an important finding, particularly because compulsive and destructive behaviors are so frustrating for family members, friends, and society in general. Why is it that an addict just can't stop? Even jail time does not result in enough motivation for some addicts to get their problem under control.

What is the evidence that the brain is altered by the compulsive use of drugs? Throughout this book, we will discuss the multitude of scientific methodologies that have been used to address this question, ranging from animal models to human brain imaging. Scientists who study psychopharmacology have been finding that drugs can change everything from brain structure (brain anatomy) to how communication occurs in the brain. Moreover, it is becoming more evident that these changes are similar to what happens with other chronic medical conditions. For example, Figure 1-4 illustrates that addiction is similar to another chronic disease, heart disease. The image shows the decreased metabolism seen in the brain of a person who is experiencing symptoms of addiction. Note that the addict's brain looks similar to the decreased metabolism seen in the heart with a person with heart disease. In both cases, the changes in the underlying organ (brain or heart) can be long lasting and devastating if left untreated (NIDA, 2010c). In both cases, treatment is not optional. Something needs to be done.

In Chapter 3 of this book, we will examine more closely what happens when dependence on a drug occurs. The physiological changes can be dramatic. A few terms used in the DSM-IV-TR criteria will be elucidated here to explain better what happens in substance dependence. First, the DSM-IV-TR criteria for substance dependence include the terms tolerance and withdrawal. Tolerance refers to the need for increased amounts of the substance to achieve intoxication or the diminished effect with continued use of the same amount of the substance.

Withdrawal refers to the characteristic illness syndrome that occurs when the substance is not used. In many cases, tolerance and withdrawal occur together. When substance use has been consistent over time, the body gets used to the drug being present. Every time a person uses a psychoactive drug, there is a change in the balance of the chemicals (neurotransmitters) in the brain. If the drug is used regularly, this change in neurotransmitter activity is noticed by the body and the body adjusts to it. As mentioned earlier in this chapter, the neurotransmitter dopamine is elevated when many psychoactive drugs are regularly taken into the body. This increase in dopamine is what makes the user of a psychoactive drug feel euphoric upon taking the drug. Increasing dopamine on a regular basis does not go unnoticed by the body. Ultimately, the body will reset itself, so that dopamine levels are somewhat lower as compared to prior to drug

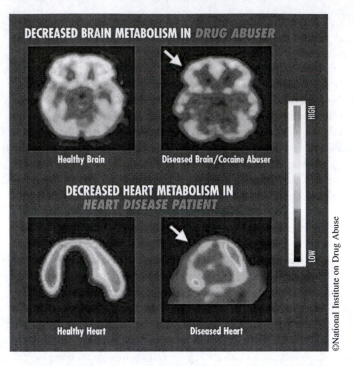

FIGURE 1-4
Addiction is like other diseases, such as heart disease. Both disrupt the normal, healthy functioning of the underlying organ (whether that is the brain or the heart) (NIDA, 2010c).

ingestion in anticipation of dopamine being increased so much with the drug. Once the body is making less dopamine, the user needs to take in more drug to raise dopamine levels to the point where the person feels high again. This need for more drug to get the same effect is tolerance. The same principle explains withdrawal. Regular drug use can result in lower resting dopamine levels since the body expects the drug to supply some dopamine. If no drug is taken, the person gets physically sick and experiences withdrawal. The exact withdrawal symptoms differ depending on which drug is being used. However, what is clear from studies of withdrawal symptoms is that the person feels physically ill. The symptoms can range from feeling irritable, depressed, and having a high fever to grand mal seizures. In some cases, withdrawal symptoms can be very nasty or even fatal, which is often why drug users avoid them by continuing to use. Moreover, withdrawal symptoms immediately dissipate upon resumption of drug use, which is how withdrawal symptoms contribute to maintenance of addiction.

Tolerance and withdrawal symptoms are two major impediments for users to discontinue their drug of choice, and both need to be addressed if an addict is going to be successful in a treatment program. Withdrawal symptoms have a psychological component since they often coincide with feelings of really wanting the drug. The term **craving** in this context refers to the strong or intense desire to use a drug. Craving is an emotional state that can be driven by the desire for the positive effect that the drug will bring or to avoid the negative effects associated with withdrawal. Craving is also called psychological dependence (Rinaldi, Steindler, Wilford, & Goodwin, 1988). For example, a person who wants to quit smoking cigarettes will find that one of the hardest parts of quitting is dealing with the intense feelings of craving for a cigarette. Craving also has a strong learned component, since environmental cues can trigger cravings. Just the sight of someone else smoking or looking at a cigarette package in a grocery store might be enough to trigger a craving state. Users also learn to associate various environmental stimuli with the drug. This learned aspect of craving is why psychopharmacologists use the terms *craving* and *psychological dependence* interchangeably.

One final note about the DSM-IV-TR criteria for substance abuse and substance dependence. If a person is using a drug, but appears not to fit the criteria for substance abuse or substance dependence, then the appropriate term to describe this is *substance use*. In other words, if use of the drug is not causing problems, including social problems, legal problems, or physiological changes, then substance use is the appropriate description. Recall from the epidemiological studies mentioned earlier that many people in the United States and worldwide use psychoactive drugs. In many cases, this use causes little concern. It is the subset of people who develop substance abuse or substance dependence who may require help.

Using the International Classification of Diseases (ICD-10)

In the United States, diagnoses for addiction typically rely on the use of the DSM-IV-TR system (APA, 2000). However, outside of the United States, diagnoses for substance-related problems more commonly use the International Classification of Diseases (ICD-10) diagnostic system. This classification system was developed by the World Health Organization for the diagnoses of all diseases, not just mental diseases (WHO, 1992). Chapter V of the ICD-10 includes the mental and behavioral disorders, with blocks F10–F19 including the disorders related to psychoactive substance use. The ICD-10 system is used by over 100 countries, and there are two main reasons for this widespread international use. First, the system is excellent, as it is clear, concise, accurate, and easy to use. Second, there is no fee for use, with everything about the classification system, including diagnostic criteria and training manuals, freely available on the Internet. It is notable that the use of the ICD-10 is similar to the use of the DSM-IV-TR in the classification of substance abuse and substance dependence. In both systems, symptoms like tolerance and withdrawal are used to assess dependence. As an illustration, Canada relies on the ICD-10 system and this does not appear to hinder the ability for U.S. and Canadian psychopharmacologists to communicate with one another. Moreover, the ICD-10's free availability facilitates use by lower-income countries. Overall, the DSM-IV-TR and ICD-10 as classification systems have considerable overlap and are similar in their approach to diagnosing addictive disorders.

More about the Science:

Moreno, M. A., Christakis, D. A., Egan, K. G., Brockman, L. N., & Becker, T. (2012). Associations between displayed alcohol references on Facebook and problem drinking among college students. *Archives of Pediatrics and Adolescent Medicine, 166*(2), 157–163.

Alcohol use is a major cause of morbidity and mortality (injury and death) among college students in the United States. However, most college students are never screened to identify if they are at risk, which is unfortunate given that brief interventions can often be very effective. Current data also suggests that up to 98% of college students maintain a profile on a social networking site like Facebook. Therefore, the researchers in this study wondered if Facebook profiles might be an avenue for identifying college students at greatest risk for problems due to drinking. In this study, publicly available Facebook profiles of students who were underage drinkers (age less than 21) were analyzed. Anything publicly accessible was viewed, including the wall, tagged pictures, and profile pictures. Profiles were categorized into one of three groups, which the researchers called Non-Displayers, Alcohol Displayers, and Intoxication/Problem Drinking Displayers. The Non-Displayers referred to profiles without any alcohol references. The Alcohol Displayers referred to profiles with one or more alcohol use references, but no references to intoxication or problem drinking. For example, a photo of the profile owner drinking from a beer bottle or a text reference to drinking alcohol at a party would be in the Alcohol Displayers category. Finally, the Intoxication/Problem Drinking (I/PD) Displayers referred to profiles that had one or more references to either intoxication or problem-drinking behaviors. For example, a text description of a profile owner "being wasted last night" or "getting drunk" would fit in this category. The researchers reported that 64% of profiles were Non-Displayers, 20% were Alcohol Displayers and 16% were I/PD Displayers. Once college students in each of these categories were identified, they were contacted to complete an alcohol screening instrument, the Alcohol Use Disorder Identification Test (AUDIT). An AUDIT score of 8 or higher indicates that the person is at risk for problem drinking and would be a suitable candidate for a brief intervention. In this study, 35% of participants scored 8 or higher on the AUDIT. The researchers found that profile owners who were classified as I/PD Displayers were more likely to score in the problem-drinking category on the AUDIT. The I/PD displayers were also more likely to report an alcohol-related injury in the past year. The researchers suggested that Facebook profiles may indicate substance use problems and this information could be used to identify at-risk students who may be appropriate for intervention.

More about the Science Thought Questions:

1. In this study, data was collected from Facebook profile owners whose information was publicly available. College students whose profiles were private were not included. Do you think that the exclusion of these individuals might have impacted the results?
2. In this study, many Facebook profile owners displayed references to alcohol use, even though they were under the age of 21. Approximately one-third of the students in this study scored as at-risk on the AUDIT. What does this indicate about alcohol use in young people?
3. It is often unclear when substance use becomes a problem requiring intervention. What do you think about the idea of Facebook profiles being used for this purpose?

Answers:

1. It is possible that exclusion of a large number of potential participants in this study might have impacted the results. For example, the choice to make a profile private may stem from individual's concerns about privacy or the individual's personality traits. These reasons may or may not be related to how much alcohol-related information is displayed on their Facebook profile. There is possible significant loss of information by not including these individuals.
2. This observation indicates that the legal ramifications of underage alcohol use are not very strictly enforced and there appears to be no social consequences regarding breaking these laws. Underage drinking appears normative in many cases for college students. In one-third of college students, their drinking may be putting them at risk for alcohol-related injuries or future alcohol problems, as measured by their AUDIT scores.
3. While there is no right answer to this question, it is clear that privacy concerns and ethics should be considered if future clinical efforts using Facebook or other social networking sites are to be successful. For example, contact from a trusted peer leader, such as a dormitory resident advisor who has received training in what to look for in a Facebook profile of at-risk students, may be far less intrusive than contact from a psychologist at the counseling center on campus.

Myth Busters: Hitting Rock Bottom

In the general public, it not uncommon to hear about someone "hitting rock bottom" as the ultimate point at which the person realized that it was time to get help for a substance abuse problem. Many times, a significant life event related to alcohol or drug use is part of this "bottom." These events can be anything from a car accident, a divorce, ending up in the hospital, a cancer diagnosis, or an intervention staged by family and friends. However, the idea of "hitting rock bottom" is a myth, in part because it is impossible to define what "bottom" really means, since such circumstances can differ among people and even over time for the same person. More importantly, the concept is problematic, since most psychopharmacologists and substance abuse experts would agree that it is foolish to wait for a problem to reach such a dramatic point before getting much needed help. Why wait for a drinking problem to result in a night in a jail before attempting to do something about the drinking? Why wait to lose custody of your children before you deal with your methamphetamine abuse? Moreover, many people who have struggled with addiction know that recovery can involve setbacks. Relapse is the norm, not the exception. Therefore, an addict can have many "bottoms," rendering the concept useless.

Throughout this book, we will examine the physical and psychological changes that accompany drug addiction. These changes become more and more pronounced over time and with greater use of the drug. Therefore, the earlier intervention occurs, the better. Think of addiction like skin cancer. Caught early, a small abnormal growth can easily be removed in a doctor's office and the problem is solved easily. Ignore the problem and the growth can cause significant health risks or even death. Why wait until dramatic treatment like chemotherapy and radiation is needed? Unfortunately, addiction is often not thought of as a medical condition since it involves behavior. Moreover, it is less clear when drug or alcohol use is abnormal because many people use psychoactive drugs recreationally and without concern. Alcohol consumption can be especially problematic in this regard because there is no clear demarcation point between social drinking and substance abuse and addiction. However, there are some ways to know when substance use is putting the person at risk for a problem.

Recall that in the Facebook study mentioned earlier in this chapter (Moreno, Christakis, Egan, Brockman, & Becker, 2012), the researchers asked participants to complete an alcohol screening instrument, the Alcohol Use Disorder Identification Test (AUDIT). In this study, an AUDIT score of 8 or higher was used to indicate that the person is at risk for problem drinking and would be a suitable candidate for a brief intervention. Using the skin cancer example again, an AUDIT score of 8 or higher is a bit like observing an abnormal looking growth on the skin. The growth may or may not be cancerous. However, it is prudent to investigate a little further and probably best not to ignore it, just in case it is a problem.

So what is the AUDIT? The AUDIT was developed by the World Health Organization (WHO) as a simple method to screen for excessive drinking and to assist in brief assessment (Barbor, Meyer, Mirin, McNamee, & Davies, 2001). Excessive drinking can cause illness and/or distress to the drinker and his or her family or friends. It is a major cause of relationship troubles, hospitalization, and even death. If a drinker seems to be engaging in hazardous or harmful drinking, the AUDIT can identify this and provide an avenue for discussion of how the harmful consequences of drinking may be avoided if drinking were reduced or even ceased. Since the test is freely available, the AUDIT is used all over the world by health care practitioners and other professionals. Table 1-2 displays some of the questions from the AUDIT.

In summary, the idea that a person has to hit "rock bottom" before getting treatment is not only a myth, but it is a dangerous myth. The concept leads people to think that dramatic problems are necessary before a person should seek help. Instead, think of behaviors with substances like any other medical problem. If symptoms arise that are somewhat disconcerting, perhaps a closer examination by an expert is warranted. Given that it is much easier to treat a substance abuse problem early on, a bit of overreaction is far better than ignoring the problem until it is extremely difficult to solve.

Table 1-2 AUDIT: The Alcohol Use Disorders Identification Test

The AUDIT consists of 10 questions. Here are some example questions. The respondent is asked to give an answer based on the consumption of alcoholic beverages during *this past year*.

How often do you have a drink containing alcohol?

How many drinks do you have on a typical day when drinking?

How often do you have six or more drinks on one occasion?

How often have you needed a first drink in the morning?

Adapted from Barbor, T. F., Higgins-Biddle, J. C., Saunders, J. B., & Monteiro, M. G. (2001). *AUDIT: The Alcohol Use Disorders Identification Test* (2nd ed.). WHO/MSD/MSB/01.6a. Geneva, Switzerland: World Health Organization, Department of Mental Health and Substance Dependence. The AUDIT is freely available on the Internet and can be retrieved from http://whqlibdoc.who.int/hq/2001/who_msd_msb_01.6a.pdf. See this document for the exact wording of the 10 questions, the response options, and scoring instructions.

A Brief History of U.S. Drug Laws

The use of psychoactive drugs can lead to harms and hazards for the user and those around the user. In recent times, society has relied on laws to regulate psychoactive drugs in an effort to mitigate these problems and to improve public health (Ryder, Walker, & Salmon, 2006). However, laws regarding restrictions or prohibitions of the manufacture, importation, sale, or possession of a psychoactive drug are a relatively recent development in the United States. A little over a hundred years ago, anyone could purchase the psychoactive drugs that are illicit today, including cocaine, heroin, marijuana, and opium. In the 1800s, all of these drugs were readily available for purchase in grocery stores or by mail order, such as through a Sears catalogue. In subsequent chapters in this book, we will examine the specific history of each drug, including the international elements to these histories. For now, it is probably fair to make the general observation that times have changed dramatically in how society views psychoactive drugs, with legislation reflecting these changes. In the past, there were no laws. Over time, the toll that addiction placed on society led to laws placing restrictions on psychoactive drugs. The toll on society from addiction was partly explained earlier in this chapter when the massive economic costs due to psychoactive drugs were elucidated. On a personal level, people find it devastating to see others become addicted to drugs, lose effectiveness, and ultimately cease functioning as productive members of society. Laws are an effort to circumvent such problems. In addition, drug use can lead to serious criminal problems that are also difficult for society to address. As such, drug laws are a means by which society has tried to reduce drug-related crime.

A few key changes in U.S. drug laws over the past century are mentioned below. At the end of this section, the current U.S. scheduling system, the basis of federal drug policy, will be introduced. It is important to note that actual drug use in the United States is not a crime under federal law, nor is it a crime to be a drug addict or alcoholic. However, there are very strict laws about manufacture, importation, sale, or possession, which makes it difficult for someone who is an addict, especially an addict of an illegal drug, to be in compliance with the law.

Well into the 1900s, any psychoactive drug was readily available in the United States, with drugs used for a variety of purposes. Psychoactive drugs were used for recreational reasons, similar to how they are used today. However, psychoactive drugs were also used for medicinal purposes, in part because medicine was less sophisticated than it is today and access to medicine was often limited. If you had a toothache, fatigue, pain, depression, or a variety of other concerns, psychoactive drugs were often used in an attempt to alleviate symptoms. In spite of their legality, drugs nevertheless caused harm during this time period. In addition, drugs have changed over time. While drug use has occurred for thousands of years, two factors distinguish drug use in the 19th, 20th, and 21st centuries from that of previous centuries (Ryder et al., 2006). First, chemical processing (legal and illegal) has made the action of a natural product more potent. Chewing the leaf taken off the coca plant is much less potent than snorting a line of cocaine (see Chapter 6 for more detail). Second, there is increasing confusion about how to deal with substance abuse and addiction, which adds to a significant public health problem. Let us examine how the United States has tried to deal with these issues, focusing on legislative efforts.

San Francisco Ordinance

The first local law regarding psychoactive drugs was passed due to citizen concern about drug-related crime. Late 1800s San Francisco featured opium dens. These opium dens were like a bar, but instead of serving patrons alcohol, opium was the psychoactive drug sold and typically smoked in these locations. Opium comes from the same poppy plant as morphine and heroin. These opium dens were frequented by Chinese men, who were in the United States as part of the labor force required for a rapid expansion in the West, including the California gold rush. Railways were being built and Chinese men were doing most of this work, although U.S. citizens were wary of these foreigners whose language, culture, and appearance was different from that with which they were familiar. Many of these Chinese laborers frequented these opium dens. In the San Francisco community, citizens became concerned about these establishments. They thought that these places were leading to drug addiction and a reduction in morals, since young people, who were not Chinese, would also visit opium dens, leading to addiction in some cases. This led to the 1875 **San Francisco Ordinance** banning opium dens. With this ordinance, only the opium den itself was banned, so that citizens could still smoke opium elsewhere. Other cities and states subsequently passed similar ordinances (Brecher, 1972, 1986).

Pure Food and Drug Act

At the federal level, the first legislation related to psychoactive drugs was the **Pure Food and Drug Act**, passed in 1906. This act not only attempted to help addicts, it also tried to stem the development of new addictions. Before the act was finally passed, nearly 200 legislative measures were proposed and rejected by Congress. However, this act was unique in that it was based on the idea that having a label on a product would prevent misrepresentation and fraud. If you look at the advertisements shown in Figures 1-5 and 1-6, you will notice that anything and everything was claimed on products containing psychoactive drugs at that time. Today, we take it for granted that we can look at the packaging of any over-the-counter medicine and see the list of ingredients. The same was not true in the past whereby a claim that a toothache medicine contained cocaine may or may not have been accurate. Even if a product did contain cocaine, which was never certain, the amount was usually unknown. The Pure Food and Drug Act emphasized that the truth about the contents must be stated on the label. The idea for incorporating labels on products came

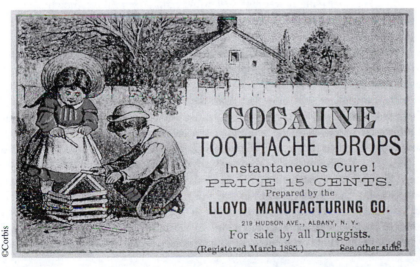

©Corbis

Figure 1-5
Advertisement for cocaine toothache drops registered March 1885.

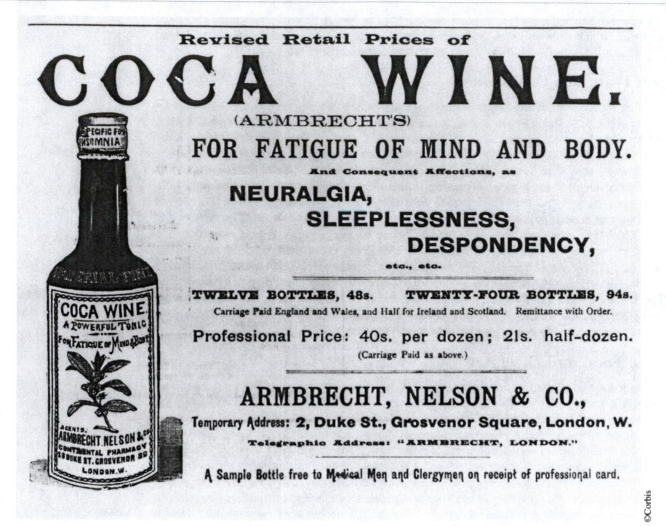

Figure 1-6
Advertisement for coca wine from the 1900 Sears Roebuck & Co. Catalog.

from the belief that addictions, particularly to opiates (heroin, opium, morphine), may have been occurring inadvertently. If people knew that certain products contained heroin, they might be cautious around such products, perhaps circumventing a possible addiction. Figure 1-7 features Harvey Washington Wiley who was instrumental in the passage of the Pure Food and Drug act and its effective administration. While the law emphasized opiates (opium, morphine, heroin), it also mandated the accurate labeling of products containing alcohol, cocaine, and marijuana. The act did not actually ban opiates or any other psychoactive drug. As a result, the legislation probably did not help many current addicts. However, the act did coincide with educational and political efforts to inform the public about the addictive potential of opiates, and it thus may have prevented the development of some new opiate addictions (Brecher, 1972, 1986). As a historical side note, Harvey Washington Wiley served as a staunch advocate for developing U.S. standards for truth in labeling. He was involved in the 1911 landmark legal action brought against the Coca-Cola company arguing that it was illegal to use the name Coca-Cola on the soft drink beverage since the product no longer contained cocaine. In addition, he contended that it was illegal for the product to contain caffeine as a drug additive. While not successful with this legal action, his work probably set the stage for greater consumer protection that we benefit from today (Pendergrast, 2000).

©B.M. Clinedinst/Corbis

Figure 1-7
Harvey Washington Wiley was instrumental in the passage of the Pure Food and Drug act in 1906 and its effective administration.

Harrison Narcotics Tax Act

Less than a decade after the Pure Food and Drug Act was passed, another piece of major legislation was introduced. The **Harrison Narcotics Tax Act** was passed by Congress and signed into law in 1914. This act strictly regulated the legal supply of certain psychoactive drugs, including opiates. Note that the term **narcotic** can be confusing when it is used differently in different contexts. Today, the term *narcotic* often refers to a psychoactive drug that induces stupor, coma, or insensibility to pain (WHO, 2012), which typically means a narcotic is often an opiate drug (also referred to as narcotic analgesics). Examples of opiates include heroin, opium, and morphine, which are all central nervous system depressants. However, the term *narcotic* is also used in common parlance and in legal settings more imprecisely to mean illicit drugs, irrespective of their pharmacology. In 1914, it was argued that narcotics (particularly opiates, but not exclusively so) could be harmful and lead to addiction. Thus, more restrictions were placed on the prescription and supply of opiates. With the passage of the Harrison Narcotics Tax Act, opiates became strictly regulated but not prohibited. To market or prescribe these drugs required a license. Thus a physician could prescribe an opiate if medically warranted, including prescribing of an opiate for an addict. Note that there were subsequently more than 50 modifications to the act in the following 50 years, with each change leading to a tougher law. It should also be noted that cocaine was included as a narcotic in this act, even though cocaine as a drug is quite dissimilar from opiates in pharmacology, effects on the user, and propensity to lead to addiction (Brecher, 1972, 1986).

Alcohol Prohibition

A mere 6 years after the passage of the Harrison Narcotic Tax Act, a dramatic change occurred in the United States. In 1920, Congress passed the Eighteenth Amendment to the Constitution, initiating the era of **Alcohol Prohibition**. This amendment very specifically prohibited the production, sale, transportation, and importation of alcohol in any part of the United States (Lender & Martin, 1982). This represented a dramatic shift in legislation of psychoactive drugs, since up until this time, only regulation was in place, via the Harrison Narcotics Tax Act. The passage of the Eighteenth Amendment was considered a victory by various facets of society, including the Women's Christian Temperance Union and the Anti-Saloon League. These groups had argued that alcohol was destructive and evil. Today, it is easy to be critical of this time period thinking that the Prohibition approach to alcohol was short-sighted. However, Prohibition should be considered in context of the alcohol consumption practices at that time, since U.S. alcohol consumption had become increasingly out of control.

Before Prohibition, per capita consumption of alcohol was very high. It is estimated that in 1790, U.S. adults drank approximately 6 gallons of alcohol per capita annually. By 1830, this number had risen to 7 gallons. In 1830, these numbers mean that a typical adult was consuming approximately 5 standard drinks per day (Mendelson & Mello, 1985). Moreover, women drank little at that time (though they represented half the population, of course). Thus if a household contained a husband and wife, average daily consumption might have been closer to 0 drinks per day for the wife and closer to 10 drinks per day for the husband.

This extreme alcohol use was taking its toll on society. Drinkers, mainly men, often gathered in saloons (bars), places known for immoral behavior of various sorts. The downing of whiskey often coincided with an increase in aggressive behavior. Prostitution and crime were prevalent. It is not surprising that there was growing frustration with these circumstances. Women who had no access to employment, ownership of property, or birth control were often also at the mercy of an alcoholic husband unable to support her and their children. Under these conditions, the eventual passage of the Eighteenth Amendment and the Prohibition Era almost seem inevitable, rather than an oddity.

As you are no doubt aware, Prohibition was ultimately not successful. With limited access to alcohol via legal means, alcohol distribution was taken over by criminal groups. We see the remnants of this era's criminal activities today. In the American South during Prohibition, moonshine runners would attempt to stay ahead of the law using the new invention, the automobile, to clandestinely distribute their whiskey. These illegal distributors would lead police on high-speed chases through curvy mountain roads in the middle of the night. The best drivers with souped-up cars were needed for this job, or else lengthy jail time or a deadly crash awaited. To perfect needed skills, drivers would practice on Sunday afternoons in friendly competitions, from which NASCAR was eventually born (Lendler, 2005).

The Eighteenth Amendment was repealed 13 years later by the Twenty-first Amendment, thus ending the Prohibition Era. Due to a rise in criminal activity and a lack of sufficient public support to continue Prohibition, this experiment in drug control came to an end. However, there were benefits observed from the Prohibition Era. First, the rate of drinking decreased dramatically during Prohibition, with estimates of consumption being one-third or one-half lower than prior to Prohibition. Second, alcohol-related deaths from complications of alcoholism, such as liver cirrhosis, were also substantially decreased (Aaron & Musto, 1981). All in all, the goals of Prohibition enthusiasts were somewhat achieved, since public health did improve. Moreover, the Prohibition Era also had lasting effects. Per capita alcohol consumption levels have never returned to those prevalent in the pre-Prohibition Era.

Legislation after Prohibition

With the experiment in Prohibition over, the trend toward increasing guidelines and penalties for possession and sale of psychoactive drugs continued. Legislative action in 1930 established the Federal Bureau of Narcotics (which is now called the Drug Enforcement Administration). Initially, the work of the Federal Bureau of Narcotics was to eradicate marijuana use (which had risen during Prohibition with alcohol not readily available). While marijuana was not outright banned, the **Marijuana Tax Act** of 1937 was federal legislation that required authorized

©SZ Photo/Scherl/The Image Works

Figure 1-8
Prohibition Era photo

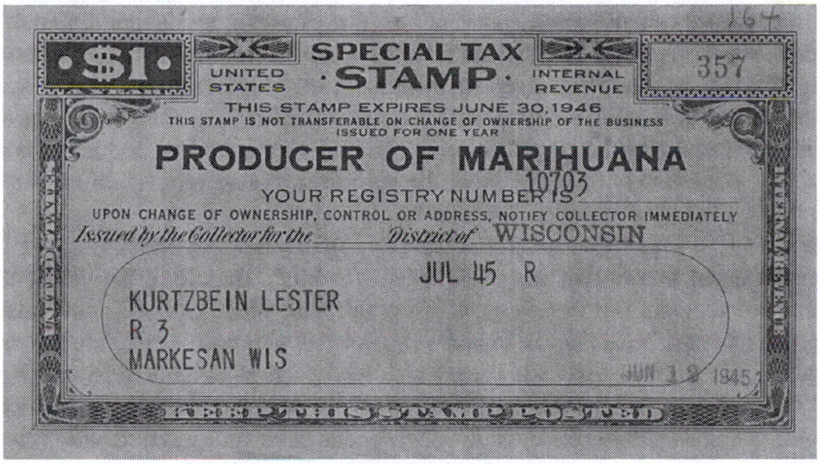

©U.S. Government

Figure 1-9
The Marijuana Tax Act of 1937 imposed an annual occupational tax, with payment reflected by a special tax stamp, on those who were authorized producers, manufacturers, importers, or dispensers of marijuana.

producers, manufacturers, importers, and dispensers of marijuana to pay an annual license fee. Only the nonmedical possession or sale of marijuana was illegal (Brecher, 1972). Figure 1-9 illustrates one of the special tax stamps used around this time. It should be mentioned that some medical uses of marijuana were accepted around this time. However, from 1937 forward, legislation regarding marijuana use grew more restrictive with increasing penalties.

From 1940 to 1970, additional federal legislation regarding psychoactive drugs was passed, which increased the severity of penalties for drug law infractions. There was increased attention to all psychoactive drugs. For example, the Drug Abuse Control Amendment of 1965 included regulation of stimulants, depressants, and hallucinogenic substances. There was also attention to treatment of substance abuse with two pieces of federal legislation. The Community Mental Health Centers Act of 1963 provided for federal funding for community-based treatment programs for addicts, as part of the deinstitutionalization movement occurring for all mental disorders. Furthermore, the Narcotic Addicts Rehabilitation Act of 1966 allowed federal courts and the criminal justice system to compel drug addicts to attend treatment.

Current U.S. Scheduling System

In 1970, the **Controlled Substances Act** (CSA) was signed into law by President Nixon. The CSA is the current U.S. federal drug policy regulating the manufacture, importation, possession, use, and distribution of certain substances. In this act, drugs are classified according to their medical use, their potential abuse, and their likelihood for producing dependence. Most psychoactive drugs have been placed in one of the five schedules, which are categories, in this act. It is noteworthy that alcohol, nicotine, and caffeine are not included in the schedules. Table 1-3 lists the five schedules together with their description, along with some example drugs. The five schedules are arranged from drugs with the most potential for abuse and no medical use (in Schedule I) to drugs with low potential for abuse and a currently accepted medical use (in Schedule V). Schedule I is the only category containing drugs with no accepted medical use in treatment in the United States.

While the statute passed by Congress created the initial listing, two federal agencies—the Drug Enforcement Administration and the Food and Drug Administration—determine which substances are added to or removed from the various schedules. Congress has additionally sometimes scheduled other substances through legislation. The CSA contains provisions for adding or rescheduling drugs as needed. Methylphenidate (Ritalin), used to treat attention deficit hyperactivity disorder, was originally classified as a Schedule III drug, but was moved to Schedule II in the 1970s. The scheduling system is also controversial. For example, marijuana is found in Schedule I, whereas Marinol (synthetic THC, which is the psychoactive chemical in marijuana) is found in Schedule III (since Marinol has accepted medical uses). We will discuss the current scientific evidence regarding the possible medical uses for marijuana and similar drugs in Chapter 10. Marijuana is one example where the classification scheme can be contentious and individuals from sectors of society will strongly disagree about the appropriate placement of drugs within various categories (Nutt, King, Saulsbury, & Blakemore, 2007).

Why put various drugs in these five schedules? This approach acknowledges that not all psychoactive drugs are equal in terms of harm and abuse potential. Therefore, the use of the schedules allows law enforcement and the courts to assess different penalties for criminal manufacture or distribution of drugs, based on the concerns associated with each drug. Penalties are greatest for Schedule I and II drugs (excluding marijuana for which penalties are slightly less severe). Penalties increase with the quantity of drug involved and the number of previous offenses. For example, a first conviction for trafficking 500 grams of cocaine mixture would carry a prison sentence not less than 5 years (up to 40 years) and a fine of up to $2 million. If there was a death or serious injury associated with the drug trafficking, the sentence is not less than 20 years. Penalties would be higher if previous offenses had occurred. While the penalties for trafficking Schedules III, IV, and V drugs are lower, the differences are only a matter of degree. For example, a first conviction for trafficking any amount of a Schedule III drug, such as anabolic steroids, is up to 5 years in prison and a $250,000 fine.

Since the passage of the CSA, additional federal legislation has been passed to control use of psychoactive drugs. In 1986, Congress passed the Controlled Substances Analogue Enforcement Act. This legislation allowed for the immediate classification of a substance as a controlled substance. This act was in response to the production of so-called designer drugs that were becoming increasingly available in the 1980s. Designer drugs were structurally similar but not identical to an illegal drug. Before this act, each time a slight change was made to the chemical

Table 1-3   Schedules of Controlled Substances and Examples of Scheduled Drugs.

Schedule	Description	Examples
I	The drug or other substance has a high potential for abuse. It has no currently accepted medical use in treatment in the United States. There is a lack of accepted safety for use of the drug or other substance under medical supervision.	Heroin Ecstasy LSD Psilocybin Mescaline Peyote Ibogaine Marijuana Synthetic marijuana (K2, Spice) Cathinone (Khat) Synthetic stimulants (bath salts) Synthetic hallucinogens
II	The drug or other substance has a high potential for abuse. It has a currently accepted medical use in treatment in the United States or a currently accepted medical use with severe restrictions. Abuse of the drug or other substances may lead to severe psychological or physical dependence.	Opium Morphine Codeine Oxycodone Cocaine Amphetamine Methamphetamine Methylphenidate PCP Methadone
III	The drug or other substance has a potential for abuse less than the drugs or other substances in Schedules I and II. It has a currently accepted medical use in treatment in the United States. Abuse of the drug or other substance may lead to moderate or low physical dependence or high psychological dependence.	Tylenol with codeine Marinol Vicodan Ketamine Anabolic steroids Rohypnol
IV	The drug or other substance has a low potential for abuse relative to the drugs or other substances in Schedule III. It has a currently accepted medical use in treatment in the United States. Abuse of the drug or other substance may lead to limited physical dependence or psychological dependence relative to the drugs or other substances in Schedule III.	Valium Ativan Librium Xanax Ambien
V	The drug or other substance has a low potential for abuse relative to the drugs or other substances in Schedule IV. It has a currently accepted medical use in treatment in the United States. Abuse of the drug or other substance may lead to limited physical dependence or psychological dependence relative to the drugs or other substances in Schedule IV.	Robitussin A-C

Source: Schedules of Controlled Substances, U.S. Department of Justice, Drug Enforcement Administration, Office of Diversion Control http://www.deadiversion.usdoj.gov/schedules/orangebook/e_cs_sched.pdf

structure of a drug, law enforcement officials would need to go through the time-consuming process required to have it certified as a controlled substance. After this legislative change, drug enforcement addressed a new drug as soon as it appeared.

Another change occurred in 1996 with the **Comprehensive Methamphetamine Control Act**. Methamphetamine is a highly addictive drug that can be made using a variety of household chemicals and pseudoephedrine (an ingredient found in cold medications). This act aimed to prevent the illegal manufacture and use of methamphetamine. Penalties for trafficking and manufacturing methamphetamine were also increased. Strong controls on bulk pseudoephedrine were implemented. To further combat the escalation in production and use of methamphetamine, the **Combat Methamphetamine Epidemic Act** was passed in 2006. This act moved all pseudoephedrine products behind the counter in pharmacies and required that purchases be tracked. Methamphetamine will be covered in Chapter 7.

More recently, a smoking-related change occurred in 2009 with the passage of the **Family Smoking Prevention and Tobacco Control Act**. This legislation authorized the Food and Drug Administration (FDA) to regulate tobacco products, including the manufacture, marketing, and sale of these products. This act has a strong focus on stopping young people from smoking. Candy-flavored cigarettes were banned following the passage of this act, as was marketing cigarettes as light, mild, or low-tar. More about this act will be discussed in Chapter 5.

The most recent piece of legislation is the **Synthetic Drug Abuse Prevention Act**, which was signed into law by President Obama in 2012. This legislation is designed to address the threat of synthetic drugs. In this legislation, synthetic compounds are banned, which includes synthetic stimulants (which on the street are called Bath Salts), marijuana (K2 and Spice), and synthetic hallucinogens. All of these are now placed under Schedule I of the Controlled Substances Act.

Finally, you may have heard that we are in a "war on drugs" or that there is a "zero-tolerance" approach to drug users in the United States. This "war on drugs" comes from the efforts of presidential administrations, starting in the 1980s and continuing today. These efforts include catching smugglers and sellers, both in United States and overseas. In addition, a zero-tolerance approach to drug users, including casual users, has also been a hallmark of our current era. Like any war, these efforts are costly. It is estimated that the U.S. government spends a billion dollars a year on antidrug operations overseas alone. Most of this money is allocated to catching drug smugglers trying to bring illegal drugs into the United States. Interestingly, the two psychoactive drugs associated with the most deaths in this country, alcohol and tobacco, are not part of the war on drugs.

In addition to expense, international relations can be complicated by international efforts to combat drugs. For example, the U.S. presence in Afghanistan was tied to the terrorist attacks of 9/11. Afghanistan is a poor barren country where poppy cultivation (which is the plant used to make opium, morphine, and heroin) remains one of the few lucrative agricultural products. An important battle in the U.S.-led war on terrorism includes combating a heroin trade supporting key terrorist groups, with Afghanistan the principal source of most of the world's opium (the source for eventual purified heroin). When Afghan President Hamid Karzai took office in 2002, he stated that "The fight against drugs is actually the fight for Afghanistan." Unfortunately, Afghanistan is losing this fight. Since its liberation from Taliban rule in 2001, Afghanistan's opium production has gone from 640 tons to 8,200 tons in 2007. A ton of heroin costs $67 million in Europe and closer to $900 million in New York city, according to Drug Enforcement Administration figures (Ehrenfeld, 2009). It has been estimated that $6 billion have been spent by the United States in the past decade on its losing efforts to combat poppies that help finance the insurgency and fuel corruption in this country (Rubin & Rosenberg, 2012). The war on drugs and the war on terrorism are intertwined. This is just one example of how devising effective drug policy is complicated by multiple forces.

As we conclude this first chapter on the introduction to psychopharmacology, it is hopefully becoming clear that there is still much to learn. I hope you share my enthusiasm for this incredibly fascinating field of study. From what happens to one individual who tries a psychoactive drug to broad international relations, substance use, abuse, and addiction permeate our society at all levels. Whether in pursuit of feeling pleasure, feeling better, or doing better, or just out of curiosity, humans seem unable to ignore the appeal of psychoactive drugs. For some, little harm occurs when psychoactive drugs are used. For others, the consequences are serious and devastating. In future chapters, we will explore the groundbreaking discoveries that are helping us understand what psychoactive drugs do to our bodies and brains. Moreover, we are making great strides in understanding how to best treat addiction and prevent it from occurring in the first place. Since psychopharmacology is a relatively new discipline, I hope that some of you reading this book will be enthused enough with the topic to consider a future career that involves psychopharmacology in some capacity. Whatever your career choices, knowledge about this topic will make you a better informed citizen as you develop your scientific literacy and critical thinking skills.

Focus on Careers: Substance Abuse Counselors

Abuse and addiction to alcohol and other drugs is a widespread problem in our society. When drug use becomes harmful, problems emerge that range from mildly disconcerting to devastating. Substance abuse counselors spend their careers helping people who have developed problems with psychoactive drugs. These professionals help clients manage and resolve their substance abuse problems using various approaches. Also called chemical dependency counselors, substance abuse counselors have in-depth knowledge about addiction and the tools that can facilitate recovery. Individuals who desire a career in substance abuse counseling should exhibit good professional judgment, be empathetic, be able to establish rapport with most clients, and be able to confront problems in a helpful manner in order to motivate clients to change. Enrollment in a bachelor's or master's degree in an addiction counseling program will provide the training required to enter this field. In addition to required coursework, supervised experience in a clinical setting and passing a standardized exam is a requirement for certification/licensure in most states. This career can be highly rewarding for those individuals who are motivated by a desire to help others. Moreover, this career path has excellent job prospects. The demand for substance abuse counselors is expected to grow by about one-third within 10 years.

Websites to explore:

Association for Addiction Professionals (NAADAC)
www.naadac.org
Many colleges and universities have bachelor's or graduate degree programs in substance abuse counseling (this one is at the University of Cincinnati)
www.cech.edu/substance_abuse_counseling

QUICK QUIZ 1-2

1. Craving is also called
   a. Physiological dependence
   b. Psychological dependence
   c. Substance abuse
   d. Substance dependence

2. In the United States, the _____ is typically used to diagnose substance-related problems, while the _____ is typically used in other countries for the same purpose.
   a. ICD-10, DSM-IV-TR
   b. DSM-IV-TR, DMS-IV

c. DSM-IV-TR, ICD-10
d. ICD-9, ICD-10

3. What is the AUDIT?
   a. An alcohol screening instrument
   b. A diagnosis for substance abuse
   c. A piece of federal legislation related to drugs
   d. None of the above

4. Which piece of federal legislation serves as the current U.S. federal drug policy?

a. The Harrison Narcotics Tax Act

b. The Marijuana Tax Act

c. The Pure Food and Drug Act

d. The Controlled Substances Act

5. Sam has been drinking more and more alcohol over time. A few months ago, he would drink approximately 4 beers per day. Now he drinks about 10 beers per day. This is an example of

a. Tolerance

b. Withdrawal

c. Craving

d. Sensitization

6. Why would having a diagnosis of substance abuse or substance dependence be helpful?

7. What does compulsive drug use refer to?

8. Explain why the notion of hitting rock bottom is a myth.

ANSWERS TO QUICK QUIZ 1-2:

1. b – psychological dependence

2. c – DSM-IV-TR, ICD-10

3. a – an alcohol screening instrument

4. d – The Controlled Substances Act

5. a – tolerance

6. It is helpful to have a diagnosis (a label) so that scientists and practitioners can communicate easily with one another, since all would be familiar with the types of symptoms that are associated with a particular diagnosis.

7. Compulsive drug use occurs when an individual is strongly involved with using a drug, getting an adequate supply of a drug, and having a strong tendency to relapse after a period of abstinence.

8. With addiction, the earlier that intervention occurs, the better. There is no need to wait until symptoms have become very serious before help can be given. The analogous situation is seeing an unusual mole on your skin. It is far better to get this checked by a professional (when treatment could be relatively easy) rather than wait until full-blown cancer is a diagnosis (when the problem could even be fatal). Overreacting is a far better course of action than waiting until the situation has led to a significant life event (the so-called rock bottom) like an arrest or a hospital visit.

CHAPTER SUMMARY

Psychopharmacology is the scientific study of the effects of drugs on behavior. Humans have used psychoactive drugs for thousands of years to alter mood, cognition, and behavior. They have been motivated initially to try drugs to make them feel good, feel better, do better, for curiosity or social influences. Both pharmacological and nonpharmacological factors contribute to a drug experience. The appeal of psychoactive drug use is widespread, as revealed by epidemiological data. Moreover, this widespread use leads to significant costs to society. In the United States alone, abuse and addiction to alcohol, nicotine, and illegal substances costs Americans half a trillion dollars a year, when the combined medical, economic, criminal, and social impacts are considered. Diagnosis of substance abuse and substance dependence allows clinicians and scientists to identify those individuals in need of treatment. Diagnosis also improves the science of psychopharmacology as it helps professionals communicate with one another about the same problem or set of symptoms. Addiction can lead to physiological and psychological changes that cause the behaviors of people who are addicted to drugs to seem compulsive and destructive. Tolerance and withdrawal are hallmark features of substance dependence. Fortunately, the notion that a person must hit "rock-bottom" before getting help for an addiction is a myth. Finally, legislation is one way that society has tried to mitigate problems with psychoactive drug use and to improve public health.

DRUGS AND THE BRAIN

Introduction

Bath salts, also called designer cathinones, are making the news lately in part because these psychoactive drugs seem to have been a factor in some really heinous crimes. These synthetic stimulants are marketed as bath salts, but as drugs they have no connection to a relaxing bubble bath. Instead, these drugs are typically sniffed or snorted, with similar reported effects to amphetamines, cocaine, Khat, LSD, and MDMA. For this reason, the Drug Enforcement Administration (DEA) placed a temporary ban on anything labeled as "bath salts," following rapid escalation in poison center reports and crimes involving these drugs (DEA, 2012a). Shortly thereafter, on July 10, 2012, President Obama signed legislation that banned all synthetic compounds, including bath salts, by placing them under Schedule I of the Controlled Substances Act. One particularly bizarre crime where bath salts may have played a role occurred in Miami, Florida, where one naked man chewed off another's face. Rudy Eugene, the attacker, was high on bath salts, and he only stopped attacking Ronald Poppo, the victim, after a police officer shot Eugene several times, eventually killing him (Brecher, 2012; CNN, 2012). Several similar bizarre crimes occurred around the same time, resulting in "Zombie Apocalypse" rising to the top of Google trends for Internet searches. While the scientific understanding of the effects of bath salts is incomplete, since the drug has only been available since the year 2010, it's clear that zombies play no role in the action of the drug. Bath salts appear to make users delirious, delusional, have intense hallucinations, and feel very paranoid. In many cases, the users take off all of their clothes because body temperature rises significantly. When violence erupts, users are not in touch with reality, a significant problem for an unsuspecting public. At the time of the attack, the outlook for Poppo was grim, given that 80% of his face was missing. Fortunately, he survived. Like his attacker, the victim appeared to be someone having a history of psychoactive drug addiction. Five decades earlier, he had been a bright high school student with an above-average IQ of 129. By the time of the attack, the 65-year-old Poppo had spent his adult life as a homeless alcoholic. His family reported that they hadn't heard from him in decades, until he became the victim of the bizarre attack making national news.

Psychoactive drugs alter brain activity and in some cases even change the structure of the brain. Understanding behavioral change from drug use first requires that we understand how the brain typically functions. Later, we consider how brain functioning is altered with drug usage. In this chapter, we will review the brain and how it functions, which will set the stage for our later examination of changes when a psychoactive drug is introduced. Importantly, contemporary evidence increasingly suggests that actual brain structure may be altered with addiction (NIDA, 2010c). So keep in mind that as we learn how neurons communicate and how the brain reward pathways function, all of this material sets the stage for understanding the changes associated with psychoactive drug use. While drug use can be merely recreational and not harmful to oneself or others, there can also be extreme outcomes at the other end of the spectrum. Behaviors, thoughts, and emotions all arise from brain activity. No matter how bizarre, behavior is a result of activity in the nervous system. For this reason, a strong foundation of knowledge regarding the nervous system is needed to understand behavioral impacts of psychoactive drugs.

LEARNING OBJECTIVES

Learning objectives can help organize your studying. Before we begin this chapter on Drugs and the Brain, keep in mind that by the end of this chapter, you should be able to . . .

1. Define various terms, such as neuron, neurotransmitter, synapse, and mesolimbic dopaminergic pathway.
2. Explain how neurons communicate and how a psychoactive drug could alter that communication.
3. Describe the major neurotransmitters involved in neural communication.
4. Describe the major divisions of the nervous system.
5. Describe the major anatomical brain structures found in the hindbrain, midbrain, and forebrain.
6. Apply your knowledge regarding which brain imaging technique could be applied to examine various questions about psychoactive drugs.
7. Evaluate the evidence that the brain can be permanently altered when psychoactive drugs are used to the point that addiction is evident.

Neurons

To better understand how drugs affect the brain, we are going to start small, at the level of cells. There are many types of cells in our body, including skin cells, muscle cells, and blood cells, among others. **Neurons** are the unique cell type that receives and transmits information. The nervous system is comprised of networks of neurons communicating back and forth to different structures within the brain, the spinal cord, and the peripheral nervous system. These nerve networks underlie everything that we feel, think, and do (NIDA, 2010c). Neuronal communication is electrochemical, which will be further explained below. We should first note that we have lots of neurons. In fact, it has been estimated that the human nervous system is made up of nearly 100 billion neurons. Figure 2-1 illustrates an idealized version of a neuron. An actual neuron may look very different depending on function and location in the nervous system. However, all neurons have here similar structures. The first is the **cell body**, within which is found the nucleus. The nucleus contains the genetic material for the neuron and other processes involved in metabolic activities. The cell body can be thought of as the command center for the cell. The second part of a neuron is the branchlike structures that extend from the cell, called **dendrites**. Dendrites tend to look like branches on a tree; appropriately the word *dendrite* is derived from the Greek word for tree. The dendrites have multiple receptor sites, which are involved in receiving

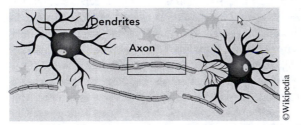

FIGURE 2-1
There are three basic parts of a neuron, including the cell body, dendrites, and axon. The figure illustrates how the message is being sent along the axon on to the next cell (from left to right).

information in neural transmissions. Later in this chapter, we will discuss how psychoactive drugs are going to bind to these receptor sites on dendrites, ultimately altering the activity of a neuron. The third part of the neuron is the **axon**, which is a long ropelike extension coming out of the cell body. While the axon looks long compared to the dendrites in the schematic shown in Figure 2-1, most axons are much longer than indicated in the picture. In fact, axons can be thousands of times longer than the diameter of the cell body. The role of the axon is to send a message on to the next cell (Julien, 2005).

To assist an axon in efficiently sending a message, particularly over long distances, many axons are covered by a layer of fatty tissue called **myelin**. A special type of cell, the glial cell, wraps itself around the axon to make up myelin. Glial cells play an important role in the nervous system's structural and metabolic functions, but glial cells are not involved in communication. Thus, glial cells are a different type of cell than neurons. Myelin acts as insulation for the axon, just like insulating wire helps conduct electricity. In fact, both axons and wires are used to conduct electrical signals as we will see below.

The presence of myelin gives the brain its unique appearance. Figure 2-2 includes two images: one of an entire human brain and the second of a human brain that has been dissected. While individual neurons are too small to see with the naked eye, what you can see is that the outside of

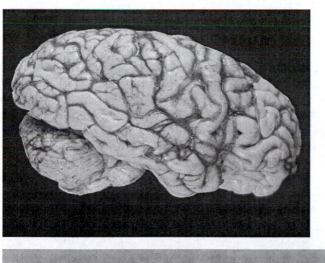

©Garry Watson/Science Source

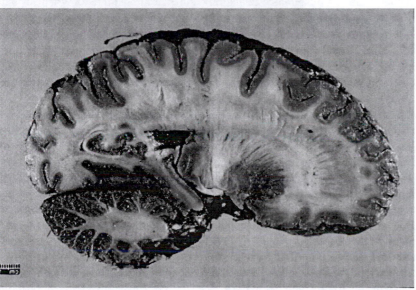

©Dr. Colin Chumbley/Science Photo Library/Photo Researchers, Inc.

FIGURE 2-2

A human brain and a human brain dissected in half (sagittal view).

the brain has a darker appearance. When dissected, the brain reveals darker and lighter regions, or gray and white matter, respectively. The white matter is composed of myelinated axons. The gray matter does not contain these myelinated axons, which results in this part of the brain's darker appearance.

Axons are a bit like wires. When a neuron transmits an electrical message, information is gathered by the dendrites and/or cell body and sent along the axon in the form of an electrical signal. This electrical signal is called an **action potential**. The action potential is produced by the flow of charged particles, called ions, through channels in the membrane that cover the axon. If a neuron is at rest (not sending a message), positively charged sodium ions are concentrated outside the axon membrane, with negatively charged chloride ions mainly inside the axon. Thus, the inside of the axon is negative in charge relative to the outside. When the neuron is ready to send a message, ion channels open. Positive sodium ions rush into the axon, which leads to depolarization of the axon. The rapid depolarization produces a change of approximately 110 millivolts. This action potential (rapid depolarization) travels along the axon rapidly and at full strength. When I say that the action potential can move fast, it really is fast! Depending on the type of axon, a speed of 100 meters per second is possible. Myelinated axons can conduct an action potential much faster than unmyelinated axons. After the neuron has fired, sodium ions are pumped out of the axon, channels close, and the neuron returns to its resting state (Julien, 2005).

The Synapse and Neurotransmitters

Thus far, we have covered the electrical part (the action potential) of electrochemical neural communication. Note that the electrical part of communication is restricted to what is occurring within an individual neuron. Beyond simple electrical communication with an individual neuron, neurons also communicate with one another via chemicals. This chemical communication is the really interesting part of neural communication, at least where psychoactive drugs are concerned. If you were looking through an electron microscope where two neurons appear to touch, you would actually see that there is space where the end of an axon and another neuron's dendrite or cell body neurons connect. This little space is called the **synapse** (or synaptic gap or synaptic cleft). When an action potential reaches the end of the axon (the axon terminal), chemicals are released. These chemicals, called **neurotransmitters**, are released into the synapse where they diffuse across space and ultimately trigger activity in the next neuron. Figure 2-3 shows the **vesicles**, which look like tiny bubbles containing the neurotransmitters. When an action potential arrives at the axon terminal, neurotransmitters are released into the synapse. So the communication of neurons is electrical along the axon and then chemical at the synapse (Valenstein, 2005). Thus, neural communication is described as electrochemical. For a little bit more terminology, the neuron releasing the neurotransmitters is sometimes called the presynaptic neuron and the neuron receiving the neurotransmitters is sometimes called the postsynaptic neuron (Julien, 2005).

Neurotransmitters released into the synapse travel across the synapse via diffusion, the process whereby particles randomly distribute in a space. For example, imagine that you have a cup of milk and chocolate powder to make a glass of chocolate milk. If you place a spoonful of chocolate powder into the milk, the powder and milk will start mixing together. If you left the glass alone for a long enough time, the liquid will eventually become chocolate milk as the particles of chocolate diffuse to locations where no chocolate was previously located. A similar process occurs in the synapse. When a presynaptic neuron releases neurotransmitters, there are many neurotransmitters on the presynaptic side and few on the postsynaptic side. Chemicals thus move toward the postsynaptic side to fill the space.

What happens when the neurotransmitters reach the postsynaptic neuron? Scattered along the dendrites and cell body of the postsynaptic neuron are **receptor sites**. These receptor sites are structures into which the neurotransmitters can fit. A receptor and neurotransmitter can be thought

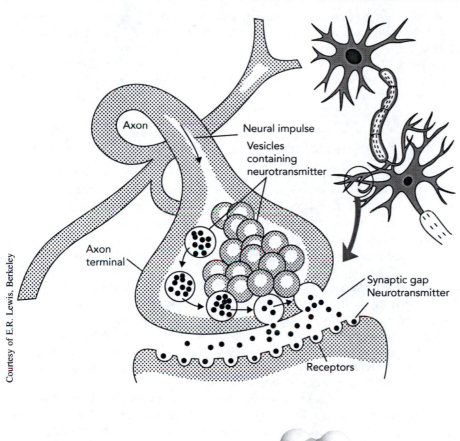

FIGURE 2-3
Neurotransmitters are released into the synapse.

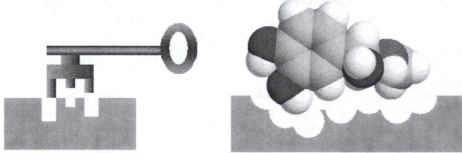

FIGURE 2-4
A neurotransmitter fits into a receptor just like a key fits into a lock.

of as a lock and a key. For the postsynaptic neuron to fire, the receptor must be unlocked with the correct key. In other words, only the correct neurotransmitter molecule can fit into a specific receptor site. Figure 2-4 illustrates how a neurotransmitter fits into a receptor just like a key fits into a lock. If a neurotransmitter fits into a receptor, the two are briefly attached; this process is called binding. Binding makes the postsynaptic neuron more or less likely to fire (produce an action potential). In **excitatory receptors**, a binding neurotransmitter is likely to result in an action potential. **Inhibitory receptors** are ones where a binding neurotransmitter is less likely to result in an action potential.

After binding, the neurotransmitter is released from the postsynaptic receptor site. The neurotransmitter may then be recycled (a process called **reuptake**), which means that the neurotransmitter returns to the presynaptic neuron via diffusion to be used again. It is also possible that the neurotransmitter is deactivated by enzymes, which break down the neurotransmitter into an inactive form (a process called **enzyme breakdown**). Note that enzymes not only are used to break down neurotransmitters, but they are also used to build neurotransmitters as well.

Since the synapse is the space into which neurotransmitters are being released, the synapse is also where psychoactive drugs have greatest effect. If a psychoactive drug is both similar to a naturally occurring neurotransmitter and also present in the synapse, the psychoactive drug could substitute for a naturally occurring neurotransmitter. Drugs can influence any of the steps involved in synaptic transmission. We will examine these possibilities after we first discuss the major types of neurotransmitters used by the brain.

Types of Neurotransmitters

There are several types of neurotransmitters involved in neural communication. The major neurotransmitters associated with the action of psychoactive drugs include dopamine, norepinephrine, serotonin, endorphins, acetylcholine, GABA, glutamate, adenosine, and anandamide. While more than 50 different chemicals have been identified as neurotransmitters, not all of these have been demonstrated to be affected by psychoactive drug use. As such, we will cover the major neurotransmitters thought to be influenced by psychoactive drugs. In addition, a particular neurotransmitter may have several different receptor sites, which are labeled using a numbering system. For example, dopamine has at least five receptor types, with the main ones labeled D_1 and D_2. Drugs often selectively act at specific receptor types. For example, many traditional antipsychotic drugs used to treat conditions like schizophrenia (a mental disorder with symptoms such as delusions and hallucinations) selectively block D_2 receptors. For now, our review of the major types of neurotransmitters will be more general. Binding of neurotransmitters at specific receptor subtypes will be important in discussing the effects of certain drugs in future chapters of this book, so being aware of the numbering system will be helpful.

Dopamine (DA) is a very important neurotransmitter that we will discuss often in this book. Most drugs of abuse either directly or indirectly target the brain's reward system by flooding circuits with more dopamine (NIDA, 2010c). Dopamine is a widespread neurotransmitter involved in the regulation of movement, emotion, cognition, motivation, and feelings of pleasure. In particular, dopamine is involved in the rewarding feelings that we experience when we eat tasty food or engage in sexual activity. When psychoactive drug ingestion results in an overstimulation of dopamine activity, the user feels high or euphoric, which encourages the user to repeat whatever behavior was associated with the euphoric feeling state. Dopamine thus helps us repeat life-sustaining activities, like eating, by associating such activities with pleasure or reward. Drugs of abuse can result in between 2 and 10 times as much dopamine being released compared with natural rewards. The release level is dependent on the type of drug, the dose, and the route of administration. Further, psychoactive drugs cause dopamine levels to become imbalanced even for naturally rewarding behaviors. For example, there appear to be similarities between elevated dopamine activity in overeating (Volkow et al., 2008) and pathological gambling (Joutsa et al., 2012) similar to dopamine overactivity in drug addiction, albeit to differing degrees.

Dopamine also plays a widespread role in other aspects of natural behavior, beyond reward mechanisms. Dopamine is the key neurotransmitter involved in many brain functions. When there is an imbalance in dopamine levels, neurological or psychiatric disorders can result (Voon et al., 2009). For example, dopamine is critical in movement regulation. If dopamine levels are insufficient, motor coordination suffers. In Parkinson's disease, dopaminergic neurons die, resulting in the primary symptom of progressive deterioration of motor control. Parkinson's disease impacts everything from walking to maintaining control over one's tongue. Patients will experience loss of fine motor control, muscle rigidity, and tremor. Patients also often experience constant shaking in their hands, something that you might have observed if you have watched recent television interviews with actor Michael J. Fox or boxing legend Muhammad Ali, two individuals suffering from this disease.

Since Parkinson's disease results in the destruction of dopaminergic neurons, treatment involves attempts to restore dopamine levels. However, the brain protects itself from toxic compounds via the **blood–brain barrier**, which filters blood before it can enter the brain. The blood–brain barrier is important because it protects the brain from all kinds of toxins to which the body might have otherwise been exposed. Ironically, dopamine cannot pass through the blood–brain barrier, even though there is lots of dopamine actually in the brain. However, L-dopa, a dopamine precursor, can pass through the blood–brain barrier. When L-dopa is administered to the patient, it crosses the blood–brain barrier. Once inside the brain, L-dopa is converted to dopamine (Deutsch & Roth, 2009). In the short term, the patient experiences some symptom relief. Unfortunately, treatment of Parkinson's disease is ultimately a losing battle, as treatment cannot yet alter the continuous loss of dopamine neurons. Moreover, side effects from elevated dopamine levels via drug treatment are systemic (throughout the body) and not targeted to only the brain region that is suffering from dopaminergic neuronal death. As such, there can be behavioral disturbances from the elevation of dopamine in other areas of the brain. Patients can experience various impulse control disorders such as compulsive eating, pathological gambling, hypersexuality, and compulsive shopping, as dopamine is involved in feelings of reward in addition to motor control (Reiff & Jost, 2011).

Atypical dopamine levels are also implicated in various psychiatric disorders. For example, schizophrenia is a mental illness characterized by symptoms such as hallucinations (perceptions not based in reality), delusions (false beliefs), loss of contact with reality, social withdrawal, and distorted emotions. Two lines of evidence suggest that elevated dopamine levels can lead to these symptoms, particularly the hallucinations, delusions, and loss of contact with reality. First, drugs that block dopamine receptors are effective in reducing these symptoms (Lodge & Grace, 2011). Second, in an individual who does not suffer from schizophrenia, similar symptoms can be drug-induced if a drug is ingested that substantially elevates dopamine levels. Elevated dopamine levels occur in cases of high levels of stimulant use, including amphetamines, cocaine, and methamphetamine (Seeman et al., 2006). Given this relationship, a stimulant drug user who has become psychotic can be treated with the same antipsychotic medications that are effective in reducing the psychotic symptoms in schizophrenia. In both cases, abnormally high dopamine activity results in psychiatric symptoms, with restoration of the appropriate level of dopamine activity resulting in symptom remission.

While dopamine is an important neurotransmitter involved in drug abuse, it should be made clear that dopamine belongs to a family of neurotransmitters known as the **monoamines** or catecholamines. The term *monoamine* is used to describe this family because the chemical structure of each of these neurotransmitters includes a single amine group. Also in the monoamine family are the neurotransmitters **norepinephrine** (NE), **epinephrine** (E), and **serotonin** (5-HT). These neurotransmitters will be mentioned often in this book because their balance is altered when psychoactive drugs are ingested. The neurotransmitters dopamine, norepinephrine, and serotonin are typically found in the central nervous system (brain and spinal cord), while epinephrine is largely found in the peripheral nervous system. Norepinephrine is synthesized from dopamine, and epinephrine is synthesized from norepinephrine, which explains why the balance of these neurotransmitters in the brain and body is so closely linked. Also, both norepinephrine and epinephrine serve several roles as hormone and neurotransmitter. For clarification, norepinephrine is sometimes called noradrenaline and epinephrine is sometimes called adrenaline, but the terms norepinephrine and epinephrine have become preferred over time in the scientific literature (Julien, 2005).

The neurotransmitter norepinephrine plays an important role in emotional arousal, including the physical changes associated with highly emotional states. Norepinephrine is also involved in the regulation of hunger and alertness. When norepinephrine is released, we are alert, focused, feel positive, and do not feel pain. Elevations in norepinephrine and epinephrine activity underlie the fight-or-flight response, which is associated with stress. For example, if you are being chased by a bear, you will feel alert, focused, and energetic, which are all necessary states to assist with your escape from your predicament. We will discuss this fight-or-flight response later in this chapter in the section on the peripheral nervous system. For now, note that when we are stressed, norepinephrine increases the rate of heart contractions and alters activity in the amygdala, a part of the brain that is important for regulation of emotion. Similar to dopamine, insufficient levels of norepinephrine lead to problems. Insufficient levels of norepinephrine have been implicated in attention deficit/hyperactivity disorder and major depression (Julien, 2005).

Serotonin (5-HT) is found throughout the brain and plays an important role in the regulation of sleep, mood, appetite, sex, and body temperature. In addition to the brain, serotonin is also found in the gastrointestinal tract and in blood platelets. The importance of serotonin is most evident when its levels are deficient, which causes significant problems. Major depression and other psychiatric disorders are associated with deficient levels of serotonin. A variety of psychotherapeutic drugs have been developed, including antidepressants and antipsychotics, which increase serotonin activity. In addition, hallucinogenic drugs such as LSD and psilocybin (hallucinogenic mushrooms) increase serotonin activity in the brain.

Since all monoamine neurotransmitters (DA, NE, E, 5-HT) are linked to mood states and emotional disorders, the discovery of psychotherapeutic drugs that alter monoamine systems has led to dramatic changes in how psychiatric disorders are treated. Dysregulation of norepinephrine and serotonin is well accepted as the biological basis for major depression. When levels of norepinephrine and serotonin are too low, depression often results. Drugs that address these imbalances lead to improved mood. Likewise, dysregulation of monoamines, particularly dopamine and serotonin, is also well accepted as the biological basis for schizophrenia. When levels of these neurotransmitters, particularly dopamine, are too high, symptoms of schizophrenia such as delusions and hallucinations become more evident. Drugs that address these imbalances result in symptoms dissipating.

While these disorders are complex, with social and psychological factors playing an important role, the biochemical balance of monoamines is nevertheless critical to mental health. Like psychotherapeutic drugs, drugs of abuse alter the balance of these same neurotransmitters. In the short term, a user may feel increased mood and euphoria with psychoactive drugs. In the longer term, constant alteration of the balance of these monoamines is not without consequences. When we examine the consequences of withdrawal from most of the psychoactive drugs in this book, a near universal observation is that depression and anxiety ensue. In many cases, patients are treated with antidepressant drugs that upregulate serotonin and norepinephrine levels, since being depressed is a complicating factor that may prevent a successful recovery from drug addiction.

The monoamines are not the only neurotransmitters influenced by psychoactive drugs. **Acetylcholine** (ACh), the first neurotransmitter discovered, is also the best understood one. While acetylcholine is found throughout the brain, it is additionally found where the axons of neurons meet skeletal muscles. Just like the synapse (where neuron meets neuron), there is also a little space where nerve meets muscle, known as the **neuromuscular junction**. After a neuron releases acetylcholine into the neuromuscular junction, the subsequent binding of acetylcholine to receptors on muscle results in muscle contraction. The binding of acetylcholine can be blocked by the deadly toxin botulinum, which is produced by bacteria that grow in environments like improperly packaged canned goods. The same toxin in carefully prepared doses is used cosmetically as Botox, which, when injected into the facial muscles, causes partial paralysis that temporarily smoothes facial lines and wrinkles. So, when you see a photo of a very smooth face on an older Hollywood actor, consider that normal acetylcholine activity is possibly being blocked.

In the brain, acetylcholine is important for memory, attention, and sensory processing. For example, substantial evidence shows that acetylcholine plays an important role in Alzheimer's disease, a degenerative dementia in the elderly. A key diagnostic feature of Alzheimer's disease is the progressive loss of memory function. In the brain, the loss of acetylcholine-releasing neurons coincides with memory loss (Parri, Hernandez, & Dineley, 2011). Moreover, drugs that elevate levels of acetylcholine, such as donepezil, are helpful in improving memory or at least preventing further declines in memory loss from Alzheimer's. Nicotine, found in a variety of tobacco products, has also been shown to improve memory, in part because nicotine binds to acetylcholine receptors in the brain (Mehta, Adem, Kahlon, & Sabbagh, 2012).

Discovered in 1973, **endorphins** function as neurotransmitters and act like naturally occurring morphine. Different from monoamines and acetylcholine, endorphins are large molecules called peptides. A peptide is a small protein, which is a chain of amino acid molecules attached in a specific order. One main role for endorphins is blocking pain, which is also called **analgesia**. When we exercise vigorously, feel excitement, experience pain, eat really spicy food, are in love or engaged in sexual activity, endorphins are released. With endorphin release, we experience little pain and feel really good. Morphine and heroin have similar effects, which is why the name *endorphin* was chosen (a contraction of endogenous morphine) (Julien, 2005; Pert & Snyder, 1973).

Gamma amino-butyric acid (GABA) is an abundant neurotransmitter that functions slightly differently from those already described. GABA is the most important inhibitory neurotransmitter in the brain and spinal cord, which means that when GABA binds with a receptor, it impedes neural firing. Outside of the central nervous system, GABA also regulates muscle tone. Increased levels of GABA activity are thought to underlie relaxation and sedation. Various psychotherapeutic drugs that are thought to act on the GABA system are effective in the treatment of psychiatric disorders where anxiety, tension, or insomnia are symptoms. Benzodiazepines (such as Valium) act on GABA and are typically used to treat generalized anxiety disorders. Barbiturates (sleeping pills) are less commonly used in current times because of risk of accidental overdose, but they also induce effects from mild sedation to total anesthesia. Alcohol is also well known to increase GABA activity, which explains some of the sedating effects that alcohol users experience.

Glutamate (Glu) is a highly abundant excitatory neurotransmitter in the brain. Glutamate receptors are so common in the brain that they are found on the surface of virtually all neurons. Glutamate is thought to be important in learning and memory. Some of the hallucinogenic psychoactive drugs, including PCP (Angel dust) and ketamine, influence glutamate activity. Glutamate is also the precursor for GABA, the major inhibitory neurotransmitter just mentioned. While there are many types of glutamate receptors, one type worth mentioning is the NMDA receptor. The NMDA receptor plays a critical role in synaptic plasticity, which at the neuronal level underlies learning, memory, and cognitive ability. Although NMDA activity is involved in synaptic plasticity, when glutamate levels become excessive, neuronal toxicity can result. For example, excessive alcohol use reduces glutamate activity, while alcohol withdrawal markedly increases glutamate activity. Too much glutamate activity can destroy neurons through overactivity of NMDA receptors. Such processes may explain why alcoholics can have widespread brain damage following repeated relapses and withdrawals (Julien, 2005).

Adenosine (ADO) is an inhibitory neurotransmitter found in the central and peripheral nervous system. Feelings of sleepiness result from the action of adenosine. Over the course of the day, adenosine levels start out relatively low and then slowly rise as the day progresses. The rise in adenosine levels is thought to suppress arousal and promote sleep. Besides leading to behavioral sedation, adenosine also regulates oxygen delivery to cells and dilates cerebral and coronary blood vessels. Alcohol has been shown to increase adenosine levels, which partly accounts for the sleepiness that accompanies drinking, although the mechanism for this occurrence remains unclear (Butler & Prendergast, 2012). What is better known is that caffeine can occupy adenosine receptors and block the action of adenosine, which is why caffeine-containing products are often associated with increased wakefulness (Fredholm, Battig, Holmen, Nehlig, & Zvartau, 1999).

The last neurotransmitter to be discussed is **anandamide** (AEA), a very recent discovery first isolated in 1992 (Devane et al., 1992). Anandamide is an inhibitory lipid neurotransmitter found in both the central and peripheral nervous systems. Anandamide binds to cannabinoid receptors, which are also sensitive to THC, the primary psychoactive cannabinoid found in marijuana. Anandamide has been an exciting discovery because this neurotransmitter may play an important role in appetite, sleep, and pain (Ameri, Wilhelm, & Simmet, 1999). For example, increased levels

Table 2-1 **Major neurotransmitters and psychoactive drugs that serve as agonists/antagonists (Carvey, 1988; Julien, 2005).**

Neurotransmitter	Type	Major roles of Neurotransmitter	Agonist Drugs	Antagonist Drugs
Dopamine	Excitatory	Regulation of motor movements, emotion, cognition, motivation, reinforcement, and feelings of pleasure; most drugs of abuse directly or indirectly target the brain's reward circuitry by increasing dopamine	Cocaine Amphetamines	Chlorpromazine
Norepinephrine	Excitatory	Regulation of hunger, alertness, arousal, and anxiety		
Serotonin	Excitatory	Regulation of sleep, mood, and appetite; hallucinations	LSD	Chlorpromazine
Endorphins	Excitatory	Modulation of pain	Heroin Morphine Opium	Naloxone
Acetylcholine	Excitatory	Activation of skeletal muscles; memory, attention, and sensory processing	Nicotine	Atropine
GABA	Inhibitory	Sedation	Alcohol Benzodiazepines Barbiturates	
Glutamate	Excitatory	Learning and memory		Ketamine
Adenosine	Inhibitory	Regulation of sleepiness		Caffeine
Anandamide	Inhibitory	Regulation of appetite, sleep, and pain	Marijuana	

of anandamide increases hunger sensation and food intake. As a result, researchers are examining if reducing anandamide activity may be a promising way to treat obesity (Engeli, 2012).

Now that we have discussed many types of neurotransmitters, you may wonder if a specific neuron produces all of these neurotransmitters or just one type. In most cases, a neuron always produces the same neurotransmitter at every one of its synapses. Since most neurons only release one kind of neurotransmitter, neurons are often classified according to the neurotransmitter released. For example, neurons that release dopamine are referred to as dopaminergic neurons. Neurons that release serotonin are serotonergic. Neurons that release acetylcholine are called cholinergic and neurons that release norepinephrine are noradrenergic. However, there are also cases where a neuron may release more than one neurotransmitter from its synapses. Note, however, that upon closer examination, each individual synapse only releases one type of neurotransmitter (Julien, 2005). In summary, there are a variety of neurotransmitters that are involved in the action of psychoactive drugs. Table 2-1 provides a summary of these major neurotransmitters.

When Drugs Look Like Neurotransmitters

Psychoactive drugs are chemicals, and neurotransmitters are chemicals. Therefore, drugs similar in chemical structure to naturally occurring neurotransmitters can tap into the brain's communication system and interfere with the normal sending, receiving, and processing of information (NIDA, 2010c). Some drugs directly activate neurons because the drug's chemical structure looks so similar to a naturally occurring neurotransmitter. This process is described as **mimicry**, since the chemical structure of the drug mimics the natural neurotransmitter. The opiate drugs (heroin,

Table 2-2   Major mechanisms by which psychoactive drugs can influence neural transmission.

Mechanism	Description	Examples
Receptor activation	A drug can activate a receptor by mimicking a neurotransmitter	Morphine occupying endorphin receptors
Receptor blocking	A drug can occupy a receptor site, making it inactive	Caffeine occupying adenosine receptors
Neurotransmitter synthesis	A drug can enhance/diminish the synthesis of neurotransmitters	Amphetamines enhance dopamine synthesis
Neurotransmitter transport	A drug can interfere with the transport of neurotransmitters to the axon terminal	
Neurotransmitter storage	A drug can enhance/diminish the storage of neurotransmitters in the vesicles of the axon terminal	Reserpine makes vesicles leaky so that neurotransmitters do not reach the synapse
Neurotransmitter release	A drug can cause the axon terminals to prematurely release neurotransmitters into the synapse	Amphetamine enhances the release of dopamine
Neurotransmitter degradation	A drug can enhance/diminish the likelihood of breakdown of neurotransmitters by enzymes	MAOI drugs prevent enzyme breakdown of serotonin
Neurotransmitter reuptake	A drug can enhance/diminish the likelihood of reuptake of neurotransmitters into the axon terminals	SSRIs decrease reuptake of serotonin

morphine, opium) mimic naturally occurring endorphins, as the structure of the drug fools receptors and allows the drug to bind to and activate endorphin receptors. Likewise, THC, which is the psychoactive chemical in marijuana, mimics the naturally occurring neurotransmitter anandamide. However, it should be mentioned that although opiates and marijuana are mimicking neurotransmitters, their activation leads to abnormal levels of activity in neural networks. This is because neurotransmitters are always in balance in the brain. By administering a drug, the balance of these neurotransmitters is inevitably altered by the external drug's influence. Table 2-2 summarizes the various ways that drugs can influence neurotransmission.

While mimicry is a clear mechanism by which a drug influences neurotransmission, one should recall that what happens when a drug fits into a receptor is similar to when a key fits into a lock. As you know, a key fits into a lock and opens a door. Similarly, a psychoactive drug fits into a receptor and acts like the naturally occurring neurotransmitter, thus activating or inhibiting the neuron. A drug that activates the neuron is called an **agonist drug**, since the drug has exactly the same effect a naturally occurring neurotransmitter would. However, you have probably had the experience of putting a key into a lock, having the key fit but being unable to open the door. The same thing can happen at a receptor. A psychoactive drug can fit into the receptor but not activate the receptor. In this case, the drug is said to be an **antagonist drug**. Antagonist drugs are also called blocking agents, because they prevent the neuron from firing. An example of agonist and antagonist drugs having opposite effects can be illustrated with the endorphin receptor. Naturally occurring endorphins can block pain and induce feelings of euphoria. Morphine and heroin also bind to the endorphin receptor and result in pain reduction and feelings of euphoria. In other words, morphine and heroin are agonist drugs acting exactly like naturally occurring endorphins. By contrast, naloxone is an antagonist drug having the opposite effect. Naloxone also binds to endorphin receptors but does not activate them. As a result, increased sensation of pain and reduction in euphoria occurs. Naloxone is extremely useful in medical settings when a patient has just taken a potentially lethal dose of heroin. When such an overdose occurs, breathing is compromised and if nothing is done, death may result. If promptly given, naloxone competes with the same receptors as the heroin, facilitating patient survival (CDC, 2012).

Psychoactive drugs can additionally alter other aspects of normal neurotransmitter activity, including how neurotransmitters are synthesized, transported, stored, and released. For example, some drugs can cause neurons to release abnormally large amounts of neurotransmitters. Cocaine and amphetamines are drugs that upregulate (increase) the release of dopamine, which has been compared to the difference between someone whispering in your ear (normal dopamine release) and someone shouting into a microphone (excessive dopamine release when the drug is present) (NIDA, 2010c).

Recall also that once neurotransmitters are released, they are deactivated in some way so that continuous messages are not sent. There are a few ways to do this, including reuptake or enzyme breakdown. In reuptake, neurotransmitters are inactivated by taking them back up into the axon terminal that released them (recycling). Drugs can prevent the normal reuptake process that recycles neurotransmitters by blocking the reuptake sites. As mentioned earlier, deficient serotonin activity has been implicated in depression. The selective serotonin reuptake inhibitor (SSRI) drugs used to treat depression block the reuptake sites for serotonin. When the reuptake sites are blocked, more serotonin is available in the synaptic gap, which results in greater serotonin binding on the postsynaptic neuron. Similarly, the enzyme breakdown process can also be altered using drugs. Enzyme breakdown is the process by which enzymes deactivate neurotransmitters after binding has occurred. The enzyme that breaks down leftover serotonin is called monoamine oxidase. Drugs called monoamine oxidase inhibitors (MAOIs) are also useful in the treatment of depression because MAOIs prevent that enzyme from breaking down serotonin and other monoamines. Increased serotonin activity results and the patient experiences relief of depression symptoms.

While the above discussion emphasized the variety of mechanisms by which psychoactive drugs immediately alter neurotransmitter activity, recognize that long-term use of a drug can have dramatically different effects versus a single instance of use. When the delicate balance of neurotransmitters in the brain is altered on a regular basis, the body adjusts to this change. For example, if drug use repeatedly increases the levels of dopamine in the brain, the brain eventually responds by reducing the amount of dopamine it produces and releases. These brain adjustments explain why individuals become tolerant to drugs (require increased doses of drug over time to get the same result) and develop withdrawal symptoms when drug use stops. Once the body makes less dopamine, the user needs to take in more drug to raise dopamine levels to the point where the person feels high or even normal again. This need for more drug to get the same effect is tolerance. The same principle explains withdrawal. Regular drug use can result in lower resting dopamine levels, since the body expects the drug to supply some dopamine. If no drug is taken, the person gets physically sick and experiences withdrawal (Nestler, 2009). In subsequent chapters of this book, we will examine the specific changes that occur for each of the psychoactive drugs when they are used on a chronic basis and then discontinued.

Myth Busters: Drugs Kill Brain Cells

In the general public, it is not uncommon to hear people say that drugs cause brain damage. Such comments often exclude the most commonly used psychoactive drugs, including alcohol, nicotine, and caffeine, since drugs in common usage most often refers to illegal drugs. We have just finished a review of neurons, neural communication, and how psychoactive drugs might influence the activity of neurons. So is the idea that drugs damage neurons and result in brain damage correct, or is it a myth?

The answer to this question may surprise you: it depends on the drug. Drug use does not appear to universally damage neurons, though certain drugs do seem to have this capacity. The most compelling evidence for damage is from alcohol (at high doses), inhalants, amphetamines, and ecstasy (MDMA).

First, let us examine the evidence for alcohol. In human alcoholics, brain shrinkage has been observed which suggests that chronic alcohol use causes neuronal death. Even a 4-day binge of alcohol is sufficient exposure to result in widespread neuronal death in rats. Fortunately, some regeneration of neurons can occur during abstinence, indicating that the damage might be reversible if it is not too extensive (Collins & Neafsey, 2012; Crews & Nixon, 2009). Further, the damage done by extremely high doses of alcohol is not uniform across ages. Both human and animal studies have shown that alcohol exposure occurring during the critical adolescent development stages can disrupt the brain plasticity and maturation processes that should be occurring during this time (Guerri & Pascual, 2010). The importance of developmental timing in the likelihood of neuronal death is dramatically illustrated by alcohol exposure in utero. A developing fetus's brain is in a critical period called **synaptogenesis**. If alcohol exposure occurs during synaptogenesis, the timing and sequence of synaptic connections is impacted, resulting in some neurons receiving an internal signal to "commit suicide," specifically referred to as **apoptosis**. When millions of such neurons experience apoptosis, a baby is born with a diminished brain, resulting in a diagnosis of fetal alcohol syndrome. The small brain size causes mental retardation and other problems that are neither reversible nor treatable (Farber & Olney, 2003). So does alcohol cause neurons to die? For an adult consuming a few alcoholic beverages in a responsible manner (not to intoxicating levels), the answer is likely not. For a developing organism, the answer is clearly yes.

What about the death of neurons from the use of inhalants? Included here are glue sniffing, inhalant abuse, and solvent abuse. Solvents including gasoline, contact adhesive (toluene), volatile hydrocarbons (found in cigarette lighter refills), and aerosol propellants are deliberately inhaled in order to achieve intoxication. Inhalant abuse is more likely among adolescents, whose brains are still developing. The evidence indicates that inhalants can cause neuronal death in the brain, in addition to other organ damage, including damage to the liver and kidneys (Flanagan & Ives, 1994).

The final group of psychoactive drugs that are likely to cause neurotoxicity are the amphetamines, which include amphetamine, methamphetamine, and ecstasy (MDMA). Use of these drugs appears to result in damage to the synapses leading to apoptosis (Cadet, Krasnova, Jayanthi, & Lyles, 2007). Recall from a few paragraphs ago that apoptosis occurs when the neurons receive an internal signal to "commit suicide." One study examined the damage that ecstasy can do to the brain. Monkeys were given ecstasy twice a day for four days and those monkeys were compared to a control group that did not receive the drug (Hatzidimitriou, McCann, & Ricaurte, 1999). The researchers stained serotonin axons in the frontal cortex (the part of the brain near the forehead that is important in thinking). There was damage (fewer neuronal axons) not just 2 weeks later, but even 7 years later! The damage 7 years later was remarkable because while there is evidence of some recovery, there is not full recovery, even though ecstasy was only given eight times in total. In other words, regeneration of the neurons occurred but was far from a complete return to the state before drug exposure. This permanent damage is quite worrisome considering that young people use ecstasy in clubs and at parties, perhaps without being aware about the negative consequences to their brains, apparently even with relatively few uses.

Other drugs do seem to cause less neuronal death. While smoking cigarettes, using marijuana, or injecting heroin can cause a multitude of physiological and psychological concerns that we will cover later in this book, the scientific evidence that these drugs lead to widespread neuronal death is debatable, and in some cases it is largely nonexistent. Like many urban legends, the notion that psychoactive drugs induce brain damage (neuronal death) is part truth and part myth.

QUICK QUIZ 2-1

1. What is released into the synapse during neural communication?
   a. Action potential
   b. Neurotransmitters
   c. Receptors
   d. Myelin

2. Drugs of abuse are most likely to directly or indirectly increase which neurotransmitter?
   a. Dopamine
   b. Acetylcholine
   c. Anandamide
   d. Glutamate

3. _____ acts like endogenous endorphins.
   a. Cocaine
   b. Nicotine
   c. Caffeine
   d. Morphine

4. _____ is an internal signal for neurons to commit suicide.
   a. Mimicry
   b. Action potential
   c. Apoptosis
   d. Synaptogenesis

5. Describe the difference between an agonist and an antagonist drug.

6. When psychoactive drugs are used long-term, what are the implications for neurotransmitter activity?

ANSWERS TO QUICK QUIZ 2-1:

1. b. – neurotransmitters
2. a. – dopamine
3. d. – morphine
4. c. – apoptosis
5. An agonist drug is a chemical that binds to a receptor and acts like the naturally occurring neurotransmitter would. By contrast, an antagonist drug is a chemical that occupies a neural receptor and blocks the normal activity that would have occurred with a naturally occurring neurotransmitter. Using the analogy of a key in a lock, the agonist drug would actually open the lock, whereas the antagonist drug is like a key that fits in the lock but does not open the lock.
6. When the delicate balance of neurotransmitters in the brain is altered on a regular basis with long-term drug use, the body adjusts to this change. For example, if drug use repeatedly increases the level of dopamine in the brain, the ultimate result will be a reduction in the amount of dopamine being naturally produced and released by the body.

The Nervous System

The most interesting action of psychoactive drugs happens at the level of the synapse of a neuron. Drugs can act like neurotransmitters or alter the balance of neurotransmitter activity. While these adjustments to neurotransmitter activity are low-level changes only visible at the microscopic level, these changes eventually impact the functioning of the entire nervous system. As such, a review of the major structures of the nervous system is necessary to understand better how drugs might impact various functions of the nervous system. Additionally, knowing some of the major brain structures can help better explain the general divisions of labor in how the nervous system operates and how psychoactive drugs might selectively impact certain tasks. For example, certain sections of the brain are responsible for breathing and heart rate, while other parts of the brain are responsible for impulse control and visual processing. One drug may decrease respiration, while another may increase impulsivity. Note also that there are pathways of neurons running through various parts of the brain that serve important functions. In particular, there is a pathway critical to feelings of pleasure and reward, with many drugs of abuse altering activity along this pathway. Keep in mind that these macrostructures (brain structures and pathways) are built up from the microstructures (neurons) that were just discussed. Long-term use of drugs eventually impact macrostructures resulting from changes in microstructures. As noted earlier in this chapter, alcohol, inhalants, amphetamines, and ecstasy can cause widespread neuronal death, changes that can lead to visible brain shrinkage from loss of matter.

To better understand the macrostructure, we'll first discuss the brain, and then we will discuss the entire nervous system. The **central nervous system (CNS)** refers to the brain and spinal cord. The **peripheral nervous system (PNS)** refers to all neural tissue outside the CNS. Neurons are sometimes bundled together, so do not be confused by the terms *neuron* and *nerve*. A **nerve** is a bundle of axons (multiple neurons in an enclosed cable-like bundle) found in the PNS. The PNS includes the **sensory nerves**, which send messages from the sensory organs (the eyes or the ears) to the brain. Likewise, nerves that send messages from the brain to muscles are called **motor nerves**. Bundles of axons are also found in the CNS. However, if a bundle of axons is located in the CNS, it is called a **tract** (Purves, Augustine, Fitzpatrick, & Hall, 2011). Also, recall from the beginning of this chapter that axons are generally covered in myelin. Since myelin is white in color, the nerves in the PNS and the tracts in the CNS appear white and are thus referred to as white matter. Unmyelinated cell bodies are referred to as gray matter.

Brain Anatomy

The human **brain** is the most complex organ in the body, as it regulates all body functions and interprets and responds to everything we experience. Billions and billions of neurons make up the brain. Surprisingly, the brain only weighs about three pounds, which does not seem like much considering the many varied parts in the brain that are needed for the coordination and performance of multiple functions (see Figure 2-5). All thoughts, emotions, and behaviors originate from the activity of the brain.

Up until recently, it was thought that the number of brain cells was fixed at birth and that with aging, cells were progressively lost. This is now known to be incorrect. The brain actually has some regenerative capacity similar to other organs in the body. Of course, the success of the body to repair itself depends on the extent of the damage. In the 1990s, it was discovered that new neurons could emerge from certain brain regions in adult mammals (Gould, Reeves, Graziano, & Gross, 1999). Today, it is widely accepted that two regions of the adult mammalian brain definitely support neurogenesis (birth of new neurons), including the hippocampus and the olfactory bulb, regions that will be further discussed below. Moreover, other areas of the brain have shown evidence of neurogenesis, including the neocortex, striatum, amygdala, and substantia nigra (Gould, 2007). Psychoactive drugs can alter the activity of various brain areas and cause damage to regions of the brain, particularly when drug use becomes chronic. Some of this damage, if not widespread, may be reversible.

We will discuss the brain from the bottom up, as the more basic functions of the brain are located closer to the spinal cord, while the more complex human activities originate further from the spinal cord. By convention, the brain is often divided into three unequal-sized sections called the hindbrain, midbrain, and forebrain. The hindbrain is located closest to the spinal cord, the forebrain is closest to the top of the head, and the midbrain is in the middle. The structures located in the hindbrain region will be described first.

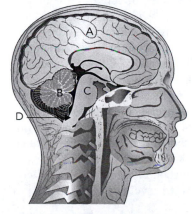

A. The Cerebrum

B. The Cerebellum

C. The Pons

D. The Medulla Oblongata

FIGURE 2-5
Schematic of the internal structures of the inside view of the human brain.

The **hindbrain**, located at the base of the brain, is the region that controls all basic functions critical to life, such as heart rate, breathing, and wakefulness/sleeping. Drugs that decrease the ability of structures in the hindbrain to function properly can result in fatalities. For example, the opiate drugs (heroin, morphine, and opium) all decrease breathing and heart rate by acting on the endorphin receptors located in the hindbrain. These drugs in high doses have a troubling propensity to result in overdose deaths. By contrast, there are no anandamide or adenosine receptors present in the hindbrain structures that regulate breathing. As a result, drugs like marijuana and caffeine, which act on the anandamide and adenosine receptors, respectively, are extremely unlikely to result in overdose deaths.

Figure 2-5 provides further detail regarding the structures located in the hindbrain, including the medulla, pons, and cerebellum. The **medulla** is just above the spinal cord. Important for the control of breathing, heart rate, swallowing, blood pressure, and digestive processes, it is also the vomit center. When toxic chemicals (including high doses of drugs) reach threshold levels in the medulla, the vomiting reflex is triggered in an attempt to clear the body of the toxin. The vomiting reflex is triggered because the brain is assessing danger to respiratory or cardiovascular capacity. In other words, when a drinker consumes an amount of alcohol that leads to vomiting, this is an indication that the alcohol dose was significant enough that the individual poisoned himself and breathing was close to being compromised.

Located above the medulla is the **pons**, which is a region that controls sleep and wakefulness. There is a pathway running through the pons and the medulla called the **reticular activating system**. This pathway regulates generalized alertness and arousal. Drugs that can induce sleep and lower arousal, such as tranquilizers and alcohol, are thought to have their effects on the reticular activating system.

The final structure of the brain stem region is the **cerebellum**, which looks like a cauliflower located separate from the rest of the brain. This highly complex structure contains several billion neurons of its own. The cerebellum is responsible for balance and coordinated motor movements, including speech. Similar to the pons and medulla, the cerebellum is also sensitive to the effects of sedative drugs, such as alcohol. When a sufficient dose of alcohol is ingested, an individual will have difficulty walking and balancing. In summary, the hindbrain, which includes the medulla, pons, and cerebellum, is a region important for many basic bodily functions such as respiration.

The **midbrain** is a relatively small region located above the hindbrain, essentially in the middle of the brain (see Figure 2-6). This small region is an important relay center for information related to vision and hearing. When we localize and have reflexive responses to sights or sounds, this processing occurs in the midbrain. Other more complex aspects of vision and audition, including the recognition and interpretation of stimuli, occur higher up in the brain. In addition to visual and auditory processing, the midbrain also contains the **substantia nigra**. The substantia nigra produces dopamine and thus is important for motivation and reward. Recall that earlier in this chapter, Parkinson's disease was discussed as a degenerative disease involving damage to the brain structures that produce dopamine, resulting in impairments in motor control. When nerve cells that should be producing dopamine die in the substantia nigra, Parkinson's disease develops. This is a slow process, since nearly 80% of the substantia nigra must be destroyed before actual motor control symptoms develop. In summary, the midbrain is a relatively small region that is important for production of dopamine, a neurotransmitter often implicated in drugs of abuse.

The final section of the brain to be discussed is the **forebrain**, which is also the largest part of the brain, located above the midbrain. This very substantial region contains a multitude of structures serving a variety of purposes from regulation of body temperature to complex planning and organization. The structures located closest to the midbrain are the **thalamus** and **hypothalamus**. The thalamus is often described as a relay station, as this is where information coming into the brain from the senses gets sent to relevant locations throughout the brain. The hypothalamus is important for the motivation of behavior. The regulation of eating, drinking, body temperature, aggression, and sexual behavior are all thought to involve the hypothalamus (Carlson, 2008).

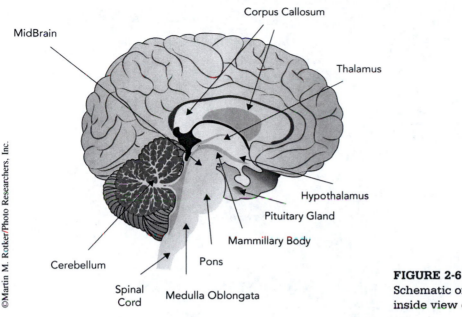

MidBrain

Corpus Callosum

Thalamus

Hypothalamus

Pituitary Gland

Mammillary Body

Cerebellum

Pons

Spinal Cord

Medulla Oblongata

FIGURE 2-6
Schematic of the internal structures of the inside view of the human brain.

Another large nearby structure is the **hippocampus**, which is thought to be involved in the formation of memories and spatial navigation. Humans and other mammals have two hippocampi located on either side of the brain (not visible in Figure 2-6 because the brain is shown in a sagittal view, meaning the right and left sides of the brain have been separated). Also found in the forebrain is the **amygdala**, which is important for strong emotions. The several structures in this section of the brain, including the hippocampus and amygdala, are thought to compose what is known as the **limbic system**, whose borders are sometimes described as the inner cortex. The limbic system is thought to be involved in the control of motivations and emotions and regulation of our ability to feel pleasure. As an example, certain behaviors critical to our existence, such as eating, are repeated due to the motivation from pleasure. Feeling pleasure encourages us to repeat eating behaviors. These areas in the limbic system can also be involved in drugs of abuse. The reason that psychoactive drug use can result in compulsive behaviors that define addiction is due to enhanced activity in these same pleasure-mediating structures in the limbic system. In general, the limbic system is responsible for emotional states, which explains why psychoactive drugs often alter mood states as part of their properties (NIDA, 2010c).

Beyond the border of the limbic system lies the **cerebral cortex**, which is comprised of everything at the top of the brain. The cerebral cortex is divided into several areas controlling specific functions. Some areas process information from our senses, which allows us to see, feel, hear, and taste (see Figure 2-7). The outer cortex is wrinkled, which makes the brain appear similar to a walnut. Given all these wrinkles, the surface of the brain appears far smaller than it actually is. If the surface were to be flattened out, it would cover an area of 2½ square feet! It should be noted that these wrinkles are not present in all species. For example, Figure 2-8 is a picture of a rat brain. Note that the brain has a cortex and a separate cerebellum similar to a human brain. However, the cortex lacks a wrinkly appearance. In addition, the rat brain has a projection seen from the left side of the image known as the olfactory bulb, which is important to the sense of smell for the rat. Recall from earlier in this chapter that the olfactory bulb is one brain region where neurogenesis has been discovered (where new neurons are created). Differences between the rat and human brain are mentioned because researchers often use animal models to better understand why drug addiction develops and how drug addiction can be treated. Fortunately, many of the lower-level structures previously discussed, particularly those involved in motivated behavior, are relatively similar across species. Therefore, the results from psychopharmacology studies with animal subjects can

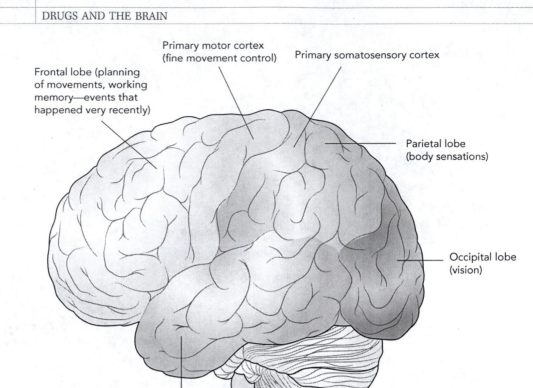

Frontal lobe (planning of movements, working memory—events that happened very recently)

Primary motor cortex (fine movement control)

Primary somatosensory cortex

Parietal lobe (body sensations)

Occipital lobe (vision)

Temporal lobe (hearing, advanced visual processing)

FIGURE 2-7
Illustration of the cerebral cortex.

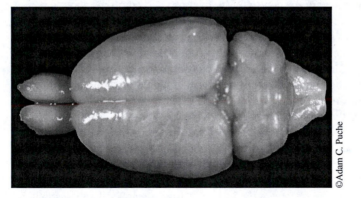

©Adam C. Puche

FIGURE 2-8
Dorsal view of adult rat brain.

most often be extrapolated to humans. However, there can be limitations to this approach, particularly for higher-order brain functions. The complexity of human thoughts and actions in part reflect our highly developed wrinkled cortex, which is not observable in some other species.

The cerebral cortex has two hemispheres, with each hemisphere controlling sensation and motor functioning on the opposite side of the body. Divided into many areas that serve various functions, each hemisphere has four lobes known as the occipital, parietal, temporal, and frontal lobes. The occipital lobes (in both the right and left hemispheres) are important for visual processing. The parietal lobes process body sensations. The temporal lobes process auditory information as well as complex visual stimuli. Finally, the frontal lobes play a critical role in the thinking center of the brain, including planning, solving problems, and making decisions. The frontal lobes perform our most complex cognitive tasks, from planning complex movements to holding information in working memory. The front section of the frontal lobes is the **prefrontal cortex**. The prefrontal cortex has been under intense investigation of late in substance abuse research because it is involved in planning, controlling impulses, and considering the long-term consequences of actions. Examination of the brain across development reveals that the prefrontal cortex is the last to develop completely. Evidence suggests that the prefrontal cortex is not fully developed until a person is 21 to 25 years of age. As such, adolescents, whose brains are still maturing, are going to find it comparatively more difficult than adults to control impulses and weigh the long-term consequences of actions. In contrast to the prefrontal cortex, the lower brain regions involved in motivated behavior have completed development by adolescence. These different rates of brain development may partially explain why adolescents are more prone to risk-taking behavior and experimenting with alcohol and drugs. The concern for adolescents is that they are undertaking those risky behaviors at a time when their brains are still developing, which makes their brains more vulnerable than adult brains to damage from psychoactive drugs (Casey & Jones, 2010).

In the News:

Jha, A. (2012, June 28). Psychedelic drugs can unlock mysteries of brain—former government advisor David Nutt says research into mental illness is hampered by the prohibition of drugs such as psilocybin and LSD. *The Guardian*.

Professor David Nutt, a British psychiatrist and neuropharmacologist, is no stranger to controversy. An avid researcher, he had until recently served as chair of the British government's Advisory Council on the Misuse of Drugs. He was fired from this government post in 2009 after publicly stating that alcohol and tobacco were more harmful than LSD, ecstasy, and marijuana. In this news interview with a *Guardian* reporter, Professor Nutt stated that scientists should have access to various illegal drugs, since such access would help scientists understand many of the deepest mysteries of the brain, including unlocking the secrets of mental illness. Nutt said, "Neuroscience should be trying to understand how the brain works. Psychedelics change the brain in, perhaps, the most profound way of any drug, at least in terms of understanding consciousness and connectivity. Therefore we should be doing a lot of this research . . . I think it's outrageous that these studies have not been done before. And they've not been done simply because the drugs were illegal." Nutt suggested that psilocybin (hallucinogenic mushrooms) and LSD's effects on the brain could be used as a model for psychosis, since these drugs produce symptoms similar to those that appear with the onset of schizophrenia. Nutt mentioned that a human subject withdrew from such a study due to concern that being in a study with a so-called illegal drug could mean he couldn't travel to some countries, including the United States. In summary, Professor Nutt called for a regulated approach that would make illegal drugs available for medical and research purposes.

Use This News Article to Test and Apply Your Knowledge:

1. In this article, Professor Nutt states that the scientific study of illegal drugs might help us understand mental illness. Based on the material from earlier in this chapter, is his statement correct?

2. If psychoactive drugs were more extensively studied to better understand processes underlying mental illness, which aspect of neurotransmission should initially be the focus of this research (such as the action potential, synapse, or myelination)?

Answers:

1. Yes, this statement is correct. Psychoactive drugs alter neurotransmitter activity. Abnormal neurotransmitter activity is also implicated in several mental illnesses, including schizophrenia, major depression, and anxiety disorders. If a drug alters neurotransmitter activity in a manner similar to that which occurs with other medical conditions, the study of the drug could inform us about the mental illness. For example, the hallucinations and delusions that are symptoms of schizophrenia are also observed with high doses of stimulants, including amphetamines and cocaine.

2. Research findings thus far have suggested that psychoactive drugs largely influence the neural activity at the synapse, either by mimicking neurotransmitters or altering neurotransmitter balance in various ways. Therefore, any research should initially examine what is occurring at the level of the synapse.

What Do You Think about This News Story?

This article highlights the ongoing controversy regarding research on psychoactive drugs, especially illegal psychoactive drugs. While this story is based in the United Kingdom, similar concerns arise in the United States and elsewhere. Many illegal psychoactive drugs can cause harms to the user. Therefore, limited research has examined the effects of psychoactive drugs due to concerns about subject safety or diversion of these drugs beyond the research lab. What do you think about researchers having access to illegal psychoactive drugs to better understand the brain? Do you think that this research should be limited to animal subjects if these drugs were to be more extensively studied? Why do you think that politicians, scientists, and the general public sometimes clash when the scientific study of drugs is being discussed? In addition, Professor Nutt argued that the legal psychoactive drugs (alcohol and nicotine) actually cause far more societal harm than the illegal ones. Do you think that Professor Nutt's opinions are very extreme, or would they be accepted by the general public?

The Mesolimbic Dopaminergic Pathway

An important discovery was made in the 1950s that has altered how people view the addiction-causing impact psychoactive drugs have on the brain. A psychologist named James Olds was conducting his postdoctoral research under the supervision of Peter Milner at McGill University in Canada. They observed that rats preferred to return to the region of the test apparatus where they received direct electrical stimulation to certain brain areas. From this observation, they concluded that the stimulation must be rewarding (Olds & Milner, 1954). In subsequent experiments, they demonstrated that they could train rats to perform novel behaviors, such as pressing a lever in an operant chamber, in order to receive the electrical brain stimulation. In essence, this research marked the discovery of the neural basis for reward. It appeared that to get the rats to press the lever for the electrical stimulation, the electrodes would have to be placed along a pathway in the brain known as the **mesolimbic dopaminergic pathway**. This pathway runs from a small subcortical area called the nucleus accumbens and travels to the frontal cortex. The nucleus accumbens is part of the striatum, which integrates information from both the cortex and limbic system to mediate behaviors that reinforce reward. The mesolimbic dopaminergic pathway is a very substantial pathway running through a large section of the brain (see Figure 2-9).

The rewarding aspect of electrical stimulation cannot be overstated. Once a rat had been trained to press a lever resulting in self-stimulation in the mesolimbic dopaminergic pathway, the rat would do so almost continuously (more than 1,000 lever presses per hour or approximately one lever press every four seconds)! Multiple studies have demonstrated that rats will lever press

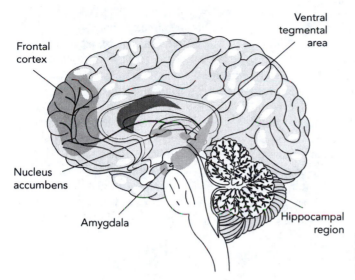

Frontal cortex

Ventral tegmental area

Nucleus accumbens

Amygdala

Hippocampal region

FIGURE 2-9
Mesolimbic dopaminergic pathway in the brain, which is important for reward and drug addiction.

to the exclusion of all other behaviors. Rats will cross electrified grids to press a lever. Rats will forgo sexual partners, water, or food (even to the point of starvation) in order to work for this brain stimulation. For this reason, Olds and others called the place in the brain where the electrode was placed the "pleasure center." Over time, it became clear that the pleasure center was actually the mesolimbic dopaminergic pathway, connecting several areas of the brain. For our purposes, the important observation is that the rewarding properties of drugs impact activity in this mesolimbic dopaminergic pathway. In particular, the nucleus accumbens contains many dopaminergic neurons, with dopamine thought to be the critical neurotransmitter in producing the rewarding properties of drugs (Koob & Le Moal, 2006). The release of dopamine in this pathway underlies the natural drives that motivate and shape behavior. For example, you see a piece of chocolate cake and taste it, dopamine is released in the mesolimbic dopaminergic pathway, and you feel good. If you see another piece of cake in the future, you are likely to repeat the behavior since your previous experience was rewarding. Electrical brain stimulation or drug injections result in similar reward experiences, just bypassing the external sensory stimulus (such as a piece of cake). As mentioned earlier, some drugs of abuse can release 2 to 10 times the amount of dopamine that natural rewards do, which illustrates the problem with psychoactive drugs. Some psychoactive drugs have such profound effects on the brain's pleasure circuit that the drug dwarfs any reward produced by naturally rewarding behaviors such eating and sexual activity (NIDA, 2010c).

More about the science:

Ersche et al. (2012). Abnormal brain structure implicated in stimulant drug addiction.
Science, *335*, 601–604.

Users who have become dependent on stimulant drugs often have structural changes indicating damage to their brains compared to similar-age control subjects. These brain changes have been observed using various brain imaging techniques. However, researchers have wondered: does the drug-taking really lead to brain abnormalities, or do brain abnormalities predate the drug taking? In other words, which came first? To answer this question, Ersche et al. (2012) studied biological sibling pairs by asking them to perform a task; additionally, the researchers imaged their brains. In each pair, one sibling had been diagnosed with a dependence on stimulant drugs (such as cocaine), whereas the other sibling had not. The subjects were asked to perform a computer task that measured impulse control. The researchers observed that both the stimulant-dependent and healthy siblings had difficulties with impulse control on the computer task. In addition, the researchers observed that the subjects (addicted or not) also had white matter abnormalities, particularly in the right prefrontal lobe. The researchers suggested that these white matter deficiencies were shared among family members and may have predisposed some subjects to take drugs. In addition, the duration of drug taking in users also influenced the integrity of the white matter in the brain. Less white matter was observed in users who had used stimulant drugs the longest. The researchers concluded that there may be familial abnormalities that create an imbalance in the limbic reward and prefrontal control systems, predisposing some adolescents to impulsive behavior and making them vulnerable to taking drugs. However, subsequent drug use does seem to exacerbate these problems in the brain.

More about the Science Thought Questions:

1. This study focused on the white matter of brains of addicted and healthy siblings. What is white matter, and what are the implications of reduced white matter in stimulant addiction?

2. Both the addicted and healthy siblings had reduced white matter in the right prefrontal lobe. What are the implications of this?

3. All research studies have limitations. What are a couple of limitations that exist with this study?

More about the Science Thought Question Answers:

1. White matter refers to brain areas that appear white in color because the axons of neurons are myelinated (insulated with glial cells) in that region of the brain. Myelination speeds neural communication. Therefore, if white matter is reduced over time via the use of stimulants, neural communication will slow down and become less efficient. Slowed neural communication should impact various aspects of cognitive processing.

2. The prefrontal cortex is the area of the brain most involved in the highest-order cognitive processes such as control of impulses and long-term planning and organization. Deficiencies in processing in this area of the brain would make it less likely that a person can weigh the long-term consequences of actions and delay gratification. These deficiencies may then predispose the individual to try psychoactive drugs. Further, there appeared to be no deficiencies in the limbic areas of the brain responsible for feeling rewards. So, while an individual with this type of imbalance will feel rewarded when using a drug, she may be unable to appropriately weigh the long-term consequences to her future health and well-being from trying the drug.

3. This study examined siblings who probably grew up in the same household and shared many experiences. Therefore, it is unclear whether genetics, shared experiences, or both contributed to the brain abnormalities in white matter in the addicted and healthy siblings. In addition, this study cannot explain why one sibling of the pair developed a stimulant addiction while the other sibling remained healthy. Since their brains looked relatively similar, other factors beyond brain structure may have played a role in differing propensity to develop an addiction. Such other factors were not addressed in the current study.

Division of the Central and Peripheral Nervous System

For the majority of this chapter, the brain has been our focus for the impact of psychoactive drugs on the nervous system. From the level of neurons up to its large structures, the brain is the origin for the majority of drug-induced changes in neural functioning, since the brain is the key organ of the nervous system. However, psychoactive drugs do impact functioning outside of the central nervous system (CNS), so the divisions within the overall nervous system will now be briefly discussed. Recall from earlier in this chapter that the peripheral nervous system (PNS) consists of all nervous tissue outside the CNS (brain and spinal cord). The PNS can be subdivided into two branches, which are called the **somatic nervous system** and the **autonomic nervous system**. The somatic nervous system consists of all the sensory and motor nerves associated with conscious senses. When you exert conscious control over your muscles, such as waving your hand to attract the attention of a taxi driver, you are using the somatic nervous system. Recall from earlier in this chapter that acetylcholine is the neurotransmitter found at most neuromuscular junctions (synapses where a neuron meets muscle). Not surprisingly, the somatic nervous system is dominated by acetylcholine activity. By contrast, the other branch of the nervous system consists of the nerves that operate outside of conscious awareness. This autonomic nervous system regulates blood pressure, as well as the functioning of the digestive system and hormone levels. When you think of the autonomic nervous system, think of anything that the body might do automatically (without exertion of effortful thinking).

Just to add further complexity, the autonomic nervous system is subdivided into two divisions. The dominant division, which keeps all internal organs functioning smoothly, is called the **parasympathetic nervous system**. The digestion of your lunch is under the control of this division. By contrast, the **sympathetic nervous system** is not active very often but it is very important in times of crisis. The sympathetic nervous system is connected to all of the same internal organs to which the parasympathetic nerves connect. However, when there is stress or danger, the sympathetic nervous system becomes active. Its function is to prepare the body for the **fight-or-flight response** to a crisis. When an organism senses danger, the body readies for a sudden expenditure of energy. Imagine that you are walking home from class one night and notice that a stranger appears to be following you. You are not certain if something is amiss, but your body prepares to fight or to run nonetheless. Blood is directed away from your digestive system and sent to your arms and legs. Your heart rate gets faster and your breathing gets heavier. You may start sweating. If you were to see the pupils of your eyes, they would be larger. If the stranger turns a corner and stops following you, you will calm down, thanks to the reactivation of the parasympathetic nervous system, which returns the autonomic nervous system back to normal.

Psychoactive drugs can influence the autonomic nervous system. In the sympathetic nervous system, the primary neurotransmitter is epinephrine. During the fight-or-flight response, the adrenal gland secretes epinephrine into the blood, which causes the physiological changes associated with the sympathetic nervous system (increased heart rate and rapid respiration). Stimulant drugs such as amphetamines and cocaine also stimulate these same synapses. Thus, the sympathetic arousal that occurs with use of these stimulant drugs is similar to what might occur if the user sensed danger and the body responded with a fight-or-flight response. Especially with high doses of stimulants, a drug user may appear to be sweating, be breathing heavily, and have enlarged pupils. There have been many cases where cocaine users have been involved in altercations with police, with the user ultimately dying. It appears that physical restraint by police in combination with the drug can lead to the death of the user. Given the body's highly aroused state from the drug, the struggle with the police officers further exacerbates an already high arousal state. Moreover, stimulants can cause heart damage over time, which makes users especially vulnerable in these highly aroused states (Pollanen, Chiasson, Cairns, & Young, 1998). The increased use of tasers to subdue individuals have limited some of these deaths, while still effectively handling combative individuals who are high on stimulants and difficult to talk down.

Techniques to Examine the Effects of Drugs on the Brain

Psychoactive drugs can have profound effects on the nervous system, both with short- and long-term use. Advances in imaging technology have made the study of psychopharmacology far more precise than it was only a few short decades ago. Technology has allowed us to examine both brain structure and brain functioning. Using technology, we can address various questions, such as whether short- or long-term use of various drugs leads to brain dysfunction. Researchers who undertake a visual study of brain structure will use one of two common techniques called **computerized axial tomography (CAT)** and **magnetic resonance imaging (MRI)**. The CAT scan (also called the CT scan) produces a three-dimensional X-ray image of the brain. To achieve this three-dimensional image, X-rays are passed through the head in a circular pattern. This results in an image of the brain that can be examined for damage to important structures. A similar, but more sophisticated, technique to create an image of the brain is MRI. In an MRI scan, a strong magnetic field is passed through the head. This results in radio waves being generated, which causes the molecules in the brain to emit energy of different frequencies depending on the type of tissue in which the molecules are located. A very detailed image is the result. Both CAT and MRI scans have been used to identify brain pathology that occurs with long-term drug use. For example, Figure 2-10 provides an MRI scan that illustrates brain atrophy or ischemic strokes observed in chronic alcoholism, an outcome also seen with heroin addicts and inhalant users (Borne, Riascos, Cuellar, Vargas, & Rojas, 2005). For the most part, the short-term effects of drugs are typically not observable on CAT and MRI scans, since brain atrophy takes time and is usually associated with long-term drug use, and some psychoactive drugs have rarely been associated with long-term brain damage. In other cases, while the MRI or CAT scan appears normal, evidence of impairments in cognitive skills such as memory and problem solving are nevertheless observable via neuropsychological testing.

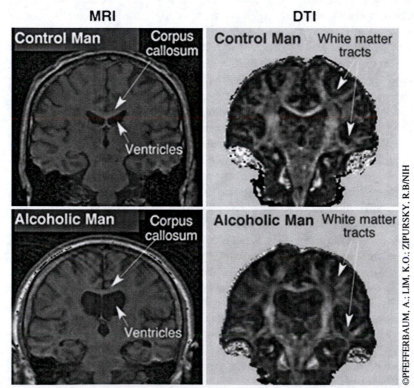

©PFEFFERBAUM, A.; LIM, K.O.; ZIPURSKY, R.B/NIH

FIGURE 2-10
MRI images of a 61–year–old healthy man (upper image) and a 60–year–old alcoholic man (lower image).

In contrast to the two imaging techniques that assess brain structure, there are other techniques that assess how the brain is functioning. One of the simplest techniques is called **electroencephalography (EEG)**. In EEG, a cap on the subject's head measures the brain's electrical activity through the scalp. The subject is often shown stimuli, and brain wave responses are recorded. Researchers look for abnormalities in EEG patterns that indicate underlying problems in brain functioning, or perhaps underlying structural damage. A similar more sophisticated approach is **positron emission tomography (PET)**. In PET, the subject is injected with weak radioactive isotopes, which then circulate through the brain. Changes in brain activity can be determined by the movement of radioactive chemicals in the brain. PET produces very detailed images of brain activity, though it does have the downside that radioactive chemicals have to be injected. While not harmful, these chemicals make some subjects wary. Fortunately, another option is available. **Functional magnetic resonance imaging (fMRI)** uses the same machine that emits magnetic fields described above for MRI. Thus, fMRI is a modification of MRI technology. With fMRI, rapid imaging of the brain across time allows the researcher to measure oxygen levels in the blood vessels of the brain. When a brain area is being utilized, oxygen is needed. Therefore, one can give subjects images to look at or tasks to perform and measure the real-time response of the brain. Use of fMRI has provided fascinating information about the acute and chronic effects of drug use. For example, fMRI has identified which brain areas are activated during drug-craving feeling states (Yalachkov, Kaiser, & Naumer, 2012). In addition, fMRI has been used in predicting which patients will be successful in drug treatment (see Figure 2-11).

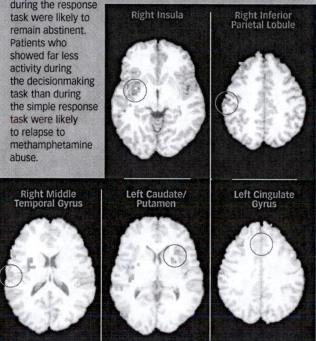

DRUG ABUSE AND DECISIONMAKING Researchers used functional magnetic resonance imaging (fMRI) to measure patterns of regional brain activity while abstinent methamphetamine abusers performed two tasks, one that required decisionmaking and one that required only a simple response. Participants who showed greater activity in selected brain regions (circled and highlighted in the brain images shown below) during the decisionmaking task than during the response task were likely to remain abstinent. Patients who showed far less activity during the decisionmaking task than during the simple response task were likely to relapse to methamphetamine abuse.

Right Insula

Right Inferior Parietal Lobule

Right Middle Temporal Gyrus

Left Caudate/ Putamen

Left Cingulate Gyrus

FIGURE 2-11
Brain activity patterns as measured with fMRI signal risk of relapse to methamphetamine.

Focus on Careers: Scientists in Academia and Industry

New discoveries about drugs and the brain occur every day. Much of the information that was included in this chapter was not even known a decade or two ago. Many new pharmaceutical drugs or equipment to image the living brain are being developed. What that means is that many people have careers in either academia (in universities) or industry (in companies) as scientists. Many scientists begin their careers as scientists immediately upon completion of their undergraduate degree. Companies hire recent graduates who have strong backgrounds in coursework including general science, neuroscience, engineering, and/or mathematics. If you enjoy courses such as research methods, statistics, and psychopharmacology, you may be well suited for a career as a scientist. One way to secure such a job is to do an internship or placement with a company while still a student. While you may not get paid for this work as a student, this experience may lead to a job offer upon graduation if your work was excellent. Another way to begin a career as a scientist is to participate in undergraduate research under the supervision of a faculty member in your department. Learning about science first-hand is the best way to determine if a career in science is a good fit for you (even if the particular research project is not your precise area of interest). If you enjoy school and research, graduate training may lead to a higher-paying and more challenging science career in academia or industry. Admittance to master's and doctoral degree programs is very competitive. Most schools require that applicants provide scores from the Graduate Record Examination (GRE), a standardized test. In addition, undergraduate GPA, letters of reference from professors, and essays describing past research experiences and future goals are considered. One very attractive aspect to pursuing graduate school training is that the cost can be minimal. Many graduate programs will waive tuition fees and even provide stipends to cover living expenses. In return, the graduate student is expected to conduct research and teach within the university. If a career in science seems like a good option for you, it is never too early to start getting some research experience to start moving in that direction.

Websites to explore:

Council on Undergraduate Research – student resources information
www.cur.org/resources/for_students/
Graduate Record Examination – Educational Testing Service
www.ets.org/gre/

QUICK QUIZ 2-2

1. A _____ is found in the central nervous system, whereas a _____ is found in the peripheral nervous system.
   a. Nerve, tract
   b. Tract, nerve
   c. Neuron, synapse
   d. Synapse, neuron

2. Which section of the human brain is largest?
   a. Hindbrain
   b. Midbrain
   c. Forebrain
   d. Cerebellum

3. Which region of the brain is the last to develop?
   a. Pons
   b. Amygdala
   c. Hippocampus
   d. Prefrontal cortex

4. Which neurotransmitter is important for activity in the mesolimbic dopaminergic pathway?
   a. Acetylcholine
   b. Serotonin
   c. Norepinephrine
   d. Dopamine

5. You hear a loud noise outside your apartment. Your heart starts racing and you begin breathing rapidly. What has been activated?
   a. Sympathetic nervous system
   b. Parasympathetic nervous system
   c. Sympathetic and parasympathetic nervous system
   d. None of the above

6. Drugs of abuse can release up to _____ times the amount of dopamine that occurs with natural rewards (such as food or sex).
   a. 1
   b. 10
   c. 100
   d. 1000

7. A scientist implants an electrode into the mesolimbic dopaminergic pathway of a rat's brain. The rat is able to press a lever to stimulate this area of the brain. What is the likely outcome?

8. Doug had many drinks one night and became so ill that he started vomiting. Why did he vomit, and which brain structure was involved in this response?

9. When would a psychopharmacology researcher choose to use MRI in a study, as opposed to fMRI?

ANSWERS TO QUICK QUIZ 2-2:

1. b – tract, nerve
2. c – forebrain
3. d – prefrontal cortex
4. d – dopamine
5. a – sympathetic nervous system
6. b – 10
7. The rat will continuously self-stimulate the mesolimbic dopaminergic pathway. The rat may press the lever at a rate of more than 1,000 lever presses per hour, to the exclusion of all other behaviors, including drinking, eating, or engaging in sexual activity.
8. Doug drank so much alcohol that he poisoned himself. When toxic chemicals reach threshold levels in the medulla of the brain, the vomiting reflex is triggered in an attempt to clear the body of the toxin. The vomiting reflex is triggered because the brain is assessing danger to the respiratory or cardiovascular system.
9. MRI is an imaging technique that examines brain structure. By contrast, fMRI examines the real-time functioning of the brain. Therefore, if a researcher is looking for brain damage associated with drug use, MRI would be used. However, if the researcher is looking for how a drug influences brain activity or if brain activity has changed with drug use, fMRI would be chosen. In addition, if the researcher wishes to see how the brain responds to drug-related cues, fMRI would be the tool of choice.

CHAPTER SUMMARY

Psychoactive drugs alter brain activity and in some cases can ultimately change the structure of the brain. Neurons communicate with one another electrochemically. Psychoactive drugs are chemicals that resemble naturally occurring neurotransmitters. Drugs impact the chemical aspect of neural communication by changing activity at the synapse, thus altering the normal sending, receiving, and processing of information. The brain is the most complex organ of the body and is made up of billions and billions of neurons. The more basic functions of the brain are located closer to the spinal cord, while the most complex things that humans can do are governed by structures located furthest away from the spinal cord. The mesolimbic pathway in the brain is the neural basis of reward. Drugs of abuse can release 2 to 10 times the amount of dopamine that natural rewards do in the mesolimbic dopaminergic pathway. Finally, various brain imaging techniques have helped us understand which brain areas are responsible for the rewarding aspects of drugs. Moreover, there can be long-term consequences of drug use, including changes to brain function and structure.

BASIC PRINCIPLES OF PHARMACOLOGY

Introduction

Doping in sports is an increasing problem because several psychoactive drugs can be used illicitly to improve athletic performance. Stimulants (such as amphetamines, ephedrine, and cocaine), opiates (such as morphine), cannabinoids, and anabolic steroids can alter human performance in the sports arena. We all know that doping is wrong. We want to see athletes compete, not cheat. However, we also know that there is an arms race between the people who cheat and those who are trying to catch the cheaters. Both sides are relying on basic pharmacological principles to achieve their goals. At the 2012 London Olympic Games, approximately 5,000 urine or blood drug tests were conducted to catch cheaters using any of the 240 drugs that were prohibited. All top five finishers in each competition were tested, in addition to other random athletes. While the final numbers have yet to be released for the London games, there were 25 cases of doping from 4,770 drug tests (0.5% doping rate) at the Beijing games and 26 cases of doping from 3,667 drug tests (0.7% doping rate) at the Athens games. Note that these are all athletes who are informed well in advance of the games that they will be drug tested! Compare these recent numbers to the 667 drug tests performed during the 1968 Olympic Games held in Mexico City, where 1 doping case was recorded (0.1% doping rate). In London, more than 150 antidoping scientists working in a laboratory the size of seven tennis courts were needed just to complete the drug testing of the athletes (IOC, 2012).

A recent story illustrates that doping can come at great personal cost, even as it improves one's performance. Lance Armstrong, a former U.S. professional road racing cyclist, was known to many as an incredible athlete. He won the Tour de France a record seven consecutive times. An implausible accomplishment for anyone, Armstrong did this after being a cancer survivor. His work for cancer awareness was well known and highly regarded, due to his tremendous athletic successes and his personal story. Millions of "Livestrong" plastic yellow wrist bracelets were sold, which raised nearly $500 million for his charitable foundation. In June 2012, the U.S. Anti-Doping Agency (USADA) charged Armstrong with having used illicit performance-enhancing drugs. These charges were based on blood samples from 2009 and 2010 and the testimony of other cyclists. While Armstrong initially challenged these charges, by August 2012, Armstrong announced that he would stop fighting the charges. Later that day, the USADA released a statement that said that Armstrong was banned for life from professional sports and would forfeit all medals, titles, winnings, finishes, and prizes since August 1998. The seven consecutive wins at the Tour de France vanished in an instant. Instead of those wins dominating his legacy, the scandal and lost wins now dominate his legacy (Pells, Dunbar, Logothetis, & Raia, 2012).

Doping in sports is just one instance where knowledge about the basic principles of pharmacology is essential to our understanding of psychoactive drug use. How do pharmacologists identify when psychoactive drugs have recently been used? Will the effects of drugs be different depending on how they are brought into the body? What are tolerance and withdrawal and how do they relate to addiction? What other social and environmental factors contribute to drug use and abuse? We will answer these questions and many more as we explore some of the basic principles of pharmacology.

©ZUMA Press, Inc./Alamy

Alamy CM7354

FIGURE 3-1
Lance Armstrong is a former professional cyclist who won the Tour de France a record seven consecutive times. In June 2012, the U.S. Anti-Doping Agency charged Armstrong with having used illicit performance enhancing drugs, based on blood samples from 2009 and 2010. In August 2012, Armstrong announced he would no longer fight the charges, and he has been banned for life from the sport.

LEARNING OBJECTIVES

Learning objectives can help organize your studying. Before we begin this chapter on the Basic Principles of Pharmacology, keep in mind that by the end of this chapter, you should be able to . . .

1. Define various key terms in pharmacology such as *pharmacokinetics*, *pharmacodynamics*, *route of administration*, *tolerance*, *sensitization*, and *withdrawal*.
2. Describe the various routes of administration and explain which routes are more likely to increase the addictive potential of a psychoactive drug.
3. Explain how the metabolism and excretion of drugs occur and how drug testing can be used to assess recent use of a psychoactive drug.
4. Understand how the dose-response curve is used to visually display data in pharmacology and how effective and lethal doses are determined.
5. Describe the different types of tolerance and the different mechanisms underlying tolerance development.
6. Explain how withdrawal is used to assess development of physical dependence.

Pharmacokinetics and Pharmacodynamics

The drug experience is a result of how the drug affects activity in the brain. When a **drug dose** (the amount of drug) is administered, the drug is transported from the point of entry into the body by the bloodstream to the site of action (the brain). **Pharmacokinetics** is the term used to describe the study of drug movement through the body. Thus, a scientist who studies how a drug is absorbed, distributed, biotransformed, or excreted is studying pharmacokinetics (Wilkinson,

2001). When the drug reaches its final site of action, the drug interacts with a receptor, which produces its effects. **Pharmacodynamics** is the study of the biochemical and physiological effects of drugs and their mechanisms of action (Julien, 2005; Ross & Kenakin, 2001). In the last chapter, we mentioned that many psychoactive drugs have a similar chemical structure to naturally occurring neurotransmitters. A drug that binds to one of the brain's dopamine receptors in a similar way to a neurotransmitter would be an example of pharmacodynamics. Obviously, pharmacokinetics and pharmacodynamics operate together ultimately to result in a drug experience. In this chapter, we will focus first on the factors that can influence pharmacokinetics.

Absorption and Distribution of Drugs

Absorption is the term that refers to the processes and mechanisms by which a drug moves from outside the body into the bloodstream. Below we will discuss a variety of ways that drugs can be absorbed, since there are many different methods for getting a drug into the bloodstream. Once absorbed by the bloodstream, the drug is moved around the body. **Distribution** is the process by which the drug is dispersed throughout the body by circulating blood. The bloodstream is a very efficient method to move a drug around the body. The heart pumps a volume of blood in every minute that is approximately equal to the total amount of blood within the circulatory system. This means that the entire blood that you have inside you circulates once a minute. Therefore, when a drug is absorbed, it only takes about a minute for that drug dose to be distributed throughout the entire circulatory system. In this rapid process, the drug may pass through various barriers to reach its site of action, the receptors. In Chapter 2 we learned that one of these major barriers is the blood–brain barrier, which protects the brain. While the effects of a psychoactive drug often arise from changes in the receptors of the brain, most of the administrated drug never reaches the brain. With any dose of drug, most ends up being circulated outside the brain. Thus, side effects of a drug are often due to the drug going to places in the body other than the primary site of action (Julien, 2005). For example, the primary sites of action for a tricyclic antidepressant drug are the serotonin and norepinephrine receptors of the brain. Individuals using these drugs often experience a variety of side effects during treatment. Side effects can include dry mouth, blurry vision, constipation, difficulty urinating, and increased body temperature. These effects occur in part because the drug alters the activity of muscarinic acetylcholine receptors in parts of the body other than the brain. The takeaway message is that the bloodstream sends a drug dose everywhere in the body. Some of the dose might alter receptor activity in the intended site of action, but receptor activity might also be altered at other locations in the body. The term **bioavailability** is used to describe the portion of the original drug dose that reaches its intended site of action (Benet, Mitchell, & Sheiner, 1990; Wilkinson, 2001).

Route of Administration

The way a drug enters the body is the **route of administration**. There are a variety of methods for getting a drug into the body, including swallowing, smoking, and injection. The route of administration is particularly important for psychoactive drugs, since the route of administration can impact the drug experience (Nelson et al., 2006). Where or how a drug is taken can greatly influence how quickly the drug reaches the brain. It is widely accepted that the more rapidly a drug of abuse can reach the brain, the greater the potential for addiction (Samaha & Robinson, 2002, 2005). For example, nicotine can be administered via smoking or through a nicotine patch placed on the skin. When nicotine is absorbed through the skin, the drug takes a long time to reach the brain, while inhalation of cigarette smoke containing nicotine results in a faster route to the brain. Thus, nicotine administered through the skin is less likely to produce addiction then the same dose of drug that is inhaled. The common methods for drug administration include oral, injection, inhalation, intranasal, sublingual, and transdermal (Beers, 2003; Porter, 2011). A summary table of these methods can be found in Table 3-1. We will discuss each route of

Table 3-1   Major routes of drug administration.

Route of Administration	Description and Factors to Consider	Examples
Oral	- Safe, convenient, and most economical - No skill required - Presence or absence of food in the stomach can dramatically alter drug absorption	Alcohol Amphetamines Barbiturates Benzodiazepines Caffeine LSD Marijuana Morphine Nicotine PCP
Injection	- Different types of needles are required for subcutaneous, intramuscular, and intravenous injections	
Subcutaneous	- Injection route requiring the least amount of skill - Faster absorption than oral administration - Slower absorption than intramuscular and intravenous injection	Barbiturates Heroin LSD
Intramuscular	- Requires skill to inject directly into muscle tissue - Potential high risk of infection in untrained professionals - Pain at injection site - Faster absorption than subcutaneous injection because of good blood flow at injection site	Barbiturates Benzodiazepines Heroin LSD
Intravenous	- Requires high level of skill to inject directly into a vein - Results in immediate drug effects because of fast absorption rate - Repeated use requires healthy vein	Amphetamines Barbiturates Benzodiazepines Caffeine Heroin LSD PCP
Intraperitoneal	- Used mainly in animals - Requires similar level of skill as subcutaneous injections - Results in fairly immediate drug effects because abdominal cavity has a rich blood supply	
Inhalation	- Rapid absorption - Little skill required - Only small amount of drug can be absorbed with one inhalation	Alcohol Cocaine Crack (freebase cocaine) Heroin LSD Marijuana Methamphetamine Nicotine (in cigarettes) PCP
Intranasal	- Rapid and effective, especially for fat-soluble drugs - Can damage the blood vessels in the nose resulting in nose bleeds	Amphetamines Cocaine Heroin Nicotine (tobacco snuff) PCP
Sublingual	- Faster absorption than oral administration	Buprenorphine

(Continued)

Table 3.1   Continued

Route of Administration	Description and Factors to Consider	Examples
	- Preferable for drugs that irritate the stomach but some drugs have an unpleasant taste making sublingual administration problematic	Heroin Naloxone
Transdermal	- Only works for some drugs because the skin is an effective barrier to many chemicals - Absorption is enhanced when drug is placed at skin location with high cutaneous blood flow - Alternative to oral route for drugs that cause gastrointestinal distress	LSD Nicotine

Notes: Some drugs (e.g., barbiturates, cocaine) can also be administered through the mucous membranes of the rectum or vagina.

THC is rarely injected because it is not water-soluble.

administration in more detail, in part because the same drug administered using different routes of administration can change the addictive potential of that drug and the risks associated with that drug. This point cannot be overemphasized. For example, cocaine administered orally rarely results in addiction, whereas the injection of cocaine is much more likely to result in addiction. In addition, the speed of each route of administration also contributes to risks associated with the drug, such as overdose. Using the cocaine example again, the oral administration of cocaine is extremely unlikely to result in a death, whereas the injection of cocaine could potentially result in an overdose resulting in death. Knowledge about each route is necessary to understand better the effects of various psychoactive drugs.

Oral

Most self-administered medications use the **oral drug administration** (swallowing). Oral administration is an easy, safe, and economical way to ingest a drug. Pills, capsules, liquids, or powders can all be swallowed. You do not need any special skills to administer drugs using this route of administration (although a pet owner struggling to get a dog or cat to swallow a pill may disagree). Moreover, oral administration is considered to be the safest administration method because it is also the slowest. When you swallow a drug, it must pass through your digestive system. The drug will pass through the stomach, which can delay the absorption further if food is also present in the stomach. When the drug reaches the small intestine, the drug can be absorbed into the bloodstream. Once in the blood, the drug is passed through the liver, which is the major site of metabolization of most drugs. Finally, the drug is delivered to the ultimate site of action via the bloodstream. For psychoactive drugs, the ultimate site of action is the brain. However, only a portion of the drug dose administered actually reaches the brain after this lengthy process. The length of this process partially explains drug safety (Beers, 2003; Porter, 2011). If you happen to orally ingest too much of a drug, there is time for an emergency room physician to implement an antidote. For a drug user wishing to experience the effects of the drug immediately, oral administration is often the last choice since it is so slow. In spite of slow absorption, orally ingested psychoactive drugs can still have potent effects. Orally administered high doses of alcohol, barbiturates, or morphine can be fatal.

Injection

Unlike oral administration, **injection** as a route of administration requires special equipment and skill. Injection requires a needle and a syringe, which is a relatively recent historical development. In 1853, physicians from Scotland and France independently pioneered the hypodermic syringe, revolutionizing modern medicine by allowing drugs to be injected into the body. In France, Dr. Charles Pravaz developed the hypodermic syringe for drug administration. His method, which

FIGURE 3-2

Scottish physician Alexander Wood (a) and French physician Charles Pravaz (b) independently pioneered the hypodermic syringe for drug administration. Dr. Wood first injected a patient with morphine in 1853. He described his invention in the paper "A New Method for Treating Neuralgia by the Direct Application of Opiates to Painful Points," published in the *Edinburgh Medical and Surgical Journal* (1855). Ironically, the first recorded fatality from a hypodermic syringe–induced overdose was Dr. Wood's wife. The tragedy arose because she was injecting morphine to excess. In 1853, Dr. Pravaz developed the first practical metal syringe.

was demonstrated using sheep and horses, was presented at a scientific meeting in Paris in 1853. In the same year in Scotland, Dr. Alexander Wood injected the first human patient with morphine. Dr. Wood described his invention in a paper titled, "A New Method for Treating Neuralgia by the Direct Application of Opiates to Painful Points," published in 1855 in the *Edinburgh Medical and Surgical Journal*. The paper describes his successful attempt of injecting an elderly woman who had suffered from severe pain (neuralgia) and who could not take opium via oral administration without vomiting. To treat her, Wood concocted a solution of morphine and sherry wine to inject into the woman. The approach was successful in treating her pain and marked a turning point in modern medicine. It appeared that Dr. Wood was aware of the implications of his findings, in part because he wrote in his paper that the narcotic had reached the brain through the venous circulation. The perils of injection of psychoactive drugs also led to a tragedy that personally impacted Dr. Wood. The first recorded fatality from a hypodermic syringe–induced overdose of morphine was Dr. Wood's wife (Mogey, 1953).

That little bit of history of how the injection of drugs was discovered illustrates some pros and cons of injection. Injection is clearly advantageous in cases where bypassing the gastrointestinal tract is required. Further, injection results in rapid and systemic onset of a drug effect. However, these positive attributes can also be viewed as negative attributes in different circumstances. In medical treatment, the rapid onset of effectiveness of pain medication via injection, such as morphine, is highly desirable. However, a recreational user will also experience an immediate "high" when the same drug is injected. This rapid onset effect for the recreational user contributes to the user wanting to repeat the experience, thus increasing the likelihood of addiction. Moreover, injection is a learned skill. If done incorrectly, hazards abound, in part because this method bypasses many of the body's normal defenses. Injecting air into a blood vessel can lead to an air embolism, which can be fatal. Injection drug users also often share needles, resulting in the spread of bloodborne disease such as HIV or hepatitis. Some of these health risks can be more or less dependent on the type of injection (subcutaneous, intramuscular, and intravenous). Different-sized needles and different skills are needed for the different types of injections described below (Beers, 2003; Porter, 2011). Finally, it should be noted that injection places the drug very close to or within the bloodstream. Proximity to the bloodstream makes injection the route of administration most likely to lead to an overdose (Bridge, 2010).

Subcutaneous Injection

When a short needle is inserted into the fatty tissue just beneath the skin to inject a drug, this is called a **subcutaneous injection**. This type of injection route requires the least skill. Once the drug has been injected, the drug will move into the small blood vessels (called capillaries) and be transported through the bloodstream to the site of action. When done properly, this type of injection rarely causes pain or discomfort. Among illicit drug users, abscesses, cellulitis, and other medical complications can be common problems for subcutaneous injectors of cocaine and other drugs (Lloyd-Smith et al., 2008). In slang terminology, this type of injection is often referred to as skin popping.

Intramuscular Injection

When a very long needle is inserted into a muscle to inject a drug, this is called an **intramuscular injection**. The needle is long because muscles lie below skin and fatty tissue. This option is typically chosen when larger volumes of drug are administered, with the location typically being the muscle of the upper arm, thigh, or buttock. Even when done properly, this type of injection can be painful, with an increased risk of infection compared to a subcutaneous injection. However, the absorption of the drug will be faster than a subcutaneous injection due to good blood flow at the injection site. In cases of heroin overdoses, first responders will often administer naloxone (an opioid antagonist) as an antidote via intramuscular injection (Wagner et al., 2010). In slang terminology, intramuscular injection is also referred to as skin popping.

Intravenous Injection

When a moderate-sized needle is inserted directly into a vein, this is called an **intravenous injection**. Most professionals would agree that intravenous injections are the most challenging to master, with a high degree of skill needed to inject directly into a vein. The benefit of intravenous injections is that drug delivery to the site of action is extremely rapid, as the drug is being delivered directly into the bloodstream. In medical settings, when time is of the essence, intravenous injection presents clear advantages. However, repeated intravenous injections can not only be painful, but sometimes impossible because they require healthy veins. In intravenous injection drug abusers, vein damage is common. One study of crack-heroin speedball injection users reported that vein damage was so common that a substantial portion of these users eventually resorted to injections in the groin (femoral vein). This groin injection approach is associated with serious health risks, medical complications, or even death due to infections and/or vascular damage (Rhodes, Briggs, Kimber, Jones, & Holloway, 2007). Beyond these concerns, likelihood of overdose is the major concern, since the drug is being directly placed within the bloodstream (Bridge, 2010). In slang terminology, intravenous injections are referred to as mainlining.

Intraperitoneal Injection

When a drug is injected into the body cavity (the peritoneum) through the abdominal wall, this is called an **intraperitoneal (i.p.) injection**. While less commonly used in humans, i.p. injections are used often in animal studies in psychopharmacology. These injections place the drug in the abdominal cavity, which contains a rich blood supply to serve the digestive system. Drug onset is more rapid with i.p. injections than with subcutaneous injections, while each type requires similar levels of skill since they are less difficult to master than intravenous or intramuscular injections. In humans, i.p. injections are often used to administer chemotherapy drugs to treat cancer.

Inhalation

When a drug is a gas or in small liquid droplets, an individual can breathe in the drug through the mouth, which is called **inhalation**. Similar to the oral route of administration, inhalation requires no special skill. Inhalants used for their psychoactive properties, such as benzene and toluene, are in a gaseous state when breathed. By contrast, small droplets of nicotine are suspended in tobacco smoke, which is inhaled. Droplets of drug must be very small to pass through the trachea (windpipe) and into the lungs. How deeply the droplets can go into the lungs depends on droplet size. Smaller droplets go deeper resulting in greater drug absorption. Once inside the lungs, the drug is then absorbed into the bloodstream. Drugs that are in particles that are too large to be inhaled can be administered via the intranasal route (see below). Typically, only a small amount of drug can be inhaled with one administration. Thus, drugs administered in this manner (such as nicotine) are typically inhaled multiple times. Despite this, inhalation is a rapid and effective route of administration for drug absorption, since the lungs have a large blood supply (Beers, 2003).

Intranasal

When a drug is breathed in via the nose, the drug can be absorbed through the thin mucous membranes that line the inside of the nose and the sinus cavities. Typically, the psychoactive drug is in the form of a powder (such as cocaine, heroin, or powdered tobacco snuff) which gets transformed into tiny droplets in air. This **intranasal** route of administration is sometimes called sniffing or snorting. For a drug to be administered in this manner, the drug should be lipid (fat) soluble, which allows the drug to be absorbed quickly. Some drugs can irritate the nasal passages enough to cause damage, particularly with habitual use. For example, recurrent nosebleeds, nasal membrane irritation, sinus problems and/or loss of olfaction (sense of smell) are localized symptoms often reported with intranasal cocaine use (Schwartz et al., 1989).

Sublingual

When a drug is placed under the tongue and dissolved in saliva, this is called the **sublingual** route of administration. The drug enters the bloodstream when it is absorbed into the small blood vessels beneath the tongue. Nicotine can be administered in this manner in the form of chewing tobacco. Since sublingual drug administration uses the bloodstream in the mouth area for absorption, it is a faster route than oral administration. It is also preferable to oral administration for those drugs that are irritating to the stomach and may cause vomiting. However, not many drugs are taken in this manner due to the aversive taste of many drugs. One common medical use of sublingual administration is the administration of nitroglycerin to treat chest pain (angina pectoris) (Beers, 2003; Porter, 2011).

Transdermal

When a drug is absorbed by placing it on the skin using a patch, this is the **transdermal** route of administration (see Figure 3-3). Through the patch, the drug is slowly absorbed and can act continuously for many hours or days. The skin is an effective barrier to most chemicals, and many drugs cannot be administered in this manner. However, in cases where this is possible, the transdermal route of administration can be preferred to oral administration for drugs, which may cause gastrointestinal distress. Absorption is enhanced by placing the drug on a skin location with high cutaneous blood flow, such as the upper arm. In addition, the drug is sometimes mixed with another chemical (such as alcohol) that enhances penetration through the skin into the

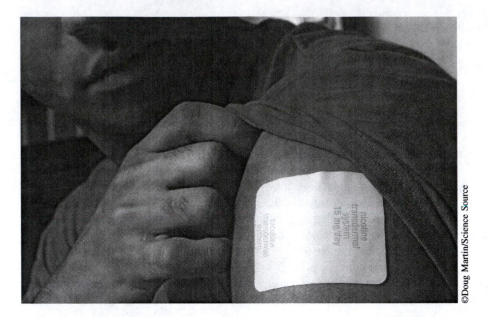

FIGURE 3-3
Illustration of trans-
dermal drug
administration.

bloodstream. However, only drugs given in relatively small doses can be given through patches. The opiate fentanyl (for pain relief), nicotine (for smoking cessation), scopolamine (for motion sickness), and nitroglycerin (for chest pain) are all drugs that can be given using the transdermal route of administration (Beers, 2003; Porter, 2011).

More about the Science:

Nelson et al. (2006). Effect of rate of administration on subjective and physiological effects of intravenous cocaine in humans.
Drug and Alcohol Dependence, 82, 19–24.

Earlier in this chapter, it was mentioned that there is wide acceptance of the notion that the more rapidly a drug of abuse can reach the brain, the greater the potential for addiction. This is referred to as the "rate hypothesis" and in part explains why route of administration can be a critical factor in the abuse liability of psychoactive drugs. For example, heroin can be administered orally or intravenously. The intravenous injection is far more likely to result in addiction than oral administration. Nelson et al. (2006) conducted a study to demonstrate how important rate of administration is to the rewarding effects of a drug. The researchers recruited 17 experienced male cocaine users (ages ranged from 21 to 40). These individuals were not in treatment. Individuals received intravenous cocaine with differing injection durations over several sessions on different days. A variety of measures were taken, including various subjective effects such as how good and stimulated they felt. The results for the positive subjective effects indicated that with faster infusion rates, subjects gave higher ratings for feeling good, stimulation, and liking the drug. Clearly, the faster the drug reached the brain (using faster infusion rates), the more rewarding the drug effect was for the user. This kind of data provides direct experimental evidence to explain the difference in abuse liability of a psychoactive drug taken by different routes of administration.

More about the Science Thought Questions:

1. In this study, cocaine was administered using intravenous infusions. What is the benefit of this experimental approach?
2. Imagine that a patient in a drug rehabilitation facility is reluctant to stop injecting their drug of choice. What could be one approach to helping this individual even if he or she is not willing to stop using the drug altogether?
3. In this study, the participants were cocaine users who were not in treatment. What do you think about the idea of recruiting users of illegal drugs for this research? What ethical concerns should be considered when designing a study such as this one?

More about the Science Thought Question Answers:

1. Intravenous infusions would prevent users from guessing how much drug they are receiving. In addition, the infusion rate could be closely monitored using this approach, which was central to the research question in this study.
2. Injection results in rapid delivery of the drug to the brain. Perhaps the patient could be encouraged to try alternative routes of administration with a slower rate of drug onset, such as oral administration. A slower rate of onset might allow the individual to reduce the amount of drug that is ingested over the course of the day. In addition, injection has many associated health hazards, making alternative routes of administration more favorable.
3. A certain amount of care should be given to the necessity of giving psychoactive drugs to individuals who are struggling with addiction. Clearly, it would be unethical to give drugs to individuals who are seeking treatment for their addiction. However, if individuals are not seeking treatment, doses of drug should remain in the range of their typical use, so that use does not escalate further. Moreover, only studies that truly help us understand addiction and may lead to better treatment should be undertaken in drug addicts, who are a vulnerable population.

Metabolism and Excretion

In Chapter 2, we discussed how drugs that reach the site of action will bind to the appropriate receptor, resulting in changes to nervous system activity. For example, the drug heroin will bind to opiate receptors, which ultimately results in changes in neural activity that makes a user feel less pain or feel high. However, once the drug has had its effect, the drug will be eliminated from the body. In many cases, drugs may be first metabolized into an inert chemical that is less likely to be reabsorbed, before elimination occurs. Drug **metabolism** refers to the biochemical modification of a drug, typically via enzyme systems, into another form. Sometimes metabolites are not inert and the newly modified chemical may impact the body. Whether the drug stays the same as its original form, or it is a metabolite, it will exit the body. Drug **excretion** refers to this process of how the chemical leaves the body. There are several routes that a drug, or its metabolite, can use to exit the body. The chemical can leave via the kidneys, lungs, bile, or skin.

When a drug uses the kidney route of excretion (also called renal excretion), the drug typically makes its final exit as a metabolite in urine. A drug can also leave the body via the lungs. This will occur with gaseous agents and to a certain extent with alcohol. The third route relies on bile, which is a substance produced by the liver aiding digestion of lipids in the small intestine. Drugs that are passed through bile and into the intestine are typically reabsorbed into the bloodstream from the intestine. Finally, a drug can exit the body via the skin as sweat. However, most drugs leave the body using the kidney route and thus end up in urine. Sometimes, researchers will describe how long it takes the body to clear a drug. One metric, **half-life**, refers to the amount of time that passes for the dose of drug in the body to be reduced by half. Psychoactive drugs that have a longer half-life can be less likely to contribute to addiction, in part because the user does not need another dose so frequently with drug elimination occurring more slowly (Julien, 2005; Warner, Bobo, Warner, Reid, & Rachal, 2006; Wilkinson, 2001).

Drug Testing

Drug testing refers to the various methods to determine if someone has used a psychoactive drug. Analyzing urine, saliva, hair, sweat, or blood samples are typical approaches to testing for the presence of many drugs, since each of these can be used to detect the drug or drug metabolite. For alcohol, breath analysis is also used. The breathalyzer is perhaps less invasive than urine testing, since most people feel comfortable blowing into a machine to give a breath sample but feel uncomfortable about producing a cup of urine (see Figure 3-4). Breath testing for alcohol is used in various scenarios, including by police for detection of impaired driving. In addition, saliva, hair, and sweat detection are increasing in popularity as the technology improves, since these techniques are low in invasiveness. Despite the highest level of invasiveness, blood testing remains widely utilized and is necessary in medical settings when injuries are an issue or upon postmortem examination (Markway & Baker, 2011; Ringmets et al., 2012).

As mentioned earlier, most psychoactive drugs or drug metabolites are detectable in urine (Miller, 1991). For this reason, pre-employment drug testing, courts/correctional drug testing, drug treatment programs, and accident drug testing have become routine. Advocates argue that drug testing in the workplace helps businesses succeed by avoiding lawsuits and maintaining

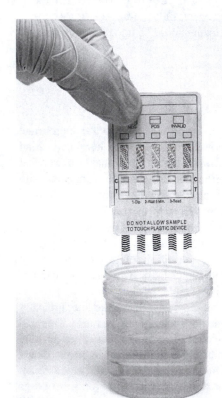

©GIPhotoStock/Science Source

FIGURE 3-4
Typical urine drug test.

safety. However, the use of drug testing is at times argued to be an infringement of personal rights. If you are sober and effective on the job, why should it matter what activities you are engaged in during nonwork hours? Despite these privacy concerns, workplace drug testing is probably here to stay.

In my laboratory, I administer drugs to human participants. For safety reasons, I need to ensure that all my participants have not used any other drugs before participating in one of my experiments. I rely on urine drug testing as a simple and easy method to test for recent use of drugs. The individual provides a urine sample in a private bathroom. A research assistant takes the urine sample, which is now in the specimen cup, and places a dipstick in it. Within 5 minutes, the results are revealed. For recent alcohol use, a breathalyzer reading is required, which takes about 1 minute to administer (see Figure 3-5). In less than 6 minutes and for less than $5.00, I can confirm that the individual who wants to participate in my study can safely do so since I have tested for the presence of 10 psychoactive drugs. However, the ability to detect the presence of a drug depends on the drug in question. Close examination of Table 3-2 reveals that the ability to detect recent use of a psychoactive drug can range from one day up to one month. This range does not coincide with the likelihood of abuse, addiction, or health risks. For example, heroin is perhaps the most difficult drug to stop use once addiction has

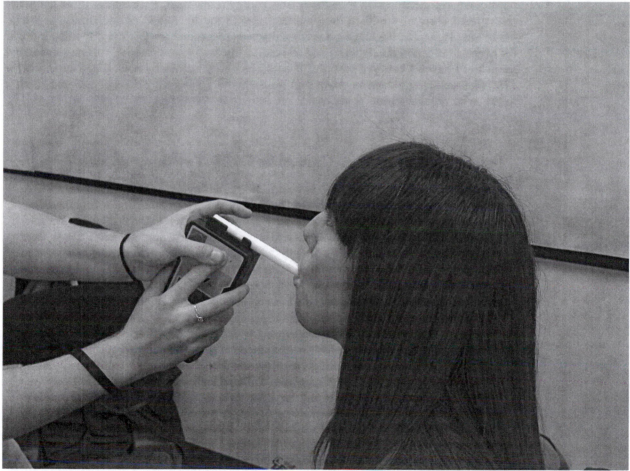

Courtesy of Cecile A. Marczinski

FIGURE 3-5
Undergraduate student researcher illustrating the use of a breathalyzer machine in my laboratory.

Table 3-2 Detection times when drug testing for psychoactive drug use.

Drug	Detection Time (days)
Alcohol	Up to 1
Amphetamine, methamphetamine	1–4
Barbiturates	2–4 for short-acting; up to 30 for long-acting
Benzodiazepines	7–42
Cocaine	1–3 for sporadic use; up to 12 for chronic use
Ecstasy	1–2
Marijuana	1–7 for casual use; up to 35 for chronic use
Opiates (Heroin, Morphine)	1–3
Phencyclidine	2–7 for casual use; up to 30 for chronic use

Note: Adapted from Chapter 9 (Drug Testing as a Tool) of the following publication:

Center for Substance Abuse Treatment (2005). Medication-assisted treatment for opioid addiction in opioid treatment programs. Treatment improvement protocol (TIP) series, No. 43. Rockville, MD: Substance Abuse and Mental Health Services Administration. This publication is in the public domain and was retrieved from http://www.ncbi.nlm.nih.gov/books/NBK64164/

In addition, information was confirmed from a drug-testing manufacturer: http://uveradiagnostics.com

taken hold, yet the detection time for opiates is only a few days. By contrast, there are many recreational users of the illicit drug marijuana, with the likelihood of addiction being relatively low. However, the longest detection times can be found for this drug. If I had a dollar for every time a potential subject had arrived in my lab, tested positive for marijuana, and said, "but I haven't used pot recently," I might be a rich woman by now. Urine detection for THC (the active ingredient in marijuana) can be up to a week after a single use and about a month with regular (chronic) use.

Focus on Careers: A Career in Drug Testing

Now that we have covered the basic principles of drug testing, let us look at all of the possible careers that are connected to this process. Drug testing has grown considerably in part because of advances in technology and in part because demand has increased with declining costs for these tests. This industry change has provided many career possibilities to consider. First, there are the companies that provide the drug tests. These companies are developing new ways to detect drugs and this requires personnel. Sales associates will often possess an undergraduate degree with a reasonable background in science given the detailed questions that arise from potential customers. For employment drug testing, customer companies sometimes prefer that a drug-testing company handle this process (by sending them urine or other specimens). Other companies will do their own drug testing on site, which requires training. Across a vast variety of sectors in the economy, employees who work in human resources or safety now have drug testing as their expertise. Moreover, pre-employment drug testing has become so common that it even is done at major job fairs. An applicant will hand in their resume and their urine sample! Beyond the corporate sector, demand for drug tests also extends to various government agencies. Drug testing itself or interpretation of drug-test results is part of the job demands for police officers, social service workers, and judges. Many court-ordered drug treatment programs incorporate drug testing. Even in school settings, drug testing is becoming increasingly common, particularly for athletes. Finally, there are the policymakers and lawyers who determine the legality of drug-testing processes and making sure that rights are not infringed upon. In sum, drug testing provides a livelihood for many people.

Websites to explore (look for the employment or careers link):

Drug & Alcohol Testing Industry Association
   http://www.datia.org
American Screening Corporation
   http://www.americanscreeningcorp.com
Arc Point Labs
   www.arcpointlabs.com

QUICK QUIZ 3-1

1. A drug that is taken sublingually is _____.
   a. Smoked
   b. Injected just below the skin surface
   c. Injected into the abdominal cavity
   d. Placed under the tongue

2. Which of the following drugs can be detected in urine for up to one month following chronic use?
   a. Opiates
   b. Marijuana
   c. Cocaine
   d. Alcohol

3. The faster the drug reaches the brain, _____.
   a. the more rewarding the drug effect
   b. the less rewarding the drug effect
   c. the faster the rate hypothesis
   d. the slower the rate hypothesis

4. Fred is applying for a job that requires preemployment drug testing. He has used one illicit drug in the past but his last use was more than a month ago. Which drug is most likely to still be detectable in a urine drug screen?
   a. Heroin
   b. Cocaine
   c. Marijuana
   d. Ecstasy

5. Explain the term "drug metabolism."

6. Bariatric surgery is a radical measure to treat obesity, whereby the stomach is reduced in size and the patient loses weight. However, recent evidence has suggested that bariatric surgery can increase the risk of alcohol use disorders (King et al., 2012). Using your knowledge about routes of administration, what is a potential explanation for this observation?

ANSWERS TO QUICK QUIZ 3-1:

1. d – placed under the tongue
2. b – marijuana
3. a – the more rewarding the drug effect
4. c – marijuana
5. Once a drug has had its effect, it will get eliminated from the body. In many cases, the drug may be first metabolized into an inert chemical that is less likely to be reabsorbed, before elimination occurs. Drug metabolism refers to the biochemical modification of a drug into this new form, called a metabolite. This change occurs with the help of enzyme systems. Finally, not all metabolites are inert since some of them will affect the functioning of the body.

6. By reducing the size of the stomach, the oral route of administration is altered by reducing the amount of time spent in the gastrointestinal tract. When alcohol is consumed postsurgery, the drug will have faster access to the bloodstream. It is known that the faster a drug reaches the brain, the greater the concern about potential for addiction.

The Dose-Response Curve

This chapter so far has focused on pharmacokinetics. Recall that pharmacokinetics refers to the study of the movement of a drug around the body, including how the drug is absorbed, distributed, and excreted. Now we will turn our attention to pharmacodynamics, the study of the biochemical and physiological effects of drugs and their mechanisms of action. To better understand how drugs have their effects, we will have a closer look at how data obtained from experiments is

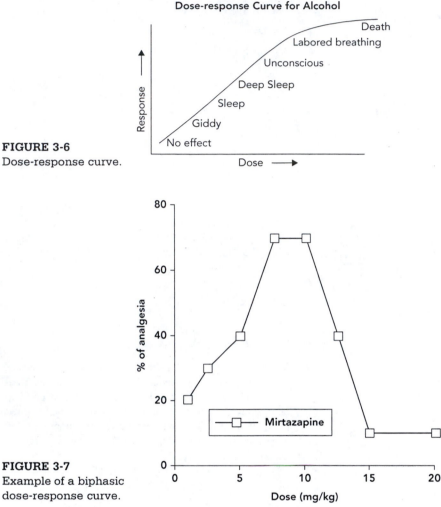

Dose-response Curve for Alcohol

FIGURE 3-6
Dose-response curve.

FIGURE 3-7
Example of a biphasic
dose-response curve.

typically presented in graphical form. Familiarity with a few of the key terms used in this area of research will be helpful in better understanding pharmacodynamics.

Researchers determine the typical responses that people or animals have to a drug by examining their responses across a range of doses. For example, a researcher may wish to study the sedative properties of alcohol. Participants may be brought into the lab on multiple occasions and be administered a different alcohol dose during each test session. The response to the dose is recorded for each session. Alternatively, animals may be administered the range of doses on different days and have their responses recorded. The response results are averaged across all participants for each dose. The data is then plotted on a graph known as a **dose-response curve**. Typically, the range of doses is placed on the *x*-axis (the horizontal line) and the average response recorded is placed on the *y*-axis (the vertical line). Figure 3-6 presents a typical dose-response curve. In this example, the drug produces increasingly larger effects on sedation as the dose of alcohol increases. After a certain point, the curve plateaus (since there is obviously no point involving higher doses where the sedation effect can be greater than death).

Not all dose-response curves will have the shape in Figure 3-6. Sometimes, there is a **peak drug effect** where the greatest response may not occur at the highest dose given. As shown in Figure 3-7, sometimes the response to the drug initially goes up with the dose, but then the response decreases as the dose continues to increase. When a dose-response curve contains a change of direction, the drug effect is described as **biphasic**. Note that a biphasic drug effect sometimes has the reverse pattern, with the response initially going down and then later reversing direction. A decline followed by an increase is described as a U-shaped function, whereas the data shown in Figure 3-7 is described as an inverted U-shaped function.

The data presented in Figure 3-7 is real data from a study that examined the analgesic response following the administration of a drug, mitrazapine, in mice. The mice were given the drug via i.p. injection. The analgesic (pain-blocking) response was investigated by placing the mice on a hot plate. The measurement of interest was the duration of time that the mouse kept its paw on the hot plate before removing it. This test is similar to the familiar situation where you put your hand under a hot water tap and then quickly remove it if the water is too hot. If pain was being blocked by the drug, the mouse would keep its paw on the hot plate longer. What is shown in the figure is that there is an optimal dose of this drug (the peak drug effect) to achieve this pain-blocking response. This optimal dose is not the highest dose of drug, but instead is an intermediate dose level.

Effective and Lethal Doses

Pharmacologists will often use the terms *effective dose* and *lethal dose* when describing a drug. The **effective dose (ED)** is the dose at which a given percentage of individuals show a particular effect of the drug. Typically, the effective dose is measured for 50% of individuals and reported as an ED_{50} value. For example, researchers may wish to determine the ED_{50} for analgesia (pain-blocking) using a new drug. For a sample of 100 patients, the ED_{50} would be the minimum dose level (such as 4 mg/kg) that blocks pain for 50 or more individuals. Note that this is just an average. There are going to be some patients who receive effective pain relief at lower doses and others who require greater doses of drug to have pain relief. However, this number will give a clinician or researcher a target that might be appropriate for most individuals (Becker, 2007).

In addition to the effective dose, a researcher will also describe the **lethal dose (LD)**, which is the dose of drug at which a given percentage of individuals die within a specific time. Similar to ED_{50}, the lethal dose is often measured for 50% of individuals (LD_{50}). For ethical reasons, humans are not used in determining LD_{50} values for drugs. Instead, a group of animals will be administered the drug at increasing levels to determine the dose level at which 50% of the animals die. The results will then be extrapolated to humans (Becker, 2007; Gable, 2004).

In the analgesic drug example above, the goal is to administer the drug to the patient at an effective dose that blocks pain while staying far away from the lethal dose. In medical settings, drugs are often characterized by a **therapeutic index**, which is an indication of how safe a drug is. It is calculated as the ratio of LD_{50}/ED_{50}. The same therapeutic index is used in the description of the recreational use of psychoactive drugs but is often called the **safety ratio**. For psychoactive drugs, the ED_{50} refers to the dose resulting in the desired effect. For example, THC (the psychoactive chemical found in marijuana) has an approximate safety ratio of 1000:1. In other words, the dose of THC that recreational users will use for its psychoactive effects is significantly lower than the lethal dose. By contrast, alcohol has an approximate LD_{50}/ED_{50} value of 10:1 (Gable, 2004). A lethal dose of alcohol is much closer to the dose used by recreational users. Larger therapeutic/safety index ratios indicate greater drug safety.

Tolerance

The response to a drug is not static across time. With repeated administration of a given dose of drug, the response may be reduced. For example, you can ask a college student the question, "How many drinks does it take for you to feel drunk?" The response might be, "three drinks." However, if this individual drinks steadily and somewhat heavily over a period of time, the response might change. A few months later, three drinks may no longer result in the feeling of being drunk. Instead, five drinks is the new reported answer. This phenomenon, called **tolerance**, is the need for increased amounts of the substance to achieve intoxication or the diminished effect with continued use of the same amount of the substance (APA, 1994). Tolerance was introduced in Chapter 1 of this book, in part because it is so central to diagnosing addiction. However, the topic of tolerance is central to pharmacology, and greater detail is now provided.

Types of Tolerance

Most researchers agree that there are three types of tolerance, called dispositional, functional, and behavioral. **Dispositional tolerance** occurs when there is an increase in the metabolism rate of a drug due to the regular use of that drug. Dispositional tolerance is sometimes referred to as pharmacokinetic tolerance since the drug may be metabolized so quickly that a portion of the dose never reaches the site of action. An example of this would be a chronic alcoholic who has had a long history of drinking. The chronic alcoholic's body will metabolize alcohol much faster than someone who has not had such a drug use history (Nuutinen, Lindros, Hekali, & Salaspuro, 1985). Dispositional tolerance is clearly problematic and will contribute to an escalation in drug use. When entering treatment, chronic alcoholics will be asked how much they typically drink in a day. The numbers are sometimes staggering. Numbers as high as 40 drinks per day are reported, which is an amount of alcohol that would almost certainly result in death for a social drinker (Vogel-Sprott, 1992).

Functional tolerance refers to the decreased behavioral effects of a drug as a result of its regular use. Functional tolerance is sometimes referred to as pharmacodynamic tolerance. With functional tolerance, it is thought that the brain and other parts of the nervous system have become less sensitive to a drug's effects. This type of tolerance can develop over many drug use sessions or even within the course of action of a single dose. The varying times over which functional tolerance may develop has led researchers to subdivide this type of tolerance into two types based on timing. **Acute tolerance** is functional tolerance that has developed within the course of a single drug dose. By contrast, **protracted tolerance** is functional tolerance that has developed over the course of two or more drug administrations.

How would a researcher determine if acute tolerance has developed? In a typical study, the drug is administered and the response across time to the single dose is recorded. The amount of drug in the body will rise as absorption occurs, peaks, and then declines, as drug elimination occurs. Figure 3-8 illustrates mean blood alcohol levels following administration of an alcohol dose. The researcher compares two time points (earlier and later in the session) when blood alcohol is similar. In the figure, this is noted by test 1 and test 2. Acute tolerance is said to be present when the response to a drug is more pronounced early in the course of the single drug dose, as compared to later, even though the level of drug in the body is the same. For alcohol use, development of acute tolerance is typically nonuniform across various brain functions. For example, individuals may report feeling less drunk and more willing to drive a car later in a session than earlier. However, actual driving ability (as measured by performance on a driving simulator) remains similarly impaired across time (Marczinski & Fillmore, 2009). This is clearly a safety concern, since individuals think they are safe to drive when they are not. This safety concern is not inconsequential, as illustrated by the results of one study that examined the status of alcohol absorption in drinking drivers who were killed in traffic accidents (Levine & Smialek, 2000). The researchers focused their analyses on driver fatality cases in which alcohol was present in the blood and death occurred shortly after the accident. They observed that only 8% of cases were in the absorption phase of the blood alcohol curve, and 25% of the cases were at the plateau. The majority of cases (67%) were on the elimination phase.

While acute tolerance is functional tolerance that is measured over the course of a single drug dose, protracted tolerance is functional tolerance that takes longer to develop. Over the course of

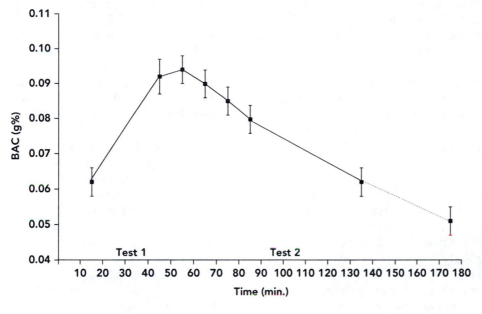

FIGURE 3-8
Acute tolerance experiments measure performance early and late in a single drug administration session when the amount of drug is the same in the body. This figure illustrates the rise and fall of blood alcohol.

two or more drug administrations, the drug response can diminish. In laboratory studies examining development of protected tolerance, drug administration sessions often occur on separate days. Functional tolerance is said to have occurred when levels of impairment diminish across those testing days. Protracted tolerance may lead to an escalation in the dose used to achieve a certain effect, which can lead to and is part of addiction to a psychoactive drug (Vogel-Sprott, 1992).

Behavioral tolerance, also called learned tolerance, is the third category of tolerance. Behavioral tolerance involves an adjustment of behavior through experience in using a drug to compensate for its effects. Drugs have various effects that can be counteracted by changes in behavior. For example, an intoxicating dose of alcohol may cause an individual to lose balance when walking or to slur when speaking. Once the individual is aware of these changes, behavioral compensation can occur. The person may walk slowly while holding on to the wall and talk really s-l-o-w-l-y (Vogel-Sprott, 1992).

While the three main types of tolerance are dispositional, functional, and behavioral, a related tolerance should also be mentioned. **Cross-tolerance** refers to the phenomenon whereby tolerance that has developed to one drug crosses over to a similar drug. Development of cross-tolerance can be problematic. For example, an alcoholic may require surgery. The alcoholic has developed significant tolerance to alcohol. However, this tolerance will also cross over to other sedative drugs, including anesthetics. When the anesthesiologist gives a dose of drug that should make most people unconscious and ready for surgery, the alcoholic may have little to no response. In this case, the anesthesiologist has a significant dilemma. What dose of anesthetic should be given that will be both effective and safe?

Mechanisms Underlying Tolerance

Why does tolerance develop? There are several explanations available, with biological changes and learning mechanisms both involved. First, the biological explanation is described. Sometimes referred to as the adaptation-homeostasis theory of drug tolerance (Cicero, 1980) or the homeostatic theory of drug tolerance (Poulos & Cappell, 1991), tolerance occurs because of the body's increasingly more efficient attempts to return to homeostasis. The term **homeostasis** refers to the stable environment in the body. The body has processes in place to regulate its internal environment and maintain a relatively constant set of conditions. A good illustration is body temperature. The body has a certain temperature that is considered ideal. If body temperature wavers above or below this level, mechanisms are in place to return the temperature back to its ideal, or set point. If the body gets too hot, sweating occurs. If the body gets too cold, shivering occurs.

Psychoactive drugs will alter the internal body environment in a direction that strays from its ideal. For example, cocaine raises body temperature. With repeated use of cocaine, the body adapts and attempts to return the body back to its homeostatic balance. The body might do this by lowering body temperature (a compensatory response). Psychoactive drugs act on neurons in the central nervous system (CNS). Thus, neurons learn to adapt to the presence of a drug with repeated exposure. As a result, a relatively normal level of functioning can occur even when the drug is present. For example, neurons that release the neurotransmitter dopamine are affected by cocaine. Cocaine increases the amount of dopamine available for neurotransmission. Thus, there is an oversupply of dopamine. With regular use, neurons adjust to this oversupply by making less dopamine. When the neurons make less dopamine, more drug is needed (which is tolerance development) to make up the deficiency and also achieve the desired effect. All of these changes are most likely to be observed with dispositional and functional tolerance.

Tolerance may also reflect learning mechanisms that you are probably familiar with. Sometimes referred to as the learning theory of tolerance (Vogel-Sprott, 1992) or the associative theory of tolerance (Siegel, Baptista, Kim, McDonald, & Weise-Kelly, 2000), tolerance is described as learned information triggering compensatory reactions in the body to return to it to a homeostatic balance. To better understand this approach, let us return to basic learning for a moment. Do you remember Pavlov and his drooling dog? Russian physiologist and Nobel Prize winner, Ivan Pavlov, had a research lab where he studied digestion in dogs. He noticed that when the lab workers came into the lab to feed the dogs, the dogs would drool, even before the food was visible. To determine if some sort of learning was involved, Pavlov designed an experiment. He decided to ring a bell and look at the reaction of the dogs. Of course, the dogs did nothing. However, if the dog was presented with food, the dog would drool in anticipation of dinner. Pavlov then provided the dog with some learning trials. He presented the food at the same time as the sound of the bell. The dog would drool (since the food was present). However, eventually the dog would drool just when the sound of the bell occurred. The dog had made the association between the two stimuli, the food and the bell. Classical (or Pavlovian or associative) conditioning reflects the process whereby an individual learns that two stimuli are associated.

The same principle underlies learned drug tolerance. A drug user learns that certain cues present at the time of drug administration are associated with drug-altered states. For example, a previously unimportant syringe becomes an important environmental stimulus for a heroin user. Recall that drugs alter the homeostatic balance in the body, as described above. Therefore, the learned associations provide the body with information that the drug is coming. When a drug-related stimulus is present, the body will prepare the appropriate compensatory response (the body response that is opposite to what the drug will do to the body). For example, cocaine administration will elevate body temperature. A regular drug user learns that the sight of cocaine and related drug paraphernalia (predrug stimulus cues) comes just before the drug effect. As such, the body will lower its temperature upon seeing the cues in anticipation of the drug administration. These conditioned (learned) compensatory responses are what mediate tolerance by counteracting the drug effect when the drug is administrated in the presence of drug-paired cues (Siegel et al., 2000). Learning can impact all three types of tolerance.

Tolerance development is driven by both biological changes and learning, and these two can be inextricably linked (Streather & Hinson, 1985). Both biological changes and learning mechanisms assist the body in dealing with disruptions in homeostasis. The effects of both mechanisms on drug tolerance can be dramatic. One example of this concerns heroin overdose deaths. When heroin is administered at too high a dose, respiratory depression and even death can occur. Anecdotal observations of human overdose deaths has revealed that the user was often in an unusual place (usual context) or some other factor was different from typical drug administrations. Given these observations, researchers have systematically investigated whether absence of typical learned environmental cues in these situations contributed to the deaths. To test this idea, researchers designed an animal experiment to see if the learned environment mattered in overdose risk. Rats were placed into three groups. Two groups of animals were given heroin injections in a specific environment for a month. The third group was given saline injections for a month. On the critical test day, all rats were given a lethal dose of heroin. One group was given this dose in the same environment that was used for the previous injections over the past month. Group two was given this dose in a brand-new environment. Group three was given the heroin dose for the first time in a familiar environment.

The mortality results were dramatic. The heroin dose was fatal for all of the rats who had never received heroin before. This was unsurprising since the dose given was intended to be a lethal dose and no tolerance would have developed in animals who had never had heroin before. The rats that had previous exposure to heroin and then received the lethal dose in the familiar environment had a mortality rate of approximately 30%. Finally, the rats that had previous exposure to heroin and then received the lethal dose in a novel environment had a mortality rate of approximately 65%. Clearly, tolerance had developed in the animals with previous exposures to heroin. Moreover, the familiar environment further triggered drug-anticipatory responses that were learned by the rats (Siegel et al., 1982). Similar findings have been observed with morphine analgesic tolerance (Siegel, Hinson, & Krank, 1978; Siegel, 1988).

One final note about tolerance is that compensatory reactions become stronger with repeated use of a given dose of drug. The body works to maintain homeostasis, and the repeated use of a drug allows the body to become more adept at handling the drug and opposing its action. Fortunately, what is learned can also be unlearned. Let us briefly return to Pavlov and his drooling dogs. What happens when the bell is presented many times and food is not presented? The dogs eventually stop drooling. This process, called extinction, is essentially unlearning. Drug users often have to incorporate this process in their treatment program to successfully deal with their addiction. Salient drug-related environmental cues must be rendered more neutral in valence. As you might expect, absence from the drug will result in biological processes being less efficient in counteracting the drug. It has been suggested that the undoing of the biological processes related to tolerance happens more readily than the learned tolerance, which is more resistant to change (given that you need opportunities for extinction episodes). However, both biological and learned tolerance can be reduced or even eliminated. Finally, resumption of use can be problematic and risky when tolerance abates. If someone is in treatment and then has a relapse, the user may think that they should use the typical dose from before the treatment (when tolerance was present). However, if tolerance has abated (due to a period of abstinence), then an overdose could occur with the previously typical dose.

Sensitization

One final phenomenon related to tolerance, but actually the reverse of tolerance, is **sensitization**. Sometimes, repeated administration of a drug results in greater sensitivity to the effects of a drug. Some researchers think that sensitization can partly explain addiction, a notion referred to as the incentive-sensitization theory of addiction (Robinson & Berridge, 1993, 2003). Far less research has been done on sensitization, but the process does seem to occur with repeated use of marijuana, cocaine, and amphetamines. In human users, the initial use of drug may not produce a remarkable subjective effect, such as "wanting more drug." However, with repeated administration of the same dose of that drug, greater responses occur. Sensitization is routinely observed in other aspects of biology as well. Allergies are a classic illustration of sensitization. A first-time exposure to poison ivy may cause only a mild skin irritation. However, subsequent exposures will elicit a painful and pronounced allergic reaction. Whenever receptors become more likely to respond to a stimulus, this more efficient response is considered sensitization.

While psychoactive drug sensitization has been less well studied than tolerance, it has been clearly observed in animal studies. For example, one reliable observation with mice is that amphetamine results in hyperactivity. With repeated exposure, greater hyperactivity will be observed even if dose administration is kept constant. Moreover, sensitization can be more pronounced in adolescent animals than adult animals. This might partly explain why adolescent humans are more likely to have drug abuse problems (Kameda et al., 2011). However, not all researchers agree that sensitization underlies the development of addiction, even for drugs like cocaine having the strongest evidence that sensitization occurs (Kalapatapu et al., 2012). It should also be noted that while sensitization appears to be the reverse of tolerance, homeostasis may not play a role in sensitization. As sensitization develops, the body is responding in ways that seem further and further from homeostatic balance. Clearly, more research is needed to understand this complicated phenomenon better.

Withdrawal Symptoms

When drug use stops, the drug is eliminated from the body. However, the person may not feel back to normal. In some cases, the individual may actually feel very ill. **Withdrawal** is the characteristic syndrome that occurs when the drug is no longer used or decreased in typical dose. The symptoms of withdrawal will differ depending on the drug that was used and the length of use. Withdrawal symptoms can range from relatively mild to life-threatening. An alcohol hangover is an example of a relatively mild withdrawal symptom. The day after excessive alcohol consumption, an individual may experience symptoms similar to having the flu. Fatigue, dry mouth, thirst, headache, drowsiness, weakness, and concentration problems are typical symptoms. Feelings of nausea and even vomiting might occur (Penning, McKinney, & Verster, 2012). While unpleasant, a hangover will go away with time. However, excessive drinking that leads to dependence results in more disconcerting outcomes. An alcoholic who attempts to cut down or quit drinking can experience life-threatening withdrawal symptoms, such as seizures, convulsions, hallucinations, vomiting, sweating, and high fever. For this reason, medications are often used to help with some symptoms, particularly in those individuals who present with high levels of recent alcohol intake and are likely to experience severe withdrawal symptoms (Cooper & Vernon, 2013; Pristach, Smith, & Whitney, 1983). In subsequent chapters, we will discuss the characteristic withdrawal symptoms for the various psychoactive drugs. While the symptoms can differ depending on the drug, it is always the case that these symptoms are aversive. Withdrawal symptoms are also observed with withdrawal of psychoactive drugs used both recreationally and therapeutically. For example, approximately 20% of patients who stop antidepressant medication taken for at least six weeks display flu-like symptoms, insomnia, nausea, imbalance, sensory disturbances, and hyperarousal. These are withdrawal symptoms in that they immediately extinguish upon reinstatement of the antidepressant medication. These symptoms are more likely with a longer duration of treatment and a shorter half-life of the treatment drug (Warner et al., 2006).

Why do withdrawal symptoms occur? The same processes underlying tolerance also underlie withdrawal. Thus, both learning and biological mechanisms play a role in withdrawal. Recall from the tolerance and learning section above that learned drug cues can mediate drug tolerance. What happens when these usual stimulus cues are presented in the absence of the drug? The unopposed compensatory responses are now evident and result in withdrawal symptoms (Siegel et al., 2000). For example, imagine that powdered cocaine is placed in front of a user who has developed high levels of tolerance to cocaine. Cocaine ingestion elevates body temperature. Just the presentation of the drug stimulus to the user will elicit compensatory processes that will counteract the effect of the drug (in this example, lowering of body temperature). If the individual does not use the drug, the user will have only experienced compensatory processes. If body temperature drops unusually low, shivering may be one withdrawal symptom that is observed. In addition to learning, the body also has biological mechanisms to return it back to its homeostatic balance. Cells in the body become adapted to the regular presence of the drug with repeated exposure. If the drug is no longer present, the body is left in an abnormal state and withdrawal symptoms may reflect this. For example, some psychoactive drugs elevate levels of monoamines (dopamine, serotonin, and norepinephrine) in the brain. With repeated use, decreased production and release of these monoamines by neurons in the brain occur because the levels of monoamines are very high due to the drug use. If the user suddenly stops using the drug, this individual will have unusually low levels of monoamines in the brain. Depression is a classic withdrawal symptom that is observed when monoamine levels are low. Mechanisms aside, the unpleasant nature of withdrawal symptoms may help to maintain drug use even in individuals who want to discontinue use. Treatments that are effective must address these withdrawal symptoms and help users manage them.

In the News:

O'Neill, J. (2012, April 28). Hospital seeing more babies born exposed to prescription drugs. *CNN*.

Tolerance and withdrawal are not limited to drug users. When a pregnant woman uses psychoactive drugs, the drug passes through the placenta to the baby. Once the baby is born, the access to the drug is gone and the newborn baby will go through withdrawal. In recent years, there has been a dramatic increase in the number of newborns experiencing withdrawal from opiates. In this news article, the director of the neonatal intensive care unit, Dr. Buchheit, reported that some opiates, such as oxycodone, are the worst offenders for the babies suffering from withdrawal in his hospital. The symptoms are clearly evident and distressing for both the baby and the observer. The babies cry constantly, are highly sensitive to light and sound, and experience seizures. Treatments must be individualized to each infant. Some treatments involve administering morphine to the infant in small doses with a gradual decrease over the following weeks to wean babies off the drugs. Morphine seems to work better than methadone (the treatment choice for adults). If the infant gets better, the question of who will take care of the infant then arises. Will the mother be able to get clean and be in a position to care for her baby? Will a relative be able to help with care, or is foster care the only answer? Unfortunately, the story mentions the widespread nature of this problem. One health department survey in Tennessee found that one-third of pregnant women in state treatment programs were addicted to prescription pain meds. The American Academy of Pediatrics notes that between 55% and 94% of babies exposed to opiates prior to birth exhibit signs of withdrawal.

Use This News Article to Test and Apply Your Knowledge:

1. In this article, the babies are experiencing withdrawal symptoms. Based on what you know about withdrawal symptoms and tolerance, what can be inferred about tolerance development to opiates in utero?
2. Two babies are admitted into a neonatal intensive care unit. Baby A had mild symptoms that did not require pharmacological treatment (morphine administrations). Baby B had severe symptoms that required pharmacological treatment that lasted over a month. In both cases, the mothers claimed that they only used a little bit of oxycodone for back pain and that they didn't realize the drug could harm their baby. Could both mothers be telling the truth (assuming that the babies and mothers were similar on all other attributes)?

Answers

1. If an infant is experiencing withdrawal symptoms upon birth, the drug use in the mother must have been sufficiently regular such that tolerance had developed in both the mother and the developing baby during the pregnancy. The more severe the withdrawal symptoms in the infant, the greater the tolerance development that must have occurred with repeated drug use by the mother. Even though the infant is not choosing to expose itself to the drug, tolerance will nevertheless occur. When the infant is born, the drug is immediately unavailable and withdrawal symptoms will occur.

2. It is very unlikely that both mothers used a similar amount of drug. More severe withdrawal symptoms occur with greater tolerance to a drug. If everything else is equal, the mother of Baby B must have been using more drug than the mother of Baby A.

What Do You Think about This News Story?

This news article highlights a growing problem, the abuse of prescription opiates. Women who are pregnant are part of the group of abusers. What do you think are possible ways to prevent this problem? Do you think that pregnant women who use opiates are aware of the harm they are doing to their developing babies? Do you think this information is widely known, just like alcohol exposure being harmful in pregnancy? Do you think that this problem has become so dire in part because people perceive that "prescription" drugs are less harmful than other street drugs? If you are interested in this problem and would like to help, some hospitals are recruiting volunteer "cuddlers." These are trained individuals who know how to hold and comfort these distressed babies, which contributes to a faster recovery process.

Physical and Psychological Dependence

Tolerance and withdrawal go hand in hand. As greater tolerance develops, more pronounced withdrawal symptoms will be observed. **Physical dependence** on a drug is a state in which the use of the drug is required just so the person can function normally. How can you tell when a person has reached the point of physical dependence? Just take away the drug. The occurrence of withdrawal symptoms is evidence of physical dependence. Moreover, if withdrawal symptoms quickly dissipate upon readministration of the drug, this is further evidence of physical dependence.

Is physical dependence central to addiction? Recall that **addiction** refers to compulsive drug use. When one is strongly invested in using a drug, getting an adequate supply of it, and having a strong tendency to resume use of it after stopping for a time period, addiction is present. Physical dependence will be present in many cases of addiction, but not always. Researchers and clinicians have noted that some patients crave drugs but do not get sick if they do not use them. **Psychological dependence** refers to the compulsive use of a drug for its pleasurable effects. Psychological dependence will lead to a compulsion to misuse a drug. Depending on the individual, the level of use and the drug of choice, among other factors, psychological and/or physical dependence may be present (Julien, 2005). Thus, in many cases of addiction, both physical and psychological dependence are present. For example, imagine an individual who wants to quit smoking cigarettes. Upon immediate cessation of smoking, the individual will experience a variety of symptoms, including irritability, anxiety, difficulty concentrating, increased appetite, insomnia, pain, and other somatic complaints. The individual will really crave a cigarette. Clearly, both physical and psychological dependence are present. By contrast, imagine an individual who has been drinking alcohol a lot lately and thinks cutting back is needed. The individual decides to stop drinking completely. Upon immediate cessation of drinking, the individual feels a strong craving for alcohol. Though this person really desires a drink, they are not physically sick in any way. In this case, there is only evidence of psychological dependence and not physical dependence. It is notable that physical dependence contributes to greater difficulty in decreasing drug use or maintaining abstinence than psychological dependence.

Researchers and policy makers have endeavored to determine which psychoactive drugs are most dangerous to society. To say this is a difficult question is a massive understatement. Many of the pharmacological variables that contribute to drug danger have been discussed in this chapter. For example, route of administration matters. A drug that reaches the brain rapidly can be more problematic than a drug administered using a slower route. Drugs that are eliminated faster (shorter half-life) may also be more problematic. Dr. Robert Gable attempted to answer this question of which psychoactive drugs are most dangerous, however difficult this question may be. He did so by examining two pharmacological variables we have covered in this chapter, dependence potential and the ratio of active dose to lethal dose (Gable, 2004, 2006). Using results from both human and animal experiments, psychoactive drugs that are used for nonmedical purposes were evaluated on these two pharmacological variables. Dr. Gable observed that heroin was highest on both dependence potential and active dose/ lethal dose ratio (meaning that it was the least safe). This places heroin towards the most dangerous on the spectrum (at least for these two examined pharmacological characteristics). By contrast, several of the hallucinogens ranked lowest on both variables. Clearly, understanding the basic principles of pharmacology is valuable knowledge to gain and is applicable to many questions, including how society should frame policies about drugs.

Myth Busters: Everyone Who Uses Cocaine or Heroin Is an Addict

In the general public, it is not uncommon to hear people say that someone who uses a so-called "hard" drug must be an addict. The use of cocaine or heroin must mean that the individual has developed an addiction and is in need of treatment. Is this notion correct or is it a myth? As discussed earlier in this chapter, various criteria need to be present to assess addiction. The compulsive use of the drug is needed. If this compulsive use is not evident, addiction is not present. Among the psychoactive drugs, heroin and cocaine are likely to result in addiction. However, addiction is not a certainty. Recreational use of these illegal drugs does occur. In fact, researchers like to study the differences between recreational and dependent users of a drug to better understand what has changed once addiction is clearly evident in individuals and how the progression from recreational use to dependence occurs. In the research literature, it appears that there are more studies comparing recreational users of cocaine as research subjects (Preller et al., 2013; Soar, Mason, Potton, & Dawkins, 2012), than recreational users of heroin (Des Jarlais et al., 2007; Eaves, 2004). This purely anecdotal observation might suggest that it is less likely that a heroin user can maintain a recreational habit without progressing to addiction. This hypothesis would be consistent with what is known about the pharmacological characteristics of heroin relative to cocaine. For example, heroin is more likely to be injected, as opposed to other routes of administration, such as intranasal or inhalation. By contrast, cocaine is somewhat less likely to be administered via injection, the route of administration with the fastest rate of onset.

QUICK QUIZ 3-2

1. A typical dose-effect, the _____ is plotted on the vertical axis and the _____ is plotted on the horizontal axis.
   a. range of doses, effect size
   b. effect size, number of participants
   c. number of participants, effect size
   d. effect size, range of doses

2. The safety of drug is sometimes described using a therapeutic index, which is calculated by the ratio of:
   a. LD_{50}/ED_{50}
   b. ED_{50}/LD_{50}
   c. LD_{100}/ED_{100}
   d. ED_{100}/LD_{100}

3. Sarah has developed an addiction to prescription pain medication and takes it all the time. When she is at work, her coworkers report to Sarah's boss that she is slurring her speech and acting high. When Sarah is questioned by her boss, Sarah manages to pull herself together and talk clearly by talking more slowly than normal. This is an example of:
   a. Dispositional tolerance
   b. Functional tolerance
   c. Acute tolerance
   d. Behavioral tolerance

4. Brandon used to smoke marijuana on a regular basis until he decided to apply for a job at a company that requires drug testing of applicants. Brandon has noticed that he really wants to smoke marijuana and he thinks about this all the time. He has not felt any illness symptoms since he stopped smoking. It is likely that Brandon exhibits _____, but not _____.
   a. physical dependence, psychological dependence
   b. psychological dependence, physical dependence
   c. addiction, psychological dependence
   d. tolerance, sensitization

5. Drug A has an ED_{50} of 2 mg/kg and a LD_{50} of 200 mg/kg. Drug B has an ED_{50} of 10 mg/kg and a LD_{50} of 100 mg/kg. What is the therapeutic index for Drugs A and B? If all things were equal, which drug is safer?

6. In the study described in this chapter, the researchers administered the drug mitrazapine to mice via i.p. injection and measured analgesic responses (Schreiber, Rigai, Katz, & Pick, 2002). Describe what this route of administration refers to and how rapid responses would be experienced. What type of dose response curve was observed?

7. Joe has a dependence on heroin. He goes to another city and stays in a hotel. After he injects his typical dose, he overdoses. Explain why this might have occurred.

8. Explain how drug sensitization is like allergies.

ANSWERS TO QUICK QUIZ 3-2:

1. d – effect size, range of doses
2. a – LD_{50}/ED_{50}
3. d – behavioral tolerance
4. b – psychological dependence, physical dependence
5. Drug A has a therapeutic index of 100. This was calculated using the therapeutic index calculation, which is LD_{50}/ED_{50} = 200/2 = 100. Using the same calculation, the therapeutic index for Drug B is 10. Therefore, Drug A is safer as indicated by the higher therapeutic index value.
6. The i.p. injection route refers to when a drug is injected into the body cavity (the peritoneum) through the abdominal wall, thus, the name intraperitoneal (i.p.) injection. While less commonly used in humans, i.p. injections are used often in animal studies in psychopharmacology. These injections place the drug in the abdominal cavity, which contains the digestive system and has a rich blood supply. For this reason, drug onset is quite rapid. The dose response curve observed was biphasic because there was a peak drug effect that did not occur at the highest dose. Instead, an intermediate dose resulted in the most pronounced analgesic response.
7. Joe has developed tolerance to heroin. Unfortunately, when he was in a novel environment (the hotel room), the absence of learned environmental cues in this novel situation prevented the body from readying itself for the typical dose. In the absence of the compensatory response that would have been normally triggered by learned environmental cues, an overdose occurred.
8. With allergies, the first-time exposure to the allergen (such as poison ivy) may only cause a mild reaction (skin irritation). However, subsequent exposures to the allergen will elicit a pronounced allergic reaction. Drug sensitization can be similar. The first exposure to a drug may elicit a very mild response (such as wanting more drug). However, with repeated exposure to the drug, greater responses occur.

CHAPTER SUMMARY

Basic principles of pharmacology help to explain the drug experience. Pharmacokinetics refers to the study of the movement of the drug in the body from the site of administration to the site of action. Pharmacodynamics refers to the study of the biochemical and physical effects of drugs and their mechanisms of action at receptors in the body. There are various ways that a drug can enter the body. Oral, injection, inhalation, intranasal, sublingual, and transdermal are all possible routes of administration for psychoactive drugs. Once the drug reaches the site of action, the drug can have its effect. After this occurs, the drug will be excreted from the body, either in its original form or as a metabolite. Drug testing refers to the various methods used to determine if someone has used a psychoactive drug. Researchers examine the effects of a drug by examining responses to that drug across a range of doses. Data are plotted on a graph, which is called a dose-response curve. The range of doses is placed on the horizontal line and the average response recorded is placed on the vertical line. This curve allows researchers to determine the effective and lethal doses of a drug. However, the individual response to a drug is not static and can change when a drug is used repeatedly. Tolerance is the need for increased amounts of a substance to achieve intoxication, or the diminished effect with continued use of the same amount of the substance. There are different types of tolerance reflecting underlying changes in both biological and learning mechanisms. The development of tolerance is particularly evident in an individual who ceases using a drug and then exhibits withdrawal symptoms. If tolerance and withdrawal are present, an individual is said to be physically dependent on that drug. Some patients crave drugs but do not get sick if they do not use them. If this is the case, the individual is said to be psychologically, but not physically, dependent on that drug.

4

CAFFEINE

Introduction

As I sit at my computer writing this chapter, I periodically stop typing and take a sip of coffee. I love the beverage, and if I had to suddenly quit drinking coffee, I would be unhappy. A sudden cessation of my typical caffeine consumption habit would probably induce a headache, make me feel fatigued, and create a generalized state of grumpiness. To avoid this, I just happily keep up my coffee drinking habit. Many of you reading this book may also be consuming your caffeine vehicle of choice, be it coffee, tea, a soft drink, an energy drink, or chocolate (Figure 4-1). Even a variety of over-the-counter medications contain caffeine. Do you have asthma, headaches, or menstrual cramps, or are you using supplements to build more muscle at the gym? Those pills and powders may have caffeine in them. The use of caffeine is so universal and found in so many products that we almost forget that we are talking about a drug.

In this chapter, we are going to explore all aspects of caffeine and how it acts as a mild central nervous system (CNS) stimulant. Caffeine is a good place to start learning about psychoactive drugs since many have personally experienced the effects of this drug. In fact, caffeine use is so universal that even age is not a factor in use. Unlike other psychoactive drugs, young children to the elderly use caffeine. For this reason, caffeine has been described as the "cradle-to-grave drug" (Kenny & Darragh, 1985). However, given that caffeine is consumed by pregnant women, it might be more appropriate to describe it as the "before-the-cradle-to-the-grave drug." You may

Figure 4-1
Caffeine is a widely used psychoactive drug found in variety of consumer products including coffee, tea, soft drinks, energy drinks, chocolate, and medications.

©pio3/Shutterstock

have many questions about caffeine. Is caffeine safe? What does caffeine do to your body? Is it addictive? Why can some people consume large amounts of caffeine without noticeable effects while others experience many negative effects? Why does it make us feel more awake and alert? How long do these effects last? Let us explore these and many other questions about caffeine.

LEARNING OBJECTIVES

Learning objectives can help you organize your studying. Before we begin the topic of caffeine, keep in mind that by the end of this chapter, you should be able to . . .

1. Describe the various sources of caffeine.
2. Define various terms associated with caffeine such as stimulant drug, alkaloid, xanthine, adenosine, and route of administration.
3. Describe how prevalent caffeine use is around the world.
4. Explain how caffeine acts on the central nervous system and how the acute effects of caffeine differ from chronic effects.
5. Apply your knowledge to calculate a typical caffeine dose for an individual.
6. Evaluate the evidence regarding the risks of consuming energy drinks.

Caffeine as a Stimulant Drug

A **stimulant drug** is a drug that increases alertness, decreases fatigue, and heightens mood. Stimulant drugs can be used for both recreational and medical reasons. **Caffeine** is a typical example of a mild stimulant drug and is the world's most widely taken psychoactive drug. Caffeine is the common name for 1,3,7-trimethylxanthine. The name *caffeine* is derived from the German word *kaffee* and the French word *café*, which both mean coffee (Heckman, Weil, & Gonzalez de Mejia, 2010). As a psychoactive drug, caffeine can improve mood and speed up thinking. Later in this chapter, we will examine the evidence that caffeine causes these changes. Caffeine can be consumed as a small but powerful component of a beverage or food product. This aspect of caffeine consumption makes it, as a drug, somewhat more interesting and difficult to study. Our experiences with this drug are frequent and typically embedded with other aspects of the food or beverage that provides the vehicle for caffeine. If you consume a sugary carbonated soft drink with caffeine in it, any changes you might experience may or may not arise from

© Kondor83/iStockphoto

Figure 4-2
Caffeine powder.

caffeine alone. However, caffeine is also a drug that can be consumed in isolation, such as in a caffeine pill. Soon after swallowing a caffeine pill, particularly if one is quite fatigued, the user will feel more awake and energized. There are other stimulant drugs, besides caffeine, that have similar but far more potent effects. Nicotine, like caffeine, is considered to be an over-the-counter stimulant. We will discuss nicotine in Chapter 5. There are also stimulants that are controlled. Cocaine, amphetamines, and methylphenidate (used in the treatment of attention deficit/hyper-activity disorder) are examples of controlled stimulants, which we will discuss in Chapters 6 and 7.

If you have taken a chemistry lab class, you might have had the experience of isolating caffeine from coffee. You start with dark coffee grounds, add several chemicals and use equipment like pipettes and Erlenmeyer flasks. After several steps and a few hours of swirling and decanting, you have as an end result a white crystalline powder that is caffeine (Figure 4-2). If you were to smell caffeine, it would be odorless. If you were to taste this powder, it would taste very bitter. However, I would strongly recommend that you not do this taste test, given that there are many ways to make errors in this process. Leave the caffeine extraction stuff to the experts, or become an expert yourself by looking at a career in psychopharmacology (see Chapter 2).

Caffeine is considered an alkaloid. **Alkaloids** are a large category of nitrogen containing organic metabolites produced by plants. Alkaloids are extremely bitter and sometimes toxic. In this textbook, we will also discuss the drugs morphine, cocaine, and codeine, which are common alkaloids. When plants produce alkaloids, they protect themselves from hungry insects by making their leaves unattractive to eat. If you were a bug, chomping on a bitter alkaloid-filled leaf is quite unpleasant, and you would move to the next plant to see if it tastes a little better. So if bugs don't like alkaloids, such as caffeine, why do we like caffeine so much? As you will see, we like the effects that caffeine has on us, and the bitter taste of the caffeine can easily be masked if it is disliked, such as by adding lots of sugar. Let's examine some of the common sources of caffeine.

Sources of Caffeine

Caffeine is found in a variety of beverages and foods. It is naturally found in coffee beans, cacao beans, kola nuts, guarana berries, and tea leaves such as yerba mate. Caffeine is also a component of several over-the-counter medications (Heckman et al., 2010). As such, most people take their caffeine orally. While quite rare, caffeine can also be injected, if the drug is mixed within an aqueous solution. Caffeine powder is also used as filler for street drugs like heroin, metham-phetamine, and cocaine. Caffeine can be made synthetically, and there is no difference between synthetic caffeine and caffeine from natural sources (Heckman et al., 2010). Let us now examine some of the most common sources of caffeine, including coffee, tea, soft drinks, energy drinks, and medications.

Coffee

Coffee is a dark-colored brewed beverage with an acidic flavor. Coffee is prepared from the roasted seeds (coffee beans) of the coffee plant. The coffee plant is a small evergreen bush or small tree of the genus *Coffea*. There are several species of this plant, such as *Coffea arabica* and *Coffea canephora*. *Coffea canephora* (also called robusta) has twice the caffeine of *Coffea arabica*, but robusta tends to be bitter, so the *arabica* variety is often preferred. Left unpruned, coffee plants may grow up to 15 feet (5 meters) in height. The leaves are dark green and glossy, and also contain caffeine, just like the seeds. The plants have white flowers, which are followed by oval berries that are brilliant red in color. The seeds (which are called beans) are found in the coffee berries, with most berries containing approximately two seeds (Figure 4-3). The berries ripen in seven to nine months, which partly explains why most coffee production occurs in countries around the equator, such as Brazil, Vietnam, Indonesia, and Columbia. When the coffee berries are ripe, they are picked, processed, and dried. One coffee plant yields five pounds of fruit, which results in one pound of dried beans. The dried beans are then roasted. The roasting process

©elpy/istockphoto

Figure 4-3
Coffee berries.

depends on the desired flavor. To make the beverage of coffee, the roasted seeds are ground and mixed with hot water long enough to extract the flavor. Coffee brewing can occur by several methods such as boiling, steeping, or pressurizing. The spent grounds are removed and the liquid final product is ready to consume and enjoy. It should be noted that coffee is big business and provides a livelihood for over 20 million people around the world. It is an incredibly labor-intensive crop, with most of the harvesting of coffee still being done by human hands. Behind oil, coffee is the second most traded export product in the world (Prendergrast, 2009).

Worldwide consumption of coffee is high. In North America and Europe, coffee consumption is approximately one-third of that of tap water (Villanueva et al., 2006). Coffee is a primary source of caffeine. It has been estimated that coffee accounted for about 75% of the total caffeine consumed by adults over the age of 18 in the United States (Ellenhorn & Barceloux, 1988; Graham, 1978). Given that there are different species of coffee plants grown in different regions of the world, and that there are a variety of ways to make coffee, it is unsurprising that the caffeine content of coffee beverages can differ. It has been estimated that a typical small cup of ground-roasted coffee (5 oz. or 150 ml) contains approximately 85 mg of caffeine (Barone & Roberts, 1996). Particularly with the rise in popularity of espresso and other specialty coffees, the caffeine content varies substantially. One research group investigated the caffeine content found in specialty coffees, by taking samples obtained from coffee shops located in one region in Maryland. They found that these coffees ranged from 58 mg to 259 mg for a typical serving (one shot of espresso). In the same study, they also examined the variability in brewed coffee within one coffee shop. Over the course of six consecutive days, the researchers went to a single Starbucks® coffee shop located in Gainesville, Florida, and acquired 16 oz. (Grande size) samples of Starbucks® Breakfast Blend coffee. Back in the lab, they determined the amount of caffeine found in the 16 oz. coffee for each day. The caffeine amounts ranged from 259 mg to 564 mg. Notice that the same order from the same coffee shop with the same type of coffee had almost double the caffeine on one day compared to another. Thus, even under highly standardized conditions found in a prominent coffee chain, the amount of caffeine varied twofold (McCusker, Goldberger, & Cone, 2003).

Tea

Tea is a beverage that has a less acidic flavor than coffee. Tea is prepared from the cured leaves of the *Camellia sinensis* plant. Similar to coffee, the tea plant is an evergreen that mainly grows in tropical and subtropical climates. It is a main agricultural product for countries such as China,

India, Kenya, and Sri Lanka. There are two popular varieties of tea. The China tea plant (*C. sinensis sinensis*) is used for most Chinese and Japanese teas. The Assam tea plant (*C. sinensis assamica*) is used for most Indian and other teas. Tea leaves are selected from the top 1 to 2 inches of a mature plant when picked, with the leaves subsequently dried. Depending on the type of tea, the leaves may also be allowed to wilt, oxidize or ferment. Dry tea is sold as black or green tea, with black tea having 97% of the share in world tea production and green tea having 3% of the share (Alkan, Koprulu, & Alkan, 2009; Weinberg & Bealer, 2001). To make tea, the dried leaves (either loose or in a tea bag) are mixed with hot or boiling water long enough to extract the flavor. Around the world, tea is typically served hot. However, in the United States and Canada, 80% of tea is consumed cold, as iced tea. Note that most herbal teas have very little or no caffeine, so we will not discuss them in this chapter.

Worldwide, tea is the most widely consumed beverage after water (Alkan, Koprulu, & Alkan, 2009). However, tea is only the second most important source of caffeine, after coffee, as tea contains less caffeine than coffee. It has been estimated that a typical cup of brewed tea (5 oz. or 150 ml) contains approximately 42 mg of caffeine, which is about half of the caffeine found in the same size cup of coffee (Barone & Roberts, 1996). Among tea beverages, yerba mate has a higher caffeine content than black and green teas. While the caffeine content in various teas can differ for the same reasons as coffee (i.e., different plant variety, different growing conditions, different preparation method), the variability in caffeine content appears to be less in tea than observed with coffee. One study was conducted to determine the concentration of caffeine in 20 commercial tea products. The researchers brewed the teas under a variety of conditions by varying the steep-times (how long the tea bag is in the cup with the hot water) and serving sizes (6 or 8 oz.). Using black, green, and white teas, the caffeine concentration per serving ranged from 14 mg to 61 mg. Not surprisingly, the longer the steep time, the greater the caffeine concentration (Chin, Merves, Goldberger, Sampson-Cone, & Cone, 2008).

Chocolate

Chocolate is a raw or processed food produced from the seed of the *Theobroma cacao* tree (Figure 4-4). This evergreen tree has been cultivated for at least three millennia in Mexico, Central, and South America. The tree grows up to 26 feet in height. The tree has white and light pink flowers. The fruit from this tree contain the seeds that are used to make cocoa powder and chocolate. The fruit, which are called cocoa pods, can grow to be quite large. Each piece of fruit is ovoid and can approach a foot in length and four inches in width. As the fruit ripens from yellow to orange, it can reach about 1 pound in weight. Inside each pod are anywhere from 20 to 60 seeds or "beans." The beans are the main ingredient for chocolate. However, do not think that you could just eat these seeds like a chocolate bar, as the seeds have an intense bitter taste. Chocolate producers allow fermentation of the seeds to improve the flavor. Then they dry the beans, clean them, and roast them. After roasting, the shell is removed to produce cacao nibs. The nibs are then ground to make cocoa mass (pure chocolate in rough form). From there, either cocoa solids or cocoa butter can be made. If you have tasted unsweetened baking chocolate, you know that it is very bitter. Unsweetened baking chocolate contains cocoa solids and cocoa butter in varying proportions. The chocolate that we like to eat is called sweet chocolate (also known as dark chocolate). In addition to the cocoa solids and cocoa butter, sugar is added to give sweet chocolate its taste. Milk chocolate is dark chocolate that also contains milk powder or condensed milk. White chocolate contains cocoa butter, sugar, and milk (but no cocoa solids) and in some countries is not considered chocolate at all.

Chocolate has become one of the most popular food types and flavors in the world. Most of our holidays are celebrated with chocolate in one form or another. In addition, chocolate or cocoa powder is used in hot and cold beverages to produce hot chocolate and chocolate milk. While cocoa was originally from the Americas, today about two-thirds of the world's cocoa is produced in Western Africa. The caffeine content of chocolate is low compared to coffee and tea. A 1 oz.

©Taylor S. Kennedy/Getty Images

Figure 4-4
Theobroma cacao tree.

serving of milk chocolate contains an average of 6 mg of caffeine. The same size serving of dark (sweet) chocolate contains about 20 mg of caffeine (Barone & Roberts, 1996). However, chocolate also contains theobromine, a chemical similar to caffeine, but with less psychoactive effects. We will discuss theobromine later in this chapter.

Soft Drinks

Soft drinks, also called sodas or pop, are beverages that contain water (which is most often carbonated), a sweetener and a flavoring agent. Manmade caffeine is added to many soft drinks, particularly cola varieties. The amount of caffeine in soft drinks is less variable than that observed in products containing caffeine from natural sources, since all of the ingredients that are included in soft drinks are part of a tightly controlled manufacturing process. The U.S. Food and Drug Administration (FDA) includes caffeine on a list of substances that are generally recognized as safe. The FDA has set the maximum concentration of caffeine in cola beverages at 65 mg of caffeine per 12 oz. bottle, which equates to 5.4 mg/oz. (FDA, 2003). Manufacturers do appear to keep their products within the FDA regulations. Researchers in one study examined the caffeine content in 19 carbonated sodas, both caffeinated and caffeine free, that were purchased from various convenience stores located in Florida. The researchers also sampled fountain Coca-Cola from nine different fast-food eating establishments (such as McDonald's, Burger King, and Steak and Shake). The authors found that for the sodas from the convenience stores, the caffeine concentrations ranged from 0–48.2 mg/12 oz. serving, which was well below the maximum allowable limit of caffeine as established by the FDA. When they examined the fountain Coca-Cola beverages, they had predicted some variability in caffeine content given that there are possible dispensing differences that could alter caffeine concentrations (more carbonated water and less syrup should lead to a less concentrated drink with less caffeine in it). Surprisingly, the caffeine concentration had little variability across restaurants and ranged from 40.9 mg to 48.4 mg/16 oz. serving (McCusker, Goldberger, & Cone, 2006).

Soft drinks are called "soft," because they don't contain alcohol, while alcoholic beverages are considered "hard drinks." Soft drinks are served chilled or at room temperature, unlike coffee and tea. Table 4-1 lists some of the popular brands of soft drinks that contain caffeine. In the United States, soft drinks account for the main source of caffeine consumed by children and adolescents, whereas coffee is the main source of caffeine for adults (Heckman et al., 2010). One nationwide 7-day food consumption survey examined caffeine consumption in children ages 5 to 18 years. The

Table 4-1 Caffeine concentration in beverages, foods, and medications.

Source	Caffeine (mg)		
	1 oz.	8 oz.	12 oz.
Coffee			
Plain, brewed	17	133	200
Plain, brewed (McDonald's)	6	50	75
Plain, brewed (Starbucks Pike Place Roast)	21	165	248
Caffe latte (Starbucks)	9	75	113
Espresso	40	320	480
Instant	12	93	140
Tea			
Plain, brewed	7	53	80
Green, brewed	6	45	68
Black, brewed	6	47	72
Yerba Mate	10	78	117
Chocolate			
Milk chocolate bar	6	48	72
Dark chocolate bar	20	160	240
Chocolate milk	1	5	8
Baking chocolate	35	280	420
Soft Drinks			
Coca-Cola	3	23	35
Pepsi-Cola	3	25	37
Diet Coke	4	31	47
Diet Pepsi	3	23	35
Mountain Dew	5	37	55
Dr. Pepper	3	27	41
Barq's Root Beer	2	15	23
Sunkist Orange Soda	4	28	42
7 Up	0	0	0
Sprite	0	0	0
Energy Drinks			
Red Bull	9	73	110
Monster	10	80	120
Amp	9	71	107
Full Throttle	8	72	108

Source	Caffeine (mg) 1 oz.	8 oz.	12 oz.
Rockstar	10	80	120
SoBe Adrenaline Rush	10	76	114
SoBe No Fear	11	87	131
Rockstar	10	80	120
NOS	16	125	187
Spike Shooter	36	286	429
Wired X 344	22	172	258
Energy Shots			
5 Hour Energy Shot	69	552	828
Red Bull Power Shot	40	320	480
Soft Drink/Energy Drink Mixes			
Mountain Dew MDX	6	47	71
Coca-Cola Blak	6	46	70
Pepsi Max	6	45	67
Tab Energy	9	72	108
Jolt Cola	6	48	72
Medications			
No-Doz	100 mg/tablet		
No-Doz Maximum Strength	200 mg/tablet		
Vivarin	200 mg/tablet		
Excedrin	65 mg/tablet		
Anacin	32 mg/tablet		
Midol	32 mg/tablet		
Dexatrim	200 mg/tablet		
Hydroxycut Hardcore	100 mg/capsule		

Notes: While all beverages are shown for caffeine content for 1, 8, and 12 oz. servings, the typical serving size for these products may differ, which influences how much caffeine is typically ingested. A standard soft drink can and a "tall" size Starbucks coffee is 12 oz. A chocolate bar is 1.5 oz. Most energy drink cans are 16 oz. in size.

Sources include Barone & Roberts (1996), Heckman et al. (2010), Reissig et al. (2009), Seifert et al. (2011), http://mayoclinic .com, http://www.energyfiend.com, and manufacturer websites for newer products. For energy drink products, manufacturers are not required to list the caffeine content that comes from other additives (such as guarana or yerba mate). Therefore, the caffeine content listed may be somewhat underestimated for some energy drinks.

researchers found that 98% of those children consumed caffeine on a weekly basis, with most of the caffeine coming from soft drinks (Morgan, Stults, & Zabik, 1982).

Energy Drinks

Energy drinks (such as Red Bull® and Monster®) are beverages marketed as providing increased energy from a combination of caffeine and other plant-based stimulants (guarana) and amino acids (taurine). Energy drinks are similar to soft drinks in that they are often carbonated and contain sugar or sweeteners. High-caffeine soft drinks have existed in the United States since the 1980s, beginning with Jolt Cola®. However, energy drinks began being marketed as a separate beverage category after the introduction of the first energy drink product, Red Bull®. This Austrian beverage was introduced in its native country in 1987 and brought to the United States in 1997 (Reissig, Strain, & Griffiths, 2009; Simon & Mosher, 2007). Energy drink consumption has since exploded. In 2011, worldwide sales were approximately $9 billion. Energy drinks have become very popular, especially with children, adolescents, and young adults. While the U.S. Food and Drug Administration (FDA) limits the caffeine content in soft drinks, which are categorized as foods, there is no such regulation of energy drinks, which are currently classified as dietary supplements (Seifert, Schaechter, Hershorin, & Lipshultz, 2011). Therefore, the caffeine content for energy drinks often far exceeds what is found in soft drinks (see Table 4-1). For example, while Coca-Cola Classic® contains 2.9 mg of caffeine/fl oz., Red Bull® contains 9.2 mg of caffeine/fl oz. It is also notable that energy drinks are often served in large-sized cans. Many of the popular brands of energy drinks are sold in 16 oz. cans as opposed to the typical 12 oz. soft drink cans. Energy shots, like energy drinks, have also been experiencing a rapid rise in popularity. Energy shots (such as 5 Hour Energy®) are similar to energy drinks but tend not to be carbonated and contain less liquid. They can contain as much caffeine as a cup of coffee in a small 2 oz. serving. It is important also to note that the variety of additives typically included in various energy drinks/shots further increases the amount of caffeine consumed. Many drinks contain guarana, a plant containing caffeine. Other additives like kola nut, yerba mate, and cocoa also increase the caffeine content of the beverage. Interestingly, manufacturers are not required to list the caffeine content for these ingredients, even though they add to the overall caffeine in the product (Seifert et al., 2011). As such, it may not be exactly clear how much actual caffeine is found in some of these products, though it is clear that the caffeine content of energy drinks can be up to three times the caffeine level that the FDA allows for cola beverages (McCusker et al., 2006).

Medications

A variety of over-the-counter and prescription medications contain caffeine. If you have a headache or cold and take over-the-counter medications to alleviate your symptoms, you may notice that caffeine is found in many of these drugs. Pain medications like Anacin® and Excedrin® are examples of such drugs. In addition, caffeine can suppress appetite due to its diuretic effects. Therefore, dieting aids like Dexatrim®, Diatac®, and Hydroxycut Hardcore® contain caffeine. Finally, several over-the-counter medications are caffeine pills meant to decrease fatigue and drowsiness. Examples of these stimulant drugs include No-Doz® and Vivarin®.

Brief History of Caffeine Use

Historians have suggested that caffeine was consumed as far back as 2737 BCE. Recall that there are a variety of plants containing mind-altering alkaloids such as caffeine. Therefore, as people sampled various plants, they would eventually discover the effect that caffeine has on the body. It is believed that China was the origin of the culture of tea planting and tea drinking. The legend behind the discovery of tea goes something like this: Chinese Emperor Shen Nung was boiling water when some leaves from a nearby bush fell into the water, giving off an aromatic odor. When the emperor tried the new drink, he liked the pleasant taste. The emperor then recommended tea for his people. The first written information about tea was recorded by Confucius in 500 BCE, who claimed drinking tea had positive effects on human health (Alkan et al., 2009).

Coffee drinking originated later than tea drinking, in 9th-century Ethiopia. The coffee shrub grew under the Ethiopian rain forest canopy in the mountains. While the story of coffee's discovery may be somewhat mythical, it is probably not too far from the truth. As the story goes, a young shepherd boy (or a holy man in some versions) was herding his goats. He watched them eat wild berries, which were coffee berries. The goats became animated and energetic soon after eating them. This prompted the boy to try the berries himself (Pendergrast, 1999). In the holy man version, the holy man had the bright idea that the berries from the plant could help him endure long nights of prayer (Blum, 1984). Once the berries were discovered to have these effects, a beverage made out of them would have arrived soon after. It should be noted that caffeine was not always well received by societies when first introduced. For example, orthodox priests were not impressed when Mohammedans used caffeine to stay awake during long prayer vigils. Apparently, they thought it was cheating. Nevertheless, official punishments for users and killing coffee trees did not stop coffee from becoming popular among Arabian Moslems. By the 10th century, coffee was mentioned as a deliberately cultivated crop in written accounts by Rhazes, an Arabian physician.

Europe around the time of Columbus knew little about tea and coffee and the effects of caffeine. Indeed, only alcohol was familiar to Europeans around the 15th century. When explorers voyaged to the east and west of Europe, they were introduced to caffeine. In Arabia, Turkey, and Ethiopia, explorers discovered coffee traded by Muslim pilgrims throughout the Islamic world. In China, European explorers found tea. In West Africa, they found the kola nut. In Mexico, Central and South America, they found the cacao plant (used to make chocolate). However, coffee and tea were expensive and rare, such that the Europeans in the upper classes used them initially as medicine. By the mid-17th century, trade with caffeine-producing countries increased and coffee and tea changed in status from medicines to drinks.

The popularity of caffeine use grew during the Industrial Revolution in the late 1700s in Great Britain and by the early 1800s in other parts of Europe and North America. At that time, the lower classes began to drink coffee and tea as prices became more affordable, thus increasing demand. As Europeans moved to the American colonies, they brought coffee cultivation with them. Intensive labor was required to grow, harvest, and process coffee. The Europeans had already brought slaves from Africa to the Caribbean to harvest sugarcane. As coffee demand increased, so did demand for more slaves for coffee cultivation, leading to an unsavory aspect of history of caffeine use in modern society. In Brazil alone, over 2 million slaves labored to support coffee cultivation on huge plantations by the mid-1800s. Brazil maintained slavery longer than any other country in the Western Hemisphere, in part because of coffee. In 1880, one Brazilian Member of Parliament declared, "Brazil is coffee, and coffee is the Negro," a statement that is offensive in current times, yet reveals the intertwined history of coffee and slavery for that country. It is notable at this point that the earlier history of coffee in Ethiopia did not involve slavery, where small farmers and their families would tend small coffee plots, making their living off the crop. The fault lies not in the coffee plant itself but in those who made economic decisions about how to harvest it (Pendergrast, 1999).

Soft drinks date back to 1798. In the United States, soft drink creation and soda fountain manufacturing were handled by local pharmacists because of their expertise in medicine and chemistry. As the local drugstore became the central attraction in many towns in the United States, the pharmacist was integral in providing beverages that were part refreshment and part pharmacology. In the late 1800s, caffeinated soft drinks appeared. Dr. Pepper® was the first such product. Soon after, Coca-Cola® and then Pepsi-Cola® were on the market. However, the "diet" versions of various soft drinks are a more recent creation. In 1952, the first official diet soft drink was introduced. Energy drinks are a recent product often from the same manufacturers that make soft drinks. Modern energy drinks first appeared in Europe and Asia in the 1960s and in the United States in the late 1990s (American Beverage Association, 2011).

The recent history of the regulation of caffeine-containing beverages in the United States is an illustration of the complexity of the regulatory issues involved (Reissig et al., 2009). The U.S. Food and Drug Administration (FDA) has historically regulated caffeine-containing soft drinks as foods. In 1980, the FDA proposed to eliminate caffeine from soft drinks, citing health concerns about caffeine (FDA, 1980). The soft drink manufacturers responded with the argument that the addition of caffeine to soft drinks was justified as it enhanced the flavor of the beverage (PepsiCo Inc., 1981). This was an odd claim given that caffeine is actually bitter and odorless. It is perhaps unsurprising that this claim has since been challenged with scientific evidence (Griffiths & Vernotica, 2000; Keast & Riddell, 2007). If caffeine were treated as a psychoactive ingredient, this would mean that the FDA would regulate soft drinks as drugs, perhaps limiting their use in children. Currently, the FDA approves caffeine and limits the maximum caffeine content of cola-type soft drinks to .02% caffeine or 71 mg/12 fluid oz., though energy drinks often exceed these maximum values for soft drinks (FDA, 2003).

This quick review of the history of caffeine ends with our consumption of caffeine and its role in society. Since coffee is the world's most popular source of caffeine, it is worth considering how our coffee arrives in our cup, even today. Author Mark Pendergrast says it most eloquently:

> *The inescapable irony of the coffee industry is that the vast majority of those . . . earn an average of $3 a day. . . . The coffee they prepare travels halfway around the world . . . where cosmopolitan consumers routinely pay half a day's Third World wages for a good cup of coffee.*

Mark Pendergrast, *Uncommon Grounds: The History of Coffee and How It Transformed Our World*

Xanthines: Caffeine, Theophylline, and Theobromine

I began this chapter saying that we would focus on caffeine. However, we need to expand our focus a bit. Caffeine has a few closely related chemical cousins that need to be introduced as they are often present in drinks, foods, and medications also containing caffeine. Theophylline and theobromine are chemical compounds that are similar to caffeine and have similar stimulatory effects on the body, albeit with different potency. These three compounds can be found in many plants in varying concentrations. In fact, over 60 species of plants have been found to contain caffeine, theophylline, and theobromine. Why would a plant contain caffeine? Well, it is not because the plant needs a pick-me-up so that it is less sleepy. The caffeine found in seeds, leaves, and fruits of some plants are natural pesticides that may paralyze and kill those pesky insects that want to eat it. However, we are not ingesting caffeine and its chemical cousins for its pesticide action. We consume it for its stimulant action on our central nervous system, which makes us feel more awake and alert. In Figure 4-5, you will see illustrations of these three chemicals (caffeine, theophylline, and theobromine) and an additional one that looks very similar, xanthine (Spiller, 1998).

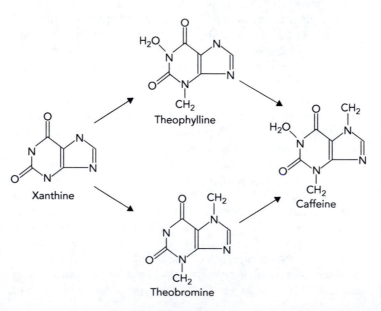

Figure 4-5
Chemical structure of caffeine, theophylline, theobromine, and naturally occurring xanthine.

Theophylline is like caffeine in that it is a white, odorless, crystalline powder that has a bitter taste. Tea contains caffeine and theophylline, but the theophylline is in a smaller proportion than the caffeine. Theophylline is used in some medications as a bronchodilator and vasodilator. Therefore, asthma is sometimes treated with theophylline, which can be manufactured in the lab or extracted from tea leaves.

Theobromine, similar to theophylline and caffeine, is also a white, odorless, crystalline powder that has a bitter taste. If you recall from earlier in this chapter, chocolate comes from the *Theobromo cocao* tree. Theobromine is the principal alkaloid that comes from this tree, and theobromine is extracted from the hulls of the cacao beans. Theobromine is found in a few other plant species as well. Theobromine is similar to theophylline in that it acts as a bronchodilator and a vasodilator so it is also used to treat breathing difficulties seen with asthma or emphysema. However, theobromine has weak central nervous system stimulant activity. Ranking the alkaloids in order of CNS stimulation, caffeine is first, theophylline second, and theobromine third. Finally, a familiar reminder of caution about theobromine and its typical source, chocolate. Dogs, cats, and even birds should not be given chocolate because they metabolize theobromine much more slowly than humans. Serious poisoning, and even death, can occur if a pet eats enough chocolate. So keep Rover away from the chocolate, even though he seems to like it.

Caffeine, theophylline, and theobromine are considered methylxanthines. So what is a xanthine? A **xanthine** is a purine base found in the body tissues and fluids of many organisms, including humans. Derivatives of xanthine are known as xanthines. Caffeine, theophylline, and theobromine are called methylxanthines, because they have methyl groups attached. Looking at Figure 4-5, you will see that the three methylxanthines look like xanthine, except that they have these methyl groups attached (as indicated by the CH_2) (Spiller, 1998). Later in this chapter, we will discuss how xanthines acting in the brain result in CNS stimulation.

In the News:

Ramer, H. (2011, September 26). UNH bans energy drinks then recants. *The Huffington Post.*

The University of New Hampshire made the news in the fall of 2011 when it decided to ban the sale of all energy drinks on campus. This decision was not insignificant given that 60,000 energy drinks were sold on that campus the previous year. Citing health and safety concerns, the university initially said that it would remove popular energy drinks, such as Red Bull, Full Throttle, Moxie Energy, and NOS from vending machines, dining halls, and convenience stores. The decision was part of the campus goal of making UNH the healthiest campus in the country by 2020. The university was also concerned about students mixing energy drinks with alcohol. However, the UNH ban on energy drinks was short-lived. After a great deal of negative student reaction and conversations with energy drink manufacturers unhappy with the decision, the university reversed its decision. University president Mark Huddleston said that conflicting reports about the caffeine and sugar content of some of the drinks, as well as negative student reaction, prompted him to call for a delay. A company spokesperson from Red Bull stated that, "These drinks have a similar caffeine content as coffee and do not contain alcohol. Since it would not be right to ban the sale of soda, coffee, or tea on a college campus, it's also inappropriate and unwarranted to single out and restrict the sale of energy drinks."

Use this news article to test and apply your knowledge:

1. In this article, the university president stated that there are conflicting reports about the caffeine of these drinks. Is this statement fully or partially correct?

2. The spokesperson from Red Bull, an energy drink manufacturer, stated that the caffeine content found in energy drinks is similar to coffee. Is this statement accurate?

Answers:

1. This statement is partially correct. The caffeine found in various energy drinks are placed in the beverage as part of a manufacturing process, just like soft drinks. For this reason, there should be little variability in the stated amount of caffeine in energy drinks provided by their manufacturers and the caffeine the manufacturer reports is found in the drinks. However, manufacturers are not required to report caffeine that comes from additives. For example, some energy drinks contain guarana, which is a plant product that also contains caffeine. Other additives like kola nut, yerba mate, and cocoa also increase the caffeine content of the beverage. If one of these additives were included, this will add to the total amount of caffeine in the product, which could result in the manufacturer's reported caffeine amount to be an underestimate. As such, the consumer may not be able to determine exactly how much caffeine he or she is consuming.

2. Yes. Table 4-1 in this chapter lists the caffeine content for various beverages. An 8 oz. cup of brewed coffee has approximately 133 mg of caffeine in it. Energy drinks listed in the same table for the 8 oz. serving contain anywhere from 71 mg to 125 mg of caffeine.

What do you think about this news story?

This article highlights an ongoing controversy about the safety of energy drink consumption and how much we should regulate access to psychoactive drugs. What do think about the university's original plans to ban energy drinks and later reversal of the decision? Do you think that these drinks might be too heavily used by students? What do you think about limiting access to certain psychoactive drugs if it might keep people healthier? Keep these questions in mind as we delve further into the effects that caffeine has both in the short and the long term on our bodies, later in this chapter.

Routes of Administration

The **route of administration** refers to the method by which a drug enters the body. The way that a drug enters the body will impact how much of the dose reaches the site of action and how quickly it gets there. In this book, we are interested in **psychoactive drugs**, because those are the drugs that have effects on mood, thinking, and behavior. For these effects to take place, psychoactive drugs need to reach the brain, with the bloodstream typically the path by which drugs reach the brain. There are many different administration routes. Some routes are fast, such as injecting a drug directly into the bloodstream. However, for caffeine, the most common route of administration is oral. Oral administration (swallowing) is familiar to everyone. Any liquid, food, pill, capsule, or powder can be swallowed. The oral administration route is considered the safest method of administering a drug. It is also convenient and economical. This is the reason that most over-the-counter medications are administered by the oral route. You do not need any special equipment or special skills to administer a drug in this manner. Moreover, the oral route is a slow route of administration, which becomes clear when the path that the drug takes is considered.

So what happens when you swallow a beverage or eat a food that has caffeine in it? When any drug is swallowed, it ends up in your stomach. The drug is then absorbed mainly through the small intestine. At this point, the drug enters the bloodstream, which transports the drug to its final site of action: the brain. The reason that you feel more awake and alert with caffeine is because of this traveling in the body to the central nervous system (CNS) receptors, where changes will take place that eventually increase alertness and arousal. How fast the drug moves along this path depends partly on how much food is in the digestive tract when the drug is ingested. If there is food in the stomach, that will delay the stomach from emptying. Food in the stomach may also dilute the concentration of the drug. Let's imagine your morning coffee. You can consume it by itself. Alternatively, you can drink the coffee with a full breakfast. If you drink it alone, you will feel the effects of the caffeine faster than if the coffee was consumed with eggs and toast. Drug administration via the oral route is considered the safest method of drug administration, because this process is slow. Therefore, if there is a problem, such as ingesting too much drug, you can undo this in a hospital more readily than for other routes of administration.

While almost all caffeine is administered by the oral route, there are rare cases where people administer caffeine by injecting it. Since this approach to drug administration bypasses the entire digestive system, the effects of caffeine are felt immediately since it does not take long for the drug to reach the brain. Moreover, caffeine is also sometimes mixed with other illegal street drugs, such as cocaine and heroin (which are also white powders). Therefore, caffeine could also be inhaled, snorted, or injected as is typical for these other drugs. In later chapters, we will discuss other routes of administration, including the different manners of injecting drugs into the body using a needle and syringe. Given that these methods are uncommon for caffeine, we will leave this topic for now.

Prevalence of Caffeine Consumption

In the United States

Approximately 90% of adults in North American consume caffeine on a daily basis (Ogawa & Ueki, 2007). Adults consume a daily dose of caffeine of approximately 4 mg/kg of body weight (Barone & Roberts, 1996). For a typical individual who weighs 75 kg (165 pounds), this amounts to a daily consumption of 300 mg of caffeine. This level equates to two cups of coffee. Of course, this is just an average. Do not be alarmed if you are far above this number. As we will see, your personal daily dose of caffeine probably depends on your tolerance for side effects from caffeine consumption.

In children and adolescents in the United States, the main source of caffeine is soft drinks. This is different than adults, for whom the main source of caffeine is coffee. Given that soft drinks have less caffeine than coffee, children and adolescents typically have lower caffeine daily doses (Frary, Johnson, & Wang, 2005). To examine caffeine intake in children, one study examined food consumption habits over a week. The authors found that 5- to 6-year-old children had an intake of 1.1 mg/kg/day. Most of the caffeine came from soft drinks (Morgan et al., 1982).

Around the World

Approximately 80% of the world's population consumes a caffeinated product every day (Ogawa & Ueki, 2007). Much of the variance that is seen in countries around the world is due in part to the rate of coffee and tea consumption in those given areas (see Table 4-2), with higher coffee consumption resulting in greater caffeine use. In the United States, Canada, and many northern European countries, coffee consumption is widespread. Coffee consumption in these countries accounts for the majority of daily caffeine ingestion among adults. By contrast, tea is the beverage of choice in the United Kingdom, Ireland, and Kuwait. The United States is also the largest per capita consumer of soft drinks, accounting for over 20% of the global total, followed by Mexico and Chile (Heckman et al., 2010). It should be noted that estimating daily caffeine use can be notoriously difficult. For example, estimates of daily caffeine use have ranged from 168 to 423 mg/day for the United States (Fredholm et al., 1999; Weidner & Istvan, 1985) and 202 to 621 mg/day for the United Kingdom (Fredholm et al., 1999; Bruce & Lader, 1986).

Table 4-2 Average daily caffeine consumption from coffee, tea, mate, and cocoa around the world[1]

Country	Population (1995) 1000 persons	Caffeine (mg/person/day)				
		Coffee	Tea	Mate[2]	Cocoa	All Sources
Algeria	28,109	79	5	0	1	85
Angola	10,816	4	0	0	0	4
Argentina	34,768	43	1	52	5	100
Australia	17,862	202	29	0	0	232
Austria	8,045	276	8	0	16	300
Brazil	159,015	26	1	10	4	40
Canada	29,402	180	18	0	12	210
China	1,220,224	2	14	0	0	16
Columbia	35,814	126	0	0	9	136
Denmark	5,223	354	15	0	21	390
Egypt	62,096	5	53	0	1	58
Finland	5,107	322	6	0	1	329
France	58,104	215	8	0	16	239
Germany	81,594	292	9	0	12	313
Guatemala	10,621	23	2	0	2	27
Honduras	5,654	160	0	0	2	162
Hungary	10,106	138	3	0	9	150
India	929,005	1	26	0	0	27
Ireland	3,546	81	127	0	5	213
Italy	57,204	198	3	0	8	210
Ivory Coast	13,694	6	1	0	13	20
Japan	125,068	119	44	0	5	169
Kenya	27,150	8	42	0	0	50
Kuwait	1,691	49	112	0	13	173
Malaysia	20,140	49	27	0	4	81
Netherlands	15,482	369	38	0	6	414
Nicaragua	4,123	219	0	0	1	221
Nigeria	111,721	1	2	0	1	4
Norway	4,332	379	8	0	13	400
Paraguay	4,828	51	1	101	3	156
Poland	38,557	100	33	0	8	141
Russian Federation	148,460	26	40	0	7	72
Saudi Arabia	18,255	14	13	0	2	28
South Africa	41,465	15	23	0	1	40
Sweden	8,788	388	12	0	7	407
Switzerland	7,166	275	11	0	1	288
Syria	14,208	35	67	5	2	108
Tanzania	30,026	3	4	0	0	7
United Arab Emirates	2,210	74	87	0	5	167

Country	Population (1995) 1000 persons	Caffeine (mg/person/day)				
		Coffee	Tea	Mate[2]	Cocoa	All Sources
United Kingdom	58,301	92	96	0	14	202
United States	267,115	143	12	0	12	168
Venezuela	21,844	135	0	0	4	139

Notes: [1]Source of this data is adapted from the 1995 food balance sheets of the Food and Agricultural Organization of the United Nations (FAO) (Fredholm et al., 1999; Heckman et al., 2010). The data provide a very rough estimate of average of consumption of caffeinated products in the population. However, this data did not include caffeine from soft drinks, energy drinks, or medicines. Despite this, the food balance sheets provide data allowing for comparisons among various countries around the world.

[2]Mate (Yerba Mate) is a type of tea that contains more caffeine than regular tea and less caffeine than coffee. The beverage is popular in Paraguay and Argentina.

Calculating Your Typical Caffeine Dose

When caffeine is consumed, the experience that a person has will depend on the dose administered. The **drug dose** is the measure of how much of the drug is consumed. The drug dose is one of the pharmacological factors that contributes to a drug experience. Scientists have a standard way to communicate a drug dose that takes into account an individual's body weight. Imagine that you have two friends who have very different body physiques. Your friend Sarah is large and weighs 200 pounds. Your friend Janice is small and weighs 100 pounds. If Sarah and Janice both consume two standard 12 oz. cans of the soft drink, Coca-Cola®, every day, their caffeine doses are not equivalent. Why? Heavier people have a greater volume of body fluid than lighter people. More body fluid results in a given amount of drug being less concentrated in the body and at the final site of action (the brain). Think of putting a teaspoon of sugar in a small cup or a big bowl filled with water. The water may taste sweeter in both cases, but you may hardly notice any effect with the big bowl, whereas the smaller cup would have a very noticeable sweet taste due to the sugar being much more concentrated.

When researchers study the effects of a drug, they often give the drug to research participants (humans or animals) using a specific dose. The desired dose is typically expressed as the amount of drug (such as the number of milligrams of the drug) per kilogram of body weight. In many of my studies on caffeine, I have found that if I want to see changes in cognitive performance, such as a demonstration that caffeine increases the speed of reactions, a dose of 4 mg/kg is sufficient to result in observable effects in human research subjects (Marczinski, Fillmore, Bardgett, & Howard, 2011; Marczinski & Fillmore, 2003, 2006).

Drug dose = milligrams of the drug/kilogram of body weight

Therefore, if your friend Sarah were to decide to participate in an experiment where caffeine was administered at the 4 mg/kg dose, the researcher would have to make a simple calculation to determine the correct dose to administer to her. The researcher would take her body weight (200 pounds) and convert it kilograms. To make this conversion, the body weight in pounds is divided by 2.2 resulting in 90.9 kg. Then the dose would be determined by multiplying her weight in kg by 4 (since the dose is 4 mg/kg). The result is a caffeine total of 364 mg.

Using the same approach, if your friend Janice were to decide to be a part of the study, her body weight would be converted to kg (100 pounds/2.2) = 45.5 kg. For Janice, the comparable dose would be 182 mg of caffeine (45.5 kg × 4 mg/kg = 182 mg). You expect that the effect caffeine has on the two research participants should be similar, even though Sarah's dose is twice as much as Janice's. It should be mentioned here that species of animals differ dramatically in the appropriate dose for various effects. For example, a fellow psychopharmacologist uses a standard

15 mg/kg dose of caffeine to see effects of this drug on speed of reactions in his mice subjects. That amount of caffeine would send my human subjects to the hospital while his mice are just fine with that dose. In general, it is assumed that a dose of 10 mg/kg in a rat is similar to a dose of 3.5 mg/kg in a human (Fredholm et al., 1999). For an individual weighing 70 kg (154 pounds), this 3.5 mg/kg dose of caffeine amounts to 245 mg of caffeine, which would be found in about 2 cups of coffee.

Dose calculations are not only for setting up well-controlled psychopharmacology studies. They are also useful in determining the self-reported consumption patterns of drug use. The same approach of correcting for body weight is often used, but not always, especially in large population studies examining caffeine use habits. One method is to give a questionnaire asking the amount of caffeinated foods and beverages typically consumed in one day. For example, Sarah might report that in a typical day, she consumes one 12 oz. cup of brewed coffee and one 12 oz. can of the soft drink brand, Diet Pepsi®. You can check Table 4-1 for the typical caffeine content for these beverages. From the table, Sarah is consuming approximately 200 mg of caffeine in her coffee and 35 mg of caffeine in her soft drink. Therefore, her daily caffeine dose, the total amount of caffeine divided by her body weight, is 2.59 mg/kg (235 mg caffeine/90.9 kg body weight = 2.59 mg/kg).

While this approach is helpful, it is far from perfect. As you notice in Table 4-1, there is considerable variability in the caffeine content for similar products, which will obviously impact the accuracy of a dose calculation. Sometimes, individuals may forget what brand or how much they had consumed, which also impacts the accuracy of the dose calculation. Nevertheless, it is helpful to get estimates of the quantity of a psychoactive drug people are using, particularly with a commonly used drug like caffeine.

QUICK QUIZ 4-1

1. Which product contains the most caffeine (assuming that the serving size is equivalent)?
   a. Coffee
   b. Tea
   c. Chocolate
   d. Soft drink

2. If you were to taste a plant that contains alkaloids, what would it taste like?
   a. Sweet
   b. Salty
   c. Bitter
   d. It would have no taste.

3. Which of the following is correct in terms of greatest to least amount of central nervous system stimulation?
   a. Theophylline, theobromine, caffeine
   b. Caffeine, theophylline, theobromine
   c. Caffeine, theobromine, theophylline
   d. Theobromine, theophylline, caffeine
   e. Theophylline, caffeine, theobromine

4. Which country has the highest per capita caffeine consumption?
   a. United States of America
   b. Nigeria
   c. Kuwait
   d. The Netherlands

5. Caffeine is often considered to be a very safe psychoactive drug. One reason for this assessment is that caffeine is typically administered using the oral route of administration. How does oral administration contribute to drug safety?

6. Your friend Janice weighs 100 pounds. She reports that on a typical day, she usually drinks a 12 oz. serving of black tea in the morning and a 16 oz. can of Monster energy drink in the afternoon. What is her caffeine dose?

ANSWERS TO QUICK QUIZ 4-1:

1. a – coffee
2. c – bitter
3. b – caffeine, theophylline, theobromine
4. d – The Netherlands
   According to Table 4-2, the Netherlands has the highest caffeine consumption of 414 mg/person/day.

5. When a drug is swallowed, it must travel through the digestive system before it can be absorbed into the bloodstream to reach the final site of action, the brain. The gastrointestinal path includes the stomach and small intestine from where caffeine is absorbed into the bloodstream, is very slow. Therefore, if you administer

too much drug, there is additional time to reach a hospital to treat an overdose.

6. 5.10 mg/kg

    To complete this calculation, first determine the amount of caffeine Janice has consumed. Since Table 4-1 only shows Monster for a maximum 12 oz. serving, take the amount of caffeine in 1 oz. (10 mg) and multiply by 16 to determine that the Monster drink contains 160 mg of caffeine. The tea contains 72 mg of caffeine. Therefore, the total caffeine consumed is 232 mg. Divide the caffeine amount by the body weight in kg (100 pounds/2.2 = 45.5 kg). Therefore, the dose is 5.10 mg/kg (232 mg/45.5 kg = 5.10 mg/kg).

Acute Effects of Caffeine

The acute effects of a drug refer to changes that take place after one ingestion of the drug. Therefore, the acute effects of caffeine refer to those immediate changes that are experienced after caffeine is administered. Acute effects can be objective (such as changes in behavior or physiology) or subjective (acquired from ratings that a participant gives about how they feel). Not surprisingly, most research with animals involves the measurement of objective changes, whereas research with human participants can include both types of measurements. While we can observe and record how active a mouse is after a dose of caffeine, we cannot infer anything about what the mouse is thinking or feeling. By contrast, human participants can be asked to perform a variety of tasks, and human subjects can also give ratings on questionnaires about how they feel. Both human and animal research can inform us about what changes take place after an acute dose of caffeine is administered.

Objective Effects

Since caffeine is a stimulant psychoactive drug, the changes that occur with caffeine in the central nervous system (CNS) reflect increased activity. There are a variety of research methods that can be used to assess changes in CNS activity. Behavioral approaches include assessing how fast humans and animals process information and perform tasks after being given a dose of caffeine. There are a variety of ways to test behaviors in a research study. Typically, a researcher will give a dose of caffeine to a human or animal subject and compare the effects of that dose to a placebo dose. (Recall that a **placebo** is an inert or chemically inactive substance that provides a control in drug research.) A **within-subjects research design** involves the same person receiving the caffeine and the placebo on different occasions and comparing outcomes. Researchers can also use a **between-subjects research design** by randomly assigning individuals to two groups, one of which would receive the active caffeine and the other would be given the placebo. The objective effects of caffeine are typically assessed in humans or animals by asking subjects to perform physical endurance tasks, motor skills, or tests that measure cognitive processing after receiving the drug or placebo (Sawyer, Julia, & Turin, 1982). For example, one recent study examined the effects of caffeine on memory performance. College students came to the lab and were given chewing gum. The experimental group of subjects received gum that contained caffeine, whereas the placebo group of subjects received gum that did not contain caffeine. The researcher then tested their memory and found that the caffeine group performed better than the placebo group (Davidson, 2011). This is an example of a between-subjects research design using a placebo control.

When humans are administered caffeine doses similar to the amount in a few cups of coffee, improvements in laboratory measures of response speed and vigilance are observed (Battig, Buzzi, Martin, & Feierabend, 1984; Childs & de Wit, 2006; Howard & Marczinski, 2010). Similarly, the administration of moderate doses of caffeine typically causes animals to become more active. Mice or rats run around and explore more with caffeine. However, the acute effects of caffeine are dose-dependent, and there is a limit on how much caffeine improves performance or increases activity levels. Lower doses have positive effects, but higher doses (500 mg or more in humans) have negative effects on performance (Kaplan et al., 1997). For several cognitive functions including attention, working memory, short-term memory, problem solving, and long-term memory, the evidence is mixed on whether caffeine can improve these cognitive processes (Davidson, 2011; Glade, 2010; James, 1991). The variability in these findings may in part be due to differences in arousal, with individuals having low levels of arousal benefiting more from caffeine. In addition, some people experience more negative side effects from caffeine, such as jitteriness and anxiety. Finally, improvements in performance are more likely to be observed in fatigued or sleepy individuals (Childs & de Wit, 2008).

In addition to the acute effects of caffeine on basic measures of motor and cognitive processes, researchers have also looked at complex tasks similar to those in the real world. For example, car driving performance benefits from caffeine in doses corresponding to one or two cups of coffee (Horne & Reyner, 1996). In one recent study, researchers examined whether a typical 250 mL can of a popular brand of energy drink would benefit subjects' performance on a long 4-hour highway drive, using a driving simulator in the lab (Mets et al., 2011). The researchers randomly assigned subjects to one of three groups. The first group drove continuously for 4 hours. The second group and third group both drove for 2 hours, took a brief 15-minute break, and then drove for another 2 hours. During the break, the second group consumed the energy drink and the third group consumed a placebo beverage not containing caffeine or any of the other functional ingredients in the energy drink. The researchers reported that swerving and straying from the speed limit occurred during hours 3 and 4 of the drive for the no break and placebo groups. However, the energy drink group maintained their safe driving performance throughout the experiment, at a level similar to that observed in all participants early in the drive.

Another real-world task common for college students is writing and proofreading papers. Staying up late to do such work is often supplemented with caffeine. Researchers determined if caffeine would benefit a commonplace language task requiring readers to identify and correct various errors, ranging from simple misspelling of one to two syllable words to complex errors such as incorrect subject–verb agreement and verb tense. The researchers also wondered if typical caffeine consumption habits might impact the results. Therefore, the researchers tested doses of caffeine ranging up to 400 mg. They also divided their subjects into two groups based on typical consumption habits, calling them high and low caffeine consumers. The researchers found that caffeine improved detection of complex errors but not the smaller misspellings. In addition, low caffeine consumers, who typically did not use much caffeine, benefited most from a 200 mg dose of caffeine, whereas the high caffeine consumers benefited most from a 400 mg dose of caffeine (Brunye, Mahoney, Rapp, Ditman, & Taylor, 2012). This study provides another example of how researchers are trying to better understand the role that commonly used psychoactive drugs play in our lives. This study also indicates that our typical use of caffeine may impact how we experience caffeine's acute effects, and we will discuss usage patterns later when we examine the chronic effects of caffeine use.

Subjective Effects

Caffeine has reliable effects on subjective state, such as mood, sleepiness, and feelings of stimulation. Subjective effects of caffeine can be more difficult to assess than objective measures. To assess a complex phenomenon such as mood, various questionnaire assessments have been developed, where research subjects are asked to rate their mood, energy, and alertness using a numbered scale. Using these approaches, researchers have found that acute doses of caffeine elevate mood and increase feelings of energy and alertness (Howard & Marczinski, 2010). Subjects also report increased ability to concentrate, motivation to work, feeling more imaginative and greater desire to socialize (Childs & de Wit, 2006; Griffiths et al., 1990). In the simulated highway driving study described above, the researcher measured ratings of sleepiness. For the subjects who drove continuously or who were given the placebo beverage after 2 hours of driving, ratings of sleepiness at the end of the drive were significantly higher compared to subjects who had consumed the energy drink (Mets et al., 2011). These acute effects of caffeine in counteracting sleepiness account for the popularity of caffeinated beverages, particularly upon wakening. Adenosine is the neurotransmitter that makes us feel sleepy. Caffeine occupies adenosine receptors and blocks action at those receptors. As a result, caffeine will be most effective in counteracting the effects of adenosine when we are fatigued, since that is when the body's adenosine activity is highest. We will further discuss the action of caffeine on adenosine receptors later in this chapter.

While caffeine appears to mitigate sleepiness and fatigue, it is less certain that caffeine alters other subjective states, such as feelings of stress. One survey study examined the relationship between perceived stress, academic performance, and energy drink consumption in college students. The authors reported a positive correlation between perceived stress and energy drink consumption. While this study only examined the relationship between two variables, the authors suggested that it might be plausible that the more stress the college students were reporting, the greater the number of energy drinks that were being consumed to try to help with the demands of schoolwork. Unfortunately, there was also a negative correlation between academic performance and energy drink consumption. Cumulative grade point average (GPA) and energy drink consumption were inversely related, with lower GPA being associated with more energy drinks consumed. The authors of the study noted that it is unclear why these relationships exist. However, they suggested that procrastination might be the mediator. Students who are not well organized have a tendency to procrastinate, resulting in cramming at the last minute. They may rely on the caffeine in energy drinks to stay up late at night to do so, even though there may be little benefit to this strategy on long-term GPA (Pettit & DeBarr, 2011). Therefore, the takeaway is clear. While caffeine may help you stay awake and improve your subjective state when you are tired, there is no guarantee that there will be benefits to your academic performance.

Effects on the Body

Adenosine receptors are found in the central nervous system (CNS), accounting for the objective and subjective effects just discussed. When caffeine is ingested, it is distributed freely throughout the body via the bloodstream. Therefore, caffeine also has effects outside the CNS, such as increasing blood pressure (Childs & de Wit, 2006). Caffeine causes the contraction of the heart muscle and relaxation of coronary arteries and bronchi (which facilitates breathing). These effects are one reason that athletes sometimes use caffeine to improve their athletic performance in events such as running. Caffeine has a diuretic effect on the kidneys, which explains why many individuals need to urinate soon after consuming a caffeinated beverage. At higher doses, caffeine stimulates respiration and elevates basal metabolism. This elevation of basal metabolism is the outcome that diet drugs are hoping to achieve by including caffeine as an important ingredient.

Caffeine delays the onset of sleep. However, caffeine's effect on sleep varies considerably among individuals. Similar to the observation that individuals prone to anxiety tend to limit their exposure to caffeine, individuals with sleeping problems, often on their own initiative, limit caffeine use (Soroko, Chang, & Barrett-Connor, 1996). As increased wakefulness is one reason why people use caffeine, poor sleep is a typical reason why people curtail their caffeine use (Fredholm et al., 1999).

Caffeinism

There are well-documented effects of caffeine on anxiety that were initially documented in psychiatric outpatients in the 1970s. Greden (1974) noticed that the patients who consumed more than 1000 mg of caffeine per day had symptoms of generalized anxiety. This observation led to the term **caffeinism**, which is listed in the *DSM-IV-TR*. There are marked individual differences in caffeinism, with some individuals prone to panic and anxiety experiencing these effects at lower doses, sometimes as low as 250 mg. However, 600 mg or more of caffeine daily increases the likelihood of experiencing caffeinism, a condition that is immediately reversible once caffeine intake is reduced (Persad, 2011).

Interestingly, individuals who are prone to anxiety may not know the term "caffeinism" but they must be aware that caffeine intake can make their anxiety symptoms worse, such that they adapt their intake accordingly, or even avoid the drug. In one large population study, there was no clear relationship between caffeine intake and anxiety, probably because highly anxious individuals avoided caffeine. Moreover, in patients with anxiety, there was no relationship between caffeine intake and anxiety, as patients with anxiety did not consume caffeine in high amounts in many cases (Eaton & McLeod, 1984).

More severe toxic symptoms occur when caffeine use increases beyond 1000 mg per day. Symptoms can range from mild to severe including muscle twitching, rambling speech, rambling thoughts, psychomotor agitation, seeing flashing lights, experiencing ringing in the ears, and cardiac arrhythmia. Sometimes a low-grade fever of about 100°F will be part of the symptoms, due to caffeine's action on the body's heat regulation (American Psychiatric Association, 2000. High levels of caffeine can induce seizures in those who have a predisposition to seizures (Fredholm et al., 1999). Cardiac arrests have occurred, particularly in individuals who have preexisting heart conditions. Some individuals are not aware of their preexisting health conditions leading to seizures or heart attacks prior to consuming high levels of caffeine.

Lethal Dose

One serious concern with psychoactive drug use is accidental or intentional overdose, which could lead to death. To measure a drug's safety, pharmacologists determine the dose at which a given percentage of individuals die within a specified period of time. This is called the **lethal dose (LD)**. It is common in pharmacology to refer to a drug's LD_{50}, which refers to the dose of drug at which 50% of animals died within a stated time. For rats, the LD_{50} for caffeine is approximately 200 mg/kg (Eichler, 1976). Therefore, if you were to administer a 200 mg/kg dose of caffeine to 100 rats, approximately 50 of them would die with 24 hours. However, researchers are aware of individual differences in both animals and humans. Lower doses might result in a particular rat's death, while a different rat may survive a much higher dose. The same variability in likelihood of death is true for other species, including humans. The lethal dose for adult humans is about 10 grams when taken orally. This lethal dose is equal to about 75 cups of coffee. Since it would be very difficult to ingest that much caffeine in one day, caffeine overdose deaths are very rare. For children, the lethal dose is approximately 100 mg/kg.

Caffeine is considered a safe drug because an extremely large amount of it would need to be consumed before the LD_{50} was achieved. It is a safe drug because the dose that people typically consume is quite low in comparison to the lethal dose. In pharmacology, the **effective dose (ED)** is the dose at which a given percentage of individuals experience a particular effect. Similar to the lethal dose, the ED_{50} is the dose at which 50% of individuals who receive that dose of drug will experience a certain effect. Caffeine is used by many individuals to improve feelings of wakefulness and to increase energy. A dose of 2 mg/kg or 1 cup of coffee would induce these changes in subjective state in 50% of individuals (ED_{50}). For a typical 70 kg (165 pound) adult, a 2 mg/kg dose results in the ingestion of 140 mg caffeine, which is far lower than the 10 grams (10,000 mg) at the LD_{50}. In later chapters in this book, we will discuss other drugs that have ED_{50} values that are much closer to their LD_{50} values, which explains why other psychoactive drugs can be far more risky to use than caffeine.

Tolerance and Withdrawal of Caffeine

In Chapter 1, recall that the *DSM-IV-TR* criteria for substance dependence were discussed. Using these criteria, one can examine whether it is possible to be clinically diagnosed as being dependent on caffeine. Drug dependence is likely when the pattern of behavior is focused on repetitive and compulsive seeking and taking of a psychoactive drug. Therefore, an individual might be dependent on caffeine if seeking caffeine is repetitive and compulsive (Nehlig, 1999). Given that a large majority of individuals seek caffeine daily, one might guess that they are dependent on caffeine (Figure 4-6). However, part of the determination of dependence involves evaluating if caffeine use leads to the development of tolerance and stopping caffeine use leads to withdrawal. The *DSM-IV-TR*'s criteria for drug dependence include the term drug "**tolerance**," which refers to a diminished drug effect with continued use. Tolerance can also refer to the increased amount of a drug needed to achieve a certain effect. Tolerance is thought to contribute to substance abuse because a user needs more and more of a drug to achieve the same effect. Therefore, drugs that are likely to lead to dependence problems are often drugs that induce rapid tolerance development. Drugs that do not lead to rapid tolerance development are thought to be safer (APA, 2000).

Tolerance develops to some, but not all, of the effects of caffeine in humans and animals (Fredholm et al., 1999). In particular, tolerance develops to some of the cardiovascular changes that occur with caffeine use. Tachycardia, heart palpitations, and increased blood pressure will sometimes occur in individuals who first use caffeine. However, these symptoms typically disappear even after a few days of use. Similarly, tolerance develops to caffeine's effects on sleep and renal effects. However, tolerance does not appear to develop to the stimulant effects of caffeine, which is one of the primary reasons why individuals continue to choose this drug (Fredholm et al., 1999). Since tolerance does not develop to the stimulant effects, the same cup of coffee can wake an individual up in the morning and increase alertness for decades. There is no need to escalate the dose of caffeine over time to compensate for development of tolerance. For this reason, individuals' caffeine use appears to remain relatively stable over time (Nehlig, 1999). The lack of tolerance development to the stimulatory effects of caffeine is another reason why scientists judge it a relatively safe psychoactive drug (Persad, 2011).

Another requirement of the *DSM-IV-TR* criteria for drug dependence is the observation of withdrawal. **Withdrawal** is a definable illness occurring when the use of a drug is stopped or decreased. Typical symptoms of caffeine withdrawal include headache, drowsiness, weakness,

"No, I don't take any drugs, but I do have a $50 a day latte habit."

Figure 4-6
Determining if someone is dependent on caffeine can be challenging.

©Harley Schwadron/Cartoonstock

apathy, decreased motor behavior, anxiety, increased heart rate, and increased muscle tension. Less commonly, more severe symptoms might occur such as tremor, nausea, vomiting, and other flu-like symptoms. The magnitude and duration of withdrawal effects from caffeine is a direct function of typical daily use. Heavy users of caffeine may report significant symptoms, whereas light users may experience nothing unusual upon cessation of their caffeine use. If withdrawal symptoms occur, they generally begin 12 to 24 hours after caffeine use is stopped. Symptoms reach a peak after 20 to 48 hours and then slowly dissipate (Fredholm et al., 1999). The withdrawal symptoms immediately disappear if the individual consumes caffeine once again. This observation has led many researchers to speculate that caffeine use is maintained because individuals wish to avoid or terminate headaches or other withdrawal symptoms, which is known as the **withdrawal reversal hypothesis** (James, 1991). Withdrawal reversal is a concern for researchers attempting to examine the acute effects of caffeine on human performance. For example, many studies ask subjects to refrain from all caffeine use for a period of time, such as 8 hours before a study begins. If the subject arrives in the lab and performs better on a reaction time task following a dose of caffeine, is it the caffeine producing improved performance, or is the alleviation of the withdrawal effects contributing to the result? This has perplexed researchers, particularly since caffeine use is so widespread among potential subjects.

Chronic Effects of Caffeine Use

There can be large differences between the acute and chronic (long-term) effects of caffeine. Caffeine is widely used and culturally accepted. Therefore, caffeine consumption does not usually have negative social consequences, which differs from many of the other psychoactive drugs covered in this book. Many individuals use caffeine daily for decades, which prompts the questions: is caffeine safe? and does its chronic use contribute to health problems? Particularly in the United States, there is some perception that caffeine is detrimental to one's health (Fredholm et al., 1999). However, it appears that, in most cases, moderate caffeine use does not negatively impact health and well-being. There is no consistent relationship between caffeine consumption and cancer, myocardial infarction, or cardiovascular diseases (Higdon & Frei, 2006). However, there is some evidence that caffeine use may be detrimental during periods of stress for some individuals with hypertension. When individuals are stressed, they increase their caffeine intake. Caffeine increases cortisol secretion by stimulating the CNS. Therefore, for a subset of individuals who have hypertension, avoiding caffeine during stressful times may prevent further increases in blood pressure (Persad, 2011).

Caffeine, in the form of coffee, might also afford some health benefits by preventing particular chronic diseases, including liver disease, Parkinson's disease, Alzheimer's disease, and type 2 diabetes mellitus (Eskelinen, Ngandu, Tuomilehto, Soininen, & Kivipelto, 2009). In one study, adult rats were fed various diets including some with coffee and some with caffeine over 80 days. The chronic caffeine intake, either in pure form or as coffee, was demonstrated to improve long-term memory when tested with object recognition. The rats did not exhibit increased locomotor or exploratory activity, indicating that the memory improvement was not due to increased activity levels (Abreu, Silva-Oliveira, Moraes, Pereira, & Moraes-Santos, 2011). Regular caffeine use might offer some protection against age-related declines in cognitive function, although this finding needs better empirical support.

Other effects of caffeine use are more complex, such as the role that caffeine might play in seizure potential. The acute effects of caffeine may precipitate seizures in humans and animals not habituated to high doses of caffeine. Long-term use of caffeine does lead to decreased seizure susceptibility, which suggests that adaptive changes occur in the brain when caffeine is used regularly. These changes may be beneficial, rather than detrimental, for particular health conditions (Fredholm et al., 1999). Clearly, more research is needed to better understand potential beneficial effects of caffeine on health. However, for healthy adults, caffeine use in moderation appears to be safe in the long term.

Focus on Careers: Health Educators

Rising health care costs have led various employers to consider how better to help their employees adopt healthier habits. In this chapter, it was noted that individuals who are stressed tend to increase their caffeine intake to sometimes excessive levels. This can lead to various health problems, many of which are entirely preventable. High levels of stress and caffeine use can result in anxiety, panic attacks, and hypertension. In some individuals, high doses of caffeine can induce seizures or lead to cardiovascular complications. All of these symptoms could lead to the need for costly medical care. To prevent some of these issues from arising, employer-sponsored wellness programs have been developed. Health educators have the job of providing employees with help with nutrition, stress management, incentives to exercise, smoking cessation options, and other programs that will improve health. In many cases, having a background in the psychopharmacology of commonly used drugs such as caffeine, nicotine, and alcohol is needed. With some of this knowledge, health educators develop materials that encourage people to make healthy decisions, such as keeping caffeine use within a moderate range. Depending on the setting (private business, university, hospital, or government), a bachelor's degree is a requirement, and the credential as a Certified Health Education Specialist is preferred. According to the Department of Labor and Statistics, the median pay in 2010 for health educators was approximately $46,000. Moreover, the number of jobs in this field is growing much faster than average.

Websites to explore:

American Association for Health Education
www.aahperd.org/aahe/
Society for Public Health Education
www.sophe.org
National Commission for Health Education Credentialing
www.nchec.org/

Caffeine Use in Pregnant Women and Children

The chronic effects of caffeine on health have been studied in healthy individuals and researchers have deemed the moderate use of caffeine to be essentially safe. However, there may be special recommendations about the health and safety of caffeine use in certain populations. In women who wish to become pregnant, there have been suggestions that high levels of caffeine consumption may have adverse effects on fertility. For example, high levels of caffeine use may lengthen the time to conceive or actually hinder conception. In pregnancy, caffeine is rapidly absorbed and crosses the placenta freely. Unfortunately, the placenta and fetus lack the enzymes needed for caffeine metabolism. The concern is that high caffeine use can cause spontaneous abortion and impair fetal growth, although these results are conflicting in the literature. In addition, the half-life of caffeine is greatly increased in pregnancy, so that a dose of caffeine remains in the body longer than would be the case pre-pregnancy (Bakker et al., 2010). Withdrawal symptoms have been reported in newborns whose mothers were heavy coffee drinkers during pregnancy. At birth, the infant of a heavy coffee-drinking mother shows symptoms that will spontaneously disappear after a few days. Symptoms include irritability and even vomiting (Fredholm et al., 1999; Heckman et al., 2010). Typically, pregnant women are advised to limit their caffeine consumption to no more than 2 cups of coffee per day to avoid these problems (Figure 4-7).

Infants who are breast-fed will be consuming caffeine that the mother consumes. While moderate caffeine consumption may not be a problem for the mother, infants have a very slow

More about the Science:

Bakker et al. (2010). Maternal caffeine intake from coffee and tea, fetal growth, and the risks of adverse birth outcomes: The Generation R Study. *American Journal of Clinical Nutrition*, *91*, 1691–1698.

Given that caffeine use is so widespread, women often consume caffeinated products before they become pregnant and continue to do so while pregnant. However, examining the health risks of caffeine use, or any other psychoactive drug use, during pregnancy is an extremely difficult task. Therefore, the effect of caffeine intake during pregnancy on the developing fetus remains unclear. However, Bakker et al. (2010) attempted to address this question. In the Netherlands, they recruited 7,346 pregnant women early in their pregnancies. They gathered caffeine intake information from the women using questionnaires during each of the three trimesters of pregnancy. Using ultrasound, they measured fetal growth. Hospital records provided birth outcomes such as height and weight. The results indicated that caffeine intake equal to or greater than 540 mg/day resulted in impaired fetal length growth. The authors additionally concluded that caffeine exposure might adversely impact fetal skeletal growth, since measurements such as birth length and ultrasound femur length were more likely to be affected in heavy caffeine users, as opposed to other measurements such as fetal weight or fetal head circumference which were not differentially impacted by heavy caffeine use.

More about the Science Thought Questions:

1. This research study involved an observational design. There are several potential confounds that may have impacted the results obtained. List a few possible confounds.
2. What would the researcher need to consider when designing a survey to assess caffeine intake in pregnant women?
3. Given that this research used an observational design, what might be a logical extension to this research using an experimental research design?

More about the Science Thought Question Answers:

1. Study confounds might have included issues such as maternal nutrition during pregnancy, maternal health, maternal lifestyle, maternal age, other drug use (nicotine, alcohol, illegal drugs, prescription medications), and access to prenatal health care.
2. The survey would need to ask about all sources of caffeine, including coffee, tea, chocolate, soft drinks, energy drinks, and medications. In addition, the researchers would need to be specific about serving sizes and brands, particularly since the caffeine content can vary widely for some caffeinated products from natural sources, such as coffee. Finally, survey instruments rely on the memory of research subjects about what they have consumed. Ideally, subject recall of this information should be close to the time when the consumption occurred, thus improving the accuracy of self-reported data.
3. Given that it would be unethical to randomly assign human pregnant women to receive high and low doses of caffeine, a study using animal subjects might be an option. Pregnant mice or rats could be given a diet during their pregnancy of high and low doses of caffeine. Birth weight and length could be measured in the pups to determine if caffeine impacts fetal growth.

©Rus S/Shutterstock

Figure 4-7
Pregnant women are typically advised to limit caffeine consumption to no more than 2 cups of coffee per day.

rate of metabolism of caffeine. Therefore, even small amounts of caffeine acquired in breast milk could accumulate, leading to toxicity (James, 1991). The ability to metabolize caffeine improves with age. However, due to their very small body sizes, children consuming caffeinated beverages, typically as soft drinks, might be consuming excessive levels of caffeine. Given the small body size of children, it is unsurprising that caffeinism and toxic reactions can occur. Caffeine can cause sleep problems in children, similar to adults, a concern that can be reversed when caffeine use is limited. Caffeine withdrawal can also occur in children. If children suddenly stop consuming soft drinks, withdrawal effects, such as headaches, can occur (Fredholm et al., 1999).

Pharmacology of Caffeine

Sites of Action

Adenosine is an inhibitory neurotransmitter found in the brain. When you feel sleepy, that is a result of the action of adenosine. Over the course of the day in all organisms, it is thought that rising adenosine levels suppress arousal and promote sleep. Adenosine receptors are found in both the central and peripheral nervous systems. Besides leading to behavioral sedation, adenosine regulates the oxygen delivery to cells and dilates cerebral and coronary blood vessels. All xanthines oppose the action of adenosine. Since caffeine has a similar molecular structure to adenosine, caffeine can bind to the same receptors as adenosine. Therefore, caffeine and other methylxanthines occupy adenosine receptors and block the action of the adenosine transmitter. When we are most sleepy, caffeine will be most beneficial, by blocking the action of sleep--promoting adenosine. Caffeine is considered an **antagonist drug** because it occupies a neural receptor and blocks normal synaptic transmission (Fredholm et al., 1999; Nehlig, 1999).

There are four adenosine receptors: A_1, A_{2a}, A_{2b}, and A_3. Methylxanthines, such as caffeine, primarily occupy the A_1 and A_{2a} receptor types. The A_1 receptors are located in all parts of the brain, including the hippocampus, cerebral cortex, cerebellar cortex, and certain thalamic nuclei. The A_{2a} receptors are located in the dopamine-rich areas of the brain, including the striatum and nucleus accumbens (Fredholm et al., 1999; Nehlig, 1999). Once caffeine attaches to an adenosine receptor, the action of adenosine is blocked. This prevents neurons in the brain that cause sleep-promoting effects from firing (Ferre, 2008). Caffeine also increases dopamine activity by its action on the A_2 receptors (Garrett & Griffiths, 1997). It is known that caffeine inhibits A_2 receptors, leading to a potentiation (increase) of dopamine activity. Why does a change in dopamine levels matter? Dopamine-rich areas of the brain, such as the nucleus accumbens, are key facilitators of drug addiction. Caffeine is thus similar to other drugs that lead to dependence problems by increasing cerebral dopamine (Lazarus et al. 2011). However, caffeine appears to cause comparatively fewer addiction-related concerns than other drugs, at least in caffeine doses commonly consumed by healthy adults. Caffeine appears to have limited effects on the dopamine-rich structures related to reward, motivation, and addiction, such as the shell of the nucleus accumbens (Nehlig, 1999). This differs from other drugs of abuse (such as heroin or cocaine) where the drug causes dramatic changes in dopamine release in the shell of the nucleus accumbens. So while the effects of caffeine in the brain do not rule it out as a potentially addictive drug, stimulant effects of caffeine are clearly different from other stimulant drugs, such as cocaine and methamphetamine, which have an addictive potential that is much greater (Fredholm et al., 1999).

Pharmacokinetics

Pharmacokinetics is the branch of pharmacology that examines the absorption, distribution, biotransformation, and excretion of drugs. Previous discussions about drug dose and routes of administration fall under the area of pharmacokinetics. Once a given amount of caffeine is ingested by swallowing, the drug is not static but rather moves around the body. First, caffeine moves via the gastrointestinal tract to reach the small intestine where it can be absorbed into the bloodstream. Once in the bloodstream, caffeine moves with the blood to reach the brain where the adenosine receptors are located. This process from swallowing to reaching the adenosine receptors takes some time. The peak effects that are experienced by a user occur 15 to 45 minutes after the drug is administered. This time to reach the peak effect will be on the faster side if the stomach is empty, leading to speeded absorption. A full stomach has the opposite effect and slows caffeine absorption. **Bioavailability** refers to the portion of the original drug dose that reaches its site of action. The bioavailability of caffeine is assumed to be almost 100% (Blanchard & Sawers, 1983), meaning that almost every milligram of caffeine ingested will probably reach an adenosine receptor.

Caffeine crosses the blood–brain barrier without difficulty. The **blood–brain barrier** is the system that filters blood before it can enter the brain. By easily crossing the blood–brain barrier, caffeine can reach adenosine receptors in the brain. Additionally, about 10–30% of caffeine in the blood becomes bound to protein and enters the circulatory system, resulting in small elevations in respiration and blood pressure (Arnaud, 1993). As discussed above, caffeine also crosses the placental barrier and is present in body fluids, including breast milk, a fact having important implications for expectant and new mothers and their infants.

Most drugs are described by their half-life, which is relevant to the last aspect of pharmacokinetics, the excretion of the drug. The **half-life** is the amount of time that is required for the dose of drug in the body to be reduced by half. While *half-life* is a term that has received some scrutiny regarding how helpful it is in understanding the body's ability to clear itself from a drug, it remains in use and is somewhat helpful in understanding the abuse potential of certain drugs. The half-life of caffeine is approximately 5 hours (Charles et al., 2008). Compare that to a half-life for cocaine (another stimulant drug that comes from an alkaloid plant), which is about 1 hour. A shorter half-life is thought to contribute to greater drug abuse and addiction, since once a drug leaves the body, the user will look for another dose. Caffeine's very long half-life is an additional reason that psychopharmacologists consider caffeine to be a safe psychoactive drug (Fredholm et al., 1999).

Caffeine metabolism is carried out mostly by the liver, and caffeine is excreted almost entirely by the kidneys. About 10% is excreted in pure form and the rest of the drug leaves the body as metabolites. Caffeine metabolism and excretion varies among individuals. People who have not regularly used caffeine typically have slower rates of metabolism and excretion. Liver disease, pregnancy, and the use of oral contraceptives slow down metabolism and excretion. By contrast, individuals who smoke cigarettes metabolize caffeine more quickly. In fact, caffeine half-life is reduced by 30–50% in heavy smokers compared to nonsmokers, accounting for the observation that smokers are often heavy consumers of caffeine, such as coffee (Fredholm et al., 1999).

Myth Busters: Consuming Caffeine in Energy Drinks Is Safe

Children, adolescents, and young adults, such as college students, often believe that energy drinks are just like soft drinks. Not knowing that the caffeine found in energy drinks can be up to three times that in soft drinks, they often consume very large quantities of these beverages. In fact, the large serving sizes of these beverages encourage the consumption of large amounts, particularly now that energy drinks are sold in 16 oz. (0.5 L) cans. So are individuals correct in assuming that energy drinks are safe, even in large quantities? The answer might be no. A recent report from one U.S. government agency, the Substance Abuse and Mental Health Services Administration (SAMHSA), provided data from emergency department admissions that address this myth.

Figure 4-8 shows the trend data reflecting a sharp increase in the number of emergency department visits involving energy drinks. To be considered a case in this tracking system, the visit must involve a drug, either as the direct cause of the visit or as a contributing factor. There was a tenfold increase between 2005 and 2009 in emergency department visits involving energy drinks. These visits were divided into two groups: those that involve energy drinks only and those that involve energy drinks in combination with pharmaceuticals, alcohol, and/or illicit drugs. About half of the visits (56%) involved energy drinks alone. When examined by the reason for the visit, more than two-thirds (67%) of visits involving energy drinks were classified as adverse reactions (including heart arrhythmias, hypertension, dehydration, seizures, sleeplessness, and nervousness). Many of these adverse reactions are a direct consequence of excessive caffeine intake. Since the majority of emergency department visits involving energy drinks alone were due to adverse reactions, this suggests that energy drink consumption by itself can result in negative health events serious enough to require a trip to the emergency room. Moreover, many individuals appear to have preexisting health conditions that might make the consumption of energy drinks particularly risky. For example, stimulants are known to lower the seizure threshold in individuals with a predisposition to seizures. While some young people may be aware of their health conditions, others may find themselves in the emergency room for the first time because they were unaware of their health condition until the consumption of energy drinks made the problem surface.

The take home message is clear: if you are going to consume energy drinks, moderation is key! Researchers and clinicians consider daily caffeine intake between 200 and 300 mg per day as moderate intake of caffeine for a healthy adult. Therefore, two typical 16 oz. cans of the energy drink Monster would be a *daily* maximum for someone who does not have preexisting medical conditions or sensitivity to caffeine (Figure 4-9). Remember, too, that caffeine is found in a variety of beverages and foods, which adds to the total daily consumption of caffeine.

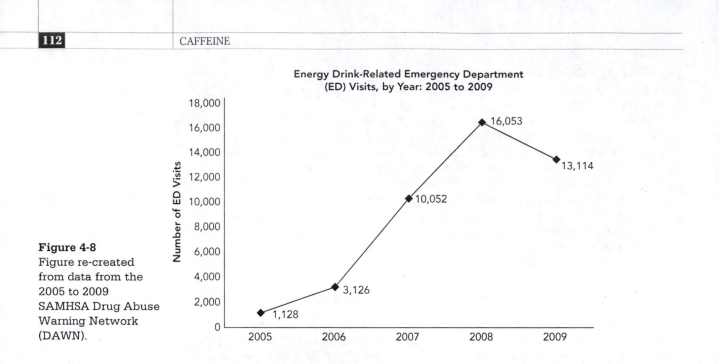

Energy Drink-Related Emergency Department
(ED) Visits, by Year: 2005 to 2009

Figure 4-8
Figure re-created
from data from the
2005 to 2009
SAMHSA Drug Abuse
Warning Network
(DAWN).

©skodonnell/istockphoto

Figure 4-9
Popular energy drink
brands.

QUICK QUIZ 4-2

1. Maribel would like to become pregnant. She knows that high levels of caffeine use can be associated with difficulties with conception and other problems in pregnancy. Therefore, she decides to stop using all caffeine. Within 24 hours, she experiences many side effects that are unpleasant, including irritability, fatigue, and a headache. What is she experiencing?
    a. Dose dependence
    b. Tolerance
    c. Withdrawal
    d. Bioavailability

2. Caffeine is considered to be an _____ drug, due to its action on _____ receptors.
    a. agonist, adenosine
    b. antagonist, adenosine
    c. agonist, serotonin
    d. antagonist, serotonin

3. The LD_{50} for caffeine is considered to be approximately equal to:
    a. 2 cups of coffee
    b. 10 cups of coffee

c. 25 cups of coffee

d. 75 cups of coffee

4. Dr. Su decides to plan a study examining the acute effects of caffeine. He asks his human volunteers to not consume any caffeinated food or drink for 24 hours before entering the lab. What is one concern that should be considered about this experimental approach?

a. Tolerance

b. Withdrawal reversal

c. Caffeinism

d. Effective dose

e. Lethal dose

5. Dr. Valdez decides to plan a study examining the acute effects of caffeine. She asks her human volunteers to not sleep for more than 2 hours the night before her study. Given this experimental approach, is she likely to observe that caffeine improves cognitive functioning? Why, or why not?

6. List two phenomena that should be evaluated when determining whether caffeine use might be considered substance dependence. What is the evaluation for caffeine for these two phenomenon?

7. Why should pregnant women limit their caffeine consumption?

ANSWERS TO QUICK QUIZ 4-2:

1. c – Withdrawal

2. b – Antagonist, Adenosine

3. d – 75 cups of coffee

4. b – withdrawal reversal

5. Yes, Dr. Valdez should observe that caffeine improves cognitive functioning. Caffeine is most effective in improving performance in fatigued individuals.

6. Both tolerance and withdrawal need to be evaluated. Tolerance refers to the reduced effect of a drug with continued use of the same dose or increased need for more drug to achieve a particular effect. For caffeine, tolerance develops to some things like sleep and renal function. However, tolerance does not appear to develop to the stimulatory effects, which is a main reason that individuals use caffeine. Withdrawal refers to a set of symptoms that are like an illness when drug use stops. For caffeine, there is a withdrawal syndrome consisting of symptoms such as headache and fatigue. These symptoms are more severe in heavier users. Most symptoms dissipate within a few days.

7. During pregnancy, caffeine is rapidly absorbed and crosses the placenta freely. The developing fetus lacks the enzymes needed for caffeine metabolism. It is possible that high levels of caffeine could impair fetal growth or lead to spontaneous abortions. In newborns, withdrawal symptoms can occur, especially in newborns whose mothers are heavy caffeine consumers.

CHAPTER SUMMARY

Caffeine is the most widely used psychoactive drug. It is found in a variety of beverages, foods, and medications, including coffee, tea, soft drinks, energy drinks, and chocolate. Caffeine use improves subjective state by decreasing sleepiness and improving mood. The neurotransmitter, adenosine, leads to sleepiness. Caffeine acts by blocking adenosine receptors in the brain, resulting in decreased sleepiness. Caffeine can also improve behavioral and cognitive functioning in certain situations. Acute and chronic caffeine intake typically has only minor negative consequences on health, with some exceptions for certain populations, such as pregnant women and children. Few users report loss of control over their caffeine intake. As such, most countries have no restrictions on the use of caffeine. While some tolerance does develop to caffeine, tolerance does not develop to the stimulation effects, which is a main reason that individuals continue to use caffeine. As a result of no tolerance to stimulation, escalation of use of caffeine is uncommon. The withdrawal syndrome from caffeine is mild and typically lasts for a few days, with symptoms such as headaches. Caffeine is used by the majority of the adult population in most countries around the world. Its use does not cause major social problems and appears to be safe in most cases. While high levels of caffeine can cause health problems, such as caffeinism and toxic reactions, the majority of individuals use this psychoactive drug safely on a regular basis.

5

NICOTINE

Introduction

I live and work in the state of Kentucky, known for race horses, fine bourbon, and tobacco farms. Kentucky also has the dubious honor of having one of the highest smoking rates in the United States. According to recent estimates, more than 1 in 4 adults in Kentucky use tobacco, a rate higher than the national average of 1 in 5 Americans (CDC, 2010b). While Kentucky is nick-named the "Bluegrass state" for its unique grassy hillsides that appear blue in the spring, one reporter quipped that the state should be called the "Blue Smoke state" because of its high rates of smoking (DeNoon, 2009). Considering the high rates of smoking in Kentucky, it not surprising that smoking-related deaths in the state are also among the highest in the nation. Today, most individuals know that smoking is harmful and that the nicotine in tobacco products is highly addictive, yet many people start the habit and then cannot quit (Figure 5-1).

In this chapter, we will discuss the psychoactive drug, nicotine, the stimulant drug found in tobacco products such as cigarettes, cigars and chewing tobacco. We will answer some of the questions associated with nicotine and smoking. What is the appeal of the drug nicotine to the user? Why is nicotine so addictive? What are the health implications of smoking? What are the most effective ways to quit smoking? In addition, we will examine some of the newer evidence about potential medical applications of nicotine. Let us explore these and many other questions about nicotine.

Figure 5-1
Most individuals know that smoking is harmful, yet many people start the habit and then cannot quit.

©Marty Bucella/Cartoonstock

LEARNING OBJECTIVES

Learning objectives can help organize your studying. Before we begin the topic of nicotine, keep in mind that by the end of this chapter, you should be able to . . .

1. Define various terms such as nicotine, reinforcer, acetylcholine, mesolimbic dopaminergic pathway, biphasic drug, and nicotine replacement therapy.
2. Describe the various sources of nicotine and the typical routes of administration.
3. Describe the prevalence of nicotine use, in the United States and around the world.
4. Explain how nicotine acts on the central nervous system and how nicotine's acute effects differ from its chronic effects.
5. Explain why smoking is harmful to health.
6. Explain tolerance, dependence, and withdrawal that occur with nicotine use.
7. Apply your knowledge of how nicotine acts in the brain to evaluate the effectiveness of various smoking cessation techniques, including the electronic cigarette.
8. Evaluate the evidence regarding potential medical uses of nicotine.

Nicotine as a Stimulant Drug

Nicotine ($C_{10}H_{14}N_2$) is the third most widely used psychoactive drug (caffeine and alcohol are the most common). Like caffeine, nicotine is an alkaloid stimulant drug. A **stimulant drug** increases alertness, decreases fatigue, and heightens mood. Stimulant drugs can be used for both recreational and medical reasons, with nicotine being used as a recreational drug almost exclusively (Julien, 2005). Produced by a plant, an **alkaloid** is a nitrogen-containing organic metabolite, which is toxic and tastes extremely bitter. Nicotine in the plant world functions as a natural antiherbivore, particularly for insects, who avoid eating leaves containing nicotine. In the tobacco plant, the biosynthesis of nicotine takes place in the roots and the accumulation of nicotine occurs in the leaves. Extremely toxic, nicotine was widely used as an insecticide in the past and is still sometimes used in organic gardening (Rodgman & Perfetti, 2009). Since nicotine is water-soluble, workers harvesting tobacco need to be careful handling green tobacco leaves. If the leaves are wet, nicotine can be drawn out of the tobacco. If nicotine touches the skin, it is absorbed and can lead to **nicotine poisoning**, which is called "**green tobacco sickness**" in the special case of harvesting overexposure to nicotine. The symptoms of nicotine poisoning include nausea, vomiting, dizziness, headache, weakness, diarrhea, breathing difficulties, fluctuations in blood pressure or heart rate, and increased perspiration. In many cases, the symptoms will go away after several days, but with more extreme cases, hospitalization may be necessary (McBride, Altman, Klein, & White, 1998). Thus, nicotine is not an innocuous chemical for humans or animals. In fact, nicotine is so toxic that it is comparable to cyanide in toxicity. Only 60 milligrams (mg) of nicotine are needed to result in death (Rose, 1991).

When humans consume nicotine in a typical form, such as smoking a cigarette, the amount of nicotine ingested is relatively low, about 1 mg. This amount of nicotine is sufficient to elicit central nervous system stimulation, without leading to symptoms of nicotine poisoning described above. However, novice smokers who try one or more cigarettes for the first time may experience symptoms like the farm workers whose skin had absorbed nicotine from the green leaves of the plant. If this is the case, why would an individual who tries nicotine ever try smoking again? One reason is that the body quickly adapts to the unpleasant effects, even as the nicotine is leading to dependence. However, as we will see later in this chapter, the true health risks of the use of tobacco products come from the delivery device (the cigarette), and not the nicotine itself (Figure 5-2). When a cigarette is burned, about 4,000 compounds are released, in addition to nicotine. The remaining chemicals account for the health risks and hazards that accompany tobacco use

Figure 5-2
While the nicotine in cigarettes will lead to addiction, it is everything else in cigarettes that may cause serious health problems and even contribute to an early death.

©Kuzma/Shutterstock

(Julien, 2005). In other words, the nicotine will get you hooked, but it is everything else in cigarettes that may cause health problems and increase your risk of early death.

Sources of Nicotine

Nicotine (Figure 5-3) is found in the tobacco plant. While there are a variety of species of tobacco plants belonging to the genus, *Nicotiana*, the principal source of tobacco today comes from *Nicotiana tabacum*. The plants of *N. Tabacum* can reach approximately 2 meters or 6 feet in height (Figure 5-4). The leaves are bright green, long, broad, and pointed. Leaves can be harvested by cutting a few leaves at a time from the bottom of the plant when mature, or by harvesting the whole plant with one cut. Cultivated tobacco tends to have a higher nicotine content compared with any wild member of the same genus (Blum, 1984).

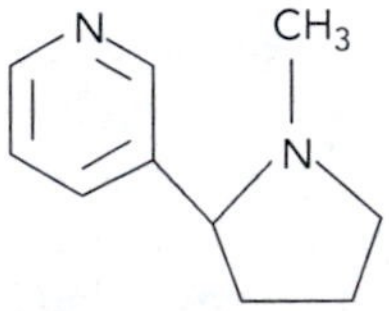

Figure 5-3
Chemical structure of nicotine.

Figure 5-4
Photograph of third-generation Kentucky tobacco farmer, Gene Witt (Shelbyville, KY).

©Ed Reinke/Associated Press

Once the leaves of the tobacco plant are harvested, they can be cured and prepared in several ways, depending on the final intended use of the tobacco. In cigarettes, cigars, or pipe tobacco, the tobacco is burned. By contrast, chewing tobacco is specially processed and flavored. Tobacco snuff that is inhaled through the nose requires the tobacco leaves to be dried, ground into a fine powder, and mixed with aromatic and flavoring agents. Most commonly, tobacco is ingested in the form of cigarettes or cigars. However, with new bans on smoking in locations such as bars and restaurants, there has been a resurgence in other forms of tobacco. Smokeless tobacco in particular has a social history with subsets of individuals such as baseball players. With some variation, once the tobacco leaf is cured, the nicotine content can reach about 6% (Blum, 1984).

Route of Administration

The **route of administration** refers to the method by which a drug enters the body. The route of administration impacts how much of the dose reaches the site of action and how quickly it gets there. Given that nicotine is a **psychoactive drug** (having effects on mood, thinking, and behavior), the final location of action is the brain. Nicotine is easily absorbed from every site on or in the body. This includes the lungs, mucous membranes of the mouth or nose, skin, and gastrointestinal tract. Most tobacco is smoked, so **inhalation** is the most common route of administration. When a drug is inhaled, the lungs are the entry point in the body. Inhalation is a fast and effective method of drug absorption. However, a drug needs to be in a gaseous or vapor state to be inhaled, which is often the case for nicotine. When tobacco is smoked, the nicotine is suspended in cigarette smoke in the form of tiny particles (tars). The nicotine is quickly absorbed into the bloodstream through the lung mucous membranes (Julien, 2005).

Nicotine in snuff and nicotine nasal spray is absorbed through the mucous membranes of the nose. While snuff is less commonly used today than other tobacco products (Regan, Dube, & Arrazola, 2012), snuff was much more common historically. Powdered tobacco can be either pinched between the fingers or placed on the back of the hand and then sniffed into the nostrils. Not surprisingly, when something goes up the nose, there is a vigorous sneeze. A drug taken through the nose is called the **intranasal** route of administration. Intranasal drug administration results in the drug entering the body through the nose and sinus cavities. Since the nose and sinus cavity have a good blood supply, this route of administration is fast and effective. For individuals who chew tobacco or nicotine gum, the mucous membranes of the mouth are the points of entry for nicotine.

Nicotine can enter the body through the skin, which is the **transdermal** route of administration. This can occur either accidentally, such as when a farm worker touches wet tobacco leaves, or with transdermal skin patches, which are typically used for the medical treatment of nicotine dependency. Transdermal patches need to be placed on a location of the body where there is high subcutaneous blood flow, like the upper arm. This is due to the role of the bloodstream's transporting nicotine to the brain, the site of action. Nicotine is unusual in making use of the transdermal route of administration, because the skin is typically an effective barrier to many chemicals.

Therefore, dependent on the route of administration, nicotine will reach the brain slower or faster, with the movement of the drug referred to as **pharmacokinetics**, which we will discuss later in this chapter. However, the route of administration, or entry point to the body, is part of pharmacokinetics and will impact how fast the nicotine reaches the bloodstream. A nicotine patch (transdermal route of administration) is slow, whereas smoking (inhalation route of drug administration) is fast (Julien, 2005).

Brief History of Nicotine Use

The origin of tobacco use appeared to have occurred long ago in the Americas. Recent evidence collected by archeologists from the Meyer-Honninger Paleontology Museum consists of a block of fossilized tobacco that dates back to the Pleistocene Era, 2.5 million years ago. The tobacco fossil was found in a river basin in northeastern Peru. Experts now think that the tobacco plant was cultivated in the Americas around 6000 BCE, as agricultural skills developed in the people living there. By 1 BCE, the people of the Americas were smoking tobacco (in various ways such as using pipes and in cigars), chewing it, and even using it in enemas. By 1 CE, tobacco was believed to be nearly everywhere in both North and South America (Borio, 2011).

The aboriginal peoples of both North and South America were the only users of the drug at the time the European explorers arrived. When Columbus landed at San Salvador Island in the Bahamas in 1492, the local people presented him with various gifts, including dry tobacco leaves. Since the Europeans did not know what the leaves were, they later threw them away. Once members of Columbus's expedition went ashore, they observed the native people smoking cigars, something they had never seen in Europe. Given that they didn't know what they were observing, the sailors reported that the local people were "perfuming themselves" or "drinking smoke." However, it did not take long for the Spanish crewmen to try tobacco. Rodrigo de Jerez picked up the tobacco-smoking habit and continued to smoke when he returned to Europe. Being the first European smoker was not without a cost. The smoke frightened his neighbors, and the Spanish Inquisition eventually imprisoned him for 7 years for his habit. The charge was that only the Devil could give a man the ability to exhale smoke from his mouth. Once released from prison, one can be certain that the sailor would have been a bit annoyed to discover that smoking had caught on in Spain during his time behind bars. The arrival of the smoking trend occurred in part because Ramon Pane, a monk who had accompanied Columbus on his second voyage, brought back tobacco leaves and seeds. The use of tobacco spread in Europe when the French ambassador to Portugal, Jean Nicot, thought that there were medical uses for the plant (Figure 5-5). He took great interest in the plant and sent tobacco and seeds from Brazil to the royal family in Paris, France, in 1560. His name was given to the plant genus, *Nicotiana*, and then to the alkaloid nicotine (Borio, 2011; Brecher, 1972).

The use of tobacco as a wonder cure spread across Europe, but tobacco also caught on as a recreational drug, mainly for the wealthy. The English were the last Europeans to acquire the use of tobacco. In the late 16th century, British sailors brought the habit home from the East Indies. A sea captain named Raleigh introduced smoking to the English court, in addition to founding the North American colony at Virginia. The colony ultimately owed its survival and prosperity to

Figure 5-5
Vintage French stamp depicting Jean Nicot who introduced tobacco to France, and gave his name to nicotine, the active ingredient in tobacco.

tobacco cultivation. The colony nearly perished initially after a shipwreck and subsequent period of starvation. Then, the colonists began to grow some Spanish tobacco seeds. The plants prospered and tobacco was sent back to Britain in 1616. Up until this time, the British had been smoking imported Spanish tobacco. Now, tobacco could come from the English colonies in North America at a more reasonable cost. In the 16th century, tobacco in England was worth its weight in silver, making it a luxury for only the rich. By the 17th century, tobacco use became widespread when the price dropped because of colonial production, such that even the poor could afford it (Blum, 1984; Borio, 2011).

However, the view of tobacco as a medical cure was not universal. In fact, King James I, in 1604, issued an antitobacco essay that resembles some of the material seen in antismoking campaigns today. In the essay, the king refuted all arguments claiming that smoking was healthful. Furthermore, the essay remarked that smoking infected man with a vicious and oily soot, which may hasten death. The king's essay turned out to be as ineffective as similar bans and punishments against tobacco use in other parts of the world, which also had limited impact on the habit. The Japanese took to smoking after Portuguese seamen brought tobacco to them in the mid 1500s. When the emperor issued a ban on smoking in 1603, the impact was negligible and smoking became commonplace. By 1639, it was customary to serve a smoke with a ceremonial cup of tea in Japan. In the mid 1600s, Pope Urban VIII and Pope Innocent X issued papal bulls against tobacco use, which the clergy and common people largely ignored. In 1633, the sultan Murad IV in Constantinople banned smoking in soldiers. When he visited his soldiers in combat during war, he delivered harsh punishments such as hanging and beheading for smoking. Even so, his soldiers continued the habit. In 1634, the first Romanoff Russian czar, Michael Feodorovitch, prohibited smoking. Punishments such as slitting the nostrils of smokers had little impact on the tobacco use of the Russian people (Blum, 1984; Brecher, 1972).

In 1828, the chemical nicotine was isolated from the tobacco plant by physician Wilhelm Heinrich Posselt and chemist Karl Ludwig Reimann of Germany, who considered it a poison. Once nicotine was isolated, the medical reputation of it declined, as it became known that the chemical was both toxic and addictive. Despite the diminished medical reputation, whenever tobacco was introduced into a region, the use of it always appeared to increase and receive general acceptance (Blum, 1984; Brecher, 1972). Increases in use occurred even though it was becoming widely apparent that the use of tobacco was not without major costs to health.

Sigmund Freud is a classic example of a user of tobacco who knew of the health risks of smoking, yet continued with the habit, thus hastening his own demise. As you probably know, Freud was an avid smoker of cigars (Figure 5-6). His doctor recommended he cease smoking due to heart troubles, and Freud made many attempts to quit but was always unsuccessful. Finally, mouth and jaw cancer struck Freud. He underwent 33 operations, during which time he continued to smoke. He finally died of cancer in 1939. His efforts over a 45-year period to quit smoking were unsuccessful, despite considerable anguish, which illustrates the extremely addictive nature of nicotine (Brecher, 1972).

Worldwide, tobacco use increased until the 1960s. At that time, views of smoking changed dramatically with the 1964 release of the U.S. Surgeon General's Report, which definitively linked smoking to cancer and other diseases. A similar report in 1971 followed from the Royal College of Physicians of London. Evidence then continued to accumulate, leaving no doubt that smoking was unhealthy. In 1988, the U.S. Surgeon General concluded that nicotine is physically addicting. The general public found that report shocking since nicotine was never thought of as a "serious" drug like heroin or cocaine. As a result of these reports, the trend in increased smoking reversed to a decline in industrialized countries. The change has been remarkable with a 50% decline in the number of smokers today compared to 1965. Even so, smoking still kills an estimated 440,000 U.S. citizens annually, with one-third of the deaths due to cancer (CDC, 2011b). In spite of the decline in the developed world, tobacco use is rising in developing countries, perhaps due the fact that these populations are not as well educated about the health risks of smoking. As such, global cigarette consumption has remained relatively stable. It is estimated that

©adoc-photos/Corbis

Figure 5-6
Sigmund Freud was
an avid cigar smoker.
He was aware of the
health risks of smok-
ing, yet continued
with the habit, thus
hastening his own
death. After 33 sur-
geries for mouth and
jaw cancer, he still
continued to smoke
until his death.

1.1 billion people currently use tobacco, comprising up to one-third of the global adult population (WHO, 1996).

Despite the known health risks of using tobacco, most Western industrialized countries have limited regulation for tobacco products. In the United States, starting with a 1984 federal law, warning labels regarding the health risks of smoking were required to be placed on packages, with each message rotating every three months. The content of the messages is based on the Reports of the Surgeon General on the Health Consequences of Smoking. Despite warning labels, before 1994, tobacco products were not regulated by the U.S. Food and Drug Administration (FDA), the governmental body that regulates drugs in the United States. Previously, the tobacco industry had avoided FDA control by claiming that tobacco products were sold for smoking pleasure only and not for the effect of the drug nicotine. However, in 1994, the commissioner of the FDA formally requested that the FDA be given the power to regulate cigarettes as drugs. During a series of hearings before a subcommittee of the U.S. House of Representatives, the commissioner outlined the scientific evidence that nicotine was addictive and that cigarette manufacturers had knowingly manipulated the nicotine delivery of tobacco products. The FDA won its case and it now regulates nicotine in tobacco products. Despite increased regulation, the FDA has not placed an outright ban on all tobacco products. Instead, it tries to control tobacco by discouraging young smokers from starting the habit, regulating images in tobacco advertising, and controlling the availability of tobacco to teenagers (Kozlowski & Henningfield, 1995). The Family Smoking Prevention and Tobacco Control Act, which became law in 2009, gives the FDA greater authority to regulate the manufacture, distribution, and marketing of tobacco products with the goal of protecting public health. This act specifically restricts retail sales and advertising to youth. Moreover, sporting and entertainment events cannot be sponsored by a tobacco company. This act also requires placing bigger and more prominent warning labels on cigarette and smokeless tobacco products. Color graphics showing the negative consequences of smoking cigarettes over the top 50% of both the front and rear panels of the package are to be implemented. However, the implementation date of these changes is currently uncertain because of ongoing legal battles between tobacco companies and the FDA (FDA, 2013c).

Prevalence of Nicotine Use

In the United States

Tobacco-related diseases in the United States cause a health burden and have a negative economic impact, which is entirely preventable. Many national surveys have examined the prevalence of nicotine use in tobacco products. Information about smoking rates is helpful to determine if various prevention strategies, such as tobacco taxes, media campaigns, and smoke-free policies, have resulted in changes in smoking rates. At the start of this chapter, I mentioned that Kentucky had one of the highest rates of smoking in the nation. The data to support this statement came from a survey that was conducted by the government agency, the Centers for Disease Control and Prevention, as part of their Behavioral Risk Factor Surveillance System. The most recent data on current cigarette use by state is shown in Table 5-1 (CDC, 2010b). While a very large and comprehensive set of data on smoking, it should be noted that this data only included adult smokers (ages 18 and older) who smoked cigarettes every day or several days a week. Underage smokers and people who used other tobacco products (such as pipes or chewing tobacco) were not included. While cigarettes are not the only vehicle for tobacco use, according to the U.S. Surgeon General's report, smoking cigarettes is the primary source of tobacco use, with six of every seven pounds of tobacco grown in the United States used to make cigarettes (USDHHS, 2010). The prevalence of cigarettes as a tobacco vehicle is one reason researchers keep their surveys simple by asking only about cigarette smoking. Table 5-1 shows that the adult cigarette smoking rates by state range from the low end of 9.1% in Utah to the high end of 26.8% in West Virginia. In general, smoking rates are higher in the Midwest and South of the United States, with men and women using tobacco at similar rates (CDC, 2010b). Overall, it is estimated that 19.3% U.S. adults, or approximately 1 in 5, are currently cigarette smokers (CDC, 2011c). While these rates seem high, they represent a significant decrease from the smoking rates seen several decades ago. In 1965, the prevalence of cigarette smoking among adults in the United States was as high as 42.4%, which means the rates of tobacco use is less than half that observed less than five decades ago (CDC, 2011b).

Table 5-1   Cigarette use in U.S. adults in the year 2010.

State	Current Cigarette Use (%)
Alabama	21.9
Alaska	20.4
Arizona	13.5
Arkansas	22.9
California	12.1
Colorado	16.0
Connecticut	13.2
Delaware	17.3
District of Columbia	14.8
Florida	17.1
Georgia	17.6
Hawaii	14.5
Idaho	15.7
Illinois	16.9

(Continued)

Table 5.1   Continued

State	Current Cigarette Use (%)
Indiana	21.2
Iowa	16.1
Kansas	17.0
Kentucky	24.8
Louisiana	22.1
Maine	18.2
Maryland	15.2
Massachusetts	14.1
Michigan	18.9
Minnesota	14.9
Mississippi	22.9
Missouri	21.1
Montana	18.8
Nebraska	17.2
Nevada	21.3
New Hampshire	16.9
New Jersey	14.4
New Mexico	18.5
New York	15.5
North Carolina	19.8
North Dakota	17.4
Ohio	22.5
Oklahoma	23.7
Oregon	15.1
Pennsylvania	18.4
Rhode Island	15.7
South Carolina	21.0
South Dakota	15.4
Tennessee	20.1
Texas	15.8
Utah	9.1
Vermont	15.4
Virginia	18.5
Washington	15.2
West Virginia	26.8
Wisconsin	19.1
Wyoming	19.5
United States	**19.3**

Smoking and tobacco use rates are collected by the State Tobacco Activities Tracking and Evaluation (STATE) System by the Centers for Disease Control and Prevention. Cigarette use in adults ages 18 and older are included in this data collected by the Behavioral Risk Factor Surveillance System (BRFSS).

When surveys are conducted, researchers typically ask demographic profile questions such as age, socioeconomic status, and race. Analyzing this type of information for drug use often reveals important differences among subgroups of the population. Moreover, this kind of information can be used to target prevention programs for subgroups having the highest rates of use of the drug in question. For smoking, it has been found that U.S. adults with less than a high school education have high smoking rates (28%). Individuals who live below the federal poverty level have high smoking rates (28%), which may exacerbate health-related issues for smoking since many of these individuals do not have access to health insurance. Finally, smoking is more common in younger people, with relatively more smokers between the ages of 18 and 24 years (24%) than in other age groups (CDC, 2011b).

While the aforementioned surveys focused on cigarette smoking, other surveys have studied all tobacco use. One nationwide study of tobacco use among 14,138 U.S. college students found that nearly half (46%) of college students had used a tobacco product in the prior year. Use of tobacco products included cigarettes, cigars, pipes, and smokeless tobacco. Current use of tobacco was about one-third (33%) of responders, which is higher than the national rate of use. Cigarettes accounted for most of the tobacco use, but cigar use was also substantial. A gender difference emerged with men reporting more total tobacco use than women, even though cigarette-smoking rates between the sexes were similar. This overall gender difference resulted from male college students being more likely to smoke cigars and use smokeless tobacco. Tobacco use was higher in white students and students who used other drugs, including alcohol and marijuana. Tobacco use was lower in students whose priorities were educational or athletic. In summary, this data suggests that tobacco use is common among college students, with rates of use higher for college students than the U.S. population as a whole (Rigotti, Lee, & Wechsler, 2000).

While the above surveys only asked adults to report tobacco use, 90% of smokers start smoking before age 18. This occurs despite the health risks associated with tobacco and age restrictions prohibiting tobacco use among youth (Leatherdale & Burkhalter, 2012). Many people cite peer pressure as a psychosocial influence leading teenagers to start the habit. However, there may also be biological underpinnings explaining adolescent smoking. First, the adolescent brain appears to be more sensitive to the rewarding effects of nicotine (Belluzzi, Lee, Oliff, & Leslie, 2004). Recent animal research has demonstrated that acetaldehyde, one of the chemicals found in tobacco smoke, dramatically increases the rewarding properties of nicotine, with this effect apparently stronger among the young. Adolescent animals displayed more sensitivity to the rewarding aspects of nicotine, which raises an additional concern that adolescents may be more vulnerable to tobacco addiction compared to adults (Belluzzi, Wang, & Leslie, 2005; NIDA, 2011a). Preventing adolescents from initiating smoking is critical, since the younger the age at which a person starts smoking, the greater the difficulty in quitting later (Breslau & Peterson, 1996). Therefore, when examining prevalence rates for tobacco use, it is important to keep in mind the demographic characteristics, especially age, of the respondents. As with adults, variables such as socioeconomic status impact smoking rates in adolescents. A recent study compared smoking rates for 12- to 14-year-old youth in the child welfare system with similar-aged peers in the community. The rates of smoking were higher for the children who were part of the welfare system (23%) relative to their peers (18%) (Fettes & Aarons, 2011). The burdens of the health risks of smoking seem to be placed on those individuals who are least able to deal with them, including children living in poverty in the United States.

Around the World

Worldwide, the use of tobacco products is far more common in developing or transitional countries than in developed countries, which perhaps echoes the observation of higher U.S. usage rates among lower income individuals. The World Health Organization (WHO) estimates that of the approximately 1.22 billion smokers in the world, approximately 1 billion of them live in developing or transitional countries. As noted above, smoking has declined dramatically in the last four decades in the United States. By contrast, tobacco consumption is rising at a rate of about 3.4% per year in the developing world. Part of the growth in the developing world coincides with general population growth in those countries. Even so, smoking rates are extremely high in various locations around the globe. Countries such as Greece, Jordan, Russia, the Ukraine, Belarus, and Malaysia have some of the highest smoking rates worldwide, with the percentage of smokers often reaching greater than 50% of the adult population. By contrast, the lowest reported rates of smoking are found in many countries of Africa and Latin America. Unlike the United States, there are dramatic gender differences in smoking rates internationally, with men reporting smoking rates sometimes five times higher than women (WHO, 2011b).

Dramatic gender differences in tobacco use can be seen in smoking rates in China. The Chinese Center for Disease Control and Prevention regularly gathers health information using large survey methodologies similar to that used by the CDC in the United States. In 2010, 13,354 participants were selected in the Chinese survey. It was observed that 28% of adults (ages 15 and older) were current smokers, with 53% of men reporting current smoking, while only 2% of women reported current smoking. In this survey, certain demographic characteristics related to smoking prevalence rates were similar to those observed in the United States. For example, higher education level was associated with lower smoking rates. By contrast, the age trends in China (for men only) were opposite to those observed in the United States, with much higher rates of smoking in people ages 45 to 64 years (63%) than in those 15 to 24 years (34%). Given that there are an estimated 301 million current smokers in China, that country is the largest consumer of tobacco in the world. Clearly, in the coming decades, China will have to bear the disease burden and risk of significant socioeconomic loss resulting from the high rates of smoking among its citizens (Li, Hsia, & Yang, 2011).

The use of tobacco products in adolescents is a persistent concern in many countries around the world, just as in the United States. When smoking begins in the young, it provides a useful indication of potential future burden among adults of that population. One recent large study from Canada examined tobacco use in 45,425 high school students. The authors asked about current tobacco use. Students who reported having smoked 100 or more whole cigarettes in their life and smoking in the previous 30 days were classified as tobacco users. The researchers reported that 7% of ninth grade students were tobacco users. By the last year of high school (12th grade), 16% were tobacco users, with more males using tobacco than females. Given the authors' fairly stringent criteria for classification as tobacco users, there is a strong possibility that the majority of these students will continue that habit into adulthood (Leatherdale & Burkhalter, 2012). However, smoking rates in Canadian youth are substantially lower than elsewhere around the world. In Latin America, adolescents seem to be acquiring smoking at much high rates. One recent survey of 10th grade students in Argentina revealed that 34% of students were current smokers (Salgado et al., 2012).

In the News:

Koch, W. (2012, January 6). Workplaces ban not only smoking, but smokers themselves. *USA Today*.

A recent article in *USA Today* discussed the controversial new practice of not hiring applicants whose urine tests positive for nicotine, whether from cigarettes, smokeless tobacco, or even nicotine patches used in the treatment of smoking. While this practice is more common for employers such as hospitals, the approach is becoming more popular given that tobacco-free hiring policies are designed to reduce insurance premiums and promote health. Financially, it makes sense (or cents) for employers to consider such policies since tobacco users tend to have health care costs that are $3,000 to $4,000 more per year than their nonsmoking peers. Many states have no rules prohibiting nicotine-free hiring and federal laws allow the practice because smokers are not recognized as a protected class. Nevertheless, smoking is legal, which leads to some outrage in the wider community regarding these policies.

Use this news article to test and apply your knowledge:

1. In this article, job applicants are eliminated from a potential job if they use tobacco products. Approximately what proportion of U.S. job applicants might be impacted by these policies?
2. The article mentions that employers test applicant urine for the presence of nicotine and use this information to screen out applicants. Is this approach appropriate if the employer is only interested in controlling health care costs?

Answers:

1. About one-fifth of job applicants might be impacted, given that the current cigarette smoking rate in the United States is 19.3%.
2. Perhaps not given that the majority of health risks from smoking come from the nicotine delivery system (cigarette), not the nicotine itself. Even though nicotine is addictive, it does not elevate health care costs. In fact, if someone uses a nicotine patch/gum/inhaler to quit smoking, their urine will test positive for nicotine, but their health should improve when they are no longer smoking. It is all the other chemicals released from cigarettes when smoking that lead to declines in health. We will discuss the health risks of smoking in greater detail later in this chapter.

What do you think about this news story?

Currently, smoking is legal for adults in the United States, even though it may increase the risks of poor health outcomes. This article raises the question of how reasonable it is for employers to monitor and control lawful behavior, even outside of the workplace. How do you feel about these employer screening techniques? Do you agree that employers should discriminate against job applicants in this manner? Do you think that there should be laws that discriminate against people who use drugs, legal or illegal? Do you think that tobacco-free hiring policies make the general public less compassionate about people who are addicted to a substance, or do you think that these policies dissuade people from smoking and promote healthy behaviors? Keep these questions in mind, particularly when we discuss the addictive potential of nicotine later in this chapter.

Focus on Careers: Social Workers

Repeated drug use can lead to physical and psychological dependence on the drug. Such changes can lead to a wide variety of problems for the user as life revolves around drug use. While less of a concern with the use of nicotine, other drug use can lead individuals to fail to fulfill normal obligations to work, family, and friends. The individual may have interactions with the criminal justice system. Social workers are on the front lines dealing with the problems that accompany substance abuse and addiction. These are caring and compassionate individuals who spend their careers helping people and promoting social justice. Social workers also assess various public policy decisions. Thus, social work as a career is very broad in scope. Some social workers protect children, whose parents are unable to properly care for them because of addiction. Other social workers interact with individuals in correctional facilities to help them get their life back on track. Social workers can be found in hospital emergency rooms intervening with cases of injuries related to alcohol or drug use. Other social workers work alongside psychologists and provide counseling for problems such as cessation from smoking and other poor health habits. The path of entry to social work as a field can vary. Some individuals with an undergraduate degree in an area like psychology may be eligible for entry-level jobs in many social service agencies. However, to be eligible for higher-paying jobs and state licensure, a bachelor's degree in social work is often required. To conduct counseling sessions or to acquire positions of greater responsibility, a master's degree in social work is advantageous. According to the U.S. Bureau of Labor Statistics, the median pay in 2010 for social workers was approximately $42,000. This field has a faster than average growth rate.

Websites to explore:

National Association of Social Workers
 www.socialworkers.org
International Federation of Social Workers
 www.ifsw.org

QUICK QUIZ 5-1

1. When an individual smokes a cigarette, what is the route of administration?
   a. Transdermal
   b. Sublingual
   c. Inhalation
   d. Intranasal

2. How have rates of cigarette smoking in the United States changed in the last four decades?
   a. They have increased.
   b. They have decreased.
   c. They have stayed about the same.
   d. They have increased at a rate that is consistent with the population growth.

3. How have rates of cigarettes smoking worldwide changed in the last four decades?
   a. They have increased.
   b. They have decreased.

   c. They have stayed about the same.
   d. There is no available data to answer this question.

4. Your friend Sam has taken a summer job picking tobacco on a farm. What might you warn your friend about regarding the job?

5. The U.S. Surgeon General in 1964 released a landmark report linking smoking to cancer and other diseases. Smoking rates declined in the decades thereafter. Was this the first time in history that people thought tobacco use might be associated with health risks?

6. Your friend is a smoker who wants to quit. She has tried to quit many times on her own but has been unsuccessful. You suggest that she try a nicotine replacement product (such as a nicotine patch) to help her quit. However, she argues that use of a nicotine patch won't help her quit because she will get the nicotine in either case. Using your understanding of pharmacokinetics and route of administration, how would you explain to your friend that the nicotine administered in the patch form might be advantageous to quitting efforts?

ANSWERS TO QUICK QUIZ 5-1:

1. c – Inhalation
2. b – decreased
3. a – increased
4. Your friend might get green tobacco sickness (nicotine poisoning) if your friend picks tobacco leaves while wet and the leaves touch the skin. Symptoms of green tobacco sickness include nausea, vomiting, dizziness, weakness, diarrhea, fluctuations in blood pressure and heart rate, and increased perspiration.

5. No, in fact King James I, in 1604, issued an antitobacco essay that resembles antismoking information common today. In the essay, it was claimed that smoking infected man with a vicious and oily soot that may hasten an early death. While the science showing that tobacco use can lead to cancer was a more recent advancement, people much earlier had seen the connection between smoking and poor health outcomes.

6. The inhalation of nicotine by cigarette smoking results in a very fast method of drug absorption. When cigarette smoke is inhaled, nicotine easily gets into the bloodstream because the lungs have a large blood supply. Therefore, nicotine administration via smoking results in rapid absorption by the brain. By contrast, nicotine administered through the transdermal route of administration using a patch will be slow. The skin is an effective barrier and thus nicotine must be absorbed relatively slowly through the skin, get into the bloodstream and then eventually reach the brain. The transdermal route of administration is dramatically slower than the inhalation route of administration. Given that nicotine is addictive, it would be better that the drug reaches the brain more slowly if the goal is the break the habit. In addition, it would be helpful to mention that the delivery device for nicotine (the cigarette) contains the harmful chemicals to health. While the nicotine is addictive, it is less able to cause health problems in an innocuous delivery device, so the patch is clearly preferable to the cigarette.

Acute Effects of Nicotine

The acute effects of a drug refer to changes that take place after one occasion ingesting the drug. The acute effects of nicotine refer to immediate changes experienced after nicotine is administered. Acute effects can be objective (such as observable changes in behavior or physiology) or subjective (such as not easily observable changes like the ratings a participant provides about how they feel). Examining the acute effects of nicotine can be a difficult task. Ideally, a researcher would wish to determine how a person responds to nicotine before that person becomes a regular user of nicotine. However, given the addictive nature of nicotine, there are ethical considerations to administering nicotine to individuals previously unfamiliar with the drug who might like it and then become smokers. As a result, the literature on the acute effects of nicotine consists of a mix of studies examining smokers and nonsmokers. In addition to ethical concerns, nicotine is a stimulant having a significant dose effect. When nicotine is administered at the normal dose, a level that would be typically used by a regular smoker, the effects may be consistent with central nervous system (CNS) stimulation. However, nicotine is a **biphasic** drug. A biphasic drug has a particular effect as utilization increases, but then the effect reverses with increased use (see Figure 5-7). Lower doses of nicotine result in CNS stimulation. However, as the dose increases, the effect reverses and causes CNS sedation. Smokers appear to be aware of the biphasic properties of nicotine and adjust their smoking style accordingly. Research has suggested that when smokers wish to achieve a stimulating effect, they take short quick puffs on a cigarette. This

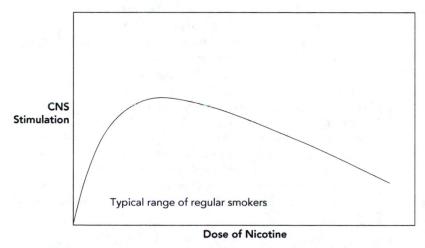

Figure 5-7
Nicotine is a biphasic drug.

produces low levels of blood nicotine, which stimulates CNS activity. However, when smokers wish to relax, they take deep puffs on a cigarette. This produces high levels of blood nicotine, which decreases CNS activity (Einstein, 1989). The biphasic properties of nicotine are interesting, since the dose administered will alter neurotransmitter activity in different ways.

Objective Effects

Since nicotine is a stimulant drug, one might predict that at doses typically used by smokers, nicotine would improve performance on objective measures. However, the results have not been consistent, in part because the acute effects of nicotine seem to somewhat depend on whether one tests a smoker or nonsmoker. When smokers are tested in laboratory studies, it appears that nicotine improves performance in behaviors that were degraded by withdrawal from nicotine. It seems that depriving nicotine-addicted smokers from nicotine not only makes them grumpy, but their attentional and cognitive abilities become impaired, too. These objective deficits quickly reverse if the person smokes or is given nicotine (Fisher, Daniels, Jaworska, Knobelsdorf, & Knott, 2012). However, it also appears that nonsmokers and nondeprived smokers show objective improvements in various skills when given nicotine. While not all studies have reliably demonstrated objective improvements in cognitive performance from nicotine, there are nevertheless indications that cognitive processes do improve following nicotine administration. Attention, working memory, short-term episodic memory, recognition memory, reasoning, information processing, learning, and even finger tapping have been shown to improve under nicotine, regardless of whether the subject in a study is a regular user of nicotine (Heishman, 1999; Heishman, Kleykamp, & Singleton, 2010; Le Houezec et al., 1994; Wignall & de Wit, 2011). Tasks that rely on multiple cognitive processes, such as simulated driving, are also improved with nicotine, particularly when the task is monotonous and leads to fatigue. For example, a study of 12 minimally abstinent smokers examined simulated driving for an hour under various doses of nicotine ranging from < 0.1 mg up to 2.1 mg. The researchers found that the brake reaction times improved after all active doses (Sherwood, 1995). Objective improvements in performance following nicotine administration seem to coincide with changes in cortical activity in the brain. One study examined EEG (electroencephalogram) activity in nonsmoking participants who were administered 6 mg of nicotine in a gum. The researchers reported that nicotine administration increased electrical activity (compared with placebo) in the frontal cortex (Fisher et al., 2012), a region of the brain used for several cognitive tasks described above.

The acute effects of nicotine appear to improve alertness, facilitate motor coordination, and enhance cognitive performance. Given these changes, a group of researchers wished to determine if nicotine would also improve athletic performance in a group of nonsmokers. The researchers had a group of men cycle to exhaustion while wearing a 7 mg transdermal nicotine patch or a placebo patch. The researchers observed that the men cycled longer following the nicotine administration compared with the placebo, suggesting that nicotine might also prolong endurance (Mundel & Jones, 2006).

It appears smokers are at least somewhat aware that nicotine can improve performance, and smokers may adjust their smoking to take advantage of nicotine's cognitive-enhancing effects. One study examined the smoking behavior of 36 subjects smoking cigarettes using different filters that altered how much nicotine they received. Subjects were given various tasks on a driving simulator and were also observed during rest periods when they were allowed to smoke. The researchers observed that smokers adjusted their nicotine intake to help them achieve an optimum level of performance on the driving task. The subjects given high-retention filters (which limited how much nicotine could be inhaled) took more frequent puffs and obtained nearly the same amount of nicotine as the smokers of cigarettes with low-retention filters (Ashton & Watson, 1970). Therefore, while many smokers may use nicotine for the subjective effects, the objective benefits to performance may be a factor contributing to initial and continued use of the drug (Heishman et al., 2010).

Subjective Effects

If you ask smokers how they feel when using tobacco, most would likely report that smoking is a pleasurable experience. Laboratory studies indicate that the good feelings smokers experience while smoking reflect the acute effects of nicotine, as opposed to the other chemicals found in cigarettes. Since subjective state reflects hard-to-measure feelings, assessing this aspect of drug use can be somewhat difficult. However, standardized questionnaires have been developed to assess reactions to nicotine. One such widely used questionnaire is the Addiction Research Center Inventory (ARCI), which asks individuals to answer 550 true–false questions regarding how they feel. The ARCI has been used in several psychopharmacology studies and has been found to differentiate the subjective effects of various drugs. In one study, nicotine was administered either by intravenous infusion or by tobacco smoke to participants who were regular smokers. The participants reported that they liked the effects of nicotine, with many of the subjective effects reported being similar to the euphoria experienced with other drugs like morphine and amphetamine. These effects peaked about one minute after drug administration and dissipated within a few minutes (de Wit & Zacny, 1995). It appears that smokers have an optimal level of nicotine resulting in the experience of positive feeling states. Ratings of drug liking are directly related to dose level, whereas desire to smoke cigarettes is inversely related to dose level, indicating that there is an optimal level of nicotine for experiencing positive subjective effects (Henningfield, Miyasato, & Jasinski, 1985).

However, smokers differ from nonsmokers in their subjective self-reports following nicotine administration. Smokers report positive effects after moderate doses of nicotine, including feeling energetic, liking the drug, feeling good, and wanting to use the drug again. By contrast, given the same dose of nicotine, nonsmokers do not report these effects. Instead, they tend to report negative subjective states, such as disorientation (Perkins, Jetton, & Keenan, 2003; Soria et al., 1996). Interestingly, certain subjective changes after nicotine administration are polar opposites for smokers and nonsmokers. A review of the literature determined that nicotine increases vigor and energy for smokers but results in feelings of fatigue for nonsmokers (Kalman & Smith, 2005). Luckily for smokers who wish to quit smoking, smokers who had quit at least one year ago report aversive feelings to nicotine, similar to nonsmokers (Perkins, Gerlach, Broge, Fonte, & Wilson, 2001).

Feeling stress is both a subjective state as well as the cause of objective physiological changes in the body. Everyone has had the experience of stress, with the associated emotions being experienced as aversive. Users of tobacco products often rely on tobacco during periods of stress and claim that smoking has a calming effect. In fact, stress results in increased smoking in a reliable manner, which led researchers to ask if nicotine reduces stress. However, there is little research evidence that smoking reduces stress. In both smokers and nonsmokers, the acute administration of nicotine decreases relaxation and increases tension and jitteriness (Kalman & Smith, 2005). Furthermore, surveys indicate that smokers have lower levels of psychological well-being than nonsmokers and ex-smokers (West, 1993). However, these findings are at odds with real-life experiences of many smokers, who, when asked about their habit, often report that smoking is relaxing and decreases stress. This perplexing observation is known as **Nesbitt's paradox**, named for the man who first studied it (Schachter, 1973). There are several possible explanations for smokers' assessment that tobacco use decreases stress. One possibility is that stress reduction from smoking is due to the relief of withdrawal-induced negative mood experienced between cigarettes (Heishman, 1999). It is also possible that some of the calming effect that smokers experience might reflect the fact that nicotine has a relaxing effect on skeletal muscles (discussed further below) (Jones, 1987). Finally, it is possible that, during stress, smokers take advantage of the biphasic properties of nicotine and use higher doses of nicotine by smoking more to induce behavioral sedation. More research on this topic is needed to help clarify this issue.

Effects on the Body

The **autonomic nervous system (ANS)** is an important regulatory system within the peripheral nervous system, which includes all nervous tissue outside of the brain and spinal cord. The ANS regulates all of the automatic functions in the body, such as breathing, heart rate, blood pressure, and digestion. The ANS is divided into two opposing branches. The first is the **sympathetic branch** of the ANS. The sympathetic branch is activated by emotional arousal via the release of epinephrine and norepinephrine from the adrenal glands. These physiological changes are responsible for the "fight-or-flight" response that occurs during emergencies. For example, imagine that you go camping and encounter a hungry bear looking at you like you might be his next dinner. What happens? You feel a sense of dread and panic. Your mind starts working quickly to figure out how to respond to the life-threatening situation. Your heart races, your blood pressure rises, you breathe faster, and you start sweating. Changes in blood flow occur, with blood shunted away from internal organs having nonessential functions, like the stomach, and moving to where blood is really needed at that moment, such as the brain and large muscle groups. All of these changes happen automatically and will facilitate you getting yourself to safety, since in this state, you can fight harder and run faster. Once the emergency is over, hopefully with a positive outcome such as you and the bear going your separate ways, you calm down. The **parasympathetic branch** of the ANS balances the actions of the sympathetic branch by exerting the opposite effect. Once the bear crisis is over, parasympathetic activity will reduce your heart rate, blood pressure, and sweating, thus bringing your body back to normal.

Many psychoactive drugs can mimic and/or elicit sympathetic arousal and nicotine is one such drug. The acute effects of nicotine impact the sympathetic branch of the ANS, particularly the cardiovascular system. Nicotine stimulates the release of epinephrine from the adrenal glands, resulting in increased arousal. An acute dose of nicotine also stimulates the heart, which leads to increased demand for oxygen. Respiration is increased from both direct and indirect stimulation of the respiratory centers in the medulla, which is located in the brainstem. While the sympathetic changes that occur during a bear attack are potentially life-saving, the constant sympathetic arousal that occurs with smoking becomes problematic. The body is not capable of frequently being in this state without incurring longer-term health consequences. When a cigarette is smoked, oxygen demanding increased heart activity accounts for some of the association between nicotine and heart disease. When insufficient levels of oxygen reach the heart, chest pain (also called angina) or a heart attack could result (Julien, 2005).

One other physiological change that occurs with increased sympathetic activity is decreased digestive activity. When a bear attack is imminent, it makes sense that the body shunts all available blood supply to where it is most needed, such as the large muscles and the brain. Where energy would be wasted, in this moment of crisis, is on digestion. The acute effects of nicotine seem to impact digestion due to sympathetic activation. One study examined gastric emptying times in smokers and nonsmokers with the researchers observing that smokers had slower emptying times than nonsmokers. This is consistent with nicotine increasing sympathetic activation, which shunts blood away from nonessential organs like the stomach. Interestingly, the researchers also observed the smokers after they quit smoking. Smoking cessation actually accelerated gastric emptying (Kadota et al., 2010). The researchers argued that changes in gastric emptying partially account for the increase in appetite and weight gain seen after smoking cessation. It should be noted that other research has demonstrated that the acute effects of nicotine decrease one's appetite for food, particularly sweet foods. In addition, nicotine also increases the amount of energy the body uses both while at rest and while exercising, indicating an upregulation in metabolism (West & Russell, 1985).

It has been consistently observed in epidemiological studies that current smokers weigh less than nonsmokers. Unfortunately for individuals trying to quit smoking, smoking cessation often results in weight gain. The gain tends to be less than 6 kg (13 pounds), which is a relatively modest increase but enough to be disconcerting to many individuals. Consequently, one commonly cited reason for initiating and continuing smoking is weight restriction. The mechanisms accounting for the relationship between smoking and weight are complex. In controlled laboratory studies using rats given free access to food, nicotine results in rats reducing total food intake and meal size, perhaps as a result of the gastric emptying effects described above. Following a period of nicotine treatment, if the nicotine is then withdrawn, the rats increased their food consumption and their weight increased. It appeared that the rats given nicotine were less hungry. However, research with human subjects has revealed that smokers actually eat the same amount or more than nonsmokers. Therefore, nicotine use may alter either metabolic rate, activity levels, or both (Donny, Caggiula, Weaver, Levin, & Sved, 2011).

Lethal Dose

A significant concern with psychoactive drug use is accidental or intentional overdose leading to death. Recall that earlier in the chapter we talked about green tobacco sickness, which is nicotine poisoning following the handling of wet tobacco leaves. Given that nicotine is fairly toxic, it is helpful to quantify the level at which the drug might be lethal. Pharmacologists determine the dose of a drug at which a given percentage of individuals die within a specified duration of time. This is known as the **lethal dose (LD)**. It is common in pharmacology to use a drug's LD_{50}, which refers to the dose of drug at which 50% of animals died within a stated time. For rats, the LD_{50} for nicotine is approximately 50 mg/kg within 24 hours. It is also useful to compare the lethal dose with the **effective dose (ED)**, the dose at which a given percentage of individuals experience a particular effect. Similar to the lethal dose, the ED_{50} is the dose at which 50% of individuals receiving the dose will experience a certain effect. For rats, the ED_{50} for nicotine has been reported to be in the range of 0.2 to 0.8 mg/kg for exhibiting increased locomotor activity (Henningfield, London, & Pogun, 2009). Therefore, there appears to be a relatively large gap between the effective dose and lethal dose, indicating that nicotine is a relatively safe drug.

For adult humans, the lethal dose of nicotine is in the range of 30–60 mg in total or 0.5–1.0 mg/kg (Gosselin, Smith, & Hodge, 1984; Rose, 1991). For children, a lethal dose is approximately 10 mg in total (Arena & Drew, 1986). For reference, recall that approximately 1 mg of absorbed nicotine is ingested from smoking one cigarette. It is quite unlikely that a person would accidentally overdose on nicotine through smoking alone, particularly since continuous smoking elicits nausea and vomiting. However, overdose could potentially occur through combined use of various sources of nicotine, such as smoking, nicotine patches, and nicotine gum. Accidental death could also occur if nicotine is spilled on the skin, given that nicotine readily passes into the bloodstream through the skin. Despite these possibilities, there are very few reported instances of nicotine-associated deaths from poisoning.

Nicotine and Reinforcement

Nicotine functions as a primary reinforcer (Donny et al., 2011). A **reinforcer** is a rewarding stimulus that increases the likelihood that a behavior will be repeated. We are surrounded by reinforcers (such as food) in our environment, and anything that we like and find rewarding might be considered a reinforcer if it causes us to repeat a behavior to obtain it again. There is no doubt that human smokers find nicotine reinforcing. In one study, human smokers agreed to have a catheter inserted into their vein so they could self-administer nicotine by pressing a lever. Responding increased on the lever when nicotine was available. When saline infusions were substituted, the research subjects stopped pressing the lever (the behavior extinguished), indicating that the nicotine served as a reinforcer (Henningfield, Lucas, & Bigalow, 1986).

Given the complexity of assessing the reinforcing effects of nicotine, many studies of reinforcement rely on animals as research subjects. Interestingly, nicotine appears to be a relatively weak reinforcer in rats. With rats, there are several methodological approaches to assess the reinforcing properties of nicotine in naive animals (animals not addicted to nicotine). While there are many approaches, I will discuss three common ones, including the Conditioned Place Preference test, the self-administration model, and the conditioned taste aversion test (Laviolette & van der Kooy, 2004). In the Conditioned Place Preference (CPP) test, the researcher creates two novel environments, one associated with nicotine and the other associated with the placebo. In a typical CPP test, on the first day, the rat receives nicotine in a unique environment having a specific color, texture, and/or odor. On the next day, the animal receives the vehicle (placebo drug) and is placed in a different environment. The two environments need to be sufficiently different for the rat to distinguish them. For example, the box that is associated with nicotine might be red with a scratchy floor and the box associated with the vehicle might be blue with a soft floor. The researcher exposes the animal to several days of alternating experiences of getting the drug or vehicle and spending time in the paired environments so that learning (conditioning) occurs. This methodological approach has its origins in the classical conditioning (learning) phenomenon made famous by Nobel Prize winner Ivan Pavlov and his observations about his drooling dogs. In Pavlov's classic experiment, dogs learned to associate food with the sound of a bell. After a few exposures, the sound of the bell alone elicited drooling. In the CPP task, after several cycles of conditioning the drug-place pairings, the rat is given the choice of the two environments. The researcher records where the animal chooses to spend most of its time. In the CPP task, it is assumed that if the animal shows a preference for the previously drug-paired environment, the drug experience must have been rewarding or reinforcing. Since nicotine is rewarding, the rat typically chooses to spend more time in the red box when that box was associated with nicotine. While helpful in determining if the animal seems to like the drug, the drawback of the CPP methodology is that the drug is not self-administered, as is the case in human drug-taking behavior.

Therefore, a second methodological approach is to allow the rat to self-administer nicotine. In a typical operant conditioning experiment, a rat is placed in an operant chamber (sometimes colloquially referred to as a Skinner box named after famed psychologist B. F. Skinner). Once inside the box, the rat will explore his surroundings and eventually find a bar that he can press. When he presses the bar, nicotine will be infused into the rat via a catheter. If the drug experience is rewarding, the rat will repeat the bar-pressing response to get more nicotine. The lever press responses are called operant responses, hence the name operant conditioning. The operant conditioning approach has been used to demonstrate that animals will self-administer nicotine. Typically, studies of nicotine reinforcement use a "fixed-ratio" (FR) schedule of operant responding, as the rat must make a fixed number of bar presses to receive the infusion of nicotine. For example, a FR10 schedule would require the rat to press the bar 10 times to get one nicotine infusion. The same FR10 schedule was also used in the human intravenous self-administration study described above. Therefore, the advantage of the animal self-administration model is that it resembles human drug-taking behavior. Once an animal is trained on the task, it will consistently and compulsively self-administer nicotine, much like a smoker standing outside in the cold clutching a cigarette and shivering while bitter winds blow.

A third task used to study the reinforcing properties of nicotine in animals is the conditioned taste aversion (CTA) task, made famous by psychologist John Garcia. The CTA task takes advantage of the robust learning that humans and animals quickly associate specific tastes with aversive states. You may have had the experience of eating a food and then getting sick soon after, perhaps due to food poisoning or some unrelated cause such as the stomach flu. From that one experience, you quickly learned the association between the food and an aversive state. As a result, you may have avoided eating that food for a long time after the one-trial learning experience. This effect is so robust that even the thought of that food might later make you feel nauseated. The CTA task takes advantage of this robust associative learning by tapping into the aversive properties of a drug. In the CTA paradigm, the researcher pairs a specific drug with a particular taste (such as cocoa) and a placebo is paired with a different taste (such as cinnamon). By pairing a specific drug with a specific taste, animals learn to avoid the taste, since the unpleasant effects of the drug become associated with the taste. Therefore, after a trial where nicotine is paired with cocoa, the rat might avoid cocoa-flavored food in the future while still continuing to eat cinnamon. CTA studies using nicotine have found that it does produce aversive effects, particularly at high doses, similar to other addictive drugs. Use of the CTA task has helped researchers uncover interesting aspects of nicotine, such as genetic differences in the likelihood that CTA for nicotine will develop (Risinger & Brown, 1996). Genotype does seem to be an important factor in propensity to become addicted to nicotine in both animals and humans (USDHHS, 2010). For example, human studies of twins have revealed that identical twins are more likely to have similar smoking habits than fraternal twins, even when not reared together (Hughes, 1986).

Results of nicotine studies using the above three paradigms illustrate that nicotine, like other drugs of abuse, can have both rewarding and aversive effects in animals, just like in humans. Moreover, combined use of these various tasks such as CTA and CPP help neuroscientists uncover which brain regions are responsible for the rewarding and aversive effects of nicotine (Sellings, Baharnouri, McQuade, & Clarke, 2008). In better understanding the acute rewarding and aversive effects of nicotine, it is hoped that better methods will be available to prevent the initiation of smoking or improve treatments for nicotine addiction. One promising aspect of the reinforcement literature for nicotine is the finding that alternative reinforcers can reduce nicotine use. For example, one study asked smokers to make choices between smoking a cigarette and receiving money. By examining various reinforcement schedules, the researchers observed smokers choosing money over cigarettes, suggesting that even in addicted smokers, nicotine is not so reinforcing that alternative reinforcers couldn't be substituted (Stoops, Poole, Vansickel, & Rush, 2011).

Chronic Effects of Tobacco Use

Components of Tobacco

Tobacco smoke causes disease. Although that statement is no longer surprising, when the first U.S. Surgeon General's report was released in 1964, people were shocked to hear it. In the nearly 50 years since the release of that landmark report, thousands of studies have now clearly substantiated the devastating effects of smoking on health. The most recent Surgeon General's report described how tobacco smoke damages every organ in the body and causes disease and death, such that there is no safe level of exposure to cigarette smoke (USDHHS, 2010). When individuals inhale cigarette smoke, they are not just inhaling nicotine, for if only nicotine were inhaled, smoking would not be as big of a problem. Nicotine is clearly addictive, but it plays a limited role in the various disease processes associated with tobacco use. There are an additional 7,000 chemicals being inhaled along with nicotine as part of the combustion emissions of burned tobacco, hundreds of which are hazardous and at least 69 of which are known to cause cancer.

Besides nicotine, which is addictive, there are two main guilty parties in tobacco smoke causing a great deal of the harm to health: carbon monoxide and tar. Carbon monoxide leads to diseases because it has the advantage over oxygen in binding to hemoglobin, which normally carries oxygen from the lungs to body tissues. The heart and brain are particularly at risk given that they need oxygen for aerobic respiration (Blum, 1984). The other component of cigarette smoke that can lead to a variety of cancers is tar, which remains in cigarette smoke once it passes through the filter. After tar was shown to be so harmful, manufacturers of cigarettes decreased the amount of tar in their products. In the late 1960s, approximately 22 mg of tar was found in one cigarette, whereas the amount of tar is about half that today. However, smokers should not be so reassured that their health is protected by less tar. The most recent U.S. Surgeon General's report reviewed the evidence over the last few decades regarding cigarette product modifications to lower emissions of a variety of toxicants. This included various changes to cigarette designs such as filtered, low-tar, and light varieties. The conclusion was that in no instance did these changes reduce the risk for major adverse health outcomes (USDHHS, 2010). However, the body does have a remarkable ability to repair itself. While tobacco exposure can cause significant harm to the body, as we will see below, the body in many cases can undo this damage once the individual quits smoking. The earlier the smoking ceases, the greater the likelihood that the damage can be undone.

Diseases Linked to Smoking

Tobacco use is the leading global cause of preventable death. Nearly 6 million people worldwide die each year from tobacco use. In addition, hundreds of billions of dollars of economic damage occur each year from tobacco use. The deaths are occurring primarily in low- and middle-income countries, a disparity that is continuing to widen further. Smoking is more prevalent in developing countries, which also typically do not employ tobacco control efforts (WHO, 2011b). When a person inhales the complex mixture of compounds found in tobacco smoke, a variety of adverse health outcomes, particularly cancer, cardiovascular, and pulmonary diseases can occur. The mechanisms causing these diseases include DNA damage, inflammation, and oxidative stress (USDHHS, 2010). The risk and severity of many diseases are directly related to the duration and level of exposure to tobacco smoke, so the sooner a person stops smoking, the better.

Cancer is caused by tar from tobacco exposure when the components of cigarette smoke individually and in combination as a carcinogenic mixture bring about the genetic and epigenetic processes resulting in cancer. The genetic and epigenetic changes lead to cancer through changes in cellular pathways fostering uncontrolled cell growth and stopping the normal mechanisms that restrain cell growth and spread. Tobacco-related cancers can occur in various places in the body, with 80% to 90% of all lung cancers attributable to cigarette smoking. Further, there is evidence for an inherited susceptibility of lung cancer, indicating that some smokers are more likely to get lung cancer. In addition, approximately 30% of cancers of the larynx, oral cavity, esophagus, bladder, pancreas, and kidneys are associated with cigarette smoking (Denissenko, Pao, Tang, & Pfeiffer, 1996; USDHHS, 2010). Unfortunately, lung cancer rates associated with smoking have increased over time, even though cigarette manufacturers have dramatically decreased the amount of tar in their cigarettes. In 1955, a cigarette contained approximately 38 mg of tar; today the value is closer to 13.5 mg. It appears that some responsibility for increasing cancer rates can be placed on the increased yield of N-nitrosamines, chemicals that are inhaled when smoking low-tar cigarettes (Wynder & Muscat, 1995). There seems to be no escaping the cancer risk. If it isn't the tar that causes the cancer, there is another chemical in tobacco smoke that will.

Cigarette smoking is also a major cause of coronary heart disease, stroke, aortic aneurysm, and peripheral arterial disease. The risk for these diseases does not increase in a linear fashion with increased exposure to smoking. Instead, even low levels of exposure to tobacco, such as a few cigarettes per day, occasional smoking, or exposure to secondhand smoke, is enough to substantially increase the risk for cardiac events. For example, one large prospective study in Norway examined the health consequences of smoking 1 to 4 cigarettes per day. The research observed that even a limited amount of light smoking was associated with a significantly higher risk of dying from ischemic heart disease (Bjartveit & Tverdal, 2005).

What causes the cardiovascular disease? It appears that carbon monoxide, nicotine, oxidizing chemicals, and particulate matter are involved. When cigarette smoke is inhaled, chronic inflammation results, which contributes to the diseases. This elevated inflammation is a powerful predictor of cardiovascular events. It should be mentioned that, while it is a part of this inflammation process, nicotine is not the biggest problem. In fact, when an individual stops smoking and relies on nicotine (in the form of patches or gums) to help with the quitting process, there is a marked improvement in the risk of myocardial infarction, sudden death, and stroke. It appears the nicotine itself poses little risk (USDHHS, 2010).

With smoking, damage and structural changes to the lung's airways and alveoli occur which can lead to chronic obstructive pulmonary disease (COPD). Smoking causes 80% to 90% of

COPD cases. Emphysema, which makes breathing difficult, is a highly prevalent component of COPD. Emphysema is a disease of the lung identified by abnormal dilution of the air spaces and distension of the lung walls. Two causative mechanisms that lead to COPD by cigarette smoking include oxidative stress (injury) and protease–antiprotease imbalance. The lungs have defense mechanisms to help with injuries from inhaled agents. These defenses can be overwhelmed by the repeated inhalation of cigarette smoke, which contains massive quantities of free radicals in its gas and tar phases. The protease–antiprotease imbalance increases destructive enzyme activity that damages the lung's structure. When the structure is damaged, the lung's elasticity decreases, leading to emphysema (USDHHS, 2010).

While the above diseases associated with smoking can lead to death, it is also important to note that exposure to tobacco smoke, either directly or via secondhand smoke, is harmful to reproduction. The harm can impact everything from fertility (the ability to get pregnant) to fetal and child development. For women, exposure to the mixture of chemicals in tobacco smoke can reduce fertility, result in earlier menopause, or lead to altered menstrual cycles via changes in hormonal functions. For men, smoking can cause chromosome changes or DNA damage to sperm. If this occurs, male fertility can be decreased, pregnancy viability may decline, and/or there may be anomalies in the child. If a couple gets pregnant, carbon monoxide is the toxicant in cigarette smoke found in the highest concentrations impacting fetal development. The major effect of carbon monoxide is to deprive the growing fetus of oxygen when the carbon monoxide binds to hemoglobin. When a baby is born to a mother who was a smoker, the baby is often small and may have neurological deficits. Besides low birth weight, fetal loss (miscarriage) and preterm delivery are also concerns (USDHHS, 2010). For adolescents who begin smoking, the future likelihood of children is typically not at the front of their consciousness. However, once addicted to nicotine, it is very difficult to stop using the drug, and during use, many of these reproduction-impacting changes can be taking place. Thus, the concerns about smoking and reproduction often occur after individuals have been addicted to nicotine for a substantial period of time and have exposed themselves to years of tobacco use.

Secondhand Smoke

In the not too distant past, people smoked in airplanes and at work. However, that changed once it became apparent that exposure to secondhand smoke (also called passive smoking) can be just as harmful as direct smoking. The most recent U.S. Surgeon General's report indicates that the scientific evidence is sufficient to conclude that there is no risk-free level of exposure to secondhand smoke. For cardiovascular disease, the immediate effects of even short exposures to secondhand smoke on cardiovascular functions appear to be as large as those seen with active smoking of one pack of cigarettes per day (USDHHS, 2010). Much of the significant risk of secondhand smoke exposure is that it can result in death in ways similar to active smoking. One longitudinal study following 32,000 healthy nonsmoking female nurses for a decade indicated that regular exposure to cigarette smoke almost doubled the nurses' chances of dying from heart disease (Kawachi et al., 1997).

Given the health consequences of secondhand smoke, legislation prohibiting smoking in public places and in cars with children is becoming increasingly common (Figure 5-8). The scientific evidence supports these changes. For example, one study sampled fine particulate matter (which could lead to diseases like cancer) in the air of the rear passenger area of cars during typical drives by smoking and nonsmoking study participants. Not surprisingly, during active smoking, the amount of particulate matter was very high in the rear passenger area, at levels that would lead to disease. However, when the same car was driven but no smoking occurred, particulate matter levels still exceeded World Health Organization guidelines for indoor air quality, even if windows had been opened during smoking drives. Therefore, children in cars where people smoke are exposed to levels of fine particulate, and such children are likely to suffer ill-health effects (Semple et al., 2012).

©JohnKwan/Shutterstock

Figure 5-8
Given the health con-
sequences of second-
hand smoke,
legislation prohibiting
smoking in public
places is becoming
increasingly common.

More about the Science:

Vansickel, A. R., Weaver, M. F., & Eissenberg, T. (2012). Clinical laboratory assessment
          of the abuse liability of an electronic cigarette. *Addiction*, *107*, 1493–1500.

Tobacco use causes various diseases. However, the nicotine in cigarettes is very addictive,
which makes it extremely difficult to quit smoking. A new product marketed to smokers to
help with their nicotine addiction is the electronic cigarette (EC). The EC looks like a
cigarette and, using a battery, produces a vapor that releases nicotine that can be inhaled.
The EC is supposed to help smokers quit or reduce smoking, improve health, or use in
locations where smoking is prohibited. In this study, the researchers wished to determine if
the EC could deliver sufficient amounts of nicotine and whether the EC was as reinforcing
as a regular cigarette. Using regular smokers, the researchers compared smoking on a
regular cigarette to smoking an EC, by assessing plasma nicotine and subjective state.
It was observed that the EC use resulted in reliable nicotine delivery after 40 puffs, a rate
that was slightly slower than a real cigarette. However, the puffs on the EC suppressed
tobacco withdrawal symptoms and increased product ratings, indicating that the
subjects thought that the EC was similar to a real cigarette. Additionally, the researchers
assessed the rewarding aspects of the EC by asking subjects to rate whether or not they
preferred to receive a puff on a regular cigarette, a puff on an EC, or an escalating amount
of money. The EC was observed to be less reinforcing than a real cigarette, since the
participants would rather have money at a lower dollar value than puffs when the EC was
the option. The findings from the multiple-choice task corresponded with the slower rate
of nicotine delivery from the EC compared to a real cigarette. Overall, the participants
found the EC to be moderately acceptable and a reasonable alternative to cigarette
smoking.

More about the Science Thought Questions:

1. This research study examined the potential usefulness of an electronic cigarette (EC) for
    smokers. What would be some of the health advantages of using an EC over a real cigarette?
2. Would use of the EC help cure the smokers' addiction to nicotine?

3. Smokers often complain that limiting their smoking impairs their ability to think (it decreases cognitive abilities), which impacts the success of smoking cessation efforts. Would use of the EC help maintain cognitive performance?

More about the Science Thought Question Answers:

1. Most of disease-causing chemicals (such as the tar and carbon monoxide) found in real cigarettes would not be inhaled with the use of an electronic cigarette. Therefore, the risks of cardiovascular disease and cancer should be minimized given that nicotine, while addictive, has less impact on subsequent poor health.
2. The EC delivers nicotine. Therefore, it is unlikely that the addiction to nicotine would go away for the smoker since the individual will still be inhaling nicotine from the EC. However, the slower delivery of nicotine from the EC may help the individual reduce the typical dose needed, which may alleviate withdrawal symptoms over time.
3. Yes, the EC delivers nicotine, and it is the nicotine in cigarettes that causes improved cognitive performance in smokers.

Tolerance, Dependence, and Withdrawal

Tolerance

Tolerance refers to an increased amount of drug needed to achieve a certain effect or a diminished drug effect with continued use. The *DSM-IV-TR* criteria for drug dependence include the term *drug tolerance*. Tolerance is thought to contribute to substance abuse when a user needs more and more of a drug to achieve the same effect. Therefore, drugs that are likely to lead to dependence problems are often drugs that induce rapid tolerance development. By contrast, drugs that do not lead to rapid tolerance development are thought to be somewhat safer (APA, 2000). For nicotine, tolerance develops quickly. Recall that at the start of the chapter, we talked about green tobacco sickness. When farm workers handle wet tobacco leaves, they can get very sick from nicotine poisoning. The symptoms of tobacco poisoning (nausea, heart palpitations, dizziness, sweating, or vomiting) can also occur when a person first attempts smoking as a recreational habit. However, signs of acute nicotine poisoning are autonomic changes that quickly go away after a person has tried smoking those first few cigarettes. If this tolerance development (diminished symptoms of nicotine poisoning) did not occur so quickly, we would not see such high rates of smoking. Tolerance to the unpleasant initial aspects of nicotine and the transition to experience the pleasurable effects of smoking a pack a day or more can be as rapid as several weeks. Tolerance development can even be observed in seasoned smokers. The effects of nicotine for the initial puffs of the first cigarette of the day are greater than the last few puffs on the same cigarette (Jones, 1987). Moreover, smokers become more efficient at metabolizing nicotine over time, which leads to increased need for the drug (Edwards, 1986).

Physical Dependence and Withdrawal

Nicotine use leads to physical dependence. To determine if the body is physically dependent on a drug, the user needs to stop using the drug, let blood levels drop, and wait until the drug is eliminated from the body. If there is no change in physical well-being, the person is likely not physically dependent. However, if a set of illness-like physical symptoms result from no drug being present, the person is likely physically dependent. Certainty about this assessment of physical dependence can be assured by administering the drug once again. If the reinitiating of drug use results in the physical symptoms of withdrawal going away, the individual is probably physically dependent on that drug. For smokers, stopping smoking results in a variety of symptoms, including craving for tobacco, irritability, anxiety, difficulty concentrating, restlessness, increased appetite, impatience, pain and other somatic complaints, and insomnia. These symptoms will go away once the person starts smoking again, or when nicotine is administered in the form of a patch, gum, or nasal spray. Researchers have suggested that as the physical addiction to nicotine becomes more apparent, the nature of the physical symptoms that occur when abstinent changes in quality from wanting to smoke to craving to smoke to needing to smoke. If abstinence from nicotine only leads to wanting to smoke, the physical dependence is mild compared to the person who needs to smoke (Difranza, Ursprung, & Biller, 2012a; Difranza, Wellman, & Savageau, 2012b).

Typically, smoking initiation begins in adolescence. Research has demonstrated that adolescent smokers exhibit symptoms of dependence even at low levels of cigarette use. Similarly, animal studies have shown that sensitivity to nicotine is increased in adolescents compared with adults. There are various patterns of progression from casual experimentation to heavy smoking and it appears that there are psychosocial, biological, and genetic determinants associated with differing trajectories regarding physical dependence on nicotine. There appears to be an inherited genetic variation in the CYP2A6 genotype that contributes to differing patterns of smoking behaviors and quitting smoking (USDHHS, 2010). Individuals who have the CYP2A6 genotype, which metabolizes nicotine more slowly, tend to exhibit less physical dependence on nicotine (Malaiyandi et al., 2006).

Myth Busters: Quitting Smoking Will Make Me Gain Weight

One fear that keeps many people from quitting smoking is a concern about gaining weight. Such fears of weight gain are not unfounded. On average, former smokers gain about 6 kg (13 pounds) following smoking cessation. Earlier in this chapter, we mentioned that there are a few reasons why stopping the use of nicotine might lead to weight gain. First, smoking cessation results in accelerated gastric emptying (Kadota et al., 2010), which means that the former smoker will feel hungry sooner. Nicotine also decreases one's appetite for food, particularly sweet foods. Once nicotine is no longer present, the motivation to consume more sweet food increases. In addition, nicotine increases the amount of energy the body uses both while at rest and while exercising, indicating that there is upregulation in metabolism (Donny et al., 2011; West & Russell, 1985). Again, with the removal of nicotine, the metabolism rate will slow. Other contributions to weight gain for former smokers include mistaking nicotine craving for food craving or using food as a coping mechanism for dealing with nicotine cravings. All of this sounds like really bad news. However, does this mean that the weight gain is inevitable when quitting smoking? The answer is no.

Researchers have been developing smoking cessation interventions with the goal in mind of limiting weight gain. When participants in smoking treatment programs are prescribed exercise along with use of nicotine replacement therapy (such as a nicotine patch), those individuals gain significantly less weight than others who don't rely on the exercise (Prapavessis et al., 2007). Another large study tracked women for 2 years, some of whom stopped smoking ($n = 1474$) and some of whom continued smoking ($n = 7832$). The researchers found that the average weight gain for the continuing smokers was 1 pound, whereas the average weight gain for the women who stopped smoking was 7 pounds. However, for the women who quit smoking *and increased their activity levels*, the weight gain was only 3 pounds (Kawach, Troisi, Rotnitzky, Coakley, & Colditz, 1996). The women who counteracted potential weight gain by increasing their exercise levels as part of their smoking cessation program were most successful in keeping weight gain minimal (a difference of only 2 pounds more than the control group who never quit smoking). A review of the literature similarly found that long-term weight gain following smoking cessation can be minimized with increased exercise or calorie restriction. Weight gain can also be minimized in the short term with the use of various smoking cessation medications, which decrease the cravings for nicotine that might lead to overeating (Parsons, Shraim, Inglis, Aveyard, & Hajek, 2009). Therefore, the take-home message is clear. Weight gain following smoking cessation is not inevitable, particularly if increased exercise is part of the treatment plan!

Pharmacology of Nicotine

Sites of Action

In the brain, nicotine stimulates the same receptors that are sensitive to the naturally occurring neurotransmitter **acetylcholine** (Figure 5-9). In the brain, acetylcholine appears to play an important role in memory and other cognitive functions. Acetylcholine was one of the first neurotransmitters to be identified. This discovery occurred because one can observe the action of acetylcholine in neurons that are located outside of the brain, since acetylcholine also activates skeletal muscles. Where a nerve meets a muscle, a small gap exists called the neuromuscular junction. When a neuron releases acetylcholine into that gap, the muscle contracts. Acetylcholine is found in neuromuscular junctions, as well as in the central nervous system (CNS).

Nicotine is called a cholinergic agonist drug, since neurons that contain acetylcholine are referred to as cholinergic neurons, and an agonist drug acts like the naturally occurring neurotransmitter would. Nicotine acts on specific acetylcholine receptors called nicotinic cholinergic receptors. Other cholinergic receptor sites are known as muscarinic receptors, but those sites do not appear to be impacted by nicotine administration. Activation of nicotinic receptors by nicotine facilitates the release of acetylcholine. In the periphery, nicotine will activate the receptors that cause increases in blood pressure and heart rate, release epinephrine (adrenalin) from the adrenal glands, and increase the activity of the gastrointestinal tract. In the brain, activation of nicotinic receptors by nicotine will improve various cognitive functions such as memory. Nicotine is a biphasic drug, so while nicotine will stimulate acetylcholine receptors at moderate doses, it will also block cholinergic transmission at very high doses (Julien, 2005).

In addition to increasing acetylcholine activity in the brain, nicotine also acts to raise dopamine levels in the **mesolimbic dopaminergic pathway**. This pathway in the brain can be thought of as the addiction pathway (see Figure 5-10). If you electrically stimulate this pathway in the brain, the subjective reaction is very rewarding. Rats that learn to press a lever to electrically stimulate their brains in the mesolimbic dopaminergic pathway appear to find the experience so reinforcing that they will press a lever more than 1,000 times per hour to receive the stimulation! No wonder this

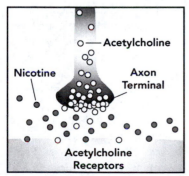

Figure 5-9
Nicotine acts as a cholinergic agonist drug.

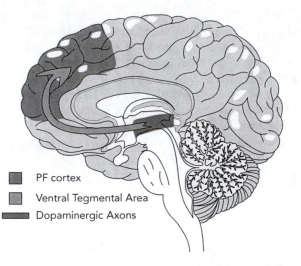

Figure 5-10
The mesolimbic dopaminergic pathway (i.e., the addiction pathway) in the brain.

■ PF cortex
■ Ventral Tegmental Area
▬ Dopaminergic Axons

part of the brain is named the pleasure center (Olds & Milner, 1954). This pathway runs from a small subcortical area called the nucleus accumbens and through the ventral tegmental area to the frontal cortex. The nucleus accumbens is a dopamine-rich structure that releases dopamine in response to nicotine. The release of dopamine explains the reinforcing/rewarding effects of nicotine. However, nicotine-induced release of dopamine from the nucleus accumbens or else-where along this pathway is not an effect unique to nicotine. Most drugs of abuse have the same effect, including cocaine and heroin (Goldstein, 2001).

Pharmacokinetics

Pharmacokinetics is a branch of pharmacology that examines the absorption, distribution, biotransformation, and excretion of drugs. We have already mentioned that nicotine is easily absorbed through most of the body's membranes, including the skin. However, nicotine is most readily absorbed from the lungs, which accounts for the popularity of cigarette smoking as a means to efficiently ingest nicotine (Blum, 1984). Once nicotine is absorbed into the bloodstream, it is distributed to various locations where it can act in the body, including the brain. Nicotine crosses the **blood–brain barrier,** the system that filters the blood before it can enter the brain, without difficulty. Smoking cigarettes results in an especially rapid rise of nicotine in the brain. One recent study examined the speed of nicotine's arrival to the brain by using an imaging technology called positron emission tomography (PET). PET scans of lung and brain regions were obtained from human subjects after single puffs from special cigarettes that contained radioactive nicotine. The radioactive nicotine was not harmful, but it allowed the movement of the nicotine in the body to be observed using the PET imaging technique. The researchers reported that the rise in nicotine concentration following a single puff was so rapid that it reached more than 50% of maximum brain levels within 15 seconds. This finding suggests that the nicotine was reaching the brain faster than what would be observed if the nicotine were directly injected into a vein (Berridge et al., 2010). Other studies have estimated that high doses of nicotine may reach the brain even faster with smoking, with time estimates of 5–10 seconds (Dar & Frenk, 2007). Given that the rate at which a drug reaches the brain influences the likelihood of addiction, it is no surprise that individuals find that use of nicotine by smoking is highly addictive.

Most drugs are also characterized by their half-life, which is relevant to the last aspect of pharmacokinetics, the excretion of the drug. The **half-life** is the amount of time that is required for the dose of drug in the body to be reduced by half. For nicotine, the half-life is 2 hours. For a smoker, nicotine is metabolized faster than nonsmokers. Over the course of a day, nicotine will accumulate in the body of a smoker. However, elimination of nicotine is sufficiently rapid that there is no day-to-day accumulation (Issac & Rand, 1972). As much as 40% of administered nicotine is eliminated in urine, with the rest of excretion relying on the enzymes of the liver (Julien, 2005).

Medical Uses of Nicotine

Given the widespread morbidity and mortality attributable to tobacco use, it may seem surprising that researchers are still trying to determine if nicotine has medical benefits. Recall that in the history section of this chapter, it was thought long ago that tobacco might have medical uses but that idea lost favor once it became apparent that tobacco use can lead to various chronic diseases or even death. As we have seen, tobacco use is separate from examining nicotine as a potential therapeutic drug. While nicotine is addictive, it does not directly compromise health like the rest of the chemicals found in cigarettes. Given that nicotine elevates acetylcholine activity in the brain, various diseases that have deficient acetylcholine levels may benefit from nicotine. Acetylcholine is important in the brain for various cognitive functions, including sensory processing, attention, and memory. Nicotine, an agonist of acetylcholine, can improve cognitive functions and may be therapeutically useful in conditions where impaired cognitive processing is a concern. Until recently, the progress made in understanding the usefulness of nicotine or similar chemicals that act on nicotinic acetylcholine receptors was hindered by the possibility of nicotine overdose (nicotine poisoning). However, given improvements in various methodological aspects of neuroscience drug research, scientists are pursuing acetylcholine agonists that could be used as possible medical treatments, while also limiting potential toxicity effects (Toledano, Alvarez, & Toledano-Diaz, 2010; Wallace & Porter, 2011).

The progressive loss of memory function that occurs in Alzheimer's disease is thought to be related to the loss of neural function in cholinergic pathways in the brain. Various drugs have been developed to prevent the decline in cognitive function with Alzheimer's disease. Drugs such as Aricept® (donepezil) and Exelon® (rivastigmine) alleviate some of the memory problems, at least initially in the disease process, by elevating levels of acetylcholine in the brain (see Chapter 14). Given the benefits of elevating acetylcholine in treating memory problems, nicotine has also been examined as a potential treatment for Alzheimer's disease. In aging lab rats and monkeys, nicotine has been shown to improve various aspects of cognition. In humans, patients with dementia like Alzheimer's disease also appear to benefit from nicotine treatment (Levin, 1992). The benefits of nicotine for the cognitive impairments associated with Parkinson's disease (PD) have also been examined. In a study that used transdermal nicotine patches in elderly patients, both with and without PD, it was determined that nicotine improved the compromised semantic processing in the PD patients, while also benefitting the semantic processing of the healthy older control patients as well (Holmes, Copland, Silburn, & Chenery, 2011).

Smoking has also been associated with a range of mental disorders, including schizophrenia, anxiety disorders, and depression. For example, individuals who meet the criteria of a mental disorder in the past 12 months smoke at twice the rate of adults without a mental disorder (Lawrence, Mitrou, & Zubrick, 2009). For schizophrenia, the data on smoking rates is shocking. Approximately 80% of patients with schizophrenia are smokers. There are two ways to look at those statistics. One can examine those statistics and think about how smoking is placing a significant health and financial burden on a set of individuals whose health is already compromised by other issues. However, another possibility is that these patients are trying to self-medicate with nicotine. Clinicians began to investigate the second possibility when they observed that patients with schizophrenia reported improvements in psychiatric symptoms following smoking, most notably the symptoms related to cognitive deficits. In schizophrenia, the delusions and hallucinations characteristic of this disorder appear not to be impacted by smoking. However, impairments in attention span and memory do improve (Winterer, 2010). As such, various studies have examined the attention improvements caused by nicotine, with the thought that nicotine

Figure 5-11
Researcher trying to
determine if nicotine
has potential medical
uses.

could be used as a new treatment for disorders where attentional impairment is a symptom, such as schizophrenia, attention deficit hyperactivity disorder, and Alzheimer's disease (Levin, Bushnell, & Rezvani, 2011). At this point, the research is still at a developmental stage, but time will tell if nicotine might be useful for a variety of health conditions (Figure 5-11). To date, there is very good evidence for the use of nicotine in the treatment of at least one medical condition, ulcerative colitis (Westman, Levin, & Rose, 1995).

Treatments to Quit Smoking

To say that quitting smoking is a difficult process would be a vast understatement. Many smokers are aware that their cigarette smoking might lead to lung cancer, cardiovascular disease, or reproductive problems. They know that if they could stop smoking, their health risks would be reduced and their quality of life improved. However, nicotine is extremely addictive, which makes the process of stopping its use so difficult. It is estimated that 17 million smokers in the United States try to quit each year and only 1 out of 10 succeed. It appears that the brain reacts to smoking-related cues even after a period of abstinence, and the smoker's brain still pays attention to these smoking cues more than other types of stimuli. The results of one study illustrate why quitting and then staying abstinent is so hard. In this study, the researchers used functional magnetic resonance imaging (fMRI) to image the brain while smoking-related or neutral pictures were shown to tobacco-dependent subjects. The researcher did this imaging before a smoking cessation attempt and again during an extended smoking abstinence of around 2 months. All of the smokers relied on nicotine replacement therapy during this abstinence period. The researchers observed that the fMRI reaction to smoking versus neutral stimuli persisted in a variety of brain areas during the abstinence. Moreover, the fMRI smoking cue reactivity was increased during the abstinence period as compared to the before measure (Janes et al., 2009). No wonder smokers are so vulnerable to relapse! They can't help but fixate on all of those smoking cues, even when they are successfully in a state of abstinence from smoking. Nevertheless, giving up smoking can be done and many people do it without help. Up to 95% of former tobacco smokers have quit without the benefit of treatment. There are many approaches, including the use of medications that can make smoking cessation successful.

There are a variety of nicotine replacement products used for nicotine replacement therapy (NRT). NRT is available in many forms, including transdermal patches, gums, nasal sprays, inhalers, sublingual tablets, and lozenges. Use of these products replaces the nicotine that previously came from a cigarette and will relieve the withdrawal symptoms, leading to a higher abstinence rate compared to placebo. Most NRT forms deliver nicotine more slowly than smoking with the increase in nicotine levels in the blood more gradual. Therefore, compared to tobacco smoking or even tobacco chewing, there are few reinforcing effects obtained from NRT use (Le Houezec, 2003). While NRT does not always lead to smoking cessation, it is common that individuals who use NRT can reduce the number of cigarettes smoked daily, achieving at least partial success and thus decreasing the health risks associated with smoking. Overall, NRT does seem to work in many cases. Compared to control subjects, individuals receiving any form of NRT are 1.7 times more likely to be abstinent from smoking after 6 months. If the NRT options are rank-ordered in effectiveness, the nasal spray and inhalers are considered most effective, following by the patch and then the gum (Silagy, Mant, Fowler, & Lodge, 1994).

In addition to NRT, there are two FDA-approved pharmacological treatments used to treat smoking. Buproprion, marketed as Zyban®, is an antidepressant that has been shown to help with smoking cessation. While an antidepressant, the effectiveness of bupriopion is not related to a history of depression. Instead, it seems to help with craving states associated with smoking cessation. Since it is not a replacement for nicotine, an individual could use bupriopion with NRT. In addition, varenicline, marketed as Chantix®, is a drug that is a partial nicotinic agonist. Therefore, this drug treats smoking by competing with nicotine in binding to the nicotinic acetylcholine receptors of the brain. The medication will decrease smoking cravings because those receptors are already occupied, and thus smoking feels less reinforcing (USDHHS, 2010).

It should be noted that there are several other drugs in development but not yet FDA-approved to treat smoking. In addition to potential new medications, nicotine vaccines are among the products seeking approval from the FDA. An antidrug vaccine is different than a medication. A vaccine is very long acting and provides protection over years. The vaccine prevents nicotine from entering the brain. Interacting with the nicotine in the blood, rather than with a nicotinic acetylcholine receptor in the brain, the vaccines are free from side effects. There are three anti-nicotine vaccines in advanced stages of clinical trials that might appear on the market soon (Escobar-Chavez, Dominguez-Degado, & Rodrigeuz-Cruz, 2011).

Finally, it should be recalled that smoking is a behavioral habit. Reliance on smoking to deal with stress or other negative emotions means that psychological approaches can be helpful for people trying to quit. Overall, treatment programs vary, ranging from self-help materials to individual cognitive-behavioral therapy. The treatments that help people tend to be most effective if they incorporate controlling nicotine withdrawal symptoms, breaking the motor behaviors that are habits involved with smoking, and learning skills to cope with the emotions, thoughts, and situations that compel smoking behavior. For example, if an individual used to deal with stress by taking a smoke break, an alternative strategy needs to be put in place when stressful experiences occur, or relapse is likely. Having an incentive to abstain, such as poor health, often works, too (Jones, 1987). Given the health care costs associated with smoking, many workplaces and health insurance companies offer smoking-cessation products and treatments for free. In 2004, the U.S. Department of Health and Human Services established a national toll-free number, 800-QUIT-NOW (800-784-8669) that serves as a single access point for smokers seeking assistance in quitting. If you are a smoker and are thinking about quitting, give them a call and see if they have suggestions to help you achieve your goal.

Preventing Smoking Initiation

Smoking results in a rapid addiction to nicotine. Smoking is associated with a variety of health problems, and quitting is very difficult. It is therefore appropriate to end this chapter with information about preventing smoking initiation. How can we dissuade individuals, specifically teenagers, from starting the habit? Prevention efforts have often focused on adolescents, as 90% of smokers start smoking by age 18. Fortunately, there have been many successes among prevention programs. In the last few years, limiting the advertising of cigarettes and incorporating warning messages on cigarette packaging have shown some successes. In some countries, warning labels have become extremely graphic, such as pictures of diseased lungs covering half the cigarette package in Canada. In addition, increasing the taxes on cigarettes and increased presence of smoke-free policies also seem to be effective approaches to preventing smoking (Freedman, Nelson, & Feldman, 2012; Szklo et al., 2012). While tobacco control policies will remain controversial in the near future, the majority of people are certainly interested in preventing young people from starting a drug habit that is so difficult to break.

QUICK QUIZ 5-2

1. What acute effect(s) does nicotine appear to improve?
   a. Motor coordination
   b. Alertness
   c. Cognitive performance
   d. None of the above
   e. All of the above

2. How does the acute effect of nicotine impact autonomic nervous system activity?
   a. It increases sympathetic arousal.
   b. It decreases sympathetic arousal.
   c. It increases parasympathetic arousal.
   d. It decreases parasympathetic arousal.

3. How much weight do smokers typically gain once they quit smoking?
   a. 4 pounds
   b. 13 pounds
   c. 25 pounds
   d. 37 pounds

4. A researcher wishes to examine the reinforcing effects of nicotine. Which of the following methods would be most similar to human smoking?
   a. Conditioned place preference
   b. Self-administration procedure
   c. Conditioned taste aversion procedure
   d. Reinforcer examination procedure

5. Smoking cigarettes can lead to cancer. What component of tobacco smoke is the biggest culprit?
   a. Nicotine
   b. Tar
   c. Carbon monoxide
   d. Carbon dioxide

6. Nicotine is a/an_____ drug.
   a. acetylcholine agonist
   b. acetylcholine antagonist
   c. serotonin agonist
   d. serotonin antagonist

7. Which of the following diseases/disorders might benefit from nicotine treatment?
   a. Alzheimer's disease
   b. Schizophrenia
   c. High blood pressure
   d. A and B
   e. All of the above

8. Bob has been smoking for 30 years. He needs to quit smoking, but he has tried many times before on his own without success. His doctor suggests a medication that might help him. The doctor explains that the drug competes with the nicotine receptors in the brain, making smoking less enjoyable. Which smoking cessation treatment is the doctor referring to?
   a. NRT
   b. Buproprion
   c. Zyban
   d. Vernicline
   e. None of the above

9. Nicotine has different effects at lower doses than it does at higher doses. Explain this.

10. Why would assessing the acute effects of nicotine be a difficult task?

ANSWERS TO QUICK QUIZ 5-2:

1. e – all of the above
2. a – it increases sympathetic arousal
3. b – 13 pounds
4. b – self-administration procedure
5. b – tar
6. a – acetylcholine agonist
7. d – answers a (Alzheimer's disease) and b (schizophrenia)
8. d – vernicline
9. Nicotine is considered to be a biphasic drug because at lower doses, CNS stimulation is typically observed. However, at higher doses, the effect reverses and CNS sedation is the result.
10. When examining the acute effects of a drug, it is ideal to examine the effects in an individual who is naive to the drug. However, nicotine is very addictive and researchers have the ethical dilemma of whether exposing a nonsmoking subject to nicotine might lead to addiction. Studies that have been conducted show that smokers and nonsmokers differ in their response to nicotine.

CHAPTER SUMMARY

Nicotine is the third most widely used psychoactive drug, after caffeine and alcohol. It is found in the tobacco plant and is administered in the form of products like cigarettes, cigars, snuff, chewing tobacco, and pipe tobacco. Nicotine is a stimulant drug, but at high doses, it has sedative properties. Nicotine can improve behavioral and cognitive functioning. These changes occur because nicotine acts as a cholinergic agonist in the brain. Given that acetylcholine is involved in a variety of cognitive processes, when nicotine increases acetylcholine levels in the brain, cognitive function improves. However, nicotine is highly addictive and tolerance develops rapidly. Moreover, there are severe health complications associated with smoking. Components of cigarette smoke, such as tar and carbon monoxide, can lead to lung cancer, cardiovascular disease, and reproductive difficulties. Given the addictive properties of nicotine, withdrawal symptoms when a person stops smoking can be aversive, a fact that makes smoking cessation difficult. Fortunately, there are a variety of nicotine replacement products and medications that can be useful in efforts to quit smoking, and other treatment options are on the horizon. Even so, most individuals who successfully quit smoking do so without help. Finally, prevention efforts such as warning labels, higher taxes on cigarettes, and smoke-free policies have been effective in reducing smoking rates over the last few decades.

6 COCAINE

Introduction

The death of 48-year-old singer Whitney Houston shocked many fans. A beautiful, talented, and hard-working pop icon, her death at a Beverly Hills hotel in California, the day before the annual Grammy Awards, required an explanation. The Los Angeles County Coroner concluded that Houston's chronic cocaine use combined with coronary heart disease led to her drowning death (Dolak & Murphy, 2012). Years earlier, Houston had been candid about her drug abuse problems. In a 2002 interview with Diane Sawyer on ABC news, Houston said, "It has been [alcohol, marijuana, pills, cocaine] at times. Nobody makes me do anything I don't want to do. It's my decision; the biggest devil is me. I'm my best friend and my worst enemy." While her use of many drugs may have contributed to her declining health, cocaine abuse may have been particularly harmful to her heart, leading to her early death. Cocaine use can interfere with the electrical system of the heart, and it can also increase the demand for oxygen by increasing the heart rate and blood pressure. A lifetime struggle with addiction to cocaine and other drugs was not a problem that Houston appeared able to resolve. Houston consumed cocaine shortly before she was found drowned in a bathtub at the hotel (Duke, 2012). Wealth, talent, beauty, and work ethic were not enough to overcome an addiction to cocaine. Her accomplishments in life were tremendous, including six Grammys and 170 million albums sold. Despite these achievements, success in solving her drug addiction problem eluded her, leading to her untimely death (Figure 6-1).

In this chapter, we will closely examine cocaine, a psychoactive stimulant drug derived from the coca plant. We will answer questions associated with cocaine use. What is the appeal of cocaine or crack to the user? Why is cocaine addictive? What happens to the health of a chronic user? How does cocaine alter brain activity? What are the most effective treatments for cocaine addiction? Let us explore these and many other questions about cocaine.

FIGURE 6-1
The use of cocaine and other psychoactive drugs contributed to the early death of singer, songwriter, and actress, Whitney Houston. Despite her tremendous accomplishments in life, including six Grammys and 170 million albums sold, she was not able to conquer her problems with drugs.

©Randee St. Nicholas/Getty Images

LEARNING OBJECTIVES

Learning objectives can help organize your studying. Before we begin the topic of cocaine, keep in mind that by the end of this chapter, you should be able to . . .

1. Explain where cocaine comes from.
2. Describe the history of cocaine from ancient times through today.
3. Describe the prevalence of cocaine use, both in the United States and around the world.
4. Describe the typical routes of administration for cocaine.
5. Explain how cocaine is treated in current U.S. drug laws.
6. Explain how cocaine acts as a stimulant in the central nervous system and how the acute effects of cocaine differ from its chronic effects.
7. Describe tolerance, sensitization, dependence, and withdrawal processes associated with cocaine use.
8. Describe how cocaine acts in the brain and for how long cocaine acts in the brain.
9. Describe the various treatment approaches to help cocaine abusers.

Cocaine as a Stimulant Drug

Cocaine ($C_{17}H_{21}NO_4$) is a powerful central nervous system **stimulant** drug. A stimulant drug increases alertness, decreases fatigue, decreases appetite, and heightens mood. Cocaine is an **alkaloid** (a nitrogen-containing organic metabolite) derived from a plant. Other stimulant alkaloid drugs include caffeine and nicotine. Note that there are dramatic differences between the mild stimulant alkaloid drug caffeine and the powerful stimulant alkaloid drug cocaine. These differences explain why cocaine is far more powerful and addictive than other stimulants, which causes cocaine to be a major illicit drug of abuse. Whether smoked, snorted, or injected, cocaine leads to strong feelings of euphoria among users. The powdered version of cocaine (**cocaine hydrochloride**), pure white in color, is snorted or dissolved in water and then injected (see Figure 6-2). **Crack** is the street name for cocaine that has been chemically processed to make a rock crystal. When heated, the crystal produces vapors that are smoked by the user. The name *crack* refers to the crackling sound that the crystal produces as it is heated. In many cases, use of cocaine in its various forms can become compulsive due to the drug's powerful effects. Repeated use of cocaine is not without repercussions, including damage to several body systems. Like many illicit drugs of abuse, cocaine also has legitimate medical uses. When biopsies or stitches need to be done in the mouth, nose, or throat, the local application of cocaine to the site is

©Science Source

©Science Source

FIGURE 6-2
(a) Cocaine. (b) Crack cocaine.

an option. Cocaine acts as a local anesthetic within two minutes after application. It does this by impeding neural firing of peripheral neurons at the location where it is placed, which numbs the area. Cocaine also causes blood vessels to narrow (vasoconstriction), leading to decreased bleeding and swelling (NIDA, 2010a,b).

The Coca Plant as the Source of Cocaine

The coca plant, *Erythroxylon coca*, is a small bush or tree that lacks any distinguishing characteristics reflecting its importance in psychopharmacology (see Figure 6-3). Not to be confused with the cacao plant (a source of caffeine and chocolate), the coca plant grows to a height of about 2–3 meters (7–10 feet), depending on light and other growing conditions. The coca plant thrives in hot and humid conditions, such as those found in tropical environments in the South American countries of Bolivia, Ecuador, Peru, Argentina, and Columbia. The branches of the coca plant are fairly straight and the leaves are oval. It is the leaves that are harvested for cocaine. When taken directly off the plant, the leaves can be chewed for a mild stimulant effect. However, purifying cocaine requires a process. Once gathered, the leaves are dried and chemically processed to make coca paste and eventually, powdered cocaine. The coca plant does produce small flowers, which become red berries. Unlike the coffee plant, which also has berries that provide the psychoactive drug caffeine, the berries on the coca plant are of little interest to coca producers.

As noted above, plants containing mind-altering alkaloids, including cocaine and caffeine, grow in the tropical regions of the globe (Pendergrast, 1999). Competition is fierce among species in the rain forest, and the lack of winter results in a continuous battle for survival. Plants that have developed psychoactive drugs as protective mechanisms can be thought of as similar to a poison dart frog using chemical self-protection. Similar to caffeine in the coffee plant, the cocaine present in coca leaves discourages predators from eating the plant. That cocaine is a widely used illicit drug of abuse for humans may seem hard to reconcile with cocaine's ecological role as an insecticide. Some researchers have suggested that the paradox may reflect fundamental differences in mammalian and invertebrate responses to cocaine. Others have suggested that the dose is important. At high doses, cocaine is toxic and operates as an effective plant compound by disrupting predator motor control. At lower doses, cocaine has similar effects in insects as in humans. For example, small doses of cocaine given to honey bees increases the rate of bees dancing after foraging, much like the stimulatory effects seen in humans. Furthermore, cessation of chronic cocaine treatment in bees results in withdrawal-like responses, just like for humans (Barron, Maleszka, Helliwell, & Robinson, 2009).

FIGURE 6-3
The coca plant.

Brief History of Cocaine Use

Cocaine is truly an ancient psychoactive drug, with a long history of use in South and Central America. Archeological evidence from thousands of years ago suggests that prehistoric native inhabitants chewed coca leaves. How do archeologists determine that cocaine was used and that coca leaves were chewed, as opposed to other routes of administration for cocaine? Evidence for use arises from carbon dating of mummies, which determines the age of their bodies, with samples from these bodies tested for the presence of cocaine. In one study, eleven bodies found in a burial site in Northern Chile were tested for cocaine. The carbon dating indicated that the bodies were 3,000 years old. Two of the 11 bodies tested positive for cocaine (Rivera, Aufderheide, Cartmell, Torres, & Langsjoen, 2005). Evidence that coca leaves were chewed comes from examination of the teeth, with cavities indicating habitual coca-leaf chewing (Indriati & Buikstra, 2001). For many native peoples from South and Central America, evidence strongly suggests that the coca plant was central to their lives, having a role in religion, medical treatment, and work (Stolberg, 2011). To this day, native peoples chew coca leaves for stimulant effects among other reasons. The coca plant is sometimes referred to as "Mama Coca" and can be considered sacred. Note that the use of cocaine via chewed leaves appears to have little deleterious effect on health and well-being, in stark contrast to the negative effects of habitual cocaine use via intranasal, inhalation, or injection routes of administration in modern society (Hurtado-Gumucio, 2000).

Even though the coca plant was cultivated by the native peoples living in Central and South America, it was unknown to the rest of the world until the arrival of the Spanish conquistadores during the 16th century. When the Europeans arrived, they encountered native people (the Incas) living in the Andes regions of Bolivia, Ecuador, and Peru. This Inca Empire was sophisticated and coca was at the center. Coca leaves were highly valued, with the Inca nobility monopolizing supply and use. The right to chew leaves was highly prized due to its spiritual significance, which made leaves more valuable than material riches. Coca also served practical purposes. Cocaine in coca leaves suppressed hunger and allowed users to withstand the effects of high altitudes and other hardships of agriculture in the Andes Mountains. Coca leaves were also used medically. As we use cocaine today, the Incas were aware of cocaine's anesthetic properties and used the drug as a local anesthetic for operations such as trephination, the oldest known surgery. Barbaric by today's standards, trephination involved a hole drilled in the skull (see Figure 6-4). The reasons for such a practice remain unclear, and may have included repair of skull fractures following hand-to-hand combat or release of demons to heal mental illness. Amazingly, some people survived this surgery, as evidenced by healed skulls with holes in them. The cocaine presumably anesthetized (as much as possible) the region of the head to be drilled.

When the Spanish conquistadores arrived, they were disturbed by the religious use of coca, which was contrary to Catholicism. After conquering the Inca people, the Spanish changed their view of coca. Although the Spanish always considered chewing coca a vice and did not partake themselves, they noticed that coca allowed the conquered people to work harder and longer. The Spanish taxed the conquered people with coca leaves serving as the monetary system. The Spanish also brought coca back to Europe, but there was initially little interest in it.

With the advent of organic chemistry techniques, the ability to isolate cocaine from the coca plant became possible. Isolation of cocaine starts with an organic solvent such as gasoline. After soaking, mixing, and mashing, the excess liquid is filtered out, leaving coca paste. In 1859, German chemist Albert Neimann discovered how to process coca paste into **cocaine hydrochloride**, a 99% pure product. Compare this to the 0.5% cocaine found in the coca leaf. Cocaine hydrochloride is a salt that mixes easily with water and is stable. With cocaine hydrochloride available, the medical use of cocaine quickly increased in both Europe and North America (Streatfeild, 2001). The popularity of cocaine also rose in part due to the 1869 invention of Vin Mariani by the European chemist Angelo Mariani. Vin Mariani was a medicinal wine made by steeping coca leaves in wine. Drinking this concoction became all the rage in Europe. The American pharmaceutical company, Parke-Davis, quickly made their own version, as did many other imitators (Kuhn, Swartzwelder, & Wilson, 2008).

©Paul Bevitt/Alamy

FIGURE 6-4
Cocaine from the coca plant was thought to be used as a local anesthetic for trephination surgeries by the Inca people.

Famous psychiatrist and historical figure in psychology, Sigmund Freud, wrote extensively about cocaine, including about his own personal use. Freud had obtained a sample in 1884; after personally ingesting it a few times, he thought he had discovered a wonder drug. In his publication, "Uber Coca," which translates to "On Cocaine," Freud advocated the use of cocaine as a local anesthetic and a treatment for morphine addiction, alcoholism, depression, and asthma (Byck, 1974). Freud was not alone in seeing the medical value of cocaine. In fact, widespread enthusiastic endorsement of cocaine by the medical establishment probably launched an era of rampant cocaine abuse. One of Freud's close friends was a fellow physician who was one such unfortunate addict. Ernst von Fleischl-Marxow suffered from chronic and excruciating nerve pain from an infection that arose after an injury that occurred during an autopsy. In an attempt to deal with his condition, von Fleischl-Marxow became addicted to morphine. Freud recommended cocaine to his friend to cure his morphine addiction. Von Fleishl-Marxow was successful in abstaining from morphine for a time while under the cocaine regime. However, he began to consume escalating amounts of cocaine and developed bizarre symptoms that would today be labeled as stimulant psychosis. He reported paranoid thoughts and a feeling of itching of the skin, as if insects were crawling underneath the skin. Eventually, von Fleischl-Marxow abandoned cocaine and returned to morphine. After a few years of living with intolerable pain, he died. Though Freud failed to help one friend, Freud also mentioned the potential local anesthetic quality of cocaine to another physician friend, Karl Koller, an ophthalmologist. Koller is now famous for his research demonstrating the usefulness of cocaine as a local anesthetic in the eye. The use of cocaine to numb the eye, ear, or nose, for procedures and operations still occurs today (Byck, 1974; Kuhn et al., 2008).

Freud's personal accounts of the usefulness of cocaine were consistent with the opinions of many others at the time. Author Robert Louis Stevenson supposedly wrote Jekyll and Hyde while taking cocaine to treat his tuberculosis. Sir Arthur Conan Doyle depicted Sherlock Holmes using cocaine to provide him energy and improve deductive reasoning (Grinspoon & Bakalar, 1976). Cocaine also made its way into a commercial product when Georgia pharmacist John Pemberton launched a tonic drink in 1886, a patented medicine containing caffeine from the cola nut with a cocaine kick from the coca leaf. Pemberton called his product Coca-Cola and marketed his drink as a brain tonic and intellectual beverage (see Figure 6-5). He also claimed it could cure everything from morphine addiction to impotence. However, the inclusion of cocaine in the beverage was brief. By the turn of the century, the cocaine had been removed (May, 1988; Pendergrast, 2000).

The removal of cocaine from Coca-Cola occurred when both the medical establishment and the general public were becoming increasingly wary of the usefulness of the drug. With a lack of regulations and product labeling, cocaine medicines, wines, and tonics began to contain more and more cocaine. The hazards of cocaine use became apparent. From development of psychosis to severe dependence to overdose deaths, the general public became wary of this wonder drug that could cure all ailments. The public also became concerned about an increasing number of violent crimes being committed while under the influence of cocaine. Further, a public health scare campaign with overt racist themes also had an impact. Reports that cocaine made African Americans powerful and uncontrollable contributed to negative views of this drug (Kuhn et al., 2008). As enthusiasm for cocaine waned, access to cocaine was controlled. With the passage of the Harrison Narcotics Act in 1914 (see Chapter 1), the legal supply of psychoactive drugs such as morphine, heroin, and cocaine became strictly regulated.

Cocaine as an illicit drug made a strong reappearance in the 1970s in the United States when cocaine flooded in through Miami, Florida, from South America. Glamorous movie stars and professional athletes snorted expensive cocaine, giving cocaine the reputation as the champagne of illicit drugs. In 1974, it was estimated that 5.4 million Americans had tried cocaine at least once in their lifetime. By 1985, when use peaked, it was estimated that 25 to 40 million Americans had tried cocaine and 3 million were dependent on the drug. By 1986, crack had become widely available in the United States, which led to a national crisis. Crack is freebase cocaine made by mixing cocaine salt with baking soda and water. The solution is heated until brittle and broken into little rocks. The rock is heated until vaporized. When the vapor is inhaled, the drug is absorbed rapidly via the lungs. The intense pleasure of the high is very short in duration, lasting only about 10 to 20 minutes. A severe crash follows, leading to a strong desire for another dose. As a result, crack is more addictive than powdered cocaine administered by snorting. The name

©Bettmann/Corbis

FIGURE 6-5
Coca-Cola was originally a patented medicine containing cocaine.

crack is derived from the crackling sound made by baking soda when the rock is heated. Crack is especially dangerous, as it is far cheaper than purified cocaine. Crack is also very potent and very addictive. Crack can be sold in small affordable rocks (as opposed to powdered cocaine that remains extremely pricey). With the increase in crack use, many overdose deaths occurred. Emergency department visits escalated with the number of cocaine-related visits rising from almost none in the 1970s to more than 80,000 cocaine-related visits in the year 1990 alone (NIDA, 1993; DEA, 2012b). As with many drugs, users became aware of the negative consequences associated with cocaine and crack. Use of both forms of cocaine declined through the 1990s and continues to decline, as we will see when we look at current prevalence rates.

Current Drug Laws in the United States

Cocaine is an illicit drug that can quickly lead to addiction but also has legitimate medical uses including local anesthesia and vasoconstriction. In clinical settings, cocaine will be used in procedures most often related to anesthesia of the eye, ear, nose, and throat. For these reasons, cocaine is considered a Schedule II drug under the Controlled Substances Act. Recall from Chapter 1 that a Schedule II drug has a high potential for abuse but has currently accepted medical uses with severe restrictions. Schedule II drugs are listed as such because they may lead to severe psychological or physical dependence.

Focus on Careers: A Career in Coca?

While the majority of this chapter will focus on cocaine as a drug of abuse, it is worth noting how widely the coca plant is used today. In fact, many people have careers that are connected to the coca plant in one way or another. When you buy a soft drink, specifically Coca-Cola, you are drinking a beverage containing coca. Of course, today there is no cocaine in Coca-Cola, but the world's best-selling soft drink is still flavored with a non-drug extract from the coca plant. The formula for Coca-Cola is a closely held secret, so the exact amount of coca in the beverage is not known by the general public. The company does confirm that coca is a necessary ingredient giving the product its distinctive taste. Where does this coca come from and who would have jobs involving coca and cocaine? The coca is grown in South America, where it has grown for thousands of years, mainly by peasant farmers (see Figure 6-6). In the United States, the Stepan Company is the only commercial entity authorized by the U.S. Drug Enforcement Administration to import dried coca leaves. Most of the approximately 100 metric tons of dried coca leaf imported each year by Stepan comes from Peru, but some also comes from Bolivia. The company has one manufacturing plant, located in Maywood, New Jersey, that is authorized to process coca leaves chemically. The non-drug extract is sold to Coca Cola. The crude extract from the coca (containing cocaine) is sold to Mallinckrodt, a pharmaceutical firm that provides the drug for medical uses. Mallinckrodt is the only commercial entity authorized to purify the product to the cocaine hydrochloride form for medicinal use. This cocaine is sold to hospitals and doctors, primarily as a local anesthetic used mainly by eye, ear, nose, and throat specialists. These processes are highly regulated and tightly controlled, which provides a multitude of jobs at various stages of the process (May, 1988).

Websites to explore (look for the careers link:

> http://www.coca-cola.com/en/index.html
> http://www.covidien.com (the parent company for Mallinckrodt, which lists career information)
> http://www.stepan.com

FIGURE 6-6
The coca plant.

©Philip Sharp/Alamy

Prevalence of Cocaine Use

In the United States

It appears that the use of cocaine, both powder and crack, has remained relatively stable over the past decade after declining from the high levels seen in the 1980s. Most national surveys ask separate questions about the use of cocaine powder and crack. Thus, the data is often separated for the two versions of the drug, even though the psychoactive ingredient is the same for both versions of cocaine. The 2010 National Survey on Drug Use and Health (NSDUH) estimated that cocaine powder use in the past month in individuals ages 12 or older was approximately 0.6% of the population, a value equating to approximately 1.5 million Americans. It is also estimated that 0.1% of the population had used crack in the past month. First-time users of cocaine have declined since the 1980s and 1990s (SAMHSA, 2011a). While rates of cocaine use are still significant and result in significant problems for society, cocaine is less of a problem than it was a few decades ago. However, keep in mind that declining trends in cocaine use may reflect increases in use of synthetic stimulants, such as methamphetamine, which will be discussed in the next chapter. The acute effects of synthetic amphetamines are similar to cocaine, with a cost that can be much lower. However, cocaine users still outnumber methamphetamine users in the United States by almost 5 to 1 (Kuhn et al., 2008).

Another way to determine the prevalence of cocaine is assessing use in young people. The Monitoring the Future survey is a national U.S. questionnaire of 8th, 10th, and 12th graders. The rate of overall cocaine past year use (powdered cocaine and crack combined) in 12th graders was 2.9%, with lower use by 8th and 10th graders. This represents a historic low compared to the high rates seen in the late 1970s and early 1980s. Similar to the NSDUH data described above, usage levels for cocaine powder were higher than for crack. The Monitoring the Future survey also asked about cocaine availability. The proportion of 12th graders who said that it would be "fairly easy" or "very easy" for them to get cocaine if they wanted was 31%. Crack was reported to be less available than powdered cocaine (Johnston, O'Malley, Bachman, & Schulenberg, 2012).

Worldwide

It is difficult to estimate worldwide use of cocaine. There is no universally accepted method of measurement, so inconsistencies pose major challenges for cross-national and cross-regional comparisons. As such, researchers seek convergence of results from different methods. By analysis of these converged results, it has been estimated that the number of past-year cocaine users worldwide is approximately 0.3 to 0.5% among individuals aged 15–64 years. This rate equates to 14–21 million people in the 15–64 age range. Moreover, ease of access to cocaine is an important factor in regional consumption rates. The greatest use occurs in North America (1.9%), followed by Western and Central Europe (1.3%), and South America (1%). Rates of cocaine use are far lower in Asia (0.2%), the Middle East (0.3%), and most of Africa (0.5%). These results may not be surprising given distribution issues associated with a coca plant only grown in Central and South America. Note that stimulants like cocaine are not inherently unappealing to potential users living in low-consumption regions of the world. The effects of amphetamines are similar to cocaine, with a major difference being that cocaine comes from a plant, whereas amphetamines are made in a laboratory (see Chapter 7). Asia has much higher rates of amphetamine use than other regions of the world, even though the rates of cocaine use in Asia are low (Degenhardt et al., 2011; Degenhardt & Hall, 2012; Pomara et al., 2012).

Routes of Administration

There are several common **routes of administration** for recreational use of cocaine, including oral, intranasal, inhalation, and injection. Recall that the method by which a drug enters the body impacts how much of the dose reaches the site of action and how quickly it gets there. For cocaine, the intensity and duration of its effects depend on the choice of drug administration route. More intense highs occur when cocaine is absorbed into the bloodstream and delivered to the brain in a faster manner. By contrast, mild stimulation occurs when cocaine is absorbed slowly. There is a long history of South American native peoples in Bolivia and Peru chewing coca leaves. This oral route of administration for cocaine is still prevalent today among native peoples. In these countries, dried coca leaves are used to make a tea, which is also an oral administration route. Whether with chewing or swallowing, these oral routes of administration result in very mild stimulant effects. Rates of abuse are extremely low with oral administration of cocaine because of the slow onset, limited intensity, and lengthy duration of effects (Hurtado-Gumicio, 2000). In South America, coca paste (processing coca leaves) is also sometimes mixed with tobacco and smoked.

In North America, cocaine for recreational use is typically administered via intranasal, inhalation, or injection routes of administration. Other routes are possible, but less common, including application in the mouth, rectum, penis, or vagina. The injection or inhalation (smoking) of cocaine typically results in a quicker and stronger high, as opposed to intranasal administration (snorting). When quickly absorbed, the duration of action for cocaine is shorter. If cocaine is inhaled, the high may only last about 10 minutes. By contrast, the intranasal administration of cocaine will result in a longer high of about 30 minutes. While the intranasal administration of cocaine can have intense effects, the drug also constricts the blood vessels in the nose. This vasoconstrictive action of cocaine slows absorption, which accounts for the longer duration of action. Recall that the route of drug administration and duration of action can be important in likelihood of abuse. In order to sustain a cocaine-induced high, an abuser will have to administer another dose of drug once the initial dose starts to subside. For this reason, injection or inhalation of cocaine may result in more drug administration episodes, as compared to intranasal administration of cocaine (Figure 6-7). Moreover, the inhalation of cocaine produces blood levels of cocaine comparable to levels observed from intravenous administration, due to the large surface area for absorption in the lungs. Through the pulmonary circulation, the cocaine-containing blood enters the left side of the heart and reaches cerebral circulation without any dilution from the rest of the blood circulation (NIDA, 2010a; O'Brien, 2001). The takeaway is that the inhalation or injection of cocaine is more likely to result in addiction than the intranasal administration of cocaine.

FIGURE 6-7
Intranasal administration of cocaine.

©Klawitter Productions/Corbis

QUICK QUIZ 6-1

1. Cocaine is a powerful nervous system _____ drug causing increased _____.
   a. sedative, fatigue and drowsiness
   b. sedative, alertness and energy
   c. stimulant, alertness and energy
   d. stimulant, fatigue and drowsiness

2. Cocaine comes from the _____ plant, which grows in _____.
   a. *Erythroxylon coca*, Asia
   b. *Erythroxylon coca*, South America
   c. *Theobroma cacao*, Asia
   d. *Theobroma cacao*, South America

3. Cocaine has been available for _____.
   a. Thousands of years
   b. Hundreds of years
   c. Only the last hundred years
   d. Only the last ten years

4. Cocaine is considered a Schedule _____ drug.
   a. I
   b. II
   c. III
   d. IV

5. The prevalence of cocaine powder use in the U.S. population is approximately _____.
   a. 0.01%
   b. 0.1%
   c. 0.6%
   d. 6%

6. In the United States, which is more commonly used?
   a. Powdered cocaine
   b. Crack cocaine
   c. Dried coca for chewing
   d. Dried coca made into tea

7. Which region of the world has more cocaine users?
   a. North America
   b. Western and Central Europe
   c. Asia
   d. The Middle East

8. Your friend decided to go on a vacation to Bolivia. While on this trip, your friend chewed coca leaves a few times. Should you be concerned about your friend becoming addicted to cocaine? Why or why not?

9. What is the difference between the recreational use of powdered cocaine and crack cocaine?

ANSWERS TO QUICK QUIZ 6-1:

1. c – stimulant, alertness and energy
2. b – *Erythroxylon coca*, South America
3. a – thousands of years
4. b – II
5. c – 0.6%
6. a – powdered cocaine
7. a – North America
8. It is unlikely that your friend will become addicted to cocaine. Chewing coca leaves involves the oral route of administration for cocaine. With this administration route, the onset of the drug effect will be slow and the intensity of the stimulant effect will be mild. Moreover, coca leaves are not purified cocaine, which makes the leaves less likely to produce dependence.
9. Even though both powdered cocaine and crack cocaine are illicit drugs that can quickly lead to addiction, there are important differences between the two types of cocaine. Powdered cocaine is snorted directly into the nose or the cocaine is dissolved in water and then injected. Crack cocaine is chemically processed freebase cocaine made by mixing cocaine salt with baking soda and water. The solution is heated until brittle and broken into little rocks. The rock is heated until it vaporizes and the vapor is inhaled. When powdered cocaine is snorted, the vasoconstrictive properties of the drug slow absorption, resulting in a typical duration of action of about 30 minutes. With crack cocaine, the high is intense but short in duration, lasting only about 10 to 20 minutes. The differences in duration of action between intranasal and inhalation render crack cocaine more addictive. Crack cocaine is also a cheaper drug to acquire on the street than powdered cocaine. Finally, powdered cocaine is more prevalent than crack cocaine in the United States.

Acute Effects of Cocaine

The acute effects of a drug are changes that take place after ingesting the drug one time. Thus, the acute effects of cocaine refer to immediate changes experienced after cocaine is administered. Acute effects can be objective, including observable changes in behavior or physiology. Acute effects can also be subjective, such as when a participant provides ratings about how they feel. Since cocaine is addictive, researchers often try to determine the acute effects of cocaine by examining responses to cocaine among recreational users. For this reason, many studies recruited participants who were intranasal users of cocaine, since these individuals are most likely to be able to use cocaine intermittently without developing symptoms of addiction (O'Brien, 2001). However, other studies have had crack cocaine users as participants (Fillmore, Rush, & Hays, 2002; Fillmore, Rush, & Hayes, 2006). In human studies, participants typically stay in a hospital setting for their own safety. The reasons for the hospital stay will become clearer when the acute effects of cocaine on the body are discussed below. While difficult to conduct, laboratory studies examining the effects of cocaine provide information about the pharmacodynamic and pharmacokinetic actions of cocaine administered by various routes. They also inform us about how people feel and act after taking the drug, which helps explain why cocaine is addictive. Animal studies are also helpful in addressing questions about the acute effects of cocaine, since control over past exposure to the drug is possible with animal models.

In general, the acute effects of cocaine are consistent with central nervous system stimulation (CNS). In the previous two chapters, we discussed caffeine and nicotine, psychoactive drugs that result in CNS stimulation. The acute effects of cocaine are more pronounced than the acute effects of caffeine or nicotine. Cocaine is a far more powerful stimulant than these other two drugs. Cocaine is also rapidly metabolized by the body. The acute effects described below are typically measured within 80 minutes of drug administration, the approximate duration of drug action for cocaine. However, recall that the route of administration can influence the duration of action. The 80-minute duration of action is an estimate for the intranasal administration of powdered cocaine. By contrast, the duration of action for inhaled crack cocaine is much shorter, lasting less than 20 minutes. However, the subjective feelings of being high are more pronounced with crack (Iversen, Iversen, Bloom, & Roth, 2009).

Objective Effects

When cocaine is administered, its stimulant effects are readily observable on several objective measures. Performance enhancements can occur for both mental and physical tasks. While the scientific data supporting these observations is relatively recent, objective changes from cocaine use have been known for thousands of years. The Inca civilization in Peru had a communication system that kept the entire empire in contact over vast distances. Runners would carry messages through the Andes mountains. Despite a difficult terrain and high altitudes, these runners would run at incredible speeds over very long distances. How was this accomplished? Cocaine helped. Runners would chew coca leaves to mitigate fatigue and allay hunger and thirst.

In more recent times, researchers have tried to assess whether cocaine can improve endurance during high-intensity activity. Endurance is tested by putting rats on treadmills (yes, there are specially designed treadmills just for little rodents—see Figure 6-8). Endurance is assessed by starting the treadmill and then increasing the speed. In one study, rats were injected with saline or differing doses of cocaine. Once the drug had taken effect, the rats were placed on the treadmill to run. The researchers increased the speed until the point at which the rat fell off the back from fatigue. Using this methodological approach, it was demonstrated that cocaine pretreatment increased speed and endurance. While the saline-treated rats ran approximately 14 minutes until fatigued, a 12.5 mg/kg dose of cocaine increased the mean run time to approximately 15 minutes. The cocaine helped the rats run an additional minute at their maximum speed. However, further increases in cocaine were actually harmful. A 20.0 mg/kg dose decreased the mean run time to only 10 minutes (Braiden, Fellingham, & Conlee, 1994).

The acute effects of cocaine can also increase alertness and arousal. A user may appear talkative, full of energy, very active in their movements, and restless. The increase in movement is

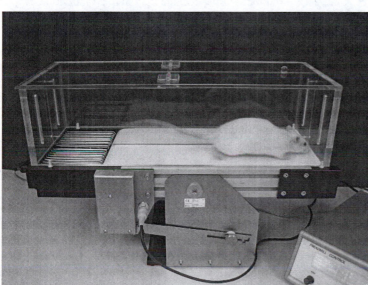

©BIOSEB USA, St. Petersburg Florida

FIGURE 6-8
Rat running on a treadmill.

clear, with the user often being in constant motion (Kuhn et al., 2008). Objective quantification of these changes can be assessed in a variety of ways. When rats are administered cocaine at doses ranging from 10 to 30 mg/kg, they become very active. How is this determination made? The rats are placed in a chamber where their movement around the box is measured. The researchers examine various aspects of motor activity, including how much distance the animals cover while moving about the box. A rat sitting in the corner hanging out and licking its paws is not going to cover much distance in 30 minutes. However, a rat that has been administered cocaine will appear visibly more active. There are typically dose-dependent increases in locomotor activity following cocaine administration. This means that with increasing doses of cocaine, the rat will travel greater distances in the box during the time allotted (Polston, Cunningham, Rodvelt, & Miller, 2006). In addition, at higher doses of cocaine, the increase in motor activity may appear more focused and repetitive. Human users may engage in repetitive tasks, such as taking apart a piece of electrical equipment and putting it back together. Animals administered high doses of cocaine may sniff back and forth in one spot of the cage environment, or else they might chew and groom compulsively (Kuhn et al., 2008).

The evidence that cocaine may improve cognitive processing is more limited than the evidence for increased locomotor activity. If individuals have the energy to engage in more activities, it might be reasonable to think that cognitive performance would also be enhanced. Increased feelings of energy may enhance the ability to stay focused and accomplish more. For this reason, cocaine has had appeal for individuals in certain occupations, such as lawyers, where a high-intensity atmosphere exists and long hours are expected (Benjamin, Darling, & Sales, 1990). Is there evidence that cocaine alters cognitive processing? One study did find that the acute effects of cocaine enhanced brain activation in drug-naive rhesus monkeys. The researchers observed that there were drug-induced changes in blood flow in the cerebral cortex following drug administration. As measured by positron emission tomography imaging, the activation was particularly robust in the prefrontal cortex region, a brain area known to be important for complex higher-order cognitive processing (Howell, Votaw, Goodman, & Lindsey, 2010). Another study that examined brain-related changes following smoked cocaine in humans also observed elevations in prefrontal cortex activity (as measured by EEG activity) (Reid, Flammino, Howard, Nilsen, & Prichep, 2006). Such observations are consistent with anecdotal human reports that cocaine enhances cognitive processing. However, other studies have found that the benefits of cocaine for cognitive performance are limited. If cocaine increases the speed of performance, this comes at a cost. In tasks where response times and errors are both recorded, cocaine may increase the speed of reactions, but more errors also occur (Iversen, Iversen, Bloom, & Roth, 2009). In other words, cocaine may help an individual respond faster, but that individual will be careless and make lots of errors too. Researchers have also found that cocaine can make an individual more careless and impulsive even when there are no benefits of cocaine on the ability to respond quickly (Fillmore et al., 2002). However, this literature remains murky, since it has also been demonstrated that cocaine can actually improve accuracy (Fillmore et al., 2006). The differences among studies could be attributable to differing doses of cocaine and different subject characteristics such as drug use histories. In general, higher doses of cocaine are more likely to result in impairments in accuracy, whereas lower doses might lead to improvements. In sum, the evidence that cocaine improves cognition is mixed, whereas the evidence that cocaine increases alertness, arousal, and endurance is fairly reliable.

Subjective Effects

Users of cocaine report a variety of subjective effects reflecting increased feelings of stimulation. They will report feeling alert, energetic, and confident. They will feel talkative and sociable. Their thinking may be grandiose in that they feel like they could accomplish anything. The most notable change is that the user experiences euphoria. They will remark that they feel high and they like the drug (Fillmore et al., 2002, 2006; Walsh, Stoops, Moody, Lin, & Bigelow, 2009). In addition, users who inject or smoke crack (the fastest routes of administration for cocaine) will report that the rush of intense physical pleasure that occurs is akin to an orgasm. Users employing slower absorption routes (intranasal or oral) will not experience the same intense pleasure, but instead report feeling good with a sense of well-being and happiness (Kuhn et al., 2008). All of these subjective changes can be quantified in research studies. Cocaine users are typically recruited, since cocaine-naive subjects could present ethical concerns given cocaine's addictive properties. The users may be admitted to a hospital unit for a week where they receive different doses of cocaine on different days. The subjects are asked to report various subjective feelings following dose administration. Users most frequently report increased feelings of rush, high, and craving (see Table 6-1). In many studies, cocaine is administered orally so that subjects are less likely to guess what dose was administered to them (Fillmore et al., 2002, 2006; Walsh et al., 2009). However, it is also important to determine the subjective effects of cocaine administered via other routes of administration, since the subjective effects are much more pronounced with faster routes of administration such as smoked crack. The high is stronger with crack, but other unpleasant symptoms are also reported, including feeling nervous and craving cocaine more (Reid et al., 2006).

Asking subjects to provide subjective ratings after drug administration allows researchers to answer various questions, such as how long the drug acts and if the euphoria experienced depends on the route of administration. Given advances in brain imaging, subjective ratings have also been used to help pinpoint brain areas underlying these feeling states. Functional magnetic resonance imaging (fMRI) technology has been used to determine which regions of the brain increase in activity that coincides with subjective ratings. When cocaine is administered, increased activity in the nucleus accumbens, hippocampus, and throughout the cortex coincides with the feelings of rush that users subjectively report. As time passes and the cocaine dose is metabolized, users report more craving for cocaine and less rush. In the brain, the signal changes and high levels of activity in the nucleus accumbens and prefrontal cortex correlate most strongly with the craving state (Breiter et al., 1997).

Table 6-1 **Mean subjective effects ratings and peak physiological effects of oral cocaine in adults with a history of cocaine use. Subjective effects were obtained one hour after the capsule was administered. Each item was scored from 0 (not at all) to 4 (very much).**

	Oral Cocaine Doses			
	0 mg (placebo)	100 mg	200 mg	300 mg
Active/alert/energetic	0.4	1.1	1.4	1.5
Good effect	0.4	0.9	1.4	1.8
High	0.3	0.9	1.8	2.1
Like	0.4	0.9	1.5	1.8
Anxious/nervous	0.2	0.5	0.4	1.0
Pay for this drug	0.2	0.6	0.9	1.1
Rush	0.1	0.6	1.0	1.5
Shaky/jittery	0.1	0.5	1.4	1.4
Take this drug again	0.4	0.7	1.7	1.7
Talkative/friendly	0.4	0.8	1.1	0.8
Heart rate (beats per minute)	71	77	89	94
Systolic blood pressure (mmHg)	121	130	136	143
Diastolic blood pressure (mmHg)	75	80	84	86

Note: Adapted from Fillmore, M. T., Rush, C. R., & Hays, L. (2006). Acute effects of cocaine in two models of inhibitory control: Implications of non-linear dose effects. Addiction, 101, 1323–1332.

Effects on the Body

Cocaine stimulates activity in the **sympathetic nervous system,** the portion of the autonomic nervous system activated in times of stress and danger (see Chapter 2). The sympathetic nervous system is not often active, but it is important in times of crisis. When a danger or stressor is present, the sympathetic nervous system prepares the body for the crisis and physiological changes result in the fight-or-flight response. The body readies for a sudden expenditure of energy by directing blood away from nonessential regions, such as the digestive system, to where the blood is needed, such as the arms and legs. Heart rate increases, breathing gets heavier, and blood pressure rises. Sweating is common. The pupils of the eyes become larger. While the fight-or-flight response is a normal reaction to danger, it can also be activated by drug use. The acute effects of cocaine result in activation of the sympathetic nervous system. All of the changes observed with the fight-or-flight response are also observed following cocaine administration (Foltin, Fischman, & Levin, 1995; Foltin & Haney, 2004). Table 6-1 illustrates how both heart rate and blood pressure increase in a dose-dependent manner following oral cocaine administration. The changes noted in the table following oral cocaine are less pronounced than observed with other routes of administration. Smoked cocaine will result in more rapid cardiovascular changes as measured by increases in heart rate and blood pressure (Reid et al., 2006).

In addition to cardiovascular changes, appetite is suppressed because of the downregulation of digestive activity coinciding with sympathetic activation. In addition, fat is broken down to help mobilize energy. Thus, cocaine use typically contributes to weight loss, with users reporting that they are not hungry. Cocaine's contribution to weight loss accounts for some of the drug's appeal to professional fashion models and other individuals who desire a low body weight (Cochrane, Malcolm, & Brewerton, 1998). Further, though food is reinforcing, cocaine is much more so. In one study, rhesus monkeys were given the choice to press a lever to receive an intravenous injection of cocaine or another lever to receive a food reward. The monkeys chose the cocaine almost exclusively. Over the eight days of the experiment, the animals decreased their food intake, lost weight, and achieved very high blood levels of cocaine (Aigner & Balster, 1978). In sum, motivation for food is suppressed with cocaine, resulting in decreased body weight.

Increases in body temperature can also occur with administration of cocaine. This can be problematic when the drug is used in combination with physical exertion. Recall from earlier in the chapter that cocaine-treated rats could run fast for a longer period of time than saline-treated rats. However, if baseline body temperature is elevated because of cocaine, the physical exertion could lead to very high body temperatures that result in heat exhaustion or heat stroke. Finally, cocaine impedes sleep, an unsurprising effect given that cocaine significantly increases alertness and arousal. Insomnia following cocaine administration is observable in both humans and animals (Kuhn et al., 2008; Walsh et al., 2009).

Users of cocaine also report that the drug increases interest in sex. Users of cocaine are more likely to engage in risky sexual behaviors and acquire sexually transmissible diseases (Ross et al., 2002). However, sympathetic activation results in downregulation of the physiological aspects of sexual activity. This is because the fight-or-flight response is about survival; sexual activity is at odds with the short-term goal of survival. Thus, experiments with animals have illustrated that cocaine can make sexual activity difficult or even impossible. For males, constriction of the blood vessels in the penis interferes with the maintenance of an erection and can delay ejaculation (Ferrari & Giuliani, 1997). Some researchers have suggested that the incidence of risky sex and sexually transmissible diseases with cocaine are a result of economic transactions (sex for money or drugs), rather than cocaine increasing sexual desire (Fullilove et al., 1993; Ross et al., 2002).

While less common, cocaine can induce seizures at doses that are not much higher than those resulting in maximal effects on mood. In animal studies, high doses of cocaine reliably induce seizures (Smith et al., 1991). Other local anesthetics can also induce seizures, indicating that seizures arise due to cocaine's anesthetic action. In the past, researchers believed that repeated use of cocaine among human users was necessary for increased sensitivity to seizures. However, the research seems now to indicate otherwise. Seizures can happen any time, regardless of length of use of the drug. Indeed, many longtime users have experienced at least one seizure. Moreover, seizures are sufficiently common with cocaine use that any adolescent or young adult arriving in an emergency room with a seizure is screened for presence of cocaine, even if the patient had no reported history of cocaine use (Kuhn et al., 2008).

Stimulant Psychosis

When blood levels of cocaine rise, energy and alertness are the typical drug responses. If blood levels continue to rise, symptoms of **stimulant psychosis** may emerge. The user may become paranoid, hostile, and belligerent. The user may be convinced that people are after them or out to get them. The individual will appear disoriented and confused. Having a rational conversation with the cocaine user may be impossible. The symptoms of stimulant psychosis resemble the symptoms accompanying paranoid schizophrenia. Sufferers may report **delusions** or thoughts inconsistent with reality. Statements such as, "I am the President of the United States" would be indicative of thinking that is not grounded in reality, in this case a delusion of grandeur. A statement like, "The FBI is out to get me" would be a delusion of persecution. Users may also report **hallucinations**, perceptions that are inconsistent with reality. Reports of hearing voices (auditory hallucination) or feeling unusual sensations such as bugs crawling under the skin (tactile hallucination) occur. Delusions and hallucinations have been reported both under the influence of cocaine and also when not using cocaine. However, these psychotic symptoms are far more likely to occur under the acute effects of cocaine (Mahoney, Kalechstein, De La Garza, & Newton, 2008; Mahoney, Hawkins, De La Garza, Kalechstein, & Newton, 2010). While there is considerable overlap in symptoms for stimulant psychosis and paranoid schizophrenia, one key distinguishing feature is violence. Violence is a major concern with stimulant psychosis but is unlikely with paranoid schizophrenia. Violence arising from stimulant psychosis may reflect the heightened sympathetic activation occurring with cocaine, since the drug readies the individual to fight. The likelihood that a user exhibits psychotic symptoms increases with use of cocaine. Longer exposure to cocaine is associated with greater severity of psychosis; individuals who have used the drug chronically for more than five years are much more likely to report psychotic symptoms (Lichlyter, Purdon, & Tibbo, 2011).

When cocaine users become psychotic, their irrational thinking is not only problematic to themselves, but also sometimes to those around them. There is a clear and unfortunate relationship between cocaine and violence. Cocaine users are more likely to commit various violent crimes such as homicides, assaults, and partner/child abuse (Degenhardt, Day, Hall, Conroy, & Gilmour, 2005; Dias et al., 2011). In addition to increased likelihood of committing violent crimes, cocaine users are also more likely to die violent deaths (Dias et al., 2011). This may reflect cocaine users spending significant time around other cocaine users. While the relationship between cocaine and violence is complicated, the various acute effects of the drug (development of psychosis and heightened sympathetic activation) contribute to this relationship. Johnny Cash's famous song, "Cocaine Blues," has lyrics directly addressing the connection between cocaine and violent crime.

Lethal Dose

Another concern with cocaine use is overdose leading to death, although the risk of death is thought to be less with cocaine than other street drugs such as heroin. In the rat, the LD_{50} dose is 1.4 mg/100 g of body weight when cocaine is given intravenously (Smith et al., 1991). Recall that the **lethal dose** refers to the amount of drug resulting in the death of 50% of animals within a stated time, such as 24 hours. In humans, it is more difficult to pinpoint an exact LD_{50} value, in part because death caused by cocaine use often involves other psychoactive drugs, with users having varying drug use histories. When medical examiners have reviewed autopsy cases that appeared to be largely due to the toxic effects of cocaine, death typically occurred because respiration ceased (the person stopped breathing). Death from cocaine is more likely with intravenous injection than other routes of administration (Di Maio & Garriott, 1978). Generalized seizures sometimes occur before death, which serve as a warning signal in many instances (Wetli & Wright, 1979). Review of overdose cases indicate that the average age of the overdose victim is 29 years old, with the victim's blood cocaine concentration averaging 6.2 mg/L, although there are a wide range in values (Mittleman & Wetli, 1984) and lower values have been reported (Di Maio & Garriott, 1978).

Cocaine use can also result in death by **myocardial infarction**, more commonly known as a heart attack (Smith et al., 1987). Myocardial infarction occurs when blood flow is completely obstructed in a coronary artery, leading to death of an area of heart tissue due to lack of blood supply. Depending on the size and location of the tissue death, sudden death of the person can occur (Tortora & Derrickson, 2012). These myocardial infarctions following cocaine use occur even though users are typically relatively young and have noninfarct vessels that are normal (Minor, Scott, Brown, & Winniford, 1991; Smith et al., 1987).

Deaths are also more likely when cocaine and alcohol are used together, since the two in combination result in greater toxicity than either drug alone (Herbst et al., 2011; Landry, 1992). In animal studies, rats or mice were given alcohol or cocaine in various doses, alone and in combination. Lethality was only observed when alcohol and cocaine were combined (Busse & Riley, 2003; Meehan & Schechter, 1995). It seems that while each drug can individually result in death, a complex chemical reaction occurs when these two drugs are mixed in the body. Researchers have determined that the human liver combines cocaine and alcohol and produces a new metabolite, **cocaethylene**. In the presence of alcohol, 17% of intravenous cocaine is biotransformed into cocaethylene, which is eliminated from the body more slowly than cocaine (Harris, Everhart, Mendelson, & Jones, 2003; McCance-Katz et al., 1993). Cocaethylene intensifies cocaine's euphoric effects, which explains why users often mix alcohol and cocaine. However, cocaethylene is also associated with greater risk of sudden death than cocaine alone (Harris et al., 2003), although the exact mechanisms underlying the heightened risk of death remain unclear.

Cocaine is also sometimes combined with drugs other than alcohol. Heroin mixed with cocaine is known by users as a speedball. Users claim that the dreaminess associated with opiates cuts some of the edginess or arousal that occurs with cocaine. Unfortunately, this is also quite dangerous. The jitteriness from a high cocaine dose is aversive, which discourages the use of a fatal amount of cocaine. Without the signal of aversive feelings, a drug overdose from the cocaine and/or heroin can more easily occur. This combination of heroin and cocaine was to blame for the overdose deaths of comedians Chris Farley and John Belushi (Kuhn et al., 2008).

One final contributor to cocaine's lethality should be mentioned. This causal factor involves substances with which cocaine is mixed. Obviously, street cocaine is not always pure, since there is no regulation of its production. The powdered pure form of cocaine is pure white. When sold illicitly, other substances may be mixed in that are similar in appearance. Some of these substances are inert, such as cornstarch, talcum powder, lactose, or mannitol. Other substances are psychoactive, including amphetamine, caffeine, and other local anesthetics. The reasons for mixing cocaine with **adulterants** (which are also called cutting agents) are purely economic. Cocaine comes from a plant that is grown in South America. The illegal importation of cocaine from Columbia and other countries is fraught with dangers and logistical problems (Kuhn et al., 2008). Adulterants are cheap and are added to increase bulk, enhance or mimic a pharmacological effect, or facilitate drug delivery. At low doses, many adulterants may have little to no impact on users' health. However, there have been cases where these adulterants have contributed to deaths, such as when cocaine has been adulterated with fentanyl (an opiate that is similar to heroin) (Cole et al., 2011). Note that the adulteration of street drugs is a concern with all illicit drugs, not just cocaine.

Chronic Effects of Cocaine Use

Cocaine is somewhat unusual in that individuals tend to use it much more irregularly than other psychoactive drugs such as opioids (heroin) or nicotine. When asked about their consumption of cocaine, regular users often report a pattern of heavy cocaine use at times and little use at other times. This is a binge pattern of drug use, with a **binge** defined as the continuous use of a drug, lasting hours to days, terminating when supply of the drug is exhausted. Even with only an intermittent pattern of use, over time various health concerns emerge (Falck, Wang, Siegal, & Carlson, 2003). Overdose, accidental injury, or violence is more likely the longer the drug is used (Siegal, Falck, Wang, Carlson, & Massimino, 2006). In addition, cardiovascular disease, cirrhosis of the liver, blood-borne infections, mental disorders, cognitive impairments, and dependence are much more likely to emerge with repeated use of cocaine (Gould, Gage, & Nader, 2012; Pomara et al., 2012).

The intranasal route of administration for a cocaine user presents unique health concerns. When cocaine is administered via the intranasal route, the drug constricts the blood vessels in the nose. When such vasoconstriction occurs repeatedly, inflammation and tissue damage to the mucous membranes of the nose results. A primary symptom that results is chronic nosebleeds. Loss of sense of smell and a constantly runny nose may also occur. Users may experience difficulties with swallowing and acquire a permanently hoarse voice. At the start of this chapter, the story of singer Whitney Houston and her battle with addiction to cocaine was described. Her beautiful voice, which built her astounding career, was ruined over time as it became hoarse and raspy. Cocaine may have played a role in these changes, in addition to the other health complications that led to her early death.

As mentioned earlier, the vasoconstriction resulting from cocaine in the nose does lengthen the duration of action of the drug, perhaps making this route of administration less likely to result in addiction for some users. Of course, not all cocaine is administered via the nose. Injection of cocaine can increase the risk of contracting blood-borne diseases, including HIV and hepatitis, since addicted users may inject with dirty needles. The injection process itself can also result in vein damage; what's more, injection of cocaine is highly likely to result in addiction.

The inhalation of cocaine, in the form of crack, also results in rapid development of addiction, since the high is achieved very quickly, as is the case with injection. Inhalation of crack cocaine presents unique health concerns, including skin damage, damage to the mucous membranes of the mouth, dental decay, and crack lung. **Crack lung** occurs when lung tissue has been scarred and damaged from crack use. When cocaine is inhaled, vasoconstriction of blood vessels in the lungs occurs, which prevents oxygen and blood from circulating, thus damaging lung tissue. The user may have a chronic cough, difficulty breathing, severe chest pain, and a fever. Many crack users also suffer from burns since the process of readying crack for inhalation can lead to fires (Dinis-Oliveira et al., 2012).

Regardless of the route of administration or frequency of use, cocaine decreases appetite, with many chronic users becoming malnourished from lack of food intake. In general, cocaine also taxes the cardiovascular and cerebrovascular systems in the body. We've discussed vasoconstriction in the nose (with intranasal administration) and in the lungs (when crack cocaine is inhaled), though vasoconstriction can also occur in blood vessels throughout the body. Arteries with or without coronary artery disease (clogged arteries) will constrict repeatedly when cocaine is used, increasing the likelihood that blood platelets will coagulate and block off the artery. Cocaine also increases blood pressure and heart rate (which both require more blood supply, not less), resulting in the worst possible scenario for constricted arteries. Given this combination of factors, it is unsurprising that repeated use of cocaine increases the likelihood of a myocardial infarction (heart attack) or stroke. Any young individual who presents to an emergency room with symptoms indicating a possible myocardial infarction or stroke is typically tested for cocaine (Rezkalla & Kloner, 2007). With chronic cocaine use, dependence on the drug, stimulant psychosis, and death all increase in likelihood. These negative consequences are much more likely when cocaine is regularly inhaled or injected, as opposed to the intranasal route of administration (NIDA, 2010a).

More about the Science:

Moeller, S. J., Maloney, T., Parvaz, M. A., Alia-Klein, N., Woicik, P. A., Telang, F., Wang, G.-J., Volkow, N. D., & Goldstein, R. Z. (2010). Impaired insight in cocaine addiction: Laboratory evidence and effects on cocaine-seeking behavior. *Brain*, *133*, 1484–1493.

Individuals who become addicted to a psychoactive drug are often the last to acknowledge the problem. Both clinicians and lay people often describe the individual as "in denial" or "lacking insight" into their problems. Recently, researchers have gathered empirical evidence suggesting that insight deficits exist in addicts, with the lack of insight extending beyond the drug problem. Moeller et al. (2010) recruited cocaine-addicted individuals and healthy controls to test for insight deficits in the laboratory. The cocaine users were divided into two groups, based on whether they screened positive or not for cocaine on a urine drug test. Since the urine drug test identified cocaine use only within the last 72 hours, the negative cocaine test group had not used cocaine within the last 3 days, while the positive cocaine test group had used cocaine within the last 3 days. All cocaine users were not using the drug at the time of testing. Once participants were in the lab, all were asked to look at a series of pictures on a computer screen and select which ones they liked. The pictures were pleasant, unpleasant, neutral, or cocaine-related. After the choice task, subjects were asked to report which type of picture they selected most often. The correspondence between a subject's self-report of their most chosen picture type with their actual most selected choice was how the researchers measured insight. The researchers found that the cocaine subjects exhibited impaired insight compared to healthy controls. Moreover, the insight deficit was most pronounced in the cocaine subjects who had a positive cocaine urine test (indicating recent use of the drug).

More about the Science Thought Questions:

1. What psychological intervention for cocaine addicts might be suggested from this study?
2. What should researchers be concerned about when interpreting data such as this?
3. Should researchers be cautious in stating that cocaine users have an "insight deficit"?

More about the Science Thought Question Answers:

1. The findings of this study suggest that addicts would benefit from interventions that enhance insight, since insight is deficient in cocaine addicts. Becoming more consciously aware of all behavioral choices (even those not related to drugs) might help these individuals deal with their addiction.
2. While the data from this study suggest that cocaine users have an "insight deficit," other factors may be involved. For example, the heavy use of cocaine may have impaired short-term memory. It could be that the cocaine user is not able to remember the choices being made at the start of the experiment. The deficit may thus not be specific to insight, but instead be indicative of widespread memory problems. In addition, individuals who are cocaine users may be different on a variety of characteristics compared to controls. The groups need to be matched as much as possible on educational attainment, intelligence, and general health, since these factors might also contribute to insight.
3. Researchers are always cautious when interpreting the results of one study. The findings from this one experiment using only one insight task are not sufficient to draw

global conclusions about insight deficits in cocaine addicts. Further, the participants in this study were presented with cocaine pictures, which may have impacted insight. It might be revealing to replicate these findings with no drug-related pictures. Such a replication would be an illustration that research is iterative, with incremental processes for acquiring knowledge about a problem. If science coming from other laboratories, using differing methodologies, leads to similar conclusions, the scientific community gains confidence in specific claims such as whether cocaine addicts have insight deficits.

Tolerance, Sensitization, Dependence, and Withdrawal

Tolerance

Tolerance refers to an increased amount of drug needed to achieve a certain effect, or alternatively it refers to the diminished drug effect with continued use (APA, 2000). Most experienced users of cocaine report requiring more cocaine over time to achieve euphoria (O'Brien, 2001). Tolerance also develops to the behavioral and cognitive impairments observed following cocaine administration, with less impairment occurring with subsequent drug administration sessions (Weaver, Dallery, & Branch, 2010). One study illustrated this tolerance development. Rhesus monkeys self-administered cocaine and initially displayed cognitive impairments following the drug administration. With repeated administration of cocaine over several sessions, tolerance developed and impairments diminished (Gould et al., 2012).

Cocaine is interesting because the development of **acute tolerance** (functional tolerance that has developed within the course of a single administration session) tends to be more pronounced relative to other forms of tolerance (see Chapter 3 for a review of the different types of tolerance). With cocaine, acute tolerance is reliably observed when cocaine is administered in a binge fashion. For example, the acute effects of cocaine are more pronounced with the first administration and reduced by the second administration, even if the second administration occurs shortly after the first. Researchers have attempted to mimic the binge administration of cocaine in the laboratory, by giving participants cocaine several times over several hours during a single session. Using this approach, researchers have found evidence of acute tolerance, such as the self-reported euphoric effect (or "high") diminishing over time despite constant plasma cocaine levels (Ambre et al., 1988). This observation confirms anecdotal reports of users stating they increasingly use more cocaine to achieve a high, but they are not able to achieve the same intense high that was experienced with the first drug administration at the start of a binge. The development of acute tolerance is problematic, since individuals will use more and more drug, with the use of escalating doses a strong contributing factor leading to addiction or possible overdose.

Sensitization

Researchers have also observed that repeating cocaine treatments results in **sensitization**. Sensitization can be thought of as reverse tolerance, with repeated administration of a drug resulting in greater sensitivity to the effects of the drug. For example, cocaine is known to increase locomotor activity. When cocaine is administered on multiple test days to animals, increased locomotor activity is observed across dose sessions even when the dose is kept the same (Polston et al., 2006). Sensitization has also been observed in cardiovascular responses. Both heart rate and blood pressure may be more elevated after many cocaine administration sessions, relative to earlier dose sessions. Since the dose is kept the same, this indicates that the body is reacting more strongly to the drug with more experience with the drug (Kollins & Rush, 2002; Walsh et al., 2009). Sensitization is also observed for subjective reactions, such as feeling jittery and stimulated (Walsh et al., 2009). However, it does not appear that "feeling high" is a subjective change that can be sensitized (Kollins & Rush, 2002). Finally, sensitization may partly explain the addictive properties of cocaine and other psychoactive drugs (Robinson & Berridge, 1993, 2003) (see Chapter 3 for a review of the incentive sensitization theory of addiction).

Physical Dependence and Withdrawal

Regular cocaine use leads to physical dependence, particularly when the drug is administered by the inhalation or injection route of administration. One simple way to assess physical dependence is to stop drug administration and observe the development of withdrawal symptoms. Typical withdrawal symptoms for cocaine users include dysphoric mood (depression), changes in appetite, fatigue, vivid and/or unpleasant dreams, increased or decreased psychomotor activity, sleepiness, bradycardia (heart rate that is too slow), and cocaine craving (O'Brien, 2001; Walsh et al., 2009). The intensity of these symptoms is most observable upon drug withdrawal, with the symptoms dissipating over time. Based on interviews of patients in treatment programs, a model of cocaine withdrawal has been developed having three distinct phases, known as crash, withdrawal, and extinction (Gawin & Kleber, 1985). The crash occurs within hours after cessation of cocaine use and is strongly characterized by depression, irritability, and fatigue. Withdrawal occurs between one and ten weeks after cessation of use and is characterized by milder symptoms accompanied by craving for cocaine. Extinction is thought to last indefinitely and is characterized as recurrent desire or craving for cocaine.

Researchers have endeavored to better understand cocaine withdrawal since withdrawal symptoms not only are unpleasant but also may interfere with successful attempts to quit or cut down using cocaine. From both anecdotal reports and laboratory-based research, users typically report that the crash phase is very aversive. Researchers have found that the development of symptoms during the crash phase coincide with declining cocaine levels in the body. For example, one study recruited nine subjects who were regular crack cocaine users and had no current intention to seek treatment. The individuals agreed to reside in an inpatient research ward in a hospital for 40 days with differing doses of cocaine being administered on different days. The researchers observed that participant ratings of crashing rise as the cocaine levels in plasma drop (Walsh et al., 2009).

While withdrawal from cocaine can be unpleasant, the symptoms are of modest severity and fairly benign, especially compared to the withdrawal symptoms that occur with psychoactive drugs such as heroin and alcohol. While the individual may feel depression, fatigue, and craving for the drug, the most unpleasant symptoms typically occur in the first 24 hours after cessation of cocaine use. Moreover, there is nothing life-threatening about these withdrawal symptoms. The evidence suggests that biological or mood disruptions associated with withdrawal of cocaine are limited in scope and dissipate somewhat rapidly (Dudish-Poulsen & Hatsukami, 2000; Walsh et al., 2009). These findings indicate that cessation of cocaine use and abuse may be easier than quitting other psychoactive drugs. However, these findings may also reflect the typical administration patterns of cocaine users, with binge use being more likely than chronic steady use. Nevertheless, it should be clarified that many users still find it extremely difficult to quit using cocaine, despite strong intentions to do so. In addition, it should not be forgotten that the route of administration matters, since route of administration coincides with the intensity of the physical dependence that develops. Users who smoke crack or inject cocaine are going to have a much harder time than intranasal users in dealing with withdrawal symptoms. Finally, users of cocaine also tend to use other drugs, including alcohol or heroin. Thus, withdrawal symptoms from cocaine may be intermingled with withdrawal symptoms from other drugs, too.

Myth Busters: A Relapse Means That Treatment Failed

Many people who use drugs such as cocaine might eventually end up in treatment, whether voluntarily or mandated by the courts. The goal of treatment programs in the United States is abstinence, since cocaine is an illicit drug. Thus, an individual is deemed successful when he or she no longer uses the drug. It is common for many users to successfully complete the treatment and go home. However, relapses are also common. Does this mean that treatment failed? The notion that a relapse means that treatment failed is certainly a myth. Clinicians who work in treatment programs know that relapses are part of the process of recovery. Falling off the wagon, so to speak, does not mean that all the successes that have been gained in treatment have been lost. Moreover, the longer an individual can go between relapses, the healthier that individual is becoming. Think of the many health risks that accompany the use of cocaine. Reducing use causes those risks to decline. With any period of abstinence from cocaine, the brain and cardiovascular system can begin to recover. Tolerance for the drug declines. Periods of abstinence also allow individuals to think more clearly and in a more long-term manner. Repair of social relationships and developing plans to support oneself with a job are only possible if a person is not moving from one drug hit to the next. Treatment programs emphasize the development of skills to address drug cravings and handle stress. If drug use begins again, for whatever reason, the individual can hopefully limit this period of restarted use by relying on the help received in treatment or at least identify that more treatment should be sought. A comparison with other psychological disorders should clarify this point. Consider a depressed person who has received treatment for his depression. If the person is well for a year but then gets depressed again, we would not think that treatment failed this person. The individual was healthy for a whole year! However, the illness has recurred and more help might be needed. One benefit of being successful in treatment (even if success was time-limited) is that the individual knows that treatment works. Persistence is the key to ultimate success in battling cocaine addiction or any other drug addiction.

Pharmacology of Cocaine

Sites of Action

In this chapter, we have discussed how cocaine acts in the body. Now we turn our attention to the site of action for cocaine in the brain. Cocaine as a chemical resembles the naturally occurring neurotransmitter **dopamine** (DA). Dopamine is a widespread neurotransmitter involved in the regulation of movement, emotion, cognition, motivation, and feelings of pleasure. Dopamine is important for those rewarding feelings that we experience when we eat tasty food or engage in sexual activity. Under normal circumstances, dopamine is released by the presynaptic neuron into the synaptic gap. When dopamine reaches the postsynaptic neuron, dopamine binds with a dopamine receptor that may result in an action potential being sent. After binding, dopamine is released back into the synaptic gap where a **dopamine transporter** on the presynaptic neuron will bind it so that it can be recycled for another use. A dopamine transporter (also called dopamine active transporter or DAT) is a membrane-spanning protein that pumps dopamine out of the synapse and back into the presynaptic neuron for storage and later release. When cocaine is administered, an increase in the amount of dopamine activity is observed. How does cocaine increase dopamine activity? Cocaine blocks the dopamine transporter, thus slowing the removal of dopamine from the synapse (Figure 6-9). This results in an accumulation of dopamine in the synapse. In other words, cocaine blocks the normal process of recycling dopamine that would have

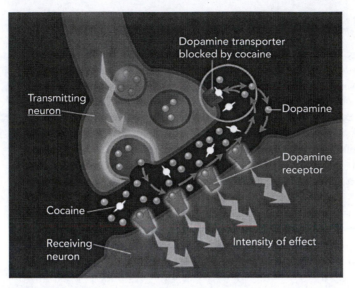

FIGURE 6-9
Cocaine blocks the dopamine transporter, which prevents dopamine from being recycled. This action increases the amount of dopamine available in the synapse, thus amplifying the signal.

occurred after postsynaptic binding. This change leaves more available dopamine in the synapse, amplifying the dopamine signal to the postsynaptic (receiving) neurons. Greater availability of dopamine accounts for the high or euphoria experienced by users (Kitty, Lorang, & Amara, 1991). In addition to subjective feelings of euphoria, elevated dopamine levels also account for the increases in behavioral activity observed with cocaine administration (NIDA, 2010a,b).

How much of the dopamine signal is amplified when cocaine is administered? One technique to address this question is **in vivo microdialysis**, in which a tiny probe (designed to mimic a blood capillary) is placed in the brain at a location of interest. Using the probe, extracellular fluid is collected and analyzed for the presence of various neurotransmitters. For psychoactive drug research, the nucleus accumbens might be one brain area to sample as it is an important part of the mesolimbic dopaminergic pathway (the addiction pathway in the brain). Since this technique is minimally invasive, a freely moving rat can be given a drug and the brain response assessed. In one study, when 10 mg/kg cocaine was administered to rats, dopamine in the nucleus accumbens increased to levels 4 times that of control animals. That is a lot of extra dopamine!

In addition to its effect on dopamine, cocaine also blocks both norepinephrine (NE) and serotonin (5-HT) reuptake (O'Brien, 2001). Recall that dopamine belongs to a family of neurotransmitters known as the monoamines. Norepinephrine and serotonin are monoamines, just like dopamine, since each of these neurotransmitters has a chemical structure that includes a single amine group. When monoamine levels are elevated as a result of cocaine use, the individual feels alert and energetic. If cocaine is used repeatedly, these drug-induced increases in monoamine activity are noticed by the body. The body adjusts to these elevated monoamine levels by producing less monoamines, in an effort to return the brain to a homeostatic balance. Deficient production of monoamines means that when cocaine is no longer administered, an imbalance will be present. One major symptom of this imbalance is depression, sometimes referred to as the "cocaine blues" (not to be confused with Johnny Cash's famous song). The depressed cocaine user will not feel normal again unless they take the drug. These effects on the brain make stopping cocaine use challenging. Fortunately, as an individual continues to abstain from the drug, the body slowly begins to elevate monoamine levels over time. Equilibrium can thus eventually be regained (Julien, 2005; NIDA, 2010a). In addition to the monoamines, cocaine also has widespread effects on other neurotransmitter systems. For example, repeated exposure to cocaine leads to dramatic changes in glutamate transmission in the nucleus accumbens of the brain (Schmidt & Pierce, 2010). Also, adenosine's modulation of dopamine activity that is increased by cocaine administration (Wells et al., 2012).

Pharmacokinetics

Pharmacokinetics refers to the absorption, distribution, biotransformation, and excretion of drugs. For cocaine, various routes of administration can be used to bring the drug into the body, as was described earlier in the chapter. Once in the bloodstream, cocaine quickly reaches the blood–brain barrier, from which cocaine penetrates the brain rapidly and easily. Metabolism of cocaine is rapid due to enzymes located in the liver and in blood plasma. As a result, cocaine has a half-life of approximately 40 minutes (Javid, Musa, Fischman, Schuster, & Davis, 1983). A urine test can identify cocaine use for approximately one to three days among sporadic users or up to 12 days for chronic users (Center for Substance Abuse Treatment, 2005; Julien, 2005).

When pregnant women use cocaine, the drug freely crosses the placental barrier such that the unborn baby experiences the drug at levels equal to those in the mother (De Giovanni & Marchetti, 2012). The use of cocaine during pregnancy is risky. Higher rates of miscarriage (20 weeks of pregnancy or earlier) and fetal death (20+ weeks of pregnancy) occur in a cocaine-using mother. At birth, infants of cocaine-using mothers are likely to be born early and/or have low birth weights (Gouin, Murphy, Shah, & Knowledge Synthesis Group on Determinants of Low Birth Weight and Preterm Births, 2011). In the majority of cases, maternal cocaine use during pregnancy is associated with a variety of other medical and lifestyle concerns that are detrimental to fetal and infant development. Fortunately, the long-term prognosis for children prenatally exposed to cocaine is good, particularly if the child grows up in a favorable and supportive environment (Singer, Garber, & Kliegman, 1991; Zuckerman, Frank, & Mayes, 2002).

In the News:

Kirkey, S. (2012, October 22). Stroke cures man of cocaine addiction, researchers report. *Vancouver Sun.*

This news story reports the curious case of a Canadian man who was apparently cured of his cocaine addiction following a stroke. The 45-year-old man had been addicted to cocaine for over two decades. His addiction was significant, as he was injecting or snorting up to seven grams of cocaine a day at the time of his stroke. The stroke affected the basal ganglia, a large cluster of nerve cells located deep in the brain that receives dopamine. After the stroke, the man reported no further craving for cocaine. While the man did experience some temporary paralysis on his right side, he recovered rapidly from this condition. No lingering deficits remain except for abnormally small handwriting (known as micrographia). In essence, he was cured of his addiction to cocaine because of a stroke. This is believed to be the first reported case of cocaine addiction "cured" by a stroke.

Use this news article to test and apply your knowledge:

1. Is it likely that the man had a stroke because of his cocaine addiction?
2. Does this report suggest that we have found a cure for cocaine addiction by just blocking off the blood supply to the basal ganglia?

Answers:

1. Yes, it is highly likely that the stroke occurred because of his chronic cocaine use. Cocaine causes vasoconstriction in blood vessels throughout the body. Arteries with or without coronary artery disease (clogged arteries) will constrict repeatedly when cocaine is used. This increases the likelihood that a blockage will occur in the heart or brain, resulting in a myocardial infarction or stroke, respectively. Cocaine also

increases blood pressure and heart rate, adding to the likelihood of a problem when arteries are already constricted.

2. To claim that a cure has been found would be premature. Although an individual case report may provide clues as to how a problem like cocaine addiction could be addressed, a variety of other factors may have played a role in this individual's outcome. Moreover, dopamine is important for several other areas of biological functioning. It would be interesting to know if the man had experienced other side effects related to motor functioning, emotional processing, cognitive processing, motivation, or feelings of pleasure. Laboratory research using animals may provide clues about whether this one observation leads to changes in how cocaine addiction is viewed.

Treatment for Cocaine Addiction

To say that quitting cocaine is difficult would be a vast understatement. The benefits from stopping use of cocaine are clear. Overall physical and mental health improve. With abstinence, the brain has the ability to recover from cocaine abuse, ranging from recovery of some cognitive deficits to a return to more normal levels of dopamine, serotonin, and norepinephrine (Gould et al., 2012). In addition, the likelihood of having difficulties with the law decrease and social relationships improve. Individuals have several options when seeking treatment, including both behavioral and pharmacological treatments. It is most common for formal treatment programs to provide both behavioral and pharmacological treatments to individuals who are seeking help for their cocaine addiction.

Behavioral Treatments

Behavioral treatments involve working with a therapist (psychologist, psychiatrist, social worker, or substance abuse counselor) so that the individual can develop coping skills that decrease cocaine use and prevent relapse. Cognitive-behavioral therapy has been shown to be particularly effective in changing behavior and modifying depressive thinking that occurs with cocaine withdrawal. Moreover, treatments that are tailored to individual needs optimize results. These treatments include a combination of therapy, increasing social support, stress management, better nutrition, and other services. In many cases, residential treatment programs can be helpful since the individual can focus entirely on getting well. Unfortunately, there are significant costs associated with a residential treatment setting. Overall, behavioral treatments may not be specific to cocaine alone, since many users have difficulties with other drugs as well (NIDA, 2010a).

Pharmacological Treatments

Given the worldwide prevalence of cocaine use disorders, drug treatments have been sought to help users, though there are currently no FDA-approved medications specifically to treat cocaine addiction. Researchers are actively investigating potential strategies that might help, such as agonist replacement therapy. Agonist replacement therapy treats the user with a drug similar to the drug of abuse, though the replacement drug is hopefully less harmful. Transporter blockers (such as the ADHD medication methylphenidate) and releasers (such as amphetamine analogs) are available for use. One promising drug that has received attention is modafinil, which increases the level of monoamines in the brain. While FDA-approved for other medical conditions such as sleep disorders (since it promotes wakefulness), the lack of compelling outcomes with cocaine users make the viability of modafinil uncertain. However, monoamine levels are low in cocaine addicts, making modafinil a promising drug treatment possibility. Of course, two questions that must be asked when applying agonist replacement therapy are: (1) will less abuse of the replacement drug occur relative to cocaine, and (2) what are the risks that the treatment will be diverted and used by others as a drug of abuse (Rush & Stoops, 2012)?

Researchers are also examining drug treatments that could help with cocaine craving and addiction by modulating glutamate transmission. There is a growing literature suggesting that repeated exposure to cocaine leads to dramatic changes in glutamate transmission in the nucleus accumbens of the brain. In the future, glutamate modulators may be used in the treatment of cocaine addiction (Schmidt & Pierce, 2010). Vaccines are also being investigated as a potential option. A vaccine would prevent cocaine in the bloodstream from crossing the blood–brain barrier and reaching the brain (NIDA, 2010a). While all these approaches hold promise, they are solutions for the future. Today, pharmacological treatments for cocaine addiction emphasize reduction in the intensity of withdrawal symptoms. In most cases, individuals report depression upon cessation of use of cocaine. Antidepressants can be helpful in mitigating these symptoms, so that individuals can focus on behavioral treatments for those skills (such as managing stress and avoiding relapse triggers) that will help them be successful at abstaining from future use (Kampman, 2010).

QUICK QUIZ 6-2

1. The typical acute effects of cocaine result in _____.
   a. Alertness and arousal
   b. Sedation and sleepiness
   c. Little change in arousal
   d. None of the above

2. The inhalation or injection routes of administration for cocaine result in _____ subjective effects, as compared to intranasal administration.
   a. less intense
   b. more intense
   c. about the same
   d. None of the above

3. Activation in which of the following brain areas correlate most strongly with cocaine-induced craving?
   a. Hippocampus
   b. Prefrontal cortex
   c. Nucleus accumbens
   d. A and B

4. Cocaine stimulates the _____.
   a. sympathetic nervous system
   b. parasympathetic nervous system
   c. fight-or-flight response
   d. A and C

5. When alcohol and cocaine are taken together, a new metabolite is formed called _____.
   a. cocaethanol
   b. cocaethylene
   c. alcococaine
   d. ethylcocaine

6. Repeated use of cocaine results in _____.
   a. tolerance
   b. sensitization
   c. no change
   d. A and B

7. Describe stimulant psychosis.

8. How is addiction to cocaine typically treated today in formal treatment programs?

ANSWERS TO QUICK QUIZ 6-2:

1. a – alertness and arousal
2. b – more intense
3. d – A and B
4. d – A and C
5. b – cocaethylene
6. d – A and B

7. Stimulant psychosis arises when blood levels of cocaine become very high, with the user becoming paranoid, irrational, and hostile. The user may report delusions (false beliefs) or hallucinations (false perceptions). Violence is major concern with stimulant psychosis.

8. The treatment of cocaine addiction often involves both behavioral and pharmacological treatment. Behavioral treatments involve working with a therapist to develop coping skills to deal with drug cravings and feelings of depression. Cognitive-behavioral therapy has been shown to be a very effective behavioral treatment. Pharmacological treatments are used to reduce the intensity of withdrawal symptoms. For example, antidepressants can be helpful in mitigating depression so that individuals can focus more effectively in counseling. There is no FDA-approved medication right now that specifically treats cocaine addiction.

CHAPTER SUMMARY

Cocaine is a stimulant drug originating from the coca plant that grows in South American countries. Cocaine's use stretches from ancient times, when coca leaves were chewed, to the present day. The use of cocaine, both powder and crack, has remained relatively stable over the past decade after declining from the high levels seen in the 1980s. Intranasal, inhalation, and injection routes of administration are typically used for cocaine. Cocaine is currently a Schedule II drug, since it has a legitimate medical use as a local anesthetic. Cocaine stimulates activity of the sympathetic nervous system, resulting in typical effects such as increased blood pressure and heart rate. Increased alertness, arousal, and motor activity are observed with cocaine use. Stimulant psychosis may emerge with high doses of cocaine. A variety of health risks are associated with cocaine use, particularly when the drug is used chronically. Myocardial infarctions, strokes, crack lung, and risk of death are among these health concerns. Both tolerance and sensitization are reliably observed with cocaine. Physical dependence can occur with cocaine, which is evident when cocaine is withdrawn and withdrawal symptoms, such as depression and drug craving, emerge. While unpleasant, these withdrawal symptoms are not life-threatening and are most problematic for the first 24 hours after cessation of cocaine use. Cocaine acts in the brain by blocking dopamine transporters, thus increasing the level of dopamine activity. Cocaine is a fast-acting drug with a half-life of approximately 40 minutes. When pregnant women use cocaine, the drug freely crosses the placental barrier and exposes the unborn baby to the drug at levels equal to those in the mother. Both behavioral and pharmacological treatments are used to treat cocaine addiction, although there is currently no FDA-approved medication specifically to treat cocaine addiction.

AMPHETAMINES

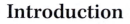

Introduction

Amphetamines are psychoactive stimulant drugs that are used and abused as recreational drugs. Amphetamines are also used therapeutically to treat individuals diagnosed with attention deficit/hyperactivity disorder (ADHD). When used appropriately, amphetamines are helpful in reducing symptoms of ADHD, such as the inability to stay focused, restlessness, overactivity, and impulsivity. Therein lays the paradox of amphetamines. As psychoactive drugs, they can be incredibly helpful and also incredibly harmful. For those with ADHD, the symptoms of the disorder can be extremely problematic. Untreated ADHD can make successful performance in school or work difficult or nearly impossible for children or adults. When properly treated with medications such as amphetamines, children and adults with ADHD often thrive. However, these very same medications are often diverted to individuals who have no medical reason for their use (NIDA, 2009). In addition, amphetamines are synthetically produced on the street. As street drugs, they have effects similar to cocaine. The risks of abuse of amphetamines are very high when used as methamphetamine, a highly addictive drug that causes substantial damage to the body (NIDA, 2006, 2010c). In this chapter, we will also discuss synthetic cathinones that are the latest amphetamine-type drugs to emerge on the street (DEA, 2012a; NIDA, 2011b). While typically known by users as bath salts, these drugs are more dangerous than suggested by their benign name. Bizarre behavior, homicides, and sudden deaths following seizures and high fever have been associated with use of bath salts (Forrester, 2012). In one recent case in Florida, Jairious McGhee, a 23-year-old caterer with no criminal record, had recently ingested bath salts when he ran through a busy intersection in the city of Tampa. Bystanders reported that McGhee was screaming rap lyrics and appeared clearly psychotic and out of touch with reality. A police officer used a taser on McGhee, with little effect. He was tased several times and fought with paramedics. His heart stopped five times before he eventually died (Vander Velde, 2012).

In this chapter, we will examine amphetamines, a class of psychoactive drugs with stimulant effects that range considerably based on type of use, whether therapeutically or as drugs of abuse. We will answer questions associated with amphetamines (Figure 7-1). What are the different kinds of amphetamines? How are amphetamines helpful to individuals who are diagnosed with ADHD? What are the effects of amphetamines on recreational users? What are the health effects of chronic use, and how do these health effects differ depending on the type of amphetamine and reason for use? What are the most effective treatment approaches for individuals with ADHD and for individuals who abuse amphetamines? How is law enforcement dealing with amphetamines, particularly since clandestine laboratories are coming up with new versions of amphetamines? Let us explore these and many other questions about amphetamines.

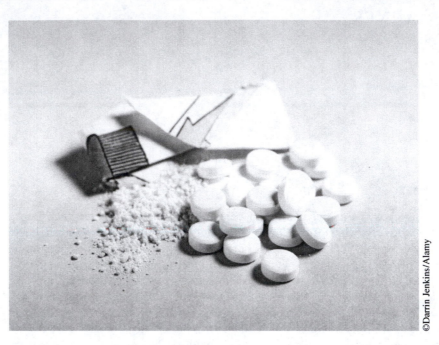

©Darrin Jenkins/Alamy

FIGURE 7-1
Amphetamines.

LEARNING OBJECTIVES

Learning objectives can help organize your studying. Before we begin the topic of amphetamines, keep in mind that by the end of this chapter, you should be able to . . .

1. Describe the various types of amphetamines, ranging from legitimate psycho-therapeutic drugs to illicit drugs of abuse.
2. Describe the various routes of administration for amphetamines.
3. Explain the brief history of where amphetamines came from and how long they have been available for use.
4. Describe the current drug laws pertaining to amphetamines in the United States.
5. Describe the prevalence of amphetamine use in the United States and around the world.
6. Explain how amphetamines act as stimulants in the central nervous system and how the acute effects differ depending on whether amphetamines are used therapeutically or recreationally.
7. Describe tolerance, sensitization, dependence, and withdrawal processes associated with amphetamine use.
8. Describe how amphetamines act in the brain and for how long.
9. Describe the various treatment approaches that are used to manage ADHD and to treat amphetamine addiction.

Types of Amphetamines

Amphetamines ($C_9H_{13}N$) are a class of powerful central nervous system **stimulant** drugs. Stimulant drugs increase alertness, decrease fatigue, decrease appetite, and heighten mood. Amphetamines result in similar changes to the brain as cocaine (covered in the previous chapter), though amphetamines typically have longer-lasting effects. Amphetamines are used therapeutically to treat various medical conditions. While the therapeutic use of amphetamines is appropriate in the majority of cases, amphetamines are also diverted for recreational use or performance enhancement by individuals who have no medically diagnosed reason to use them. The line between therapy and illicit use can be murky, as illustrated by the recent spate of National Football League (NFL) suspensions of players using Adderall® without a prescription (McNally, 2013). Amphetamines are also street drugs that are used illicitly and abused. Amphetamines are typically found in pill form or appear as a white, odorless, bitter crystalline powder or rock crystal. Whether use is medically warranted or illicit, amphetamines are produced synthetically. All of the amphetamines described in this chapter, both therapeutic and illicit, are made in a laboratory. This is in contrast with other stimulant drugs, which have their origins in plant sources (caffeine, nicotine, and cocaine).

Therapeutic Use

While many of us have difficulty paying attention or feel a little hyperactive from time to time, some children and adults struggle with these symptoms continuously. When inattention and/or hyperactivity is persistent (that is, more frequently displayed and more severe than typically observed in age-matched peers), a diagnosis of **attention deficit hyperactivity disorder (ADHD)** may be made. ADHD is typically diagnosed in preschool or in the early elementary years. For many, ADHD symptoms improve with age, although a subset of children become adults still experiencing symptoms. Fortunately, prescription amphetamines are helpful in mitigating ADHD symptoms. With medication, children are often better able to focus in class, with grades subsequently improving. There are several medications available, with the preferred choice often determined by trial and error. For some patients, the most effective drug is Adderall®, a mix of amphetamine ($C_9H_{13}N$) salts (Figure 7-2). For others, methylphenidate ($C_{14}H_{19}NO_2$) is more effective. Methylphenidate is sold as Ritalin® and Concerta®, a longer-acting version of the drug. Methylphenidate is the most commonly used stimulant treatment for ADHD. Other brand-name medications that contain or metabolize into amphetamines include Dexedrine®, Dextrostat®, Desoxyn®, Didrex®, ProCentra®, and Vyvanse®. Later in this chapter, we will discuss the paradox of why an individual who lacks focus and is hyperactive may be calmed and more focused after stimulant administration. While amphetamines are used medically to treat ADHD, they have other uses as well. For example, amphetamines are effective in treating **narcolepsy**, a chronic sleep disorder characterized by excessive sleepiness and falling asleep at inappropriate times (such as falling asleep at work). In addition, amphetamines are used in the short-term treatment of morbid obesity (NIDA, 2009).

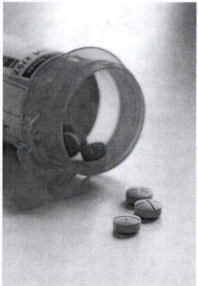

©Getty Images/Photo Researchers RM

FIGURE 7-2
Adderall® is a psychotherapeutic drug used to treat attention deficit/hyperactivity disorder (ADHD). It consists of a mix of amphetamine salts.

Illicit Use

The illicit use of amphetamines comes in two forms. First, medications such as Adderall®, Ritalin®, and Concerta® may be used by individuals who have no legitimate medical reason to do so. **Drug diversion** is the term the U.S. Drug Enforcement Administration (DEA) uses for the recreational consumption of legitimately prescribed medication. When diverted, amphetamines can be used to improve performance as a cognitive enhancer, or they can lead to feeling high or euphoric. On college campuses, drug diversion of ADHD medications is a serious concern, one which will be discussed in greater detail later in this chapter.

In addition to diverted prescription medications, there are a variety of amphetamine variants found on the street. Amphetamine ($C_9H_{13}N$) has two stereoisomers. **Stereoisomers** are molecules having a similar molecular formula and sequence of bonded atoms but different three-dimensional orientation of their atoms. The two stereoisomers for amphetamine are dextroamphetamine (*d*-amphetamine) and levoamphetamine (*l*-amphetamine), which are mirror images of one another. The *l*-form is less impactful in the central nervous system, but it has stronger cardiovascular effects. The *d*-form (dextroamphetamine) is used more commonly to feel euphoric or high, but both versions are used illicitly and are found in street amphetamine. An equal proportion of the *d* and *l* forms is referred to as a **racemic mixture**. In many cases, a user may not know whether *d*-amphetamine, *l*-amphetamine, or the racemic mixture is being ingested. Interestingly, the mechanism of action for methylphenidate, the drug most widely used to treat ADHD, is similar to *d*-amphetamine. In this chapter, a common theme will be that the amphetamines used therapeutically and illicitly are the same drugs, though the doses and motivations for use are dramatically different. When used illicitly, amphetamines are sometimes referred to as speed or uppers (Sagvolden & Xu, 2008; Yang, Atkins, & Dafny, 2011).

Methamphetamine ($C_{10}H_{15}N$) is another amphetamine drug structurally similar to $C_9H_{13}N$ amphetamine. Referred to as crank, crystal, crystal meth, ice, and speed on the street, it has a significant potential for abuse since users experience an intense high after use, particularly when smoked or injected. This intense high is followed by a similarly intense and aversive crash, leading to the user wanting another dose of drug. Thus, methamphetamine is thought of as being potentially very addictive. Just like amphetamine, methamphetamine has two stereoisomers (*d* and *l*). When *d*-methamphetamine is used, it results in more potent physiological and behavioral effects than a similar dose of *l*-methamphetamine. Abuse potential is also higher for *d*-methamphetamine since it is the more potent dopamine releaser, as will be explained in greater detail later in this chapter. Samples obtained by law enforcement in 2010 revealed that approximately 62% of abused methamphetamine was *d*-methamphetamine only, with 25% being the racemic mixture of methamphetamine and the remaining 13% being *l*-methamphetamine (Maxwell & Brecht, 2011).

Methamphetamine looks like a pill or powder, whereas crystal methamphetamine resembles glass fragments or shiny blue-white rocks (Figure 7-3). Methamphetamine can smell like ammonia, cat urine, or even burning plastic. The recent rise in methamphetamine use has been due in part to the ease with which ordinary household products and cold medications can be used to make the drug. The acute and chronic effects of methamphetamine can result in serious damage to the body and brain. Compared to amphetamine, higher levels of methamphetamine reach the brain. Thus, methamphetamine is a more potent stimulant drug than amphetamine. Excluding diverted amphetamines, methamphetamine represented 95% of the amphetamines found on the street in the year 2010. While methamphetamine is typically used illicitly, there is a legitimate medical use for it in the treatment of morbid obesity (DEA, 2011, 2012a; Maxwell & Brecht, 2011; NIDA, 2010c; Salter, 2012).

Finally, **cathinones** ($C_9H_{11}NO$) are synthetic amphetamine-like chemicals that are more commonly referred to as **bath salts**. Street names like Cloud 9 and Bliss make bath salts seem benign, but bath salts are potent stimulants causing serious health problems. The key psychoactive ingredients in bath salts, cathinones, occur in nature as an alkaloid in the leaves of the khat plant, *Catha edulis*. This plant grows in East Africa and the Arab Peninsula. The leaves of this

©DEA

FIGURE 7-3
Crystal methamphetamine.

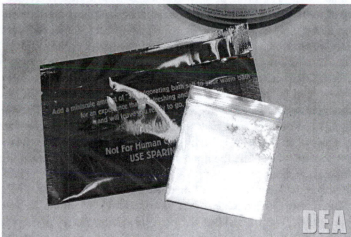

©DEA

FIGURE 7-4
Bath salts (designer cathinones).

plant have psychoactive chemicals including cathine and cathinone, which are structurally similar to but less potent than amphetamines (Kalix, 1981; Kelly, 2011). When people chew the leaves of this plant, they are using the stimulant drug **khat**. The use of khat is uncommon in North America, since the leaves must be fresh when chewed to achieve stimulant effects. However, cathinone is used in several synthetic forms in the United States. Indeed, there is an ever-expanding pool of designer cathinones being developed in clandestine laboratories. Chemicals such as methcathinone, mephedrone, MDPV (3-4 methylene-dioxyprovalerone), and methylone are common. Methcathinone ($C_{10}H_{13}NO$) in particular appears to be highly addictive, much like methamphetamine. Bath salts are found typically in tablet/capsule form or as a fine white or slightly yellow-colored powder (Figure 7-4) (DEA, 2012b; NIDA, 2011b). Many cases of toxicity or sudden death have been associated with bath salt use. There are no legitimate medical uses for cathinones (Kelly, 2011).

Routes of Administration

The route of administration for amphetamines depends on how the drug is used. Several common routes of administration for amphetamines include oral, intranasal, inhalation, and injection. When used as a legitimate medical treatment for ADHD, narcolepsy, or extreme obesity, amphetamines are administered orally as pills or capsules. Recall that the oral route of administration results in a slow onset, limited intensity, and lengthy duration of effect. All of these properties are a result of the drug needing to pass the digestive system before being absorbed into the bloodstream, the ultimate path for the drug to reach the brain. Thus, oral administration is ideal for the therapeutic use of amphetamines. For example, a child diagnosed with ADHD exhibits chronic and consistent deficits in the ability to pay attention and/or control his or her behavior in school. A medication that works for up to 6 hours will be effective in helping the child keep symptoms in check for the duration of the school day.

The recreational use of amphetamines, either for performance enhancement or for the high, also can occur via the oral route of administration. In addition, intranasal administration may be used, when amphetamines are snorted in powder form. In some cases, diverted pharmaceutical drugs are crushed in order to be administered intranasally. As street drugs, amphetamines are also commonly ingested intranasally, including baths salts (designer cathinones). For subjective responses and likelihood to produce dependence, the type of amphetamine seems to matter less than the route of administration. One study had methamphetamine users snort doses of methamphetamine and d-amphetamine. There were no significant differences between the two types of amphetamines on the majority of measures collected by the researchers, including amphetamine plasma levels, cardiovascular, mood, and psychomotor performance effects. However, methamphetamine produces a slightly increased heart rate more and greater ratings of feeling high than d-amphetamine (Kirkpatrick et al., 2012a,b).

With methamphetamine, inhalation (smoking) is a common route of administration. The crystal form of methamphetamine is suitable for vapor inhalation, which results in rapid absorption of the drug into the bloodstream from the lungs. In the last chapter, it was discussed that crack is cocaine in a form that can be smoked. Crack leads to a pronounced high associated with abuse and dependence, more so than intranasal administration of cocaine. The same is true with methamphetamine. When crystallized methamphetamine hydrochloride (referred to as ice by users) is smoked, it results in pronounced highs and significant problems with abuse and dependence. It has been reported that the bioavailability of methamphetamine is up to 90% when smoked, while the bioavailability of methamphetamine is 79% when the route of administration is intranasal (Cruickshank & Dyer, 2009). Over the last decade, users have increasingly preferred to smoke crystal methamphetamine, rather than inhale or inject powdered methamphetamine (Maxwell & Brecht, 2011). Cost may be an additional factor in these trends, since crystal methamphetamine can be cheaper than powder methamphetamine, much like crack became more popular than powder cocaine in the 1980s due to crack's lower cost.

Amphetamines of all types, including bath salts, can also be injected. If this is the case, amphetamines will be put into a solution that can be injected into a vein using a syringe. Amphetamines are typically dissolved in water or alcohol. Injection of amphetamines is the route of administration associated with very high rates of abuse and dependence, as well as co-occurring physical and psychological problems (Novak & Kral, 2011). Users of methamphetamine who partake in a binge (also called a run), typically inject up to a gram of methamphetamine every two or three hours over several days. The user continues using, without sleeping or eating, until he or she runs out of methamphetamine or becomes too disorganized and confused to continue (NIDA, 2010d). Additionally, injecting any drug of abuse is fraught with a variety of health risks. HIV and other infectious diseases spread when contaminated syringes or needles are reused. Vein damage is common as well (NIDA, 2006).

Brief History of Amphetamine Use

Amphetamines are synthetic (laboratory-produced) psychoactive drugs. However, the history of amphetamines goes back to plants of the genus *Ephedra*, used in Chinese medicine for millennia to help treat breathing problems associated with asthma. In the 1920s, scientists at the Eli Lilly

Company identified the chemical ephedrine as the active plant ingredient that dilated bronchioles, making breathing easier for those with asthma. **Ephedrine** is an alkaloid that has a similar structure to amphetamines and methamphetamine. Once ephedrine was isolated, it quickly became widely used. Scientists extracted ephedrine from plants, though the supply from plants was limited. Researchers thus worked on producing synthetic ephedrine in the laboratory, but they were initially unsuccessful. One researcher working on this problem was Gordon Alles, a young chemist living in Los Angeles. In one attempt to synthesize ephedrine in 1929, he actually synthesized amphetamine. Typical of the time, Alles tried out his new drug on himself. He took 50 mg (a dose five times what would be the standard dose once the drug was medically approved eight years later). That dose made his blood pressure go up sharply (it reached 164/96, a clear change from his baseline of 130/78). However, he was optimistic about this new chemical because his nose felt clear (a desired outcome since he was hoping to develop a new allergy medication). He also reported feeling in good spirits and having difficulty sleeping that night. Thus began the age of speed. News of Alles's discovery spread quickly. As Alles had found, further laboratory experiments demonstrated that amphetamine was effective in dilating bronchioles, just like ephedrine. Amphetamine was found to have other reliable effects, such as producing stimulation and euphoria. By the 1930s, amphetamine was being used for these various effects (Kuhn et al., 2008; Rasmussen, 2008).

Also in the 1930s, Japanese scientists were trying to synthesize ephedrine when they synthesized methamphetamine instead. Similar to amphetamine, methamphetamine has bronchiole dilation and stimulant properties. Methamphetamine was soon marketed to the Japanese people and became widely used and abused. When World War II began in 1939, amphetamines and methamphetamine became widely used by soldiers of many countries, including Germany, Japan, and the United States. Millions of tablets were distributed during the war, across all ranks and divisions. Bomber pilots were given amphetamine and methamphetamine to fight fatigue and enhance focus during long flights. Unfortunately, the effects of amphetamines were not entirely beneficial to those pilots. Agitation, impaired judgment, and uncontrolled aggression were problems that pilots experienced when using amphetamines. Even Adolf Hitler was said to have been given daily intravenous injections of methamphetamine by his personal physician from 1942 until his death in 1945 (Kuhn et al., 2008; Rasmussen, 2008). Despite the problems associated with amphetamines, the military still uses them even today, albeit in more limited capacity. The practice continues to come under scrutiny, such as during the Persian Gulf War and Afghanistan conflict. When military pilots make judgment errors, appear reckless, or violate rules of engagement, there is speculation regarding the role amphetamines may have played. Nonetheless, the U.S. military affirms that amphetamines are effective in allaying fatigue and enhancing focus on long missions when fatigue is a concern and sleep is not possible (Miller, 2003).

After World War II, amphetamine and methamphetamine use was common, with amphetamine tablets available in the United States without a prescription until 1951 (Maxwell & Brecht, 2011). Amphetamine was used by athletes to improve performance. Amphetamine was used by physicians to treat patients with depression. Amphetamine was also the first diet pill. Popular for use as an appetite suppressant in the 1950s and 1960s, amphetamine did help users lose weight. However, negative side effects of use of these stimulant drugs also became apparent, from addiction to psychosis. Japan in particular experienced significant stimulant addiction problems. By the 1960s, it was clear that amphetamines were dangerous; slogans such as "Speed kills" became widely used in public health campaigns. While overdoses did occur, the more common reason that amphetamines resulted in death was paranoia leading to violence. Despite concerns about addiction, amphetamines were originally placed on Schedule III of the Controlled Substances Act in 1970 (see Chapter 1). Schedule III drugs today include Tylenol® with codeine and Marinol®. In 1971, amphetamines were moved to Schedule II given the awareness of high potential for abuse, the position where methamphetamine had always been listed. Amphetamine use declined during the 1980s, when cocaine and crack became more popular. Amphetamines subsequently reemerged in various new forms. In 1986, the U.S. Congress passed the Controlled Substances

Analogue Enforcement Act, which allowed for the immediate classification of new controlled substances. This legislation was enacted in response to the production of designer drugs, notably amphetamines, which were becoming increasingly available in the United States. Previously, every slight change to the chemical structure or a drug required law enforcement officials to go through the time-consuming process required to have it certified as a controlled substance. After this legislation, drug enforcement could more easily address a new drug as soon as it appeared, although that did not appear to impact the demand for amphetamines (Bovett, 2006).

In the mid-1990s, methamphetamine first appeared on the West Coast of the United States and moved eastward. All forms of methamphetamine became widely used, including ice, a volatile version of the drug that can be heated and inhaled (a process similar to the use of crack, the volatile form of cocaine). Use of ice resulted in dramatic increases in addiction and toxicity. Emergency department admissions related to amphetamines soared; California saw a 460% increase in such admissions from 1985 to 1994. In 1996, the Comprehensive Methamphetamine Control Act was passed. This legislation increased penalties for the manufacture and trafficking of methamphetamine. At the time, methamphetamine production and trafficking was controlled by organized criminal groups. This legislation did seem to curb the effectiveness of these large criminal groups, but it had the unintended consequence of encouraging methamphetamine production in small individual labs (Bovett, 2006).

In both the United States and Asian countries, there continues to be widespread concern about methamphetamine, with the term "meth epidemic" often used. In 2006, U.S. law enforcement personnel listed methamphetamine as the number one drug problem facing the nation (Kuhn et al., 2008). Part of the recent rise in methamphetamine use has been due to the drug being easily made in clandestine domestic laboratories using basic household products. A small methamphetamine laboratory can be set up in a shed or trailer. Household products such as pseudoephedrine (found in over-the-counter cold medicine), anhydrous ammonia (an agricultural fertilizer), and red phosphorus (used in matches) all have legitimate uses, but in combination they can be used to make methamphetamine. The ease of manufacture of methamphetamine is in contrast with the production process for cocaine and crack cocaine, which have similar stimulant effects as amphetamines. Production of cocaine depends on the growth, harvesting, and processing of the coca plant, grown in South America. Transporting cocaine to a buyer in the United States is relatively difficult. The production and distribution issues associated with cocaine are generally absent with amphetamines. Thus, synthetic amphetamines can be cheaper than cocaine. Unfortunately, making methamphetamine can be extremely hazardous, particularly for those who have no background in chemistry. Inappropriate mixing of chemicals results in explosions and fires. Some of the chemicals used to make methamphetamine are highly toxic, with illicit drug producers often unconcerned about dumping biohazards into the environment. Unsuspecting neighbors may be unaware of the health risks (Bovett, 2006; Office of National Drug Control Policy, 2012).

Since pseudoephedrine is an important ingredient in the illicit drug methamphetamine, one approach to preventing methamphetamine production has been to increasingly limit sales of pseudoephedrine. In 2006, the Combat Methamphetamine Epidemic Act was passed, implementing restrictions on the sale of products containing pseudoephedrine and ephedrine. Sales are now restricted to pharmacies, with cold medications containing these ingredients kept behind the counter. If a consumer wishes to purchase a medication containing pseudoephedrine, no prescription is required, since pseudoephedrine is a legitimate, effective decongestant. However, the pharmacist records each purchase and purchaser and this information is tracked electronically. Other chemicals that can be used to manufacture methamphetamine are also closely monitored (Bovett, 2006). Professionals in public health, law enforcement, and medicine all support restricting access to the methamphetamine precursors, but there is also a legitimate decongestant use for pseudoephedrine, which makes restricting access challenging. States have also developed specific laws to limit pseudoephedrine sales. As one example, Kentucky law limits pseudoephedrine sales to 7.2 g/person/month. This is a sufficient amount to allow a legitimately sick patient to take the maximum daily dose (240 mg/day). Sales are tracked electronically to ensure compliance with the law. Despite these restrictions, it has been estimated that one-third of the illicitly produced methamphetamine is still made from legitimately purchased pseudoephedrine. As an illustration, a recent study examined the relationship between pseudoephedrine sales and the number of clandestine methamphetamine laboratory seizures in Kentucky in the year 2010. Law enforcement defines a "laboratory" as having two or more chemicals or two or more pieces of equipment used in manufacturing methamphetamine. The researchers found that, the more pseudoephedrine sold, the more meth labs police were seizing (Talbert, Blumenschein, Burke, Stromberg, & Freeman, 2012).

As law enforcement becomes more effective at finding and shutting down domestic methamphetamine labs, Mexican "superlabs" have increasingly provided methamphetamine to fill the void. Where there is demand for illicit stimulant drugs, such as currently exists for methamphetamine, producers and distributors fill the need. In addition, laboratories (legal or not) making amphetamines and methamphetamine are also making other amphetamine derivatives. Synthetic stimulants are referred to as "designer drugs" because chemists alter the molecular structure of the original drug to make a new drug with a different profile of action. In some cases, structural variants are synthesized for legitimate research or medical purposes. In other cases, these new variants appeal to users wanting a novel drug experience and/or to evade law enforcement. While all of these are related to amphetamine, there is an ever-evolving diversity of chemicals appearing on the street. Some, more similar to hallucinogens, will be discussed along with ecstasy (MDMA) in Chapter 11. However, the classification of chemicals as amphetamines or hallucinogens can be somewhat difficult in some cases. For example, bath salts (designer cathinones) may appear more amphetamine-like or more hallucinogenic, depending on slight alterations the chemist makes to the drug. Regardless of how bath salts are classified, recent data suggests that use of bath salts is escalating. Calls to poison control centers related to bath salts in 2011 were 20 times the number recorded in 2010 (American Association of Poison Control Centers, 2012). Clearly, there is a strong current appeal of amphetamines and amphetamine-like stimulant drugs.

Current Drug Laws in the United States

Amphetamines are used as illicit drugs that quickly lead to addiction and cause significant health problems. Amphetamines also have legitimate medical uses, such as the treatment of ADHD, narcolepsy, and extreme obesity. While less common, methamphetamine is sometimes prescribed off-label for treatment-resistant depression. Thus, amphetamines, methamphetamine, and methylphenidate are all listed as Schedule II drugs under the Controlled Substances Act. Recall from Chapter 1 that a Schedule II drug has a high potential for abuse but also has currently accepted, albeit significantly restricted, medical use. Schedule II drugs are listed as such because they may lead to severe psychological or physical dependence. Cathinone (found in bath salts and also the key psychoactive ingredient from the khat plant) is a Schedule I drug, since cathinone has no currently accepted medical use (DEA, 2012b).

In the News:

Salter, J. (2012, October 11). Mexican cartels fill demand for meth in USA. *USA Today*.

The demand for the inexpensive and highly addictive drug, methamphetamine, seems insatiable in the United States. Despite efforts to crack down on American-made methamphetamine, the number of American labs continues to rise, albeit at a much slower rate than a few years ago. However, the demand for methamphetamine continues to increase, with Mexican drug cartels quickly filling any void left behind as domestic production decreases. Approximately 80% of methamphetamine found in the United States today comes from these Mexican superlabs. Authorities report that Mexican cartels are expanding methamphetamine distribution in the United States, using pipelines for distribution that already exist for marijuana and cocaine. Seizures of methamphetamine along the southwestern border of the United States have quadrupled over the last several years, from 4,000 pounds of methamphetamine in 2007 to more than 16,000 pounds in 2011. Mexican methamphetamine is more pure than domestically produced methamphetamine, since the Mexican product is made on an industrial scale by professional chemists. Federal authorities report that the influx of methamphetamine from Mexico illustrates a difficulty of waging the drug war; when one source of drug is curtailed, other suppliers step in to satisfy demand.

Use this news article to test and apply your knowledge:

1. What efforts have been made to crack down on American-made methamphetamine?
2. What is a main message this article conveys regarding drug policy?

Answers:

1. Pseudoephedrine, a key ingredient in over-the-counter cold medications, is also a key ingredient in the illicit drug methamphetamine. One way that domestic methamphetamine production has been halted has been limiting sales of pseudoephedrine. Medications containing pseudoephedrine are kept behind the counter in pharmacies. All sales are tracked by pharmacists, and consumers are only allowed to purchase an amount of pseudoephedrine that is appropriate for personal use. Other chemicals that can be used in the manufacture of methamphetamine are also closely monitored.
2. It appears that efforts to combat drugs have limited effectiveness unless demand decreases. As long as there is strong demand for methamphetamine in the United States, someone will provide the drug to users who want it.

Prevalence of Use of Amphetamines

In the United States

The prevalence of amphetamine use has been studied separately for therapeutic and recreational uses. Among therapeutic uses of amphetamines, the most common is the treatment of attention deficit/hyperactivity disorder (ADHD). In the United States, approximately 9% of children are diagnosed with ADHD, with rates twice as high for boys than girls (Merikangas et al., 2010). Since ADHD often leads to impaired academic performance and behavior problems at school, pharmacological treatment is common. In 2010, analysis by the U.S. Food and Drug Administration (FDA) indicated that approximately 20 million prescriptions for ADHD medications were dispensed to pediatric patients (ages 17 and younger). Analysis of drug utilization trends indicate that prescriptions for ADHD medications have been increasing significantly over the last decade. Methylphenidate (used to treat ADHD) is the top prescription of any type dispensed to adolescents! Methylphenidate (Ritalin®) is thus more common even than allergy medications, antibiotics, or antidepressants (Chai et al., 2012). This development of widespread and increasing use of ADHD stimulant medications has caused concern among medical professionals and the general public. In particular, concerns about the long-term use of amphetamines in a developing child are frequently raised. Later in this chapter, we will examine the scientific data addressing this issue.

Nontherapeutic use of amphetamines includes both diverted prescription medications and illicit street drugs (amphetamines, methamphetamine, and synthetic cathinones). The National

Household Survey, conducted annually by the Office of Applied Studies in the Substance Abuse and Mental Health Services Administration (SAMHSA), gives information about drug usage rates in the United States. Details of the survey methodology were provided in Chapter 1. The data from the 2010 survey indicate that there are approximately 1.1 million current (past month) users (ages 12 and older) of diverted prescription stimulants in the United States. This corresponds to approximately 0.4% of the population. When survey respondents were asked how they got diverted medications, approximately half reported that they got the medication from a friend or relative, and they did not pay for it (SAMHSA, 2011a).

The use of diverted prescription medications is four times more common than the use of illicit amphetamines. Data from the 2010 National Household Survey indicate that there were approximately 353,000 current (past month) users of methamphetamine in the United States, about 0.1% of the population. By contrast, it is estimated that there are approximately 1.5 million current users of cocaine (including crack) in the United States (SAMHSA, 2011a). While there are several illicit amphetamines, use of methamphetamine is the most common. In fact, data from law enforcement indicates that methamphetamine constitutes about 95% of illicit amphetamine-type drugs identified on the street, while 5% is amphetamine. This data does not include diverted medications (Maxwell & Brecht, 2011). A promising piece of news is that the number of new users of methamphetamine seems to be declining. From the National Household Survey in 2010, it was estimated that there were approximately 105,000 new U.S. users of methamphetamine. These numbers have been declining every year from a peak of 318,000 in 2004 (SAMHSA, 2011a). Unfortunately, there is no data to ascertain current prevalence rates for synthetic cathinones (bath salts). Indirect evidence indicates that use is rising, but reliable survey data is lacking (American Association of Poison Control Centers, 2012; DEA, 2012b). Therefore, the decline in use of methamphetamine may reflect increasing use of synthetic cathinones. Further research is clearly needed to more effectively address this question.

Given that a large percentage of illicit amphetamine use is from diverted medications, it is unsurprising that use of amphetamines is predominant in adolescents and young adults, who also have high rates of legitimate prescriptions. The Monitoring the Future surveys have been used to examine the prevalence of amphetamine and methylphenidate use in high school students. The 2008 survey data indicated that past-year use of diverted methylphenidate was 1.6% of 8th graders, 2.9% of 10th graders, and 3.4% of 12th graders. Amphetamine use (including diverted prescription and street amphetamine) was measured separately from methylphenidate. Approximately 6.8% of 12th graders reported past year amphetamine use. While these numbers may seem high, they are in fact lower than levels seen in the mid 1990s (NIDA, 2009). Nontherapeutic use of diverted ADHD medications is also widespread among college students. Survey data from 2006 and 2007 indicate that full-time college students (ages 18 to 22) are twice as likely as their non–college-attending peers to have used Adderall® nonmedically in the past year (6.4% versus 3.0%) (SAMHSA, 2009).

Worldwide

It is difficult to estimate worldwide use of amphetamines. There is no universally accepted method of measurement, and inconsistencies pose major challenges for cross-national and cross-regional comparisons. Many surveys from other countries do not include the use of diverted pharmaceutical amphetamines. Moreover, some surveys examine amphetamine and methamphetamine use together, while others do not. Further, use of synthetic cathinones has largely not been studied. Despite these challenges, researchers seek convergence of results from different methods. Using various approaches, it has been estimated that between 14 million and 56 million people ages 15–64 years have used an amphetamine-type drug at least once in the past year. This represents approximately 0.3–1.3% of the world's population. Not surprisingly, amphetamine use rates are much higher near amphetamine-manufacturing countries, such as those found in Southeast Asia and North America (Degenhardt & Hall, 2012). In several countries, rates of

FIGURE 7-5
Chewing of khat leaves resulting in ingestion of naturally occurring cathinones.

dependence on amphetamine/methamphetamine are rarely studied, in part because dependence on cocaine and amphetamines are not separated but rather combined as stimulant use disorders. However, one cross-national comparison reported relatively similar rates of dependence on amphetamines/methamphetamine in many countries from surveys conducted between the years 2000–2007. Approximately 0.2% of the population in the United States was dependent, 0.28% in the Czech Republic, 0.38% in the United Kingdom, and 0.73% in Australia (Degenhardt et al., 2011).

Khat, which contains the naturally occurring stimulant cathinone, is not emphasized in this chapter because it is rarely used in North America. However, khat is widely used elsewhere in the world. An estimated 10 million individuals worldwide chew khat. Use is higher in regions where the plant grows, such as the Arabian Peninsula and East Africa. For example, 82% of men and 43% of women in Yemen reported at least one lifetime episode of khat use (NIDA, 2011b). Khat use involves chewing leaves, which limits the ingestion of high quantities of stimulant cathinones, and this route of administration results in a slow drug onset (Figure 7-5). Even among habitual users, dependence risk is probably mild, although there appear to be no studies that have investigated prevalence rates for dependence on khat (Manghi et al., 2009; Nencini & Ahmed, 1989).

QUICK QUIZ 7-1

1. Amphetamines are used therapeutically to treat which of the following medical conditions?
   a. Morbid obesity
   b. Narcolepsy
   c. Attention deficit/hyperactivity disorder
   d. All of the above
   e. None of the above

2. The active psychoactive chemicals in bath salts are similar to the psychoactive drug found in the plant _____.
   a. *Cannibas sativa*
   b. *Erythroxylon coca*
   c. *Nicotiana tabacum*
   d. *Coffea Arabica*
   e. *Catha edulis*

3. What are the common routes of administration for illicit amphetamines?
   a. Oral
   b. Inhalation
   c. Injection
   d. b and c
   e. All of the above

4. Amphetamines have been in use for how long?
   a. Less than 10 years
   b. Less than 100 years
   c. Less than 1000 years
   d. More than 1000 years

5. Amphetamines are listed as Schedule _____ drugs, methamphetamines are listed as Schedule _____ drugs, and cathinones are listed as Schedule _____ drugs.
   a. II, II, I
   b. I, I, II
   c. I, I, I
   d. II, II, II
   e. IV, IV, V

6. Most illicit amphetamine found on the street by law enforcement is _____.
   a. amphetamine
   b. methamphetamine
   c. racemic mixture amphetamine
   d. isometric mixture amphetamine

7. What is drug diversion? When illicit amphetamines are used, what proportion of use is from diverted drugs?

8. Describe the role that amphetamines have played in the military.

9. Explain the relationship between cold medications containing pseudoephedrine and methamphetamine.

ANSWERS TO QUICK QUIZ 7-1:

1. d – all of the above
2. e – *Catha edulis*
3. e – all of the above
4. b – less than 100 years
5. a – II, II, I
6. b – methamphetamine
7. Drug diversion refers to the recreational use of prescription medications. An example of drug diversion is the use of Adderall® to get high, even though the medication was legitimately prescribed by a physician for the treatment of attention deficit/hyperactivity disorder. The use of diverted prescription medications is four times more common than use of illicit amphetamines. Clearly, drug diversion is a big concern with amphetamines.
8. Amphetamines have been used in the military since World War II. Millions of tablets were distributed during World War II, across all ranks and divisions to soldiers in Germany, Japan, and the United States. Bomber pilots were given amphetamine and methamphetamine to fight fatigue and enhance focus during long flights. The military still uses amphetamines today, albeit in more limited capacity. This practice has come under scrutiny from time to time. When military pilots make judgment errors, appear reckless, or violate rules of engagement, there is speculation regarding the role played by amphetamines. Nonetheless, the U.S. military affirms that amphetamines are effective in allaying fatigue and enhancing focus on long duration missions when exhaustion is a concern and sleep cannot occur.
9. Pseudoephedrine is a key ingredient in over-the-counter cold medications. It is also the key ingredient required to make the illicit drug methamphetamine. For this reason, medications containing pseudoephedrine are kept behind the counter in pharmacies. All sales are tracked by pharmacists and consumers are only allowed to purchase an amount of cold medication that is appropriate for personal use.

Acute Effects of Amphetamines

The acute effects of a drug are changes that take place after ingesting the drug one time. Thus, the acute effects of amphetamines refer to immediate changes experienced after amphetamines are administered. A typical acute dose of amphetamine is approximately 10 to 30 mg, while a typical acute dose of methamphetamine is approximately 5 to 10 mg (Verstraete, 2004). Acute effects can be objective, including observable changes in behavior or physiology. Acute effects can also be subjective, such as when a participant provides ratings about how they feel. Dramatic differences in acute effects are observed when amphetamines are used therapeutically or recreationally. The type of amphetamine and the route of administration are also important in leading to the observed acute effects. At the end of this section, the considerable overlap in the acute effects of recreational use of amphetamines and cocaine is reviewed.

Therapeutic Outcomes for Children and Adults with ADHD

When amphetamines are given to a child or adult with ADHD, the acute effects of the drug are observable within 30 to 60 minutes of oral dose administration. The individual may report better ability to pay attention, stay focused, and control his or her own behavior. With children, parents and teachers can often acutely observe these changes as well. Prescription stimulant medications robustly suppress symptoms of ADHD, though these observations seem paradoxical. Why does a stimulant drug actually make an inattentive and hyperactive child seem more focused and less active? Studies of the disorder have systematically found that the areas of the brain that are important for paying attention are hypoactive (underactive) in children and adults with ADHD. Advances in brain imaging have shown that brain areas such as the frontal and parietal cortices are less active during cognitive tasks in children and adults with ADHD. The lower levels of activity coincide with poorer objective cognitive performance. When amphetamine-based medications are administered, brain-imaging studies have demonstrated increased activity in these same frontal and parietal cortex regions of the brain. This upregulation in cortex activity coincides with better cognitive task performance, such as improved sustained attention and working memory. In summary, amphetamines bring brain areas that are exhibiting too little functioning up to a level of functioning closer to approximately normal for individuals with ADHD (Bush et al., 2008; Franzen & Wilson, 2012; Wong & Stevens, 2012). Moreover, the effects of ADHD medications are immediate with the first use. For example, one study examined medication-naive boys with ADHD who were given their first dose of methylphenidate. Before the drug treatment, the boys with ADHD displayed the typical hypoactivity in the attention networks in the brain when compared with control boys of the same age. Then, when the boys with ADHD received their first dose of methylphenidate, activity increased in the brain regions that had previously had too little activity. The boys with ADHD appeared normal after one dose of methylphenidate, and they were not different from controls. One dose of drug is all that is needed to see these dramatic changes in brain activation (Rubio, Halari, Mohammad, Taylor, & Brammer, 2011).

The recreational use of amphetamines results in acute physiological changes, such as increased blood pressure, that are typically not observed with therapeutic doses of amphetamines. Cardiac output is not reliably altered when amphetamine medications are used as prescribed. Moreover, the therapeutic drugs chosen to treat ADHD are those that mainly have prominent central nervous system (CNS) stimulant effects and few other effects (Sagvolden & Xu, 2008). Methylphenidate (Ritalin®) has a chemical structure similar to amphetamine, with mainly prominent CNS effects. Dextramphetamine (Dexedrine®) or mixed salts amphetamines (Adderall®) likewise have greater CNS action and less peripheral action than amphetamine or methamphetamine (Hoffman, 2001).

How long do these medications last? Short-acting stimulant medications have a duration of action of approximately 4 to 6 hours, whereas the extended release formulations are effective for up to 14 hours. Since extended-release formulations do not require dosing during the day, they are often preferred for children attending school. Further, there are no residual effects of stimulant medications once they wear off. If stimulant treatment ceases, symptoms of ADHD may reemerge within hours. Parents and teachers are often quick to notice if a child missed even one dose (Schachar & Tannock, 1993).

Acute Effects Associated with Illicit Use

There are several acute manifestations of the illicit use of amphetamines. There is drug diversion, where individuals use ADHD medications for cognitive enhancement or to get high. There is also the use of illicit street amphetamines. When diverted ADHD medications are used for cognitive enhancement, research suggests that the effects are similar to those observed with therapeutic use. The ability to pay attention, focus, and control behavior is improved even in individuals who do not have a disorder (Berridge & Devilbiss, 2011). Such outcomes account for why diverted medications are illicitly used for improved focus and longer study sessions, thus leading to improved test scores and grades. Unfortunately, illicit use of prescription medications can also lead to abuse of amphetamines, especially when individuals feel high with an increased dose. Moreover, significant health risks are associated with nontherapeutic use of amphetamines, such as cardiovascular complications including myocardial infarctions or strokes (Schwartz, 2012).

At higher doses, amphetamines lead to a variety of changes. Objective changes include further performance enhancement effects such as increased endurance, alertness, and arousal. Increases in motor stimulation are observed. Physical performance is enhanced in part because fatigue is delayed, with amphetamines often abused for this very purpose (Hoffman, 2001). However, enhanced endurance, alertness, and motor stimulation are often accompanied by impairments in accuracy and poor self-control of one's behavior (Fillmore, Rush, & Marczinski, 2003). In animals, increased motor stimulation may include running around over greater distances or compulsive chewing and grooming. In humans, gross and fine motor stimulation can be apparent. Users may be more active or pace back and forth. Human users may also engage in repetitive tasks such as taking apart a phone and putting it back together again. Psychomotor stimulation is reliably observed following administration of all amphetamines, particularly at higher doses. However, methamphetamine is a stronger motor stimulant than the designer cathinones (bath salts) (Baumann et al., 2012).

Amphetamines stimulate activity in the **sympathetic nervous system**, the portion of the autonomic nervous system activated in times of stress or danger (see Chapter 2). When a crisis emerges, the sympathetic nervous system becomes active to prepare the body to deal with the situation. Physiological changes include readying the body for a sudden expenditure of energy by directing blood flow to essential regions of the body and away from nonessential regions or activities such as digestion or salivation. Heart rate increases, breathing gets faster, and body temperature and blood pressure rise. Sweating occurs and pupils become larger. These changes are referred to as the fight-or-flight response. Amphetamines can induce these changes in the body, especially at nontherapeutic doses. Note that some amphetamines, such as *l*-amphetamine and methamphetamine, are more likely to produce such sympathetic nervous system stimulation effects.

Among subjective impacts, the acute effects of amphetamines result in increased feelings of stimulation and feeling high. Users will feel alert, energetic, and confident. They think faster and work harder, which explains the street name "speed." Users also feel talkative and sociable. Thinking may be grandiose and speech may reflect such grandiosity, with the individual saying that they can accomplish anything. The most notable change is the experience of euphoria. Users feel high and like the drug. Fatigue is opposed by amphetamines; the use of amphetamines can interfere with sleep. Unpleasant subjective effects also occur, including nervousness or craving the drug. Some amphetamines are far more likely to induce these subjective effects. For example, a variety of doses of methamphetamine and *d*-amphetamine result in increased ratings of feeling stimulated, alert, and liking the drug. By contrast, methylphenidate induces such changes only at high doses (Rush et al., 2001). Since studies administer the various amphetamines using the same route of administration, observed differences might be affected by the chosen route of administration. Methamphetamine and amphetamines are often administered by inhalation or injection, which results in a fast drug onset and higher peak effect. Methylphenidate is orally administered, which results in a slow drug onset and lower peak effect.

High levels of amphetamine use can lead to symptoms of **stimulant psychosis**. Users may become paranoid, hostile, and belligerent. The user may be convinced that people are after them or out to get them. The user may be disoriented and confused. Delusions (false beliefs) and hallucinations (perceptions not based in reality) also both occur. Hallucinations could include seeing people who are not there or feeling bugs are crawling on or under the skin. Methamphetamine users are particularly prone to the tactile hallucinations of feeling bugs, a symptom that users often refer to as **crank bugs** (crank is another name for methamphetamine). This tactile hallucination may result in compulsive scratching leading to skin damage. Violence is also a major concern with stimulant psychosis, in part because the drug induces heightened sympathetic nervous system activation. Heightened sympathetic activation results in problems for users hearing voices or otherwise not thinking clearly.

When a dose of amphetamine is too high, toxicity may result. Symptoms of toxicity include restlessness, dizziness, tremor, fever, confusion, stimulant psychosis, and/or suicidal or homicidal tendencies. When poisoning is fatal, while it is somewhat less common with stimulants than other drugs of abuse, it may be precipitated by convulsions and coma. Cerebral hemorrhages or evidence of myocardial infarction may be evident on autopsy (Hoffman, 2001). While less common with amphetamines, the designer cathinones (bath salts) can lead to very high body temperature, which in some cases leads to death (Baumann et al., 2012). The toxicity of designer cathinones has physicians concerned because cases of exposure that require medical attention tend to be quite serious. In particular, options for treatment are limited to supportive measures such as administration of intravenous fluids, benzodiazepines, and oxygen. In other words, there is no antidote to a toxic dose of designer cathinones (Forrester, 2012). However, most fatalities associated with amphetamines and amphetamine-like drugs are due to accidents, suicides, and homicides that were precipitated by psychosis or other psychological disturbances coinciding with high drug doses (Cruickshank & Dyer, 2009).

Similarities with and Differences from Cocaine

Little distinguishes cocaine from amphetamines, and the consequences of use of both tend to be remarkably similar (Ciccarone, 2011). In fact, if time of testing is constrained, users of both drugs can rarely distinguish amphetamine from cocaine when both are administered in a blind fashion (Oliveto, McCance-Katz, Singha, Hameedi, & Kosten, 1998). Both cocaine and amphetamine increase attention and alertness; use results in pleasurable effects that may lead to abuse. Sympathetic nervous system activation occurs following use of both drugs, although methylphenidate is less likely to lead to changes in the sympathetic nervous system (Kuhn et al., 2008). One difference between cocaine and amphetamines is that amphetamines have a longer duration of action. For example, one study administered cocaine or methamphetamine intravenously to subjects. The results indicated that the subjective effects of cocaine (feeling high) tended to peak and decline earlier than those produced by methamphetamine, which seems to have a longer duration of action. Likewise, cardiovascular effects (faster heart rate, higher blood pressure) tended to return to normal more rapidly with cocaine than methamphetamine (Newton, De La Garza, Kalechstein, & Nestor, 2005). The longer duration of amphetamines has also been observed in animal models, with d- and l-amphetamine resulting in longer durations of action compared with cocaine (Jarbe, 1993). The longer duration of action of amphetamines may explain why amphetamine users are more than a third more likely than cocaine users with similar drug use histories to experience a psychiatric hospitalization resulting from stimulant psychosis (Leamon, Gibson, Canning, & Benjamin, 2002). Finally, there has been little research comparing duration of action of synthetic cathinones (bath salts) to amphetamines and cocaine. However, one study with rats found that cathinone exerted an onset of action that was more rapid and had a much shorter duration of action than both amphetamine and cocaine (Schechter, 1989). One final difference between amphetamine and cocaine is that cocaine can easily induce seizures at doses only slightly higher than needed for maximal effects of mood. Amphetamines rarely induce seizures, suggesting that cocaine's local anesthetic action may be related to its seizure potential (Kuhn et al., 2008).

Focus on Careers: A Career in Law Enforcement

The use of psychoactive drugs leads to many societal problems. In many situations, law enforcement intervenes (see Figure 7-6). The number of available career paths addressing drug use and related to law enforcement may surprise you. There are police officers who are charged with protecting lives and property. There are detectives and criminal investigators (also called agents and special agents) who gather facts and collect evidence of possible crimes. In all roles, knowledge about pharmacology can be critical in helping citizens or solving crimes. Careers in law enforcement range from working in a police department of your local town to working for federal law enforcement agencies. If law

©Mikael Karlsson/Alamy

FIGURE 7-6
Psychoactive drugs lead to many societal problems. In many situations, law enforcement intervenes.

enforcement and psychoactive drugs interest you, federal agencies such as the Drug Enforcement Administration, the U.S. Bureau of Alcohol, Tobacco, Firearms, and Explosives, the U.S. Customs and Border Protection, or the Federal Bureau of Investigation may appeal to you. While work in law enforcement can be physically demanding, stressful, and dangerous, it can also be highly rewarding. Moreover, the possibilities are endless. If you enjoy science but dislike risk, there are several suitable career paths available in law enforcement. A laboratory-based job might fit perfectly. What are the requirements to begin a job in law enforcement? It is becoming increasingly common for entry-level law enforcement officers to have a college degree. In addition, a background check, drug test, and psychological screening are required. Most agencies have a training academy that recruits must successfully complete before starting on the job training. In addition, many police departments have a full-time psychologist that conducts preemployment evaluations and provides counseling to officers and agents when needed. Thus, graduate study in psychology, particularly in clinical psychology, may ultimately lead to a career in law enforcement. In sum, there are endless possibilities to consider.

Websites to explore (look for the careers link):

http://www.fbi.gov
http://usdoj.gov/dea
http://atf.gov
http://cbp.gov
Most local police departments have their own website.

Chronic Effects of Amphetamine Use

Therapeutic Use

Attention deficit/hyperactivity disorder (ADHD) is a chronic condition. Since the ability to focus, pay attention, and control one's behavior is important for success in school, many children with ADHD are treated for years with stimulant medication administered daily. This begs the question: What are the implications of chronic therapeutic amphetamine treatment, especially for children? In many cases, researchers and parents alike have been concerned about the long-term use of amphetamines on the developing child, particularly since amphetamines are also a drug of abuse. Even if the long-term use of amphetamines is not harmful, the efficaciousness of this approach needs to be addressed.

First, there does seem to be reliable evidence that students with ADHD treated with stimulant medication perform much better in school over the long term. For example, one study recruited children with and without ADHD when they were 7–11 years old. The researchers compared children who did and did not receive stimulant medication treatment for ADHD. Approximately 9 years later, high school grade point average (GPA) and performance on the Wechsler Individual Achievement Test-II (WIAT-II) was recorded. The researchers statistically controlled for severity of childhood ADHD symptoms (since this is an obvious confounding factor as children with more symptoms are also more likely to receive medication). The results indicated that the adolescents who did not have ADHD performed best academically (highest mean GPA). However, adolescents with ADHD that were treated with stimulants had much higher GPAs and WIAT-II scores at follow-up than those adolescents with ADHD that did not get treated with stimulant drugs. At least as far as academic performance is concerned, treating ADHD with amphetamines leads to long-term benefits (Powers et al., 2008).

In addition to academic performance, chronic treatment with amphetamines has been shown to help with other aspects of functioning in individuals with ADHD, ranging from maintaining better family and peer relationships to driving a car. For example, young drivers with ADHD are more likely to have accidents, since being inattentive or impulsive is not consistent with safe driving. One study randomly assigned adolescent active drivers to a methylphenidate or no medication condition for 3 months, after which the assigned drug treatment was reversed for subjects for another 3 months. Each driver's car had in-car video monitoring for the 6-month study. When methylphenidate was being used, individuals with ADHD reported fewer ADHD symptoms, reported less risky driving, and exhibited fewer video-recorded driving errors and collisions, as compared with no drug treatment. Long-term methylphenidate treatment improved driving safety in individuals with ADHD (Cox et al., 2012). The evidence for improved social relationships is a little less impressive. However, it does appear that chronic treatment with stimulant medications helps children with ADHD interact with their peers more effectively (Hoza et al., 2005a,b).

While there are benefits of chronic therapeutic use of amphetamines for ADHD, as described above, one concern about long-term use of ADHD medications has to do with growth. Children who take amphetamines experience suppressed appetite (a common occurrence whether amphetamines are taken therapeutically or recreationally). Recall that amphetamines were originally used in the treatment of obesity, with methamphetamine still used today in the treatment of morbid obesity. If children eat less while taking stimulant medication, they tend to gain less weight, or even lose weight. This is concerning since these children may not grow to their full height potential, and short adult stature may result. Some studies have found that the problem of weight loss or lack of weight gain in children treated with amphetamines occurs primarily early on in treatment, such as during the first 4 months (Spencer et al., 2006). Longer-duration studies have found that methylphenidate or mixed salts amphetamines have more deleterious effects on weight and height gain when doses were high (Pliszka, Matthews, Braslow, & Watson, 2006). Due to these concerns, physicians frequently suggest that children with ADHD keep their dose at the lowest effective level. In addition, physicians frequently recommend **drug holidays**, which are time periods off from taking a therapeutic drug. For children given ADHD medications, drug holidays are typically weekends and/or summer vacations. The goal of a drug holiday is to regain appetite and catch up on growth. Drug holidays are sometimes also used when sleep disruption becomes a side effect of treatment. However, studies that have systematically examined the role of drug holidays on weight/height gain and sleep improvement have found that drug holidays do not have any significant impact on either (Pliszka et al., 2006; Spencer et al., 2006). Thus, height and weight gains need to be closely monitored in children with ADHD who are being treated with stimulant medications.

Finally, it should be noted that even with chronic treatment with stimulant medications, the symptoms of ADHD do not disappear. While many children experience symptom remission as development progresses, others still experience symptoms of ADHD into adulthood. Continuous drug treatment increases the likelihood that the therapeutic drug will become less effective with time, since tolerance may develop. Switching medications can help address tolerance, but switching is not always effective (Schachar & Tannock, 1993). Given concerns about long-term amphetamine use (and problems with drug ineffectiveness with long-term use), alternative medications have been developed. For example, Strattera® (atomotoxine) is used to treat ADHD, but it is not an amphetamine drug. It acts in the brain to increase norepinephrine, which helps in behavioral control. However, it takes many weeks for Strattera® to become effective, whereas stimulant amphetamine medications are effective in under an hour. In general, Strattera® seems less effective than amphetamines, which still remain the first choice in the therapeutic treatment of ADHD. Despite their benefits, stimulant medications are not without concerns. Children and adolescents with ADHD often experience poor peer relationships, academic underachievement, and low self-esteem, concerns that have been observed repeatedly in studies. Children with ADHD tend to be less well liked by peers and are more likely to suffer from social rejection. For this reason, psychotherapy, as well as therapeutic drug treatment, is recommended to improve outcomes for children with ADHD (Hoza et al., 2005a,b; Schachar & Tannock, 1993). In sum, stimulant psychosis from methamphetamine is associated with many poor long-term outcomes, ranging from relapses of psychosis and chronic psychotic state to suicidal thoughts and death.

Illicit Use

The long-term illicit use of amphetamines can lead to a variety of problems. As with cocaine, users tend to take amphetamines somewhat more irregularly than other psychoactive drugs such as heroin or nicotine. However, irregular use may become more frequent over time, and doses may be increased as tolerance develops. When high levels of amphetamines (or cocaine) are used, symptoms of **stimulant psychosis** may emerge. This psychotic state can occur following one initial high dose of amphetamines, but psychosis becomes far more likely among chronic users (Ujike & Sato, 2004). Stimulant psychosis is characterized by paranoia, hostility, and violence. When suffering from stimulant psychosis, an individual will be out of touch with reality. Hallucinations (false perceptions) and delusions (false beliefs) are hallmarks of this psychotic state. In the short term, psychosis can result in many problems, including injuries and death. Over the longer term, repeated episodes of psychosis are likely with chronic use. Deterioration in mental state can have negative long-term outcomes. In Thailand, there has been a methamphetamine epidemic that afforded researchers the ability to determine long-term outcomes for methamphetamine users who developed their first episode of psychosis resulting in a hospitalization. Over 1,000 patients were initially admitted to hospital in the years 2000 or 2001. In the year 2007, the researcher tracked down these same patients and interviewed them again, where possible. Unfortunately, a second interview was not possible for 8% of the participants, who had died. Cause of death was most likely due to suicide, accident, or AIDS. For those who were still living, nearly half had experienced a relapse of psychosis. Approximately one-quarter of the sample had been readmitted to hospital for psychosis. Approximately 10% of the living sample was experiencing persistent psychosis (the drug was no longer the main cause of the psychosis) and had been given a diagnosis of schizophrenia (Kittirattanapaiboon et al., 2010). Similar outcomes have been reported from studies conducted in North America, which suggests that the availability of psychiatric care is not the reason for such poor prognosis (Lev-Ran, Imtiaz, & Le Foll, 2012). In addition, persistence of psychosis in abstinent former users is more likely in abstinent methamphetamine users as opposed to abstinent cocaine users (Mahoney et al., 2008).

Stimulant psychosis can be problematic for a variety of reasons. One particularly common tactile hallucination is the feeling that bugs are crawling underneath or on the skin, which is called

formication syndrome. This sensation is unpleasant, and users will chronically pick and dig at their skin. Skin lesions are common and can become seriously infected over time. Users may often experience a similar sensation in their scalp, and they shave their heads to get rid of the feeling.

In addition to the serious concern of stimulant psychosis, there are additional health problems associated with chronic use of amphetamines. Individuals who chronically abuse methamphetamine often develop serious dental problems. The term **meth mouth** is used to describe the severe tooth decay (dental caries), enamel erosion, and loss of teeth accompanying methamphetamine use. While the exact mechanism explaining such terrible dental outcomes remains a mystery, it is thought that methamphetamine induces a few harmful changes. First, the drug inhibits saliva flow, which makes the mouth become very dry. Saliva protects the teeth from some bacteria; insufficient levels of saliva increase the likelihood of dental caries (cavities). When the mouth is dry, methamphetamine users will often consume sugary drinks to allay thirst. Poor oral hygiene is common, which exacerbates the problem, although poor oral hygiene is a concern for all drug users. In addition, the acute effects of methamphetamine induce teeth grinding, or **bruxism**, which wears down enamel. Dentists are wary about treatment of active methamphetamine users, as local anesthetics that have vasoconstrictive properties can result in myocardial infarctions (heart attacks). Other cerebrovascular accidents can also occur when combined with recent use of methamphetamine. Clearly, the most important component in treating dental problems associated with methamphetamine is to stop using methamphetamine (Hamamoto & Rhodus, 2009).

Since they can be unpleasant to see, images of chronic methamphetamine users are not included in this book. However, a Google search will bring up images of methamphetamine users with self-injurious skin lesions and dramatic dental decay. Chronic users also tend to appear malnourished, an unsurprising outcome since amphetamines suppress appetite. Images of addicted users have been used extensively in public awareness campaigns, such as the Montana meth project. Public awareness campaigns are largely motivated by police officers, who repeatedly arrest the same individuals and are shocked at the dramatic aging and deterioration in appearance over a matter of months in methamphetamine users. However, presenting images of methamphetamine users and their skin/dental conditions has not been conclusively shown to impact rates of methamphetamine use (Anderson, 2010).

One final concern associated with chronic illicit amphetamine use is brain damage. Both human and animal studies have shown that biochemical and structural changes occur in the brain with long-term abuse of amphetamines. For example, chronic methamphetamine administration damages dopamine and serotonin nerve terminals, which alters the balance of these important neurotransmitters in the brain (Volkow et al., 2001). Decreased availability of these important monoamine neurotransmitters corresponds with higher rates of depression in abstinent or actively using methamphetamine abusers. In addition, widespread structural damage has been observed across the brains of long-term amphetamine abusers (Nakama et al., 2011). This is disconcerting, since it is unknown how much this damage can be reversed if the drug use ceases. For example, one study recruited individuals in their 30s who had used methamphetamine for at least a decade. They compared the brains of the methamphetamine abusers to controls who were of similar age and matched on a variety of other demographic characteristics. The researchers found that methamphetamine abusers had 8% smaller hippocampal volumes compared to control subjects. In the same study, atrophy of limbic structures, which are important for emotional regulation, was observed in methamphetamine abusers. As the brain shrinks, ventricles expand to fill the empty space in the skull, and this was also observable in the methamphetamine abusers. Researchers have described these structural changes as similar to early Alzheimer's disease (Blakeslee, 2004; Thompson et al., 2004). Given these changes in the brain, cognitive impairments are unsurprising. Deficits in memory and executive functioning (planning, problem solving) are observed in chronic abusers of amphetamines (Marshall & O'Dell, 2012).

What causes the amphetamine-induced damage in illicit users of these drugs? While the exact mechanisms are somewhat in dispute, researchers have hypothesized that amphetamines are neurotoxic because the drug induces neuroinflammation in the brain (Coelho-Santos, Goncalves, Fontes-Ribeiro, & Silva, 2012). Cell death occurring in the brain following chronic amphetamine use seems to be similar to the cell death that follows a head injury (Gold et al., 2009). However, brain damage is strongly dependent on amphetamine dose. Indeed, very low concentrations of methamphetamine can be protective to the brain, even though high doses of the same drug can cause widespread damage (Coelho-Santos et al., 2012; Rau, Kothiwal, Rova, Brooks, & Poulsen, 2012). This distinction may provide some clue as to why the very same drug provides excellent therapeutic outcomes for individuals with ADHD and terrible harm for illicit chronic users. The dose is critical in understanding likely outcomes with chronic amphetamine use.

Myth Busters: Amphetamine Treatment for ADHD Increases Risks of Drug Abuse

Perhaps the most persistent and salient concern about using amphetamines to children and adolescents with ADHD is the future risk of substance abuse and dependence. Amphetamines are not benign drugs. Amphetamines are illicit street drugs, with the same chemicals used to get high also being used to treat children. Doesn't amphetamine use in children lead to future drug abuse problems? This question worries parents, teachers, and physicians. Fortunately, it is a myth that amphetamine treatment for ADHD leads to higher risk of later drug abuse. There is no indication that long-term use of amphetamines, when used as directed to treat ADHD symptoms, results in any greater risk of future use of other drugs of abuse. There are two reasons why this is a myth. First, while a drug used to get high by recreational users is often the same drug used to treat ADHD, the therapeutic doses in treating ADHD are far lower. The oral route of administration is used to administer therapeutic ADHD medications, while many users of illicit amphetamines use inhalation or intranasal routes of administration. The inhalation or intranasal route of administration increases the abuse potential of any drug, including amphetamines. Since the dose is low and the route of administration results in a slow onset, abuse of therapeutically-prescribed ADHD medication is unlikely. Second, perceptions of misuse of amphetamines have to be disentangled from the data that substance abuse rates are typically higher in individuals with ADHD compared to the general population. ADHD is a disorder of behavioral control; higher impulsivity and lack of future planning are traits that increase the risk of drug abuse. Various studies using both human and animal models have found that duration of stimulant treatment does not appear to be associated with frequency of any form of psychoactive drug experimentation, use, dependence, or abuse by adulthood (Barkley, Fischer, Smallish, & Fletcher, 2003; Gill et al., 2012). To be clear, individuals with ADHD are more likely than the general population to experiment with legal and illegal drugs, as well as use, be dependent on, or abuse psychoactive drugs. This is particularly true if individuals have also been diagnosed with comorbid conduct disorder (Gudjonsson, Sigurdsson, Sigfusdottir, & Young, 2012). However, the use of stimulant medications (or the lack thereof) makes no contribution to these trends. In fact, one meta-analysis (a study combining findings from several other studies) determined that the risk of developing a substance use disorder was significantly *lower* in adolescents with ADHD who were treated with stimulants, as compared to adolescents with ADHD who remained untreated (Wilens, Faraone, Biederman, & Gunawardene, 2003). Thus, as long as stimulant medications are used properly by individuals with ADHD, the risk of developing drug abuse problems may actually be reduced compared with the risk of no treatment.

Tolerance, Sensitization, Dependence, and Withdrawal

Tolerance

Tolerance refers to the need for increased amount of drug to achieve a certain effect, or alternatively to a diminished drug effect with continued use of the same amount of drug (APA, 2000). Tolerance develops when amphetamines are used repeatedly, and tolerance development is more pronounced with the higher doses when amphetamines are used to get high than with the lower doses associated with therapeutic use. For example, patients with narcolepsy have been treated for years with amphetamines without requiring an increase in the initially effective dose (Hoffman, 2001). Children and adults treated with amphetamines for ADHD will at times develop tolerance to their medications. Physicians typically deal with tolerance by increasing the dose to achieve symptom control, in the following ways: incorporate drug holidays to allow for tolerance reversal or switch to a different amphetamine medication or non-amphetamine drug (such as Strattera®). Tolerance development is always a risk when amphetamines are used therapeutically, so keeping patients on the lowest effective dose is important.

Tolerance development is more likely among amphetamine abusers as compared to users of amphetamines for medical reasons (McClure, Saulsgiver, & Wynne, 2009). Amphetamine abusers take higher doses and their preferred route of administration (inhalation or injection) results in faster drug onset, both of which contribute to tolerance. While a typical initial dose of amphetamine is 10 to 30 mg, tolerant users may ingest as much as 2000 mg per day of the drug (Verstraete, 2004). As tolerance develops, higher doses of amphetamines are used, which often leads to a variety of problems. Use becomes compulsive, as withdrawal symptoms become pronounced when the typical dose increases. Health declines and stimulant psychosis develops (Danaceau et al., 2007; Hoffman, 2001).

One concern with tolerance development is that it occurs rapidly across time. In pregnant abusers of amphetamines, tolerance development can lead to dramatic increases in dose levels during the nine months of pregnancy. Amphetamines easily cross the placental barrier, exposing the developing fetus to these drugs (White et al., 2009). Thus, tolerance development can be particularly harmful during pregnancy when the mother ingests increasing doses of amphetamines, in the process also exposing the fetus to higher and higher doses (White et al., 2009). The outcomes for children prenatally exposed to amphetamines, such as methamphetamine, have not received much research attention. However, some negative outcomes are clear with in utero exposure to amphetamines. Children prenatally exposed to methamphetamine have higher rates of ADHD, externalizing behavior problems, anxiety, and depression. Heavier exposure is more strongly related to attention problems (LaGasse et al., 2012). Even though prenatal exposure to amphetamines is problematic, outcomes are less devastating than those associated with other psychoactive drugs such as alcohol. Unfortunately, amphetamines are frequently used with alcohol, and tolerance readily develops to both these psychoactive drugs (Kirkpatrick et al., 2012a,b). Fortunately, tolerance to amphetamines seems to be readily reversible with abstinence (Danaceau et al., 2007).

Sensitization

The reverse of tolerance is sensitization. With sensitization, repeated administration of a drug results in greater sensitivity to the effects of a drug. Sensitization often develops when amphetamines are used repeatedly. For example, amphetamines increase locomotor activity in animals. When the same dose is repeatedly administered, locomotor activity increases, even though the dose has been kept the same. Moreover, cross-sensitization is observable among the amphetamine drugs. Cross-sensitization occurs when sensitization develops to one drug and then crosses over to another similar drug. For example, sensitization that develops to amphetamines will also be observable when methylphenidate is administered, and vice versa (Yang, Atkins, & Dafny, 2011).

The development of psychiatric symptoms, such as psychosis, in amphetamine users is thought to be due to sensitization processes. Initial mental health in amphetamine users will often be reasonably healthy (nonpsychotic). Progressive use of amphetamines will lead to a progressive deterioration in mental health. Initially, prepsychotic symptoms emerge; with continued use, there is an eventual progression to a severely psychotic state. If a person manages to stop using for a period of time, that individual nevertheless remains at an enhanced vulnerability to relapse back into psychosis if use of the drug resumes. This vulnerability persists for a long time after stopping use. As such, researchers have argued that sensitization develops during abuse and underlies the susceptibility to and onset of psychosis and vulnerability to relapse (Ujike & Sato, 2004).

Dependence and Withdrawal

Regular amphetamine use leads to physical dependence, particularly when the drug is administered by routes of administration other than oral, such as inhalation or injection. One simple way to assess for physical dependence is to cease drug administration and observe if withdrawal symptoms appear. For amphetamines, typical withdrawal symptoms include depression, fatigue, agitation, and cognitive impairment. These symptoms occur because chronic use of amphetamines results in depletion of monoamine neurotransmitters and neurotoxicity. Depression tends to be the most pronounced withdrawal symptom. Abstinent users may also report other withdrawal symptoms such as headaches, heart palpitations, dizziness, confusion, delirium, or psychosis. The duration of withdrawal symptoms is fortunately time-limited. For methamphetamine abusers, most psychiatric symptoms such as depression and psychosis resolve within a week of abstinence, although heavier users may experience severe depression that persists much longer, and suicidal ideation is a concern among heavier users. Feelings of craving for the drug persist for a long period of time; possibly lasting six weeks or longer. While physical dependence also occurs with amphetamines, it is less pronounced than for other drugs of abuse. Moreover, withdrawal symptoms, while aversive, are generally not life-threatening (Cruickshank & Dyer, 2009; Hoffman, 2001; Pennay & Lee, 2011; Zorick et al., 2010).

Pharmacology of Amphetamines

Sites of Action

Amphetamines act in a complex manner to increase the activity of monoamine neurotransmitters (dopamine, serotonin, and norepinephrine) in the brain. All amphetamines increase dopamine activity. Each amphetamine may increase the activity of serotonin and norepinephrine to varying degrees, depending on the type of amphetamine. Overall, amphetamines are structurally similar to the neurotransmitter dopamine. Therefore, amphetamines bind to dopamine receptors and mimic the action of this neurotransmitter. In addition, amphetamines block dopamine reuptake sites. When dopamine transporter reuptake sites (see Chapter 6) are blocked, these changes leave more dopamine available in the synapse, thus increasing the likelihood that receptor binding will occur. Amphetamines also enhance the release of dopamine, leading to much higher concentrations in the synapse. Finally, amphetamines prevent the normal enzyme breakdown process that typically occurs to eliminate excess monoamine neurotransmitters. By inhibiting the action of enzyme breakdown, more monoamine neurotransmitters will be available for binding. In sum, it seems that amphetamines act in four ways to increase dopamine activity: (1) amphetamines mimic dopamine, (2) amphetamines block dopamine transporter reuptake sites, (3) amphetamines enhance the release of dopamine, and (4) amphetamines block enzyme breakdown of dopamine. Elevations of dopamine levels via all of these mechanisms (Figure 7-7), especially in the mesolimbic dopaminergic pathway in the brain, are thought to underlie the addictive aspect of amphetamines (Cruickshank & Dyer, 2009; Hoffman, 2001; NIDA, 2006).

Amphetamines also increase norepinephrine and serotonin activity to varying degrees. For example, methamphetamine blocks norepinephrine transporter reuptake sites and serotonin transporter reuptake sites, in addition to dopamine transporter reuptake sites. Methamphetamine also enhances release of norepinephrine and serotonin in the synapse (in addition to enhancing

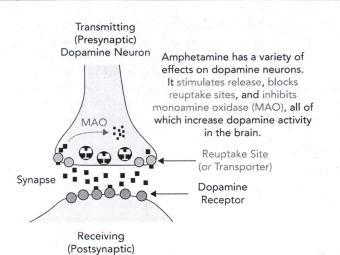

Transmitting
(Presynaptic)
Dopamine Neuron

Amphetamine has a variety of
effects on dopamine neurons.
It stimulates release, blocks
reuptake sites, and inhibits
monoamine oxidase (MAO), all of
which increase dopamine activity
in the brain.

MAO

Synapse

Reuptake Site
(or Transporter)

Dopamine
Receptor

Receiving
(Postsynaptic)
Neuron

FIGURE 7-7
Mechanism of action
for amphetamines.

release of dopamine). It has been estimated that methamphetamine is twice as potent as dopamine at releasing norepinephrine. Also, methamphetamine is 60 times more potent at releasing norepinephrine than serotonin (Cruickshank & Dyer, 2009). Methylphenidate (Ritalin®) appears to act primarily by increasing dopamine and norepinephrine activity (by blocking reuptake and enhancing release), but does not change serotonin activity (Sulzer, Sonders, Poulsen, & Galli, 2005). The pharmacological action of designer cathinones (bath salts) is somewhat poorly understood, in part because new chemicals are constantly being developed in clandestine laboratories that may have unique pharmacological profiles. However, researchers have generally found that cathinones act similarly to other amphetamines in that they act as nonselective monoamine reuptake inhibitors. The chemicals cathinone and methcathinone seem to block dopamine and norepinephrine transporter reuptake sites and enhance dopamine release. Other variations of designer cathinones, such as mephedrone, also have the additional effect of enhancing release of serotonin. It seems that designer cathinones that more strongly increase serotonin activity tend to be most similar to MDMA (ecstasy; see Chapter 11) in their pharmacological action and reported effects (Baumann et al., 2012; Simmler et al., 2013).

Different amphetamines can differentially elevate amine levels. Researchers have determined which changes in dopamine, norepinephrine, and serotonin levels accompany observed effects on behavior. Elevations in norepinephrine are thought to be largely responsible for increased attention and alertness. Elevated norepinephrine and dopamine levels are thought to underlie increased locomotor activity. Elevated serotonin and dopamine levels (particularly when high doses of amphetamines are administered) are thought to be responsible for symptoms of psychosis (Cruickshank & Dyer, 2009; Hoffman, 2001; NIDA, 2006).

Where elevations of monoamine levels occur in the brain depends on how amphetamines are used. Stimulant medications, such as methylphenidate and amphetamine, are administered at low doses, compared to the illicit use of amphetamines. At low doses, amphetamines increase dopamine and norepinephrine activity in a somewhat localized fashion in the brain, particularly in the prefrontal cortex area. These changes underlie the improvements in attention and calming of behavior resulting from the therapeutic action of ADHD medications (Arnsten, 2006). Thus, amphetamines administered at low therapeutic doses tend to increase monoamine activity regionally in the brain. By contrast, when doses of amphetamines are increased, large and widespread increases in the activity of all monoamine neurotransmitters (dopamine, norepinephrine, and serotonin) can be observed throughout the whole brain (Berridge & Devilbiss, 2011; Devilbiss & Berridge, 2008).

While the action of amphetamines in the brain is clearly important, both for therapeutic and illicit users, amphetamines also act in the periphery (outside of the brain). Amphetamines increase epinephrine activity in the periphery, which results in increases in blood pressure, heart rate, respiration, and pupil dilation. Recall that epinephrine was formerly known as adrenaline, but the term *epinephrine* has become preferred over time (Julien, 2005). However, users on the street will describe how amphetamines cause an "adrenaline rush," a description that would be accurate if the old term *adrenaline* was still in use.

Finally, mention should be made about the differences between amphetamines and cocaine. Amphetamines and cocaine can appear to be similar in behavioral and physiological effects. Both drugs are chemically similar to dopamine. However, there are key differences in the basic mechanisms of how both drugs alter the site of action in the brain. Cocaine has a simple mechanism: blocking dopamine transporter reuptake sites (see Chapter 6). As described above, amphetamines act in a variety of ways to increase dopamine activity. These multiple actions of amphetamines are the underlying reason why amphetamines have a significantly longer duration of action than cocaine. In addition, the multiple ways that amphetamines increase dopamine mean that dopamine reaches higher levels with amphetamines compared to similar doses of cocaine. Researchers have argued that higher dopamine levels achieved with amphetamines explains why brain damage is more likely in methamphetamine abusers than cocaine abusers, since extremely high concentrations of dopamine are toxic to nerve terminals (NIDA, 2006).

Pharmacokinetics

Pharmacokinetics refers to the absorption, distribution, biotransformation, and excretion of drugs. Amphetamines can be brought into the body via several routes of administration, described earlier in the chapter. Once in the bloodstream, amphetamines quickly reach the blood–brain barrier, which amphetamines easily penetrate to reach sites of action. Metabolism of amphetamines occurs because of the action of enzymes located in the liver. The various amphetamines have a wider half-life range than seen in other psychoactive drugs. Methamphetamine has a half-life of approximately 10 hours. The half-life of racemic amphetamine is approximately 12 hours. Methylphenidate has a half-life ranging from 2½ to 5½ hours, dependent on whether the formulation is immediate- or extended-release (Childress & Berry, 2010). Since amphetamine medications are prescribed for children and adults with ADHD, the physician must keep in mind that half-life is shorter in children than adults. When amphetamines are eliminated from the body under normal circumstances, approximately 30% of the ingested amphetamine is eliminated in urine in unchanged form. Amphetamines can be detected in urine for up to 1 day in sporadic users and up to 4 days in chronic users. Methamphetamine has a slightly longer detection time, with detection in urine for up to 3 days in sporadic users and up to 7 days in chronic users (Cruickshank & Dyer, 2009; Verstraete, 2004).

More about the Science:

Volkow et al. (2001). Loss of dopamine transporters in methamphetamine abusers recovers with protracted abstinence. *The Journal of Neuroscience, 21*, 9414–9418.

Repeated use of methamphetamine results in very high levels of dopamine activity in the brain. Methamphetamine is neurotoxic to dopamine transporter reuptake sites. In methamphetamine abusers, up to 30% loss of dopamine transporters occurs with heavy use over time. Loss of these dopamine transporters has measurable effects, ranging from decreased memory ability to slower motor functioning. In this study, the researchers wanted to know if this damage was reversible when methamphetamine abusers stopped using the drug. The researchers recruited 12 methamphetamine abusers who were in treatment and hoped to be continuously abstinent. A subset of only 5 of these subjects remained drug-free and were able to complete the study. Using positron emission tomography, the researchers imaged the brains of these individuals earlier and later in the abstinence time period.

Figure 7-8 illustrates the dopamine transporter binding for one subject at 1 and 24 months of abstinence. A control subject's brain is presented for comparison. At one month of abstinence, the brain displays significant impaired dopamine transporter functioning. With time, dopamine transporter functioning improved. By two years of abstinence, some recovery in dopamine functioning occurred such that the dopamine transporters appeared closer to a normal functioning brain. In summary, the brain can recover from methamphetamine-induced neurotoxicity, but this recovery does not happen very quickly.

More about the Science Thought Questions:

1. What are some considerations for researchers when selecting control subjects for this study?
2. The researchers recruited 12 methamphetamine abusers who had hoped to complete the study. Unfortunately only 5 were able to stay abstinent. The findings were presented for these 5 subjects. Should subject attrition (those dropping out of the study) be considered when interpreting these results?

More about the Science Thought Question Answers:

1. Selecting appropriate control subjects is challenging because control subjects need to be as similar as possible to methamphetamine abusers on all other characteristics, except for methamphetamine abuse history. Therefore, attempts would need to be made to find control subjects who were similar to the patients in variables such as intelligence, brain size, and other drug use (alcohol, tobacco, and marijuana).
2. Yes, subject attrition is an issue in this study because attrition was very high due to more than half of the subjects dropping out. Importantly, the individuals who dropped out of the study were individuals who could not stay abstinent. Individuals who relapse are likely to have had a more severe addiction to start with than individuals who remained successfully abstinent. Therefore, it may be overly optimistic to conclude that dopamine transporter function can fully recover after two years of abstinence, since the individuals who possibly had the most damage to dopamine transporters from drug use were dropped from the study.

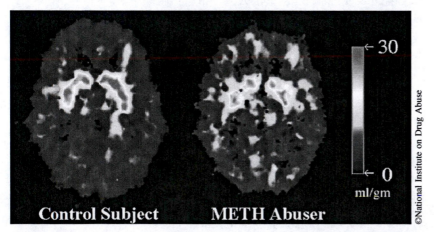

FIGURE 7-8

Chronic methamphetamine use causes damage to the neurons in the brain that release dopamine. Fortunately, some of this damage is reversible with long-term abstinence. While the methamphetamine abuser's brain still shows evidence of impairments in dopamine activity at 1 month of abstinence, most of this damage appears to be reversed by 2 years.

Treatment

Amphetamines are unusual in that they can be used therapeutically to treat psychological conditions such as ADHD, but treatments also have been designed to combat amphetamine abuse. Not surprisingly, the treatment approaches differ considerably for these two treatment groups.

Treatment Plans for ADHD

The treatment plan for an individual who has ADHD should ideally be multifaceted and not just limited to medication (Figure 7-9). Symptoms of ADHD impact multiple aspects of a child or adult patient's life. The goal of treatment should be improvement in all of these areas. In school, improving academic performance is almost universally a goal. Medication should help academic achievement by improving attention and decreasing disruptive behaviors in the classroom. In addition, behavioral interventions can be extremely helpful in the classroom setting. A teacher can implement various strategies that will limit distractions and help a child with ADHD sustain attention and control his or her behavior. For example, the child's desk might be moved to the front of the classroom and away from the door. The teacher can limit large-group work for a child with ADHD and instead students may work in smaller groups or pairs. Children with ADHD respond better to immediate feedback than delayed feedback. As such, computer programs have been developed to teach certain skills incorporating lots of immediate feedback, which can help a child master difficult material. Additional specific interventions for ADHD may include organizational skills training and reinforcement for goals obtained (such as stickers on a chart for time on task). Extra tutoring by a special education teacher may be needed, especially if the child has fallen far behind his or her peers. All of these behavioral efforts, in combination with appropriate medication, frequently improve overall academic performance (Fiks et al., 2012).

In addition to issues at school, children with ADHD symptoms may display behaviors that are problematic at home and with peers. Social skills training can help with these issues. A family

©Digital Vision/Getty Images

FIGURE 7-9
Effective treatment for ADHD should ideally be multifaceted. The classroom teacher can implement various strategies that can help the child manage their symptoms more effectively.

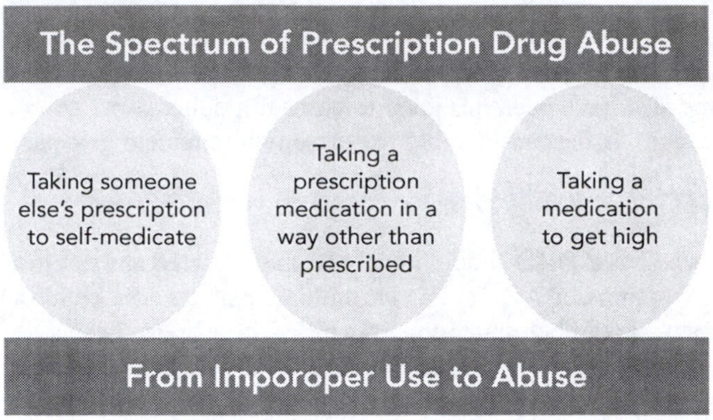

The Spectrum of Prescription Drug Abuse

Taking someone else's prescription to self-medicate

Taking a prescription medication in a way other than prescribed

Taking a medication to get high

From Imporoper Use to Abuse

FIGURE 7-10
One treatment goal for patients with ADHD is to ensure that amphetamine medications are used as prescribed and are not diverted.

approach to treatment can decrease stigma and increase medication compliance (Abikoff et al., 2013; Fiks et al., 2012). Parents of children with ADHD are more likely to be depressed and feel ineffective as parents. Specific training for parents can help them be more effective at parenting, such as increasing the amount of positive reinforcement for good behavior (Cunningham & Boyle, 2002). Improving social skills in the individual with ADHD is generally important in order to improve relationships with family members and peers. It is also a good way to prevent the development of other psychiatric complications, such as depression, anxiety, or other addictions, which are often comorbid with ADHD (Barkley et al., 2003).

One final concern not always receiving enough consideration is that effective treatment planning for ADHD should address drug diversion. Patients must be properly informed about the importance of taking their medication exactly as prescribed and never giving their medication to anyone else. While amphetamines can be very effective therapeutic drugs, these same drugs can be easily misused and abused. A patient must be clearly informed that they must only take their medication as prescribed, never take anyone else's ADHD medication, and never take more medication than prescribed, particularly to get high. Parents are critical in ensuring that children and adolescents are using their medications only as directed. Physicians are essential in ensuring that the individual being prescribed medication to treat ADHD symptoms is receiving the lowest possible dose to manage symptoms appropriately (Figure 7-10). Note that a large proportion of ADHD cases resolve by adulthood. Physicians need to periodically reduce the dose or stop the medication altogether (drug holiday) to see if favorable transition is taking place given that patients may outgrow ADHD (Barkley et al., 2003).

Treatments for Illicit Users

Behavioral interventions remain the primary treatment approach for illicit amphetamine abusers (Pennay & Lee, 2011). Cognitive behavioral therapy and contingency management have been demonstrated to be most effective. Contingency management refers to a program where incentives are given to the patient when engaged in treatment and staying abstinent. Drug-court monitoring rehabilitation programs are an example of contingency management, in that individuals can avoid jail time by attending treatment sessions and providing drug-free urine tests on a regular basis. Similar to treatments for patients with ADHD, effective interventions for amphetamine abusers are multifaceted, since drug addiction is a complex problem. One approach that has been successfully used with methamphetamine abusers is called the Matrix Model. This treatment approach includes behavioral therapy, individual counseling, a 12-step support, drug testing, encouragement for activities that do not involve drug use, and family education (NIDA, 2006; Petry et al., 2005; Rawson et al., 2003). Both inpatient treatment programs and outpatient treatment programs are available for amphetamine abusers. Of course, cost is a consideration when selecting a treatment program. Outpatient programs are far less expensive than intensive inpatient programs (Zorick et al., 2010).

Unfortunately, there are no currently available medications that specifically help amphetamine abusers. Patients are often prescribed medications that address withdrawal symptoms. For example, antidepressants are frequently prescribed, since depression is a common withdrawal symptom. Researchers have endeavored to find medications that would be suitable to treat stimulant abusers. Substitution therapy has recently become the approach of interest. The goal would be to provide a drug to the patient that is similar to the amphetamine being abused, with the treatment drug less likely to provide a high and thus less likely to be abused. To date, no drug has proven viable, but researchers are still searching for a candidate (Pennay & Lee, 2011). In addition, researchers have considered a vaccine treatment as another treatment approach. One vaccine against methamphetamine has been shown to be effective in mice, but has yet to be tested in humans (Shen et al., 2013). Hopefully more options will soon be available for abusers of illicit amphetamines.

QUICK QUIZ 7-2

1. Chronic methamphetamine use can alter the appearance of users. How is appearance altered?
   a. The user has less visible wrinkles.
   b. The user's teeth may fall out.
   c. The user may develop skin lesions from chronically picking at the skin.
   d. b and c
   e. a, b, and c

2. How long does a typical amphetamine stimulant medication need to be taken for it to be effective (better attention and focus) for an individual with ADHD?
   a. Less than one hour
   b. Less than 24 hours
   c. Less than 7 days
   d. 4–6 weeks or longer

3. _____ is a medication used to treat ADHD symptoms but is not an amphetamine drug. It is _____ effective than amphetamines in the treatment of ADHD symptoms.
   a. Ritalin®, more
   b. Ritalin®, less
   c. Strattera®, more
   d. Strattera®, less
   e. Adderall®, more

4. Methamphetamine abusers will often grind their teeth, which is called _____.
   a. meth mouth
   b. bruxism
   c. stimulant psychosis
   d. formication
   e. crank bugs

5. Amphetamines _____ the level of monoamines in the brain.
   a. increase
   b. decrease
   c. do not change
   d. None of the above

6. What is a contingency management program? Give an example of how contingency management could be used to treat amphetamine abusers.

7. Can the chronic use of amphetamines result in brain damage? Explain your answer.

8. What is a drug holiday? Why do physicians recommend drug holidays for children with ADHD using stimulant medications? Are drug holidays effective?

ANSWERS TO QUICK QUIZ 7-2:

1. d – b and c are both correct
2. a – less than one hour
3. d – Strattera®, less
4. b – bruxism
5. a – increase
6. Contingency management refers to a program where incentives are given to the patient engaged in treatment and staying abstinent. Drug courts often use contingency management. The individual can stay out of jail (the incentive) by being involved in therapy sessions and demonstrating that he or she is not using drugs via clean urine drug tests.
7. Amphetamines can result in brain damage. Cell death can occur in the brain following chronic amphetamine use. However, damage is dependent on dose. High doses induce neuroinflammation, which causes damage to the brain. By

contrast, very low concentrations of methamphetamine can be protective to the brain, in spite of the same drug causing widespread brain damage at higher doses. The dose is critical for understanding what outcomes are likely with chronic use of amphetamines.

8. A drug holiday is a period of time where a prescribed medication is not used. Physicians will prescribe drug holidays for children using stimulant medications to treat ADHD symptoms. Weekends and summer vacations are thought to be time periods when the use of stimulant medications is less necessary, since the children are not in school. The purpose of a drug holiday would be to catch up on growth, gain weight, or get more restful sleep. However, studies have found that drug holidays do not have any impact on growth or sleep quality. Nevertheless, a drug holiday might be a good way to assess if a child or adolescent with ADHD is outgrowing the disorder and no longer experiencing symptoms.

CHAPTER SUMMARY

Amphetamines are a class of powerful central nervous system stimulant drugs. They increase alertness, decrease fatigue, and heighten mood. They are used therapeutically to treat various conditions such as attention deficit/hyperactivity disorder, narcolepsy, and extreme obesity. They are also used illicitly and abused, which can occur either when prescription medications are diverted or when these drugs are purchased on the street. The typical routes of administration for amphetamines include oral, inhalation, and injection. When amphetamines are used therapeutically, one dose is effective in under an hour. These medications, as long as used appropriately, can be very effective and can be used safely for years. The abuse of amphetamines can cause considerable harm to the individual. Addiction can develop, as can serious psychiatric symptoms, brain damage, and other health problems. Amphetamines act by various mechanisms to increase the level of monoamines in the brain. Elevated levels of dopamine, in particular, account for the addictive potential of amphetamines.

ALCOHOL

Introduction

Suppose you were sitting at the kitchen table, eating dinner with your family. Out of your window, you see the flashing lights of two police cruisers in front of your house. The police had followed your neighbor home. Shortly thereafter, the police bring your neighbor out onto her driveway, a reflection of privacy being a luxury when in trouble with the law. Your intoxicated neighbor fails a field sobriety test, in that she cannot stand on one leg and walk a straight line. After a poor Breathalyzer result, your neighbor is handcuffed, put into the back of the police cruiser, and taken to the jail. That would make for a dismal dinner, would it not? Not long ago, my family was sitting at dinner one night and watched these events unfold. Kids playing basketball in the street, riding their bikes, or walking their dogs were not safe as she negotiated her way home around dinner time. Given the charges, our neighbor stayed in jail for 2 weeks, lost her driver's license for a year, and was mandated to attend a treatment program. While I wish this was an isolated incident, the fact is that my neighbor is far from alone in society. However, unlike other medical issues, her problem with alcohol can seriously harm others, especially unwitting bystanders. It is challenging to sympathize with a disease that can cause harm, or even death, to innocent people. Such is the paradox of alcohol (Figure 8-1). While many people enjoy alcoholic beverages and drink responsibly, the same is unfortunately not true for everyone. Why is it that some cannot keep their drinking under control, yet others have no problem with consuming alcohol? As is often the case, I had no idea my neighbor has a serious drinking problem; she is always cheerful and pleasant to be around. Her inner battle with the bottle was not readily apparent, at least until she spent a fortnight in jail.

©pixhook/istockphoto

FIGURE 8-1
Alcohol is a widely used psychoactive drug.

Learning objectives can help organize your studying. Before we begin the topic of alcohol, keep in mind that by the end of this chapter, you should be able to . . .

1. Describe different types of alcohol.
2. Describe various routes of administration for alcohol.
3. Explain the brief history of alcohol including how long alcohol has been available for use.
4. Describe the prevalence of alcohol use and abuse in the United States and around the world.
5. Explain the acute effects of alcohol and how it acts as a sedative in the central nervous system.
6. Describe the different effects of moderate and chronic drinking on health.
7. Describe tolerance, dependence, and withdrawal processes associated with alcohol use.
8. Describe how alcohol acts in the brain, and for how long.
9. Describe various treatment approaches to treat alcohol problems.

Alcohol as a Sedative Drug

Alcohol (C_2H_6O) is a central nervous system **sedative drug**. A sedative drug decreases alertness, increases fatigue, and slows cognitive processing. To some extent alcohol is biphasic in nature, meaning that alcohol induces both stimulation and sedation, dependent on the dose. In small doses, alcohol induces euphoria and diminishes inhibitions. In larger doses, alcohol induces classic sedative effects ranging from impaired motor function to coma and death as the dose escalates. Alcohol is a clear, colorless, and volatile liquid that is rapidly absorbed from the gastrointestinal tract and distributed throughout the body. It is the primary ingredient found in alcoholic beverages such as beer, wine, and spirits (hard liquor). Alcohol is widely used and has a long history of use (Gately, 2008). The terms *ethanol*, *ethyl alcohol*, and *grain alcohol* are used interchangeably to refer to alcohol (Fleming, Mihic, & Harris, 2001). Psychopharmacology studies using humans typically use the term *alcohol*, while animal studies more frequently use the term *ethanol*. In this chapter, the term *alcohol* will be used.

Certain types of alcohol refer to substances that are not drinking alcohol (ethanol). Isopropyl alcohol (rubbing alcohol) is used for industrial purposes, including as a solvent for paint. Isopropyl alcohol is also a gasoline additive, and it can be found in various personal care products such as hand sanitizer. Methanol is used as antifreeze (found in windshield washer fluid), as a solvent, and as fuel. A large percentage of methanol is used industrially to make other chemicals. Ingestion of other kinds of alcohol is extremely hazardous because they are so toxic to humans. Ingestion of as little as 10 ml of methanol can result in permanent blindness and ingestion of as little as 30 ml can result in death (Vale, 2007).

Types of Alcohol

Beer, Wine, and Spirits

Drinkable alcohol (ethanol) is found in three classes of beverages including beer, wine, and distilled spirits (hard liquor). The manufacture of endless variations of alcoholic beverages can be quite sophisticated. A visit to a winery, brewery, or distillery allows one to see the care and detail that goes into a great bottle of wine, beer, or spirits. The merger of art and science is palpable. However, the making of alcohol is actually a fairly simple process. All that is needed are four things: sugar, water, air, and yeast. Yeast is a unicellular organism found in the wild, which is used to make bread and alcoholic beverages. When sugar, water, air, and yeast are present, the yeast eats the sugar, and the yeast multiplies. The by-products of this metabolism are alcohol and carbon dioxide. This process is called **fermentation**. Fermentation results in a high-calorie substance. One ounce of pure ethanol contains 224 calories, which is 75% more calories than found in refined sugar (Gately, 2008). Many living creatures seem to be attracted to naturally occurring fermented beverages. For example, wild yeast found on rotting fruit or nectar on plants can lead to fermentation. While not widespread in the animal kingdom, some species of animals have been observed imbibing naturally occurring alcohol. One fascinating example of this is the tiny pen-tailed treeshrew, a small mammal from Malaysia that looks like a rodent with a long tail. These little animals consume the fermented flower nectar from the bertam palm tree on a daily basis. They drink so much that researchers have determined their daily consumption of alcohol is the human equivalent of 10 to 12 glasses of wine! Despite high doses of alcohol, the shrews appear not to be intoxicated; they are not falling out of the trees (Graber, 2008; Wiens et al., 2008).

Fermentation:

$$\text{Yeast} + \text{Sugar} + \text{Water} + \text{Air} \Rightarrow \text{Alcohol} + \text{Carbon Dioxide}$$

The manufacture of alcohol by fermentation is simple. However, the constituent ingredients may differ for various alcohols, particularly the sugar source. The sugar source comes from plant material, with the choice of plant material determining the type of alcohol made. Grapes, and less commonly other fruits, are used to make wine. Grains from barley, rice, or corn can be used to make beer. The grains provide starch with the enzyme amylase needed to convert the starch into sugar so that fermentation can occur. Amylase occurs naturally in barley malt, which is why many beers are barley-based. In addition, the metabolic process from yeast produces alcohol. The longer the yeast is allowed to grow, the more alcohol that will be present in the resulting beverage—at least to a point. The largest percentage of alcohol reached with fermentation is 10% to 15%. Beers tend to contain approximately 2% to 8% alcohol by volume, with light beers having lower percentages of alcohol. Wines tend to contain approximately 10% to 12% alcohol by volume. In addition, carbon dioxide may or may not be retained in the final beverage. For example, table wine does not contain carbon dioxide, but carbon dioxide provides the little bubbles in champagne (Lea & Piggott, 2003).

Fermentation leads to a maximum final alcohol content of 15% by volume. The alcohol content of spirits (hard liquor) exceeds this amount of alcohol by volume. To exceed 15% alcohol by volume, a second process after fermentation is needed. **Distillation** involves heating the fermented beverage to increase the alcohol content. Why would heating the beverage increase its alcohol content? Alcohol has a lower boiling point than water. When a fermented beverage is heated, the steam that rises has a higher alcohol content than does the liquid mixture being heated (since the water has not boiled yet). The steam vapor containing alcohol is collected and cooled, leading to a liquid with a higher alcohol content than the original fermented beverage. Sometimes alcohol manufacturers repeat distillation many times to increase the alcohol content in the final product. There are many types of distilled spirits, including bourbon, brandy, gin, rum, scotch, tequila, vodka, and whiskey. When wine is distilled (increasing the alcohol content to closer to 20% alcohol by volume), it is converted into either dessert wine (fortified wine), port, or sherry. The other distilled spirits tend to have upwards of 35% alcohol by volume. Distilled spirits are sometimes aged (stored) for years, or even decades, to improve taste. Aging can remove any harsh flavors; if stored in wood barrels, the wood can add to the flavor of the beverage. Higher-quality spirits are often aged for longer periods, with the price of the product often reflecting the cost of storage. Typically, vodkas and gins are not aged (Lea & Piggott, 2003).

The source of sugar dictates the type of distilled spirit that results. Brandy comes from the distillation of a fermented fruit beverage. Scotch comes from the distillation of fermented corn and malted barley. Bourbon comes from the distillation of fermented corn, malted barley, and rye. Rum is distilled from fermented molasses from sugarcane. Gin is distilled from various sources, such as potatoes, barley, corn, wheat, or rye. Vodka is distilled from fermented potato. When beer is distilled, the fermented grain beverage becomes whiskey. Finally, tequila is distilled from the fermented center of the agave plant. There are endless possibilities, but the starting point for a distilled spirit is always a plant-based sugar source (Lea & Piggott, 2003; Lendler, 2005).

Beers, wines, and distilled spirits can vary dramatically in quantity of alcohol. There are two ways this information is communicated to consumers. First, the alcohol percentage is reported as alcohol by volume, which may be listed on the product label using a short form such as ABV or alc/vol. For example, a 12 oz. (355 ml) standard beer bottle may be labeled as 5% alc/vol. This means that there is 17.75 ml of alcohol in the bottle, calculated as 355 ml × .05. In addition to labels representing alcohol by volume, alcoholic beverages can also be labeled by proof. **Proof** also refers to proportion of alcohol in the beverage and corresponds to twice the alcohol by volume (ABV). For example, a bottle of vodka could be labeled as 80 proof or 40% ABV. Conventionally, many distilled spirits are labeled using proof instead of alcohol by volume. The use of the term *proof* is a holdover from an earlier era, with its origins in the British navy yards in Jamaica. The British sailors wanted to determine if their alcohol (usually rum) was strong enough, as they were always concerned that their rations of rum were being watered down by their superiors. To test whether their rum was unadulterated, the sailors poured a small amount of the alcohol on gunpowder and lit it on fire (note to the reader – do not try this at home!). If the rum's percentage of alcohol was too low, the flame would fizzle out. If the rum's percentage of alcohol was high enough, the blue flame would burn and the gunpowder would explode. The explosion would be "proof" of the rum being sufficiently strong, which translated to approximately 100 proof or 50% ABV (Lendler, 2005).

Given that various alcohols have different percentages of alcohol by volume, a system has been devised to define what constitutes a single alcoholic beverage. A **standard drink** (Figure 8-2) contains 14 grams of pure alcohol (about 0.6 fluid ounces of alcohol or 1.2 table-spoons). One standard drink is typically found in 12 fluid ounces (355 ml) of 5% ABV beer, 5 fluid ounces (148 ml) of 12% ABV wine, or 1.5 fluid ounces (44 ml) of 40% ABV/80 proof liquor (such as vodka, bourbon, or rum). A mixed drink containing a 1.5 fluid ounce shot of spirits mixed with some other nonalcoholic beverage is also considered a standard drink, for example a rum and coke or a vodka tonic (NIAAA, 2012b). In practice, mixed drinks often contain one to three standard drinks, as many bartending recipes use more than one distilled spirit. Given that different brands and types of beverages vary in their actual alcohol content, the definition of a standard drink is treated with some leeway in both research and practice.

FIGURE 8-2
One standard drink of alcohol.

Vaporized Alcohol

While alcohol is almost universally ingested via oral administration of an alcoholic beverage, a brief mention about vaporized alcohol is warranted. Distilled spirits can be inhaled if the liquid is placed in a machine that vaporizes the alcohol and mixes it with oxygen. The process of inhaling a fine alcoholic mist is sometimes referred to as **alcohol without liquid (AWOL)**. First introduced in Asia and Europe, the machine for this purpose was brought to the United States in 2004. It quickly became clear that there are health and safety risks from breathing in alcohol instead of drinking it. Since vaporized alcohol bypasses the normal digestive processes associated with drinking alcohol, a greater blood alcohol concentration and high is achieved and overconsumption can easily occur (Kruhoffer, 1983). Today most states have made it illegal to possess, sell, or use an AWOL machine, a legislative change that was supported by alcohol industry groups such as the Distilled Spirits Council of the United States. However, vaporized alcohol is sometimes used in animal studies, since exposure to vaporized alcohol can ensure that the animals achieve high blood alcohol concentrations. Vaporized alcohol is also effective in demonstrating alcohol-induced brain damage (Pfefferbaum et al., 2008).

Alcohol for Medical Uses

Alcohol has four main medical uses. First, alcohol stimulates appetite and contains calories. Alcohol is sometimes prescribed by physicians for underweight elderly patients to drink before dinner to stimulate appetite. Alcohol has also been used to increase appetite and weight in cancer patients who are experiencing cancer-associated loss of appetite and weight (Jatoi et al., 2011). Of course, the benefits of the medical use of alcohol would need to be weighed against any potential adverse drug interactions or other considerations for sick and frail patients. Second, alcohol is an excellent solvent, so it is included in products such as cough syrups. Third, dehydrated alcohol can be injected near nerves to mitigate pain, such as in cases of advanced cancer or pain after limb amputation (Lim, Kim, & Kim, 2012; Roberts & Henderson, 1981). Finally, alcohol has antibacterial properties, which allow mouthwashes to rid the mouth of excess bacteria. Alcohol can also be placed on the skin to decrease bacterial counts and cause a cooling sensation. Interestingly, the antibacterial medical use of alcohol is not exclusive to humans. Fruit flies are those tiny insects that like to hover over a fruit bowl. When fruit flies acquire nasty bugs such as parasitic wasps, they seek environmental alcohol to fight the infection. Alcohol can be found near rotting and fermenting fruit that has naturally occurring yeast on it. When enough alcohol is consumed by the fruit flies, it kills the wasps growing inside of them (Michel, Kacsoh, & Schlenke, 2012).

Routes of Administration

The **route of administration** refers to the method by which a drug enters the body. The route of administration impacts how much of the dose reaches the site of action and how quickly it gets there. For alcohol, the most common route of administration is oral. When alcohol is orally administered (swallowed), it ends up in the stomach. The alcohol then passes through the stomach and travels to the small intestine. If food is in the stomach, the food will delay stomach emptying, and food also dilutes the concentration of alcohol. An interesting illustration of the importance of the stomach can be seen when the stomach is reduced in size via bariatric surgery. One study found that patients who underwent this surgery for weight loss were more likely to develop an alcohol-use disorder (Conason et al., 2013). It appears that keeping alcohol in the stomach helps delay alcohol from reaching the small intestine, which is where alcohol enters the bloodstream. Once in the bloodstream, alcohol is transported around the body and to the brain. While most alcohol is orally administered, inhalation and injection are also possible (described earlier in reference to medical uses of alcohol and vaporized alcohol).

Brief History of Alcohol Use

In the beginning, there was a grape. And then a winged insect came, accidentally carrying some yeast . . . the yeast got on the grape . . . A bird in search of food came along and ate that grape . . . the bird started feeling pretty good about his life . . . And ancient man saw this.

Ian Lendler, Alcoholica Esoterica (2005)

The history of all psychoactive drug use begins with alcohol. Given that alcohol occurs naturally in the environment, it is unknown when the first animal or human consumed the first alcoholic beverage, but the practice is certainly ancient. Historians tend to trace the origin of the history of alcohol to the time that alcohol production became intentional rather than accidental. It seems that it was during the Neolithic period, or approximately 7000 BCE, when the making of alcohol began. Important transitions taking place in human culture at that time facilitated the discovery of alcohol. Humans abandoned their nomadic lifestyles and instead took up agriculture, which allowed a more stable existence. Food processing techniques were emerging among the Neolithic people living in the ancient East, Near East, and Egypt, including heating, spicing, soaking, and fermentation. In addition, pottery vessels were being made for the first time, allowing liquids to be stored. Several key archeological discoveries indicate that it is indeed around 7000 BCE that humans initiated the production and consumption of alcohol. The evidence includes pottery jars discovered in northern China dated from approximately 7000 BCE. Chemical analysis of the residues inside these jars indicated that they kept a fermented drink made with rice, honey, grapes, and hawthorn berries. Another important archeological discovery occurred in the Zagros mountains of western Iran. Again, large pottery jars were discovered that had yellowish and reddish residues inside. Chemical analysis indicated that an alcoholic beverage had been stored inside. The jars were found in a kitchen of a Neolithic brick building dated about 5400 BCE, and one of these artifacts is now displayed at the University of Pennsylvania Museum of Archeology and Anthropology. Some evidence suggests that beer may have made its first appearance in Egypt around 6000 BCE. Researchers disagree about what came first: beer or wine. The archeological evidence seems to suggest that both types of alcoholic beverage emerged around the same time (Michel et al., 1993). Notably, whenever alcohol was discovered, no society abandoned it. Instead, the production process became increasingly sophisticated with time. The brewing process of beer appears to have become very sophisticated by 2000 BCE, with beer residue found in Egyptian tombs (Williams, 1996). The making of distilled spirits seems to have first arisen in China around 1000 BCE. Europe did not seem to have distilled spirits until much later, about 800 CE (Gately, 2008).

Since alcohol has been part of our society for thousands of years, human history and the history of alcohol are intertwined. Alcohol has been integral to everything from nourishment, to celebrations, to religion. However, the negative consequences associated with heavy alcohol consumption have been written about and discussed for as long as alcohol has been used. The epic Sumerian poem *Gilgamesh*, written in approximately 2000 BCE, is considered to be the oldest and greatest surviving work of early Mesopotamian literature. Gilgamesh features a character named Enkidu, a wild man, who is persuaded to join civilization. Part of Enkidu's education in the ways of civilized men was to eat the food and drink the beer that was the custom of the land. The poem states that, "*Enkidu ate the food until he was sated, He drank the beer—seven jugs! and became expansive and sang with joy!*" Gilgamesh provides evidence that at least as far back as 2000 BCE, humans knew about alcohol's potential psychoactive effects (drunkenness) and were not just consuming alcohol for nourishment (Gately, 2008).

The demarcation between wine and beer drinkers was clear in Egyptian society by about 3100 BCE. The elite drank wine, while the workers drank beer. The elite clearly were connoisseurs of their alcoholic beverage of choice. Pictographs depicting wine-making techniques have been found in tombs in the ancient capital of Thebes, Egypt (Figure 8-3). Moreover, jars found in

©Ann Ronan Picture Library/HIP/The Image Works

FIGURE 8-3
Pictograph showing wine making found inside a tomb at Thebes, Egypt, around 1500 BCE.

Egyptian tombs provide evidence that the making and drinking of wine was a great pleasure for the elite. Archeologists have found jars that are clearly labeled with the type of wine, year, vineyard, and vintner; jars that are intended for consumption in the afterlife. Among beer consumers, papyrus scrolls list financial accounts for laborers who built the famous Egyptian pyramids of the Giza Plateau. The daily ration of beer per worker was 1⅓ gallons. Scientists have re-created Egyptian beer using both written and pictorial evidence as guides. The beer made in 3100 BCE was approximately similar to many beers today, about 5% ABV. Apparently laborers constructing the pyramids were consuming approximately 16 bottles of beer daily (Gately, 2008).

Northern Europeans learned how to make alcohol via knowledge that spread from the Middle East. Around 5000 BCE, the cultivation of cereals that could be used to make beer was occurring in Europe. Beer was being made in Scotland by 3800 BCE, although it is unclear whether the Scottish discovered fermentation independently or if that knowledge arrived from the Middle East. On the other side of the Atlantic Ocean, the sophisticated Mayan culture had also independently discovered fermentation during the Neolithic era. By 1000 BCE, the Mayans were drinking mead (honey wine) in addition to building sophisticated cities. The Mayans developed an additional fermented drink using corn as the plant source. Similar to other cultures at the time, the Mayans knew that over-consumption of alcohol caused drunkenness, depicted on scenes of glazed cups or pottery figurines looking intoxicated. By about 1000 BCE, if humans were no longer nomadic and living a relatively stable agricultural lifestyle, they were probably making and consuming alcohol (Gately, 2008).

Ancient Greece generated the first coherent debate about the pros and cons of alcohol consumption, as wine was central to Greek culture. In this Hellenic society, wine was used as an offering to gods, as currency, as medicine, and consumed as a beverage to allay thirst. In Athens, wine consumption was even a civic duty. Hippocrates (d. 370 BCE) is the father of Western medicine, whose Hippocratic Oath is recited by medical students to this day. Hippocrates's writing on wine was quite positive. He advocated the use of wine to treat almost every illness, except depression (which he characterized as patients suffering from an overpowering heaviness of the brain). Not everyone was positive, as other Greeks also wrote about the hazards of too much alcohol, including death. The Greeks attributed the hazardous aspects of drinking to a god called Dionysus (also referred to by his Roman name of Bacchus). However, the Greeks also believed that amethyst (a violet-colored quartz stone) could ward off intoxication. Drinkers would wear talismans made of amethyst and drink from amethyst cups so that they could enjoy wine without the negative effects of intoxication. The concern about overuse of alcohol also led to legislative ideas to encourage safe consumption. Plato initially proposed a minimum drinking age of 18, stating that the young had excitable dispositions and that to add wine to such dispositions would be like pouring fire on fire. In his later writings, Plato seemed to recant his position, arguing that the youth must learn how to drink since wine was a necessary part of culture. Early experiences with wine were necessary to learn how to be disciplined in consumption. Rome was also a drinking civilization with wine at the center of culture. The Romans did not allow young men under the age of 30 to drink alcohol. Both the Greeks and Romans asserted that women should not drink (Gately, 2008).

As the Common Era (CE) began, the major religions had strong opinions about whether alcohol was a virtue, a vice, or both. Judaism viewed wine as a holy beverage integral to the religion. The two major meals of every Sabbath were and still are begun with a blessing over a cup of wine. Blessings over wine play a role in other major celebrations of the faith, such as weddings and circumcisions. However, the faithful were warned not to consume in excess. The biblical story of Noah describes how Noah left his ark and immediately planted a vineyard, made some wine, got drunk, and then lay uncovered in his tent. The description seems to warn that Noah's excessive alcohol consumption led to an embarrassing outcome. Christianity also incorporated wine in its most important ritual, the Eucharist (bread and wine, which transubstantiated the body and blood of Jesus, the son of God). However, not all religions embraced alcohol. Islam arose with the prophet Mohammed (d. 632 CE) in Arabia. Instructions on how Muslims were to behave were contained in the Koran, which prescribed a total ban on the consumption of alcohol. Interestingly, it was Muslims who perfected the extraction of alcohol from wine, leading to the discovery of distilled alcohol. Jabir Ibn Hayyan (d. 815 CE) discovered that heating alcohol and collecting the vapor made for a stronger drink (Gately, 2008).

By the 13th century, alcohol was widely consumed in Western Europe. Everyone drank regularly, including children, in part because safe drinking water was not readily available (so alcohol was sought for its antibacterial properties). Beer or wine was consumed with breakfast, lunch, and dinner. When Europeans came to North America, they brought alcohol and the knowledge of how to make it with them. The Pilgrims are thought to have landed their ship, the *Mayflower*, on Plymouth Rock in 1620 in part because they had run out of beer. The new nation of America arose, and Americans were very heavy drinkers. Every town that sprung up had a tavern at the center, a place where politics, business, and pleasure mixed with drink. The Europeans traded with native peoples who lived in America without alcohol before the Europeans arrived. When the British began trading with the native peoples for animal furs in the 1600s, alcohol was provided in return. Native people quickly became enamored with alcohol and drank excessively. Many succumbed to devastating alcohol problems, a concern that still plagues native people today (Mancall, 1997). However, the native people were hardly the only ones struggling with drinking problems in early America.

America over time became dominated by extreme drinking. The escalation in use was tremendous. By 1830, per capita consumption was the equivalent of 5 standard drinks per day per adult. Given that women drank very little, that meant that men were drinking closer to 10 drinks per day (Mendelson & Mellow, 1985). By today's standards, that level of consumption would make a physician cringe. Not surprisingly, there were repercussions associated with that level of drinking. With women not able to vote, own property, or control reproduction, a drunkard husband was a disaster. Eventually, public sentiment grew increasingly negative about alcohol, and the temperance movement gained strength. Dr. Benjamin Rush was a signer of the Declaration of Independence, but he is best remembered for his support of temperance in his 1785 masterpiece "*Inquiring in to the effects of ardent spirits on the human body and mind.*" In this writing, the physician Rush seemed to express little concern with beer and wine. However, he wrote that the consumption of distilled liquor over time could be lethal and that chronic drunkenness (alcoholism) was a disease. Eventually, the frustration from alcohol's problems led to Alcohol Prohibition (discussed in greater detail in Chapter 1), with the Eighteenth Amendment to the Constitution prohibiting the production, sale, transportation, and importation of alcohol in any part of the United States. Alcohol Prohibition did limit access to alcohol and Americans drank less during those years, with public health improving due to lower incidence of diseases like liver cirrhosis. However, the rise of clandestine alcohol manufacture, sales, and consumption, combined with lack of public support for Prohibition, eventually led to the repeal of Prohibition. Prohibition was repealed with the Twenty-first Amendment in 1933, 13 years after the Eighteenth Amendment prohibited alcohol (Lender & Martin, 1982). Today, states have much discretion over the regulation of the sale and consumption of alcohol. Moreover, society's view of alcohol worldwide remains mixed, much as it has always been.

Prevalence of Alcohol Use and Abuse

In the United States

Alcohol is widely consumed by a large portion of the U.S. population. Findings from the 2010 National Household Survey indicate that slightly more than half of Americans reported that they were current drinkers of alcohol (52%), with current drinking defined as having had an alcoholic beverage within the past 30 days. The survey was conducted with participants 12 years and older, so the rate of current alcohol use does include underage drinkers (see Chapter 1 for more information about the survey methodology). The data suggests that approximately 131 million people in the United States have consumed an alcoholic beverage in the past month. The survey also asks how much alcohol is consumed and how often. The researchers found that nearly one-quarter (23%) of respondents reported binge drinking, which was defined as having five or more drinks in a row on at least one day in the past 30 days. In addition, 7% reported heavy drinking, which was defined as binge drinking on at least five days in the past 30 days. Thus, approximately 17 million people in the United States are drinking heavily, which is putting their brains and livers at risk for serious problems. Given that the consumption of alcohol is illegal for persons under the age of 21 in the United States, it is also interesting that the survey data suggested that there are an estimated 10 million underage drinkers nationwide. Finally, the survey asked about driving under the influence. Approximately 11% of all survey respondents reported driving under the influence in the past year. The highest rate of impaired driving was for ages 21 to 25, where the rates of driving under the influence was 23% (nearly 1 in 4 people for this age group!) (SAMHSA, 2011a).

Worldwide

Alcohol is widely consumed around the world, but despite widespread consumption, most people do not drink. About half of all men and two-thirds of women worldwide do not consume alcohol on a regular basis. Among the rest of the world's population, the majority of people consume alcohol safely, but harmful use of alcohol is still widespread. Nearly 4% of all deaths worldwide are related to alcohol, including injuries, cancer, cardiovascular disease, and liver cirrhosis. Among young people between the ages of 15 and 29, approximately 9% of all deaths are due to alcohol-related causes. The United States ranks in about the middle of all countries in alcohol consumption. There are regions of the world that drink far less than the United States (Northern Africa and the Middle East) and other regions that drink far more than the United States (Northern Europe and Northern Asia). Note that the countries that consume the most alcohol also have the most alcohol-related problems. The heavy drinking that occurs in the Russian Federation and neighboring countries (sometimes described informally as the "vodka belt") results in 1 in 5 men dying from alcohol-related causes. Countries including the Russian Federation, Ukraine, Belarus, Finland, Norway, Iceland, Sweden, Greenland, Lithuania, Estonia, Latvia, Poland, and Slovakia have populations that consume high levels of distilled spirits and also experience disproportionate levels of alcohol-related health and social problems. By contrast, countries such as Afghanistan, Iran, Kuwait, Libya, Saudi Arabia, Sudan, and Yemen experience almost no alcohol-related harms, as alcohol consumption is incompatible with Islamic religion, social norms, and/or laws in these countries (WHO, 2011a).

Binge Drinking in Adolescents and College Students

Epidemiology

Even though adolescents and most college students are not of the legal age to drink in the United States, many do so anyway. College life seems to have special status when it comes to alcohol use. College students have always had higher rates of drinking than similarly aged peers who do not attend college. As far back as the 1950s, researchers provided data from a U.S. national survey documenting the widespread use of alcohol by college students (Straus & Bacon, 1953). Clearly, college drinking has long been considered a rite of passage and integrated with the college experience. However, the high level of drinking that occurs on college campuses is disconcerting. Approximately 80% of college students have consumed alcohol in the past year, though most of these students are underage. More importantly, it is estimated that almost one-half of all college students are considered binge drinkers, which in many studies is defined as the consumption of five or more alcoholic beverages on one drinking occasion in the past two weeks for males and four or more alcohol beverages on one drinking occasion in the past two weeks for females (Wechsler, Dowdall, Davenport, & Castillo, 1995; Wechsler et al., 2002). Binge drinking is associated with intoxicating doses of alcohol and leads to many problems. The culture of college drinking is obviously not to drink moderately! College students often aim to drink frequently, heavily, and with the goal of getting drunk (Marczinski, Grant, & Grant, 2009). Note, however, that heavy alcohol consumption is not universal on college campuses. One-fifth of college students do not drink at all (Wechsler et al., 1995, 2002).

Some people perceive a stereotype of the heavy college drinker: white, male, athletic member of a fraternity who views parties as important to the college experience. There is some truth to this stereotype. Binge drinking is more common among freshman students, males, individuals involved in varsity athletics, and/or members of fraternities/sororities (Wechsler et al., 1995, 2002). The type of college matters as well. College students at religious or commuter schools drink less than similar peers attending other colleges (Dowdall, 2009). Binge drinking in college students is also now well understood as a pattern of drinking that is established before entrance to college. Underage drinking in high school students is common and contributes to the main causes of death among high school students (Miller, Naimi, Brewer, & Jones, 2007). Drinking in adolescents, especially with an early age of onset, is a strong predictor of college drinking habits and a subsequent alcohol-use disorder diagnosis (Morean, Corbin, & Fromme, 2012). Moreover, underage drinking is associated with cognitive deficits and brain damage (McQueeny et al., 2009). See the "More about the Science" feature for further evidence of this.

The high rate of extreme drinking in high school and college populations is interesting, in part because there has been an overall general decline in drinking in society as a whole. Moreover, college students in other countries similar to the United States seem not to engage in binge drinking to the same degree. For example, researchers have compared the drinking patterns of U.S. and Canadian college students (who are relatively similar except that the drinking age is 18 or 19 in Canada, depending on the province). Canadian college students had higher lifetime and past-year rates of alcohol use compared to the U.S. students. However, binge alcohol use for past-week and past-year drinkers was significantly higher among U.S. students than their Canadian counterparts (41% versus 35% for past-week binge alcohol use, 54% versus 42% for past-year binge alcohol use). Hence, the authors concluded that while Canadian students are more likely to drink, it was the U.S. students who drank more and to excess, with a variety of possible social and environmental causes (Kuo et al., 2002).

Negative Effects on Health and Well-being

When alcohol is consumed at high levels by adolescents and college students, there can be serious and sometimes deadly consequences. Binge drinking is associated with a host of social and personal problems. Binge drinkers are more likely to have poor academic performance, drive while intoxicated, damage property, suffer injuries, and engage in violence and risky sexual behavior (Wechsler et al., 1994). A continued pattern of binge drinking also poses immediate and long-term health consequences. Immediate consequences include alcohol poisoning, which may result in a trip to the emergency room or could even be fatal. The same outcomes occur with driving after drinking. Additionally, there are the preventable injuries. For example, college students have fallen out of upper story windows, walked into traffic, or choked on their own vomit because they passed out from drinking too much. In some cases, these are close calls, but in other cases these incidents result in funerals—a terrible shame, since they are entirely preventable. Moreover, there are a subset of individuals who binge drink in college and then experience long-term consequences, including alcohol dependence and liver cirrhosis (Wechsler et al., 1995).

Prevention and Intervention

Drinking is integrated into college life, which makes combating excessive drinking with prevention and intervention programs extremely challenging, given the "culture of alcohol" on college campuses (NIAAA, 2002, 2008). However, colleges and universities have achieved some successes. Prevention programs vary, but many try to alter awareness and encourage students to think about the consequences of drinking heavily (cognitive approach). Other prevention programs attempt to alter the college environment. This is achieved by decreasing alcohol availability for underage students, having strong penalties for underage students who are caught drinking on campus, raising alcohol prices and taxes, limiting bar locations by mandating that they be located at least a certain distance from campus, having alcohol-free residences, and limiting kegs in residences to students who are of the age to drink (environmental approach) (NIAAA, 2002, 2008). Colleges will often work with local businesses and local government to enact these environmental changes. When college students have problems with alcohol, there are several interventions available. Alcohol expectancy challenge interventions work by altering how students think about drinking. For example, a student may think that alcohol makes him more attractive to the opposite sex. The intervention would challenge this notion by examining recent incidents of being rebuffed by the opposite sex for being too drunk, aggressive, and out-of-control. This intervention approach can change expectations about alcohol but may have limited long-term effectiveness in reducing risky drinking practices (Scott-Sheldon, Terry, Carey, Garey, & Carey, 2012). A more effective intervention is motivational interviewing with feedback. In motivational interviewing, the individual receives personalized feedback about the harms associated with her recent drinking activity (Cowell, Brown, Mills, Bender, & Wedehase, 2012; Riper et al., 2009). Typically, the student is asked to provide information about his or her own recent drinking behavior. The student's own drinking habits are then compared to the normal drinking patterns of other students at the school by the clinician. The health risks of the student's own drinking habits are then discussed. These individual face-to-face interventions, while more expensive to implement, tend to result in much greater reductions in drinking over time as well as greater reductions in alcohol-related problems (Carey, Scott-Sheldon, Carey, & DeMartini, 2007). In sum, a comprehensive plan that incorporates both prevention and intervention strategies can reduce harmful drinking on a college campus.

In addition to the prevention and intervention efforts discussed above, it is important that college students generally know what scientists perceive as safe levels of drinking for an adult 21 and older. Based on research that has examined health risks (liver cirrhosis) and likelihood of developing alcohol dependence, guidelines for low-risk drinking have been developed (Figure 8-4). Low-risk drinking for men constitutes no more than 4 standard drinks per day and no more than 14 drinks per week. Women are more likely to experience alcohol-related harms at lower thresholds of drinking, thus the low-risk drinking limits are lower. It is recommended that women consume no more than 3 standard drinks per day and no more than 7 drinks per week. Keeping within these limits will considerably decrease the likelihood of developing problems with alcohol. However, individuals under the age of 21 should not drink, because high doses of

Low-risk drinking limits		MEN	WOMEN
On any Single DAY		No more than **4** 🍺🍺🍺🍺 drinks on any day	No more than **3** 🍺🍺🍺 drinks on any day
		AND	**AND**
Per WEEK		No more than **14** drinks per week	No more than **7** drinks per week
To stay low risk, keep within BOTH the single-day AND weekly limits.			

FIGURE 8-4

Keeping within these recommended limits constitutes low-risk drinking (NIAAA, 2012b). However, avoid alcohol altogether if you are: (1) underage, (2) pregnant or planning to become pregnant, (3) planning to drive a vehicle or operate machinery, (4) taking medications that interact with alcohol, and/or (5) managing a medical condition that can be made worse by drinking.

alcohol can cause serious damage to their still-developing brains. This risk has been clearly demonstrated in both human and animal studies (Coleman, He, Lee, Styner, & Crews, 2011; Crews, Braun, Hoplight, Switzer, & Knapp, 2000; Lisdahl, Thayer, Squeglia, McQueeny, & Tapert, 2013; McQueeny et al., 2009; Parada et al., 2012; Vetreno & Crews, 2012). In addition, the age of drinking onset is a predictor of later alcohol dependence, with adolescents who start drinking at earlier ages being more likely to develop serious problems with alcohol (Lee, Young-Wolff, Kendler, & Prescott, 2012). For individuals who are of the legal age to drink, various strategies can help keep drinking in a safe range. Simple things like keeping track of the number of drinks consumed, pacing drink consumption to one per hour, alternating alcoholic drinks with nonalcoholic drinks, eating food while drinking, and finding alternative ways to have fun with friends not centering on alcohol are a few suggestions.

More about the Science:

McQueeny et al. (2009). Altered white matter integrity in adolescent binge drinkers. *Alcoholism: Clinical and Experimental Research*, *33*, 1278–1285.

Binge drinking is common in high school students. However, the adolescent brain continues undergoing structural maturation until age 21. Thus, heavy alcohol consumption may be damaging to a developing brain, even though similar doses of alcohol may not cause problems for an adult brain. McQueeny et al. (2009) examined the impact of alcohol use on the adolescent brain by imaging the white matter in the brain of adolescents. The researchers focused on white matter (myelin) since myelin insulates the axons in the brain, which leads to improved neural conduction (see Chapter 2). In addition, white matter maturation continues into late adolescence, with chronic adult alcoholics tending to have reduced white matter. The researchers used an MRI technique called diffusion tensor imaging to assess the integrity of the white matter in the brains of adolescents who did or did not binge drink. The two groups were otherwise matched on a variety of other demographic characteristics. The researchers observed that the binge drinkers had reduced white matter integrity compared to the non–binge drinkers. This white matter deficiency was observed throughout the brain, including in the major fiber tract pathways found in the frontal, temporal, and parietal lobe regions, as well as the cerebellum. In addition, the intensity of binge drinking mattered. Greater self-reported drinking (peak blood alcohol concentrations) and a greater frequency of hangovers were associated with reduced white matter integrity.

More about the Science Thought Questions:

1. Given the results of this particular study, can one conclude that binge drinking in adolescence damages white matter (myelin)?
2. What might be practical implications of reduced white matter in the brains of binge drinking adolescents?

More about the Science Thought Question Answers:

1. It would be slightly premature to conclude that white matter deficits result from binge drinking. It is possible that decreased white matter integrity predisposes an adolescent to binge drink. Only animal studies can conclusively determine if the binge use of alcohol damages white matter.
2. White matter improves the speed of neuronal conduction because it insulates axons. Therefore, less white matter would result in slower neural conduction. As a result, thinking might be slowed. School performance could be affected when binge drinking adolescents would be less able to think as quickly as their peers.

QUICK QUIZ 8-1

1. Alcohol is a central nervous system _____ drug.
   a. sedative
   b. stimulant
   c. excitatory
   d. amphetamine-like
   e. None of the above

2. _____ consume fermented beverages.
   a. Humans
   b. Treeshrews
   c. Fruit flies
   d. a and b only
   e. All of the above

3. The maximum alcohol content that can be achieved with fermentation alone is _____.
   a. 2%
   b. 5%
   c. 15%
   d. 20%
   e. 100%

4. Distillation can increase the alcohol content of a fermented beverage. Why?
   a. Alcohol has a lower boiling point than water.
   b. Alcohol has a higher boiling point than water.
   c. Yeast multiply in the presence of sugar.
   d. Carbon dioxide release increases the alcohol content.

5. Historically, the intentional production and consumption of alcohol first occurred around
   a. 17,000 BCE
   b. 7,000 BCE
   c. 700 BCE
   d. 700 CE

6. According to the 2010 U.S. National Household Survey, _____ of Americans are current drinkers of alcohol.
   a. 72%
   b. 62%
   c. 52%
   d. 42%

7. According to NIAAA, what is considered low-risk drinking?

8. Where does the United States rank in worldwide alcohol use?

ANSWERS TO QUICK QUIZ 8-1:

1. a – sedative
2. e – all of the above
3. c – 15%

4. a – alcohol has a lower boiling point than water
5. b – 7000 BCE
6. c – 52%

7. According to NIAAA, low-risk drinking for men constitutes no more than 4 standard drinks per day and no more than 14 standard drinks per week. Women are more likely to experience alcohol-related harms at lower thresholds of drinking, thus the low-risk drinking limits for women are lower. It is recommended that women consume no more than 3 standard drinks per day and no more than 7 drinks per week. Keeping within these limits will considerably decrease the likelihood of developing problems. Moreover, no alcohol consumption should occur in individuals ages 20 and younger, because alcohol can be particularly harmful to the developing brain. In addition, individuals who are pregnant or who have medical conditions that contraindicate alcohol use should abstain.

8. The U.S. ranks in about the middle of countries in alcohol consumption. There are regions of the word that drink far less than the United States (Northern Africa and the Middle East) and other regions that drink far more than the United States (Northern Europe and Northern Asia).

Acute Effects of Alcohol

The acute effects of alcohol are changes that take place after ingesting alcohol one time. Acute effects can be objective, including observable changes in behavior or physiology. Acute effects can also be subjective, such as when individuals report how intoxicated (drunk) they feel. Researchers have determined that the acute effects of alcohol are strongly dependent on **blood alcohol concentration (BAC),** or the amount of alcohol that is circulating in the bloodstream. A BAC of .10 g% translates to one part of alcohol per thousand parts of blood. There are various ways to assess BAC. Direct methods include taking breath or blood samples. Techniques to assess BAC were described in greater detail in Chapter 3. Police officers routinely rely on breath samples to ascertain whether drivers are over the legal limit (.08 g%). Breath samples tend to be reasonably reliable, as there is a direct 2000:1 relationship between the amount of alcohol observed in blood and the amount of alcohol in expired alveolar air (Fleming et al., 2001). Using research that relied on direct blood or breath methods to assess BAC, researchers have developed mathematical calculations to estimate BAC based on a variety of factors. These calculations are used in both research and practice. In the real world, BAC calculations can be used to estimate approximate BAC in legal cases. For example, an individual may be suspected of committing a crime under the influence of alcohol, but no Breathalyzer reading was obtained at the time of the incident (Figure 8-5). Experts may gather information about amount of alcohol consumed, timing of alcohol consumption, body weight, gender, food consumed, and a variety of other factors to estimate BAC at the time of the crime. Several equations are available; the updated Widmark equation is the most widely used in forensic cases (Watson, Watson, & Bat, 1981). These same

FIGURE 8-5
The Breathalyzer machine is a device can be used to assess breath alcohol concentration.

©James Shaffer/Photo Edit

calculations are also used in research for a variety of reasons or as part of safe drinking intervention programs. Some calculations are very basic, including only the number of standard drinks consumed and the time since drinking was initiated.

For example:

$$BAC = (NSD)(.025) - (NHD)(.015)$$

NSD = number of standard drinks (12 oz. beer, 5 oz. wine, or 1.5 oz. shot of liquor)

NHD = number of hours since drinking began

Example: You consumed 4 bottles of beer and you started drinking 3 hours ago. Your BAC is approximately (4)(.025) − (3)(.015) = .1 − .045 = .055 g%.

The above calculation allows an individual to quickly estimate BAC. This calculation makes a few important assumptions. First, the formula assumes the individual weighs approximately 160 pounds. Therefore, the first part of the formula, or (NSD)(.025), is the estimate of how much BAC rises (.025 g%) per standard drink consumed given a body weight of 160 pounds. The first part of the equation estimates that BAC will rise approximately .05 g% if 2 standard drinks are consumed. However, body weight is an important variable not included in this equation. Thus, the first part of the calculation can be slightly unreliable if the individual is extremely light or heavy. A small body size would lead to an underestimation of BAC and a large body size would lead to an overestimation of BAC.

The second part of the formula estimates how much BAC drops over time. Alcohol is metabolized by the liver at a steady rate that causes a drop in BAC of .015 g% per hour. Therefore, the second part of the formula uses time to estimate how much BAC has been reduced due to alcohol metabolism. Unlike the first part, body weight has no impact on the accuracy of the second part of the equation. Moreover, the calculation illustrates that BAC drops very slowly, since every standard drink needs more than an hour to be metabolized out of the body.

Two factors deserve special mention in discussing BACs. First, women tend to achieve higher BACs than men, even when the amount of alcohol given is proportional to body weight. Women tend to have a higher percentage of body fat and different levels of the enzymes that break down alcohol, which will be explained further later in this chapter (Pikaar, Wedel, & Hermus, 1988). Second, consumption of food is important in lowering BAC. When food is present in the stomach, there is a delay in stomach emptying. As a result, food and alcohol do not reach the small intestine and ultimately the bloodstream as quickly as would have occurred if no food had been present. If a male consumes three standard drinks on an empty stomach, BAC may reach somewhere between .067 g% and .092 g%. The same male who eats a full meal with the same amount of alcohol may reach a BAC of only between .030 g% and .053 g% (Fleming et al., 2001). As such, a meal might make the difference whether this male would be over or under the legal driving limit (.08 g%). Even what you mix in your alcohol can affect BAC. If alcohol is mixed with a diet drink, BAC will be higher than if the same amount of alcohol is mixed with a sugar-sweetened beverage (Wu et al., 2006). Again, the differences can be dramatic, with peak BACs being over the limit (.091 g%) when alcohol is administered with a diet drink mixer even though the same amount of alcohol mixed with a sugar-sweetened beverage would result in a lower BAC (.077 g%) (Marczinski & Stamates, 2013).

The acute effects of alcohol depend on the BAC. Table 8-1 illustrates some of the effects associated with various BACs. However, specific outcomes differ for individuals based on several factors. How much alcohol an individual typically drinks, how quickly alcohol is consumed, gender, body weight, percentage of body fat (physical condition), drugs and medications, and the amount of food in the stomach are all factors that influence BAC. Despite this variability, changes in brain and body functioning consistently occur as BAC rises since alcohol alters activity in various body systems.

Table 8-1   Blood alcohol concentration and typical acute alcohol effects.

BAC (g%)	Typical Effects		
	Objective	Subjective	Physiological
.01–.02	Little changes; a driver's ability to divide attention between two tasks (talking on a cell phone while driving) can be impaired	Slight changes; feeling of well-being	Little changes
.03–.04	Mild impairment of motor skills such as tracking & steering when driving	Feeling relaxed, slightly exhilarated, more talkative	Skin may be flushed in some individuals
.05–.06	Impaired judgment; Motor coordination impairments are more noticeable; Visual and hearing acuity decreased; Mild working memory impairment such as forgetting someone's name after an introduction; Reduced inhibitory control over behavior; **.05 g% is the legal limit for driving in many countries around the world**	Exaggerated emotional reactions (happy or sad); Feeling disinhibited and impulsive; Feeling of warmth, relaxation; Stimulation and sedation (may be dependent on whether BAC is rising or falling)	Increased urination
.07–.09	Impaired judgment, motor coordination & reaction times; Speech is slurred; Some disturbance of balance; **.08 g% is the legal limit for driving in U.S. and Canada**	Clearly intoxicated; May not recognize impairment	Numbness of senses (face and limbs); Increased urination
.10–.13	Balance is clearly impaired (person may stagger when walking); Uncoordinated behavior; Significant increases in reaction time; Pronounced impairments in judgment & memory	Clearly intoxicated	Decreased pain perception; Jerky eye movements
.14–.19	Significant impairment of all physical and mental functions; Difficulty standing and talking; Profound impairments in judgment, perception, reaction time	Blackouts (failure to recall events for a portion of time) coincide with BAC of .15 g% and higher	Vomiting or nausea can occur
.20–.29	Difficulty staying awake; Double vision, slurred speech, cannot walk or stand without assistance	Confused, dazed	
.30–.39	Loss of consciousness (passing out); Cannot comprehend what is going on; General suppression of all cognitive abilities	Confusion and stupor	Loss of consciousness; Vital reflexes like gagging & breathing become compromised; considered lethal dose (LD_1) since 1 in 100 people die at this BAC level
.40 – .44	Unconscious/coma	Unconscious/coma	Unconscious/coma; skin is sweaty and clammy;

BAC (g%)	Typical Effects		
	Objective	Subjective	Physiological
			Alcohol has become an anesthetic
.45 – .50+	Deep coma/death	Deep coma/death	Deep coma/death; circulation & respiration ceases to function; considered lethal dose (LD_{50}) since 50 out of 100 people would die at this level

Quick calculation to estimate **BAC = (NSD)(.025) – (NHD)(.015)**

NSD number of standard drinks (12 oz. beer, 5 oz. wine, or 1.5 oz. shot of liquor)

NHD number of hours since drinking began

e.g., You consumed 4 bottles of beer and you started drinking 3 hours ago. Your BAC is approximately (4)(.025) – (3)(.015) = .1 – .045 = .055 g%.

Note that body weight and gender are not taken into account in this quick calculation.

Table adapted from Marczinski et al. (2009) and Wechsler & Wuethrich (2002).

Objective Effects

Alcohol is a sedative drug. Therefore, the acute effects of alcohol result in impairments in cognitive and motor performance. As the amount of alcohol increases in the body, so does the impairment that can be easily observable in a variety of laboratory tasks, including psychomotor performance, working memory, and attention. When blood alcohol rises to very high levels in the body, unconsciousness, coma, and even death can result. However, at low doses, it appears as if alcohol has a stimulant effect. Drinkers may appear more talkative, more willing to engage in conversations with strangers, more aggressive, and have greater libido (enhanced sexual interest). How do all of these behaviors, which appear to be stimulatory in nature, occur if alcohol is a sedative drug? When a small amount of alcohol is consumed, the sedative effects initially decrease functioning of brain areas responsible for control over behavior (which is sometimes referred to as **inhibitory control**) (Figure 8-6). Brain regions such as the prefrontal cortex and the anterior cingulate are important for engagement of self-control, and they are also susceptible to the impairing effects of alcohol from a few drinks (Anderson et al., 2011). As a result, an individual will appear less in control of his or her own behavior and will appear more impulsive after a few drinks (Fillmore, 2003). Additionally, weakened inhibitory control can also lead to further alcohol consumption. As an illustration, imagine that a college student goes to the bar with some friends. In advance of entering the bar, he plans to have only one beer, since he needs to go home and write a paper due the next morning. However, one drink later, inhibitory control is being diminished. His friends urge him to have one more beer before he has to leave, and so he consumes another. The ability to weigh the short-term gain of staying with friends versus the long-term consequences of having no paper written becomes increasingly difficult as self-control is diminished with every additional sip of alcoholic drink.

It may seem counterintuitive that a sedative drug, alcohol, has stimulant effects at low doses. In the previous chapter on amphetamines (Chapter 7), we discussed how hyperactive children experience a calming effect with low doses of amphetamines, even though amphetamines are stimulant drugs. In children with ADHD, the prefrontal cortex of the brain is hypoactive (underactive). When amphetamines are given at low doses, the stimulant effect brings this region of the brain to a more "normal" level of functioning, such that children are better able to control their behavior. However, excessive doses of amphetamines result in classic stimulant effects in children with ADHD and others who do not have ADHD. The areas of the brain responsible for control over behavior are important and can account for some counterintuitive observations regarding low doses of psychoactive drugs, including amphetamines and alcohol.

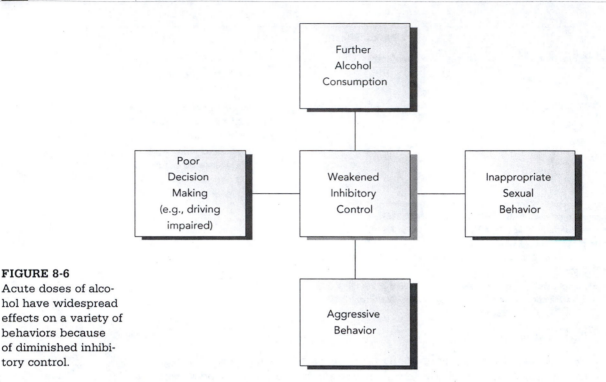

FIGURE 8-6
Acute doses of alcohol have widespread effects on a variety of behaviors because of diminished inhibitory control.

Alcohol and Driving

Driving is a complicated skill requiring one's full faculties. The acute effects of alcohol diminish all aspects of cognitive performance, with driving no exception. Even at low BAC levels, driving ability is impacted, in part because driving requires one to engage in more than one task simultaneously. A driver must: monitor the visual field, pay attention to the constantly changing surroundings, look for unexpected events and respond accordingly, track his or her own vehicle on the road, make decisions about when to change lanes or make a turn and signal accordingly, manipulate gas and brake pedals to maintain the posted speed limit or stop as required, and make continuous other judgments. All of these skills are diminished at BAC levels well below the legal limit (.08 g%) and are even reduced at a BAC level under .05 g%. More alcohol in the system (particularly above .08 g%) leads to greater diminishment of vision, and the ability to stay alert is dramatically reduced. Alcohol-induced impairment is clearly evident in driving, perhaps more than any other cognitive task (Verster, Pandi-Perumal, Ramaekers, & de Gier, 2009).

Since the acute effects of alcohol impair driving ability, it comes as no surprise that alcohol remains one of the principal risk factors for motor vehicle crashes. Earlier in this chapter, statistics on impaired driving were presented. Findings from the 2010 National Household Survey indicated that the highest rate of impaired driving was for ages 21 to 25, where impaired driving rates were 23% (nearly 1 in 4) (SAMHSA, 2011a). The National Highway Traffic Safety Administration reported 10,288 U.S. fatalities in crashes involving a driver with a BAC of .08 or higher in the year 2010. That corresponds to 31% of the total traffic fatalities for the year. Drivers with a BAC level of .08 or higher who were killed in a crash were four times more likely to have had a prior conviction for driving while impaired than were drivers who consumed no alcohol. Moreover, it cannot be overlooked that innocent individuals are harmed or killed by impaired drivers. In 2010, 17% of children who were killed in motor vehicle traffic crashes were victims of drunk driving. This includes children who were either in a vehicle that was hit by a drunk driver, in a vehicle driven by a drunk driver, or pedestrians/bicyclists hit and killed by a drunk driver. It goes without saying that these deaths are preventable if people would not mix drinking and driving (NHTSA, 2012).

Grassroots organizations such as Mothers Against Drug Driving (MADD) have been instrumental in changing public opinion as well as legislation regarding drunk driving over the last several decades. Analyzing the impact of public policy changes is challenging, in part because hundreds of laws have been implemented in the United States, reducing alcohol-impaired driving and accidents. Despite challenges, it is fairly well accepted that lowering state BAC limits has been an effective approach in reducing impaired driving accidents and deaths. The move from a .10 g% to a .08 g% legal limit for driving in the United States has lowered the number of alcohol-related crashes, fatalities, or injuries between 5% and 16% (Fell & Voas, 2006; Voas et al., 2002; Wagenaar et al., 2007). Other analyses have determined that raising the minimum legal drinking age (MLDA) to 21 and reinforcing this by making it illegal for underage drivers to have any alcohol in their system (zero tolerance laws) have been effective and have prevented an estimated 732 deaths each year (Fell et al., 2009; Voas, Tippetts, & Fell, 2003). In most other countries, the legal BAC limit for driving has been lowered to .05 g% or below (Bernhoft & Behrensdorff, 2003). These changes have occurred because research findings always suggest that lowering the limit saves lives. The risk of a fatal crash is 4 to 10 times higher for drivers with BACs between .05 g% and .07 g% than for sober drivers (Fell & Voas, 2006). In Brazil, zero tolerance for drinking is now the standard for driving, which has resulted in significant reductions in alcohol-related traffic fatalities (Andreuccetti et al., 2011). It remains to be seen whether the United States will consider further lowering the legal limit, though scientific evidence seems to suggest that such a policy could save lives and reduce costs (Phillips & Brewer, 2011).

Alcohol and Aggression

Alcohol and aggression often coincide with alcohol-related violence, which is a serious and common societal concern. Crimes of murder, attempted murder, manslaughter, sexual assault, and child/partner/spousal abuse often involve alcohol consumption on the part of perpetrator and even sometimes the victim (Abbey, 2011; Foran & O'Leary, 2008). Bars, parties, and athletic events can be environmental contexts in which alcohol-induced aggression is more likely (Moore, Shepherd, Eden, & Sivarajasingam, 2007; Treno, Gruenewald, Remer, Johnson, & Lascala, 2008). The acute effects of alcohol result in diminished judgment and heightened emotionality, which facilitates aggressive behavior, especially in conflict-filled situations (Heinz, Beck, Meyer-Lindenberg, Sterzer, & Heinz, 2011). Moreover, alcohol-induced aggression is not limited to humans, since it has also been observed in a variety of animal models, including mice, rats, and monkeys. As one example, researchers presented male mice with an intruder male mouse in their home cage. Mice dislike an intruder on their home turf, which makes this a good paradigm to study aggression. Mice who were under the influence of alcohol displayed large increases in the frequency of bite attacks and other hostile behavior (de Almeida, Rowlett, Cook, Yin, & Miczek, 2004). Moreover, aggression increases with the alcohol dose. In a study with male and female college students, researchers demonstrated that there is a clear alcohol dose-dependent rise in aggression, as measured by intensity and duration of shocks administered to a fictitious opponent (Duke, Giancola, Morris, Holt, & Gunn, 2011). However, alcohol does not universally induce aggression. Many people drink and never so much as make a nasty comment to another. Researchers attempt to identify individual differences to understand better who is more or less likely to become aggressive when drinking. Typically, males are far more likely to be aggressive than females when drinking. Moreover, individuals who are generally more impulsive, uninhibited, hostile, and antisocial are more likely to be aggressive under the influence of alcohol (Birkley, Giancola, & Lance, 2013; Borders & Giancola, 2011; Giancola, Godlaski, & Roth, 2012). Likewise, being unconcerned about the future consequences of one's actions is also a baseline trait that leads to greater aggression when combined with alcohol (Bushman, Giancola, Parrott, & Roth, 2012). In sum, aggression results when alcohol interacts with personality and aspects of the environment (Abbey, 2011; Dewall, Bushman, Giancola, & Webster, 2010).

Subjective Effects

The acute effects of alcohol alter one's subjective state in several ways, and some of these changes are primary motivators for individuals to consume the drug. Individuals feel euphoric when drinking. They also may feel more emotional, an outcome that can be positive or negative depending on the circumstance. The subjective emotions of happiness, sadness, or anger depend on the dose of alcohol and a variety of other cognitive and environmental factors. If one is already sad to begin with, alcohol may lead to heightened feelings of sadness and dysphoric mood. However, if one is already happy, alcohol may facilitate further happiness as well. Drinkers also have preexisting expectations of how they will feel when drinking. If one thinks that drinking alcohol will make them happier, less stressed or more sexually aroused, they may perceive these changes as occurring after consuming alcohol (or act accordingly, even though they were only given a placebo beverage in a study). Subjective state changes under alcohol also result in feelings of stimulation and sedation. The outcome somewhat depends on whether BAC is rising or falling. Typically, individuals report more stimulating effects when BAC is rising (early in the drinking session). By contrast, individuals report more sedating effects when BAC is falling (later in the drinking session) (Martin, Earleywine, Musty, Perrine, & Swift, 1993). Enhancement of subjective stimulation may partly explain why mixing energy drinks or other stimulants with alcohol results in greater risks associated with drinking, such as longer drinking sessions, higher BACs, and increased likelihood of needing emergency medical treatment (Marczinski et al., 2011, 2012; O'Brien, McCoy, Rhodes, Wagoner, & Wolfson, 2008; Thombs et al., 2010).

Subjective feeling states contribute to cognition and behavior. For example, how one feels can contribute to decision making about whether to drink more or whether to engage in risky behaviors. A drinker's self-perception of how they feel is part of an assessment of whether they are intoxicated. For example, such efficacy judgments can be the basis upon which a drinker decides if he or she is able to drive. Researchers have clearly demonstrated that both social and dependent drinkers are very poor estimators of intoxication, with judgments becoming less accurate as BAC increases (Beirness, 1987). Moreover, the more frequently one drinks, the more likely one will be inaccurate in judging driving ability, even when driving ability is extremely impaired. For example, college students who binge drink are more likely to report being willing to drive, especially as BAC is declining, compared to similar college students who drink more moderately (Figure 8-7; the * indicates a significant difference between the groups). However, both groups are equally poor drivers when intoxicated (Marczinski et al., 2008; Marczinski & Fillmore, 2009).

In the News:

Granderson, L. Z. (2012). Drunken driving is not about the NFL. *CNN*.

The National Football League (NFL) has undergone criticism in the wake of the DUI arrest and charges of intoxication manslaughter against Dallas Cowboys player Josh Brent, age 24. Brent was apparently out drinking with his friend and teammate Jerry Brown, age 25, in Dallas, TX. At approximately 2:20 a.m., Brent was intoxicated when he drove his car at high speeds and hit a curb. The car flipped over and caught on fire. Brown died in the crash. Brent has had previous DUI charges and may spend up to 20 years in prison. Critics of the NFL have argued that driving drunk seems to be a persistent problem among players. The author of this news article argues that drunk driving occurs because our culture promotes a casual attitude toward intoxication and driving. While the arrest of a professional athlete may make headlines, the author argues that the problem is far more widespread than any of us likes to admit, especially among young adult males.

Use this news article to test and apply your knowledge:

1. The author of this article argues that impaired driving is common in society, especially among young adults. Is this assertion correct?
2. The crash in this incident was very serious. The car flipped over and caught on fire. What does alcohol intoxication do to an individual's ability to drive?

Answers:

1. Yes, the author is correct. Findings from the 2010 National Household Survey indicated that the highest rate of impaired driving was among individuals ages 21 to 25, where past year rates of impaired driving were 23% (nearly 1 in 4). Both individuals in this incident were in the age group most likely to engage in impaired driving (and also most likely to binge drink).
2. Driving is a complicated skill that is significantly compromised by alcohol intoxication. All driving skills are diminished at BAC levels well below the legal limit (.08 g%) and are even reduced at BAC levels under .05 g%. With more alcohol in the system (particularly above .08 g%), vision is diminished and the ability to stay alert is dramatically reduced. In addition, alcohol diminishes impulse control and increases aggression, which could have contributed to the crash that led to the death of Jerry Brown.

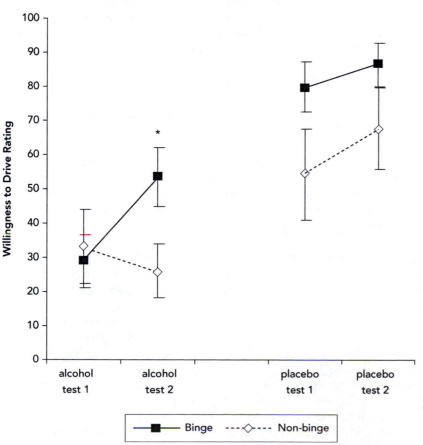

FIGURE 8-7

College students who are binge drinkers are more likely to report that they are willing to drive when blood alcohol is declining (test 2) as compared to when blood alcohol is rising (test 1), which indicates development of acute tolerance to the subjective effects of alcohol. Non-binge social drinkers do not report any differences when tested at the same time points. Both groups are poor drivers under alcohol when tested at both time points (Marczinski & Fillmore, 2009).

Effects on the Body

The acute effects of alcohol have a variety of effects on the body. Pain perception is reduced. Balance and coordination are also reliably reduced with increasing BAC. The ability to stand still is diminished when the balance controls in the inner ear are impacted by alcohol. Assessment of balance and coordination impairments serves as the basis for field sobriety testing that police officers use to assess possible alcohol intoxication in drivers. While the field sobriety test may differ from state to state, three tests make up the battery that has been approved by the National Highway Traffic Safety Administration and appears to be the most reliable (NHTSA, 2001; Stuster, 2006). The battery consists of (1) the one-leg stand, (2) the walk-and-turn, and (3) horizontal gaze nystagmus. As the name suggests, the one-leg stand requires the individual to stand on one leg. Individuals with a BAC of .08 g% or higher will have great difficulty in doing so. The walk-and-turn test includes both a motor and cognitive component. The individual is instructed to walk a straight line using 9 heel-to-toe steps. The individual must count out loud. Those with BACs above .08 g% typically fail this step when they are unable to follow instructions and/or unable to keep their balance while walking the line. Finally, the horizontal gaze nystagmus assessment asks the individual to look at a pen moving in front of their eyes from left to right. When BACs rise above .08 g%, individuals are no longer able to smoothly move their eyes to follow the moving object. Instead, eye movements appear involuntarily jerky when vision is impaired by alcohol. Note that officers typically administer the field sobriety test for suspicion of alcohol use and then follow up with a breath alcohol test.

In addition to changes in balance and coordination, alcohol stimulates gastric secretions and induces sensations of hunger. Alcohol also reduces the amount of body fat that can be oxidized. As such, regular use of alcohol can result in weight gain, since the alcohol itself contains calories, alcohol stimulates appetite, and alcohol alters body fat oxidation. If the alcohol dose is sufficiently high, the alcohol begins to harm the stomach, leading to gastrointestinal problems. Nausea and vomiting may occur at BACs greater than .15 g%, but there are significant individual differences in response to alcohol, with vomiting often occurring below the .15 g% level (Fleming et al., 2001).

Drinkers sometimes perceive that alcohol increases sexual interest, but the effect on the body is actually the opposite. While a subjective change of increased sexual interest may be due to alcohol's disinhibiting effect on libido, most research on the acute effects of alcohol and sexual function indicates that alcohol interferes with sexual ability. Increased BAC is associated with decreased sexual arousal, increased ejaculatory latency, and decreased orgasmic pleasure. In fact, such concerns escalate with increasingly heavy use of alcohol, and rates of impotence are as high as 50% in chronic alcoholics. Alcohol also acts as a peripheral dilator, meaning it increases blood flow to the skin. As a result, alcohol induces a feeling of warmth. Sweating may result, which leads to lost heat and a lower body temperature. If a large amount of alcohol has been consumed, the fall in body temperature can be quite pronounced. Alcohol is a major risk factor in hypothermia deaths. Alcohol also has a diuretic effect, resulting in urination above and beyond that which would occur due to the consumption of the fluid. This effect occurs because alcohol inhibits the release of the antidiuretic hormone vasopressin. Interestingly, tolerance develops to this effect, with chronic alcoholics actually having less urine output than control subjects in response to a challenge dose of ethanol (Fleming et al., 2001).

Alcohol as a sedative drug has reliable effects on sleep and consciousness. Even at low doses, alcohol interferes with high-quality sleep, and drinkers may not feel rested upon awakening. Poor sleep results from alcohol suppressing the REM (rapid eye movement) portion of sleep, which is when dreaming occurs. REM is very important for memory consolidation, when experiences from the recent day (short-term memories) are transferred into long-term memory for permanent storage. With low doses of alcohol, REM is suppressed early in the night, and some rebound of REM occurs later in the night. For higher doses of alcohol, REM is suppressed for the whole night. When REM is suppressed, a blackout may occur. A **blackout** refers to alcohol-induced amnesia or a failure to recall a period of time during drinking in spite of no loss of consciousness. For example, a drinker may seem to have no memory for going to a new bar with friends between midnight and 2 a.m., yet the friends assert that the drinker was indeed awake and alert during that time. There are two distinguishable forms of blackouts: en bloc and fragmentary blackouts. **En bloc blackouts** are instances of full and permanent memory loss for intoxicated events. In contrast, **fragmentary blackouts** are instances of incomplete memory loss for intoxicated events where poor memories can be aided by the provision of cues to help reconstruct events to "fill in the blanks." All blackouts can be disconcerting, but en bloc blackouts tend to be experienced as very negative, more so than fragmentary blackouts (Hartzler & Fromme, 2003; Nash & Takarangi, 2011; Rose & Grant, 2010). Blackouts are reported frequently by college student drinkers. One survey of college undergraduates asked the question, "Have you ever awoken after a night of drinking not able to remember things that you did or places that you went?" Of the students who have ever consumed alcohol, 51% reported a blackout at some point in their lives and 40% reported a blackout in the past year. Some of the students reported later learning that they had participated in a range of undesirable or dangerous activities, including engaging in unprotected sex, driving, or vandalizing property (White, Jamieson-Drake, & Swartzwelder, 2002). Simple things like slowing down alcohol consumption and drinking less help prevent blackouts from occurring.

Lethal Dose

As blood alcohol rises very high, alcohol becomes an anesthetic, and loss of consciousness can result. When loss of consciousness occurs, medical intervention is a necessity since all vital reflexes like gagging, coughing, and breathing can be compromised. Without these basic reflexes, and given the predisposition to vomiting when acutely intoxicated, unconscious intoxicated individuals are at significant risk of choking or aspirating stomach contents into their lungs. Upon admission to hospital (where the unconscious person needs to be), endotracheal intubation is sometimes needed to maintain an airway and protect the lungs (Marczinski et al., 2009). In far too many cases of college-drinking deaths, an individual lost consciousness and there was no one with the good sense to call an ambulance and have the individual properly assessed by medical personnel. Never leave someone alone who has lost consciousness; allowing someone to "sleep it off" is a recipe for disaster! This cannot be emphasized strongly enough. Alcohol is a powerful sedative drug that at high doses results in death. The lethal dose of alcohol (LD_{50}) coincides with a BAC range of .45 g% to .50 g% however, there are many instances of lethal intoxication far below a BAC of .45 g%. For example, an analysis of 175 fatal cases of acute alcohol intoxication (uncomplicated by other factors) found that the mean BAC at death was .355 g%. BACs were even lower in cases were aspiration occurred (choking on vomit) as opposed to cases with no aspiration. In addition, BACs were lower in individuals who did not have a long history of prolonged heavy alcohol consumption, suggesting that tolerance may be a factor in identification of the lethal dose (Heatley & Crane, 1990). In sum, alcohol is the primary psychoactive substance found in postmortem toxicology tests, since alcohol is widely used and can result in fatalities (Jones & Holmgren, 2009).

Myth Busters: Drinking Isn't All That Dangerous

Alcohol is widely available in our society. Many college students believe that alcohol is generally safe and that concerns about drinking are overstated. It is true that alcohol, when consumed responsibly, is unlikely to lead to major problems. However, it is clearly a myth that alcohol is not dangerous, particularly when used in high doses. Just ask any emergency department physician about their typical caseload, and he or she will tell you that alcohol was a causal factor in many admissions. Between the years 1992 and 2000, an estimated 68.6 million patients were seen in U.S. emergency departments with alcohol as a factor, a rate of 28.7 cases per 1,000 patients (McDonald, Wang, & Camargo, 2004). In fact, recent data has suggested that alcohol-related emergency department visits in the United States have increased significantly over the past 15 years, even though other drug-related emergency department visits have remained essentially stable (Cherpitel & Ye, 2012). One in three 18- to 24-year-olds who end up in an emergency room is intoxicated. Up to 9% of college student freshman per academic year require an emergency department visit for an alcohol-related reason (Wright, Norton, Dake, Pinkston, & Slovis, 1998; Wright & Slovis, 1996). Alcohol use is associated with homicides, suicides, accidents, assaults, and drownings. It is estimated that 1,825 college students between the ages of 18 and 24 die each year from alcohol-related unintentional injuries (NIAAA, 2012b). One recent example might make these statistics seem more real. Northern Illinois University freshman student David Bogenberger attended an alcohol-infused party at Pi Kappa Alpha fraternity. He was found dead in a fraternity house bed the following morning. His blood alcohol content at autopsy was found to be greater than .40 g% (five times the legal limit). His family and friends grieve the loss of this young man's life. The 22 members of the fraternity who were present at the party have been criminally charged with felony hazing, and 17 other members face misdemeanor charges. A felony hazing charge can result in a possible prison sentence of up to three years and a misdemeanor hazing charge carries a possible prison sentence of up to 364 days (Walberg & St. Clair, 2012).

Focus on Careers: Lawyers

The use of alcohol leads to many societal problems. Impaired driving, underage drinking, assaults, child abuse or neglect cases, and homicides often involve alcohol. In many cases, clients on various sides of these cases need lawyers. Lawyers can advise clients and act as their advocates. The number of available career paths related to the legal profession is large, even for those wishing to specialize in a career with a psychopharmacology focus. Moreover, understanding human behavior is essential to the daily work of lawyers, making this career path an attractive option for talented undergraduate psychology majors. Knowledge of psychology can be beneficial for tasks ranging from jury selection, eye-witness testimony, to interviewing and counseling clients.

What is involved in becoming a lawyer? Application to law school involves a rigorous admission process largely based on undergraduate grades and performance on the stan-dardized Law School Admissions Test (LSAT). Applicants also provide a personal statement that can be used to illustrate qualities such as evidence of leadership or com-munity involvement. Three strong letters of recommendation are also needed. Law schools are obviously looking for applicant characteristics typically found in good lawyers. Strong oral and written communication skills, strong analytical skills, being able to work well under pressure, having a strong work ethic, and being able to be empathetic to a client's situation and needs are all desirable. All undergraduate majors are acceptable when applying to law school. Some law schools recommend undergraduate classes in logic (found in a philosophy department), writing, or critical thinking as good preparation. If admitted, law school is three years in duration. Upon completion of law school, students must pass the bar exam in their state in order to practice law. While three-fourths of lawyers work in private practice, others work in private industry, in the government, in the judiciary, or in public interest organizations. A career in law can be stressful and involve long hours. However, it can also be extremely rewarding, including financially rewarding. The Bureau of Labor Statistics estimates that the 2010 median pay for lawyers in the United States was approximately $112,000. Besides a high salary, many lawyers often feel much rewarded in helping people in difficult situations.

Website to explore:

http://www.lsac.org
The Law School Admission Council website provides a wealth of information about the law school admissions process and various career options for lawyers.

Moderate Drinking and Health

There has been much debate among researchers regarding whether regular moderate consumption of alcohol is protective to health. The debate arose from the initial observation that French citizens consume high-fat diets and yet have low rates of cardiovascular disease (an observation that has been labeled the French paradox). Typically, a high-fat diet is a risk factor leading to cardiovascular disease. However, French citizens consistently consume alcohol, which led researchers to wonder if there is something in wine or alcohol generally protecting the cardiovascular system. Researchers have examined resveratrol (abundantly present in red wine) to see if it acts as a cardioprotective agent (Wu et al., 2001; Wu & Hsieh, 2011). The jury is still out about whether low to moderate alcohol consumption protects against cardiovascular disease. Those who abstain from alcohol have a variety of reasons for not consuming alcohol, including preexisting health conditions or concerns about genetic risks for alcoholism. Moreover, alcohol use tends to elevate the risk of death from a variety of other diseases. For example, one study using 2005 data determined that approximately 26,000 deaths from ischemic heart disease, ischemic stroke, and diabetes were averted by current alcohol use, but these were outweighed by 90,000 alcohol-related deaths from other cardiovascular disease, cancers, liver cirrhosis, pancreatitis, alcohol dependence, injuries, and violence (Danaei et al., 2009). Physicians do not currently advocate the ingestion of alcohol solely to prevent coronary heart disease, as the evidence for the benefits of alcohol for cardiovascular health remains equivocal. While the moderate consumption of alcohol may provide enjoyment, the scientific evidence remains relatively weak for any treatment benefit for medical conditions like cardiovascular disease (Fleming et al., 2001).

Chronic Effects of Alcohol Use

The chronic use of alcohol can lead to a variety of problems. Chronic use of alcohol has such widespread deleterious effects on the body that it would be difficult to find a body system exempt from harm. The contribution of alcohol consumption to disease, injury risk, and alcohol dependence is largely determined by two separate but clearly related aspects of drinking. First, the volume of alcohol consumed is important, with higher volumes associated with greater problems. Second, the pattern of drinking is important, with binge drinking more problematic than drinking that is evenly spaced across time (WHO, 2011a). As alcohol use becomes chronic and consistently heavy over time, changes occur that alter how one thinks and how one's body functions. Alcohol problems occur to varying degrees, and it is uncertain where the line between heavy social drinking and alcohol abuse should be drawn, particularly since alcohol is omnipresent in our society. However, there are clear cases where problems have developed that require medical intervention, including dependence and physiological manifestations of excessive use of alcohol.

ALCOHOLISM

FIGURE 8-8
The amount of drinking can differ for an individual who fits the criteria for alcohol abuse or alcohol dependence.

Alcohol Dependence

An individual is diagnosed as being dependent on alcohol when three or more of the following has occurred in the past year: (1) tolerance (use of more alcohol to achieve intoxication or diminished effect with continued use of the same amount of alcohol); (2) withdrawal (characteristic syndrome when alcohol is not used); (3) escalation of use; (4) persistent desire or unsuccessful efforts to cut down; (5) great deal of time spent in activities necessary to obtain alcohol or recover from use; (6) important social, occupational, or recreational activities given up because of drinking; or (7) continued drinking despite knowledge of psychological or physical problems it is causing (APA, 2000). Recall from Chapter 1 that an individual who does not meet the criteria for dependence might fit the criteria for abuse (a maladaptive pattern of drinking that leads to clinically significant impairment or distress). The amount of drinking can differ widely for individuals who fit the criteria for abuse or dependence. In one study, the dependence criteria fit for women who drank approximately 63 drinks in a 28-day period (~2 drinks/day) and men who drank approximately 103 drinks in a 28-day period (~4 drinks/day) (Brown, Saunders, Bobula, Mundt, & Koch, 2007). However, in some extreme cases, alcohol consumption may be almost continuous, with 20 drinks or more a day being the observed pattern. In summary, the loss of control over drinking, escalation in use, withdrawal symptoms, and other listed criteria are far more important that the number of standard drinks consumed (Figure 8-8).

Tolerance

The *DSM-IV-TR* criteria for substance dependence include tolerance as a symptom, as tolerance develops readily to alcohol. In fact, individuals who have become highly dependent on alcohol will often drink an amount of alcohol on a daily basis that would harm or possibly kill a social drinker. Family members and friends are often shocked at how much alcohol an individual struggling with dependence had been consuming in spite of appearing largely functional until the problem was revealed. While tolerance may develop over years of use, tolerance can also be observable in short periods of heavy use. Acute tolerance is even observable within one dose, when behavioral impairment and subjective feelings of intoxication are more pronounced with BAC rising compared to a similar BAC when it is falling. Tolerance also develops across alcohol consumption episodes. College student drinkers may perceive changes in tolerance development across time, with the ability to consume more alcohol developing as drinking occurs regularly. In fact, laboratory investigations with social drinkers have observed that acute and chronic tolerance can be observed within as little as five consecutive days of alcohol exposure (Bennett, Cherek, & Spiga, 1993). Even in social drinkers, heavy alcohol use and its associated tolerance development can result in a variety of subjective changes that lead to an escalation in alcohol consumption. For example, heavier social drinkers report less pronounced subjective effects and less activity in the nucleus accumbens (the reward center in the brain) compared to more moderate drinkers, even when alcohol dose is the same (Gilman, Ramchandani, Crouss, & Hommer, 2012). When the amount of alcohol being consumed remains relatively steady across time, clinicians are somewhat less concerned. More concerning is when use has become compulsive and there is an escalation in use across time (see Chapter 3 for a review of types of tolerance, dependence, and withdrawal).

Physical Dependence and Withdrawal

Consistent alcohol use leads to physical dependence in part because the mechanisms underlying tolerance allow the body to become more efficient at handling the drug. To ascertain whether the body has become dependent on alcohol, just remove the alcohol to identify whether physical symptoms emerge when the drug leaves the body. Physical dependence can occur easily and can even be observed after one heavy drinking session. If you have ever overindulged in alcohol and suffered a **hangover** the next day, you have actually experienced minor alcohol withdrawal symptoms from short-term physical dependence on alcohol. Symptoms of a hangover are many of the same ones associated with feeling ill, such as upset stomach, fatigue, headache, thirst, depression, and anxiety. A hangover is due to withdrawal symptoms; consuming more alcohol may relieve some of the symptoms. However, relief is temporary and only delays the inevitable. There are no cures for a hangover except time, rest, fluids, and perhaps some analgesic medication for the headache. The symptoms of a hangover are thought to be partly due to the metabolism of alcohol when it is broken down into acetaldehyde. Acetaldehyde is a more toxic substance than alcohol, generating headaches, nausea, fatigue, and sensitivity to loud noises.

While a hangover may largely be an annoyance, withdrawal symptoms following chronic heavy use of alcohol are severe. In fact, the withdrawal syndrome from alcohol is more likely to cause death than the withdrawal syndrome from any other psychoactive drug, including opiates. If not medically supervised, severe cases of withdrawal may result in death rates as high as 1 in 7 cases. Referred to as detoxification, withdrawal from alcohol is the necessary, albeit unpleasant, first step in treatment. In many cases, detoxification occurs in a hospital setting, given that alcohol dependent individuals may often have severe or even life-threatening withdrawal symptoms. Withdrawal symptoms from alcohol are so consistently observed that they have been staged. They have also been well studied in animals, although the stages typically progress faster in animal models. In humans going through Stage 1, symptoms that emerge within a few hours of the last drink include tremors, rapid heartbeat, hypertension, excessive sweating, loss of appetite, and insomnia. These symptoms often reflect central and autonomic nervous system overarousal, which occurs when alcohol is withdrawn, since alcohol is a sedative drug. By Stage 2, within 24–48 hours, hallucinations emerge which can be auditory, visual, and/or tactile. For example, a

Table 8-2   Progression of alcohol withdrawal syndrome.

Stage	Symptoms
1	Central and autonomic nervous system hyperactivity; Tremors, rapid heartbeat, hypertension, excessive sweating, loss of appetite, insomnia
2	Hallucinations
3	Delusions, disorientation, delirium, amnesia
4	Seizures

patient may report that bugs are all over their skin or voices are talking to them. If an individual is in medical treatment, administration of a sedative benzodiazepine drug such a diazepam can mitigate some of the worst symptoms from the next two stages. In Stage 3, delusions, disorientation, delirium, and amnesia occur. While the use of the term is somewhat inconsistent, **delirium tremens** refers to severe cases of withdrawal with symptoms of hallucinations, delusions, and tremors; it typically peaks around 72 hours. In Stage 4 (the final stage), seizures may occur. Through all four stages, the patient will crave alcohol and may experience anxiety, dysphoria, insomnia, nausea, and vomiting. Medical personnel are most concerned about withdrawal seizures and delirium tremens, but fortunately these can be medically managed and can be predicted based on both personal history measures (prior drinking history and prior history of withdrawal seizures) and medical assessments (imaging to identify structural brain lesions and blood work to identify low serum potassium levels and lower platelet count). If patients go through detoxification in the hospital, the stay does not need to be too lengthy and may be less than 8 days in duration. Withdrawal symptoms may still be experienced for up to several weeks after cessation of alcohol use (Corfee, 2011; Eyer et al., 2011; Heilig et al., 2010). In sum, withdrawal from alcohol can be an aversive experience for the patient, but medical management can mitigate some of the most unpleasant and potentially harmful aspects.

Chronic Effects on the Body

Chronic abuse of alcohol leads to a variety of medical problems. Perhaps the most significant problem involves damage to the brain (Figures 8-9). In about half of individuals who are diagnosed with alcohol dependence, some neurological difficulties are identified, including memory problems, blunted emotional responsiveness, and difficulty with balance. Fortunately, most patients exhibit some improvement in brain structure and functioning within one year of abstinence. However, approximately 1 in 10 alcohol-dependent individuals exhibit permanent and debilitating brain damage, even if treatment for alcohol dependence is successful. Generalized brain shrinkage can be seen in alcohol-dependent individuals compared to the brains of similarly aged control individuals. Moreover, older alcoholics exhibit more cortical tissue damage than younger alcoholics. The prefrontal cortex (important for impulse control and other aspects of higher-order executive processing) seems to be particularly vulnerable to damage from chronic heavy alcohol use (Oscar-Berman & Schendan, 2000; Pfefferbaum, Sullivan, Mathalon, & Lim, 1997; NIAAA, 2004.

FIGURE 8-9
Alcohol and the brain.

©DNY59/istockphoto

Brain damage from chronic heavy use of alcohol may occur for several reasons. Clearly, there is the direct effect of alcohol on the brain. However, there are also indirect causes of damage that are associated with a drinking problem, including poor general health and severe liver disease. In individuals who drink large amounts of alcohol over long periods of time, the alcohol provides a large portion of daily needed calories. However, calories from alcohol are deficient in vitamins and minerals required for health. Thiamine deficiency (vitamin B_1 deficiency) is a common outcome of overall poor level of nutrition among alcoholics. Thiamine is an essential nutrient found in many foods and needed by all tissues, including the brain. Up to 80% of alcohol-dependent individuals have a deficiency in thiamine, and some will go on to develop a very severe form of dementia called **Wernicke–Korsakoff syndrome**. Wernicke–Korsakoff syndrome is actually a combination of two diseases. Wernicke's encephalopathy is a short-lived and severe condition that includes symptoms such as mental confusion, paralysis of the nerves that control the eyes, and impairment in muscle coordination. In up to 90% of alcoholics with Wernicke's encephalopathy, individuals also develop Korsakoff's syndrome, which is a long-lasting and debilitating condition characterized by learning and memory problems. Patients with Korsakoff's syndrome are easily frustrated and have difficulty with motor control, including walking and coordination. These patients can experience psychosis, and their memory problems are quite pronounced. They experience retrograde amnesia (problems remembering old information). However, the most pronounced problem with Korsakoff's syndrome is anterograde amnesia, the inability to encode new memories. This is very frustrating for family members, since one can have a long conversation about care options or finances only to discover an hour later the patient has no recollection of the conversation. If Wernicke-Korsakoff syndrome is diagnosed early enough, the patient can be treated with thiamine to improve brain function. Unfortunately if damage is more severe, little can be done. Care shifts to being more supportive as the brain damage is permanent.

While the brain can be easily damaged by chronic alcohol abuse, the liver is another internal organ that is very susceptible to damage from chronic alcohol abuse. The liver breaks down alcohol into metabolites and clears them from the body. Chronic heavy drinking taxes the liver and can result in liver dysfunction. There are three alcohol-induced liver diseases, ranked in ascending order of severity: (1) fatty liver, (2) alcohol hepatitis, and (3) cirrhosis. The most benign condition is fatty liver, which arises when fat accumulates on the liver. Some fat in the liver is normal, but when fat begins to exceed 10% of the liver, problems emerge. Fatty liver tends to manifest in few symptoms, though fatigue and localized pain may develop. Most cases of fatty liver are only diagnosed with routine blood work that accompanies an office visit to a general physician. Fatty liver is common not only due to its occurrence with heavy alcohol use, but also as a medical complication associated with obesity. With abstinence from alcohol, fatty liver is entirely reversible. A second, more serious liver problem is alcohol hepatitis. Alcohol hepatitis occurs when liver cells became inflamed, causing some cells to die. An outward indication of alcohol hepatitis is the skin looking oddly yellow. The yellow color of the skin all over the body (jaundice) occurs due to bile accumulating. Alcohol hepatitis can be reversible if medically treated and the patient becomes abstinent. Alcohol hepatitis can be fatal if left untreated and the patient continues drinking. Finally, the most serious and life-threatening alcohol-induced liver damage is cirrhosis. Cirrhosis occurs when chronic inflammation in the liver results in widespread cell death, leaving hard scar tissue behind. The liver becomes increasingly unable to metabolize toxins, such as ammonia, which damages the body. Up to 20% of alcohol-dependent patients develop cirrhosis of the liver. Cirrhosis is a grim diagnosis, in part because the condition is not reversible and it often becomes quickly fatal. Only half of patients who receive this diagnosis are alive five years later. In the United States, a 6-month abstinence from alcohol is required before a patient with severe liver damage can be considered for liver transplantation. Unfortunately, most patients do not live long enough to receive a transplanted liver (Fleming et al., 2001; Mathurin et al., 2011).

Organs in the body are interconnected, so damage to the liver can also cause damage to the brain. When liver cells are damaged, the liver allows excess amounts of ammonia and manganese, which are both toxic, to enter the brain and damage brain cells. This process results in a serious and potentially fatal brain disorder called **hepatic encephalopathy**. Symptoms include changes in sleep patterns, mood (anxiety/depression), and personality. Significant cognitive effects such a shortened attention span occur. Problems with coordination result, including flapping or shaking of the hands. In very serious cases, the patient may slip into a coma, which can be fatal. Treatments focus on lowering blood ammonia concentrations, providing liver-assist devices to clear the blood of toxins, or liver transplantation in rare cases (NIAAA, 2004). Chronic alcohol abuse also leads to damage to other body organs, including the stomach, intestines, pancreas, skeletal muscles, and heart muscle. Chronic alcohol abuse also increases the likelihood of developing various cardiac problems, having a stroke, and experiencing sexual difficulties such as impotence (Fleming et al., 2001). While it does not appear that women are any more likely than men to experience alcohol-induced brain damage, the same cannot be said for most other medical consequences of alcohol use. Women are more likely to develop alcohol-induced cirrhosis of the liver, cardiomyopathy (heart muscle damage), and peripheral neuropathy (nerve damage), even though women may have fewer years of drinking history than men (NIAAA, 2004).

Fetal Alcohol Syndrome

Alcohol is a **teratogen**, which means that it is an agent causing developmental defects in an embryo. Alcohol is by far the number one fetal teratogen, especially for women still drinking during pregnancy despite public health campaigns warning of the risks. The diagnosis of **fetal alcohol syndrome (FAS)** is given to a child who was prenatally exposed to alcohol and exhibits clear damage from this exposure. There are three key characteristics of FAS: (1) craniofacial abnormalities, (2) central nervous system (CNS) dysfunction, and (3) pre- and/or postnatal growth deficiencies. Long before the scientific method was known, humans may have been aware of the connection between maternal heavy drinking and birth defects. Some scholars argue that the link has been known since ancient Greek and Roman times, as evidenced by writings from antiquity. However, modern scholarship argues that historical understanding of the problem of maternal drinking and resultant birth defects was limited at best. Other writings from antiquity seem to indicate a belief that intoxication at the moment of conception led to deformity, with the father's drunkenness being the primary concern (Abel, 1999; Calhoun & Warren, 2007). The modern-day understanding of fetal alcohol syndrome stems from a largely overlooked French paper in 1968, followed by influential papers published in the Lancet in 1973 that firmly laid the foundation for diagnosis of fetal alcohol syndrome (Jones & Smith, 1973; Jones et al., 1973; Lemoine, Harousseau, Borteyru, & Menuet, 1968). There is no other drug coming close to the harm caused by alcohol when exposed in utero with the effects of this exposure being permanent. In the United States, fetal alcohol syndrome is the most common cause of mental retardation and believed to occur in approximately 1 per 1000 live births. *It is also the most common preventable cause of birth defects.*

Alcohol exposure in utero can result in a variety of pregnancy complications. Rates of miscarriage or stillbirth are much higher in drinking mothers. If the baby is born, it is likely delivered early; often the baby is small even when corrected for gestational age. There are a variety of complications associated with fetal alcohol syndrome. The most noticeable to the casual observer are the characteristic facial features associated with FAS, including a thin upper lip, sunken nasal bridge, and lack of definition of facial features (Figure 8-10). The CNS dysfunction is characterized by mental retardation (IQ < 70) resulting in widespread deficits in not only intelligence, but also speech, movement, and social skills. Other symptoms include poor postnatal growth (following deficient prenatal growth), decreased muscle tone, and poor coordination. Heart defects, malformed limbs, genital abnormalities, brain damage, and/or reduced brain size are also serious manifestations of FAS. Behavioral problems include hyperactivity, inability to concentrate, extreme nervousness, and an inability to understand cause-and-effect relationships (Fleming et al., 2001; Tortora & Derrickson, 2012).

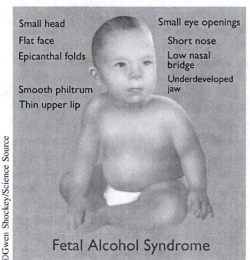

Small head
Flat face
Epicanthal folds

Small eye openings
Short nose
Low nasal bridge
Underdeveloped jaw

Smooth philtrum
Thin upper lip

Fetal Alcohol Syndrome

©Gwen Shockey/Science Source

FIGURE 8-10
Facial characteristics typical of fetal alcohol syndrome.

Alcohol freely crosses the placenta, in the process harming the development of the baby. Prenatal exposure to alcohol occurs on a continuum, so different children will have different development issues from exposure in utero. Large amounts of alcohol increase the severity of FAS, while children having less alcohol exposure in utero may not exhibit all three characteristics that define FAS. The diagnosis of fetal alcohol effects (FAE) is reserved for less severe cases where maternal alcohol use during pregnancy is suspect and the child exhibits at least one of the diagnostic symptoms of FAS. Typically, abnormal intellectual or behavioral development is a problem associated with FAE, whereas the characteristic facial features are more likely to occur with FAS (Kuehn et al., 2012). The prognoses for FAS and FAE vary. None of the babies with FAS are going to have normal brain development. There is no cure for FAS. The multiple problems associated with FAS are difficult to manage, and a team of health care providers is typically needed to handle the various problems. Children do better when diagnosed early, which allows various educational and behavioral strategies to be developed to help the child function to the best of his or her ability. The prognosis is better for FAE, but these children nevertheless often struggle intellectually and socially (Carlo, 2007).

Researchers have determined the aspects of maternal drinking most likely to result in FAS. Animal research has been instrumental in helping make these determinations. First, binge drinking appears much more harmful than drinking smaller amounts of alcohol distributed over time. High maternal BACs result in more fetal damage. Second, timing is important. While alcohol use any time in pregnancy can cause harm, the first three months are a particularly risky window for exposure. It is during the first three months that the central nervous system is being laid down in the developing fetus and alcohol does the most damage (Cunningham et al., 2010). Unfortunately, many women may be unaware of a pregnancy in the early months and may inadvertently expose a developing fetus to alcohol. Caution regarding alcohol consumption is recommended in women of child-bearing age who may become pregnant.

Myth Busters: Genetics Is Destiny for Alcoholism

Some people can have a beer or glass of wine without feeling the urge to drink more. For other people, the first glass of alcohol is the starting point to loss of control over drinking; they can't seem to stop drinking once they start. Many people believe that genetics is destiny when it comes to alcohol dependence. If your father was an alcoholic, you will become an alcoholic too. While genetics plays a role, it is a myth that genetics is destiny when it comes to alcoholism. Research indicates that both your genetic makeup and your environment influence your risk for alcohol abuse and alcoholism. Your genetic makeup is the information stored in your DNA inherited from your parents. Genes do play a role in how your body responds to alcohol. However, there is no single gene that determines if you will develop alcohol dependence. Instead, there are many genes involved in the risk of developing alcohol problems. Researchers have studied large families with alcoholic and nonalcoholic members. They have compared identical and fraternal twins. They have studied adopted children and their biological and adoptive families. Combining all of this research, it's been determined that about half of our risk for alcoholism is influenced by genetics. Some genes play a straightforward role in alcohol, such as influencing how effectively the body breaks down alcohol. Other genes play a role in how pleasant or rewarding one perceives alcohol to be. Even some genes that seem to be unrelated to alcohol use play a role. For example, "clock" genes control the body's daily rhythms, including changes in body temperature or when you want to fall asleep and wake up. Clock genes both influence and are influenced by alcohol use. If you do have a genetic risk for alcoholism, the environment in which you live is important. If you surround yourself with people who drink heavily and encourage you to drink heavily as well, you raise your risk for alcohol problems. In contrast, protective factors include being married or being religious. For adolescents carrying high-risk genes, having parents that monitor their activities and friends closely decreases their risk of developing alcohol problems. Parents who do not monitor activities as closely are associated with increased risk for alcohol problems among adolescents who have a genetic predisposition to have such problems. In sum, lifestyle choices can be extremely important for alcohol dependence risk. Even without a genetic risk, poor lifestyle choices can result in alcohol dependence. There are many individual and psychosocial variables that influence when and how much we drink, which ultimately influences our risk for alcohol problems. While genetics is certainly important, it is far from destiny when it comes to alcoholism (Foroud & Phillips, 2012; Heath et al., 1997; NIAAA, 2012a).

Pharmacology of Alcohol

Sites of Action

The acute effects of alcohol result in changes to almost every major neurotransmitter system in the brain. These changes lead to decreased excitatory activity and enhanced inhibitory activity in the central nervous system. Moreover, alcohol also alters the activity of many functions in the brain. For example, alcohol dissolves in lipid membranes and alters their internal structure. This change increases membrane fluidity, which results in loss of membrane potential and decreased conduction of messages by neurons. Decreased cell growth can also result from these changes to the lipid membranes, underlying some of the teratogenic effects of alcohol (Huffer, Clark, Ning, Blanch, & Clark, 2011). Alcohol changes so many aspects of neural processing that it is reasonable to assert that it affects most cell membranes and neurotransmitters (Fleming et al., 2001; Julien, 2005). Despite the complexity, researchers have determined some of the specific changes from both the acute effects of alcohol and also changes with alcohol administered in a chronic fashion.

Glutamate is a major excitatory neurotransmitter in the brain. Even small amounts of alcohol interfere with the activity of glutamate. This interference may result in memory problems, including blackouts. Chronic alcohol consumption increases the number of available glutamate receptor sites in the brain such that when alcohol is withdrawn, glutamate receptors adapted to the constant presence of alcohol become overactive. This overactivity causes neurons to die, which can lead to seizures, strokes, and brain damage. Moreover, thiamine deficiencies that commonly occur in chronic heavy drinkers may also contribute to glutamate overactivity (Crews, 2000; Ward, Lallemand, & de Witte, 2009).

GABA is a major inhibitory neurotransmitter in the brain. Alcohol increases GABA (especially by acting as an agonist at the $GABA_A$ receptor), which leads to some of the sedation and decreased anxiety that is experienced by users of alcohol. GABA receptors are sensitive to alcohol at doses attained during social drinking or severe intoxication. However, with chronic use of alcohol, the number of GABA receptors in the brain is reduced. If a person stops drinking, the brain becomes overexcited, since the deficiency in GABA receptors leads to deficient levels of inhibition. Withdrawal seizures may also arise due to deficient GABA activity. In certain areas of the brain, activity is dependent on the balance between the excitatory action of glutamate and the inhibitory action of GABA, with alcohol impacting the activity of both systems (Kumar et al., 2009; Valenzuela, 1997).

Alcohol stimulates the release of serotonin, which is the neurotransmitter important for emotional expression. Alcohol also increases the release of endorphins (which function as naturally occurring morphine, possibly contributing to the high of intoxication and the craving to drink). When alcohol is consumed, endorphins are released in the nucleus accumbens, the reward center of the brain, accounting for the pleasure reported by alcohol consumers (Mitchell et al., 2012). Endorphins block pain thus alcohol-induced increases in endorphin activity underlie the analgesic effects of alcohol. Interestingly, the hyperalgesia that is experienced in alcohol-dependent patients undergoing withdrawal seems to be comparable to that experienced by opiate-dependent patients undergoing withdrawal from opiate drugs like heroin or morphine (Gatch, 2009). Alcohol also leads to increases in the release of dopamine, which contributes to motivation and the rewarding effects of alcohol (Weiss & Porrino, 2002).

Alcohol increases adenosine, an inhibitory neurotransmitter. Increased adenosine activity leads to sleepiness, which is how alcohol induces sedation. Adenosine regulates the brain's glutamate levels, which are also impacted by alcohol (Nam et al., 2012). Both enhancement and inhibition of nicotinic acetylcholine receptor function have been observed, possibly dependent on the dose of alcohol. Effects of alcohol on these receptors are important, as alcohol-dependent individuals are often also smokers, and the nicotine in cigarettes binds to nicotinic acetylcholine receptors (Fleming et al., 2001). Finally, alcohol increases cannibinoid neurotransmitter activity, which results in greater motivation to consume alcohol and underlies some of the reinforcing properties of alcohol (Pava & Woodward, 2012). In sum, consumption of alcohol seems to impact every major neurotransmitter system in the brain.

Pharmacokinetics

Pharmacokinetics is the branch of pharmacology examining the absorption, distribution, biotransformation, and excretion of drugs. The acute effects of alcohol are a function of blood alcohol level. When an alcoholic beverage is swallowed, alcohol begins to be absorbed in the stomach. The majority of the alcohol then moves to the small intestine. In the small intestine, the rate of absorption is much faster than in the stomach, since the surface area available for absorption is smaller. As such, the longer the alcohol stays in the stomach, since the slower the rise in blood alcohol concentration (BAC). BAC rises more slowly when the stomach is full, and particularly when fat-rich foods such as pizza have been ingested. Once in the bloodstream, alcohol first travels to the liver before it quickly distributes into all of the body fluids (Fleming et al., 2001).

The metabolism of alcohol occurs because the enzyme, **alcohol dehydrogenase**, present in gastric mucosa cells and liver cells, breaks down alcohol into **acetaldehyde** and then ultimately acetate. Acetaldehyde does not cause intoxication, but buildup of acetaldehyde in the body is thought to lead to the many unpleasant symptoms associated with a hangover. Acetate is relatively inert. The process of alcohol metabolism begins in the stomach. This first-pass metabolism occurring in the gastrointestinal tract lowers blood alcohol levels compared to the same dose of alcohol administered intravenously, which bypasses the digestive system. When the rate of gastric emptying is slow, more alcohol will be absorbed and converted to acetaldehyde in the stomach, and less alcohol will reach the bloodstream. Less gastric metabolism of alcohol has been observed in women than men, which can result in women having higher BACs than men, even though the alcohol dose is the same. Aspirin inhibits the activity of the alcohol dehydrogenase enzymes. When aspirin is administered with alcohol, first-pass metabolism is decreased up to 40% due to inhibition of gastric acetaldehyde. This can result in substantially elevated BACs, so never take aspirin while drinking alcohol. Most alcohol is metabolized in the liver, where the alcohol is first metabolized into acetaldehyde and then into acetate (Fleming et al., 2001; Gentry et al., 1999; Tortora & Derrickson, 2012).

An interesting application of the important role of acetaldehyde is the **Asian flushing response**, a physical reaction occurring to some people when drinking alcohol. The skin gets red and flushed and other symptoms may emerge, such as heart palpitations, tachycardia, sweating, and headache. This response is seen in people of Asian descent who have a deficiency in the acetaldehyde enzymes. When alcohol is consumed, acetaldehyde builds up in the body and the metabolism of alcohol is markedly diminished. Since the symptoms of the Asian flushing response are aversive, people who experience these symptoms tend to drink very little. Alcohol dependence is somewhat rare in Asia compared to other parts of the world, partially due to this biological phenomenon (Kitano, 1989).

Treatment for Alcohol Addiction

Alcohol is omnipresent in our society, and drinking is socially acceptable. For someone who has difficulty controlling their drinking, there are constant environmental cues eliciting craving. At least 14 million Americans meet the criteria for alcohol dependence or alcoholism and would benefit from treatment. More effective treatment could reduce the current U.S. economic burden from alcohol problems of about $170 billion each year. Moreover, effective treatment could reduce the more than 100,000 annual alcohol-related deaths. Far too frequently, medical diagnosis and treatment are delayed until the problem is extreme (Fleming et al., 2001). Challenges notwithstanding, many individuals are successful in conquering their drinking problems. Some people who drink heavily are able to reduce their alcohol intake to a more reasonable level of their own accord. Others utilize the variety of treatment options available, ranging from brief interventions to intensive inpatient treatment. There are even web-based options. Inpatient hospital treatment tends to be less common today, since the costs of inpatient treatment can be prohibitive. Thus, inpatient hospital treatment tends to be reserved for serious alcohol dependence cases when there are medical risks from alcohol detoxification. However, once detoxification has been completed, the remaining treatment is most commonly administered via outpatient settings. What is clear from the scientific literature is that treatment works and people do get better. The process can sometimes be challenging, especially if relapses occur. With persistence, success can be achieved in part because there are so many treatment options that are available.

If you or someone you know is in need of substance abuse and mental health treatment, talk to your local primary care physician, campus health center, or utilize the SAMHSA treatment locator on the web. You can also call SAMHSA to discuss various options:
http://www.samhsa.gov/treatment/
1-800-662-HELP

Abstinence

The goal of the majority of treatment programs for alcohol dependence in the United States is abstinence. The largest and most widely known group embracing the abstinence model is **Alcoholics Anonymous (AA)**. As an international organization, AA has a primary goal of helping its members stay sober and helping other alcoholics achieve sobriety. In AA, men and women come together on a regular basis to share their experiences, strength, and hope with one another to solve their common problem: alcoholism. The only requirement for membership is a desire to stop drinking. There are no dues or fees to be part of AA, with the organization supporting itself through its own contributions. The success of AA as an organization is truly remarkable. Founded in 1935 by two recovering alcoholics, it is estimated that there are now more than 2 million people in the United States who are members belonging to one of the 100,000 AA chapters. It is estimated that over half of the people in the United States who received treatment for alcohol or drug use problems did so through a self-help program like AA (SAMHSA, 2011a).

AA subscribes to a disease model of alcohol dependence, in particular alcohol dependence is seen as a disease that can never be cured. Members are encouraged to maintain constant vigilance against taking even one drink. AA's famous slogan is, "One drink, one drunk." Members are also encouraged to work the 12 steps to achieve sobriety (Table 8-3). What is being a member of AA like? Typically, members attend regular and frequent meetings held by an AA chapter. During meetings, established and sober members give testimonials about their experiences, such as stories of their problems with alcohol and how their lives have improved now that they have conquered their addiction. New members are encouraged to assert that they are alcoholics and work on the 12 steps. New members are paired with a sponsor who has been successful in working the 12 steps and will act as a mentor to the new member. As a self-help group, all members are there to provide emotional support and counseling to one another. The companionship that develops is close, in part because members are urged to call one another at any time of day when struggling and trying not to relapse. Researchers have noted that it is notoriously difficult to conduct empirical research on AA and its effectiveness. Thus, it remains unclear what specific aspects of AA lead to sobriety. However, randomized controlled trials that have examined AA have found that subjects who consistently attended AA had better drinking outcomes than individuals who did not attend AA (Greenfield & Tonigan, 2012; Magura, McKeen, Kosten, & Tonigan, 2013).

AA has been so successful that there are now AA-like programs for other substances, such as Cocaine Anonymous and Marijuana Anonymous. AA clearly has many positive features and has been helpful to many people. However, AA will not work for everyone. One key concern for many is that AA subscribes to the abstinence model. Therefore, individuals who are not ready to

Table 8-3   The twelve steps of alcoholics anonymous.

1. Admit powerless over alcohol
2. Believe that God will restore person
3. Turn over life to God
4. Make moral inventory
5. Admit wrongs
6. Have God remove defects of character
7. Ask God to remove shortcomings
8. Make list of persons harmed
9. Make direct amends to persons harmed (where possible)
10. Continue personal inventory
11. Improve conscious contact with God
12. Have spiritual awakening as the result of these Steps

Adapted from The Twelve Steps and Twelve Traditions by Alcoholics Anonymous World Services, Inc. (1952). More information about AA can be found on their website, http://www.aa.org

give up alcohol for life will be strongly deterred by AA. In addition, drinking problems can vary in intensity. The AA approach seems well suited to the older chronic alcoholic who has struggled for a lifetime with a drinking problem. What about the college student who is having trouble controlling their drinking? For that college student, the AA approach may be extreme. In addition, some individuals suffering from serious alcohol dependence may disagree with the core notion of AA that a person must label themselves an alcoholic for life. Even if sober for several decades, the approach of AA is that the person is not cured and will carry the disease forever (hence, the need for constant vigilance of never taking a drink).

Further, some individuals who prefer the AA abstinence model may nevertheless find the religious overtones of the 12-step program incompatible with their personal beliefs. Among the 12 steps of AA, half have a reference to God. For individuals who do not believe in God or are not actively religious, the AA model may be a bad fit. Consequently, alternative 12-step programs similar to AA but not involving a religious component have arisen (Ogbourne, 1989). For those who perceive that AA is not an appropriate treatment approach for them, the good news is that there are a variety of alternative abstinence approaches to treatment that are also very effective.

One effective alternative to AA is cognitive-behavioral therapy. This approach to treating alcohol dependence involves the client meeting regularly with a therapist to work on decreasing drinking. The goal is to reinforce behaviors inconsistent with drinking and avoid situations that were previously associated with drinking. The underlying belief of cognitive-behavioral treatments is that environmental contingencies can either encourage or discourage drinking. For example, if a client decides to enter a bar, that choice increases the likelihood that drinking will occur. By contrast, if the client removes all alcohol from the home, that decreases the likelihood that drinking will occur. Sometimes, the therapeutic approach is practical—for example, improving social skills like improving assertiveness in refusing drinks. In addition, clients are encouraged to spend time with people who are supportive and not associated with drinking. One variation of cognitive-behavioral therapy interprets relapses differently than AA. In relapse prevention treatment, the therapist encourages the client to view any lapse back into drinking as a learning experience. Instead of seeing a drink as the battle of alcoholism having been lost, the individual is encouraged to understand that lapses occur but do not necessary lead to a total relapse (Marlatt & Gordon, 1985). While relapse prevention treatment is a cognitive-behavioral approach, the clinician does not discount the physiological aspects of alcohol dependence. However, the cognitive-behavioral approach is different to the AA disease model's view of a relapse as a lost battle, with the disease taking over. In essence, the relapse prevention model takes the catastrophes and drama out of recovery by teaching clients to change how they think and help them learn new healthy behaviors.

Moderated Drinking

Drinking problems fall on a continuum. Thus, the abstinence approaches to treatment may be excessive for individuals who have less severe problems. Moreover, some individuals simply cannot imagine not drinking, even if their drinking is causing them current harm. It is socially difficult to avoid alcohol altogether, in part because alcohol is so common in our society. Researchers and clinicians are learning that abstinence is not the only option for alcohol-dependent individuals. It is possible to teach a person not to use alcohol in an extreme fashion but rather to drink in moderation. Controlled drinking was initially described by Mark and Linda Sobell as an approach to guide individuals toward more moderate drinking (Sobell & Sobell, 1993). The basic premise underlying the controlled drinking model is that individuals may be unaware of how much control they have over their behavior and alcohol consumption. By helping a client become aware of the costs of drinking and the benefits of cutting down drinking (or even abstaining), the client can slowly cut down. Some of the techniques of controlled drinking seem exceeding simple and yet are extremely effective. For example, a client may first consume a drink. The clinician may encourage the client to delay consuming another drink for 20 minutes. The delay provides an opportunity to reflect on the costs and benefits of having another drink as well as the costs and benefits of drinking to excess. Beyond the strategies to address specific drinking behaviors, the client is also encouraged to examine how sources of stress at work, with family members, and with friends all contribute to the likelihood of drinking. When these sources of stress are identified, the client can anticipate them and resist them to keep control of behavior. This approach seems to work well either as an individual treatment or in groups (Sobell, Sobell, & Agrawal, 2009). In sum, abstinence is not the only option.

Moderated drinking interventions have also been found to be effective in brief interventions. For example, college students are a large demographic group that drinks heavily. Some college students find that their drinking has gotten out of control. Moderated drinking approaches can help individuals decrease their drinking so that their alcohol consumption is no longer jeopardizing their health and well-being. These interventions are often very brief. For example, individuals may be asked to report on their drinking over the past 3 months using a calendar. After carefully assessing drinking over the past 3 months, a brief motivational intervention is given, which includes individualized feedback. For example, the feedback may include information about how excessive alcohol use can be harmful and how moderating drinking can reduce these harms. Comparisons of the individual's past 3-month drinking to community and national averages also provides feedback about an individual's drinking. Even though the intervention is limited in scope, individuals who participate in the intervention exhibit reduced drinking behavior up to a year after the intervention (Sobell & Sobell, 1996).

Pharmacological Approaches

Pharmacological treatments can be particularly helpful to some individuals attempting to resolve their alcohol dependence problems. Craving for alcohol is a constant concern for individuals trying to control their drinking. Individuals who receive medication as part of their treatment program are more likely to stay with the program (Fonsi Elbreder, de Souza e Silva, Pillon, & Laranjeira, 2011). There are three FDA-approved drugs that are options for pharmacological treatment of alcohol dependence. First, **disulfiram** (Antabuse®) is a drug that induces violent vomiting when a user also consumes alcohol with the drug (Figure 8-11). Antabuse® is inert in the

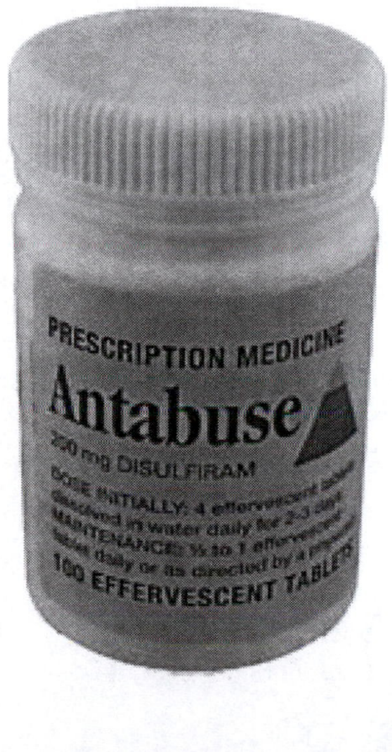

Courtesy of Teva Pharmaceuticals

FIGURE 8-11
Antabuse® is used to treat alcohol dependence.

absence of alcohol. However, if Antabuse® is taken with alcohol, blood acetaldehyde concentrations rise up to 10 times their normal levels, leading to illness (Fleming et al., 2001). Therefore, pharmacological treatment with disulfiram strongly discourages drinking. The effectiveness of disulfiram in discouraging drinking appears to be due to a taste aversion learning mechanism. Humans and animals are likely to develop a taste aversion when a food or drink results in nausea or other gastrointestinal illness. In the natural world, it makes sense that if an animal eats a novel food and then becomes ill, the animal should avoid that food in the future. Disulfiram is therefore inducing a learned taste aversion by pairing the taste of alcohol with extreme gastrointestinal illness. When used as directed, disulfiram works to deter drinking. However, it is only effective as a deterrent to drinking when the individual takes the medicine regularly as directed. Unfortunately, in many instances, when alcohol-dependent individuals crave alcohol, they will cease taking their medication so that they do not vomit once they start drinking. For this reason, the evidence that disulfiram is effective in helping combat alcohol problems is equivocal. Researchers have found that up to 80% of patients stop taking disulfiram for a variety of reasons. In fact, the results of one clinical trial indicated that if disulfiram was taken as prescribed, it was more effective than the other medications available for the treatment of alcohol dependence (Laaksonen, Koski-Jannes, Salaspuro, Ahtinen, & Alho, 2008). The issue is not with the effectiveness of disulfiram but with patient compliance.

Since patient compliance is a serious concern with disulfiram, it is fortunate that other pharmacological options are available. A second pharmacological treatment option is **naltrexone** (ReVia® or Vivitrol®), which is an opiate antagonist drug. As mentioned earlier in the chapter, alcohol consumption results in the release of endorphins. The drug naltrexone blocks endorphin activity, thus reducing the craving for alcohol (Miller, Book, & Stewart, 2011). A third pharmacological option for treatment is **acamprosate** (Campral®). This drug also reduces craving for alcohol but through a different mechanism than naltrexone. Acamprosate antagonizes both glutamate and GABA receptors. Despite having a different mechanism, acamprosate and naltrexone appear to be equally effective at reducing drinking. Moreover, the different mechanisms of drug action for acamprosate and naltrexone allow clinicians to prescribe both at once. One study reported that patients who were given both medications were more successful in staying abstinent than patients who received only acamprosate or naltrexone (Feeney & Connor, 2011).

QUICK QUIZ 8-2

1. Approximately _____ of alcohol dependent patients exhibit permanent and debilitating brain damage.
   a. 1%
   b. 5%
   c. 10%
   d. 20%

2. Diagnosis of fetal alcohol syndrome requires which of the following symptoms?
   a. Craniofacial abnormalities
   b. Central nervous system dysfunction
   c. Pre- and/or postnatal growth deficiencies
   d. a and b only
   e. All of the above

3. Your friend decides to go out drinking, but he has a headache. He decides to take an aspirin. What is the likely outcome if he consumes his typical dose of alcohol?
   a. His blood alcohol level will be higher than normal.
   b. His blood alcohol level will be lower than normal.
   c. His blood alcohol level will be the same as always.
   d. He will be less likely to have a hangover the next day.

4. Which of following drugs are FDA-approved medications for the treatment of alcohol dependence?
   a. Disulfiram
   b. Naltrexone
   c. Acamprosate
   d. a and b are correct
   e. All of the above

5. Even small amounts of alcohol will _____ glutamate activity.
   a. increase
   b. decrease
   c. not change
   d. None of the above

6. You consumed 5 shots of liquor over 2 hours. What is your estimated BAC? Show your work. Would you be legal to drive? Why, or why not?

7. University and college presidents often have the difficult task of dealing with binge-drinking on their campuses. One very controversial initiative that has been put forth to address hazardous drinking among student populations is the Amethyst Initiative. The initiative argues that the drinking age should be lowered to 18 from 21. The idea is that an 18-year-old adult who can vote, sign a contract, serve on a jury, and enlist in the military should also be able

to have a beer. If alcohol were freely available, students might make better choices and might drink more moderately. Why would the proponents of this idea call it the Amethyst Initiative? A hint: The answer has something to do with history.

8. Stimulant and sedative drugs sometimes have paradoxical effects at low doses. For example, amphetamines help calm the behavior of children suffering from attention deficit/hyperactivity disorder (ADHD), while alcohol can stimulate behavior. How are these two observations related and what does that inform us about the brain?

ANSWERS TO QUICK QUIZ 8-2:

1. c – 10%
2. e – all of the above
3. a – His blood alcohol level will be higher than normal.
4. e – all of the above
5. b – decrease
6. Using the basic calculation to estimate BAC, this scenario would result in a .095 g% BAC. The calculation to estimate BAC is (Number of Standard Drinks)(.025) – (Number of Hours Since Drinking Began)(.015) = (5)(.025) – (2)(.015) = .095 g%. Given that the legal limit for driving in the United States is .08 g%, it would not be legal to drive in this scenario.
7. In ancient Greece, large amounts of alcohol were known to induce intoxication. However, the Greeks believed that amethyst (the stone) could ward off intoxication. If wine was consumed from an amethyst cup, for example, the drinker would not get drunk. Therefore, this initiative is being thought of as an approach that might limit the number

of college-age intoxicated drinkers while still allowing them access to alcohol.

8. Low doses of stimulant and sedative drugs impact the functioning of the prefrontal cortex of the brain, which is the brain region important for control over behavior. In children with ADHD, the prefrontal cortex is hypoactive. When amphetamines are given at low doses, the stimulant effect brings this region of the brain to a more "normal" level of functioning, so that children are better able to control their behavior. Alcohol is a sedative drug. At low doses of alcohol, sedation effects occur in the same area of the brain responsible for control over one's behavior. As such, a slightly intoxicated individual will appear less in control of his or her own behavior, more talkative, more hyperactive, and have poorer judgment. These behaviors may appear to result from overstimulation but in fact reflect the sedating effect of alcohol on a specific region of the brain.

CHAPTER SUMMARY

Alcohol is a central nervous system sedative drug that can be found in beer, wine, and distilled spirits. Alcohol has a long history of use in part due to fermentation occurring in nature. The acute effects of alcohol are strongly dependent on blood alcohol concentration. At lower doses, alcohol appears to result in increased stimulatory effects, in part because alcohol first decreases the functioning of the areas of the brain that are important for control over behavior. At higher doses, alcohol becomes an anesthetic, and at very high doses alcohol can result in fatalities. When alcohol is used chronically, a variety of health concerns emerge, including alcohol dependence, brain damage, and liver damage. Alcohol is a teratogen. When used during pregnancy, alcohol causes permanent developmental defects in the developing embryo, leading to fetal alcohol syndrome. Alcohol results in widespread changes to almost every neurotransmitter in the central nervous system. Individuals who become dependent on alcohol face a difficult process of withdrawal, including hallucinations and seizures. Fortunately, a variety of treatment options are available to individuals who wish to control their drinking, including self-help groups, psychological therapy, and medications.

9

OPIATES

Introduction

My first experience studying opiate drugs was a slimy one. I was an undergraduate psychology student with a fun summer job as a research assistant in a neuroscience research lab. One of my responsibilities involved maintaining the snail colony. The snails were subjects of several experiments determining the effects of opiates on pain perception. I spent much time cleaning the very slimy and somewhat smelly snail aquarium and feeding the snails their diet of romaine lettuce. The snails often escaped their aquarium, and I would sometimes find a slime trail leading in all directions across the room. When they weren't escaping, the snails seemed amenable to drugs like morphine, despite my inept injection efforts. You may be wondering why snails are used to study opiate drugs. The land snail (*Cepaea nemoralis*), which is found in damp locations of backyard gardens, has a similar opioid system to humans (Figure 9-1). Pain perception is fundamental to all living things. From invertebrates to humans, avoiding things that cause us harm is essential to our well-being. Pain is aversive and can be debilitating. While pain clearly has a psychological component for humans, the basic opiate system functions similarly in vertebrates and invertebrates, with the methodology to test pain also being similar. Just as a human who puts a foot in an overly warm bathtub will retract it quickly, a snail will also retract its body from an overly warm surface, which makes the snail a good animal model for studying pain perception. After injecting psychoactive drugs into the snail, it can be determined whether pain is being enhanced or blocked by timing the subsequent withdrawal reflex (Kavaliers & Ossenkopp, 1993; Kavaliers & Perrot-Sinal, 1996). Scientists devote much effort to developing new approaches to deal with pain because the best pain-blocking opiate drugs, such as

FIGURE 9-1
Withdrawal reflex observed in a land snail, *Cepaea nemoralis*, when in pain. An opiate drug, such as morphine, will lengthen the amount of time before a snail will show this response, indicating that pain perception is reduced.

©crystalfoto/Shutterstock

heroin and morphine, also elicit euphoria. Euphoria makes these painkillers extremely addictive. Tolerance also develops rapidly to opiate drugs, causing them to lose effectiveness over relatively short periods of time. In the last few decades, newly developed high-strength prescription opiate painkillers have increasingly been abused as psychoactive drugs when diverted from intended use. The recreational use and abuse of OxyContin® made headlines when teenagers and high-profile celebrities became addicted (Meier, 2012). It is a great challenge in our society to keep legal opiate drugs available for those with a legitimate medical need, while keeping opiates out of the hands of those who will abuse them. Opiate drugs bring many people great relief from terrible pain, yet they also cause many others great harm from addiction. In this chapter, we will explore why this is the case.

LEARNING OBJECTIVES

Learning objectives can help organize your studying. Before we begin the topic of opiates, keep in mind that by the end of this chapter, you should be able to . . .

1. Describe the sources of opiate drugs.
2. Explain the brief history of opiates, including how long opiates have been available for use.
3. Describe the various routes of administration for opiates.
4. Describe how opiates are used to treat various medical conditions.
5. Explain the acute effects of opiates and how they act as sedatives in the central nervous system.
6. Describe tolerance, dependence, and withdrawal processes associated with opiate use.
7. Describe how opiates act in the brain and for how long.
8. Describe the various treatment approaches used to treat opiate addiction.

Opiates as Sedative Drugs

Opiates are powerful psychoactive sedative drugs that block pain and induce euphoria. Opiates include a variety of pharmaceutical drugs (morphine, methadone, and fentanyl) and illicit drugs (heroin and opium). When used appropriately to treat severe pain, opiates can be incredibly effective drugs in alleviating suffering. When abused, opiates can result in severe dependence. **Morphine** ($C_{17}H_{19}NO_3$) is the principal alkaloid found in opium. Opium comes from a plant source, and its isolated chemical morphine is widely used in medicine to treat severe pain. Medical treatment of severe pain from cancer, accidents, and heart attacks often involves administration of morphine or similar opiates. **Heroin** ($C_{21}H_{23}NO_5$) is a purified version of morphine that is very addictive and is highly likely to be abused. Heroin has no acceptable medical use in the United States. Other synthetic or semisynthetic opiate drugs include codeine, Demerol®, Dilaudid®, OxyContin® (oxycodone), Percodan®, Sublimaze®, and Vicodin®. These opiates are used both medically and abused when diverted from original intent (Gutstein & Akil, 2001; Kuhn et al., 2008). **Drug diversion** is used to describe any case where a legitimately prescribed medication is used for illicit recreational purposes. Currently in the United States, diverted opiate prescription medications result in more overdose deaths than deaths attributable to heroin and cocaine (CDC, 2011a). Drug diversion is a very serious problem with opiates, more than any other psychoactive drug.

Opiates have been used for thousands of years to treat pain. All living organisms are exposed to a range of stimuli and conditions in both their internal and external environment that can lead to pain. While pain can be a difficult concept to define, **pain** in humans is often described as an unpleasant sensory and emotional experience associated with actual or potential tissue damage (Merskey, 1983). The ability to perceive pain is referred to as **nociception**, and the ability to block pain without loss of consciousness is referred to as **analgesia**. Pain is often the most aversive medical symptom leading a patient to seek help from a physician (Meier, 2003). While pain may appear solely to cause problems, the ability to perceive and respond to aversive stimuli is a basic and necessary biological function. Pain can protect us from harm, such as the pain you feel when you touch a hot stove. Pain can also be debilitating, such as when a cancer patient experiences constant and worsening pain as a tumor grows and presses on nerves or damages bone. Severe pain is also common in diseases such as sickle-cell anemia, rheumatoid arthritis, shingles, and diabetes. In the medical treatment of pain, there is no test to inform a physician about how much pain a patient is actually experiencing, and pain can vary considerably from person to person. Obviously a severe injury would induce pain in most individuals. However, chronic pain can be particularly difficult to assess, as some cases may not have any measurable injuries. In some cases, the nervous system just seems to have gone awry in how it processes pain signals (Del Seppia et al., 2007).

Opiates are psychoactive drugs that result in profound analgesia and can relieve extreme human suffering. It is hard to conceive of the time when morphine and other opiates were not available. Medicine relies heavily on opiate drugs to improve the human condition when severe injuries or illnesses occur. However, opiates can also be the source of extreme human suffering. Individuals who become addicted to opiates are faced with the almost insurmountable task of trying to stop use. Opiates are extremely addictive. As sedative drugs, opiates can also lead to death, with overdoses a serious concern among individuals who abuse opiates. Opiates are also sometimes referred to as **narcotics** (DEA, 2012c). Narcotics are any psychoactive drug with sleep-inducing properties, but the term has been used imprecisely and sometimes refers to all illegal drugs, including cocaine or marijuana. Given that opiates and cocaine or marijuana are extremely dissimilar, the use of the term narcotics has been slowly falling out of favor. Consequently, the term *opiates* will be used throughout this chapter.

Sources of Opiates

Opiates can be natural, synthetic, or semisynthetic. Opiates from natural sources come from the opium poppy, *Papaver somniferum*, a beautiful flowering plant growing naturally and cultivated in Middle Eastern countries like Afghanistan (Figure 9-2). The plant can reach a height of up to 5 feet (150 cm) depending on growing conditions. The Latin botanical name means *sleep-bringing poppy*, an apt description for a plant with sedative psychoactive properties. The bold yet delicate flowers of the poppy plant can vary widely from white to dark red in color. Flowering occurs approximately 90 days after germination, and the flowers only last a few days. When the petals drop, a round seed pod the size of a large pea remains. The seed pod grows larger until it is about the size of your thumb. At this point, it is ready for harvesting, at approximately 2 weeks after the petals have dropped. The psychoactive properties of the plant come not from the flowers but rather from the sap found inside the seed pod. If the green seed pod is cut with a knife, a milk latex sap will ooze from the cut. When dried, the sap turns dark brown, and the dried sap results in **opium**. Sometimes referred to as raw opium, opium contains the alkaloids morphine, codeine, and other alkaloid compounds (Figure 9-3). The dried sap can be smoked or eaten. In fields of cultivated poppy plants, the plants can also be mowed like grass and then dried to make poppy straw, which contains the same compounds. The poppy seeds from the plant contain very little of the opiate compounds, and they are often used in baked goods or made into poppy seed oil. While certain poppies are widely used in gardening, the true poppies, genus *Papaver*, are the plants with the psychoactive properties that grow readily in the Middle East (Booth, 1996; Grey-Wilson, 2002).

Opium contains several important chemicals that contribute to its effects. Morphine can be isolated from opium, as can codeine and thebaine. Morphine and codeine are widely used in medicine as analgesics. Thebaine is the starting material used to make oxycodone (Meier, 2003).

©AFP/Getty Images

FIGURE 9-2

Local poppy farmers harvest the opium sap from the bulb of the plant during a ten-day harvest period in Fayzabad, Afghanistan (Getty Images, May 31, 2011).

©Neil Howard/Getty Images/Flickr RF

FIGURE 9-3

The mature seed pod (after the flower blooms) of the opium poppy plant (*Papaver somniferum*). If cut with a knife, milky sap will ooze out. This sap contains the alkaloids morphine and codeine.

Once morphine is isolated, it is approximately 10 times more potent than the original opium. Morphine can also be chemically processed further to make heroin, which is a far more powerful opiate than morphine (Figure 9-4). The quality of heroin available on the street can vary enormously, ranging in color from black to white. Pure heroin is a white, odorless powder, whereas black tar heroin is quite impure. Black tar heroin from Mexico appears tarlike and is too impure to

FIGURE 9-4
Heroin (purest version is the white powder on the right).

be smoked, so it is often melted to be injected (Ashton, 2002). Since heroin is extremely expensive, it is often adulterated (cut) with other similar-looking compounds such as caffeine or talcum powder.

Production and distribution of clandestine naturally occurring opiates is limited by various factors impacting all agricultural crops. Poppy crops may have bumper yields in some years in the Middle East and may be impacted by drought or additional problems in others. The world demand for opium, the raw material for heroin, remains strong in spite of this variability. Afghanistan is the world's largest producer of opium, and its farmers harvest 80% of the world's supply. According to the United Nations, poppy cultivation is estimated to have increased 18% in Afghanistan between 2011 and 2012. The Afghan counternarcotics minister, Zarar Ahmad Mugbil, estimated that the Taliban made over $150 million from the poppy crop in 2012. Most Afghan heroin ends up in Russia, Iran, and Europe (Rubin, 2012). In the United States, heroin use escalated during the 1990s but has remained somewhat level since the 2000s. However, abuse of other opiate drugs has increased during this same period in the United States.

Chemists, legitimate or not, have developed chemical analogues to naturally occurring morphine and heroin. Examples of synthetic opiates made entirely in a lab include fentanyl and methadone. There are also semisynthetic opiates that start from an opium plant source but require elaborate processing to reach the final product, such as oxycodone. The illicit manufacture of laboratory-made opiates includes a variety of compounds. Examples include designer heroin and variations of fentanyl (which users refer to as China White). Some of these laboratory-made opiates can be 10 to 1,000 times more potent than plant-based heroin, which increases the likelihood of overdose. However, the most important recent trend among opiate abusers is the dramatic escalation in the abuse of diverted prescription opiate medications made by pharmaceutical companies. When used appropriately to treat severe pain, these medications are extremely effective. However, individuals who are not in severe pain use these same drugs with hazardous outcomes. The problems with diverted opiate medications emerged in the early 2000s. **OxyContin**® (which arrived on the market in 1996) was initially considered just another opiate medication, since it contained oxycodone, a well-known opiate used in medicine. However, the breakthrough with OxyContin® was its 12-hour duration of action, where other opiates only lasted up to 4 hours. OxyContin® contained relatively high doses of oxycodone to generate the long duration of action. Initially used by cancer patients, the controlled-release formulation helped many patients sleep comfortably and free from pain. By the early 2000s, OxyContin® became more widely used for other chronic pain conditions, such as severe back pain or severe arthritis. More legitimate widespread use of the drug coincided with drug diversion. Abusers learned that they could crush the high-dose oxycodone-containing tablet to snort the drug. Alternatively, they could dissolve the drug in water and inject it for a powerful and immediate high, just like heroin. Abusers nicknamed the drug Oxy or Hillbilly Heroin (referencing its widespread use in Appalachia). The drug appealed especially to young people such as high school students. In addition to the problem of obviously illegitimate use of OxyContin®, there is also the thorny issue of individuals using OxyContin® or other similar opiate medications for chronic pain and then becoming addicted. Cases of prescription opiate addiction arising from legitimate prescriptions have physicians concerned about how to properly treat pain, without inducing addiction. Conservative talk show host Rush Limbaugh completed a rehabilitation program after becoming addicted to OxyContin®, with his initial use of the drug apparently for debilitating back pain following spinal surgery. Other high-profile celebrities, such as actor Matthew Perry, also claim to have become addicted after treatment for legitimate pain. Studies of the increase in OxyContin® abuse have suggested that perhaps many patients and physicians were misinformed about the risks of OxyContin®. The original label on the drug, which had FDA approval, stated that the reported risk of addiction was small. This product label was changed in 2008, after the risk of addiction became evident. Despite increasing concern about both legitimate and diverted prescription opiates, retail prescriptions have tripled in the past two decades (Meier, 2003; Whoriskey, 2012).

Brief History of Opiate Use

The poppy plant, *Papaver somniferum*, is native to the Middle East. Humans seem to have been aware of the plant's pain-relieving and euphoric effects for at least 7,000 years. Historically, opium was more often used as an analgesic than for its psychoactive properties. Among all psychoactive drugs, only alcohol seems to have been intentionally used earlier than opium. Recall that the seed pod of the poppy plant need only be cut open to reveal the latex milky sap that constitutes raw opium. This sap can be dried and then smoked or eaten. As such, neither scientific knowledge nor much technical prowess is needed to access the plant's powerful effects. Archeological evidence suggests that around 5000 BCE, the Sumerian and Assyrian civilizations in lower Mesopotamia (modern-day Iraq) began cultivating the poppy plant and extracting opium from it. The Sumerians referred to the poppy as Hul Gil, which roughly translates to "joy plant" or "plant of happiness." The Sumerians passed along the plant and knowledge of its euphoric effects to the Assyrians, who did the same for the Babylonians, who in turn passed the knowledge to the Egyptians. By approximately 1600 BCE, the Egyptians began cultivating their famous poppy fields in the ancient capital city of Thebes. The papyrus of Eber, dated approximately 1550 BCE, notes that opium could calm the cries of children and the abdominal pain from worms. The opium trade flourished when ships brought opium across the Mediterranean to Europe. In 460 BCE Greece, Hippocrates (the father of medicine) wrote that opium was a useful pain-reliever, but he dismissed any magical (psychoactive) characteristics of opium. Hippocrates advocated the use of opium for treating various diseases. Alexander the Great introduced opium to Persia around 330 BCE. Roman civilization absorbed knowledge from Greek culture, including the uses of alcohol and opium. Arab use of opium was extensive while Roman civilization was declining. Opium was frequently used to treat diarrhea and other medical conditions. Trade routes that initially reached Persia eventually reached India and China thus expanding the use of opium (Aragon-Poce et al., 2002).

By 400 CE, China had received knowledge about opium from Arab traders. The Chinese initially used opium mainly as medicine. Interestingly, opium disappeared from Europe for about 200 years starting in the 1300s. During the time of the Inquisition, anything from the East (where poppy cultivation and opium use originated) was linked to the Devil. The hiatus from opium use ended around 1500 CE, when Portugese traders arriving in China became enamored with smoking opium. In China, the practice of mixing opium with tobacco for smoking became widespread. European physicians began treating their patients' pain with opium and after 1680, with laudanum (a mixture of opium in sherry wine). Also in the 1600s, residents of Persia and India were eating and drinking opium mixtures for recreation. Europeans became increasingly interested in obtaining opium, and trade flourished. Ships chartered by Elizabeth I in England were instructed to go to India, purchase opium and bring it back to England. The British were quick to dominate the opium trade between India and China. The first edict prohibiting opium use came from Chinese emperor Yung Cheng in 1729. He prohibited the smoking and domestic sale of opium, except when used as medicine (Aragon-Poce et al., 2002; Santoro, Bellinghieri, & Savica, 2011).

In 1753, Linnaeus, the father of Botany, first classified *Papaver somniferum* (the opium poppy) as "sleep-inducing" in his book *Genera Plantarum*. By the end of the 1700s, the British completely dominated the opium trade. All poppy growers in India were forbidden to sell opium except to the British East India Company. In 1799, China's emperor Kia King banned opium completely. In 1803, German pharmacist Friedrich Seturner identified the active ingredient in opium, the alkaloid morphine. Seturner was the first person to isolate a plant alkaloid. Seturner named the chemical morphium (which later became morphine) after the Greek god of dreams, Morpheus. The name was chosen due to the dreamlike state that morphine induced in the user. Fifty years after Seturner's discovery, morphine was widely available in both Europe and the United States. The discovery of the hypodermic syringe at that time led users to inject morphine, contributing to an escalation in dependence. Users were taking morphine to combat pain, but also for purely recreational reasons (Aragon-Poce et al., 2002; Hamilton & Baskett, 2000; Santoro et al., 2011; Scott, 1998).

While the war on drugs may seem like a modern development, there have been several intense conflicts about drugs historically. The First Opium War commenced on March 18, 1839, when the imperial Chinese commissioner ordered all foreign traders to surrender their opium. The British were obviously unhappy with this pronouncement, given British dominance of the opium trade. In response, the British sent warships to the Chinese coast. By 1841, the British had defeated China in this first drug war. China was forced to pay a large indemnity to Britain and Hong Kong was ceded to the British. China wouldn't resume sovereignty over Hong Kong until 1997, following 156 years of British colonial rule. After the First Opium War (1839–1841), hostilities restarted in 1856 when both Britain and France began the Second Opium War (1856–1860) against China. Like its predecessor, the Second Opium War arose from British/French grievances about Chinese control of the opium trade. Once again, China was defeated and forced to pay an indemnity. Opium importation into China was legalized, and opium production increased all over Southeast Asia.

In the United States, the American Civil War (1861–1865) was a gruesome conflict in which many soldiers needed limbs amputated or other surgeries performed. The liberal use of morphine by soldiers, justified on humanitarian grounds, also led to widespread addiction, an outcome labeled "Soldier's disease." Addiction to opiates grew following a discovery in 1874 by an English researcher, Charles Wright. He boiled morphine with acid on a stove and isolated heroin. His goal was to develop a nonaddicting version of morphine, but instead he discovered a much more addictive opiate (though the addictive properties of heroin were initially unclear). Also in 1874, the smoking of opium within the city limits of San Francisco was banned (see Chapter 1). In 1890, U.S. Congress imposed a tax on opium and morphine. In 1898, the German chemical company Bayer launched its new medicine, heroin (Figure 9-5). Heroin's name arose from German doctors describing the drug as heroisch (which translates to heroic). In a move that illustrates how little understood were the addictive properties of opiates in the early 1900s, the Saint James philanthropic society mounted a campaign to help morphine addicts give up their addiction by supplying them with free samples of heroin through the mail. Medical journals also published papers in which physicians argued that heroin was an effective treatment as a step-down cure for morphine. By 1903, heroin addiction was rising to alarming rates, and the medical establishment was beginning to reverse its position on the addictive potential of heroin. Many physicians were nevertheless reluctant to change their view of heroin, since the drug was such an effective strong analgesic. The rise in addiction to opiates could no longer be ignored in the United States. By the turn of the century, over a quarter of million Americans (from a population of 76 million) were addicted to opiates (Scott, 1998).

With the passage of the Pure Food and Drug Act in 1906 (see Chapter 1), the availability of opiates declined in part because companies were required to label the contents of medicines for

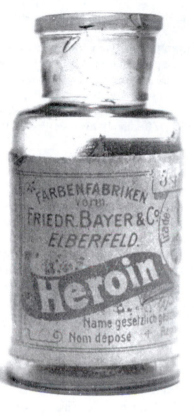

©Mpv_51/English Wikipedia

FIGURE 9-5
Bayer's heroin bottle contained 5 grams of heroin.

the first time. President Woodrow Wilson signed the Harrison Narcotic Act in 1914, which taxed and regulated opiates. With the Harrison Narcotics Act, doctors and pharmacists were required to register and pay a tax if they prescribed narcotics. In 1919, legal interpretation of the Harrison Act outlawed medical prescription of narcotics to addicts, thus forcing drug abusers to be dependent on black-market distributors. Interestingly, it was only around this time that heroin addicts began injecting heroin (even though soldiers during the American Civil War had done so with morphine). The term "junkies" arose when a group of addicts in the 1920s supported their heroin habit by collecting scrap metal from industrial dumps. The manufacture of heroin was banned in the United States in 1924. By the 1930s, heroin manufacture had become largely an underground enterprise. The exception was Japan and the territories it occupied, where pharmaceutical companies produced heroin for the Chinese until the end of the Second World War. Also in the United States in the 1930s, pharmaceutical companies were working on developing less addictive opiate drugs. Dilaudid® (hydromorphine) was introduced as a nonaddictive substitute for heroin. Abuse became widespread, and Dilaudid® was nicknamed drugstore heroin. The U.S. involvement in Vietnam (1965–1970) led to widespread use of heroin among service members stationed in Southeast Asia. Heroin was sold openly in South Vietnam and was relatively inexpensive ($10 would buy enough heroin for 10 injections, which would have cost $500 in the United States at that time). In 1971, the Pentagon released a report showing approximately 5% of personnel in Vietnam had opiate-positive urine drug tests. Vietnam also was blamed for the surge in illegal heroin coming to the United States, with estimates of 750,000 U.S. heroin addicts at that time. The heroin epidemic subsided in the mid-1970s. Interestingly, follow-up of service members who had returned to the United States found that only about 1% to 2% of them were using opiates 12 months later. Those rates were consistent with those found in individuals going into the service (Robins, 1974). It seemed that the combination of heroin availability, low cost, and stress in Vietnam led to widespread heroin use. When contributing factors changed as service personnel returned home, many no longer used heroin, which suggests that compulsive use of heroin is not inevitable.

More than 200 years ago, morphine was isolated from opium. Morphine remains the most widely used analgesic, particularly in the treatment of severe pain. Heroin remains primarily in the hands of criminals worldwide, except in rare cases of its medical use in certain countries outside of the United States. Heroin is also fully or partly responsible for many overdose fatalities, including celebrities such as singer Janis Joplin (d. 1970), comedian John Belushi (d. 1982), actor River Phoenix (d. 1993), and singer Kurt Cobain (d. 1994) (Booth, 1996; Hamilton & Baskett, 2000; Meier, 2003; Scott, 1998).

Pharmaceutical companies have recently been developing a variety of new opiates for the treatment of severe pain. The most notorious of these for drug diversion is OxyContin®, with its controlled-release of oxycodone over a long duration of action (12 hours). First released in the 1990s, Oxycontin® was a result of the increasing focus on better pain treatment in patients. However, pain is an elusive concept, and drug abusers realized that the same opiate drug that was so helpful to chronic pain sufferers could also be abused by snorting, inhaling, or injecting it (Whoriskey, 2012). Moreover, a subset of pain patients will subsequently develop an addiction to their medication. Society is currently having a difficult time deciding how to handle opiates. Medically, they are needed. Opiates are not only extremely helpful for severe pain, but they decrease diarrhea and suppress coughs. However, opiates are easily abused due to their strong addictive potential.

Current Drug Laws in the United States

The current legal scheduling of narcotics ranges from Schedule I to Schedule V (see Chapter 1 for information about the Controlled Substances Act). Heroin is located on Schedule I due to its high potential for abuse and lack of medical use in the United States. Morphine, opium, codeine, oxycodone (OxyContin®, Percocet®), and many other opiate medications are found in Schedule II. Various medications containing very small doses of codeine, such as Robitussin AC® (a cough syrup containing codeine) are located on Schedule V, since they have low potential for abuse and currently accepted medical uses. Researchers in both academia and industry are intensely interested in discovering new ways to treat chronic pain, either by modifying opiate drugs so that they are less likely to be abused or by finding drugs that act differently in the body from opiates.

Prevalence of Opiate Use

In the United States

Most national surveys ask separate questions about the use of heroin and use of diverted prescription opiate medication. The 2010 National Survey on Drug Use and Health (NSDUH) estimated that there were approximately 200,000 past-month users of heroin in the U.S. population (ages 12 and older). By contrast, there were approximately 5.1 million past-month users of diverted prescription opiates. Thus, diverted prescription opiates are approximately 25 times more prevalent than heroin. In 2010, approximately 1.9 million individuals in the United States were estimated to be abusing or dependent on diverted opiate drugs, a rise from the 1.5 million reported in 2002. The pattern of greater problems with diverted prescription medications is also reflected in new initiates (new first-time users). In 2010, there were approximately 140,000 individuals who used heroin for the first time in the past 12 months, while there were approximately 2 million new users of diverted opiates. The use of diverted opiate medications is more common in 12- to 17-year-old youths, with past-month rates of 2.5%, and in 18- to 25-year-old young adults, with rates of 4.5%. Diverted prescription opiates are the second most prevalent illicit drug used in these age groups, behind only marijuana (Johnston et al., 2012). Diverted prescription opiates are more widespread in rural areas, particularly in Appalachia, compared to similarly located urban areas (Young, Havens, & Leukefeld, 2012). Interestingly, there is a gender reversal in use of diverted prescription medications. While males typically use more illicit drugs than females, among youths ages 12 to 17, females had past-month use rates of 3.0%, versus males with rates of 2.0% (Johnston et al., 2012). Over the past two decades, while heroin use has remained relatively stable, both the legitimate use and illicit abuse of prescription opiate medication have escalated. In 2011, approximately 238 million prescriptions were written for opiate medications. These opiate medications are now responsible for more deaths than the number from both suicide and motor vehicle crashes, or deaths from cocaine and heroin combined (Manchikanti et al., 2012). Interestingly, the acquisition of opiate medications for illicit use follows atypical patterns compared to other illicit drugs. When asked where they get medications used illicitly, more than half of abusers state that they got it from a friend or relative for free, whereas only 4% reported getting the pills from a drug dealer (Johnston et al., 2012).

Around the World

It is somewhat difficult to estimate worldwide use rates of opiates. However, it has been estimated that in 2009, there were approximately 12–21 million people (approximately 0.4% of the population) who were opiate users, having used opiates at least once in the past year. More than half of these users were residents of Asian countries, with the highest levels of use along the main drug-trafficking routes coming out of Afghanistan. There are also newer opium production and heroin-trafficking routes utilizing African countries to ship illicit opiates to European markets. Wherever these drugs are being shipped, use of opiates is increasing. Illicit opiate use contributes to more deaths than all other illicit psychoactive drugs. It has been estimated that approximately 100,000 deaths occur worldwide each year that are attributed to the illicit use of opiates. These deaths are opiate overdoses and the numbers do not include deaths from HIV/AIDS, a major concern for heroin injection drug users (Degenhardt & Hall, 2012).

In the News:

Meier, B. (2012, April 8). Tightening the lid on pain prescriptions. *The New York Times*.

The use of prescription opiate medications is rising in the United States. Approximately 15 years ago, opiates were reserved for extreme medical cases such as cancer, end-of-life care, or postoperative pain. However, pain experts changed their view on the utility of opiates and extended their use to treat chronic pain conditions. The resultant change in use of opiate medications has been dramatic. In 2011, sales of opiate drugs totaled approximately $8.5 billion, up from $4.4 billion in 2001. Early indications of the escalation in use came from workers' compensation claims, when injured workers prescribed opiate medications for pain had died from overdoses. Increasing rates of drug diversion also made many stakeholders concerned. In an effort to stem the tide of overuse, an aggressive effort was undertaken in Washington state. In the new Washington law, any patient taking an opiate medication (hydrocodone, fentanyl, methadone, oxycodone) in a daily dose equivalent in strength to 120 mg of morphine, and not improving, will need to be evaluated by a pain specialist. Advocates of the new law argue that the change will stem the rise in overuse of opiates. Detractors argue that patients with chronic pain conditions such as degenerative joint diseases, lupus, sickle-cell disease, back injuries, and arthritis are notoriously difficult to treat, so withholding access to opiate pain medications will restrict patient access to adequate care.

Use this news article to test and apply your knowledge:

1. Lawmakers in the state of Washington felt that the use of opiate medications was a concern and created a new law to address it. Is the observation in Washington consistent with U.S. national data?
2. Why might chronic pain patients be difficult to treat?

Answers:

1. Yes, national data indicates that the use of diverted prescription opiates is a major and escalating problem. Recent survey data indicates that there are approximately 5.1 million past-month users of diverted prescription opiates in the United States.
2. Chronic pain patients tend to be difficult to treat in part because pain is a subjective experience that is difficult to assess. There is no medical test that can inform a physician how much pain a person is experiencing. Chronic pain is debilitating, which may lead to other problems such as depression, anxiety, loss of employment, or inability to maintain social relationships. Moreover, the same medications that help treat pain medications can also be abused to get high. A physician is faced with the difficult task of determining if a patient's symptoms reflect pain treatment or drug-seeking behavior.

What do you think about this news story?

Do you think that this new law will help or hurt patients? Do you think that this new law will stem the rising tide of diversion of opiate medications?

There are no right or wrong answers to this question. It is only with time that we will learn if it is effective or if it interferes with patient care.

Medical Uses for Opiates

Opiate drugs are widely prescribed for severe acute and chronic pain. There has been a shift in how physicians prescribe opiates over the past 15 years. While opiates were in the past reserved for extreme cases of cancer, terminal illness, and postoperative pain, the medical establishment has increasingly changed its view about patient pain and suffering and identified many cases of debilitating chronic pain warranting the use of opiates. However, this shift in approach has been controversial, in part because the escalation in availability of opiates to the general public has coincided with increased drug diversion. One issue that complicates the diagnosis and treatment of pain is that no medical test accurately measures patient pain level. While the physician or nurse can take into consideration other diagnostic indicators, such as how much a tumor has spread or how much pain is likely after a particular surgical procedure, the patient ultimately needs to verbally communicate what he or she is feeling. A comprehensive pain assessment might ask various questions about the pain, such as where it is located, how intense it is, how aggravating it is, when it started, and how long it has lasted. The physician or nurse may also assess pain using behavioral observation such as body language or oral expression. Some medical professionals might use formal assessments such as a rating scale in which a patient indicates a number representing how he or she currently feels. The rating scale may range between 0 and 10, with 0 indicating no pain and 10 indicating terrible pain. In children, the rating scale might use pictures of faces, ranging from very happy to crying (Wong & Baker, 1988). While all of this input can be helpful in assessing if opiates are warranted and whether the dose of opiate is effective, the diagnosis and treatment of pain with opiates can also be fraught with problems. Patients may be overmedicated or alternatively undertreated for their pain. Moreover, individuals seeking opiates for reasons other than pain control can take advantage of the process, given the importance of subjective reporting in treating pain. Finally, pain patients often also have a concurrent addictive disorder, which complicates how properly to treat patients who are in pain but are also likely to abuse opiate medications. Moreover, pain patients with a prior history of psychoactive drug use may choose not to disclose that information for fear that they will be denied care (Gourlay, Heit, & Almahrezi, 2005).

Table 9-1   Opiate drugs available for medical use.

Generic Name	Trade Name	Typical Oral Dose (mg)	Potency Compared to Oral Morphine[1]
Natural			
Morphine	Avinza® MS Contin®	10–30	1
Codeine		30–60	0.1
Semisynthetic			
Diamorphine (heroin)[2]		5–10	4–5
Synthetic			
Buprenorphine	Butrans® (patch)	5–20 mcg/hr	40
Fentanyl	Sublimaze® Duragesic® (patch)	.05–.10	50–100
Hydrocodone	Vicodin® Lortab®	1–1.5	1
Hydromorphone	Dilaudid®	2–4	5
Methadone	Dolphine®	2.5–10	3–4 (acute)[3] 7.5 (chronic)
Meperidine	Demerol®	50–150	0.2
Oxycodone	Percocet® Percodan® OxyContin® Roxicodone®	2.25–5 10–80 (extended release)	1–2
Oxymorphone			7
Pentazocine	Talwin®	30	
Propoxyphene	Darvon®	32–65	

[1]The reliability of comparing the analgesic (pain-blocking) action of differing opiate drugs to morphine has been questioned, in part because inter- and intraindividual differences in pharmacology can influence the accuracy of dose calculations. While an estimate is provided, this chart is only intended to provide potency comparisons to morphine. Duration of drug action is not included, which must be factored into dosing decisions. Given that opiates are drugs that can result in very serious side effects, including overdose deaths, clinicians should always use great caution in administering any opiate drug.

[2]Diamorphine is heroin. Diamorphine is not used medically in the United States, but it is used in many European countries to treat severe pain cases.

[3]Methadone is more potent than other opiates when used chronically. It is approximately 7× stronger than morphine when used for a week or longer, but is only 4× stronger than morphine when used for up to 3 days. Methadone is stored in fat tissue, which accounts for higher potency with longer use.
Source: Shaheen et al. (2009).

There are a number of possible drugs available for the appropriate medical use of opiates. Pain is present in 50% of individuals suffering from advanced cancer and in more than 80% of individuals who are terminally ill. Pain is obviously distressing and a feared symptom of advanced disease. Morphine is widely regarded as the prototypical opiate analgesic, so opiate drugs are often compared to morphine (see Table 9-1). Typically, short-acting opiates (duration of action of 4–6 hours) are used in acute and postoperative pain. When pain is chronic, the long-acting opiates (duration of action of up to 12 hours) may be more effective. Since tolerance develops rapidly to opiates and pain can worsen or abate, astute physicians should be constantly assessing their patient for changes in symptoms. Physicians may switch drugs frequently and/or change routes of administration to adapt to changing symptoms and avoid adverse consequences (possibly even including death from overdose). In addition to pure opiate drugs, a variety of drugs are available that combine opiates with other pain relievers like acetaminophen, including Tylox® and Percocet®. Given that non-opiate pain relievers are less potent than opiates, these combination medications are used for more moderate cases or as symptoms improve (Shaheen, Walsh, Lasheen, Davis, & Lagman, 2009).

Opiates are very effective in treating severe pain. Following administration of an opiate drug for pain, many patients report that they are still aware of the pain being present but that the pain is no longer as aversive. Opiate drugs also reduce the emotional suffering accompanying pain. The patient appears calmer and less agitated. Interestingly, the physical effect of opiates tends to be fairly specific to reducing pain. Mental and motor abilities may remain relatively intact even though pain may be dramatically reduced. At therapeutic doses used in medical settings, many patients are not too drowsy unless the dose is quite high, which occurs with cancer and other terminal illnesses. However, side effects are a significant concern. The patient needs to be monitored for signs or complaints of nausea, vomiting, constipation, urinary retention, confusion, sedation, cognitive impairments, impaired sexual performance, and respiratory depression (impaired breathing). Especially with the chronic use of opiates, patients may also develop **opiate-induced hyperalgesia**, in which the patient becomes increasingly sensitive to pain over time (Chau, Walker, Pai, & Cho, 2008).

Routes of Administration

The **route of administration** refers to the method by which a drug enters the body. The route of administration impacts how much of the dose reaches the site of action and how quickly it gets there. Opiates are administered by various routes of administration. Oral administration of

Focus on Careers: Clinical Trials Careers

While knowledge in medicine has led to tremendous achievements helping patients every day, there is still much that is not known. This is particularly true in the area of pain management. The scientific process is slow, complex, and expensive, but eventually various new drugs and devices move from the laboratory to the market. Many people pursue careers in clinical research, helping biotechnology get translated from bench to bedside. There are a variety of entry points to start a career in clinical research. For many such jobs, an undergraduate degree and some experience in research (such as with a faculty member in your department) may be all that is needed to launch your career. The most popular entry to a clinical trials career is as a clinical research associate (CRA) or a clinical research coordinator (CRC). Employed by companies, contract research organizations, universities, and hospitals, these individuals monitor research trials activities, coordinate documentation, and meet with physician investigators leading various studies. They recruit, screen, and enroll patients in studies. Having excellent organizational and people skills are key. Meticulous attention to detail is also a necessity, especially given that patient lives may be at stake. CRC jobs have a median salary of approximately $50,000 in the United States.

Another popular way to enter the field of clinical research is as a data manager. The clinical trials process involves the collection of lots of data. A data management team ensures that data is collected accurately and handled with integrity. If you like statistics, you might start as a biostatistician, where you will analyze the data that has been collected. There are also careers as clinical quality assurance auditors, regulatory affairs specialists, and clinical safety specialists. Given that clinical trials are heavily regulated, these jobs ensure that studies comply with all rules and regulations. Clinical safety specialists tend to be nurses, since their main responsibility is to track adverse events (unwanted side effects from a drug or device), although having some experience in the clinical research field might be sufficient. Finally, medical writing is another great career path. Volumes of information come out of clinical trials, and good writers are needed to help communicate this scientific information in an easy-to-understand format to physicians, patients, caregivers, and the general public. While there are various certification programs that have been developed for clinical trials careers, certifications are often not necessary for entry-level jobs. For many people in clinical trials careers, the ultimate reward is seeing new therapies benefitting people for the first time. Given that pain management is such a central concern in medicine, development of new medications to treat pain conditions will remain a high priority.

Some websites to explore:

Society of Clinical Research Associates
http://www.socra.org
CenterWatch is a leading source of clinical trials information for professionals and patients.
http://www.centerwatch.com

opiates in pill form is widely used in medicine for the therapeutic treatment of pain. Transdermal administration via a patch on the skin is also used in treating chronic pain with opiates. Illicitly used opiates are sometimes administered intranasally (snorted) or by inhalation (smoking). Finally, opiates can also be administered by various types of injections, including subcutaneous, intramuscular, and intravenous. Opiate administration by injection is common in both medical settings and among abusers. On the street, low-purity heroin is too impure to be smoked, so users melt it to inject it. Abusers also inject heroin because it achieves the most immediate and potent high. In medical settings where patients are in extreme pain, intravenous administration of opiates can provide near-immediate relief, while intramuscular injections tend to be avoided (since the injection process itself can cause pain). Heroin addicts often prefer intravenous injection, also known as mainlining, because the drug takes almost immediate effect. Some heroin users start the injection habit with subcutaneous injections, given that they require less skill. However, most users proceed to intramuscular injections and then ultimately acquire the skill of self-administering the drug with intravenous injections. A major concern with intravenous administration of heroin and other opiates is the sharing of needles. This practice is risky because it results in the spread of various diseases, such as hepatitis C and AIDS (acquired immunodeficiency syndrome) (Harrell, Mancha, Petras, Trenz, & Latimer, 2012). A study of injection drug users in New York City found that most of them inject heroin (though other drugs like cocaine and methamphetamine are also injected). In the sample from New York City, almost a quarter of the injection drug users were infected with HIV (human immunodeficiency virus) that causes AIDS (Davis, Johnson, Randolph, & Liberty, 2006). Babies born of mothers infected with HIV as well as sexual partners of these individuals will be infected with HIV as well, spreading the problem beyond just the injection drug user. Sterile needles eliminate the risk of disease transmission among injection drug users. Various cities have developed needle exchange programs, in which users can properly dispose of dirty needles and receive clean needles. Public health campaigns also encourage users to clean dirty needles with bleach if a needle exchange program is not available. While needle exchange programs are at times viewed negatively by the general public, researchers have found that these programs do reduce disease transmission and improve public health. Also, needle exchange programs can provide bridges for users that ultimately lead them to enroll in treatment programs (Kidorf, King, Gandotra, Kolodner, & Brooner, 2012).

Myth Busters: Patients Given Morphine Are Certain to Become Addicted

Physicians and patients alike are concerned about opiate drug use and addiction. While the risk of addiction is clearly a concern, it is a myth that patients given morphine or any other opiate for legitimate reasons of severe pain will inevitably become addicted. This myth is prevalent not only in the United States but also around the world. It is so common that it has been labeled **opiophobia** (Glare, 2011; Motov & Khan, 2008). Studies of cancer patients have found that opiate medication can be stopped when patients are no longer in pain with no evidence of drug craving or other symptoms of addiction being present. Even among cancer patients using very high doses of morphine for severe pain, the patients did not report feeling euphoria after being given the drug. Moreover, opiates are very safe when used as directed, and they are less toxic than some other drugs used in medicine, such as chemotherapy medications. The myth that opiate use inevitably leads to addiction is widely held and contributes to much unnecessary suffering. Elderly patients in particular are often untreated or undertreated for severe pain by physicians. These elderly patients are not only in severe pain, but they may also become depressed, experience social isolation, and exhibit cognitive impairments because of poor pain management (Auret & Schug, 2005; Varner, 2012). Patients may also be noncompliant with physician instructions because of unnecessary fear of addiction from opiates. For example, a patient may delay taking opiates, take less than the amount prescribed, or not take the prescribed medication. Poor pain control can also slow recovery after surgery if pain prevents mobility (Zenz & Willweber-Strumpf, 1993).

Laboratory research using animal models and healthy individuals provides clues to why addiction is unlikely to develop when opiates are used to treat pain. Pain can be induced in several ways that do not cause bodily damage in research settings, such as the cold pressor test in which the subject places a hand in an ice bucket. The subject tells the researcher when pain is present and pulls their hand out of the ice when pain becomes unbearable. The researcher records how long the subject was able to withstand the icy water. The hot water immersion test is identical to the cold pressor test except that the pain induction involves hot water. Similar procedures can also be used on laboratory rodents, such as the tail flick test. Rats and mice have sensitive tails. If they feel too much heat on their tail, they will flick it away (which can be timed by the researcher). In these various paradigms, morphine (or other opiates) decreases pain perception, so that the hand/tail can stay in the cold/hot water longer. Importantly, the presence of the aversive painful stimulus prevents the development of tolerance to morphine, which is a key concern in the rise of addiction (Cooper et al., 2012; Vaccarino & Couret, 1993; Vaccarino et al., 1993). Likewise, human studies do not report significant euphoria when opiates are taken while the subject is in pain. This result is noticeably different from the recreational user experiencing strong subjective effects of euphoria (feeling high) after opiate administration. The subjective feeling of euphoria is a key motivation for users to take the drug. In sum, opiates are sometimes considered "bad drugs" because of their association with addiction. However, opiates are also extremely good drugs that are incredibly useful in medicine. Both physicians and patients can work together to ensure that pain control is achieved when using opiates, while simultaneously minimizing the risks of addiction. In medicine, the goal of the prescribing physician is to find a minimal dose of opiate drug that will block pain without eliciting euphoria in the patient.

QUICK QUIZ 9-1

1. In the United States, abuse is more prevalent for _____.
   a. heroin
   b. diverted prescription drugs
   c. both heroin and diverted prescription drugs equally

2. Opiates are classified as Schedule _____ drugs.
   a. I
   b. IV
   c. IV and V
   d. V
   e. All of the above

3. Opium comes from which plant?
   a. *Cannibas sativa*
   b. *Erythroxylon coca*
   c. *Papaver somniferum*
   d. *Nicotiana tabacum*
   e. *Camellia sinensis*

4. Morphine is _____ times more potent than opium.
   a. 2
   b. 5
   c. 10
   d. 20
   e. 50

5. Opiates induce _____.
   a. nociception
   b. analgesia
   c. anesthesia
   d. laudanum
   e. diarrhea

6. Explain why the term *narcotic* can be confusing.

7. What is opiophobia? Why does it exist?

8. What are two benefits of needle exchange programs?

ANSWERS TO QUICK QUIZ 9-1:

1. b – diverted prescription drugs
2. e – all of the above
3. c – *Papaver somniferum*
4. c – 10
5. b – analgesia
6. The use of the term *narcotic* is intended to refer to opiate drugs. However, narcotic is also used in some contexts to refer to all illegal drugs, including drugs with vastly differing effects from opiates, such as cocaine and marijuana. In practice, the use of the term can be somewhat imprecise.
7. Opiophobia refers to the fear of using opiate medications to treat pain due to concerns about addiction. Opiophobia exists in physicians and patients because opiates are drugs of abuse. However, opiates are also extremely useful drugs in the medical treatment of severe pain. When opiates are used properly and as directed by a physician, the risk of addiction is relatively small.
8. Needle exchange programs provide injection drug users with clean needles in exchange for dirty needles. These programs limit the transmission of various diseases such as HIV-AIDS and hepatitis C. In addition, needle exchange programs may provide a contact point for drug users to find treatment, since they ensure users regularly come into contact with health professionals. Both the needle exchange and contact with professionals will contribute to general public health.

Acute Effects of Opiates

The acute effects of a drug are changes that take place after the ingestion of one dose of the drug. The acute effects of opiates can be objective, including observable changes in behavior or physiology. The acute effects can also be subjective, such as when the user reports how they feel. The baseline state of the individual matters greatly for the acute effects of opiates. For users in pain, opiates will induce analgesia, which will lead to a significant reduction in pain. For users not experiencing pain, potent subjective effects occur, including feelings of euphoria. Nevertheless, high doses of opiates can be fatal for both medical patients and drug abusers alike.

Objective Effects

Opiates are sedative drugs that decrease activity and induce sedation and sleepiness. Used in the medical treatment of pain, opiate administration leads to decreased objective evidence of pain. Associated changes in behavior include less grimacing, moaning, clutching at body part in pain, or verbal complaints of pain. Except at extremely high doses, motor coordination tends to be relatively intact, though behavioral activity may be significantly reduced following opiate administration. However, users sometimes report feeling restless. Speech may be slightly slurred and confusion or poor judgment may be evident, although these changes are more likely at higher doses. Cognitive impairments are also evident, such as decreased ability to learn and remember information (Farahmandfar, Naghdi, Karimian, Kadivar, & Zarrindast, 2012; Fishbein et al., 2007). Individuals feel less sociable under the influence of opiates and thus are less likely to talk to and seek out social interactions with others. The lack of sociability includes lack of sexual drive and interest (Kuhn et al., 2008). In one laboratory-based study, heroin users were studied in an inpatient setting where they were allowed to self-administer heroin for a month. The researchers recorded information about a variety of behaviors. Following self-administration of heroin, one key observable change involved social interaction. The acute effects of the drug resulted in individuals withdrawing from social contact, even though there were no changes in overall activity levels during waking hours (Barbor et al., 1976).

Subjective Effects

If you ask a user who snorts or injects opiates how they feel, they will typically report feeling an initial rush of pleasure, after which a dreamy and pleasant feeling takes over. A general sense of well-being is experienced, accompanied by reduction in tension, anxiety, and aggression. There is little sensitivity to pain. All of these characteristics contribute to the usefulness of opiates in treating extreme pain in medical settings, although feelings of euphoria are unlikely when pain is treated with the appropriate dose of opiate drug. It is the euphoria experienced with opiates that contributes to the drug's abuse potential. When an opiate is swallowed, the user may experience less of a rush, instead experiencing a feeling of pleasant drowsiness. By contrast, injection or smoking of heroin and other opiates typically results in a significant euphoric effect. Users also report a feeling of floating, a wave of relaxation that overtakes the body. Other subjective effects can be unwanted, including feelings of drowsiness, nausea, inability to concentrate, and apathy. Users may also report vivid dreamlike experiences (DEA, 2012a; Kuhn et al., 2008).

The dreamy sleep-inducing effects of opiates were portrayed in the classic MGM 1939 film, *The Wizard of Oz*. Dorothy and her friends are on their way to the Emerald City when the Wicked Witch of the West conjures up a poppy field, preventing the group from reaching their destination. Dorothy and the Cowardly Lion become drowsy and fall asleep while walking through the poppies. The Scarecrow and Tin Man are unable to carry Dorothy. Fortunately, the Good Witch Glinda had been watching over them and created a snowfall to offset the poppies' sleep-inducing power. Dorothy and the Lion awaken and the four skip happily to the Emerald City to see the Wizard of Oz.

The subjective effects of opiates strongly contribute to an inward focus and a decreased interest in others. Users report feeling uninterested in interacting with others and a dramatic reduction in sexual interest. The rush that comes with intravenous injection of opiates like heroin is often compared by users to an orgasm. For many users, the drug apparently feels better than actual sex.

Effects on the Body

Opiates have several acute effects on the body. Pain perception is markedly reduced due to the potent analgesic effect of opiates. Respiration is depressed, so breathing may be more shallow or slow. Blood pressure is not altered markedly, indicating that opiates act primarily on the respiratory functions of the body. The skin may appear flushed and feel itchy. The pupils of the eyes constrict, with pinpoint pupils considered to be a hallmark feature of opiate use. Opiates also induce gastrointestinal distress. Nausea, vomiting, and constipation can occur. Vomiting occurs because opiates act on the medulla in the brain, which is the center of the brain sensitive to toxins. Opiates are prescribed by physicians in the treatment of extreme pain, to suppress cough, to cure diarrhea, or to induce sleep. Extreme cases of diarrhea can be fatal; opiates can save lives by increasing the tension of various muscles in the digestive tract, so that the normal movement of food through the digestive tract is significantly slowed. In both abusers of opiates and medical patients being treated with opiates, constipation is highly likely (DEA, 2012a; Kuhn et al., 2008).

Lethal Dose

Opiates can easily lead to overdose and death (Figure 9-6). Even when opiates are used in medical settings to treat severe pain, physicians are constantly vigilant about symptoms of overdose. Suppressed respiration is the primary symptom of concern. Death is imminent when breathing slows, and death occurs when respiration ceases. Other effects indicating a possible overdose include extreme drowsiness, muscle weakness, confusion, cold and clammy skin, pinpoint pupils, slow heart rate, and coma (DEA, 2012a). An opiate overdose can occur with chronic use of opiates or even with the first use of the drug. Heroin users are at high risk for overdose, with the injection route of administration for heroin most associated with overdose deaths (Degenhardt et al., 2010a). However, overdose deaths occur with both legitimate and diverted opiate prescription pain medications (oxycodone, methadone, hydrocodone), with the problem significantly larger in the past decade. The Centers for Disease Control (CDC) analyzes patterns of drug overdose deaths attributable to both legal and illegal drugs. In the year 2008, there were a total of 36,450 overdose deaths in the United States attributable to drugs. An astounding 74% of these overdose deaths were found to be caused by prescription opiate medications. Deaths involving opiate prescription pain medications now exceed those involving heroin and cocaine. The CDC labels this change a public health epidemic that is worsening over time (CDC, 2011a).

When opiates are used medically, a potential overdose can be averted by quickly injecting the opiate antagonist **naloxone** (Narcan®) or **nalmefene** (Revex®). These same drugs are also used to treat drug abusers who experience an overdose (Figure 9-7). Injection of the antagonist blocks the effects of the opiate drugs and will quickly and safely save the patient from an overdose. The approach is so effective that many large cities in the United States have implemented programs in which drug users in needle exchange programs are given naloxone and trained how to administer it. Such programs, while controversial, do save lives since time is of the essence when an opiate overdose occurs. Proponents of naloxone distribution programs argue that if too much time elapses before emergency personnel can reach a victim, that

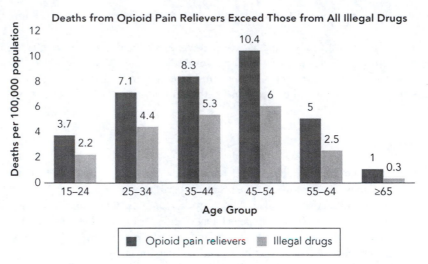

Deaths from Opioid Pain Relievers Exceed Those from All Illegal Drugs

FIGURE 9-6
One serious problem with drug diversion of opiate pain medications is the risk of death (CDC, 2011a).

FIGURE 9-7
Naloxone injection kit to treat an opiate overdose.

person may die. Access to naloxone promotes health and reduces the harms associated with drug use. However, opponents see naloxone administration programs as encouraging opiate use, if the life-saving potential of naloxone leads users to perceive opiate use as less risky (Piper et al., 2007).

The risk of overdose and death is significant for opiates. The risk can be exacerbated when users mix opiates with other drugs. Users sometimes inject a combination of heroin and cocaine, referred to as a **speedball**. Users claim that the dreaminess associated with opiates cuts some of the edginess or arousal occurring with cocaine. Unfortunately, this drug combination can also be quite dangerous. The signal of the aversive feelings of each drug (jitteriness from too much cocaine and excessive sedation from too much heroin) is masked by the other drug. Drug overdoses can thus more easily occur. Speedball use was to blame for the overdose deaths of comedians Chris Farley and John Belushi (Kuhn et al., 2008). Overdose deaths are also likely when opiates are combined with other sedative drugs, such as heroin and alcohol or heroin and benzodiazepines. The death of actor Heath Ledger illustrates the problem of combining various prescription medications, each of which may be perfectly safe when used separately. An autopsy revealed that he had consumed several opiate painkillers and antianxiety medications, including oxycodone, hydrocodone, diazepam, alprazolam, and temazepam. The brand names associated with these drugs include OxyContin®, Vicodin®, Valium®, Xanax®, and Restoril®. All of these prescription sedative medications would have had a cumulative effect on the body resulting in Ledger's death (Barron, 2008).

Chronic Effects of Opiate Use

Individuals who become dependent on opiates tend to quickly establish a near-daily chronic pattern of use. They use the drug despite significant social and health problems. Heroin users who inject their drug will often do so four or more times per day. A habit might cost $30 to $100 per day, though the constant use of heroin makes employment almost impossible. Being arrested for drug or property crimes, prison time, exposure to disease, and even overdoses are often not enough to dissuade users. Even opiate users who seek treatment may still continue to use for decades. Chronic users of opiates struggle to control their drug use and are at significantly elevated risk of dying prematurely, with the primary cause of death being from overdose (Degenhardt et al., 2010a).

Researchers have determined that the likely outcome for a chronic opiate user is somewhat grim. An early death is a strong possibility, sometimes because the drug use itself results in an overdose. Illnesses related to drug injection, such as HIV-AIDS, can also result in death. One longitudinal study followed 581 male heroin addicts over a period of 33 years. The researchers recruited heroin addicts admitted to the California Civil Addict Program from 1962 to 1964. The California program was a compulsory drug treatment program for heroin-dependent criminal offenders. Individuals were interviewed at 10-year intervals. The latest interview occurred in 1996–1997, when the mean age of the sample was approximately 57 years. During the study period, approximately half of these individuals had died, with the main causes of death being drug overdose or accidental poisoning. This death rate is almost 100 times that would have occurred in the general population among individuals of the same age. Among those still alive after 33 years, 20% were still using heroin and another 14% were in jail (Figure 9-8). For individuals who were still alive, high rates of physical health problems, mental health problems, and criminal justice

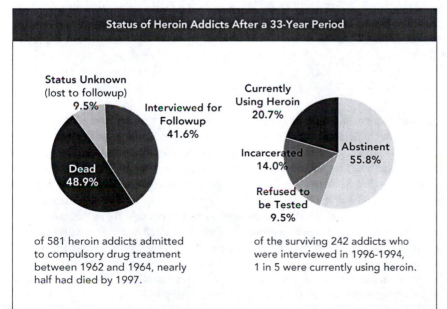

Status of Heroin Addicts After a 33-Year Period

Status Unknown (lost to followup) 9.5%

Interviewed for Followup 41.6%

Dead 48.9%

Currently Using Heroin 20.7%

Incarcerated 14.0%

Abstinent 55.8%

Refused to be Tested 9.5%

of 581 heroin addicts admitted to compulsory drug treatment between 1962 and 1964, nearly half had died by 1997.

of the surviving 242 addicts who were interviewed in 1996-1994, 1 in 5 were currently using heroin.

FIGURE 9-8

Status of heroin addicts after a 33-year period (Hser et al., 2001).

system involvement were observed (Hser, Hoffman, Grella, & Anglin, 2001). While the findings from this sample may not be representative of all chronic opiate users, in part because the sample was recruited from a corrections-based treatment program, the findings do parallel other observations that opiate addicts tend to struggle for a lifetime with their addiction and have significantly higher mortality rates (Khademi et al., 2012; Larney, Randall, Gibson, & Degenhardt, 2013). Chronic opiate use may cause more problems than the chronic use of most other psychoactive drugs.

Injection drug users are also likely to acquire nasty infections from frequent injections into skin that has not been cleaned properly. Localized infections can easily become systemic, and with pain perception being blocked, the user may not be initially aware (or not care) that illness is developing. The skin on arms becomes marked with scar tissue from all of the injection sites. Veins collapse with frequent injections. Many users initiate injection drug use by subcutaneous injection (referred to as **skin-popping**) and then progress to intravenous injection (referred to as **mainlining**). Tetanus infections are more likely with subcutaneous injections, while HIV and hepatitis C infections are more likely with intravenous injections. These problems are an issue for all injection drug use. Compared to injectors of other psychoactive drugs, heroin users inject most frequently and consistently, which results in greater risk from these problems. While some of these risks are mitigated when opiates are injected in medical settings, vein collapse and infections at injection sites are concerns in frail sick patients whose immune systems have been compromised either by illness or chemotherapy treatments (Gutstein & Akil, 2001).

The chronic use of opiates, in either a medical or abuse context, can also lead to other concerns. One serious concern is opiate-induced hyperalgesia, which refers to increased sensitivity to pain developing over time. Among pain patients, opiate-induced hyperalgesia is a problem because patients need increased doses of opiate medication to control their pain. Likewise, abusers of opiates escalate doses to avoid painful sensations (Compton, Canamar, Hillhouse, & Ling, 2012). Chronic opiate use also leads to a decreased production of sex hormones, which is likely to result in impotence in men. Sexual and reproductive problems arise in both men and women. Women of reproductive age cease having menstrual cycles and men have decreased sperm production. Many female and male addicts engage in sex in exchange for drugs or money to buy drugs. However, this sexual activity seems generally not to be motivated by strong sexual interest. If women are pregnant and using opiates, the developing fetus is exposed to the same drug. Numerous medical complications are likely, some due directly to the drug and others arising because of problems with the addict lifestyle. Babies born to addicted mothers have lower birth weights and exhibit withdrawal symptoms within 72 hours of birth. Withdrawal from opiates in newborn babies is similar to adult withdrawal symptoms. Symptoms include tremors, respiratory distress, irritability, yawning, sneezing, difficulty sucking and swallowing, and a distinctive high-pitched cry indicative of great distress. Some babies also have seizures. Symptoms typically subside within 8 weeks (Finnegan, 1982).

Weight loss and chronic constipation also occur in chronic users of opiates. Compared to other sedative drugs such as alcohol, opiates seem to cause little damage to internal organ systems. However, heroin addicts do develop neurocognitive deficits somewhat similar to those observed in chronic alcoholics. The ability to problem solve, remember information, and perform other cognitive tasks can be deficient in individuals who have been addicted to heroin, even if the subjects are abstinent when tested (Fishbein et al., 2007). The mechanism for cognitive problems developing in opiate users is unclear, in part because opiates themselves do not appear to be too harmful to individual neurons. It has been suggested that suppression of breathing during opiate use results in low blood oxygen levels that can damage the brain. Prolonged heroin-induced respiratory depression can lead to strokes that result in significant cognitive deficits. In addition, among heroin addicts infected with HIV, a variety of neuropathological changes occur which are associated with the disease process from AIDS (Buttner, Mall, Penning, & Weis, 2000).

Tolerance, Dependence, and Withdrawal

Tolerance

Tolerance refers to an increased amount of drug needed to achieve a certain effect or a diminished drug effect with continued use. The *DSM-IV-TR* criteria for drug dependence include the term *drug tolerance*. Tolerance is thought to contribute to substance abuse when a user needs more and more of a drug to achieve the same effect. Therefore, drugs that are likely to lead to dependence are drugs that induce rapid tolerance development. By contrast, drugs that do not lead to rapid tolerance development are thought to be somewhat safer (APA, 2000). For opiates, tolerance develops extremely quickly, which is why opiates can be so addictive. The rate of tolerance development for opiates strongly depends on the baseline state of the individual. Among those in intense pain, such as terminal cancer patients, not much tolerance development occurs. The same dose of morphine may be equally effective across time, as long as the underlying medical condition causing the pain does not change much. By contrast, individuals who use opiates to achieve euphoria tend to experience faster development of tolerance to the euphoric effects of opiates. As a result, increasing doses are needed across time to achieve the desired subjective effects. For all users, both medical and recreational, tolerance develops to the respiratory suppression occurring with opiates. Thus, users may be able to increase their typical dose without decreased breathing being a concern. Tolerance to the respiration-suppressing effects of opiates can be dramatic. A chronic user may consume a daily quantity of opiate drug that would result in certain death for a casual user. Tolerance does reverse with abstinence. When an individual resumes the use of opiates after periods of abstinence (drug treatment, prison time), the individual may resume use at a level that may lead to an overdose or even an overdose fatality (Degenhardt & Hall, 2012). The difference between the effective dose and lethal dose is small for opiates, which leads to an increased likelihood of a fatal consequence. Finally, constipation is a concern with opiate use, with chronic use not resulting in tolerance for the constipating effects of opiates (Kuhn et al., 2008).

Both biological changes and learning mechanisms explain tolerance development to opiates (see Chapter 3). The body becomes increasingly efficient at returning itself to homeostasis, its stable ideal environment. As mentioned earlier, opiates suppress respiration. Over time and with frequent exposure to opiates, the body gets more efficient at counteracting the respiration suppressing action of opiates. Thus, users may be able to use higher and higher doses of opiates without ceasing respiration. Learning mechanisms also play an important role in tolerance to opiates. Environmental cues that are typically associated with opiate use become associated with drug-altered states. If the heroin user typically injects the drug in a particular location, the sight of the syringe and cues in the environment inform the body of the user to increase respiration in anticipation of drug administration. These conditioned (learned) compensatory responses mediate tolerance by counteracting the drug's effects in the presence of drug-paired cues (Siegel et al., 2000). The effects of both biological and learning mechanisms on drug tolerance can be dramatic for opiates. Heroin overdose deaths are much more likely when the user has not used recently (such as following a time in jail) or when the drug is used in an unusual context (such as in a hotel room) (Siegel et al., 1982).

Physical Dependence and Withdrawal

Regular opiate use leads to physical dependence, in which the individual's body needs the drug to function and taking the drug away results in symptoms of illness. Physical dependence can occur extremely rapidly with opiates and can be established within weeks of regular use. Physical dependence can easily be assessed by ceasing administration of the opiate drug. In physically dependent individuals, withdrawal symptoms usually appear shortly before the time of the next typical dose. For regular heroin users, feelings of illness may emerge 6 hours after the last use of the drug. Thus, addicted heroin abusers are often injecting the drug 3 to 4 times per day to minimize

Table 9-2   Acute effects of opiates and opiate withdrawal symptoms.

Acute Effects of Opiates	Opiate Withdrawal Symptoms
Analgesia	Pain
Euphoria	Depression
Sedation	Restlessness
Relaxation	Irritability
Respiratory depression	Yawning, panting
Hypothermia	Hyperthermia
Peripheral vasodilation, skin warm and flushed	Piloerection (goose bumps), skin feels chilled
Constipation	Diarrhea
Pupil constriction	Pupil dilation
Decreased blood pressure	Increased blood pressure
Drying of secretions	Runny nose, watery eyes
Decreased sex drive	Spontaneous ejaculations and orgasms

Note: Adapted from Gutstein & Akil (2001).

withdrawal symptoms. Early in the withdrawal process, flu-like symptoms including watery eyes, runny nose, and sweating may arise. If the drug is not administered, withdrawal symptoms become more aversive and intense. Drug craving, pain, nausea, tremors, restlessness, irritability, anorexia (loss of appetite), and severe depression may be reported. The pupils of the eyes dilate. The individual will look flushed and sweat excessively. Blood pressure and heart rate will be elevated, and the individual will report feeling chilled. Sexual ability redevelops, with spontaneous ejaculation or orgasms often experienced. However, this recovery of sexual activity may result in limited enjoyment due to the individual feeling miserable from diarrhea. Piloerection (goose bumps) become visible, causing the patient to look a bit like a plucked turkey, hence the colloquialism "going cold turkey." Likewise, the patient may have spastic arm and leg movements, hence the other popular expression, "kicking the habit." Depending on how often and how much drug was used, withdrawal symptoms disappear within days or weeks (DEA, 2012a). Withdrawal symptoms are opposite in direction to the acute effects of the drug described earlier in the chapter. For example, the acute effects of opiates result in respiratory depression. When opiates are withdrawn, the individual may yawn or pant, resulting in more oxygen in the respiratory system. Increasing oxygen in the respiratory system is directly opposite to the acute effect of opiates (see Table 9-2).

While opiate withdrawal symptoms can make an individual feel miserable, symptoms of withdrawal are not usually life-threatening. The main concern is a possible severe loss of fluids, which in extreme circumstances could be fatal. Note that opiate withdrawal is different from withdrawal from alcohol, another sedative drug, in that alcohol withdrawal symptoms can more easily result in death (see Chapter 8). Withdrawal from opiates is similar to a really bad case of the flu. If the individual can persist through the symptoms, the unpleasantness from withdrawal reduces considerably after a few days. Unfortunately, for many opiate users there is a long-lasting dysphoria (depression) and drug craving that persists for up to 6 months, long after the acute physical symptoms of withdrawal have gone away (Kuhn et al., 2008).

Pharmacology of Opiates

Sites of Action

Discovered in 1973, **endorphins** are chemicals that function as neurotransmitters and act like naturally occurring morphine (Figure 9-9). The discovery of endorphins has an interesting history

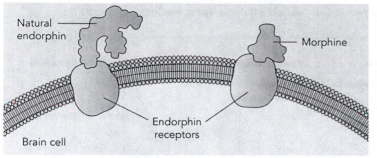

FIGURE 9-9
Natural endorphins and exogenous opiate drugs will both bind to endorphin receptors.

since it is tightly tied to our current war on drugs. In response to President Nixon's call for a war on drugs in 1972, Congress appropriated money that led a neuroscientist at Johns Hopkins, Dr. Solomon Snyder, and his graduate student Candace Pert, to discover the opiate receptor. Heroin and morphine molecules fit into this receptor just like a key fits into a lock (see Chapter 2). The subsequent discovery of the brain's own opiate-like chemicals, endorphins, was a similarly great achievement. Unlike other neurotransmitters, endorphins are large molecules called peptides. A peptide is a protein, which is a chain of amino acid molecules attached in a specific order. One main role for endorphins in the nervous system is to block pain. When endorphins bind to their receptors, neurotransmission is inhibited or blocked, mainly by blocking neurotransmitter release. This action dampens pain messages being sent through the nervous system. Endorphin activity increases when we exercise vigorously, feel excitement, eat really spicy food, engage in sexual activity, or experience pain. Increased endorphin activity both blocks our pain and makes us feel really good. Endorphins are responsible for the so-called "runner's high," which is the euphoria resulting from long-distance running. The amount of euphoria experienced with a runner's high corresponds to the number of opiate receptors occupied with endorphins, particularly in the cortex and limbic brain areas (Boecker et al., 2008). The same result also occurs when the fight-or-flight response is induced during situations of extreme stress. Morphine and heroin have similar analgesic and euphoric effects, hence the name endorphin, a contraction of endogenous morphine (Julien, 2005; Pert & Snyder, 1973).

It is interesting that the endogenous opiate system was unfamiliar to researchers until the 1970s, even though humans have been using opiate drugs for thousands of years. However, the groundwork for the discovery of endorphins was laid in the 1960s, when chemists altered the morphine chemical and created naloxone. Earlier in this chapter, the importance of naloxone in treating opiate overdoses was discussed. Naloxone reverses an overdose due to its action as an opiate antagonist. While physicians quickly adopted naloxone as a treatment for opiate overdoses, researchers also became interested in naloxone. Researchers were interested in naloxone's similar chemical structure to morphine, suggesting both chemicals could possibly act at the same receptor site. In research and practice, it was clear that naloxone had an opposite effect to morphine, increasing pain rather than decreasing it. Moreover, when both drugs were administered at the same time, no change was experienced, suggesting that the drugs were cancelling each other out. Scientists thought that there must be natural brain chemicals structurally and functionally similar to morphine and naloxone. By 1975, such chemicals—endorphins—had been discovered. Shortly thereafter, it became clear that all vertebrate and invertebrate animals have endorphins binding to opiate receptors widely distributed throughout the central nervous system. There are three distinct families of opioid peptides called the enkephalins, endorphins, and dynorphins. All of these peptides are found in the brain and are together referred to as endorphins (Pert, 1997; Snyder, 1989).

There are at least three types of receptors that bind to endorphins, referred to as *mu*, *delta*, and *kappa* (see Table 9-3). Drugs that are agonists of *mu* receptors display the strongest analgesic effects but are also the most addictive. Morphine is a prototypical *mu* receptor agonist drug. *Mu* receptors are found throughout the brain, spinal cord, and the periphery. They are highly

Table 9-3   Receptor types upon which endogenous endorphins and exogenous opiates act.

Receptor Type	Analgesic Action	Abuse Potential	Emotional Response
mu (μ)	Excellent for *mu* agonist morphine	Very high for *mu* agonists like morphine	Euphoric
delta (δ)	Poor	Low	Strong antidepressant effects
kappa (κ)	Moderate	Low	Dysphoric

concentrated in the nucleus accumbens, the reward center in the brain, which explains why opiate use so easily becomes compulsive. *Mu* receptors are also present in the brain stem regions that are responsible for initiation of vomiting and control of respiration. When a *mu* agonist drug like morphine is administered, nausea, vomiting, and decreased respiration may occur. Chemicals that bind to *delta* receptors (*delta* agonists) tend not to be very addictive, but they also result in poor analgesic action. As a result, researchers think that *delta* receptors largely function to modulate the activity of *mu* receptors. *Delta* receptors may also play a role in neuroprotection and cardioprotection. For example, extreme stress can induce neuronal death, but delta receptor activation can protect neurons under conditions of extreme stress. Activation of *mu* and *delta* receptors also increases immune reaction intensity. *Delta* receptor agonists also stimulate robust antidepressant effects, which has led researchers to wonder about the therapeutic potential of delta agonists as a new way to treat depressive disorders. The action of *kappa* receptors seems to be between the action of *mu* and *delta* receptors. *Kappa* agonists tend to be not very addictive and have a modest analgesic action. *Kappa* agonists could potentially make great analgesic drugs since they are not very addictive while they block pain. The problem with *kappa* agonists is the induction of a strong dysphoric (depressive) response. Patients tend to dislike feeling depressed, even if their pain goes away. This renders *kappa* agonists not practically useful. Researchers think that the action of *kappa* receptors might function to antagonize *mu* receptor activity in the brain. There is still a lot to learn about these different types of receptors. For example, the differential distribution of the three receptor types in the nervous system remains under intense investigation (Feng et al., 2012; Idova, Alperina, & Cheido, 2012; Julien, 2005; Jutkiewicz, 2006; Kieffer, 1999; Trezza, Damsteegt, Achterberg, & Vanderschuren, 2011).

When brain chemistry is altered, there can be widespread repercussions. When opiates are used regularly, tolerance develops rapidly. It is now thought that the biological basis of opiate tolerance involves a type of glutamate receptor called the **NMDA receptor**. Researchers have examined whether NMDA receptor antagonists can be mixed into opiate medications to cause analgesia, yet not result in tolerance. Some promising findings have been observed in animal studies (Fischer et al., 2008). Another approach to reducing the abuse potential of opiate medications is to combine a low dose of naltrexone (an opiate antagonist) with the opiate agonist drug. This strategy seems counterintuitive, since naltrexone is an opiate antagonist. However, naltrexone together with opiates results in enhanced pain relief, while the naltrexone blocks the rewarding effects of the drug and limits tolerance development. Given the strong demand for opiate drugs to treat severe pain, new medications are needed that retain the effective analgesic properties in *mu* receptor agonist drugs, but are less likely to result in tolerance, dependence, and addiction (Whistler, 2012).

Pharmacokinetics

Pharmacokinetics is a branch of pharmacology examining the absorption, distribution, biotransformation, and excretion of drugs. Opiates can reach the bloodstream via various routes of administration described earlier in this chapter (oral, transdermal, inhalation, intranasal, and injection). Once in the bloodstream, opiates are distributed throughout the body, including in the brain. Only a portion (50%) of orally administered morphine passes through the blood–brain barrier and reaches the brain. Heroin is more lipid-soluble and has an easier time than morphine crossing the blood–brain barrier. Once inside the brain, heroin is converted to morphine, making the two drugs identical at their site of action. The enhanced lipid-solubility of heroin is a result of heroin being the morphine molecule with two acetyl groups attached. The acetyl groups allow heroin to penetrate the blood–brain barrier more easily, making heroin 2 to 3 times more potent than morphine. Thus, a far smaller dose of heroin is needed to achieve a similar effect as morphine in the brain. In end-of-life medical treatment (**hospice care**) of patients in extreme pain, morphine is the opiate of choice in the United States. However, when death is imminent, a patient can be so frail that veins can collapse. Administering a smaller volume of drug is therefore advantageous. In countries such as the United Kingdom and other European nations, physicians may administer heroin, though the drug is known as **diamorphine** in a medical setting. The term *heroin* is reserved for illicit use, but heroin and diamorphine are the exact same drug (Higginson & Gao, 2012; Klepstad et al., 2005). Physicians who treat patients in hospice settings sometimes advocate for the use of diamorphine in the United States, but it remains to be seen if a significant policy change will occur, since heroin is a major drug of abuse in the United States.

Once opiate drugs have bound with their appropriate receptors, opiates are metabolized by the liver and excreted by the kidneys. Metabolism and excretion happen fairly rapidly with opiates. Approximately 90% of administered opiates are excreted within 24 hours, although traces of opiates in urine will remain for a few more days. The half-life of morphine is about 2 hours, while the half-life of codeine is 3 to 6 hours. The typical detection window for morphine or heroin in a urine drug test is approximately 48 hours, although chronic users have tested positive for opiates up to 5 days later when very sensitive tests have been used (Verstraete, 2004).

Treatment for Opiate Addiction

To say that quitting use of opiates is a difficult process would be a vast understatement. The initial phase of stopping opiate use is very unpleasant, with withdrawal symptoms resembling a really bad case of the flu. These acute symptoms usually last a few days. The concern with treating opiate addiction is a very long-lasting **abstinence syndrome** plaguing patients for up to 6 months. Dysphoria (depression) and drug craving persist long after the acute physical symptoms of withdrawal have subsided (Kuhn et al., 2008). Users are consumed with thoughts of wanting to use opiates again, and they feel terrible all the time. Every part of them wants to resume using, which makes treatment a challenge. Fortunately, there are a variety of pharmacological approaches that can be helpful to patients. The most common approach to treat opiate addiction is to substitute another opiate less likely to be abused and monitor the substitute drug through a medical clinic or physician's office. Methadone, LAAM, or buprenorphine/naloxone maintenance therapy allows a former addict to still have an opiate drug binding to opiate receptors, thus eliminating withdrawal symptoms. However, the pharmacological treatment medication is less likely to be abused because it tends to lead to less euphoric effects. Methadone, which is also used to treat pain, has long been used in the treatment of opiate addiction. Methadone treatment was initiated in the United States in 1963, after failed attempts at using morphine as a substitute for street heroin. Methadone treatment has slowly received increased acceptance over time, although the prospect of a methadone clinic in one's own neighborhood often brings the ire of local residents. Despite logistical issues, including societal resistance, methadone treatment has become standard practice for treatment of opiate addiction. The advantage of methadone is an extremely long half-life, 10 to 25 hours. Methadone's long duration of action is far preferable to other opiates whose half-life is substantially shorter. The long half-life means the methadone patient will not experience withdrawal symptoms, so dose administration need not be frequent. LAAM is another drug that can be used like methadone. The duration of action for LAAM is even longer than methadone, allowing the recovering addict the advantage of not visiting the clinic as frequently. Given that methadone clinics are not easily accessible in some locations, LAAM is a preferable pharmacological treatment in many cases. The third option for substitution treatment is the newer drug, Suboxone®, a patent medication that combines buprenorphine and naloxone. Buprenorphine is a partial *mu* opiate agonist and a *kappa* opiate antagonist. Buprenorphine is a drug derived from thebaine, the compound in opium used to make OxyContin®. Buprenorphine is 25 to 50 times more potent than morphine, and it has a much longer duration of action than morphine. Naloxone is a *mu* opiate antagonist. While Suboxone® is much more expensive than methadone, many patients have found Suboxone® to be very effective (Fareed, Casarella, Amar, Vayalapalli, & Drexler, 2010; Gutstein & Akil, 2001; Ling et al., 1994; Martinez-Raga et al., 2012; Uchtenhagen, 2011).

The goal of substitution therapy is the extremely slow reduction in dose over a long period of time. During this time, the patient reenters society by working or going to school, rather than maintaining a drug habit that possibly involved criminal behavior and risky injection drug use. For some patients with severe opiate addictions, substitution therapy may be a lifelong medical treatment. In addition to pharmacological treatment for opiate addiction, psychological treatment is also important. Support is needed to help the patient deal with drug craving and reenter society. For example, a support group that meets weekly to help with job search strategies and emotional support benefits patients during recovery. Moreover, the rate of comorbid psychological disorders is extremely high in patients dependent on opiate drugs. If patients are experiencing another disorder, such as depression, recovery may be hindered if the other disorder is not treated as well (Julien, 2005).

Treating patients dependent on opiates is difficult. Relapse is common, and lifelong substitution therapy is necessary for many individuals. In some countries, individuals dependent on opiates like heroin receive their drug of choice in treatment settings. Heroin clinics can be found in countries such as Switzerland, the Netherlands, Germany, England, and Denmark. Patients visit the clinic and inject their heroin in a closely regulated setting. Crime is reduced and public health improves because addicts are no longer committing crimes to obtain their drug, using dirty needles to inject their drug, engaging in prostitution for drug money, or living on the street (Uchtenhagen, 2011). However, heroin clinics illustrate the difficulty, once addicted, of getting off opiates. Obviously, preventing individuals from reaching the point of needing treatment is preferable. Avoiding the negative outcomes from addiction requires that the initial appeal of opiates must decline for potential users. In the near future, the greatest challenge surrounding opiate use will be addressing the issues of the diversion of prescription opiate medications. Obviously, physicians and lawmakers want to strike an appropriate balance in which opiate abuse is deterred, while patients who are in severe pain receive access to these critical medications. The abuse of diverted opiate medications is on the rise, making this issue ever more urgent. Opiate abuse has harmful ramifications for the legitimate and appropriate use of opiates in treating pain. Physicians may insufficiently treat severe pain if they avoid prescribing these medications. Alternatively, if physicians prescribe opiates frequently, they may find themselves under scrutiny from law enforcement. Patients experiencing severe pain may worry about addiction and feel stigmatized if they use opiates (Figure 9-10). Clearly, novel approaches to pain treatment provide more options to patients. Devising opiate medications with lower abuse potential would help limit diversion (Walwyn, Miotto, & Evans, 2010; Zacny et al., 2003). What else do you think can be done to decrease the appeal of opiates for non-therapeutic uses?

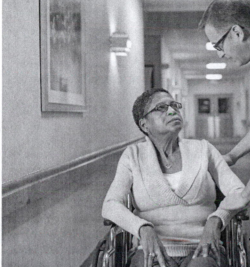

©Yellow Dog Productions/Getty Images

FIGURE 9-10
A patient experiencing chronic pain may worry about addiction if using opiate drugs.

More about the Science:

Drdla-Schutting et al. (2012). Erasure of a spinal memory trace of pain by a brief, high-dose opioid administration. *Science, 335,* 235–238.

Researchers are constantly discovering new things about opiates, even though opiates have been used by humans for thousands of years. One of the latest discoveries may lead to changes in how opiates are used to treat chronic pain. The treatment of chronic pain has often been difficult, in part because it sometimes appears that the body is sending pain messages after the cause of the pain is no longer present. Pain messages are blocked by opiates when the drug binds to specific *mu*-opiate receptor sites in the central nervous system. However, recent thinking suggests that cellular changes might also be taking place in the nervous system, creating memory traces of pain that contribute to chronic pain. The researchers in this study wondered if opiates not only relieve pain but also at the correct dose actually erase memory traces of pain. To test this question, the researchers created a memory trace of pain in the spinal cord of rats by applying stimulation to nerve fibers. Normally, this procedure induces increased neural activity resulting in a spinal memory trace of pain, the model of chronic pain. This memory trace is thought to be triggered by a variety of mechanisms, including the potentiation (amplification) of signal transmission between synapses where neurons meet. The researchers found that a brief intravenous infusion of a high dose of morphine after the nerve fiber stimulation prevented the normally increased neural activity from occurring. In other words, a high dose of morphine over a short period of time prevented the development of the pain signal. To determine if giving a brief high dose of opiates will help human chronic pain patients, patients with chronic pain are being tested to see if a high dose of opiate over 60 minutes might help their pain. The brief high dose would be in contrast to a more moderate dose over a longer time, which is typically how chronic pain has been treated.

More about the Science Thought Questions:

1. What safety considerations will the researchers need to consider when attempting to translate these findings from animals to humans?
2. Typically, chronic pain patients are treated with opiate drugs like OxyContin® (Figure 9-10). How is the approach to chronic pain treatment different in this study?

More about the Science Thought Question Answers:

1. Opiates can lead to a variety of side effects, especially when used at high doses. A particular concern might be respiratory depression (decreased breathing) since opiates at high doses can be fatal. Human patients would need to be monitored carefully given the risks of high doses of opiates.
2. Many long-acting opiates such as OxyContin® have a 12-hour duration of action with a low to moderate dose. These researchers are suggesting that a very short duration (1 hour) of opiate exposure and a high dose would be more effective. This would represent a radical shift in how opiates are typically used to treat chronic pain.

QUICK QUIZ 9-2

1. What are three kinds of opiate receptors?
   a. Mu, delta, beta
   b. Mu, delta, kappa
   c. Beta, delta, kappa
   d. Beta, kappa, mu
   e. None of the above

2. A new treatment for opiate addiction is called Suboxone®. What two drugs are included in this medication?
   a. Buprenorphine and naloxone
   b. Methadone and naloxone
   c. Methadone and buprenorphine
   d. Morphine and naloxone
   e. Morphine and buprenorphine

3. The opiate receptors in the brain will respond to _____.
   a. dopamine
   b. glutamate
   c. serotonin
   d. endorphins
   e. norepinephrine

4. A heroin overdose can be treated with _____.
   a. morphine
   b. diamorphine
   c. naloxone
   d. L-dopa
   e. None of the above

5. Tolerance to the effects of opiates occurs for the following:
   a. Respiratory suppression
   b. Euphoria
   c. Constipation
   d. a and b
   e. All of the above

6. The acute effects of opiates result in
   a. Stimulation
   b. Sedation
   c. Analgesia
   d. a and c
   e. b and c

7. Is opiate withdrawal life-threatening? Why or why not?

8. Describe the abstinence syndrome for opiates.

9. What is diamorphine? How and where is it used?

ANSWERS TO QUICK QUIZ 3-2:

1. b – *mu, delta, kappa*
2. a – buprenorphine and naloxone
3. d – endorphins
4. c – naloxone
5. d – a and b
6. e – b and c
7. Opiate withdrawal is not life-threatening except in extreme cases of dehydration. The withdrawal symptoms typically resemble a really bad case of the flu.

8. The abstinence syndrome refers to the dysphoria (depression) and drug craving that persists for up to 6 months after the acute phase of opiate withdrawal. These symptoms are aversive, which is one reason that substitution therapy (such as methadone) is used to help patients with an opiate addiction.

9. Diamorphine is heroin used in a medical setting. Diamorphine is reserved for cases of extreme pain, such as found in terminal cancer cases. It is not legal in the United States, but it is used in various European countries.

CHAPTER SUMMARY

Opiates are sedative drugs that have potent analgesic effects. Opiates resemble naturally occurring endorphins that function with the same purpose of blocking pain. Recreational users of opiates often report that drug administration results in euphoria and a dream-like pleasant state. Opiates have been used for thousands of years, initially as opium. Currently, most illicit users of opiates are using diverted prescription medications, although heroin is still used frequently as a street drug. There is significant risk of overdose with opiates because high doses suppress respiration. Tolerance to opiates develops rapidly, and individuals who use opiates regularly become physically dependent on them. Withdrawal symptoms resemble a bad case of the flu. There is a pronounced abstinence syndrome that can last for up to 6 months. Individuals in withdrawal experience dysphoria and drug craving, which makes abstinence challenging. Treatment often incorporates opiate substitution, allowing the individual to resume a productive life while avoiding withdrawal symptoms. The challenge for medical professionals is appropriately to treat patients for severe pain while avoiding unnecessary addiction and drug diversion.

10   MARIJUANA

Introduction

Pot and politics certainly go hand in hand these days. On Internet websites, you may have noticed that most stories about medical marijuana or the legalization of recreational marijuana attract an incredible number of reader comments. Everyone has an opinion, and those opinions are usually pretty strong ones. Not every opinion is grounded in scientific knowledge about marijuana. This is probably true for every psychoactive drug, but marijuana seems to elicit especially strong opinions, even among those lacking in-depth knowledge of the drug.

Mitch Earleywine is an addiction researcher whose specialty actually *is* marijuana policy. Earleywine suggested three principles for critically examining research on marijuana. His ideas are good ones:

1. *everything should be made as simple as possible but no simpler,*

2. *distinguish research and its meaning as data separate from interpretation, and*

3. *some things are neither good nor evil.*

Earleywine, 2002

In this chapter, I will do my best not to share my personal opinions about marijuana as a psychoactive drug so that we might focus on the science. Some things are relatively clear about marijuana, though many others still need to be better understood. As you work through this chapter, I encourage you to set aside your preconceived ideas about marijuana, focusing instead on the science. In addition, we'll try to connect scientific knowledge to the practical reality of life in our society. Science is wonderful in helping us understand many things, but it would be naive to think that only science matters within the broader social context. We'll be dealing with quite a bit of complexity in this chapter, since there are many pieces to the puzzle of marijuana. However, I am confident that by the end of the chapter you will have a better knowledge base about marijuana. At a minimum, you will hopefully be more knowledgeable about the issues surrounding marijuana. Even if your views are unchanged by the end of this chapter, my goal is for you to better understand the complexity associated with this very controversial psychoactive drug.

LEARNING OBJECTIVES

Learning objectives can help organize your studying. Before we begin the topic of marijuana, keep in mind that by the end of this chapter, you should be able to . . .

1. Describe the source of marijuana.
2. Explain the brief history of marijuana, including how long marijuana has been available for use.

3. Describe the various routes of administration for marijuana.
4. Describe the various medical uses for marijuana.
5. Explain the acute effects of marijuana and how the drug acts in the central nervous system.
6. Describe tolerance, dependence, and withdrawal processes associated with marijuana use.
7. Explain how marijuana acts in the brain and for how long.
8. Describe the various approaches that are used to treat marijuana abuse and dependence.

Marijuana as a Sedative Drug

Marijuana is an illicit psychoactive sedative drug from the cannabis (hemp) plant. The name marijuana is thought to have its origins in the Portuguese word *mariguango*, which translates as intoxicant. Marijuana consists of the dried and crushed leaves from the cannabis plant, which are typically smoked, but can also be eaten in baked goods or consumed as tea. In the United States, marijuana is typically smoked in rolled cigarettes ("**joints**"), in pipes or water pipes, or in hollowed-out cigars ("**blunts**"). When smoked, a distinctive and pungent sweet-and-sour odor is emitted. Marijuana is known by many names including pot, reefer, grass, weed, and many others. Marijuana is the most widely used illicit drug both in the United States and worldwide. People's experiences with marijuana can differ considerably depending on the potency of the drug. Sedative effects such as relaxation and drowsiness are experienced by many users. The psychoactive chemical in marijuana is delta-9-tetrahydrocannabinol (delta-9-THC or **THC**). THC is also the active ingredient in several FDA-approved medications such as dranabinol (Marinol®) and nabilone (Cesamet®). These medications are used to treat medical conditions including glaucoma, severe nausea, vomiting, weight loss, and pain. THC and similar chemicals are also the psychoactive ingredients in illicit street substances with names like "Spice" and "K2." There is likely no other psychoactive drug more controversial than marijuana and its psychoactive chemical, THC (Earleywine, 2002, 2007; Gunderson, Haughey, Ait-Daoud, Joshi, & Hart, 2012; Johnston et al., 2012; Kuhn et al., 2008; NIDA, 2012a). Understanding the various facets of this drug will help disentangle fact from fiction.

The Marijuana Plant

The cannabis (hemp) plant, *Cannabis sativa*, is the source of marijuana and hashish. The cannabis plant contains more than 400 chemicals (Figure 10-1). At least 60 of the chemicals are **cannabinoids** (as they bind to cannabinoid receptors in the brain), but the most important of these cannabinoids is delta-9-tetrahydrocannabinol (THC). THC is the plant's main psychoactive chemical, although researchers are examining some of the other chemicals found in this plant for potential additional medicinal use. Various marijuana plants can significantly differ in how much THC is contained in each. Marijuana can contain 1% to 3% THC all the way up to 20% THC in the sinsemilla variety (Earleywine, 2002).

The cannabis plant is a hardy plant that grows quickly in a variety of environments (Figure 10-2). Cannabis is highly resistant to pests and grows easily. In favorable environments, the plant can reach a height of 20 feet. The leaves consist of five or more narrow leaflets extending from a slender stem attached to a thick, hollow stock. The leaflets are arranged palmately, which means they radiate from a common center like fingers of a hand spreading apart. Closer examination of the jagged edge of each leaflet reveals a resemblance to the blade of a serrated knife. Cannabis is considered an herbaceous annual, since it both has nonwoody stems and will die at the end of the growing season if in the natural environment. The plant has flowers from late summer to mid-fall. There are male and female varieties of cannabis, which are partly distinguishable because the

FIGURE 10-1
Marijuana plant.

FIGURE 10-2
Marijuana plants (*Cannabis sativa*).

female plant tends to be shorter than the male. The male and female also have different types of flowers. The male has flowers that are elongated clusters that turn yellow and die after blossoming. The female has flowers that grow in spike-like clusters and retain their green color after blossoming. The female plant's flowers are larger than the male's, which help the female plant catch pollen. The female plant produces seeds and a sticky resin that protects those seeds. **Hashish** is produced by removing and drying resin found on the tops (flowers) of the hemp plant. Hashish is much more potent than marijuana, because it contains a higher proportion of the main psychoactive ingredient in the plant, THC. The plant produces this resin as a protective mechanism against sun, heat, and dehydration, which partly explains why cannabis is hardy in a variety of growing conditions (Earleywine, 2002).

The stiff and fibrous stalks of the cannabis plant can be used to produce various consumer products. The fiber (also referred to as hemp) is used to make rope, cloth (used in clothing), canvas (used for ship sails), paper, and shampoos. The fiber tends to be stronger and more resistant to mildew than similar fibers such as cotton. The seeds can be eaten as food and are often found in granola and cereal. The seeds can also be made into oils. Both hemp oils and seeds contain trace amounts of THC. Industrial hemp (cannabis) plants grown for industrial uses have very low concentrations of THC (less than .15% THC as compared to 2% THC found in psychoactive cannabis plants). Thus, a person might try to smoke a whole field of industrial hemp plants and still be unable to get high. Owning hemp products such as clothing or food items is legal. While dozens of products are made from industrial cannabis, industrial cannabis is a far smaller agricultural product than it was one hundred years ago. Currently, it is illegal (per U.S. federal law) to grow or possess marijuana in plant or drug form (DEA, 2011).

Brief History of Marijuana Use

The cannabis plant is thought to be native to India, from a region north of the Himalayan Mountains. The use of the *Cannabis sativa* plant has a long history, with its first use occurring about 10,000 years ago. Archeologists have discovered pots made of cannabis fibers at a site on the island of Taiwan off the coast of mainland China. While the plant may have initially been used for its fiber, the psychoactive and medicinal usefulness of the plant were also known early in history. References to the plant by Chinese Emperor Shen Nung are dated to 2737 BCE. In the emperor's writings, the cannabis plant was recommended for its sedative and analgesic effects. The plant at this time was not cultivated but rather was collected in its natural habitat. The emperor recommended that cannabis tea would be beneficial for gout, malaria, and rheumatism. He also recommended cannabis tea for poor memory, an odd assertion given marijuana's typical effects of inducing memory impairment, which will be described later in this chapter. Cannabis also served a religious purpose, as it was thought to counteract evil spirits. Thus, the cannabis plant has been known as a psychoactive drug for almost five millennia. Early deliberate cultivation of the plant is dated from 28 BCE, with early Chinese writings indicating that the plant was mainly grown for its fibers (Abel, 1980; Bostwick, 2012).

Knowledge of the cannabis plant's characteristics spread from China to nearby countries. In India, cannabis was considered one of the five sacred plants according to *Atharva Veda*, one of the oldest books of Hinduism (Aldrich, 1977). From Asia, cannabis use spread eastward to the Middle East and then North Africa. The Greek physician, Galen, prescribed marijuana for various medical conditions around 120–200 CE. In 300 CE, young women in Jerusalem received marijuana for pain during childbirth. In the 10th century, hashish was first used among the Arabs, who also made paper from the cannabis plant. The Egyptians were using hashish in the 11th century. Despite long-standing use of cannabis for its psychoactive effects around the world, the West only recently adopted cannabis for its psychoactive effects. However, the plant had been cultivated for its fiber. In fact, King Henry VIII fined his farmers in England if they did not raise hemp. The Spanish brought cannabis to Chile in 1545. The plant was cultivated in North America as soon as the British arrived, in the Virginia colony of Jamestown. The hemp plant was a widely cultivated staple crop, including by presidents George Washington and Thomas Jefferson, to make clothing and rope. Jefferson even invented a device for processing hemp (Earleywine, 2002; Johnson, 2012).

Not until the 1800s did descriptions appear in medical writings and the Western press describing the psychoactive effects of marijuana and hashish use. In Great Britain, cannabis was introduced by an Irish physician, Dr. William O'Shaughnessy, who had been to India and had seen cannabis used as medicine. He conducted experiments on animals and then on people to better understand marijuana's effects. He found that marijuana eased the pain of rheumatism, a broad term historically used to refer to conditions today known as rheumatoid arthritis. O'Shaughnessy's observations were similar to those from a few millennia earlier by Emperor Shen Nung. French physician Dr. James Moreau advocated use of cannabis to treat mental illness. From the mid-1800s to the 1930s, European and American physicians prescribed cannabis for a variety of medical conditions. However, cannabis use never became widespread, although various groups did adopt the drug from time to time. In the mid-1800s, intellectuals became marijuana users, inspired by books such as *The Arabian Nights* and *The Count of Monte Cristo*, which included favorable descriptions of hashish highs in the exotic Orient (Abel, 1980; Bloomquist, 1971; Johnson, 2012).

> *"When you return to this mundane sphere from your visionary world, you would seem to leave a Neapolitan spring for a Lapland winter—to quit paradise for earth—heaven for hell! Taste the hashish, guest of mine—taste the hashish."*
>
> Alexandre Dumas, *The Count of Monte Cristo* (1844)

At the turn of the 20th century, cannabis smoking was relatively unknown in the United States but prevalent in Mexico. Stories of marijuana-induced violence were reported in Mexican papers and subsequently translated for U.S. consumption. The Mexican Revolution (1910–1920) pushed immigrants and their marijuana smoking northward. U.S. newspaper stories decried marijuana and described how the drug led to homicidal violence. In the 1920s, jazz musicians such as Louis Armstrong adopted marijuana smoking. New Orleans was a central dispensing area of marijuana to Mexican laborers and black Americans who followed the lead of jazz musicians in adopting marijuana smoking. Marijuana use increased further during Alcohol Prohibition (1920–1933), since the drug provided an alternative for a dry society. When Prohibition ended, marijuana use subsided. Opposite to the U.S. experiment with Alcohol Prohibition, in the late 1800s India, British taxes made marijuana so expensive that many Indian people turned to alcohol as an alternative (Abel, 1980; Earleywine, 2002; Johnson, 2012).

In the United States, prohibition against marijuana began in 1937 when the U.S. Congress passed the Marihuana Tax Act (note that the spelling of marijuana has changed over time). Spearheaded by the efforts of Harry Anslinger, the head of the federal Bureau of Narcotics, the act levied a tax of approximately $1 on anyone who dealt commercially in marijuana. While possession and usage of hemp or cannabis was not criminalized, there were penalty and enforcement provisions to which handlers were subject. Fines or prison terms could result for individuals who violated procedures outlined in the act. Passage of the Marihuana Tax Act may have been prompted by several causes. The timber industry was lobbying for a smaller hemp industry, which had been supplanting commercial timber interests, including supplying paper for newspapers. In addition, public hysteria regarding marijuana had been on the rise, as captured in propaganda films such as *Reefer Madness*. In that cult classic film, first released in 1936, nice responsible young adults descend into violence and insanity after smoking marijuana. Somewhat contrary to the public hysteria, the American Medical Association opposed the passage of the Marihuana Tax Act, as it taxed physicians and pharmacists who prescribed or cultivated cannabis for medical reasons. The Marihuana Tax Act did still allow medical use of marijuana, although taxes surely dissuaded medical professionals from prescribing marijuana. The act also outlawed possession or sale of marijuana for recreational reasons. After the Marihuana Tax Act, stricter penalties for the sale and possession of marijuana would be imposed over time (Johnson, 2012).

In the 1960s, marijuana was a famous symbol of the hippie counterculture. Challenging authority, embracing social change, and experimentation with drugs, including marijuana, all symbolized the era. Also at that time, Harry Anslinger introduced the rhetoric that today is referred to as the **"gateway drug theory."** Anslinger argued that control of marijuana was necessary to prevent users from moving to other highly addictive drugs such as heroin. In 1964, the active psychoactive chemical in marijuana, THC, was first isolated by chemists. Increasing federal government restrictions on marijuana use culminated with the 1970 classification of marijuana as a Schedule I drug (meaning that it is illegal and has no medical value). By the 1970s, some states had begun to take a more liberal approach to marijuana use, including eliminating jail time as punishment for marijuana possession arrests. The more liberal era was short-lived, as marijuana again became widely regarded as a dangerous drug in the 1980s. Between 1978 and 1987, the percentage of high school seniors who reported daily use of marijuana dropped considerably, from 10% to 3% (Bostwick, 2012; Johnson, 2012).

The current movement for using marijuana as medicine only seems like a radical change if one ignores history. Recent examinations of marijuana's therapeutic potential for certain medical conditions began in the mid-1980s, in part because the active ingredient, THC, was isolated and examined for potential medical uses. In 1985, the FDA approved the drug dronabinol (synthetic THC) for the medical treatment of cancer patients. In 1995, the state of California became the first of 18 states to legalize plant-based medical marijuana, in the process going against federal law. Medical marijuana dispensaries have arisen almost overnight in states where its use has been legalized at the state level, even though marijuana use continues to be a crime at the federal level. Drug diversion is a serious concern, with the Drug Enforcement Administration (DEA) shutting down the worst offenders who claim to be medical marijuana dispensaries yet are clearly fronts for illicit drug dealing, rather than for treating people with legitimate medical issues such as cancer or AIDS. In the November 6, 2012, election, the states of Washington and Colorado voted to legalize the recreational use of marijuana, with possession of up to an ounce being decriminalized in adults over the age of 21. In Colorado, an individual is permitted to grow up to six plants at home. These state-level changes are of course in opposition to federal law; time will tell how these inconsistencies will be resolved. In sum, marijuana remains the most widely used illicit drug, both in the United States and worldwide, with the pendulum swinging widely in how the drug is viewed (Bostwick, 2012; DEA, 2011; Johnson, 2012).

Current Drug Laws in the United States

Synthetic THC-based medicines including dronabinol (Marinol®) and nabilone (Cesamet®) are used medically to treat vomiting, weight loss, pain, and other conditions. These medications are considered Schedule III drugs (see Chapter 1 for a review of the U.S. Controlled Substances Act). There are several synthetic THC drugs found on the street, known by names such as Spice, K2, or Blaze. Though they are disguised as natural herbal incense mixtures, users know and refer to them as "fake pot." These drugs are Schedule I drugs, with some containing THC and others containing chemicals extremely similar to THC. Plant-based cannabis in any form is a Schedule I drug, which means it has no accepted medical use in the United States. As mentioned above, state and local laws do differ from federal law with respect to marijuana (Figure 10-3). In principle, federal law trumps state law. In 2012 alone, state or local marijuana laws changed to become more lenient in Colorado, Connecticut, Massachusetts, Rhode Island, and Washington State. In Colorado and Washington State, residents voted to legalize recreational marijuana use, illegal under federal law since marijuana is a Schedule I drug (the same category as heroin). This raises interesting questions for the road forward. Federal law doesn't have jurisdiction over a street robbery or even a murder. However, federal officers could jail a person for possession of marijuana (in part because this is essentially a commerce issue), even when the state or local law has no prohibition against the drug (Osler, 2012). How will this

©Image Source/Corbis

FIGURE 10-3
Marijuana is
a Schedule I drug.

inconsistency be resolved? The answer is unclear. However, the reader should understand the stance of the Drug Enforcement Administration, which clearly states that marijuana is a Schedule I drug, and using it is breaking federal law.

> *"Marijuana is properly categorized under Schedule I of the Controlled Substances Act . . . evidence supports this classification . . . smoked marijuana has a high potential for abuse, has no accepted medicinal value in treatment in the United States, and . . . lack of accepted safety for its use even under medical supervision."*
>
> The DEA Position on Marijuana (DEA, January 2011, page 2)

Focus on Careers: Lobbyists and Political Consultants

There have been many periods in history during which public opinion has undergone significant shifts. Dramatic shifts in public opinion can lead to changes in law. While not impossible, it can be quite difficult for an individual citizen to influence politicians in a way that leads to legislative change. Enter the **lobbyists**, individuals who make their careers understanding the political system, and whose job it is to persuade legislators to vote for legislation favoring the lobbyist's employer. With marijuana, there are two national organizations whose lobbying efforts have been instrumental to the recent state-level legislative changes: the National Organization for the Reform of Marijuana Laws (NORML) and the Marijuana Policy Project (MPP) (visit www.norml.org and www.mpp.org to see more about these particular organizations). What do lobbyists do? Lobbyists directly meet with elected officials to provide information pertinent to a bill. Lobbyists also do less glamorous jobs such as writing letters, phoning, and organizing community meetings that rouse public support for an issue. Lobbyists can advocate for just about any group in society including researchers, pharmaceutical companies, or universities. Successful lobbyists tend to be extremely adept at the art of persuasion. They may do extensive background research on a complicated issue and then provide a simple story about how a problem might be solved by laws appealing to legislators and/or the general public. The path to a career in lobbying (or political consulting or even public relations) is different for everyone. While most lobbyists have college degrees, there is no specific background or certification/licensing requirement. However, experience in a government-related internship would be helpful to enter the field. A lobbying career does require superb written/oral communication skills. The ability to network is critical, so a charismatic personality and the ability to connect quickly with strangers are important job requirements. Thus, a lobbyist career might not be the best fit for an introvert who dislikes talking to strangers. The salary range for lobbyists is variable and can be low if working for a grassroots organization. However, many of these jobs can be valuable even though the pay may not be very good. For example, President Barack Obama served as a community organizer in Chicago before earning his law degree. The job of advocating for the poor and disenfranchised was surely a difficult one, but it launched President Obama's ultimately extremely successful political career. Thus, advocating for others can lead to other exciting career opportunities. Moreover, lobbying can also be a financially lucrative career, particularly for those working for major firms in Washington, D.C. The downside to a lobbying career can be long and irregular hours, frequent travel, and election uncertainty impacting demand for your services. The benefits of a career as a lobbyist include working in an exciting and rewarding job, especially if working to promote a cause in which you believe.

Some websites to explore:

American League of Lobbyists
http://www.alldc.org
American Association of Political Consultants
http://www.theaapc.org
In addition, contact your local elected officials to find out about internships or other opportunities available in your area.

Prevalence of Marijuana Use

In the United States

Marijuana is the most widely used illicit drug and the third most commonly used recreational drug after alcohol and tobacco. The *2010 National Survey on Drug Use and Health (NSDUH)* estimated that there were approximately 17.4 million current (past-year) users of marijuana in the United States. This number includes users of hashish and accounts for approximately 6.9% of the population ages 12 and older. Males and females differ in marijuana use, with approximately 9.1% of males and 4.7% of females using marijuana in the past year in the United States. Moreover, 15.7% of past-year marijuana users had used marijuana on 300 or more days within the past 12 months. This translated to approximately 4.6 million individuals being daily or almost daily users of the drug. Finally, the survey found that 2.4 million individuals used marijuana for the first time in the past 12 months. These new initiates were largely young, with 59% of them being age 18 and younger (SAMHSA, 2011a).

Marijuana is the most prevalent illicit drug used by adolescents. Data from the *2011 Monitoring the Future* study revealed that 36% of high school seniors (12th graders) reported past-year use of marijuana and 11% of seniors reported past-year use of synthetic marijuana (Figure 10-4). While these numbers seem high, they are lower than those observed in 1979, when 51% of seniors reported past-year use of marijuana. In 2011, 6.6% of seniors reported daily use of marijuana. When asked about access to marijuana, 82% of seniors reported that marijuana would be fairly easy or easy to get, indicating that while illicit, marijuana is a highly accessible drug (Johnston et al., 2012).

Around the World

Similar to the U.S. pattern of drug use, marijuana is the most widely used illicit drug worldwide and the third most commonly used recreational drug worldwide after alcohol and tobacco. An estimated 125–203 million individuals (2.8% to 4.5% of the global population age 15–64 years) have used marijuana (including hashish) at least once in the past year. Regional differences exist, with the highest rates of marijuana use occurring in North America, Western Europe, and Oceania

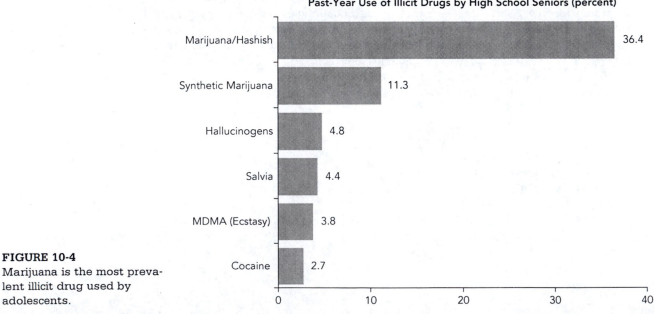

FIGURE 10-4
Marijuana is the most prevalent illicit drug used by adolescents.

(Australia, New Zealand). The burden of marijuana use on health is limited compared to other illicit drugs. While marijuana is associated with dependence and mental disorders, marijuana use (unlike heroin use) is not associated with increased mortality rates (Degenhardt & Hall, 2012).

Rates of cannabis use among adolescents are relatively similar across countries despite substantially different laws and policies governing its use. For example, laws regarding cannabis are strictest in the United States, somewhat less so in Canada, and least strict in the Netherlands. Despite these differences, rates of cannabis use among 10th graders are similar in all three countries (Simons-Morton, Pickett, Boyce, ter Bogt, & Vollebergh, 2010).

Worldwide, most marijuana use involves plant-based marijuana. However, a recent global survey of almost 15,000 participants found that 17% of marijuana users had reported use of synthetic marijuana (synthetic THC) at least once in their lifetime. Among those who had reported use of synthetic marijuana, 41% had done so in the past 12 months. However, 93% of synthetic marijuana users reported a preference for plant-based natural marijuana. Reasons for preferring plant-based marijuana included greater pleasure, better high, and better functioning after use. Synthetic marijuana was associated with greater paranoia and more significant hangovers (NIDA, 2012c; Winstock & Barratt, 2013).

Routes of Administration

The **route of administration** refers to the method by which a drug enters the body. Marijuana is typically administered either by inhalation or oral administration. Inhalation of marijuana via smoking is the most rapid and efficient means of drug administration. Marijuana can be smoked with joints or blunts. Marijuana can also be smoked using pipes (also referred to as bowls) or water pipes, colloquially referred to as bongs. The drug is absorbed through the lungs, and users experience the effects of THC within minutes. Peak blood levels of THC are experienced about 10 minutes after initiation. The duration of drug action for smoked marijuana is 2 to 3 hours.

The other major route of administration for marijuana is oral. Marijuana can be eaten in food such as brownies or taken in pill form, such as in synthetic THC medications. The onset of the drug effect with orally administered marijuana is much slower and less efficient than smoked marijuana. Oral administration requires the drug to be passed through the digestive tract until THC is absorbed in the small intestine. The onset of drug action for orally administered marijuana is 30 to 60 minutes after swallowing. Peak blood levels of THC are observable at 2 to 3 hours after oral administration. The duration of drug action for orally administered marijuana is approximately 4 to 6 hours. It is estimated that the dose must be three times higher to achieve the same effect with oral administration as experienced when marijuana is smoked (Iversen, 2008; Julien, 2005).

Medical Uses for Marijuana

Marijuana has a long history as a medicine, dating back to Chinese Emperor Shen Nung (2737 BCE), who recommended the plant for its sedative and analgesic properties. Up until the 1930s in the United States, marijuana was found in medicines to treat pain and other symptoms. Passage of the Marihuana Tax Act in 1937, and the increasing sophistication of pharmaceutical research, led marijuana largely to lose its status in modern medicine. The pendulum of medical opinion may be currently swinging back in the other direction, with researchers and physicians once again considering the possible therapeutic use of marijuana for certain medical conditions. While research on this topic is ongoing there are a few conditions for which treatment with THC and other compounds found in marijuana seem to be helpful. Moreover, the recent discovery of the endocannabinoid system in the brain, upon which THC acts, has led scientists to reexamine the potential of marijuana to manage chronic pain, muscle spasticity, cachexia, glaucoma, and other problems (Aggarwal et al., 2009).

Given marijuana's status as a Schedule I drug, only synthetic medications that include THC as an active ingredient are administered to patients, although there are exceptions in which plant-based marijuana is smoked or orally consumed by patients in locations where use is legal at the state level. Many other countries take a more liberal approach to the medical use of marijuana. In the United States, FDA-approved synthetic THC medications include dranabinol (Marinol®) and nabilone (Cesamet®). Both contain THC as an active ingredient and are thus listed as Schedule III drugs under the Controlled Substances Act. These synthetic medications are administered in pill form. Oral administration results in slow drug onset and relatively long duration of action. While oral administration contributes to drug safety and decreases the abuse potential of these medications, patients sometimes dislike the slow onset, particularly for conditions like pain or muscle spasms. An oral cannabinoid spray (Sativex®) has been developed, which is a combination of THC and cannabidiol (another chemical found in the marijuana plant). The spray has a faster onset, which is desirable for some medical conditions. Although not yet FDA-approved, it has received approval in other countries (Canada, United Kingdom, and Spain) to treat muscle spasms and pain from multiple sclerosis. Various studies have found this cannabis spray to be effective in treating pain, and FDA approval may be shortly forthcoming (Wilsey et al., 2013). While not legal at the federal level, many states have also approved plant-based marijuana for medical purposes. Smoked marijuana or marijuana found in food products have been used by many patients. Smoked marijuana results in a faster onset of effect than oral administration, but it can also lead to adverse reactions. Panic or anxiety attacks can occur in some patients, as can feelings of disorientation. Patients are not able to drive after smoking marijuana. While descriptions of medical conditions that seem to be treated by THC are described below, realize that the systematic study of marijuana in well-designed and controlled clinical trials remains woefully deficient (Pertwee, 2012; Williamson & Evans, 2000).

Glaucoma is a disorder resulting from increased pressure in the eye (ocular hypertension) that can lead to blindness. When too much pressure builds in the eyeball, the optic nerve can be damaged. Glaucoma is a serious irreversible condition that is the leading cause of blindness in the United States. In the 1970s, data suggested that marijuana might be a beneficial treatment for glaucoma. Successful treatments already existed for glaucoma, including medications and surgical options to release the pressure in the eyeball, but blurred vision, headaches, and other problematic side effects occurred for some patients. It was determined that marijuana decreased intraocular pressure. It's uncertain why marijuana decreases intraocular pressure, though it has been suggested that marijuana dilates the vessels that drain excess fluid from the eyeball. When fluid is drained from the eyeball, pressure in the eyeball drops. Treating ocular hypertension with marijuana can prevent the rise in blood pressure, which can lead to blindness (Crandall et al., 2007). The use of marijuana is not a cure however, since stopping use of marijuana (or synthetic THC), results in pressure in the eyeball increasing once again. Current ophthalmologists generally prefer other approaches to treating glaucoma, such as medications or surgery, to marijuana. Glaucoma is a medical condition affecting more than 2 million Americans over age 25, with marijuana being one potential means of treating the condition.

Multiple sclerosis (MS) is an autoimmune disease that affects the central nervous system. The disease process leads to inflammation that damages myelin, the glial cells that insulate axons. Damage to myelin slows neural transmission. Unfortunately, MS is a chronic disease with no known cure. One symptom of MS that can be difficult to manage is muscle spasticity (muscle spasms). Patients often experience episodes where muscles contract and become very tight, mainly in the arms and legs. These muscle spasms can sometimes be very painful and uncontrollable. Muscle spasticity can be debilitating and leave some individuals unable to walk. Existing drug therapies for spasticity have been limited in effectiveness. However, anecdotal observations from patients who had self-medicated with the illicit drug of marijuana described some relief from muscle spasticity. Systematic studies have now demonstrated that marijuana-based medicines can improve symptoms of muscle spasticity (Pryce & Baker, 2012). Randomized, clinical trials have found that treatment with the oral cannabinoid spray (Sativex®) or oral cannabis has led patients to experience less severe symptoms of spasticity, which leads to a better ability to perform daily activities (Oreja-Guevara, 2012; Zajicek et al., 2012).

Another serious and debilitating symptom of MS is neuropathic chronic pain. Chronic pain is also a difficult symptom to manage in a variety of other medical conditions. Opiate drugs (described in Chapter 9) are effective in inducing analgesia, but they are also likely to lead to tolerance, which can create dependence. Marijuana may be an alternative analgesic drug for chronic pain, since THC also induces analgesia. Although THC may be less potent than opiates, the action of THC may be sufficient to help patients in chronic pain. Several randomized control trials have examined the analgesic efficacy of a cannabis oral spray inhaled by neuropathic pain patients, both with and without MS as the underlying disorder causing the pain. Given that neuropathic pain is chronic and resistant to treatment, a new way to treat this pain is desirable. Patients who had received the cannabis oral spray reported less pain after drug administration. Psychoactive effects were minimal and well tolerated. Patients reported better sleep, given that pain interferes with the ability to experience restful sleep. While patients experienced some cognitive detriments or symptoms like dizziness, these problems typically dissipated over time (Rog, Nurmikko, Friede, & Young, 2005; Wilsey et al., 2013).

Treating pain with opiates or marijuana need not be an either/or proposition, given that the two classes of drugs act on different receptor systems in the brain. Thus, researchers have investigated if marijuana can be used in addition to prescription opiates. When both opiates and marijuana are used, patients experience greater relief from pain than if either drug is used alone. Additionally, patients are often able to reduce the typical dose of opiates required to control pain when marijuana/THC is also administered. Dose reduction for opiates is important, as opiates are likely to induce tolerance and may potentially lead to addiction (Lucas, 2012). Moreover, tolerance development and addiction are less concerning for marijuana/THC. Since opiates and marijuana act on different neurotransmitter systems, it is not surprising that opiates and marijuana seem to have different analgesic outcomes. Opiates directly block pain. While patients may still notice their pain, it is less intense after opiate administration. By contrast, marijuana tends not to result in a perceived reduction in pain intensity. Rather, patients report that the unpleasantness of pain is reduced following marijuana administration. There tends to be a shift in the emotional reaction to the pain (Lee et al., 2013). The combination of marijuana-based medications and nonsteroidal anti-inflammatory drugs (NSAIDs) has also been found to be an efficacious way to treat pain (Anand, Whiteside, Fowlder, & Hohmann, 2009).

While pain is an aversive symptom, so is vomiting. Among patients undergoing chemotherapy for cancer, nausea and vomiting are likely side effects of treatment. Synthetic THC decreases vomiting (**emesis**), and so it is used as an antiemetic drug. Systematic investigations of the antiemetic properties of marijuana began in the 1970s. It became clear that marijuana decreases nausea and vomiting and increases appetite (Schwartz & Beveridge, 1994). Lack of appetite (**anorexia**) is another symptom related to emesis. Cancer patients undergoing chemotherapy may experience both emesis and anorexia. **Cachexia** is the term physicians use to describe a patient who "wastes away" from weight loss, often due to cancer, AIDS, or congestive heart failure. Cachexia is worrisome because it is a risk factor for death. Moreover, significant weight loss can also impact treatment options. Chemotherapy or other drug treatments may have to be delayed if the patient continually vomits and does not eat. Surgeries to remove tumors may need to be delayed if the patient is too frail and has lost too much weight. In these situations, the appetite-stimulating effect of marijuana or THC medications is a good choice with few effective alternatives. Clinical trials have demonstrated that dronabinol (Marinol®) increases appetite and decreases vomiting among cancer patients (Aggarwal et al., 2009). Similarly, one randomized, double-blind, placebo-controlled study involving AIDS patients demonstrated that a dose of 5 mg/kg of dronabinol resulted in significant appetite increases at 4 and 6 weeks into the study. Unpleasant side effects were reported for approximately 20% of patients, with feeling high, dizziness, confusion, and difficulty sleeping being the major concerns. These side effects, while unpleasant, are generally acceptable, given that these patients are experiencing a variety of other

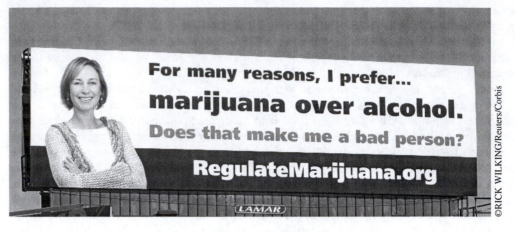

FIGURE 10-5
Marijuana and synthetic THC medications are known to be efficacious for several medical conditions.

unpleasant symptoms from their illness. Moreover, unpleasant side effects tend to dissipate with time on the THC medication.

Although marijuana and synthetic THC medications are known to be efficacious for several medical conditions, there may be still other conditions that could benefit from its use (Figure 10-5). Disorders that could potentially be treated include epilepsy, neurodegenerative disorders, and affective disorders. Recall that the *Cannabis sativa* plant contains many chemicals. While THC is the prevalent and widely studied therapeutic agent, the other compounds in marijuana should also be more thoroughly investigated, particularly since THC results in psychoactive effects that some patients find unpleasant. More understanding of the constituent ingredients in marijuana, and more knowledge about the human cannabinoid system upon which marijuana acts, will better inform us if marijuana should have a place in modern medicine (Hill, Williams, Whalley, & Stephens, 2012).

One final important consideration in the potential medical use of marijuana is whether physicians support use of the drug. Interestingly, few studies answer this question. Studies that have been done indicate a general consensus among physicians that marijuana, natural or synthetic, is *not* medically useful. The increased use of legal medical marijuana at the state level has not altered physician opinion over time. One national survey of family physicians, general internists, obstetrician-gynecologists, psychiatrists, and addiction specialists asked about the legal prescription of marijuana as a medical treatment option. Only 36% believed prescribed marijuana should be legal, a rate less supportive of medical marijuana than found in the general American public (Charuvastra, Friedmann, & Stein, 2005). A more recent survey of family physicians in Colorado (where medical marijuana is legal) indicated that only 19% thought that medical marijuana should be recommended to any patient. The majority of physicians thought marijuana posed significant mental (64%) and physical (61%) health risks (Kondrad & Reid, 2013). Another survey specifically examined the prescribing practices and professional opinions of clinical oncologists, physicians who treat cancer. This survey inquired about the usefulness of synthetic THC (dronabinol or Marinol®) or smoked marijuana as antiemetics for nausea and vomiting accompanying chemotherapy treatment. The researchers found that oncologists rarely prescribed dronabinol (only 6% of oncologists prescribed the drug at least five times in a 3-year period). Moreover, only 30% of oncologists supported the idea of rescheduling smoked marijuana from Schedule I to another level that would allow it to be used in medical treatment of cancer patients. Even oncologists in favor of plant-based cannabis as a treatment option estimated that they would prescribe marijuana cigarettes less than once per month, if they were available (Schwartz, Voth, & Sheridan, 1997).

There are a variety of explanations for the lukewarm response of physicians to FDA-approved synthetic THC medications or medical marijuana. Some of the hesitation may arise from legitimate professional concern about prescribing a drug that is clearly illegal at the federal level (Figure 10-5). Even though synthetic THC medications are Schedule III drugs, and thus fully legal for medical use under a doctor's supervision, their association with marijuana's Schedule I status may prompt concerns about drug diversion or abuse. The worry of drug diversion has some basis. Recent analysis of medical marijuana patient medical records in California clinics found that most patients presented with difficult-to-assess subjective symptoms such as pain, insomnia, and anxiety (rather than conditions like cancer, multiple sclerosis, or AIDS, which are objectively observable with medical tests) (Nunberg, Kilmer, Pacula, & Burgdorf, 2011; Reinarman, Nunberg, Lanthier, & Heddleston, 2011). Physicians may also be less familiar with synthetic THC medications if sales representatives from pharmaceutical companies promote them less than more lucrative patent medications. This would not be unique to the medical use of marijuana compounds, but instead it may reflect that medicine, and medical knowledge, tends to get commercialized. Professional development opportunities for physicians are often supported by pharmaceutical companies. Furthermore, new drug development is lengthy and expensive and thus depends heavily on lucrative patent medications at the end of the long discovery process. Pharmaceutical companies may not be motivated to conduct research examining the medical usefulness of marijuana compounds, given that they cannot obtain a patent for a plant that a patient can grow themselves (Abramson, 2008). A third explanation for lack of physician enthusiasm about medical marijuana may be a legitimate concern about not causing additional harm to their patients. Physicians are taught in medical school to "first, do no harm," a tenet from the Hippocratic Oath, taken by physicians committing to practice medicine ethically and honestly. With marijuana, there are legitimate worries about doing harm. As an example, smoked marijuana has been linked to cancer growth, particularly smoking-related malignancies. A physician may feel uneasy about treating nausea and vomiting from chemotherapy with an agent that may escalate cancer in a patient who is struggling to battle cancer (Bowles, O'Bryant, Camidge, & Jimeno, 2012; NIDA, 2012a). Of course, these are only a few of the reasons physicians might be hesitant about the medical use of marijuana. Can you think of a few additional reasons?

QUICK QUIZ 10-1

1. Marijuana comes from which plant?
   a. *Papaver somniferum*
   b. *Cannabis sativa*
   c. *Erythroxylon coca*
   d. *Nicotiana tabacum*
   e. *Camellia sinensis*

2. What seems to be the opinion of physicians about the medical usefulness of marijuana?
   a. It is very useful as medicine.
   b. It is not very useful and its use may cause other medical problems.
   c. More research regarding its medical usefulness is needed.
   d. a and c
   e. b and c

3. There is some evidence that THC may be medically useful as a treatment for_____.
   a. anorexia
   b. pain
   c. emesis
   d. a and b
   e. All of the above

4. According to the 2011 Monitoring the Future survey, approximately _____ of high school seniors reported using marijuana at least once in the past year.
   a. 3%
   b. 13%
   c. 36%
   d. 56%

5. In the United States, marijuana use typically involves
   a. Joints
   b. Pipes
   c. Blunts
   d. a and b
   e. All of the above

6. The FDA has approved medications that contain _____.
   a. anandamide
   b. THC
   c. *Cannabis sativa*
   d. dopamine

7. Worldwide, marijuana is most likely to be used as _____.
   a. plant-based marijuana
   b. synthetic marijuana
   c. plant-based and synthetic marijuana in equal amounts
   d. None of the above

8. What is multiple sclerosis? How is marijuana therapeutically useful for this condition?

ANSWERS TO QUICK QUIZ 10-1:

1. b – *Cannabis sativa*
2. e – b and c
3. e – all of the above
4. c – 36%
5. e – all of the above
6. b – THC
7. a – plant-based marijuana

8. Multiple sclerosis is an autoimmune disease that affects the central nervous system. The disease process elicits inflammation, which damages myelin and slows neural transmission. It is a chronic disease with no known cure. Marijuana has been shown to have therapeutic potential in treating muscle spasticity and neuropathic pain from this disease.

Acute Effects of Marijuana

The acute effects of marijuana are changes that take place after ingesting the drug one time. Acute effects can be objective, including observable changes in behavior or physiology. Acute effects can also be subjective, such as when individuals report how high they feel. Of course, the baseline state of the individual can influence response to the drug (Figure 10-6). Individuals who use marijuana (or THC medications) primarily for medical reasons are often nauseous or in pain at the time of drug administration. The baseline state will have an effect on the individual's response to the drug. For those who are nauseated or in pain, relief from aversive symptoms may be central to the acute experience of the drug. Recreational users of marijuana may be primarily motivated to achieve a subjective state such as feeling high, although the drug also produces several objective changes, including changes to the body. Regardless of the reason for use of marijuana, the risk of fatal overdose is extremely small when marijuana is used alone.

Objective Effects

Marijuana is a sedative drug, with acute effects impairing both cognitive and behavioral functions. Multiple aspects of cognitive processing are impaired by marijuana (Kelly, Foltin, Emurian, & Fischman, 1990; Ranganathan et al., 2012). The ability to pay attention in a sustained manner is decreased. In addition, errors on psychomotor tasks tend to increase. When marijuana users drive, their driving skill is impaired in part because they are less able to concentrate on the driving task and avoid distraction (Kelly, Darke, & Ross, 2004). Road-traffic accidents are more likely for individuals having used marijuana, with higher risk for individuals having had higher doses of marijuana. The problem of impaired driving under the influence of marijuana is a serious concern. However, statistics do indicate that alcohol-impaired driving is a much greater societal problem, in part because marijuana is used less frequently than alcohol. A study in France between 2001 and 2003 found that 3% of fatal road-traffic accidents were attributable to marijuana, whereas 30% of

©Ruben Koerhuis/Alamy

FIGURE 10-6
The acute response to marijuana depends on whether the individual is using the drug for recreational or medical reasons.

accidents were attributable to alcohol (Laumon, Gadegbeku, Martin, Biecheler, & the SAM Group, 2005). Of course, either type of fatal crash (marijuana- or alcohol-related) is entirely preventable. Researchers have estimated that the impairment resulting from a 2.6% to 4.0% THC concentration is comparable to a blood alcohol concentration of .05 g% (Liguori, Gatto, & Robinson, 1998; Ramaekers, Berghaus, van Laar, & Drummer, 2004).

The decrements in attention following marijuana administration lead to impairments in memory. When one does not pay attention, new information is not stored in memory for later retrieval. Marijuana's contribution to interference with memory processing is highly reliable, particularly in relation to the ability to form new memories, rather than recalling old well-learned memories (Kuhn et al., 2008). For example, an individual who has smoked marijuana may have a conversation with a friend and mutually decide to meet at 7 p.m. at a certain restaurant. This memory may be poorly encoded and the individual who smoked marijuana may not remember the time, the location, or anything else about the conversation. However, the marijuana-smoking individual would still be able to recall information from earlier events when not under the influence of marijuana, such as how the friends had decided to attend a concert and had purchased tickets for the event earlier that week. Thus, the acute effects of marijuana decrease attention, which limits how much new information can be encoded and stored in long-term memory during the time marijuana is in the body.

Beyond memory impairment, individuals who are under the influence of marijuana exhibit diminished motor activity. Marijuana users also tend to interact with others less frequently in social situations, although that observation can depend on context. In laboratory settings, decreased verbal interactions occur among research subjects who have smoked marijuana, although these individuals may still spend time with others. However, some users also demonstrate the opposite outcome, in which talkativeness increases, even while most other aspects of motor behavior are reduced. In addition, aggression is reduced, and subjects in research studies are less likely to exhibit aggressive responses to highly provoking actions by others. Finally, another reliable outcome with marijuana administration is increased appetite. Individuals feel hungry and eat more food when using marijuana (Kelly et al., 1990). This objective change in appetite stimulation is sometimes referred to as "the munchies" and is therapeutically useful in medical patients. Increased food intake can also lead to weight gain among recreational users of the drug. Increases in food intake tend to be similar whether marijuana is smoked or orally administered as THC in pill form (Hart et al., 2002).

Subjective Effects

The acute effects of marijuana can cause several changes in subjective state. However, the one constant about the acute effects of marijuana on subjective state is that reported experiences are highly variable. Thus, conclusions about the typical subjective effects for users are somewhat difficult to make (Kuhn et al., 2008). For example, many who use marijuana may report feeling almost nothing the first few times they tried marijuana. It has been argued that the lack of subjective change among initial users could reflect anything from inexperience in smoking technique to the necessity for sensitization to occur in the brain. When subjective effects are experienced, users report euphoria or a feeling of being high, but the effects tend not to be dramatic and the users may also characterize themselves as feeling mellow, drowsy, relaxed, or carefree. Users tend to be prone to laughter and **loquaciousness** (talkativeness) (Hart et al., 2002). Subjective effects from smoking marijuana tend to be experienced within a few minutes after initiation of smoking. Subjective effects may peak at approximately 15–30 minutes and then dissipate within 2–3 hours (Grotenhermen, 2003). The experience of marijuana intoxication is routinely described as intellectually interesting or emotionally pleasant. Users may describe transient perceptual alterations whereby visual images may seem more intense, colorful, or meaningful. Others describe a relaxed and open experience in which normal feelings and thoughts can be processed more fully. The user's perception of time may also seem to slow down. Subjective changes tend to be similar whether marijuana is smoked or administered orally as THC in pill form (Hart et al., 2002; Wachtel, ElSohly, Ross, Ambre, & de Wit, 2002). However, not all subjective effects are positive, and some users report anxiety, panic attacks, or other negative symptoms (Grotenhermen, 2003; Ranganathan et al., 2012). Less commonly, paranoid thoughts and other psychotic symptoms occur. The acute effects of synthetic illicit THC and similar compounds, found in Spice and K2, are similar to marijuana. However, in some cases acute anxiety and psychosis have been reported to be higher with synthetic marijuana than with plant-based marijuana (Gunderson, Haughey, Ait-Daoud, Joshi, & Hart, 2012).

Effects on the Body

The most observable effect of marijuana use is bloodshot eyes. The acute effects of marijuana result in vasodilation, which leads to bloodshot eyes about an hour after smoking. In addition, the acute effects of marijuana result in changes in cardiovascular functioning. Users may experience slight increases in heart rate, pulse rate, and blood pressure. The peak heart rate is experienced approximately 20 minutes after smoking and may be elevated for about an hour (Kelly, Foltin, & Fischman, 1993). These cardiovascular changes are relatively mild and inert, but they can be problematic for individuals with preexisting heart disease. Individuals may also experience dry mouth, thirst, hunger, headache, nausea, or dizziness (Grotenhermen, 2007).

One important consideration for any psychoactive drug is whether a dose of the drug can be lethal. Note that the brain receptors that bind to THC, the active ingredient for marijuana, are not located in the brain stem. The brain stem is the region of the brain critical for control of respiration, and thus THC does not seem to alter basic biological functions such as breathing. Since marijuana does not alter breathing and heart rate, it is essentially impossible to take a fatal overdose of marijuana (Kuhn et al., 2008).

Chronic Effects of Marijuana Use

Despite the widespread use of marijuana, the literature on the chronic effects of marijuana is oddly sparse. However, there are indications that chronic use of marijuana leads to several important health concerns. First, chronic marijuana use can result in various cognitive deficits. Cognitive impairments can be observed, from basic motor coordination to more complex executive functions such as planning, organizing, solving problems, and making decisions. Memory problems and difficulty controlling emotions and behavior have also been reported. Of course, the deficits vary considerably in severity, with one's history of drug use playing an important role. Quantity, recency, and duration of use, as well as age of onset of use, are all factors that contribute to the likelihood that cognitive deficits emerge. Users who have used more marijuana, more recently, for a longer duration of time, and with a younger age of initiation are more likely to experience problems (Crean, Crane, & Mason, 2011). Moreover, chronic marijuana users may also use other drugs that increase the likelihood that cognitive deficits develop.

One study illustrated the cognitive deficits experienced by chronic marijuana users. Heavy marijuana users who had been abstinent for a month still exhibited deficits in decision-making tasks compared to similar controls. Poorer cognitive performance and decreased brain activation measured by brain imaging during cognitive tasks appeared to be dose-related. The deficits in brain activation and decision making were most pronounced in users that smoked 53–84 joints/week, compared to users who smoked 8–35 joints/week, although the more moderate users of marijuana did still exhibit deficits (Bolla, Eldreth, Matochik, & Cadet, 2005). Other research indicates that heavy marijuana users process reward information abnormally, showing a bias toward immediate rewards in a simulated gambling task. This bias is correlated with future drug use, with marijuana users showing the greatest bias toward immediate rewards having the greatest probability of escalating drug use over time (Cousijn et al., 2012).

As is found with other psychoactive drugs, the chronic use of marijuana has been demonstrated to result in lost insight about one's behavior. The ability to process errors in the environment can be measured by various computerized tasks, with a diminished capacity to detect errors linked to symptoms such as loss of insight. One study compared 16 active chronic marijuana users and 16 controls matched on a variety of demographic characteristics except for marijuana use. The researchers measured impulse control and awareness of errors. Interestingly, the marijuana users and controls performed similarly on impulse control, but the marijuana users were less aware of their behavior and their errors. The researchers also imaged subjects' brains using fMRI, and they discovered that cannabis users had decreased functioning in the anterior cingulate and right insula regions, the parts of the brain known to correlate with error awareness (Hester, Nestor, & Garavan, 2009). In sum, decreased awareness about one's own behavior may occur for chronic users of marijuana. Of course, these cognitive deficits associated with chronic marijuana exposure may lead to problems at work or school.

A second significant concern with chronic marijuana use is the increased risk of serious mental health problems such as psychosis. **Schizophrenia** is a serious mental disorder characterized by disturbance in thought, emotion, and behavior. Schizophrenia affects approximately 1% of the world's population. Individuals suffering from schizophrenia experience psychotic symptoms like delusions (false beliefs) and hallucinations (false perceptions). As a disorder, schizophrenia is difficult to treat, even though various antipsychotic drugs are available (see Chapter 12). Schizophrenia is a chronic condition that typically begins in late adolescence or early adulthood. The cause of schizophrenia is not well understood, and genetics clearly play a role (Kring, Johnson, Davison, & Neale, 2012). However, the environment matters as well. Many clinical studies have reported an association between marijuana use during adolescence and development of schizophrenia. Patients presenting in an emergency room with first-time psychotic symptoms are asked about drug use, and many (though certainly not all) psychotic patients report marijuana use. This suggests that marijuana may be the trigger for psychosis among vulnerable individuals (Tosato et al., 2013). Establishing a causal relationship between marijuana use and schizophrenia is difficult due to the uncertain interaction between marijuana and schizophrenia. One possibility is that marijuana causes schizophrenia to develop. This outcome could be more likely in a patient with a preexisting genetic vulnerability to developing the mental disorder. Marijuana might also induce schizophrenia in a person with no biological predisposition. However, there is another possible explanation that reverses the causal direction of the relationship between marijuana and schizophrenia. As a psychoactive drug, marijuana may appeal to adolescents developing schizophrenia, since the drug may help with the emergence of preclinical symptoms of schizophrenia. This other explanation seems equally plausible given that individuals predisposed to developing schizophrenia are sensitive to stress (and marijuana use leads to feelings of relaxation). Clearly, understanding the relationship between marijuana and schizophrenia is complicated. Fortunately, researchers are making progress.

One symptom of schizophrenia is a deficit in **sensorimotor gating** (or sensory gating). Sensorimotor gating refers to normal neurological processes that filter out redundant or unnecessary environmental stimuli so that the motor system does not need to respond to them. For example, imagine that you move into an apartment right near the train tracks. When you first move into your apartment, you may notice every train that goes by during the day and be awoken at night by every train that passes. The train is so loud that it might startle you a bit each time it passes. You wonder if you should move! However, a short time later you no longer "hear" the train. Your brain has learned that the sound of the train, and even the rumbling in the walls of your apartment, are irrelevant. As such, sensory processing of the train stimulus is diminished and a motor reaction (startle response) to the stimulus ceases to occur.

One reliable observation among patients with schizophrenia is a deficit in sensorimotor gating. That train will endlessly bother the patient. The inability to filter out irrelevant information (an attentional dysfunction) means that the schizophrenia sufferer experiences constant sensory overload. Both human and animal models of schizophrenia have demonstrated that excessive dopamine levels are responsible for the failure of sensorimotor gating (Braff & Geyer, 1990). Interestingly, and relevant to our discussion, patients with schizophrenia (who are nonusers of marijuana) and otherwise healthy, chronic marijuana users (not using the drug at the time of the study) both show sensorimotor gating failures (Kedzior & Martin-Iverson, 2007). This observation is consistent with other findings that otherwise healthy, chronic marijuana users and patients with schizophrenia both show similar generalized attention and executive functioning problems, although the deficits tend to be far more pronounced in schizophrenia (Johnstone, Humphreys, Lang, Lawrie, & Sandler, 1999; Solowij, 1998). Deficits in generalized attention are not persistent among chronic marijuana users if they stop using the drug; the attention problems tend to subside when users are abstinent for 12 months or longer (Solowij, 1998).

In humans, it is unclear what causes what in the schizophrenia–marijuana relationship. Fortunately, animal studies help establish the causal direction of the relationship. In one study, researchers administered a cannabinoid receptor agonist drug (whose action would be like THC in marijuana) or a placebo drug to mice during the mouse-equivalent of adolescence or early adulthood. Once the mice were fully grown, the researchers looked for deficits in sensorimotor gating. The researchers found that the mice that had exposure to the marijuana-like drug during the adolescent period had deficits in sensorimotor gating in adulthood. Drug-exposed animals also showed reductions in both cannabinoid and glutamate receptor activity as compared to control animals. This suggests that exposure during adolescence to a marijuana-like drug had long-term effects on neural functioning and resulted in symptoms (sensorimotor gating deficits) resembling schizophrenia symptoms (Gleason, Birnbaum, Shukla, & Ghose, 2012). In sum, while the marijuana–schizophrenia relationship needs to be better understood, animal studies do suggest that frequent exposure to marijuana in adolescence enhances later vulnerability to psychotic symptoms such as those seen in schizophrenia.

Among chronic marijuana smokers, there is also a risk of damaging lung functioning and developing cancer. Marijuana smoke is irritating to the lungs and can induce various respiratory problems such as chronic cough and frequent chest infections (NIDA, 2012b). Also, tar exposure is carcinogenic, and marijuana cigarettes contain more tar than tobacco cigarettes. Moreover, lung damage is greater for marijuana users smoking blunts (a cigar emptied of its tobacco and refilled with marijuana). A cigar wrapper is a tobacco leaf, so users are inhaling both marijuana and tobacco when smoking a blunt. Evidence suggests that smoking a blunt increases carbon monoxide exposure and heart rate more than smoking the same amount of marijuana in a joint (Cooper & Haney, 2009). Marijuana smokers often also smoke cigarettes, so separating the contribution of marijuana and tobacco to lung damage can be difficult. Whether an individual is smoking marijuana or tobacco, they are inhaling tar, carbon monoxide, cyanide, and benzopyrene. Exposing lung cells to these chemicals causes DNA damage, which can be a precursor to cancer. Similarly, chronic bronchitis occurs among smokers of three to four marijuana joints per day or smokers of a pack or more of cigarettes per day. Either type of smoking puts the lungs at risk for damage (Kuhn et al., 2008).

Reproductive functioning is also negatively affected by chronic marijuana use. Among both male and female chronic marijuana users, a loss of libido (decreased sexual interest and arousal) can occur. Both men and women also experience objective decreased reproductive capacity (decreased fertility). For men, chronic marijuana use can result in decreased sperm production and decreased sperm motility (the sperm that are present tend not to be very good swimmers). Men may also experience ejaculation problems or impotence. For women, chronic marijuana use can result in nonovulatory menstrual cycles in which menstruation occurs with no egg released. In the event that a sperm does meet an egg, embryo implantation and development tends to be impaired, which decreases the likelihood of a successful pregnancy. Among adolescent and young adult users of marijuana, decreases in fertility may seem unimportant if they are not planning on having children any time soon. However, men may not like the hormonal effect of marijuana, which increases the secretion of the hormone prolactin, leading to the development of breast tissue (gynecomastia). Keep in mind that it is unknown why these reproductive changes occur, how reversible they are, or how permanent such changes might be (Bari, Battista, Pirazzi, & Maccarrone, 2011).

If a successful pregnancy occurs, marijuana exposure in utero can have negative consequences. In utero marijuana exposure has deleterious effects on brain development, leading to subtle impairments in cognitive abilities later in life (Grotenhermen, 2007). The effects of in utero marijuana exposure may be similar to in utero cigarette exposure, with infants born preterm (early) and at a smaller size than would be expected given gestational age. Hyperactivity disorders are elevated in children exposed to both kinds of smoking in utero (Brown & Graves, 2013). Children exposed to marijuana in utero are also more likely to smoke cigarettes or marijuana themselves, when assessed in their adolescent or young adulthood years (Porath & Fried, 2005). While the above concerns caution against marijuana exposure during pregnancy, it does not appear that marijuana is a devastating teratogen like alcohol (Day & Richardson, 1991).

One final concern with chronic marijuana use is motivation. **Amotivational syndrome** refers to the lack of motivation, associated with chronic marijuana use, to achieve conventional goals. First described in the late 1960s, clinicians often described chronic marijuana users as apathetic and without ambition or goals. The apparent relationship between lack of motivation and chronic marijuana use is sometimes cited as a reason for opposing more liberal marijuana laws. There is no doubt that many young chronic marijuana users appear to lack motivation. Educational attainment is lower among chronic marijuana users. Adolescents who frequently use marijuana tend to have lower grade point averages, less satisfaction with school, negative attitudes toward school, increased rates of absenteeism, and overall poor school performance compared to their peers (Lynskey & Hall, 2000; Macleod et al., 2004). However, it is unclear whether the drug use itself caused the loss of motivation. It may be that preexisting personality traits leading to poor school performance also make marijuana appealing. There are many adolescents and young adults who seem to lack motivation and goals and yet are not users of marijuana. Moreover, amotivational syndrome is not a robust observation among chronic marijuana users. Other studies have found that daily use of marijuana in adults does not impair motivation and some researchers have argued that it may even enhance well-being (Barnwell, Earleywine, & Wilcox, 2006). Again, studies with animal subjects can be instructive to this complicated issue. In one study, researchers trained rhesus monkeys to perform a cognitive task having a motivation component called the progressive-ratio task where the monkey had to work harder over time to achieve treats. The monkeys were also trained to smoke marijuana (or a placebo). Drug exposure lasted for 2 months or an entire year and could occur daily or only on weekends. The researchers found that a year of daily or weekend-only marijuana exposure resulted in monkeys earning fewer reinforcers (treats) than monkeys who had only recent exposure to marijuana or none at all. The researchers seem to have found that chronic marijuana exposure might have induced an amotivational syndrome in monkeys. The amotivational syndrome disappeared once the monkeys were no longer given access to marijuana for a few

Myth Busters: Marijuana Is Harmless

The nationwide effort to decriminalize marijuana and increase the medical use of marijuana has led to widespread assertions that marijuana is a harmless drug. Teenagers are now more likely to report being past-month smokers of marijuana than cigarettes. Surveys of teenagers reveal a perception that marijuana smoking is less harmful than cigarette smoking (NIDA, 2012b). However, it is a myth that marijuana use poses no risks to health and well-being. First, there are clear legal risks from using marijuana, given that plant-based marijuana is a Schedule I drug. Beyond the legal concerns, there are also health risks. Whenever one alters brain chemistry with a psychoactive drug, there will be repercussions, particularly for a brain that is still developing. In this chapter, research was described that has found that chronic marijuana users may have memory deficits that persist after the drug leaves the body. While these deficits may reverse with abstinence, one recent study suggested that this reversal is less likely to occur when marijuana use was initiated in adolescence. A large prospective study followed individuals from birth until their fourth decade of life. The researchers found that individuals who began smoking marijuana heavily in their teenage years lost as many as 8 IQ points between age 13 and 38. The loss of cognitive abilities did not reverse, even when the adults stopped smoking marijuana (Meier et al., 2012). In addition to concern about neuropsychological deficits, smoking marijuana also irritates the lungs and can cause various respiratory problems or even cancer. Marijuana use can also lead to a variety of sexual problems, including loss of libido, impotence, and decreased reproductive capability. Finally, there is the association between chronic marijuana use and serious mental illness, particularly psychosis. Given that schizophrenia is a very serious, chronic, and difficult-to-treat mental disorder, it is a concern that marijuana may be a precipitating factor increasing the likelihood that schizophrenia develops. While individuals with a preexisting genetic vulnerability may be more at risk for schizophrenia, many individuals who would use marijuana probably have no idea if they are genetically vulnerable to schizophrenia. In sum, marijuana may not be as addictive as heroin, another Schedule I drug. However, marijuana is far from harmless, and it is a myth that marijuana use is not associated with risk.

weeks to a few months (Paule et al., 1992). Thus, the monkey study shows it is possible that chronic marijuana use may induce an amotivational syndrome. However, the evidence is equivocal in humans, and it is possible that chronic marijuana exposure elicits cognitive deficits that are problematic when combined with naturally diminished motivation.

Tolerance, Dependence, and Withdrawal

Tolerance

Many psychoactive drugs can result in tolerance when used regularly. Users may find that their typical dose results in a suboptimal effect, and such users may therefore escalate their dose to achieve the desired effect. However, whether tolerance to marijuana actually develops is currently unclear. In some cases, users do not appear to escalate their dose over time, which suggests that tolerance development may not be a major concern for recreational users or medical patients (O'Brien, 2001). Other evidence suggests that tolerance does develop to marijuana. Frequent marijuana smokers may report that they feel less high than an infrequent user given the same dose. This might indicate that tolerance has developed among frequent marijuana users (Kuhn et al., 2008). In one study examining tolerance in a controlled laboratory inpatient setting, marijuana smokers were given 20 mg of THC every 3.5–6 h for a week. The subjective ratings of intoxication following the first THC dose of the day declined over the week, indicating that the subjects had developed some tolerance to the high that the dose of marijuana induced. Tolerance was limited to subjective effects, however. While THC lowered blood pressure and elevated heart rate over the six days, it did so in a similar manner on each test day, suggesting that tolerance did not develop to the cardiovascular effects of the drug (Gorelick et al., 2012). However, behavioral studies with animals have demonstrated tolerance to THC (Desai et al., 2013). If tolerance to marijuana develops, it seems to go away rapidly with abstinence from the drug (O'Brien, 2001).

Dependence and Withdrawal

Dependence on marijuana can lead individuals to seek treatment. However, clinical drug abuse populations tend not to be dominated by exclusive marijuana users since few patients ever seek treatment for marijuana addiction alone. Individuals who need treatment for drug abuse problems may use marijuana, but it is unlikely that marijuana was the major concern requiring treatment. However, there does tend to be a natural history of drug initiation, a pattern that has been documented in various countries around the world (Degenhardt & Hall, 2012). Typically, individuals initiate the use of drugs in the following order: alcohol and tobacco first, marijuana second, and then other illicit drugs such as cocaine and heroin. Earlier in this chapter, we discussed the gateway drug theory, which is based on the premise that marijuana control is necessary in order that users not proceed to other highly addictive drugs such as heroin. The gateway drug theory is difficult to study, since it requires prospective cohort studies. For example, researchers might design a prospective cohort study that involves recruitment of children before any of the children had tried marijuana and then follow those children into adulthood to see who became addicted to other drugs. Despite the lack of good prospective cohort studies, it does seem clear that marijuana is frequently a stepping stone to dependence on other more highly addictive illicit psychoactive drugs. However, a large majority of marijuana users do not proceed to use or become dependent on other drugs, which has led researchers to question the validity of the gateway drug theory.

There are also clearly cases of dependence on marijuana. The risk of dependence on marijuana has been estimated to be approximately 9% among lifetime marijuana users, which is a significant concern but a rate that is far lower than the risk of dependence for other illicit drugs (Degenhardt & Hall, 2012; NIDA, 2012b). Most often, marijuana leads to a psychological dependence rather than a physical dependence. The marijuana user may crave the drug. They may feel irritable, depressed, restless, and agitated if they do not use the drug. However, there are limited illness-like physical withdrawal symptoms indicating physical dependence on the drug. Some patients may report insomnia, nausea, anorexia, and cramping. If withdrawal symptoms develop, they tend to follow a time-course similar to other drugs like nicotine. The onset of withdrawal symptoms from marijuana begins after 1–3 days of abstinence. Peak effects occur on or before day 6. After 2 weeks of abstinence, withdrawal symptoms have dissipated for most individuals (Haughey, Marshall, Schacht, Louis, & Hutchison, 2008). Both psychological and physical withdrawal symptoms are not particularly aversive, at least in comparison to withdrawal symptoms following abuse of other psychoactive drugs. Even compulsive marijuana users do not appear to continue to use the drug out of fear of withdrawal symptoms (O'Brien, 2001). This makes marijuana quite different than other drugs of abuse. For example, individuals who become dependent on alcohol or opiates will become extremely sick, even fatally so, if they suddenly cease use of their drug of abuse. Such users of alcohol or opiates may continue use of their drug just to avoid the development of withdrawal symptoms (see Chapters 8 and 9).

Withdrawal symptoms can be variable among chronic marijuana users. Some of this variability is a direct result of the typical use pattern. Heavier users are more likely to experience withdrawal symptoms. However, even after typical use variability is taken into consideration, some users experience almost no withdrawal, while others experience significant psychological and physical withdrawal symptoms. Recent research suggests that genetic factors may play an important role in the variability of withdrawal from marijuana. There are natural variations in the gene that regulates the endocannabinoid system, which is the receptor system upon which THC acts. In one study, researchers recruited 105 college students who were daily marijuana smokers. Participants were tested once at baseline and then again 5 days after abstinence. As expected, withdrawal symptoms differed considerably. The researchers found a difference among subjects in their cannabinoid receptor 1 (*CNR1*) genotype. Subjects either had a T/C SNP (single nucleotide polymorphism) or a T/T SNP on the *CNR1* gene. The individuals with the T/C genotype had far more pronounced withdrawal symptoms after abstinence. In sum, there is a genetic contribution to withdrawal symptoms from marijuana (Haughey et al., 2008).

Pharmacology of Marijuana

Sites of Action

The cannabinoids are a diverse group of chemicals that activate cannabinoid receptors in the brain. Cannabinoids can be produced naturally by the body (endocannabinoids), come from the cannabis plant (phytocannabinoids like THC), or be produced synthetically by humans (synthetic cannabinoids). The naturally occurring endogenous fatty acid that binds to cannabinoid receptors is **anandamide**, which is an inhibitory lipid neurotransmitter thought to play a role in appetite, sleep, memory, concentration, time perception, pleasure, and pain perception (Ameri et al., 1999). Anandamide was first isolated in 1992 and is found in both the central and peripheral nervous system (Devane et al., 1992). Increased levels of anandamide increase hunger and food intake. Since THC, the active ingredient in marijuana, acts like anandamide, THC binds to the same receptors as anandamide, thus mimicking the action of the naturally occurring neurotransmitter (Julien, 2005; NIDA, 2012a,b; Pertwee, 2005).

The modulatory activities of the cannabinoid system in the body have been a relatively recent discovery (Bostwick, 2012). Thus, much is yet to be understood about cannabinoid receptors and the role that endocannabinoids play in the normal functioning of the nervous system. However, some things are known. First, there are a huge number of cannabinoid receptors in the brain. In fact, cannabinoid receptors may outnumber opiate receptors by a factor of 10 to 20. Indeed, there may be more cannabinoid receptors than any other type of receptor. Cannabinoid receptors are located throughout the brain, with large numbers found in the cerebral cortex, basal ganglia, hippocampus, and cerebellum. However, one area is curiously devoid of cannabinoid receptors. The brain-stem structures that regulate basal body functions such as respiration do not appear to have any cannabinoid receptors. As discussed earlier, this explains why marijuana is relatively nonlethal. There are two types of cannabinoid receptors, referred to as CB_1 and CB_2. Anandamide binds to both CB_1 and CB_2 receptors. CB_1 receptors are found in both the brain and the periphery. Overactivation of central CB_1 receptors by THC induces psychotropic effects such as feeling high and disrupted memory or distorted perceptions. CB_2 receptors are thought to be located mainly outside of the central nervous system. CB_2 receptors are found in the heart and other body tissues involved in inflammatory and pain responses. Anandamide can block painful and inflammatory responses, playing a similar role to endogenous opiates. While CB_2 receptors were originally thought to be restricted to the immune system, there is now evidence that these receptors can also be found in primary sensory neurons. Increased levels of CB_2 receptors have been found in human peripheral nerves after an injury, especially painful neuromas. Agonists of CB_2 receptors induce analgesia, which can also result in activation of the endogenous opiate system (Anand, Whiteside, Fowlder, & Hohmann, 2009). Activation of cannabinoid receptors also has been shown to alter the activity of other neurotransmitters, such as opiates and GABA (Farquhar-Smith & Rice, 2003; Julien, 2005; Valverde, Karsak, & Zimmer, 2005).

The chronic use of any psychoactive drug may alter the delicate balance of receptor and neurotransmitter activity in the brain. Marijuana is no exception. Chronic daily marijuana smokers show a downregulation (reduction) in brain CB_1 receptor activity. In one recent study, the downregulation in CB_1 receptors was reversible with an abstinence of about a month (Hirvonen et al., 2012). The implication of reduced CB_1 receptor activity is debatable, but depression is one significant concern. Interestingly, researchers have developed genetically modified mice that lack CB_1 cannabinoid receptors and are considered to be a genetic model for depression (Valverde & Torrens, 2012). These mice not only act depressed, but they also have a variety of other symptoms associated with depression. They are anxious, have difficulty learning and remembering, are more sensitive to pain, and do not eat well (Valverde et al., 2005). In sum, cannabinoid receptors obviously play an important role in a variety of aspects of health and well-being.

Pharmacokinetics

Pharmacokinetics refers to the absorption, distribution, biotransformation, and excretion of drugs. Marijuana can reach the bloodstream via the routes of administration described in this chapter, oral and inhalation. The dose absorbed after a typical smoked marijuana joint can vary from 5 mg to 30 mg. Once in the bloodstream, the active ingredient in marijuana, THC, is distributed throughout the body, including in the brain. Some of the THC will be broken down by the liver before it reaches the brain. Metabolism of THC is fairly slow. Moreover, THC can be stored in the fatty deposits of the body. THC that is stored in fat is released from these tissues slowly over a long period of time before finally being eliminated. THC is detectable for approximately 10 hours in urine, but its metabolite THCCOOH can be detected far longer. In a recreational user, detection of marijuana use may be feasible for 3 to 7 days, and detection may be possible for up to 3 weeks in chronic users. Smoked marijuana tends to have a shorter detection time than marijuana ingested orally, such as when consumed in brownies (Kuhn et al., 2008; Verstraete, 2004).

More about the Science:

Neumeister et al. (2012). Positron emission tomography shows elevated cannabinoid CB_1 receptor binding in men with alcohol dependence. *Alcoholism: Clinical and Experimental Research*, 26, 2104–2109.

Researchers know that the active ingredient in marijuana, THC, stimulates cannabinoid receptors in the brain. However, marijuana may not be the only psychoactive drug that alters cannabinoid receptor activity. Various animal studies have indicated that manipulations of CB_1 receptors alter alcohol intake. For example, administration of CB_1 receptor agonists (drugs that bind CB_1 receptors and act exactly like naturally occurring anandamide) enhances alcohol consumption, whereas decreased CB_1 receptor functioning decreases alcohol intake (Femenia et al., 2010; Vinod et al., 2008). The researchers in this study wanted to know if cannabinoid receptor activity, particularly the signaling of CB_1 receptors, is linked to alcohol dependence. To answer this question, the researchers recruited 8 male individuals who were dependent on alcohol and had not had a drink for 4 weeks. An additional 8 males of similar age were recruited as healthy control subjects. None of the subjects were marijuana users. **Positron emission tomography (PET)** was used to scan the subjects' brains and a CB_1 receptor selective radiotracer [^{11}C]OMAR was administered to subjects. The radiotracer allowed researchers to examine CB_1 receptor density. The researchers observed that alcohol dependent subjects had 20% more CB_1 receptors than healthy control subjects. This higher CB_1 receptor density was found in brain regions such as the amygdala, hippocampus, anterior and posterior cortices, and orbitofrontal cortex.

More about the Science Thought Questions:

1. Why did the researchers exclude marijuana users?
2. Based on the results of this study, can the researchers conclude that alcohol dependence causes elevated CB_1 receptors?

More about the Science Thought Question Answers:

1. Heavy marijuana users tend to show downregulation of brain CB_1 receptors. The researchers wanted to understand the relationship between elevated CB_1 receptor binding and alcohol dependence. Regular marijuana use could have altered cannabinoid receptor activity and could have been a confounding factor in this study.
2. The researchers can only conclude that elevated CB_1 receptor density occurs in alcohol-dependent men who have been abstinent for one month. It remains to be determined, perhaps in animal studies, whether alcohol dependence causes elevations in CB_1 receptor density, whether abstinence after cessation of heavy drinking results in upregulation of CB_1 receptors, or whether elevated numbers of CB_1 receptors are a preexisting vulnerability for alcohol dependence.

Treatment

Few patients seek treatment for marijuana addiction. Many patients in drug treatment programs are marijuana users, but it is fairly uncommon for an individual to seek treatment just to stop marijuana use. As such, there are limited specific treatments reserved for patients who are abusing or dependent on marijuana. The main concern for treating heavy marijuana users is that cessation of drug use may lead to depression and drug craving. Those attempting to stop use of

In the News:

Frum, D. (2013). Marijuana use is too risky a choice. *CNN*.

Journalist and political commentator David Frum wrote an opinion piece for CNN opposing marijuana legalization. His article described the efforts of a new organization, headed by former U.S. Representative Patrick Kennedy, to oppose marijuana legalization called *Smart Approaches to Marijuana* (see www.learnaboutsam.com). The new group rejects the war on drugs model, specifically opposing prison sentences for casual marijuana use. However, the group has a clear message: Marijuana is a bad choice. Frum argues that marijuana damages brain development in young people. Heavy users become socially isolated and perform poorly at work and school. Marijuana smoke harms the lungs, and marijuana use may trigger psychotic symptoms in individuals predisposed to mental illness. Frum states that when writing social rules, we need to consider the audience. While some people can cope with complexity, others need clarity. Some people will snap back from an early bad choice, while others may not. Frum states that "just say no" is an easy rule for everyone in society to follow. In an interesting angle on this question, Frum argues that the question of marijuana legalization is a bit like the mortgage industry (the analogy seems stretched, but consider the argument). In the past, the rule was that a prospective home-buyer was required to put 20% down on a house and sign up for a mortgage with fixed payments over the next 30 years. However, bankers in a loosely regulated industry developed some novel ways to skirt those rules and get potential buyers into houses. No money down, interest-only, balloon, or adjustable rate mortgages afforded flexibility. While these newer mortgages allowed some people to become homeowners who might have been unable to buy a home under the old approach, others got in over the heads and became trapped in houses that they could not afford, especially in a declining housing market. We live in a world that has many abundant and potentially risky choices. Frum asks whether we want to introduce legalized marijuana into this mix, and he concludes we should not. In a world where people prone to make bad choices are the ones most likely to be hurt, he thinks that marijuana legalization will punish the vulnerable in our society for making bad choices and deluding themselves into thinking they are managing their drug use. What do you think?

Use this news article to test and apply your knowledge:

1. In this news story, Frum argues that marijuana use can damage brain development, result in social isolation, harm the lungs, and trigger psychotic symptoms in individuals predisposed to mental illness. Are his assertions correct?
2. Frum argues that people can delude themselves into thinking that they are managing their drug use. Based on what you know about psychoactive drug abuse, is this assertion correct?

Answers:

1. Yes, there is scientific evidence supporting the connection between marijuana use and the various health and social problems described by Frum.
2. Research findings do indicate that individuals who abuse psychoactive drugs tend to be slow to realize how harmful their behaviors are to themselves. It is common for drug abusers to think that they are effectively managing their drug consumption. In Chapter 6 (Cocaine) of this book, a study was presented showing that individuals addicted to cocaine lack insight into their own behaviors. Earlier in this chapter, we discussed evidence that cannabis users lack insight even when making faulty decisions.

What do you think about this news story?

One question that obviously arises from this news story is the relationship between marijuana and other psychoactive drugs, legal or not. Both nicotine and alcohol can also cause significant health problems (see Chapters 5 and 8), but they are legal. Proponents from the *Smart Approaches to Marijuana* argue that the experiment with Big Tobacco suggests a public health disaster may await full legalization of marijuana. Medical marijuana is already available in the prescription medications dronabinol and nabilone, rendering any further legalization efforts unnecessary, according to their website. Thus, this group argues that allowing everyone free access to a potentially harmful psychoactive drug will definitely result in harmful consequences for some. What do you think is the answer for society? Do you agree with Frum's assertions, or not? What do you think will happen with marijuana in the United States over the next 5 or 10 years?

marijuana may also be irritable, anxious, and have trouble sleeping. Antidepressant medication and psychological therapies can be helpful (O'Brien, 2001). Cognitive-behavioral therapy and motivational incentives (such as providing vouchers as rewards to patients who remain abstinent) have been successful in treating marijuana dependence. There are no specific psychotherapeutic medications that are used for marijuana addiction, although the increase in knowledge regarding the cannabinoid system in the brain suggests that new alternatives may be on the horizon (NIDA, 2012b).

QUICK QUIZ 10-2

1. Which of the following are acute effects of marijuana?
   a. Improved memory
   b. Impaired memory
   c. Loquaciousness
   d. a and c
   e. b and c

2. What is one visibly outward sign that someone has used marijuana?
   a. Profuse sweating
   b. Pinpoint pupils
   c. Bloodshot eyes
   d. Panting
   e. Pale skin

3. Both _____ and _____ bind to cannabinoid receptors.
   a. anandamide, THC
   b. anandamide, opiates
   c. THC, opiates
   d. LSD, serotonin
   e. None of the above

4. Marijuana cigarettes contain _____ tar than/as tobacco cigarettes.
   a. more
   b. less
   c. about the same amount of

5. Chronic use of marijuana can result in _____.
   a. memory problems
   b. decreased libido
   c. reproductive difficulties
   d. deficits in sensorimotor gating
   e. All of the above

6. Chronic users of marijuana may have a positive urine drug test up to _____ after the last use of the drug.
   a. 2 days
   b. 3 days
   c. 7 days
   d. 2 weeks
   e. 3 weeks

7. Explain how marijuana acutely affects appetite in both recreational users and medical patients.

8. Is a fatal overdose possible with marijuana? Explain your answer.

9. Are individuals who are dependent on marijuana likely to seek treatment? Why or why not?

ANSWERS TO QUICK QUIZ 10-2:

1. e – b and c
2. c – bloodshot eyes
3. a – anandamide, THC
4. a – more
5. e – all of the above
6. e – 3 weeks
7. The acute effects of marijuana induce hunger and increase food intake. In recreational users, this is referred to as "the munchies" and can be associated with weight gain. In medical patients, marijuana or synthetic THC can be used to increase appetite, which may be important for an underweight patient suffering from nausea, vomiting, or cachexia.
8. A fatal overdose is not possible with marijuana. THC binds to cannabinoid receptors. These receptors are not found in the brain stem structures that regulate breathing and heart rate. Therefore, even high doses of THC will not alter breathing or other basic functions, which is why marijuana is a nonlethal drug.
9. Individuals who are dependent on marijuana are unlikely to seek treatment. One reason might be that withdrawal from marijuana is relatively inert compared to the withdrawal processes associated with other psychoactive drugs. The main problems for heavy marijuana users, when they discontinue their use, are depression and drug craving. They may also be irritable, anxious, and have trouble sleeping. These are relatively benign symptoms that most individuals may be able to deal with on their own, without the intervention of a professional.

CHAPTER SUMMARY

Marijuana is a psychoactive illicit sedative drug that comes from the *Cannabis sativa* plant. THC is the psychoactive chemical in marijuana, and THC can be found in several FDA-approved medications. Marijuana has a long history of use going back 10,000 years, both for its fiber and for its psychoactive properties. Routes of administration for marijuana are inhalation (smoking) or oral (eating foods containing marijuana). There are a variety of medical reasons why THC is prescribed for patients, including the treatment of nausea, vomiting, pain, muscle spasms, and glaucoma. The acute effects of marijuana result in feelings of relaxation, well-being, and being high. Cognitive and motor impairments are observable when users have used marijuana. If marijuana is smoked, the drug begins to act within minutes and may last a few hours. Metabolism is slow and urine detection of THC can persist for as long as 3 weeks in chronic users of the drug. THC acts like naturally occurring anandamide in the brain and body. Both THC and anandamide bind to cannabinoid receptors. The lack of cannabinoid receptors in the brain stem structures controlling respiration explains why marijuana is a nonlethal drug. The chronic use of marijuana has been associated with a variety of health concerns including cognitive deficits, reproductive difficulties, lung damage, and risk of development of schizophrenia.

HALLUCINOGENS

Introduction

Hallucinogens belong to a category of psychoactive drugs resulting in bizarre acute drug effects. The brain responds to such drugs with distorted perceptions and hallucinatory experiences. A **hallucination** is a perception in the absence of a stimulus. Seeing blobs of colors or people who don't exist are examples of hallucinations. Hallucinogenic drugs also alter one's thoughts and mood. Hallucinogenic drug use is so ancient that it predates written history. In the 1960s, hallucinogenic compounds were widely used with the intent of expanding the mind or treating mental illness. While much has been written about halluci-nogenic experiences, Dr. Oliver Sacks provided fascinating detail about hallucinations in a recent book, aptly named *Hallucinations*. As a neurologist, Sacks has seen many patients having hallucinations as a symptom of underlying neurological conditions such as mental illness, blindness, and even migraines. However, it's his description of his own experience using hallucinogenic drugs during the 1960s that capture some reasons users experiment with hallucinogenic drugs.

> *"As I drew nearer to look at it, the spider called out, "Hello!" It did not seem at all strange to me that a spider should say hello . . . I said, "Hello, yourself," and with this we started a conversation, mostly on rather technical matters of analytic philosophy."*
>
> *Oliver Sacks, Hallucinations* (2012)

LEARNING OBJECTIVES

Learning objectives can help organize your studying. Before we begin the topic of hal-lucinogens, keep in mind that by the end of this chapter, you should be able to . . .

1. Describe the various types of hallucinogenic drugs.
2. Explain the brief history of the various hallucinogens and how long they have been available for use.
3. Describe the various routes of administration for hallucinogens.
4. Describe the prevalence of hallucinogen use in the United States and around the world.
5. Explain the acute effects of the various hallucinogens and how they act in the central nervous system.
6. Describe the chronic effects of hallucinogen use.
7. Describe tolerance, dependence, and withdrawal processes associated with hal-lucinogen use.
8. Describe treatment approaches to treat hallucinogen users.

Hallucinogens

Hallucinogens are psychoactive drugs that alter one's perceptions, mood, and cognitive processes (thoughts). The word *hallucinogen* is derived from the Latin word *alucinor*, which roughly translates as "I wander in mind, talk idly, and dream." Hallucinogenic experiences can vary widely depending on the type of hallucinogen (LSD, psilocybin mushrooms, PCP, MDMA/ecstasy, or salvia). Even with the same drug, separate experiences can differ dramatically. While sensory experiences without relevant or adequate external stimuli (**hallucinations**) are the hallmark of these drugs, hallucinogens can also induce a variety of other effects including heightened emotional states and altered senses of space and time. A user may feel a sensation of being separate from one's body, a heightened sense of insight, or believe that time is standing still. Users typically refer to the experience of being under the influence of a hallucinogenic drug as a **trip** (DEA, 2013a; Kuhn et al., 2008).

There are over 90 species of plants and synthetic chemicals in the category of hallucinogenic psychoactive drugs. These hallucinogens are typically administered orally or, less commonly, smoked. Hallucinogens can alter consciousness in very profound and bizarre ways or induce milder effects that do not necessarily lead to false perceptions. For centuries, humans have ingested hallucinogenic drugs during religious experiences. By the 1960s, these drugs rose in fame and notoriety. Hallucinogens were referred to as psychedelic drugs—a reference to their apparent mind-expanding or mind-revealing attributes. These drugs are still used illicitly, and they are sometimes referred to as **psychotomimetics** because they mimic the functional psychosis characteristic of the serious mental disorder schizophrenia. For example, hallucinations such as hearing voices or seeing things not physically present can either be symptoms of schizophrenia or be drug-induced (Kring et al., 2012). Generally, hallucinogens are somewhat less likely than other psychoactive drugs to produce dependence and addiction in users. Note, however, that use of hallucinogens can lead to health concerns that will be described later in this chapter (Nichols, 2004).

Almost all hallucinogens are chemical compounds containing nitrogen and classified as alkaloids. Many hallucinogens have chemical structures similar to naturally occurring neurotransmitters such as serotonin or acetylcholine. Given the wide variety of hallucinogenic drugs, it is helpful to group them based on how they act in the central nervous system. By this approach, there are five classes of hallucinogens: (1) serotonergic hallucinogens, (2) methylated amphetamines, (3) anticholinergic hallucinogens, (4) dissociative anesthetics, and (5) kappa opiate hallucinogens. Each of these classes of hallucinogen will be described in this chapter. Hallucinogens are somewhat less well understood than other psychoactive drugs, in part because the wide variety of hallucinogens means that research on each type is somewhat limited (Nichols, 2004; NIDA, 2009).

Types of Hallucinogens

Serotonergic Hallucinogens

Serotonergic hallucinogens are psychoactive drugs that powerfully alter perception, mood, and cognitive processing by increasing the action of serotonin in the brain. These drugs typically produce very vivid visual hallucinations. Other effects on consciousness also occur. The most common serotonergic hallucinogen is the synthetic drug **lysergic acid diethylamide (LSD)**, which is sometimes referred to as acid. LSD is produced in clandestine domestic laboratories. On the street, LSD may be found in several forms that are orally administered. LSD can be produced as tablets, capsules, or in liquid form. Dealers also package LSD by placing drops of solution on absorbent blotter paper or a sugar cube (Figure 11-1). The blotter paper may be divided in small decorated squares with each square representing one dose. Within an hour of ingestion, users experience vivid visual hallucinations and extreme changes in mood. The visual distortions can include distorted perceptions of object shape or size, depth, movements, colors, sounds, touch, and the user's own body image. These changes will profoundly impair judgment, such that users are susceptible to accident or injury. LSD is a Schedule I substance under the Controlled Substances Act, since it has no currently accepted medical use (DEA, 2013a,b).

LSD is a synthetic drug. However, there are several plants with similar properties to LSD. **Psilocybin** is a serotonergic hallucinogen that comes from specific mushrooms (Figure 11-2). There are more than 200 species of psilocybin mushrooms, with most found in the genus,

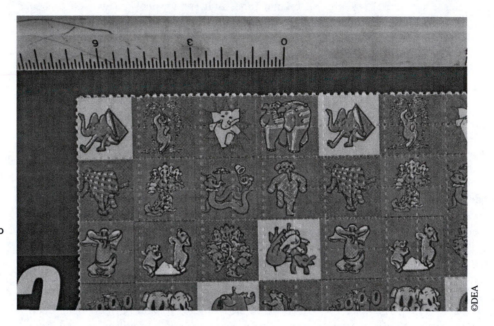

©DEA

FIGURE 11-1
LSD is often added to absorbent paper (blotter paper) and divided into decorated squares. Each square is one dose.

©PETER DEJONG/AP/Corbis

FIGURE 11-2
Psilocybin mushrooms.

Psilocybe. Most psilocybin mushrooms are found in subtropical humid forests, but the mushrooms can also be grown indoors. In the wild, psilocybin can easily be confused with poisonous mushrooms, which can be lethal if consumed. Users of psilocybin mushrooms usually consume the dried plant orally. If available, fresh mushrooms are also consumed. The mushrooms taste bitter and may be mixed with other foods or brewed in a tea to disguise their taste. Dried mushrooms can also be crushed into a powder and placed in capsules for swallowing. Psilocybin mushrooms contain two active compounds: psilocin and psilocybin, both resembling LSD in the effects they produce. The potency of mushrooms varies, but most have .2% to .4% psilocybin and trace amounts of psilocin. Similar to LSD, users of mushrooms experience varying degrees of hallucinations, illusions, altered perceptions of space and time, and altered body image. Euphoria is reported, which is sometimes followed by anxiety. Psilocybin and psilocin are listed as Schedule I substances under the Controlled Substances Act since neither has a currently accepted medical use in treatment (DEA, 2013c; Kuhn et al., 2008).

Another serotonergic hallucinogen is **mescaline**, which is a hallucinogen that comes from the peyote cactus, *Lophophora williamsii* (Figure 11-3). Mescaline can either be extracted from the peyote cactus or produced synthetically. The peyote plant is a small spineless cactus that has been used historically by native peoples in northern Mexico and the southwestern United States for religious purposes. The portion of cactus that is above the soil is referred to as the crown and looks like a disc-shaped button that can be cut off at the root. These buttons (dried or fresh) are chewed or soaked in water to produce a liquid that can be ingested. The extract is very bitter, so a tea is often prepared, which requires boiling the cacti for several hours. The peyote buttons can also be ground

©Susan E. Deginger/Alamy

FIGURE 11-3
The peyote cactus is the source for the hallucinogenic drug mescaline.

into a powder and placed in capsules for swallowing. Mescaline is also a Schedule I substance. There are several other less well-known drugs that are also serotonergic hallucinogens. Ibogaine, harmaline, and dimethyltrptamine (DMT) are serotonergic hallucinogens found in plants from Africa and South America, but less commonly found in North America (DEA, 2013c).

Methylated Amphetamines

Scientists frequently disagree about which drugs belong in the hallucinogen category. Such controversy exists for **methylated amphetamines**, with **MDMA** (**ecstasy** or molly) being the most widely used methylated amphetamine (Figure 11-4). MDMA is methylene-dioxy-methamphetamine and is one of several synthetic drugs chemically similar to other amphetamines (discussed in Chapter 7). MDMA does induce stimulant effects and elevate sympathetic nervous system activity, resulting in increased heart rate and blood pressure. Unlike other amphetamines, methylated amphetamines do induce psychoactive effects such as hallucinations. The halluci-nations resulting from use of methylated amphetamines such as MDMA tend to be less pro-nounced than the bizarre hallucinations occurring with serotonergic hallucinogens. For example, recreational use of MDMA can result in subjective effects such as altered time perception and mild changes in visual perception (Nichols, 2004). MDMA (ecstasy) is sometimes referred to as a **club drug**, which is a drug popular at night clubs and raves. A **rave** is a large gathering of people who get together to party and dance to electronic music. Casual sex and use of hallucinogenic drugs including MDMA (and also LSD) may be common in these environments.

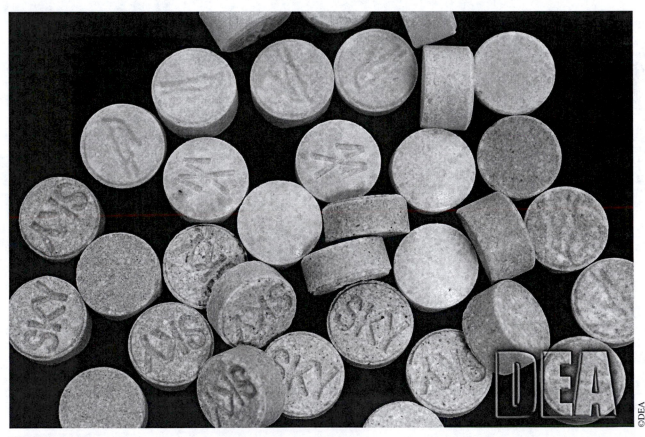

FIGURE 11-4
MDMA (ecstasy) is a methylated amphetamine.

Anticholinergic Hallucinogens

Anticholinergic hallucinogens are psychoactive drugs that induce hallucinations but are also used in medicine for several reasons. Found in a variety of plants, these drugs are alkaloids that act as acetylcholine receptor antagonists. Atropine and scopolamine are the two most common anticholinergic hallucinogens, which can be found in plants including deadly nightshade/belladonna (*Atropa belladonna*), Jimson weed (*Datura stramonium*), and angel's trumpet (*Datura sauveolens*). Ingestion of these plants induces hallucinations, delirium, agitation, and memory disturbances. The user experiences a dreamlike trance state and then awakens with no memory of the drug experience. Higher doses can lead to paralysis, convulsions, and death. Some of the plants are extremely poisonous and likely to induce fatalities from respiratory suppression (the person stops breathing). For example, consumption of up to five berries or one leaf from the nightshade can be lethal for an adult (Hall, Popkin, & McHenry, 1977; Muller, 1998).

Dissociative Anesthetics

Dissociative anesthetics are drugs producing feelings of detachment (dissociation) from the environment and one's self. Dissociative anesthetics also induce distortions of visual and auditory perceptions. There are many drugs that can be included in the category of dissociative anesthetics, but phencyclidine (PCP) and ketamine are the two most frequently used street drugs. **Dextromethorphan**, the cough-suppressing ingredient in over-the-counter cough and cold medications, is also a dissociative anesthetic. Dextromethorphan is safe at the dose recommended on cold medications. A typical recommended cold medication dose might be one-third of an ounce of medication, containing 30 mg of dextromethorphan. Consumption of four or more ounces of medication would induce dissociative effects from dextromethorphan (NIDA, 2001).

In medical treatment requiring surgical anesthesia, a dissociative anesthetic may be administered because it induces anesthesia while still leaving the patient semiconscious. Dissociative anesthetics act in the brain by antagonizing NMDA glutamate receptors. Phencyclidine (PCP or angel dust) was initially tested as an anesthetic because of its tranquilizing effects. A white crystal powder, PCP can be dissolved in water or alcohol. It is very bitter, and it is found on the street in tablet, capsule, and colored powder forms. Users typically administer PCP by oral, intranasal, or inhalation routes of administration. If smoked, users often place the powder in marijuana or other plant material (NIDA, 2009).

Ketamine is a similar drug to phencyclidine. Ketamine is more widely used than PCP as an anesthetic in veterinary and pediatric medicine. Much of the ketamine on the street has been diverted from veterinarians' offices. It is manufactured as a liquid for injection. When used illicitly, ketamine is typically evaporated to form a powder that is subsequently administered either by intranasal or by oral administration. Ketamine has no odor or taste. A victim may be unaware that ketamine has been added to a beverage, with the drug inducing amnesia in the unsuspecting victim. Thus, ketamine has also been used as a "date rape" drug. Ketamine induces similar effects to another date rape drug, flunitrazepam (Rohypnol® or roofies), but ketamine's mechanism of action in the brain is different than flunitrazepam's, since flunitrazepam is a benzodiazepine drug (see Chapter 13).

Kappa Opiate Hallucinogens

Finally, **kappa opiate hallucinogens** are drugs that act as kappa opiate agonists and produce hallucinogenic effects. Salvia is a kappa opiate hallucinogen having an interesting status as a hallucinogen, since it currently is not controlled under the U.S. Controlled Substances Act. As a result, anyone can use salvia, even though it induces hallucinogenic effects, although some states have local laws prohibiting use. Salvia is ingested by chewing or smoking the plant material from the *Salvia divinorum* plant (Figure 11-5). This perennial plant is native to Mexico and has been used there for both religious purposes and as medicine. Salvia has large green leaves and can grow to over three feet in height. The plant has white flowers. The active

FIGURE 11-5
Salvia divinorum.

ingredient thought to be responsible for its hallucinogenic effects is Salvinorin A (also called Divinorin A). Most of this active ingredient is found in the leaves of the plant. Users of salvia report hallucinogenic experiences similar to those of the classic serotonergic hallucinogens such as LSD. However, the acute effects of salvia are typically brief and dissipate within 20 minutes after the drug is inhaled (DEA, 2012d; Johnson, MacLean, Reissig, Prisinzano, & Griffiths, 2011).

Brief History of Hallucinogen Use

The use of hallucinogens predates written history (Table 11-1), as hallucinogens were used by various early cultures in rituals and religious ceremonies (Nichols, 2004). In ancient India, references to the use of hallucinogens (particularly serotonergic hallucinogens from plant sources) can be found in various Vedic hymns, the oldest scriptures of Hinduism, from 1500 to 1000 BCE. Native people living in Central and South America, including the Aztecs and Mayans, also used hallucinogenic mushrooms as part of religious rituals to produce visions and to contact the spirit world. Mushroom icons dated from around 1000 BCE have been found in Mayan ruins. Peyote cactus (mescaline) was ingested as a sacrament during services of the Native American Church, with the practice still occuring today. Use of hallucinogens as part of secret all-night ceremonies occurred in ancient Greece, although hallucinogen use was far less common than use of other psychoactive drugs such as alcohol. Scholars believe the doses of plant-based hallucinogens used in

Table 11-1   Examples of drugs that fall within the five classes of hallucinogens.

Class of Hallucinogens	Drug Name	Source (if relevant)
Serotonergic hallucinogens	LSD (lysergic acid diethylamide)	Synthetic (can be derived from ergot)
	Psilocybin	*Psilocybe* mushrooms
	Mescaline	Peyote cactus; also synthetic
	Ibogaine	*Tabernathe iboga* shrub
Methylated amphetamines	MDMA (ecstasy)	Synthetic
Anticholinergic hallucinogens	Atropine	Synthetic or found in various plants including Jimson weed, deadly nightshade/ belladonna, and Angel's Trumpet
	Scopolamine	
Dissociative anesthetics	PCP (phencyclidine)	Synthetic
	Ketamine	Synthetic
Kappa opiate hallucinogens	Salvinorin A (salvia)	*Salvia divinorum* plant

religious ceremonies were generally low; such doses would not have resulted in dramatic effects beyond spiritual activities. Hallucinogens may also have been used in medicines (Nichols, 2004).

The use of plant-based anticholinergic hallucinogens has been prevalent in nearly every culture. The ancient Romans were aware that some plants induced hallucinations and at sufficient doses were fatal poisons. It's believed that anticholinergic hallucinogens were the active substances in medieval anesthetics, witches' brews, and poison arrows used in warfare. Interestingly, women used the anticholinergic hallucinogen belladonna as an eye drop to dilate their pupils and make them more seductive. When Spanish explorers arrived in Central and South America in the 1500s, they were surprised by the widespread use of hallucinogens in religious ceremonies among the Aztecs and Mayans. However, the return of the Spanish explorers did not result in European adoption of hallucinogens (unlike what occurred with cocaine and tobacco) (Muller, 1998).

LSD is probably the most widely known hallucinogenic drug, yet it was discovered far more recently than most other plant-based hallucinogens. Albert Hoffman, a Swiss chemist, is credited with discovering LSD while working for Sandoz Pharmaceuticals in 1938. Hoffman was researching ergot, a fungus that infests grains like rye. Ergot poisoning causes a potentially fatal disease (called St. Anthony's Fire) in those who eat bread made with the infected grain. St. Anthony's Fire induces hallucinations and psychosis, but the more serious health problems associated with this disease include convulsive seizures, vomiting, and gangrene. The victim's skin breaks out in blisters that eventually turn black. While working with chemicals derived from ergot, Hoffman experienced odd mental effects following accidental exposure to one of the derivative chemicals. To determine if these effects were due to the chemical on which he was working, he deliberately exposed himself to the chemical and again experienced intoxicating effects. The chemical that he had discovered was LSD. LSD is manufactured from lysergic acid, which is found in ergot. Hoffman later isolated the active ingredients in psilocybin mushrooms in the 1950s (Hoffman, 2009; Nichols, 2004).

During the Cold War, hallucinogens, including the newly discovered chemical LSD, were of interest in the U.S. biological warfare research program. This aspect of hallucinogen history is controversial even today. For example, a mass poisoning incident took place in a picturesque village, Pont-Saint-Esprit, in southern France in 1951. Residents who had eaten bread from the same baker developed pronounced hallucinations, with some also developing psychotic symptoms. Terrifying hallucinations of beasts and fire were reported. Hundreds of people developed symptoms of psychosis, and dozens had to be hospitalized and placed in straitjackets at the local asylum (this was at a time when antipsychotic drugs were not yet available). Five people died from suicides stemming from psychosis, not from drug overdoses. The mystery of the poison source was referred to by locals and the world media as Le Pain Maudit (Cursed Bread). Many theories circulated about the source of the hallucinogenic poison. One widely favored explanation held that the flour from a local baker was unintentionally contaminated by ergot such that the villagers had experienced ergot poisoning. While plausible, this seems less likely given that Europeans had been aware of ergot poisoning for hundreds of years and typically were careful to avoid contamination. However, investigative journalist H. P. Albarelli Jr., has more recently claimed that the outbreak was not an accident but instead a covert experiment directed by the U.S. Central Intelligence Agency and the U.S. Army's Special Operations Division. In the last few years, Albarelli has uncovered old CIA and White House documents that suggest that these organizations were involved in the Pont-Saint-Esprit incident, as well as other cases where American servicemen were drugged in experiments with hallucinogens like LSD without their awareness between 1953 and 1965 (Albarelli, 2009; Samuel, 2010). While the pertinent details remain unclear, the Cold War use of hallucinogens may have resulted in disastrous consequences for individuals unaware that a drug was the cause of their frightening experiences including visual hallucinations.

Hallucinogens gained wide prominence in the 1960s. Sandoz Pharmaceutical (Hoffman's company) promoted LSD as a drug that could be helpful to psychiatrists in psychotherapy. The rationale for adding LSD to talk-therapy treatment was its ability to break down normal barriers to communication and facilitate therapy. Psychiatrists were also encouraged by the medical establishment and pharmaceutical companies to try LSD themselves so that they could experience psychosis and thus be more empathetic to patients suffering from schizophrenia or other psychotic disorders. In both the 1950s and 1960s, numerous clinical studies were conducted to determine if hallucinogenic drugs were efficacious in the treatment of a variety of medical conditions, especially psychiatric conditions (Nichols, 2004).

Outside the medical realm, LSD was embraced by the general public in the 1960s. Some acceptance resulted from influential advocates of the drug, including two Harvard professors, Timothy Leary and Richard Alpert (Alpert would later change his name to Ram Das after he became a religious writer). Both Leary and Alpert thought LSD could enhance spiritual and psychological health and well-being. While some experiments during their tenure at Harvard University were conducted, Leary and Alpert abandoned the scientific method in favor of leading a social and religious movement. Leary's fame escalated, and he quickly became a media celebrity. Both Leary and Alpert's academic careers imploded when they were both fired from Harvard in 1963. The demise of their academic careers proved no hindrance to their very effective proselytizing of LSD to the general public (de Saint Phalle, 1969).

Hallucinogen use also greatly influenced music and culture during the 1960s. By the end of the 1960s, 2 million people in the United States had tried LSD. Not all reports were favorable. News articles claiming that LSD caused chromosomal damage or induced homicidal behavior dissuaded some users (even though those claims eventually were shown to have no basis in scientific evidence). Both LSD and psilocybin mushrooms became illicit drugs in the United States following legislation in 1968. Use of LSD then declined in the 1970s and 1980s (Lattin, 2011). Medical research on hallucinogens also ceased around 1970. Interestingly, the potency of LSD found on the illicit market has actually declined since the 1960s. Today, a typical LSD dose may be 0.04 mg to 0.06 mg. In the late 1960s, tablets of LSD were available containing 0.25 mg of LSD or more. Note that the decreased potency for hallucinogens is different than trends for other psychoactive drugs. Unlike hallucinogens, the potency of most other psychoactive drugs (such as marijuana) has increased over time (Nichols, 2004).

The history of PCP (phencyclidine) somewhat parallels the history of LSD. PCP was developed in the 1950s as an intravenous anesthetic. PCP was discontinued from widespread medical use in 1965 after it became clear that patients were often delusional, irrational, and agitated while recovering from anesthesia. Ketamine was developed in 1963 as an anesthetic drug similar to PCP but lacking some of PCP's adverse effects. Also in the 1960s, PCP gained popularity as a street drug, with users often calling it "angel dust." Users reported PCP inducing feelings of strength, power, and invulnerability, while the drug also had a numbing effect. The appeal of PCP declined after many users had bad reactions. Psychotic symptoms often resulted in hospital admissions. Some abusers of PCP experienced long-term cognitive and psychiatric symptoms that persisted up to one year after last use of PCP. Today, ketamine is a somewhat popular club drug and its use seems to be increasing, with users sometimes referring to it as "special k" (NIDA, 2009).

The history of MDMA (ecstasy) is also brief. Merck Pharmaceuticals in Germany patented MDMA in 1913. While Merck originally intended to market MDMA as a diet drug, this never came to pass and the drug was abandoned for many decades. In the 1960s, other methylated amphetamines (DOM, MDA) were used with varying effects. However, users rediscovered MDMA in the 1970s as LSD use declined. Users claimed that MDMA was a love drug due to enhanced positive feelings and empathy toward others. Night clubs and raves were places where the drug was often used. Interestingly, MDMA was legal until 1985, in part because MDMA was thought to be useful as an adjunct in psychological talk therapy. However, the Drug Enforcement Administration (DEA) quickly acted to make MDMA an illicit drug after animal research showed that MDMA may cause brain damage. MDMA remains a popular club drug, and it is currently more widely used than any other hallucinogenic drug, including LSD (Holland, 2001).

Finally, salvia was a virtually unknown hallucinogenic drug in the United States until about 10 years ago. However, the use of salvia (from the *Salvia divinorum* plant) for psychoactive properties may go back centuries among people living in southern Mexico, where it was used in religious ceremonies. Salvia knowledge is limited because it is a new drug, with our lack of knowledge extending to its historical use (Casselman & Heinrich, 2011; Cunningham, Rothman, & Prisinzano, 2011).

Current Drug Laws in the United States

Many hallucinogens are currently categorized as Schedule I drugs (see Chapter 1 for information about the Controlled Substances Act). The lack of therapeutic utility of most hallucinogens, such as LSD, psilocybin, and MDMA (ecstasy), combined with their potential for abuse, account for the illicit status of these drugs. However, other hallucinogens are used in various medical contexts and thus have a different scheduling status. For example, the dissociative anesthetics phencyclidine (PCP) and ketamine are legitimately used medically as anesthetics. PCP is listed as a Schedule II drug, while ketamine, more widely used as an anesthetic in veterinary and pediatric medicine, currently has a Schedule III status. Scopolamine is used in the treatment of extreme motion sickness and also has a Schedule II status. Interestingly, salvia is not scheduled at this writing, though it induces brief hallucinogenic effects when chewed or smoked by users. Various states have passed legislation to place regulatory controls on the salvia plant itself or its active hallucinogen chemical, salvinorin A (DEA, 2012a, 2013a).

Prevalence of Hallucinogen Use

In the United States

Data from the 2010 National Survey on Drug Use and Health (see Chapter 1 for methodology) indicate approximately 1.2 million individuals in the United States ages 12 and older reported hallucinogen use in the past month. This equates to approximately 0.5% of the U.S. population. Use of hallucinogens is much less common than that of other illicit psychoactive drugs. Compare the 1.2 million hallucinogen users with the 17.4 million individuals who reported past month use of marijuana. MDMA (ecstasy) was the most common hallucinogen, with 695,000 (0.3% of the population) reporting past month use of that drug. The 2010 survey also asked about new initiates (new first-time

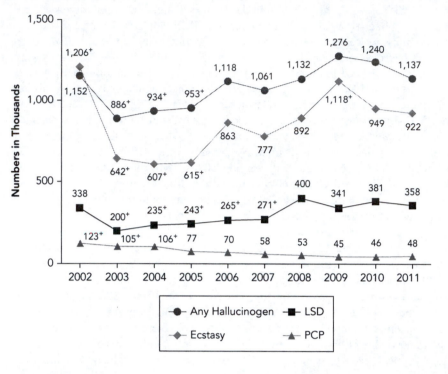

FIGURE 11-6
Past-year first-time U.S. users of a hallucinogenic drug from the National Survey on Drug Use and Health (SAMHSA, 2011a).

users of hallucinogens within the past year). There were 1.2 million new initiates of hallucinogens in the past year (yes – this number is the same as the past month users). New initiates of hallucinogens most frequently reported use of MDMA (ecstasy) followed by LSD (Figure 11-6) (SAMHSA, 2011a). Most surveys do not ask about use of hallucinogens other than MDMA and LSD. Therefore, it is difficult to determine how common use is of psilocybin, peyote (mescaline), and other hallucinogenic drugs. Most researchers believe that use of these other hallucinogens is infrequent (NIDA, 2009).

One consistent finding is that hallucinogen use is most common among adolescents and young adults, with use rarely persisting beyond the late 20s (Chilcoat & Schutz, 1996). Thus, it is helpful to focus on prevalence of hallucinogen use in adolescents. The Monitoring the Future Survey is a national U.S. questionnaire completed by 8th, 10th, and 12th graders. The 2011 survey indicates that MDMA is more frequently used than LSD, a trend that has held constant over the last few years. Approximately 5% of 12th graders reported at least one use of MDMA in the past 12 months. By contrast, 3% of 12th graders reported at least one use of LSD in the past 12 months. Interestingly, the researchers also asked about use of salvia for the first time in the 2011 survey. Remarkably, 6% of 12th graders reported use of salvia in the past year, which indicates that salvia has now become more popular than MDMA (ecstasy). Given that this was the first year that salvia use was questioned, it will be interesting to see in future surveys whether use of salvia remains popular among adolescents (Johnston et al., 2012).

Around the World

Similar to the U.S., worldwide hallucinogen use is much less frequent than that of other illicit drugs. Moreover, the disease burden associated with hallucinogen use is low, especially compared with other illicit drugs such as opiates (which can result in overdose deaths and are also associated with needle-associated disease transmission). For these reasons, researchers interested in global use rates of various psychoactive drugs often omit questions about hallucinogen use. However, evidence from more limited studies indicates that the most widely used hallucinogen worldwide is MDMA (ecstasy), similar to U.S. findings (Degenhardt & Hall, 2012).

While researchers often use surveys to identify global use patterns for illicit drugs, surveys can be extremely expensive and present many challenges. As a result, researchers have increasingly adopted different methodologies to assess patterns of illicit drug use. For example, researchers have analyzed untreated wastewater (sewage) from water purification plants for urinary bio-markers indicating drug consumption. One of the most recent and largest studies analyzing untreated wastewater was conducted in Europe. Researchers from 11 European countries sampled urban wastewater from 19 large cities during the course of one week in 2011. The researchers examined the water samples for the presence of a variety of illicit psychoactive drugs, including MDMA (ecstasy). The scientists found that MDMA use was far lower than other psychoactive drugs, including cocaine and marijuana. In some cities in Spain, MDMA use was so low that there was no evidence of it in the wastewater. MDMA was measurable and much higher in large cities in Holland, Belgium, and England, although evidence of MDMA use was still lower than for other illicit drugs. Interestingly, MDMA loads in wastewater were higher on weekends than weekdays, which fit its equity as a club drug (Thomas et al., 2012). A 2010 study in Australia also analyzed wastewater, finding approximately 0.08 doses of MDMA per week consumed per 1,000 people (Chen et al., 2011).

In some areas of the world, hallucinogen use may be more or less common than in the United States, with access to the drug sometimes being a main consideration. Adults and adolescents in Taiwan are less likely than their U.S. peers to use MDMA, in part because ketamine is a popular hallucinogenic drug in Taiwan (Chen et al., 2009; Joe Laidler, 2005). In general, our under-standing of worldwide use rates for newer hallucinogens remains woefully deficient. However, one study did report that salvia use among Canadian adolescents is high, similar to data from U.S. adolescents (Currie, 2013).

Hallucinogens are a large category of drugs, many of which come from plants that grow in different areas of the world. For this reason, there are several hallucinogens rarely used in the United States but much more common elsewhere. One example is the hallucinogen, **ibogaine**, found in the shrub, *Tabernathe iboga*, which grows in West Africa (Figures 11-7). Ibogaine is a serotonergic hallucinogen, like LSD, but ibogaine also induces a broad variety of effects on other neurotransmitter systems beyond serotonin. The bark of the root of the iboga plant is sometimes eaten in traditional African religious ceremonies to induce visions and commune with ancestors. Induction of a near-death experience is sought for spiritual and psychological purposes. Prevalence of ibogaine use is unknown but thought to be relatively high among some ethnic groups in West Africa. Moreover, there has been a global increase in ibogaine use as the drug has gained a reputation as a treatment for other addictions such as alcohol or opiate dependence. Systematic studies of ibogaine's efficacy are lacking, but that has not stopped individuals struggling with addiction from trying it (Alper, Lotsof, & Kaplan, 2008; Strubelt & Maas, 2008).

©Emilie CHAIX/Photononstop/Corbis

FIGURE 11-7
Tabernathe iboga plant.

In the News:

Carey, B. (2012). A "party drug" may help the brain cope with trauma.
The New York Times.

The widespread systematic study of hallucinogens to treat various medical conditions largely ended in 1970 (Nichols, 2004). However, ongoing research indicates that a hallucinogenic drug might be medically useful. For example, posttraumatic stress disorder (PTSD) is a condition experienced by individuals following a severe traumatic event. The traumatic event may be experienced again as memories or nightmares, with accompanying feelings of anxiety and arousal. PTSD can be debilitating, chronic, and lead to suicide. PTSD is common among soldiers returning from war. Unfortunately, traditional approaches of prescription medication and counseling do not help all patients with PTSD. In this article, the researchers (who were also clinicians) wanted to know if MDMA (ecstasy) could help patients recover from PTSD. The researchers prepared the patients for the drug exposure during several weekly therapy sessions. Then, MDMA was administered in one long therapy session that lasted up to 10 hours. In the altered drug-induced state, the patient was encouraged to talk about and focus on the trauma. After the drug session, the patients completed several additional weekly therapy sessions. Another day-long drug-assisted session occurred, followed by weekly therapy sessions that completed the treatment protocol. At the completion of the study, the researchers found that scores on standard measures of PTSD symptoms (anxiety, depression, nightmares, and hyperarousal) decreased approximately 75% by the end of treatment. This was twice the relief experienced by patients undergoing a similar treatment protocol without the MDMA. Two veterans with PTSD explained the benefit of MDMA as follows: the MDMA produced a mental sweet spot allowing them to feel and talk about the trauma without being overwhelmed by it. The researchers believe that this feeling state is due to the hormone oxytocin being released following MDMA administration. Elevated oxytocin is thought to increase sensations of trust and affection. MDMA also seems to decrease brain activity in the amygdala, the region of the brain that is active during fearful and threatening situations.

Use this news article to test and apply your knowledge:

1. What would need to change if MDMA were to be widely used in the treatment of PTSD? (Hint—think of the Controlled Substances Act)
2. What might be some health risks accompanying MDMA administration that the researchers would need to consider?

Answers:

1. Currently, MDMA (ecstasy) is a Schedule I drug and thus has no accepted medical use in the United States. If MDMA were deemed medically useful, its position in the Controlled Substances Act would need to be changed to at least Schedule II status.
2. MDMA can induce sympathomimetic effects including increases in blood pressure and heart rate. Individuals who have preexisting heart conditions or other cardiovascular complications would need to be carefully monitored during treatment.

What do you think about this news story?

Do you think that treatment with a "club drug" is a good approach for patients with PTSD? Do you think that the use of MDMA would be embraced by physicians and patients if the drug was demonstrated to be effective in treating PTSD?

QUICK QUIZ 11-1

1. Which of the following is a serotonergic hallucinogen?
   a. Ketamine
   b. MDMA
   c. Mescaline
   d. PCP
   e. Salvia

2. Salvia is currently listed as a _____ drug under the U.S. Controlled Substances Act.
   a. Schedule I
   b. Schedule II
   c. Schedule III
   d. Schedule IV
   e. It is not scheduled

3. _____ comes from a mushroom, and _____ comes from the root of a shrub.
   a. Psilocybin, ibogaine
   b. Ibogaine, psilocybin
   c. Psilocybin, mescaline
   d. Mescaline, psilocybin
   e. Mescaline, ibogaine

4. What is the most common hallucinogen in the United States, according to the most recent National Household Survey?
   a. LSD

   b. Psilocybin mushrooms
   c. MDMA (ecstasy)
   d. Salvia

5. What is the most common hallucinogen among adolescents, according to the most recent Monitoring the Future study?
   a. LSD
   b. Psilocybin mushrooms
   c. MDMA (ecstasy)
   d. Salvia

6. Prevalence rates for drug use in a population are often established using survey methodology. What is another way that scientists can estimate illicit drug use rates?

7. During the 1950s and 1960s, hallucinogens played a role in medicine. At that time, why did physicians view hallucinogens as medically useful? When did systematic research on the medical applications of hallucinogens end?

8. There was a mass poisoning incident in Pont-Saint-Esprit, France, in 1951. Many people experienced psychotic symptoms including intense hallucinations. It remains unclear whether the people had been accidentally or intentionally poisoned. Why might it be difficult to determine whether the poisoning was intentional (beyond the problem that the incident occurred several decades ago)?

ANSWERS TO QUICK QUIZ 11-1:

1. c – mescaline
2. e – it is not scheduled
3. a – psilocybin, ibogaine
4. c – MDMA (ecstasy)
5. d – salvia
6. Researchers can also analyze wastewater (sewage) for urinary biomarkers of illicit drugs.
7. During the 1950s and 1960s, psychiatrists believed that hallucinogens (especially LSD) would be helpful in talk-therapy treatment, as the drug would break down the normal barriers to communication and facilitate therapy. Psychiatrists were encouraged to try LSD themselves so that they could experience psychosis and be more empathetic to patients suffering from schizophrenia or other psychotic

conditions. Systematic research on the medical usefulness of hallucinogens ended in around 1970.

8. Ergot is a fungus that grows on rye and can induce hallucinations. It is possible that the local baker inadvertently included ergot in bread consumed by the people in the town, accidentally poisoning them. LSD is the hallucinogen that can be derived from ergot, as LSD is manufactured from lysergic acid found in ergot. At the time of the poisoning, the CIA was conducting experiments on LSD as part of their biological weapons program during the Cold War. Uncovered documents suggest that the townspeople might have been intentionally exposed to LSD as part of one of these experiments. Without further evidence, it is probably impossible to determine whether the poisoning incident was accidental or intentional.

Acute Effects of Hallucinogens

The acute effects of psychoactive drugs are a result of both pharmacological and non-pharmacological factors (see Chapter 1). An example of a pharmacological factor is drug dose, with a higher dose typically inducing a more pronounced effect. However, hallucinogens are somewhat unique among psychoactive drugs in that their effects are unpredictable relative to dose. This unpredictability partly arises from nonpharmacological factors being incredibly important in the hallucinogen drug experience. User expectations and the environment (setting) where the drug is taken are primary determinants of the acute effects after hallucinogen dose administration. For example, if a user takes a hallucinogenic drug in a religious setting and expects to have a spiritual experience, it is likely that the user will experience acute effects consistent with that expectation and environment. The same drug at the same dose might result in significantly different effects if expectation and/or the environment are different, such as taking the same drug dose at a night club. Use of hallucinogens in unstructured or unwise ways can result in unpredictable or even disastrous consequences (Nichols, 2004). Variability of acute effects of hallucinogens helps explain why research on hallucinogens is deficient.

Serotonergic Hallucinogens

Serotonergic hallucinogens such as LSD, mescaline, and psilocybin induce vivid visual hallucinations within an hour of ingestion. Colors may appear brighter and visual scenes may seem to have sharper definition. People and objects can appear altered in orientation or size. Little creatures (elves, dwarfs, or fairies) or giants may be observed. Hallucinations differ from internal imagery in that users tend to look at or scan imagined scenes when hallucinating, as opposed to closing their eyes or having an abstract gaze with mental images. Brain imaging reveals that visual hallucinations activate the same visual areas and pathways in the brain as real visual perception (ffytche et al., 1998). Perception of visual motion may not appear continuous but rather be experienced as a series of snapshots. Stroboscopic (cinematic) vision is a common acute effect of mescaline. In addition to visual hallucinations (the most common drug experience), the acute effects of serotonergic hallucinogens can also induce distortions or enhancements of the other senses (auditory, olfactory, and gustatory hallucinations). The user may report increased hearing acuity or more intense tastes. In sum, users report seeing images, hearing sounds, or feeling sensations that seem real but have no basis in reality. **Synesthesia**, the melding of the senses, may also be experienced. As an example, the user may report seeing music or hearing colors. The user may be unable to concentrate or focus attention. Perceptions may also become disconcerting. The **Capgras delusion** occurs when a user thinks that a friend or family member has been replaced by an identical imposter (DEA, 2013a; NIDA, 2001; Sacks, 2012).

Serotonergic hallucinogens impair judgment largely because the user becomes preoccupied with trivial thoughts, experiences, or objects. The boundary between the body and surroundings may blur, and the user may report a sense of detachment. Perceptions of space and time may seem altered, and past experiences may seem to merge with the present. The user may be unable to distinguish fantasy from reality. The user may also feel intensely spiritual and in unity with the environment. Labile (constantly changing) mood state and euphoria are also common. Serotonergic hallucinogens also induce a variety of physical changes consistent with sympathetic nervous system activation. Blood pressure, heart rate, and body temperature may all increase. Sweating may also occur. Dilated pupils, loss of appetite, sleeplessness, dry mouth, and tremors are also physical effects that may be experienced. Motor coordination is impaired, since these drugs grossly alter the ability to perceive visual stimuli (DEA, 2013a; NIDA, 2001; Sacks, 2012).

Serotonergic hallucinations can result in a wide variety of experiences. Sometimes, highly adverse reactions occur, referred to by users as **bad trips**. Frightening hallucinations, confusion, paranoia, disorientation, agitation, panic, and feelings of terror have been reported. When a bad trip occurs, the experience can be frightening and induce panic due to the experience being so vivid. A feeling of loss of control, despair, fear of insanity, and death can be problematic given the long duration of action of these drugs. In some cases, an emergency department admission is warranted for the safety of the patient and others around the patient. Treatment typically involves talking to the patient to calm them down (talk-down therapy) and administration of benzodiazepines (antianxiety medications) to calm the patient. Cases requiring a hospital visit seem to be somewhat rare but are more likely in those having a preexisting vulnerability to developing psychosis (Nichols, 2004). More commonly, users report the effects of serotonergic hallucinogens are unpredictable, with many trips including both pleasant and unpleasant aspects. For example, the opposing emotional states of euphoria and fear may transition so rapidly that the user experiences both emotions simultaneously. As such, a bad trip is dominated by unpleasant aspects but may still have a few pleasant aspects (NIDA, 2001). Death from use of hallucinogens such as LSD, psilocybin mushrooms, and mescaline is extremely rare. However, drug-related injuries or deaths occur in part because the hallucinogenic experience contributes to errors in judgment. For example, a user may think that he or she can fly and proceed to jump out of a window. Bad trips can be terrifying experiences that lead to disasterous choices (DEA, 2013b).

The duration of action for serotonergic hallucinogens varies depending on the type of drug administered. The duration of action for LSD is up to 12 hours. The duration of action for mescaline (synthetic or from the peyote cactus) can be up to 12 hours. The duration of action for psilocybin (from mushrooms) can be up to 6 hours (Nichols, 2004).

Methylated Amphetamines

Methylated amphetamines such as MDMA (ecstasy) result in various acute effects. Some effects appear similar to other hallucinogenic drugs, while others appear dissimilar to other hallucinogens and more like amphetamines. Subjective effects such as altered time perception and limited changes in visual perception following MDMA use are similar to those experienced by users of serotonergic hallucinogens such as LSD. In contrast to serotonergic hallucinogens, which produce pronounced visual hallucinations, MDMA tends to elicit fairly mild hallucinations. Even when hallucinations are absent with MDMA, other cognitive impairments are observed. One study administered comparable doses of MDMA and methamphetamine to research participants who were then asked to complete a computerized driving simulation task. The researchers found that performance in the MDMA condition was worse on all aspects of driving compared to the methamphetamine condition, which was worse than the placebo condition (Stough et al., 2012). Thus, MDMA may interfere with cognitive abilities more than other amphetamines.

The acute effects of MDMA include a variety of subjective changes that account for the appeal of this drug. Users report a mild euphoria. They also report feelings of warmth, empathy, openness, and diminished defensiveness. Users report that these subjective changes enhance a party atmosphere, since they feel sociable and talkative. Similar to both serotonergic hallucinogens and amphetamines, methylated amphetamines induce sympathetic nervous system activation. Increased heart rate, increased blood pressure, pupil dilation, insomnia, and appetite suppression all occur. Use of MDMA also induces muscle tension and **bruxism** (teeth grinding) (Figure 11-8). At night clubs and raves, adults may sometimes be observed sucking on baby pacifiers to mitigate bruxism. Users may also wear little clothing at raves. While a large number of people in one location may generally elevate the ambient temperature, which partly explains the lack of clothing, the other explanation is that MDMA substantially elevates body temperature (Parrott, 2012). At night clubs and raves, dancing further increases body temperature. Dehydration can be a serious concern since MDMA has a long 8-hour duration of action. Dehydration may also be worse for users who combine MDMA with alcohol. Acute health risks can even emerge, such as heat exhaustion and heat stroke. Further, toxic effects such as liver damage and kidney failure have also been reported. Similar to amphetamines, MDMA can result in various cardiovascular complications, which can lead to myocardial infarctions (heart attacks). There have been cases where these factors result in fatalities from MDMA (Nichols, 2004; Parrott, 2012; Turillazzi, Riezzo, Neri, Bello, & Fineschi, 2010).

FIGURE 11-8
Bruxism (teeth grinding) is an acute effect of MDMA (ecstasy). Users will suck on pacifiers at clubs to mitigate this effect of the drug.

Anticholinergic Hallucinogens

Atropine and scopolamine, either from a plant such as Jimson weed or as isolated drugs, are fairly uncommon as street drugs. The primary reason is that the effective dose tends to be only somewhat smaller than the lethal dose. Thus, it is very easy to accidentally administer a fatal dose. Even so, there are cases of intentional use or accidental poisonings (CDC, 1995, 2010a; Wiebe et al., 2008). When a low dose is administered, anticholinergic hallucinogens induce a variety of acute effects similar to those observed with serotonergic hallucinogens. Hallucinations, delirium, agitation, loss of motor control, and memory disturbances may occur. The sympathetic nervous system is activated, as evidenced by increased heart rate, increased blood pressure, dilated pupils, rapid respiration, and elevated body temperature. Users report a dreamy trance or stupor, and recollection of the drug experience is poor. If the dose is high enough, paralysis, convulsions, and death may occur. Given that anticholinergic hallucinogens are found in a wide variety of plants such as deadly nightshade, Jimson weed, moonflower, and angel's trumpet, there have been cases in which children and adults have consumed plant material and become extremely ill. Prompt intravenous administration of physostigmine can reverse the toxic effects of anticholinergic hallucinogens (DeFrates, Hoehns, Sakornbut, Glascock, & Tew, 2005; Hall et al., 1977). Interestingly, scopolamine at low doses is an effective antiemetic (antinausea) drug in the treatment of motion sickness. When used to treat motion sickness, scopolamine is typically administered using a transdermal patch that releases the drug slowly into the body through the skin (Renner, Oertel, & Kirch, 2005).

Dissociative Anesthetics

The acute effects of PCP and ketamine depend on the dose, with ketamine far less potent than PCP at comparable doses. At low and moderate doses, dream-like feelings occur with pleasant sensations such as floating, a trance, or separation from the body (an out of body experience). Dissociative anesthetics are used recreationally for these effects. Arms and legs may become numb and muscle coordination may be lost. At low doses, dissociative anesthetics impair basic cognitive processes such as attention, learning, and memory. Physiological changes at low doses include sympathetic nervous system activation. Slightly increased respiration and pronounced rises in blood pressure and heart rate are observed. The individual may appear flushed and be sweating. As the dose is increased, amnesia (no memory for the drug experience) will occur. Given that ketamine induces amnesia, is odorless, tasteless, and commonly found on the street, it is sometimes used as a date rape drug. Unsuspecting victims may be sexually assaulted after unknowingly consuming ketamine with a beverage. As ketamine is becoming more widespread as a club drug, patrons of such environments should never leave drinks unattended (NIDA, 2001, 2009).

At higher doses of dissociative anesthetics, hallucinations, anesthesia, amnesia, impaired motor functioning, psychosis, and depression can occur. Blood pressure and heart rate can drop, and potentially fatal respiratory problems can occur. Nausea, vomiting, and drooling may be apparent. Users may have odd muscle contractions that lead to bizarre postures. These muscle contractions can be so severe that bone fractures sometimes result. Bad trips may occur and be terrifying for users, such as a feeling of complete sensory detachment that is described as a near-death experience. Sometimes, users of ketamine refer to these bad trips as the "k-hole." Typically, PCP and ketamine users are brought to an emergency department when a bad trip has led to violent or suicidal behaviors. Treatment is typically supportive. The patient is placed in a quiet room with little sensory stimulation. Benzodiazepines (antianxiety medications) might be administered to control agitation and prevent seizures. While PCP was widely abused in the 1960s and 1970s, its use has since declined precipitously. Users became aware that the acute effects of PCP are especially unpredictable, even when compared to other hallucinogens. Thus, users moved to other illicit drugs when it became clear that bad trips were a likely outcome when using PCP (NIDA, 2001, 2009).

In medicine, ketamine is a preferred anesthetic when reliable ventilation equipment is not available, since respiratory suppression effects, while present, are less of a concern with ketamine than for other anesthetics. However, ketamine is not typically ideal as an anesthetic because of the hallucinations it induces. The duration of action for PCP and ketamine is up to 6 hours, depending on the route of administration. Oral administration of a dissociative anesthetic results in the longest duration of action, while injection, intranasal, or inhalation administration of these drugs greatly shortens the duration of action (NIDA, 2009). When death from overdose of PCP or ketamine has occurred, the cause is respiratory arrest (the person stops breathing). Coma, convulsions, and seizures may occur before the actual death. However, the primary cause of death from dissociative anesthetic use among recreational users is accidental injury or suicide, rather than a direct drug effect (DEA, 2013a; NIDA, 2009).

Kappa Opiate Hallucinogens

When the leaves of the salvia plant are chewed, users often keep the plant material in the cheek, which facilitates absorption through the oral mucosa. As a result, effects appear relatively quickly, within 5 or 10 minutes. When dried leaves are smoked, effects may be experienced in approximately 30 seconds and may last about 20–30 minutes. Users report various hallucinogenic experiences such as bright lights, vivid colors and shapes, and hallucinations of objects not present. Similar to other hallucinogens, out-of-body experiences or body distortions may occur with kappa opiate hallucinogens. Users may also experience dizziness, lack of coordination, and slurred speech (DEA, 2012d).

Research on the acute effects of kappa opiate hallucinogens such as salvia is limited. Studies examining the acute effects of inhaled salvinorin A (the active chemical in the salvia plant) have found subjects reporting enhanced feelings of a mystical-like experience. Other subjective effects similar to serotonergic hallucinogens (such as LSD) have also been reported. Subjects additionally report intense experiences such as pressure on the body, change in spatial orientation, revisiting of childhood memories, cartoon-like imagery, or contact with entities. The drug also interferes with memory. Unlike serotonergic hallucinogens, salvinorin A does not induce changes in heart rate and blood pressure, even though subjects may characterize subjective changes as being intense. There appears to be little concern about persisting effects (flashbacks) among subjects assessed a month after use (Johnson et al., 2011; Maclean, Johnson, Reissig, Prisinzano, & Griffiths, 2013).

Focus on Careers: Physicians

A patient who is hallucinating for some unknown reason can provide quite a challenge to a physician. Are the hallucinations drug-induced, or are they due to an underlying organic condition? Mental disorders such as schizophrenia can have hallucinations as a symptom. Developing blindness in an elderly patient can also result in hallucinations. Even if the physician can narrow down the source of hallucinations to a drug, the specific drug may be difficult to identify due to the patient's altered mental state leaving them extremely frightened or irrational (Woo & Hanley, 2013). In these cases, the physician will need to act like a detective by consulting poison control centers and specialized laboratories with expertise in horticulture, especially since many different drugs can induce hallucinations. Physicians who specialize in emergency medicine, neurology, and psychiatry are all likely to treat patients experiencing hallucinations.

There is no doubt that medicine is rewarding, which is why it is an appealing career to individuals who both love science and want to help people. So how does one become a physician? The process is lengthy and difficult. First, an individual must complete a 4-year BS or BA undergraduate degree program. A pre-med undergraduate degree is ideal but not necessary for admission to medical school. However, any candidate must complete several undergraduate introductory courses in biology, chemistry, physics, English, and calculus. An inevitably challenging organic chemistry class is required. In addition, the Medical College Admissions Test (MCAT) must be written, the standardized test for admission to medical school. Medical schools are highly selective in choosing applicants, looking for strong students who would also make compassionate doctors. For the lucky applicants who are admitted, medical school lasts 4 years. Upon completion of medical school, a residency is completed in a hospital setting so that physicians are highly trained in their chosen specialty (family medicine, pediatrics, psychiatry, and many others). The training period of 3 to 8 years in length is intensive, requires long hours, and pays relatively little. After residency is over, physicians write their board exams and are finally able to practice medicine! A handsome salary is a financial reward for the lengthy and demanding training. However, many physicians would argue that no dollar compensation amount can match the intellectual challenges of new medical cases and the reward of helping patients.

Some websites to explore:

American Medical Association's requirements for becoming a physician:
http://www.ama-assn.org/ama/pub/education-careers/becoming-physician.page
Medical College Admissions Test:
https://www.aamc.org/students/applying/mcat/

Chronic Effects of Hallucinogen Use

As mentioned earlier in this chapter, hallucinogen use tends to be most common among adolescents and young adults, with use rarely persisting beyond the later 20s (Chilcoat & Schutz, 1996). Hallucinogens are used far less consistently than other psychoactive drugs. For this reason, the chronic effects of hallucinogen use tend to be limited compared to other psychoactive drugs. However, a few concerns seem to be specific to frequent use of hallucinogens. Some concerns apply to all hallucinogens and others are specific to a particular hallucinogen such as MDMA (ecstasy). One serious concern for all hallucinogens is the experience of **flashbacks**, which are fragmentary recurrences of the drug experience even after the drug is no longer present in the body. A flashback typically involves a reexperiencing of one or more of the perceptual effects that were induced when the hallucinogenic drug was used previously. Visual symptoms such as seeing objects that are not physically present can persist for either a short time or for months. The timing of flashbacks is very unpredictable. However, stress may induce a flashback, and flashbacks are also more common in younger individuals. After users discontinue use of the drug, flashback episodes typically diminish in frequency and intensity over time (DEA, 2013a). Interestingly, there appears to be no clear relationship between the rate of flashbacks and prior frequency of hallucinogen use (Nichols, 2004). For a small subset of individuals, flashbacks can persist and induce impairment in social or occupational functioning. When this occurs, a diagnosis of **hallucinogen-induced persisting perceptual disorder (HPPD)** may be made. It is currently unclear how prevalent HPPD is in chronic users of hallucinogens. However, many clinicians would argue that HPPD is relatively rare. When HPPD does occur, there is little specific treatment except supportive psychotherapy and pharmacological treatment with antidepressants or antianxiety medications (Nichols, 2004; NIDA, 2001).

The chronic use of any type of hallucinogen is also problematic for individuals predisposed to develop various psychological disorders such as psychosis and depression. Recall that this was also a concern with marijuana use (Chapter 10). While individuals with a preexisting vulnerability to a mental disorder may eventually develop symptoms of the disorder, use of hallucinogens may hasten the onset of the disorder. However, among otherwise emotionally healthy individuals, use of hallucinogens may not cause long-term problems (Nichols, 2004). The concern is always whether an individual is aware of a preexisting vulnerability. A genetic history of schizophrenia or major depression in a family may be evident in some cases but not in others.

The chronic effects of MDMA (ecstasy) use tend to differ from other hallucinogens. The risk of persistent psychosis is relatively unlikely, as is a diagnosis of hallucinogen-induced persisting perceptual disorder (HPPD). However, other concerns emerge when MDMA is used repeatedly. Frequent MDMA use elevates the risk of cardiovascular problems, similar to repeated use of amphetamines. In addition, MDMA has immunosuppressive properties. For a frequent user, the body becomes less able to withstand illness over time as immunity becomes impaired (Boyle & Connor, 2010). Finally, frequent users may also experience brain damage. MDMA is neurotoxic, especially when administered repeatedly at high doses. The neurotoxicity seems to be selective to serotonin axon terminals (Gudelsky & Yamamoto, 2008). Deficient serotonin levels will lead to depression and sleep problems. Fortunately, abstinence from the drug may allow the brain to recover some functioning (Selvaraj et al., 2009). Though recovery is possible, one longitudinal study following MDMA users for several years after they became abstinent reported that memory was still impaired more than two years after abstinence (Thomasius et al., 2006).

When psychoactive drugs are used chronically, there is always the concern about addiction development. Addiction seems to be less of a problem with most hallucinogens than other psychoactive drugs, with the exception being the dissociative anesthetic, PCP. Regular use of PCP results in drug craving and withdrawal symptoms such as depression and memory loss. Withdrawal symptoms may persist for as long as one year after a chronic PCP user discontinues use (NIDA, 2001). Fortunately, use of PCP seems to have diminished over time. As mentioned, other hallucinogens tend not to cause such concerns regarding addiction. In fact, regular use of some hallucinogens may not lead to any chronic problems whatsoever. For example, peyote (mescaline) is used regularly by Native Americans in religious settings. Researchers examined the long-term residual psychological and cognitive impacts of peyote use. No evidence was found that the use of peyote, at least in a very specific religious context, caused any problems (Halpern, Sherwood, Hudson, Yurgelun-Todd, & Pope, 2005). However, most scientists would agree that research is deficient on this topic.

Myth Busters: LSD Stays in Your Body Forever

Hallucinogenic drugs have a mysterious equity perhaps because they induce some pronounced odd psychoactive effects. This may explain myths surrounding hallucinogens, some of which are also odd. One persistent and widespread myth is that LSD stays in the body forever. Another version frequently mentioned by students is that LSD is stored in the spinal fluid. If you crack your back, the story goes, you will release the LSD and cause a trip. I should note that at least one student every semester I teach this course has asked me about this myth. Let's address the question: can LSD remain in your body to be released at a later time, thus inducing hallucinogenic effects? The answer is no. This is clearly a myth. While it is true that some psychoactive drugs can be stored in the body (for example, THC in marijuana can be stored in body fat), LSD is not such a drug, nor for that matter are any other hallucinogens. LSD is a long-acting drug with a duration of action of up to 12 hours. However, LSD is also rapidly metabolized and eliminated from the body. A urine drug screen is only capable of detecting LSD or its metabolites for about 72 hours after use (Hawks & Chiang, 1986).

Given that this myth is so widely held, it is good to question the source of this myth. It is likely that the myth persists because users of LSD (or other hallucinogens) sometimes experience flashbacks. While flashbacks may feel like a repetition of a drug-induced experience, flashbacks may actually occur because of inappropriate memory retrieval. It's even possible that brain damage results in memories of the hallucinogenic experience feeling very real. In some cases, the flashbacks are frequent and distressing enough that a diagnosis of hallucinogen persisting perception disorder (HPPD) is warranted. Flashbacks, either mild or distressing, are not occurring because LSD is being released from various storage locations in the body. A similar psychological disorder, posttraumatic stress disorder (PTSD), also has flashbacks as symptoms. A soldier may reexperience the trauma of a war situation in flashbacks even after the soldier has returned home safely. In sum, vivid memories sometimes intrude upon daily experiences; retrieved hallucinogenic experiences are often examples of such vivid memories.

Tolerance, Dependence, and Withdrawal

Hallucinogens induce a variety of potent psychoactive effects. Tolerance can develop very rapidly when hallucinogens are administered repeatedly, such as seen in the daily administration of LSD to rats (Buckholtz, Freedman, & Middaugh, 1985; Buckholtz, Zhou, Freedman, & Potter, 1990). However, humans do not often administer hallucinogens so frequently, and tolerance development is less of a concern with intermittent use. For those who repeatedly take various hallucinogens, tolerance may develop. Progressively higher doses will be required to elicit the desired state of intoxication. If tolerance develops, cross-tolerance may also develop, especially among hallucinogens in the same class. For example, a user may develop tolerance to psilocybin mushrooms and simultaneously become tolerant to LSD, despite little or no use of LSD. However, tolerance does not cross over to unrelated psychoactive drugs having different underlying brain mechanisms, such as marijuana and PCP. When tolerance does occur, it appears to reverse rapidly with even a few days of abstinence (NIDA, 2001).

Though tolerance may develop with repeated use of hallucinogens, users do not report craving hallucinogens. Hallucinogens are not especially reinforcing (rewarding). This makes them dissimilar to other psychoactive drugs such as cocaine or heroin, which result in strong cravings after repeated use. As a result, compulsive drug-seeking behavior is not typically observed among hallucinogen users. One exception is phencyclidine (PCP) for which repeated use can induce craving and compulsive drug-seeking behavior, despite adverse consequences. For all hallucinogens, dependence is unlikely and long-term use is uncommon.

Despite evidence that frequent hallucinogen use can induce tolerance, there is little evidence of significant withdrawal symptoms when use ceases. While some users may self-report negative withdrawal symptoms upon cessation of MDMA (ecstasy), these symptoms appear relatively transient. Most typically, individuals will report symptoms such as feeling depressed, having difficulty sleeping, and experiencing pain. These withdrawal symptoms seem to be relatively minor, given that most individuals never seek treatment for them (Degenhardt et al., 2010a; McCann et al., 2011).

Pharmacology

Sites of Action and Pharmacokinetics for Serotonergic Hallucinogens

The serotonergic hallucinogens (LSD, psilocybin, and mescaline) stimulate serotonin (5-HT receptors), specifically the 5-HT$_{2A}$ receptors. While the precise mechanism by which serotonergic hallucinogens induce hallucinations is still unclear, serotonergic hallucinogens activate 5-HT$_{2A}$ receptors in the cerebral cortex and locus ceruleus. The cerebral cortex plays an important role in cognition, perception, and mood. Activation of 5-HT$_{2A}$ receptors is most pronounced in the frontal and temporal cortex. The locus ceruleus receives signals from all areas of the body and can be thought of as the body's novelty detector for external stimuli. The activation of 5-HT$_{2A}$ receptors also results in increased glutamate levels in the cerebral cortex of the brain (Nichols, 2004; NIDA, 2001). Rapid tolerance can be observed when serotonergic hallucinogens are used repeatedly. It appears that some of this tolerance development correlates with downregulation of 5-HT$_{2A}$ receptors. For example, studies of daily administration of LSD in rats have demonstrated that daily drug exposure selectively decreased the numbers of 5-HT$_{2A}$ receptors in the rat brain (Buckholtz et al., 1985, 1990).

Pharmacokinetics refers to the absorption, distribution, biotransformation, and excretion of drugs. Serotonergic hallucinogens such as LSD are absorbed within 60 minutes of oral administration. Peak blood levels may occur around 3 hours. The duration of action can range from 6 to 12 hours, depending on the type of serotonergic hallucinogen. LSD and mescaline have longer durations of action than psilocybin. Psilocybin mushrooms contain significant amounts of the chemical psilocybin and trace amounts of psilocin. Once in the body, psilocybin becomes unstable and converts to psilocin. Psilocin is 1.4 times more potent than psilocybin and is thought to be the source of the physical and psychological changes occurring in users. The liver acts to metabolize the serotonergic hallucinogen before it is excreted from the body in urine. However, LSD is difficult to detect in typical urine drug screening. A specialized ultrasensitive radioimmunoassay would need to be performed on the urine sample to verify the recent use of a serotonergic hallucinogen. Even so, such assays can typically detect use only within the last 24 hours (Nichols, 2004; Julien, 2005; Verstraete, 2004).

Sites of Action and Pharmacokinetics for Methylated Amphetamines

Methylated amphetamines like MDMA (ecstasy) act in a variety of ways similar to the action of both amphetamines and serotonergic hallucinogens. MDMA promotes the release of monoamines, including dopamine and serotonin (5-HT), in multiple brain regions. Thus, MDMA acts like other amphetamines by increasing the release of dopamine in areas of the brain such as the nucleus accumbens, striatum, and prefrontal cortex. MDMA also acts like serotonergic hallucinogens by elevating serotonin activity. In addition to MDMA stimulating the release of monoamines, MDMA also enhances the release of acetylcholine in the prefrontal cortex, hippocampus, and striatum. Finally, repeated administration of high doses of MDMA can result in selective neurotoxicity to serotonin (5-HT) axon terminals (Gudelsky & Yamamoto, 2008). The typical route of administration for MDMA is oral, and peak drug effects are experienced 1½ to 3 hours after swallowing the drug. The duration of drug action is typically 8 hours. Urine detection of MDMA is possible for 3 to 4 days (de la Torre et al., 2000; Verstraete, 2004).

Sites of Action and Pharmacokinetics for Anticholinergic Hallucinogens

The anticholinergic hallucinogens like atropine and scopolamine are antagonists at muscarinic acetylcholine receptors located in both the central and peripheral nervous system. When acetylcholine receptors are blocked, hallucinations, a dreamlike trance, and loss of motor control occur. The recreational use of atropine and scopolamine is limited because it is risky. While atropine induces hallucinations and altered consciousness, the effective dose is only slightly smaller than the lethal dose. In medicine, low doses of scopolamine are an effective treatment for nausea associated with motion sickness. The duration of action for atropine is approximately 3 to 4 hours, with scopolamine having a longer duration of action than atropine. While urine drug testing is useful for most psychoactive drugs, it is rarely conducted for anticholinergic hallucinogens. The urinary concentrations available to test for presence of atropine or scopolamine may be too low for detection, even in cases where an overdose has occurred (Renner et al., 2005).

Despite limited recreational and medical use of anticholinergic hallucinogens for safety reasons, atropine plays an important role as an antidote for nerve gas attacks. Exposure to deadly nerve gases (including cholinesterase inhibitors such as sarin) leads to death when these gases inhibit the breakdown of acetylcholine. As a result, too much acetylcholine will be available in synapses. If a victim of sarin exposure is quickly administered atropine, atropine blocks acetylcholine receptors and counteracts the effect of the nerve gas. Military personnel on the front lines are issued atropine injectors since nerve gas attacks are more likely in such environments. Interestingly, scopolamine has been found to be slightly less effective as an antidote to a nerve gas attack. Researchers have discovered that atropine has anticholinergic properties but also antiglutamatergic properties. Scopolamine only has anticholinergic properties. When counteracting nerve gas, an antidote having both anticholinergic and antiglutamatergic properties appears most effective. While atropine is used most widely, newer similar drugs such as benactyzine and caramiphen have also been found to be effective as nerve gas antidotes (Weissman & Raveh, 2008).

Sites of Action and Pharmacokinetics for Dissociative Anesthetics

The dissociative anesthetics like PCP and ketamine act as NMDA receptor antagonists. The NMDA receptor is a type of glutamate receptor important for the perception of pain, emotions, responses to the environment, learning, and memory. Blockage of the NMDA receptor accounts for anesthetic and analgesic properties of dissociative anesthetics. In addition, PCP increases dopamine activity by blocking dopamine reuptake, which elevates dopamine levels in synapses. Elevated dopamine activity is responsible for the euphoria associated with many abused drugs and provides some explanation why frequent PCP use leads to addiction, more than any other hallucinogenic drug. Ketamine is structurally similar to PCP but 10 to 50 times less potent in antagonizing NMDA receptors (NIDA, 2001, 2009).

PCP and ketamine may be administered via various routes of administration. Peak effects for PCP are experienced within 15 minutes if smoked and within 2 hours after oral administration. The duration of action for PCP may typically be up to 6 hours, but a return to normal may not occur for about 24 hours. The duration of action is much shorter for ketamine, up to 2 hours after oral administration and only up to 45 minutes if injected. Urine detection of PCP can occur for about a week following a high dose, whereas ketamine can only be detected in urine for about 3 days (Clements, Nimo, & Grant, 1982).

Sites of Action and Pharmacokinetics for Kappa Opiate Hallucinogens

Salvinorin A is the psychoactive ingredient in the salvia plant that induces hallucinogenic effects. Salvinorin A is a kappa opiate receptor antagonist. The various opiate receptors were covered in greater detail in Chapter 9. Drugs that are agonists of kappa receptors tend not to be very addictive and have a modest analgesic action. Kappa agonists also induce a strong dysphoric (depressive) response. Salvinorin A blocks the action of kappa receptors and thus may be responsible for some mood elevating effects of salvia. Why salvinorin A induces hallucinations remains unclear. Researchers have confirmed that the hallucinogenic effects of salvia use are not mediated by the 5-HT_{2A} receptor, the target of other hallucinogens such as LSD. The duration of action for salvinorin A ranges from 20 minutes to 1 hour, with oral ingestion resulting in a longer duration than smoking. Given that salvia is a new drug that is not controlled, there is no reliable urine drug test to identify recent use of salvia (Cunningham et al., 2011).

More about the Science:

> Killinger et al. (2010). Salvinorin A fails to substitute for the discriminative stimulus effects of LSD or ketamine in Sprague-Dawley rats. *Pharmacology, Biochemistry and Behavior, 96,* 260–265.

Use of salvia as a hallucinogen has only recently become a trend in the United States. As a result, the drug is not regulated under the Controlled Substances Act. Salvinorin A is the active chemical in salvia that induces hallucinations. Salvinorin A is chemically and structurally unique, as it is a highly potent and selective kappa opiate receptor agonist. However, researchers and physicians have wondered if salvinorin A is similar in acute effects to other controlled hallucinogens such as LSD or ketamine. One way to address that question is to conduct a **drug discrimination study** using animals. Drug discrimination studies are widely used in psychopharmacology research. In this type of study protocol, drugs serve as discriminative stimuli to indicate how reinforcers (rewards) are obtained. Animals are trained to use interoceptive (internal) cues of a training drug (such as LSD) as the cue for performing a specific operant response (such as pressing a lever to get a food reward). A rat is injected with the drug (or placebo) and then placed in an operant chamber with bars that can potentially provide food rewards. Over several training sessions, the rat is taught the relationship between the internal drug-induced feeling state and the lever that should be pressed to receive the food reward. For example, the rat may be taught that pressing the left lever will result in a food reward if no drug was given and pressing the right lever will result in a food reward if LSD was given (Solinas, Panlilio, Justinova, Yasar, & Goldberg, 2006). After training, the rat is then tested. The rat receives a test drug (generalization test) to determine which lever the rat will press.

In this study, 8 rats were trained initially to discriminate between 2 drug stimuli (exposure to LSD versus placebo), and 8 were trained to discriminate ketamine versus placebo. The researchers only proceeded to the test day once the rats were clearly responding to the drug-associated lever when given LSD (or ketamine) and responding to the placebo-associated lever when given saline (no drug). On the generalization test day, all trained rats were administered salvinorin A. The researchers recorded which lever the rat pressed. The question in this study was whether the rat perceived salvinorin A to be like LSD or ketamine. The rats did not respond either to the LSD or ketamine associated lever when given salvinorin A. Given these observations, the researchers inferred that salvinorin A does not "feel like" LSD or ketamine. The rat does not think to press the trained drug-associated lever to get the food reward after receiving salvinorin A.

More about the Science Thought Questions:

1. The results of this study suggest that the acute effects of salvinorin A are perceived as being different from the acute effects of LSD or ketamine to rats, even though all of these drugs are considered hallucinogens. Is this surprising, given the known mechanisms of action of these drugs?
2. What other drugs given on the generalization test might result in high levels of lever pressing, assuming the rat has been trained to associate lever-pressing with LSD?

More about the Science Thought Question Answers:

1. These results are not surprising given that salvinorin A, LSD, and ketamine all have differing mechanisms of action. Salivorin A is a kappa opiate agonist. LSD is classified as a serotonergic hallucinogen because it activates serotonin (5-HT$_{2A}$) receptors. Ketamine is a dissociative anesthetic and acts as an NMDA receptor antagonist. Therefore, the mechanisms of actions of these three drugs are all different, even though they are all hallucinogens.
2. Psilocybin and mescaline might also result in a pronounced response on the drug-associated lever. LSD, psilocybin, and mescaline may lead to similar effects given that they are all serotonergic hallucinogens.

Treatment

Few patients seek treatment for problems with frequent use of hallucinogens. While patients in drug treatment programs use hallucinogens, it is uncommon for an individual to seek treatment just to stop using hallucinogens. Users do not report craving hallucinogens, even those who have become tolerant to the drug and have escalated their dose over time. Hallucinogens are typically not reinforcing (rewarding), and compulsive drug-seeking behavior is not typically observed among hallucinogen users. Dependence is unlikely and long-term use is uncommon. There is little evidence that significant withdrawal is present when use of hallucinogens ceases (Chilcoat & Schutz, 1996; Nichols, 2004; NIDA, 2009). Treatment may be sought where hallucinogen persisting perception disorder (HPPD) has developed and frequent flashbacks are distressing. In those cases, psychological therapy to help manage stress, and pharmacological therapy with antidepressants and/or antianxiety medications may be warranted. Finally, hallucinogens do not hold a prominent place currently in medical treatment. However, recent small studies suggest that MDMA may be helpful in the treatment of PTSD (see the In the News feature earlier in this chapter). Likewise, researchers have found that ketamine rapidly improves depressive symptoms in patients experiencing treatment-resistant major depression (Diazgranados et al., 2010; Ibrahim et al., 2011). With time, it will be interesting to see if scientists discover other medical uses for hallucinogens.

QUICK QUIZ 11-2

1. A user of a hallucinogenic drug may report seeing music or hearing colors. What is this phenomenon called?
   a. Flashback
   b. Bad trip
   c. Synesthesia
   d. Hallucinogen-induced persisting perceptual disorder (HPPD)

2. Which hallucinogen is the least likely to produce pronounced visual hallucinations?
   a. MDMA (ecstasy)
   b. LSD
   c. Psilocybin
   d. Mescaline

3. Which of the following is true about hallucinogens?
   a. Tolerance can develop rapidly with repeated use.
   b. Frequent users report craving hallucinogens.
   c. A significant withdrawal syndrome occurs when frequent use ceases.
   d. All of the above

4. Serotonergic hallucinogens activate _____ receptors, whereas salvinorin A is a _____ antagonist.
   a. 5-HT_{2A}, NMDA
   b. 5-HT_{2A}, kappa opiate
   c. NMDA, kappa opiate
   d. NMDA, 5-HT_{2A}
   e. NMDA, mu opiate

5. Blockage of the NMDA receptor accounts for anesthetic and analgesic properties of _____.
   a. serotonergic hallucinogens
   b. methylated amphetamines
   c. anticholinergic hallucinogens
   d. dssociative anesthetics
   e. kappa opiate hallucinogens

6. You are a soldier who is stationed in the Middle East. Which drug might you carry in case of a deadly nerve gas attack?
   a. LSD
   b. MDMA
   c. Mescaline
   d. Ketamine
   e. Atropine

7. Frequent use of MDMA (ecstasy) elevates the risk of developing several health problems. List three such problems.

8. Are anticholinergic hallucinogens widely used in society today? Explain your answer in reference to the effective and lethal doses of anticholinergic hallucinogens.

9. Are frequent hallucinogen users likely to seek treatment for their drug use? Explain your answer.

ANSWERS TO QUICK QUIZ 11-2:

1. c – synesthesia
2. a – MDMA (ecstasy)
3. a – tolerance can develop rapidly with repeated use
4. b – 5-HT_{2A}, kappa opiate
5. d – dissociative anesthetics
6. e – atropine
7. Frequent use of MDMA can result in cardiovascular problems, suppression of immune system functioning, and brain damage.
8. Anticholinergic hallucinogens such as atropine and scopolamine are not widely used. One primary reason is that the effective dose tends to be only somewhat smaller than the lethal dose. It is very easy to accidentally administer too high of a dose that results in a fatality. This makes anticholinergic hallucinogens very risky.
9. Frequent users of hallucinogens are very unlikely to seek treatment for their drug use. Users do not report craving hallucinogens when they stop use. Compulsive drug-seeking behavior is not typically observed among hallucinogen users. Dependence is unlikely and long-term use is uncommon. There is little evidence of a significant withdrawal syndrome. All of these factors contribute to a low probability that a frequent user of hallucinogens will need treatment.

CHAPTER SUMMARY

Hallucinogens are psychoactive drugs that alter one's perceptions, mood, and cognitive processes, sometimes in profound ways. Sensory experiences without relevant external stimuli are hallmarks of these drugs. There are five classes of hallucinogens, each having a different mechanism of action. The five classes are serotonergic hallucinogens, methylated amphetamines, anticholinergic hallucinogens, dissociative anesthetics, and kappa opiate hallucinogens. Human use of hallucinogens predates recorded history, since many hallucinogens (psilocybin, mescaline, ibogaine) are found in a variety of plants. Some synthetic hallucinogens (LSD, MDMA) have only been available for less than one hundred years. Today, use of hallucinogens is less common than use of other illicit psychoactive drugs. Hallucinogens are largely used by adolescents and young adults, with use rarely persisting into adulthood. The acute effects of hallucinogens can be unpredictable, and nonpharmacological factors (setting, expectation) can be incredibly important in the drug experience. Highly adverse reactions, such as frightening visual hallucinations or paranoia, are referred to by users as bad trips. Chronic users of hallucinogens can experience some long-term consequences of hallucinogen use including flashbacks, hallucinogen-induced persisting perceptual disorder (HPPD), and development of psychosis or depression (among vulnerable individuals). Frequent use of hallucinogens may also result in tolerance development. However, users will not typically report craving, compulsive drug-seeking, or a withdrawal syndrome upon cessation of use. For these reasons, hallucinogen users rarely seek treatment. In conclusion, hallucinogens are poorly understood compared to other psychoactive drugs, in part because there are so many hallucinogens and the research on most types is limited.

ANTIPSYCHOTIC DRUGS

Introduction

Elyn Saks by all accounts has had an illustrious career (Figure 12-1). A graduate of Yale Law School, she currently serves as a professor at the prestigious Gould School of Law at the University of Southern California. She is known for her work as a legal scholar and a mental health policy advocate. She has played a major role in society's effort to deal with complicated mental health issues such as the right to refuse treatment, involuntary commitment, and competency to be executed. She is not only professionally successful but also happily married. For these reasons, she surprised many colleagues and friends when she revealed her lifelong

©Damian Dovarganes/AP

FIGURE 12-1
Elyn Saks is a legal scholar and mental health-policy advocate. Her 2007 memoir, *The Center Cannot Hold: My Journey through Madness*, describes her lifelong struggle with schizophrenia, including severe episodes of psychosis. Her life is an illustration of how patients who are provided with therapy, medication, and support can live highly successful lives.

struggle with schizophrenia in her memoir called *The Center Cannot Hold: My Journey through Madness*. Published in 2007, her memoir quickly became a national bestseller because her life story is fascinating. Her first symptoms of schizophrenia emerged when she was only 8 years old. While in law school, her first psychiatric hospital admission occurred after a full-blown psychotic episode in which she experienced both delusions and hallucinations. Over the years, her debilitating illness included many severe episodes of psychosis leading to several misguided or harmful treatment experiences. Despite the perception that schizophrenia carries a grim prognosis, Saks makes clear there is no reason this needs to be so. Though doctors told her that she would never live independently, hold a job, find a loving partner, or get married, all of these good things have happened for her. Doctors informed her that her work life would consist of menial part-time jobs manageable when symptoms were quiet. Her career is nothing of the sort! Her memoir is profound and hopeful. Her memoir is also realistic in acknowledging that her medical condition is chronic, and she will need treatment (medication and psychological therapy) and support for the rest of her life. There is no doubt that the discovery of antipsychotic drugs has been instrumental in helping people like Saks live productive, healthy, and happy lives (Saks, 2007, 2013).

LEARNING OBJECTIVES

Learning objectives can help organize your studying. Before we begin the topic of antipsychotic drugs, keep in mind that by the end of this chapter, you should be able to . . .

1. Describe the various kinds of antipsychotic drugs.
2. Explain the brief history of antipsychotic drugs and how long they have been available for therapeutic use.
3. Describe the various medical conditions that might result in psychosis and how prevalent these conditions are in society.
4. Explain the acute effects of antipsychotic drugs, including how they act in the central nervous system.
5. Explain the chronic effects of antipsychotic drugs.
6. Describe how tolerance and withdrawal might impact treatment regimens using antipsychotic drugs.
7. Describe how psychosis is treated.
8. Describe how new psychotherapeutic drugs are developed using the FDA process.

Psychosis

The brain is wonderful when it works properly. However, sometimes the brain does not work as it should. Throughout this book, we have focused on how psychoactive drugs alter brain functioning in relatively healthy individuals. In this chapter and the next, we shift our focus to psychoactive drugs used to help return a brain to normal when it is experiencing dysfunction due to a mental disorder. A **mental disorder** is defined in the *DSM-IV-TR* as a clinically significant behavioral or psychological syndrome or pattern. Key features of a mental disorder include distress, disability or impaired functioning, violation of social norms, and dysfunction (APA, 2000). Mental illness can range from mild concerns to a devastating disconnect with reality. In this chapter, we will focus on the therapeutic psychoactive drug treatment of serious mental disorders that have psychosis as a symptom.

Psychosis is a loss of contact with reality, typically characterized by delusions and hallucinations. **Delusions** are false beliefs about what is taking place or who one is. An example of a delusion might be that an individual feels like the FBI is following him or her everywhere. As long as the person has not committed a serious crime, such thoughts probably have no basis in reality. However, this false belief could evoke considerable paranoia, fear, suspicion, and anxiety. The person may fear leaving his or her home due to this delusion. Such behavior could prevent that person from being able to attend school or work. Moreover, social isolation may lead to increasing loss of contact with reality. **Hallucinations** are false perceptions (such as seeing or hearing things not actually present). Hallucinations might include hearing voices talking to you even though there is no one else in the room. Like delusions, hallucinations can evoke fear and anxiety. In addition to delusions and hallucinations, a psychotic individual might exhibit disorganized thoughts and speech. While we may all feel a bit scattered in our thinking at times, disordered thinking in psychosis is significantly more disorganized. Thoughts jump between unrelated topics and a logical conversation cannot occur. All of these symptoms (delusions, hallucination, and thought disorder) are serious. Loss of contact with reality causes people to stop caring for themselves or otherwise function normally. In extreme cases, escalating psychotic symptoms can result in the patient harming himself or someone else. In such cases, medical treatment is necessary to help the individual resume normal functioning within society (Freudenreich, Weiss, & Goff, 2008; Kring et al., 2012).

There are a variety of underlying causes of psychosis, although something is amiss with the brain in all cases. Psychosis may be drug-induced, either during use or during withdrawal. The hallucinogenic drugs (described in Chapter 11) will induce delusions and hallucinations to varying degrees. High doses of stimulant drugs such as cocaine and amphetamines will also induce psychotic symptoms, referred to as stimulant psychosis (described in Chapters 6 and 7). In most of these cases, symptoms abate when the drug is eliminated from the body, leading to no further harm. Likewise, drug withdrawal can also lead to psychosis. Individuals who are chronic alcohol drinkers may experience psychosis when ceasing use of alcohol. Symptoms of delirium tremens include hallucinations, delusions, and tremors (described in Chapter 8). Several organic mental disorders also share psychosis as a symptom. **Schizophrenia** is a serious mental disorder characterized by disturbance in thought, emotion, and behavior. Psychosis is central to the diagnosis of schizophrenia (Freudenreich et al., 2008; Kring et al., 2012).

Other mental disorders less commonly have psychosis as a symptom. These include mood disorders (major depressive disorder and bipolar disorder) and some personality disorders. Mood disorders are typically thought of as persistent states of extreme sadness (**major depressive disorder**) or general disturbances of emotion including both extreme sadness and mania, which is extreme elation and irritability (**bipolar disorder**). While these disorders are typically treated with other psychotherapeutic drugs including antidepressants and mood stabilizers (described in the next chapter), sometimes psychosis emerges as a symptom. For example, postpartum depression sometimes emerges within days or up to 4 weeks after a mother gives birth. In extreme cases, psychosis may be a symptom that develops along with extreme sadness. Dramatic changes in hormone levels, among other factors, are part of the reason that new mothers may be more at risk at developing psychotic symptoms. Psychosis is also a problem more common in old age. Psychosis may emerge after a surgical procedure, stroke, brain tumor, or progression of dementia (such as Alzheimer's disease). Psychosis can occur with various other neurological problems including HIV-AIDS, epilepsy, Parkinson's disease, and Huntington's disease. When psychosis emerges for whatever reason, whether the primary disorder or not, antipsychotic drugs can be extremely helpful in getting the symptoms under control (Doucet, Jones, Letourneau, Dennis, & Blackmore, 2011; Freudenreich et al., 2008; Kring et al., 2012).

Finally, it should be noted that there are several medical conditions not having psychosis as a core symptom that are nevertheless frequently treated with antipsychotic drugs. In pediatric patients, antipsychotic drugs are used to lessen symptoms from autism. **Autism spectrum disorder** is a disorder beginning in childhood that includes deficits in social communication and social interactions, repetitive and restricted behaviors, and speech deficits, which sometimes can be severe. Children with this disorder rarely initiate social contact with others and may not look at (or even turn their backs on) other children or adults who are trying to communicate with them. These children can become extremely upset over small changes in their typical daily routine or surroundings. Stereotyped motor behaviors and harmful behaviors such as self-mutilation and aggression can be very problematic. For example, a child may bang his or her head repeatedly, which is clearly very dangerous. Antipsychotic drugs are used to decrease problem behaviors such as aggression in pediatric populations (Dove et al., 2012; Kuehn, 2009). However, antipsychotic drugs are largely used to treat severe symptoms, and there is no one drug treatment that has been effective at reducing most of the symptoms of autism spectrum disorder. In sum, there are a wide variety of medical conditions where antipsychotic drugs may be applicable and helpful (Freudenreich et al., 2008; Kring et al., 2012).

Types of Antipsychotic Drugs

Antipsychotic drugs are psychotherapeutic drugs that can be used to reduce psychotic symptoms. These drugs can be incredibly effective for patients who have lost contact with reality. Antipsychotic drugs reduce hallucinations and delusions and improve thinking and behavior. All antipsychotic drugs antagonize dopamine D_2 receptors in order to control psychotic symptoms. The **dopamine hypothesis of schizophrenia** posits that excess dopamine release and/or excess sensitivity of dopamine neurons causes the psychotic symptoms (also called positive symptoms) of schizophrenia. Antipsychotic drugs act in various ways to decrease dopamine levels in the brain. Antipsychotic drugs also have other uses. They are used to treat bipolar disorder and severe major depression. They are used to decrease aggressive and self-injurious behavior in children with autism. There are various antipsychotic drugs that are available to patients experiencing psychosis. While effective in the treatment of psychosis, antipsychotic drugs are far from a panacea. Each of the available drugs can have short- and long-term side effects (Figure 12-2). Some long-term side effects can be serious enough that they resemble symptoms of neurological diseases (Freudenreich et al., 2008; Kring et al., 2012). For clarification, **psychotherapeutic drugs (psychotropic drugs)** are psychoactive drugs designed to improve mood state and mental functioning. Psychotropic drug is a term that can be used interchangeably with psychotherapeutic drug. There are four classes of psychotherapeutic drugs: antipsychotics, antidepressants, antianxiety drugs, and mood-stabilizing

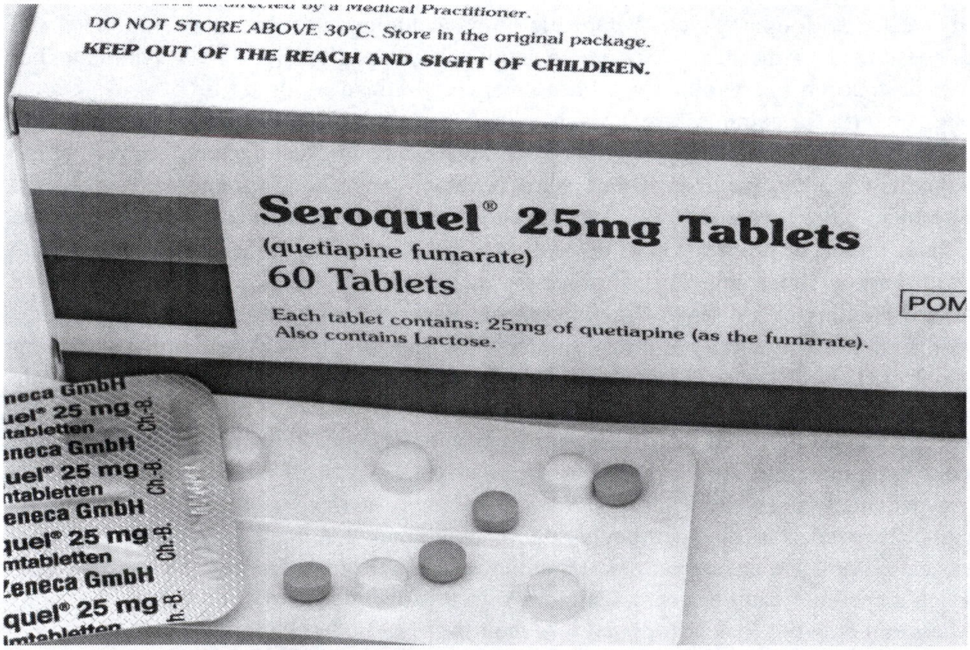

FIGURE 12-2 Antipsychotic drugs reduce psychotic symptoms but can also have serious long-term side effects.

drugs. Antipsychotic drugs will be discussed in this chapter and the remaining three classes will be discussed in the next chapter. Antipsychotics and **neuroleptics** refer to the same drug class, with the former being the preferred term in North America and the latter being preferred in Europe.

Antipsychotic drugs account for a large portion of the entire prescription drug market in the United States. The fifth best-selling prescription drug for the entire prescription drug market is Abilify® (aripiprazole) and the sixth best-selling prescription drug is Seroquel® (quetiapine), both of which are antipsychotic drugs. In 2011, antipsychotic drugs of all kinds were prescribed to 3.1 million Americans at a cost of $18.2 billion. Moreover, the antipsychotic drug market is growing, with 2011 sales reflecting a 13% increase over the previous year (Friedman, 2012). Even though there are many antipsychotic drugs available and several recent additions to the market, most of these psychiatric drugs are subtle variations of drugs that have been available since the 1950s. Sometimes these updated versions have more favorable side-effect profiles. For example, the antipsychotic drug clozapine was developed in the 1960s. In rare cases, clozapine could result in dangerously low white blood cell counts. Pharmaceutical companies worked to develop drugs that acted like clozapine yet did not lower white blood cell counts. Although some new drugs were successful in mitigating issues with clozapine, other side effects arose with these newer versions. Substantial weight gain or serious metabolic problems emerged in place of the risk of lower white blood cell counts. Nevertheless, researchers argue that despite the many available antipsychotic drugs, newer and better drugs are still needed (Sanders, 2013).

Traditional (Typical) Antipsychotics

Starting in the 1950s, **traditional (typical) antipsychotic drugs** were the first drugs available to reduce the symptoms of psychosis (Table 12-1). Chlorpromazine was the first traditional antipsychotic. That drug revolutionized the treatment of patients experiencing mental illness,

Table 12-1 Antipsychotic medications.

Class	Generic Name	Trade Name
Traditional (typical) antipsychotics	Chlorpromazine	Thorazine
	Fluphenazine	Prolixin
	Haloperidol	Haldol
	Mesoridazine	Serentil
	Perphenazine	Trilafon
	Pimozide	Orap
	Prochlorperazine	Compazine
	Promazine	Prazine
	Trifluoperazine	Stelazine
	Trifluopromazine	Psyquil
	Thioridazine	Mellaril
Second-generation (atypical) antipsychotics	Amisulpride	Solian
	Clozapine	Clozaril
	Loxapine	Loxitane
	Molindone	Moban
	Olanzapine	Zyprexa
	Paliperidone	Invega
	Quetiapine	Seroquel
	Risperidone	Risperdal
	Sertindole	Serlect
	Thiothixene	Navane
	Ziprasidone	Zeldox
Third-generation antipsychotics	Aripiprazole	Abilify

allowing them to function and leave a psychiatric hospital. Treatment with a traditional antipsychotic drug reduces delusions, hallucinations, and other symptoms of schizophrenia. Traditional antipsychotics block dopamine receptors, as they are dopamine antagonists. This action in the limbic system is thought to reduce psychotic symptoms. A traditional antipsychotic drug (such as pimozide) may also be used to control symptoms of **Tourette syndrome**. The medication will decrease the frequency of uncontrolled movements (motor tics) or vocal outbursts (vocal tics). However, while traditional antipsychotic drugs are effective at blocking dopamine receptors, this action can lead to undesirable side effects. Some of these side effects include motor problems that are permanent; they do not abate even after drug treatment has ceased. In light of the serious side effects, the action of blocking dopamine was almost too effective with traditional antipsychotics, and other approaches have been found to be more favorable. Even so, traditional antipsychotic drugs are still used, especially in cases of short duration treatment (Chakos, Mayerhoff, Loebel, Alvir, & Lieberman, 1992; Julien, 2005; Mailman & Murthy, 2010).

Second-Generation (Atypical) Antipsychotics

Second-generation (atypical) antipsychotic drugs are in several respects similar to the traditional (typical) antipsychotic drugs. The difference in second-generation (atypical) antipsychotic drugs is that the dopamine-blocking action is less potent and is balanced by other actions on serotonin receptors. Antagonism of dopamine receptors reduces psychotic symptoms. Antagonism of serotonin receptors relieves other symptoms of schizophrenia such as blunted affect, impaired emotional responsiveness, apathy, loss of motivation, and social withdrawal. Until recently, experts believed that development of motor and other side effects may be less likely with second-generation antipsychotics, because the dopamine blockage is less efficient (Friedman, 2012; Julien, 2005; Mailman & Murthy, 2010). Very large clinical trials, such as the Clinical Antipsychotic Trials for Intervention Effectiveness (CATIE), have failed to show that the second-generation antipsychotics were any more effective or better tolerated by patients than older first-generation antipsychotics (Jayaram, Rattehalli, & Adams, 2012; Stroup et al., 2007; Swartz et al., 2007). However, these conclusions remain controversial. Prescribing patterns indicate that second-generation antipsychotics are more likely to be prescribed than older (and cheaper) first-generation antipsychotic drugs (Friedman, 2012; Koranek, Smith, Mican, & Rascati, 2012). It is interesting to speculate how much habit or advertising plays a role in these prescribing patterns; clear data to address this question is absent from the literature. Currently, second-generation antipsychotic drugs are also frequently chosen in treating pediatric patients, with their use having grown tenfold in recent years. Risperidone is the most widely used antipsychotic drug for children and adolescents (Curtis et al., 2005).

Third-Generation Antipsychotics

Third-generation antipsychotic drugs include the new drug Abilify® (aripiprazole) and a few others under development. Instead of simply antagonizing dopamine receptors, third-generation antipsychotic drugs exert a stabilizing influence on dopamine receptors, referred to as functional selectivity. In this way, third-generation antipsychotics may exert different effects at a single receptor by acting as a full agonist at one pathway and an antagonist at a second pathway. Abilify® (aripiprazole) is also used in combination with an antidepressant drug in patients who are not experiencing relief from depression with the antidepressant drug alone (Mailman & Murthy, 2010).

Brief History of Antipsychotic Drugs

Our modern understanding of mental illness and its appropriate treatment is a relatively new phenomenon. Historically, hearing voices or experiencing delusions was thought to be caused by evil spirits or the devil. This possession could only be treated with **exorcism**. The ritualistic casting out of evil spirits included prayers, noisemaking, and barbaric acts including flogging and starvation, were thought to render the body uninhabitable by the devil. Over time, the persecution of individuals experiencing psychosis diminished, but care did not improve. The first **asylum** (a hospital where people with mental illness would be confined and cared for) was the Priory of St. Mary of Bethlehem, founded in 1243. In 1403, records indicate that six men with mental illness were housed there, which suggests that it was not a large place. In 1547, Henry VIII gave the hospital over to the city of London so that it could be devoted to the confinement of the mentally ill. The word *bedlam* has its origin in the state of those found at Bethlehem. Conditions were deplorable and chaotic. Patients were chained to walls in rooms that were dungeons, given horrible food, and generally poorly cared for. The patients were seen as animals rather than humans. Perhaps most sad is that the asylum served as a tourist attraction until the 19th century; visitors viewed the patients for entertainment. Vienna had a similar asylum with windows for tourists, named the Lunatics Tower. Physicians treated patients in these asylums, but they did so with unscientific and sometimes inhumane methods. Bloodletting was frequently used, as it was thought that excess blood caused mental illness. Hot irons, flogging, revolving chairs, and other odd approaches were employed in hopes of cleansing the patient of maladies (Kring et al., 2012).

Dr. Phillipe Pinel (d. 1826) is thought to be a key historical figure advocating for the mentally ill (Figure 12-3). At a large asylum for insane women in Paris (La Bicetre), he was the physician in charge during the French Revolution. Pinel is regarded as the first physician to view patients as sick and not as beasts to be chained and controlled. It is claimed that Pinel unchained the patients at La Bicetre and allowed them access to the outdoors. Historical evidence does dispute whether Pinel was actually responsible for unchaining the patients. Jean-Baptiste Pussin, a former patient who became an orderly in the asylum, may have done so. Regardless of whose idea it was to unchain the patients, Pinel received the credit and was in favor of the changes. He became an advocate of this radical new approach to treating patients experiencing psychosis and other symptoms of mental illness. Following Pinel's infrastructure changes at La Bicetre, some of the patients responded so well that they were able to be discharged after years of incarceration. While

FIGURE 12-3
Dr. Phillipe Pinel freeing the patients from chains at the Paris Asylum for insane women. This point in history is considered to be a transition point when treatment of mental illness became more humane. Painting by Robert Fleury (1795).

Pinel was clearly a reformer, his views of compassion rather than incarceration were largely reserved for his affluent patients. For poor patients, little progress was made in treatment, with straightjackets replacing chains (Kring et al., 2012).

For a time, asylums adopted Pinel's more humanitarian approach to treatment, which became known as moral treatment. Asylums also increased in size and number. Patients experiencing psychosis and other mental disorders were increasingly housed permanently in these facilities. The first U.S. public psychiatric hospital, Publick Hospital, was opened in 1773 in Williamsburg, Virginia. Given the lack of specific medications to treat the mentally ill, it was unsurprising that asylums slowly slipped back into their previous brutal methods by the late 1800s. In the United States, a Boston schoolteacher named Dorothea Dix (d. 1887) became another crusader for improved treatment of patients in asylums. She helped see that state hospitals were built to treat all those suffering from symptoms of mental illness. Unfortunately, these hospitals eventually become overcrowded and understaffed. Physicians who worked in these hospitals were trying various treatments to help their patients. In the 1840s, marijuana (cannabis) was systematically investigated as a treatment for depressed and manic patients. In the early 1900s, amphetamines were given to depressed patients. Electroshock therapy was developed around this time and is still used in cases of severe depression unresponsive to drug treatment. Lithium was discovered in 1949 as a possible treatment for bipolar disorder, but interestingly was not approved until much later (Kring et al., 2012; Talbott, 2004).

The turning point in the history of treating psychosis was the discovery of **chlorpromazine**, the first antipsychotic drug. Chlorpromazine was synthesized in 1951 by Paul Charpentier in France and became available for prescription in 1952. It was initially used as an anesthetic, and its first use was in general surgery. The drug was given before surgery and was found to decrease the patient's anxiety and prevent shock during the actual surgery itself. The calming effect of chlorpromazine was soon thought to be useful for patients experiencing mental illness. At the Val-de-Grace military hospital in Paris, psychotic patients were given chlorpromazine. When the drug took effect, the patients became calm and their thoughts appeared less disorganized. Importantly, the patients did not lose consciousness but rather seemed detached and disinterested in their surroundings. Straightjackets could be removed and the noise level in the patient areas diminished. With chlorpromazine, psychiatry was instantly revolutionized. Chlorpromazine was clearly more effective in treating psychosis than previously used drugs such as morphine scopolamine combinations. Psychiatrists on the front lines with patients viewed chlorpromazine as a miracle drug. Not surprisingly, within three years the use of chlorpromazine spread rapidly to the rest of Europe, the United States, and then worldwide (Ban, 2007).

Chlorpromazine led to a dramatic reduction in the number of patients experiencing psychosis requiring hospitalization. In the United States, the population in psychiatric hospitals peaked at 560,000 patients in 1955 (Stroup & Manderscheid, 1988). Chlorpromazine was introduced in 1955, and the number of psychiatric inpatients subsequently dropped dramatically. Today, there are only about 150,000 hospitalized psychiatric patients, despite a substantially larger U.S. population. Shortly after chlorpromazine became available, other antipsychotic drugs were used, such as clozapine and haloperidol (as well as other psychiatric medications including antidepressant and antianxiety drugs). All of these new psychotherapeutic drugs contributed to the deinstitutionalization trend. This historical change in how society cares for the mentally ill is largely favorable. When patients are taking antipsychotic drugs, they are more functional and can return to society rather than live long term or even permanently in a mental hospital. However, the number of psychiatric beds has declined so much recently that patients needing a brief inpatient stay are sometimes unable to access appropriate care. Moreover, people experiencing psychosis (or other mental illness) may also find themselves without medication or medical care for a variety of reasons, including lack of health insurance, and may slip into dire circumstances including homelessness. Many mental health advocates argue that there are great deficiencies in community outpatient mental health

Myth Busters: People Who Are Psychotic Are Also Dangerous and Violent

It is common for people to think that those experiencing symptoms of psychosis are dangerous and violent. This is largely a myth. The incidence of violence in people with schizophrenia or another medical condition is not much higher than in the general population. In most cases, individuals experiencing symptoms of psychosis are frightened and confused, and thus unlikely to become violent. However, there is a small subset of patients with schizophrenia who do become violent. In those cases, the diagnosis also typically includes a comorbid disorder associated with violence. **Conduct disorder** is often diagnosed in childhood when a pattern of extreme disobedience is observed including theft, vandalism, lying, and early drug use. Childhood conduct problems predict adult violence. Individuals who are suffering from both schizophrenia and conduct disorder are the most likely to exhibit aggressive behavior. This suggests that childhood conduct problems and violence are linked, with or without schizophrenia present. Comorbid substance abuse with schizophrenia is also associated with an increased likelihood of violence (Swanson et al., 2008).

When an individual is psychotic as a result of drug abuse, the risk of violence may be higher. Earlier in this book, **stimulant psychosis** was discussed (see Chapters 6 and 7). Stimulant psychosis arises after high doses of cocaine or amphetamines are ingested. Similar to the symptoms of schizophrenia, stimulant psychosis causes individuals to become paranoid and experience other psychotic symptoms such as delusions and hallucinations. One key difference between drug-induced stimulant psychosis and organically based schizophrenia is that stimulant psychosis is much more likely to be associated with hostility and violence. The escalation in violence with stimulant psychosis may be partly due to heightened sympathetic nervous system activity (also referred to as the fight-or-flight response). The influence of the drug elevates heart rate and blood pressure and readies the person to run away or fight. This highly aroused state is more conducive to aggression. Beyond differences in violence, other hallucinations such as crank bugs (formication syndrome) are rarely observed in schizophrenia, indicating that psychosis that is drug-induced can be extremely different than psychosis with an underlying cause that is organic. When psychosis has an organic basis, the risk of violence is no different than that would be observed in the whole population.

care, transitional housing, and vocational training programs needed by patients during transition times. Despite problems accompanying the deinstitutionalization movement, antipsychotic drugs are the primary treatment today for patients experiencing psychosis (Ban, 2007; Blader, 2011; Talbott, 2004).

Currently, there are many psychotherapeutic drugs available to treat mental illness. In the United States alone, there were $25 billion in sales of psychiatric medications in 2011. U.S. pharmacies filled about 55 million prescriptions for antipsychotic drugs in 2011. Despite advances in drug development, some scientists argue that no new drug designed to treat psychiatric illness in a novel way has reached patients in more than three decades. Antipsychotic drugs are not a panacea for treating schizophrenia. Some serious symptoms of schizophrenia are not addressed by antipsychotic drugs. Moreover, these medications sometimes have serious side effects that can be so objectionable that patients will cease using the medications and slip back into a psychotic state. In addition, antipsychotic drugs are now much more widely used than ever before. Some uses are less controversial, such as psychosis associated with dementia in elderly patients. In other cases, the use of antipsychotic drugs remains highly controversial, such as the use of these drugs by children with autism. While history suggests that we have made dramatic progress in understanding and treating serious mental illness, still more progress is needed in the future (Sanders, 2013).

Epidemiology of Psychosis

The main target population for antipsychotic drugs is patients suffering from schizophrenia. Schizophrenia is a serious mental disorder affecting approximately 1% of individuals over a lifetime. There are approximately 2.4 million Americans who suffer from chronic schizophrenia. Men are slightly more likely to suffer from schizophrenia than women. In 2011, antipsychotic drugs of all kinds were prescribed to 3.1 million Americans. While a large portion of these prescriptions were related to schizophrenia, antipsychotic drugs are also sometimes used in patients with other disorders, such as bipolar disorder. The lifetime prevalence of bipolar disorder is 1.5% (Friedman, 2012). Pediatric patients are becoming increasingly likely to receive prescriptions for antipsychotic drugs, especially for autism. Autism spectrum disorder affects about 1 of every 88 children when assessed at 8 years of age. Males are four times more likely than girls to have autism spectrum disorder (CDC, 2009). In the past three decades, diagnoses have increased dramatically. One study from California noted that diagnoses for autism increased 300% during a 25-year time period (Maugh, 2002).

In the News:

Brodie, L. (2013, February 27). Cramer smells opportunity in biopharma. *CNBC*.

Jim Cramer is a fast-talking and humorous television personality who hosts CNBC's *Mad Money*. In his television show, Cramer attempts to identify stock investment opportunities for his viewers. In this article, Cramer mentions several pharmaceutical companies he thinks are currently a "buy, buy, buy." One company, Alkermes, has made its mark developing long-lasting formulations of existing drugs. For example, Risperdal Consta® is a long-acting antipsychotic drug (risperidone) administered via injection in a doctor's office every 2 weeks. Thus far, patients seem to do well with this medication compared to others requiring daily oral medication. Alkermes is working on a new extended-release version of Abilify® that would also be injectable (Figure 12-4). If this new version of Abilify® makes it to the market, patients would only need to receive an injection once a month in the doctor's office, instead of taking pills every day. The company would receive two decades of patent protection for developing this new injectable version of a previously existing drug. The article mentions that these drugs are used to treat people with severe mental illnesses like schizophrenia.

Use this news article to test and apply your knowledge:

1. Considering the symptoms of schizophrenia, what might be one advantage of using injections that are needed less frequently than daily oral administration of pills?
2. The article mentions that these antipsychotic drugs are used in the treatment of schizophrenia. List two other disorders for which these medications might be useful.

Answers:

1. Symptoms of schizophrenia include delusions, hallucinations, and thought disorder. These symptoms may make it difficult for patients to be compliant on a daily basis with taking antipsychotic medications. The thought disorder may make planning to take medication every day at a certain time challenging, especially for those patients who do not have a great deal of social support. A bimonthly or monthly injection could potentially make medication compliance easier for some patients.
2. Antipsychotic drugs are also used in the treatment of bipolar disorder and autism.

What do you think about this news story?

Shortly after this article was published, the FDA approved Abilify Maintena®, the once-monthly injection version of Abilify® (Edney, 2013). In 2012, sales of Abilify® were $2.8 billion, but the patent expires in 2015. Do you think the extra cost of an injectable version of Abilify® will be a beneficial switch compared to a daily dose of the same medication in a cheaper generic form?

Important note to the reader:

Stocks are highly volatile and views about whether a stock is a good buy are subjective and may vary even in the course of one day. This article is used purely as a means for you to test and apply your knowledge and should not be viewed as an investment recommendation. Critics of Jim Cramer would say that his record on correctly predicting buying opportunities for stocks is spotty at best! If you are interested in investing in the pharmaceutical industry, talk to an investment professional about the pros and cons of doing so. The main message of this portion of the chapter is that the development of new psychiatric medications does not occur in a vacuum. Rather, companies develop these new drugs because they are in the business of making money.

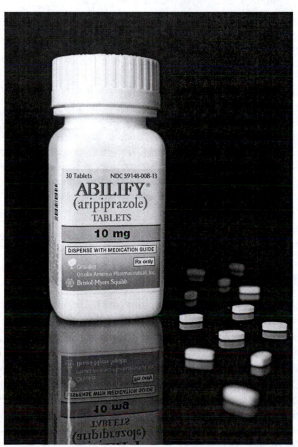

© Bloomberg/Getty Images

FIGURE 12-4

On March 1, 2013, the FDA approved a long-acting injection version of the antipsychotic drug Abilify®. Patients would receive a monthly injection to control symptoms, instead of taking oral medication daily.

QUICK QUIZ 12-1

1. What is the lifetime prevalence of schizophrenia?
   a. 0.1%
   b. 1%
   c. 5%
   d. 10%

2. How many prescriptions for antipsychotic drugs were filled by U.S. pharmacies in 2011?
   a. 55,000
   b. 550,000
   c. 5,500,000
   d. 55,000,000
   e. 550,000,000

3. The primary mechanism by which all antipsychotic drugs control symptoms of psychosis is by antagonizing _____.
   a. dopamine receptors
   b. serotonin receptors
   c. acetylcholine receptors
   d. glutamate receptors

4. _____ are false perceptions and _____ are false beliefs.
   a. Delusions, hallucinations
   b. Delusions, thought disorders
   c. Hallucinations, thought disorders
   d. Thought disorders, delusions
   e. Hallucinations, delusions

5. Which antipsychotic drug is most likely to be prescribed for children and adolescents?
   a. Risperidone
   b. Clozapine
   c. Olanzapine
   d. Chlorpromazine
   e. Haloperidol

6. When was the first antipsychotic drug discovered? Was this drug developed initially to treat psychosis?

7. What has been the trend in the number of inpatients in psychiatric hospitals in the United States over the last century?

8. Currently, physicians are more likely to prescribe second-generation antipsychotics instead of first-generation antipsychotics. Why does this occur? Does the scientific evidence support the view that second-generation antipsychotics are superior to first-generation antipsychotics?

ANSWERS TO QUICK QUIZ 12-1:

1. b – 1%
2. d – 55,000,000
3. a – dopamine receptors
4. e – hallucinations, delusions
5. a – risperidone
6. Chlorpromazine was discovered in 1951. It was not developed initially to treat psychosis. It was developed as an anesthetic in surgery.
7. The population in psychiatric hospitals was increasing until 1951, when chlorpromazine was introduced. After, the number of inpatients declined precipitously (even as the general U.S. population was increasing).
8. The prevailing wisdom among physicians who prescribe second-generation antipsychotics is that there are reduced side effects with these drugs. However, recent large clinical trials have revealed that there appears to be little difference in effectiveness or side effects for either antipsychotic drug class. Both types control symptoms, and both may lead to serious side effects.

Acute Effects of Antipsychotic Drugs

Patients experiencing psychosis may have symptoms such as delusions and hallucinations. They may be agitated and experience other concerns such as confused thinking (thought disorder) and difficulty sleeping. Antipsychotic drugs decrease the problematic symptoms of psychosis in serious mental disorders such as schizophrenia. Antipsychotic drugs act relatively quickly compared to other psychotherapeutic drugs for the treatment of mental illness. Within a few days of drug treatment, a patient may start to feel better and experience decreased psychotic symptoms. A rapid response is more likely if the medication was an appropriate choice and administered at an appropriate dose. By contrast, a slower response is typical of psychotherapeutic drugs such as SSRI antidepressants (discussed in the next chapter). SSRIs may only start to become effective after several weeks of treatment (Baldessarini & Tarazi, 2001).

Once the antipsychotic drug has taken effect (after several days of treatment), the patient may report that various distressing symptoms such as hearing voices and paranoid thoughts are slowing dissipating. Patients may appear a little drowsy and slow to respond. Motor activity is diminished. However, the patient will find himself or herself able to answer questions and think clearly. Agitation diminishes and the patient may be less withdrawn. Aggression and impulsive behavior (if present) may also decrease. Among individuals who take antipsychotic drugs to treat autism, the medication may lead to increased communication and more responsiveness. Self-injurious behaviors and other evidence of agitation may decline (Baldessarini & Tarazi, 2001).

In addition to the acute effect of controlling psychotic symptoms, antipsychotic drugs have various other effects on the body. Antipsychotic drugs decrease the release of stress hormones such as corticotrophin-releasing hormone (CRH), coinciding with the calming effect experienced by patients. Clinical doses of antipsychotic drugs do not appear to alter respiration. However, slight decreases in blood pressure (hypotension) may occur, with decreases being more evident in systolic blood pressure readings than diastolic blood pressure. Tolerance develops to the hypotensive effects of antipsychotic drugs. After a few weeks of treatment, blood pressure may return to normal levels. Antipsychotic drugs decrease gastric secretion and motility. Patients may complain of constipation. Decreased sweating and salivation may be reported, as well as impaired sexual functioning. Even early in treatment, neurological side effects may be visible such as motor rigidity, shuffling gait, tremors, and restlessness. Finally, each antipsychotic drug may have particular side effects that can in some cases be quite serious. For example, agranulocytosis is a rare but serious complication of clozapine treatment. When agranulocytosis occurs, the bone marrow stops producing white blood cells, leading to very serious infections. Patients maintained on clozapine need to have regular blood work to test for agranulocytosis. If left unchecked, agranulocytosis can result in death. Another serious side effect of clozapine is inflammation of the heart lining (myocarditis), which can also be fatal if not detected by regular monitoring of heart functioning (Baldessarini & Tarazi, 2001).

Antipsychotic drugs are also powerful mood-stabilizing drugs (in addition to decreasing psychotic symptoms). They are therefore also used in treatment of bipolar disorder and severe major depression. Suicide is always a concern with mood disorders. Antipsychotic drugs, even when taken in large quantities in a suicide attempt, will not lead to a life-threatening coma or suppression of vital functions such as breathing or heart rate (Baldessarini & Tarazi, 2001).

The choice of antipsychotic drug for any individual clinical case is complex. Clinicians often must try several kinds of drugs at different doses before a patient is stabilized. In addition, the many possible side effects warrant constant vigilance. In certain cases, side effects may be innocuous or even beneficial. For example, some antipsychotics (such as chlorpromazine) have the pronounced side effect of increasing sedation, while others are less likely to result in this concern. In a highly agitated patient, the sedative quality of some antipsychotics may help the patient get some rest (Baldessarini & Tarazi, 2001; Friedman, 2012).

Chronic Effects of Antipsychotic Drugs

Schizophrenia is a chronic disorder likely requiring antipsychotic drug treatment for a lifetime. There are several chronic effects that emerge from very long-term use of antipsychotic drugs. Chronic antipsychotic drug treatment can alter metabolism and lead to weight gain. Weight gain is also a function of the sedative action of antipsychotic drugs. If a person feels sedated and a bit sleepy, lower activity levels may contribute to weight gain. In pediatric patients treated with antipsychotic drugs, rapid weight gain is a common side effect of drug treatment that can lead to other significant health problems (Dove et al., 2012; Sharma & Shaw, 2012). Interestingly, while weight gain is often observed in humans, other animals treated with antipsychotics often experience weight loss. Researchers believe that metabolic differences between humans and other animals explain these observations. It is also possible that weight loss in animals occurs because antipsychotics are sedating, which decreases the amount of active feeding time (Bardgett et al., 2013; Correll et al., 2009).

Patients maintained on traditional antipsychotics may eventually develop serious and permanent motor problems resembling the symptoms of Parkinson's disease. Tremors, rigidity, muscle spasms, and problems with gait and balance emerge (and don't cease even after drug treatment is stopped). The person may shuffle when they walk. Their face may appear mask-like, and they may drool because of excessive salivation. In addition, patients may exhibit **tardive dyskinesia**, which is characterized by involuntary movements of the mouth, tongue, trunk, arms, and legs. Tardive dyskinesia is most likely to develop when antipsychotic drugs have been used for two years or longer, although there are infrequent cases where only a few months of treatment can induce symptoms. Tardive dyskinesia is more likely to be observed in female than male patients. These motor problems stem from reduced dopamine activity in the extrapyramidal tract (the region of the brain outside of the pyramidal tracts that originate in the basal ganglia). This area of the brain is important for movement initiation, smoothing out movements, and stopping movements. Up to half of patients maintained on antipsychotic drugs develop motor problems to varying degrees (Baldessarini & Tarazi, 2001; Chakos et al., 1992).

Since antipsychotic drugs are dopamine antagonists, some endocrine changes occur related to dopamine activity. Most antipsychotic drugs increase the secretion of prolactin, although this effect will vary depending on the type of antipsychotic drug. When prolactin is chronically elevated, male patients may develop breasts and female patients may experience engorged breasts. Antipsychotic drugs also inhibit the release of growth hormone, which can be an issue for pediatric patients being treated with these drugs (Baldessarini & Tarazi, 2001).

Women who are pregnant or breast-feeding may require treatment with antipsychotic drugs. Postpartum psychosis is one condition where the health of the mother and her infant depend on getting psychotic symptoms under control. However, antipsychotic drug treatment in women who are pregnant or nursing is not without concern. Animal studies have demonstrated long-term behavioral effects of antipsychotic drug exposure in utero or through breast milk. Hyperactivity, impaired impulse control, and greater behavioral sensitivity to dopamine agonist and antagonist drugs have all been reported in adult animals that have early exposure to antipsychotic drugs. There is also an elevated risk of birth defects in women who used antipsychotic drugs during pregnancy (Cuomo et al., 1981, 1983; Scalzo & Spear, 1985; Shalaby & Spear, 1980).

Tolerance and Withdrawal

Tolerance develops with repeated use of antipsychotic drugs. A patient that previously had good symptom control may start to experience symptoms of delusions and hallucinations. When these symptoms occur, the clinician may raise the dose or switch the patient to another antipsychotic drug. Given that schizophrenia is a chronic condition that probably requires lifetime treatment with medication, tolerance development is an ongoing concern. If a patient abruptly ceases using medication, some withdrawal symptoms may emerge. Difficulty sleeping and malaise are commonly reported, which may indicate that some physical dependence on the drug has developed. Note, however, that antipsychotic drugs are not addictive. Patients do not crave them if they no longer have access to them (Baldessarini & Tarazi, 2001).

Pharmacology

Sites of Action

When chlorpromazine was introduced in 1952, the mechanism of action by which the drug decreased psychotic symptoms was unclear. By the 1960s, scientists had determined that the mechanism of action of chlorpromazine was the blocking of dopamine receptors. Psychosis results from an excessive level of dopamine in certain regions of the brain, especially the basal ganglia and limbic areas of the forebrain. All antipsychotic drugs decrease levels of dopamine activity, although different types of antipsychotic drug do so to varying degrees. The traditional antipsychotic drugs (such as chlorpromazine) act as high-affinity dopamine D_2 receptor antagonists. This means that these drugs are extremely effective at blocking dopamine activity in the brain. However, this effectiveness, while helpful in reducing psychotic symptoms, will also result in potent and sometimes permanent side effects when these drugs are used chronically (Baldessarini & Tarazi, 2001; Julien, 2005; Mailman & Murthy, 2010).

The second-generation (atypical) antipsychotic drugs (such as clozapine, olanzapine, and risperidone) also act as D_2 receptor antagonists. However, the dopamine-blocking agent is less potent in second-generation antipsychotics than the traditional antipsychotic drugs. Further, dopamine-blocking in second-generation antipsychotics is also balanced by other actions on serotonin receptors. As mentioned, the action of blocking dopamine receptors reduces psychotic symptoms. The antagonism of serotonin receptors relieves some of the other negative symptoms of schizophrenia such as flattened affect. The likelihood of motor and other side effects may be reduced with second-generation antipsychotics, as compared to the traditional antipsychotics, because the dopamine blockage is less efficient. Studies have been conducted to determine the ideal D_2 receptor occupancy levels to decrease psychotic symptoms while minimizing the likelihood of side effects such as motor problems. It appears that D_2 receptor occupancy levels should be below 80% to make the drug most effective, while also reducing the risk of extrapyramidal side effects (Sakurai et al., 2013).

Finally, the new third-generation antipsychotic drugs (aripiprazole and other drugs in development) act differently than simply antagonizing dopamine receptors. They exert a stabilizing action on dopamine receptors, which is referred to as **functional selectivity**. Instead of acting as a dopamine receptor antagonist only, these drugs may exert different effects through a single receptor. These drugs may act as a full agonist at one pathway in the brain and act as an antagonist at a second pathway (Julien, 2005; Mailman & Murthy, 2010).

Currently, second-generation antipsychotic drugs are frequently chosen in the treatment of pediatric patients. Their use has grown tenfold in recent years. Risperidone is the most widely used antipsychotic drug for children and adolescents, with aripiprazole and quetiapine also being used. While use of antipsychotics may be necessary for a child whose brain is developing, there is always a concern about the implications of drug exposure during development. It appears that chronic administration of antipsychotic drugs decreases dopamine activity, which results in changes to dopamine receptor density. In essence, the brain compensates for deficient dopamine levels by making more dopamine receptors. Increases in forebrain dopamine receptor density are much more likely during antipsychotic drug treatment that occurs while the brain is still developing (Curtis et al., 2005; Moran-Gates, Grady, Shik Park, Baldessarini, & Tarazi, 2007). The specific implications of these increased numbers of dopamine receptors in the forebrain of an adult need to be determined in future studies. It is also unknown how readily these changes might be reversed once drug treatment ceases.

Pharmacokinetics

When compared with other psychoactive drugs, antipsychotics are surprisingly unpredictable in patterns of absorption. The oral route of administration is most common, as these medications are administered in pill form, although long-acting injections have recently become available. Peak serum levels for most antipsychotics are obtained within 2 to 4 hours of drug administration. Once in the body, antipsychotics accumulate in the brain, lung, and other tissues that have a good blood supply. These drugs also cross the placenta and are transmitted through breast milk. As such, antipsychotic drug treatment is typically limited to extreme cases of psychosis in pregnant or nursing women (Baldessarini & Tarazi, 2001).

The typical duration of action of these drugs is at least 24 hours. Thus, a daily dose is typical for a patient not experiencing considerable side effects. Drug metabolism by the liver is very slow for antipsychotics. Half of the amount ingested is typically eliminated within 20 to 40 hours. Urine detection of antipsychotic drugs occurs months after the last dose, although this test is rarely performed since antipsychotics are almost never abused. The developing fetus, the infant, and the elderly have diminished capacity to metabolize and eliminate antipsychotic drugs. Careful dose selection should occur with these age groups. Children may metabolize antipsychotics slightly faster than adults (Baldessarini & Tarazi, 2001)

More about the Science:

Bardgett et al. (2013). Adult rats treated with risperidone during development are hyperactive. *Experimental and Clinical Psychopharmacology, 21, 259–267.*

Antipsychotic drugs have been used in pediatric patients for the treatment of various disorders including autism spectrum disorder and bipolar disorder. There has been a dramatic escalation in the use of antipsychotic drugs by children in the past two decades. In the United States, nearly 20% of antipsychotic drug users are children ages 18 and younger (Curtis et al., 2005; Domino & Swartz, 2008). Researchers have questioned the implications of treating a developing brain with powerful drugs that have many known serious side effects. Fortunately, animal studies can provide efficient answers to the long-term effects of pediatric antipsychotic drug administration on brain development. In this study, researchers assigned juvenile rats to various drug conditions (1 mg/kg risperidone, 3 mg/kg risperidone, or vehicle/placebo) (Figure 12-5). The rats were administered these doses daily from postnatal days 14 to 42, which is considered analogous to early childhood through early adolescence in humans. The risperidone-treated rats had lower body weight than vehicle rats during the active drug treatment. However, body weight differences were no longer significant by postnatal day 45, when all rats were no longer being treated with the drug. After drug treatment was complete, the adult rats were tested repeatedly from postnatal day 49 to 365 by measuring locomotor activity for 20 minutes on each test day. Only 4 weeks of daily early-life risperidone treatment resulted in hyperactivity that persisted well into adulthood. Such hyperactivity lasted as long as 6 months after the cessation of treatment.

More about the Science Thought Questions:

1. Why might the researchers report body weight in the rats?
2. What might be the underlying cause of the observed elevated hyperactivity in adulthood?

More about the Science Thought Question Answers:

1. Antipsychotic drugs have various side effects including weight gain or weight loss. Activity levels may be related to weight. For example, a fat rat may move around a lot less than a thinner rat. It would be important to rule out whether body weight was a factor in the observed long-term hyperactivity.
2. Antipsychotic drug treatment decreases dopamine activity. Continuous suppression of dopamine activity could result in an upregulation in the number of dopamine receptors in the brain (a rebound effect). Once the rats are adults, dopamine activity may be high in their brains due to a large number of dopamine receptors. Elevated dopamine activity is associated with hyperactivity.

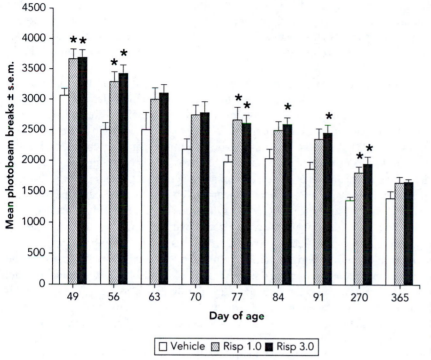

FIGURE 12-5
When juvenile rats are treated with the antipsychotic drug risperidone, they grow up to be hyperactive adults. Locomotor activity was measured in adult rats for 20 minutes at various ages. * indicates change from vehicle.

Treatment for Psychosis

Symptoms of psychosis emerge for a variety of medical reasons. Treatment can only be initiated once a proper diagnosis has been made. Typically, a diagnosis relies on a psychiatric evaluation and various other forms of testing. A psychiatric interview involves a clinician interviewing a patient and asking about symptoms. In a patient out of touch with reality, great clinical skill is needed to acquire as much background information as can be reasonably obtained given the patient's condition. In addition, laboratory testing might include urine or blood drug screens to determine if psychosis was drug-induced or related to drug withdrawal. Current or recent use of hallucinogens, cocaine, amphetamines, marijuana, or alcohol might contribute to psychotic symptoms. If psychosis was caused by drug use, treatment may be limited, since psychotic symptoms may abate as the drug of abuse is metabolized out of the body. Other blood tests may also be used to determine if hormone levels and electrolyte levels are normal, with such tests also ruling out syphilis or other infections that can also induce psychosis. Depending on the results of other diagnostic tests, an MRI scan of the brain may determine if a stroke, brain tumor, or other neurological problem is leading to psychotic symptoms (Freudenreich et al., 2008; Kring et al., 2012).

Once a proper diagnosis has been made, the treatment plan will depend on the cause of the psychosis. Interestingly, antipsychotic medications are not specific to the type of psychosis being treated. The same drug may be appropriate for a patient suffering from schizophrenia, autism spectrum disorder, postpartum psychosis, or bipolar disorder. Thus, choice of medication is largely by trial and error. However, other aspects of treatment may be tailored to the patient's symptoms. Inpatient hospital care is typically warranted until the patient has stabilized or appears not to be a danger to others and the patient himself. Once a patient has been stabilized on antipsychotic medication and symptoms of psychosis have abated, the patient may return home. For many patients, a supportive living environment may be needed. That environment may be provided by family members. Alternatives such as group homes and halfway houses are also possibilities. Given the chronic nature of many psychotic disorders, social and vocational rehabilitation may be ongoing. Higher-functioning patients will benefit from psychological treatment with a therapist. Almost all patients will be under the care of a psychiatrist on a permanent basis, given that administration of antipsychotic drugs will be ongoing (Baldessarini & Tarazi, 2001; Kring et al., 2012; Talbott, 2004).

The prognosis for an individual experiencing psychosis largely depends on the cause of the psychosis. A correctable cause (recent drug use, infection, or hormone imbalance) has the best prognosis and may not even require therapeutic treatment with antipsychotic drugs. If drugs are required, treatment may be quite brief. Chronic conditions may require long-term or even lifelong antipsychotic drug treatment. Schizophrenia is a chronic condition requiring constant effort to keep psychotic symptoms under control. Moreover, clinicians need to be highly vigilant in assessing for various side effects, some of which can result in permanent complications. Tardive dyskinesia and other motor problems are always a concern given that development of symptoms resembling Parkinson's disease is very serious. When symptoms of motor problems emerge, the clinician may reduce the dose of the drug. However, the clinician must also remain cognizant of keeping the drug at levels sufficient to keep psychotic symptoms at bay. Drug holidays can also provide some relief, by allowing the body to take a break from the drug. Drug holidays can be risky and must be closely monitored to prevent the resumption of a full-blown psychotic episode. There are also a few medications to treat side-effect symptoms (such as benztropine and trihexyphenidyl). In addition to the development of side effects, patients will sometimes become tolerant to their medication. When tolerance develops, symptoms of psychosis return. When this occurs, the prescribing physician will typically increase the dose as long as side effects remain tolerable or switch the patient to another antipsychotic drug (Stroup et al., 2007).

While many view the prognosis of schizophrenia as a grim development, this does not have to be the case. While the onset of the disorder is often debilitating, some individuals will end up prospering with appropriate treatment (as illustrated by the life story of Elyn Saks at the opening of this chapter). Like all mental disorders, different cases of schizophrenia can have different onsets, courses, and outcomes. Dementia and senile neurodegenerative disorders are likely to result in increasing psychosis over time. Development of drug tolerance or side effects will typically require constant monitoring by the health practitioner. Changing the antipsychotic drug or altering dose levels help minimize some of the long-term problems that emerge with chronic antipsychotic drug treatment regimens (Freudenreich et al., 2008; Kring et al., 2012; Talbott, 2004). Antipsychotic drug treatment helps patients in a variety of ways. Limiting psychotic symptoms is only one part of the benefit. Once patients are stabilized, they tend to achieve a better quality of life and improved psychosocial functioning in the community. All antipsychotic drugs seem to be similar in achieving this improved patient well-being. Moreover, patients who show gains in psychosocial functioning with antipsychotic medications tend to be those patients most impaired at the outset. Even so, medication should not be the only approach in improving functioning. Intensive rehabilitative intervention and constant outreach are needed to ensure that medications are taken as directed and the patient does well in a community setting (Swartz et al., 2007).

Finally, a brief mention about medication cost should be made. Some patients respond extremely well to some of the newer antipsychotic drugs that are still under patent. These newer drugs, while effective, are prohibitively expensive. This is a serious concern for a patient struggling to maintain their mental health in order to keep their employment and health insurance (Figure 12-6). Given that large studies have not conclusively found that certain antipsychotic drugs are more effective than others in treating schizophrenia, many patients could potentially do just as well using the generic versions of traditional first-generation antipsychotic drugs. Interestingly, 90% of antipsychotic prescriptions in the United States are written for second-generation antipsychotics. On average, patients spend at least 30% more on medication if they are maintained on a second-generation drug, even though symptom relief and side effects may not be much different between the first- and second-generation classes of antipsychotics (Rosenheck et al., 2006).

©Ghislain & Marie David de Lossy/cultura/Corbis

FIGURE 12-6
Family members are instrumental in the treatment of schizophrenia and other psychotic disorders.

Development of New Psychotherapeutic Drugs

Clinical Trials and FDA Approval

Psychosis remains difficult to treat with existing medications. Better psychotherapeutic drugs to treat mental illness are clearly needed. This section of the chapter discusses the process by which new psychotherapeutic drugs reach consumers. In general, it is fair to assert that drug discovery is a tough and slow business. Despite huge advances in science, it remains challenging to find novel compounds that have therapeutic potential. When a promising compound is identified, there are still many hurdles to overcome before that drug ever reaches a patient. As mentioned earlier in this chapter, most of the antipsychotic drugs currently available on the market are modifications of chlorpromazine, the first antipsychotic drug available since the 1950s. While it is possible to synthesize a brand-new drug that has an entirely novel mechanism of action, most of the time pharmaceutical companies will be recombining known compounds or trying to use an existing drug for a new purpose. In rare cases there are breakthroughs or novel approaches. For example, ibogaine was described in the last chapter as a plant used in religious ceremonies by native people living in West Africa. Scientists have been interested in ibogaine's potential to treat alcohol or opiate dependence. Ibogaine, while promising, has yet to pass all of the rigorous steps required for it to reach patients (Alper et al., 2008; Strubelt & Maas, 2008).

The following steps are required to get a drug from bench to bedside (Table 12-2). First, scientists must identify a drug that might be therapeutically useful. Bench work is needed to identify the new chemical compound and how it might act in the body. If the drug looks promising after bench work has been completed, preclinical studies are conducted. In these studies, animals are given the drug to determine drug effects and to establish safety parameters. Two species of animal must be tested before a drug reaches a human subject. Ideally, one of the species should be an animal model of the disease in question. If the scientists are examining a new antidepressant, it would be ideal to test this new drug on a special strain of depressed mice to see if they act less depressed while taking the drug. If the results of the animal studies from

Table 12-2 U.S. Food and Drug Administration (FDA) process of moving a drug from bench to bedside.

Stage	Description
Initial drug synthesis	Identifying a drug that might have clinical value and preliminary laboratory testing
Preclinical studies	Testing drug on at least two species of animals; Apply for Investigational New Drug (IND) label from FDA
Phase 1 clinical trials	Establish safety of drug using up to 50 healthy normal volunteers
Phase 2 clinical trials	Determine if drug is effective to treat medical condition using 50–200 patients with target disease
Phase 3 clinical trials	Determine if drug is effect to treat medical condition using 1,000 or more patients with target disease using more lax selection criteria; used to establish appropriate doses and labeling requirements
FDA review and approval	New Drug Application (NDA) submitted to FDA
Postmarketing testing	Once drug is being used by consumers, researchers evaluate the effectiveness of the drug and any unforeseen side effects

both species are promising, the pharmaceutical company or drug developer will contact the U.S. Food and Drug Administration (FDA) to request that the label **Investigational New Drug (IND)** be applied to the drug. If the FDA agrees to the labeling, clinical trials can begin (Walters, 1992).

Clinical trials are experiments designed to determine drug effectiveness in human subjects. There are three phases to the clinical trials process. In Phase 1, healthy human volunteers without the disease are recruited ($n = 50$). The goal in Phase 1 is to determine that the drug does not induce adverse effects in a small sample of healthy individuals. In Phase 2, individuals with the target disease (such as schizophrenia) are recruited ($n = 50$ to 200). The goal in these closely controlled clinical trials is to see if the drug is effective. If the drug is being used to decrease psychotic symptoms, the patients should experience these benefits. Note that Phase 2 involves tightly controlled subject recruitment. Only individuals who have the target disease and few other problems would be recruited. If Phase 2 is successful, Phase 3 commences. Phase 3 is used to determine if a broad sample of patients with the disease experience symptom remission with the drug. Phase 3 involves a much larger sample ($n = 1,000$ or more) than Phase 2. Consistent with the larger sample size, Phase 3 subject selection criteria are intentionally less stringent. In other words, patients with schizophrenia who also have other medical problems would be recruited. An obese patient or one with diabetes may not be allowed to participate in Phase 2 but would be included in Phase 3. One objective of Phase 3 is to determine if there are subsets of patients who experience adverse events while taking the new drug. For example, patients with schizophrenia who also have diabetes may have adverse side effects not experienced by patients without diabetes (Walters, 1992).

The FDA monitors all three phases of clinical trials closely. If the drug has been promising throughout, the pharmaceutical company or drug developer will file a **New Drug Application (NDA)** with the FDA. This application is extensive and compiles all that is known about the drug from both preclinical and clinical testing. The FDA will respond to this application within 6 months. If the FDA determines that the drug seems safe and effective, the drug is approved. With FDA approval, the drug can be marketed and sold both in the United States and around the world. If the FDA denies the NDA, the pharmaceutical company can go back and collect more data or resolve concerns with the drug and later submit another NDA (Walters, 1992).

The testing and approval process for a new drug may fail at any stage. The likelihood that any particular drug will succeed in all stages and eventually receive FDA approval is extremely low. While this is true for every drug, it is especially the case for drugs that target the central nervous system. While many patients are anxious for new medications to treat problematic diseases, the reality is that the basic bench research alone may take years. The preclinical (animal) studies can also be slow to conduct. Moreover, the likelihood of failure is still high once the trials move to the human phases. Side effects may emerge in human subjects that were not identified in the animal studies. Moreover, a drug that is very effective in mice and rats just may not work in humans. It has been estimated that drugs targeting the brain take on average about 18 years to go from preclinical experiments to FDA approval. Drugs that target the brain spend an average of 8½ years in the human clinical testing portion alone, more than 2 years longer than the average for other drugs. Clinical trials that assess new psychiatric medications are typically viewed as difficult and expensive by those in the industry. Partly this is due to the brain being more complex than any other organ. The complexity makes it difficult to determine what is going on in the brain. By contrast, researchers can use blood pressure readings to quickly identify what is happening in the heart. When the brain is not functioning properly, symptom descriptions are often the primary way researchers assess what has gone wrong. For these reasons, pharmaceutical companies are often hesitant to invest heavily in the research and development of psychiatric drugs (Sanders, 2013). Pharmaceutical companies need to make money or they will go out of business. Therefore, economic considerations alone dictate that pharmaceutical companies should be wary of spending too much time and money on trying to develop brand new psychiatric drugs.

Distribution and Marketing of FDA-Approved Drugs

After a drug receives approval from the FDA, the pharmaceutical company begins to market the drug. The company gives the drug a brand name, which is the commercial name used in advertising. A drug is also given a generic name. For example, Abilify® is the brand name for the drug with the generic name aripiprazole. In return for all the time, money, and effort that went into a new drug, the pharmaceutical company is granted sole rights to market the drug for 20 years from the date the patent was filed. The lengthy development process accounts for the high cost of brand-name drugs. The company needs to make a profit beyond recouping not only the development cost for drugs that make it to market, but also all of the drugs that fell out of the pipeline after failing at some step in the development process. Finally, even as sales of the newly approved drug commence, the process of evaluating the new drug continues. Postmarketing testing involves tracking possible unforeseen side effects of the drug and assessing the effectiveness of the drug. This postmarketing data occurs for about 2 years and can be used to add warning labels or even withdraw drugs from the market if unexpected problems emerge (Sanders, 2013).

Generic Drugs

Once the patent expires on a new drug, generic versions can then be sold. **Generic drugs** are cheaper versions of a drug sold by companies that did not pay for the original drug development and FDA approval process. While expiry of the patent allows other companies to sell generic versions of a drug, these others can only use the generic name in the market, not the brand name. The company that holds the patent may still market and sell the brand-name drug, although sales typically diminish as patients switch to the generic and less-expensive version of the drug having the same effect. According to the FDA, a generic drug is a copy of the brand-name drug with the same safety, strength, route of administration, quality, performance characteristics, intended use, and dosing. While a generic drug may look different than the brand-name drug (e.g., a pink circle pill instead of a yellow diamond pill), the medication is the same. Generic drugs are generally much less expensive (at least 80% less on average) than the corresponding brand-name drug. For this reason, it is not surprising that nearly 8 in 10 prescriptions filled in the United States are for generic drugs. The FDA monitors adverse events for generic drugs, just like it does for brand-name drugs. Thus, patients should not be concerned that generic drugs are any less safe or effective than their pricier branded counterparts (FDA, 2013b).

Focus on Careers: The Pharmaceutical Industry

One in four Americans suffers from a diagnosable mental illness in any given year (Sanders, 2013). The pharmaceutical industry tries to address this problem by developing medications that alleviate patient suffering. Investments in drug development for psychiatric medications are risky for pharmaceutical companies. Therefore, it is becoming common for pharmaceutical companies to work collaboratively with each other as well as with academic centers in hospitals and universities. This approach spreads the risk so that a drug falling out of the pipeline does not impose lost research and development costs on one company alone. In addition, universities can provide a great deal of the preliminary bench work and preclinical testing. The bench work and preclinical testing is quite risky, since the majority of drugs never make it past these initial steps. If a career in the pharmaceutical industry is appealing, there are a variety of places that an entry point can be made. For many, graduate school is the bridge to this industry. Many graduate programs with a neuroscience and/or psychopharmacology focus provide the necessary background for the bench and preclinical work of the pharmaceutical industry. Graduate programs with a neuroscience/psychopharmacology focus may be found in a variety of departments including psychology, biology, behavioral science, and pharmacy programs. All graduate programs have varying requirements, but most require the Graduate Record Examination (GRE), a standardized test. GRE scores, grades, reference letters, and statements of interest are all submitted to programs for consideration. Many graduate students conduct research studies that become master's theses and doctoral dissertations. Theses and dissertations often constitute an important part of the preclinical testing portion of drug development. With strong training, graduates of these programs will find it relatively easy to find work with pharmaceutical companies. In addition, moving from graduate school to industry is not the only option with these graduate degrees. Regulatory affairs are also an important part of the pharmaceutical industry. The Food and Drug Administration (FDA) is the federal agency responsible for oversight of the development of new drugs. The FDA has various summer and internship programs, including some that are designed for undergraduate students. In sum, developing new drugs that help patients live better lives can be a highly rewarding career path for individuals who enjoy science.

Note: See the Focus on Careers section in Chapter 9 for more information about starting a career in human clinical trials.

Some websites to explore:

The Educational Testing Service provides details about the GRE.
https://www.ets.org/gre/

U.S. News and World Report provides some preliminary information about graduate programs.
http://grad-schools.usnews.rankingsandreviews.com/best-graduate-schools

The FDA provides information about careers, including internships for students.
http://www.fda.gov/AboutFDA/WorkingatFDA/default.htm

QUICK QUIZ 12-2

1. Chronic use of antipsychotic drugs can result in a syndrome that includes involuntary movements of the mouth, tongue, trunk, arms, and legs. This syndrome is called
   a. Postpartum psychosis
   b. Tardive dyskinesia
   c. Stimulant psychosis
   d. Parkinson's disease

2. All antipsychotic drugs decrease _____.
   a. dopamine
   b. serotonin
   c. acetylcholine
   d. glutamate
   e. adenosine

3. Which of the following are the most potent D_2 receptor antagonists?
   a. First-generation (traditional) antipsychotics
   b. Second-generation (atypical) antipsychotics
   c. Third-generation antipsychotics
   d. Fourth-generation antipsychotics

4. A Phase 1 clinical trial typically includes _____.
   a. 2 species of animals
   b. 50 patients with the disease of interest
   c. 50 healthy individuals
   d. 50 to 200 patients with the disease of interest
   e. 1,000 or more patients with the disease of interest

5. Sally has been admitted to the hospital because she is experiencing psychotic symptoms. Her physician believes that schizophrenia is the cause of her symptoms and starts her on antipsychotic medication. When should she start to experience relief from her psychotic symptoms?
   a. A few hours
   b. A few days
   c. A few weeks
   d. A few months

6. An antidepressant drug has been available for sale for about a year. The FDA has been tracking suicides in adolescents who take this drug. They decide to put a black box warning on this drug given this data. Where did this data come from?
   a. Preclinical trials

   b. Clinical trials
   c. Premarketing testing
   d. Postmarketing testing
   e. None of the above

7. Generic drugs typically cost _____ less than brand name drugs.
   a. 20%
   b. 40%
   c. 60%
   d. 80%
   e. 100%

8. Fred and Jim both are experiencing symptoms of psychosis. A physician determined that the cause of Fred's psychosis is drug-induced since he had recently taken a large dose of cocaine. A physician determined that the cause of Jim's psychosis is due to the mental disorder of schizophrenia. What is the probable prognosis for these two individuals?

9. Your mother goes to the pharmacy to fill a prescription. The pharmacist tells her that the brand-name drug will cost $32, while the generic version costs $4. She wants to save the money and take the generic, but she is worried that the brand-name drug will work better. What would you say to her?

10. Dr. Edwards and Dr. Ruiz both work for a pharmaceutical company doing bench research. Both scientists are presenting an idea about a new drug to their boss. Dr. Edwards proposes trying something radically different such as examining whether a different neurotransmitter system (not dopamine) can be targeted to reduce psychotic symptoms. Dr. Edwards argues that his new approach could result in a hugely successful blockbuster drug. By contrast, Dr. Ruiz proposes a slight modification of an existing drug that the company already makes. Dr. Edwards acknowledges that investing money in developing his drug is risky although a huge payoff may occur if the drug works. Dr. Ruiz acknowledges that investing money in developing her drug is much less risky although the payoff may be more limited since there are already several drugs on the market that are like hers. The boss only has so much money to spend on research and development. Which scientist's idea will probably get the boss' approval? Why?

ANSWERS TO QUICK QUIZ 12-2:

1. b – tardive dyskinesia
2. a – dopamine
3. a – first-generation (traditional) antipsychotics
4. c – 50 healthy individuals

5. b – a few days
6. d – postmarketing testing
7. d – 80%

8. Fred's prognosis is better than Jim's prognosis. The cause of Fred's psychosis is correctable. Once the cocaine leaves Fred's body, his psychotic symptoms should abate, and he may not even need treatment with an antipsychotic drug. By contrast, Jim's prognosis is more serious given that schizophrenia is typically a lifelong mental disorder that will probably require continuous antipsychotic drug treatment to keep symptoms under control.

9. You would tell her that the generic drug is a copy of the brand-name drug. The Food and Drug Administration (FDA) ensures that all generics are the same in terms of safety, strength, route of administration, quality, performance characteristics, intended use, and how dosing should occur. You can reassure her that 8 in 10 prescriptions filled in the United States are for generic drugs, and the FDA tracks adverse events for generics in the same way it tracks adverse events for brand-name drugs.

10. The boss is very likely to agree to Dr. Ruiz's proposal of a slight modification of an existing drug that the company already makes. While the boss would love to have a blockbuster drug, as suggested by Dr. Edwards, it is likely too risky a strategy. Most psychiatric medications in development never get to the point of receiving FDA approval. The process of developing psychiatric medications is much more difficult and expensive than developing any other type of prescription medication.

CHAPTER SUMMARY

Psychosis is a loss of contact with reality which can include delusions and hallucinations. Antipsychotics are psychotherapeutic drugs that reduce psychosis and other problematic symptoms of mental illness. These drugs are used to treat schizophrenia, postpartum psychosis, bipolar depression, serious major depression, and autism. Antipsychotic drugs are effective in reducing psychosis but can induce various side effects, some of which can be quite serious. There are three classes of antipsychotic drugs: (1) traditional, (2) second generation, and (3) third generation. The traditional antipsychotics (such as chlorpromazine) have been available since the 1950s and act as potent dopamine D_2 antagonist drugs. The second-generation antipsychotics act similarly to the traditional antipsychotics, but the dopamine-blocking action is less potent. The third-generation antipsychotics exert a stabilizing action on dopamine receptors. All antipsychotics decrease psychotic symptoms. Symptom relief occurs within a few days of treatment in most cases. However, with chronic use, various motor problems and other side effects emerge. Tardive dyskinesia is a syndrome with symptoms such as involuntary movements of the mouth, tongue, trunk, arms, and legs that are permanent. Treatment for patients must be multifaceted since schizophrenia tends to be a lifelong condition. Finally, the process of approving new drugs involves many steps, including preclinical testing and clinical trials (Phases 1, 2, and 3). If the FDA approves a new drug, an additional phase of postmarketing occurs. Drug development for psychiatric medications is particularly difficult and lengthy. The average time for testing and approval of drugs targeting the central nervous system is almost 20 years in many cases. Largely for this reason, the currently available antipsychotic drugs are mostly variants of the first drugs that became available in the 1950s.

ANTIDEPRESSANT, ANTIANXIETY, AND MOOD-STABILIZING DRUGS

Introduction

I grew up in Canada, where folks are obsessed with hockey. Not surprisingly, I also enjoy watching hockey games. They are fast-moving and fun. However, my enjoyment of hockey over time has declined somewhat, replaced by growing concern for player well-being. Hockey is an aggressive contact sport in which players incur concussions. Though all players wear helmets, concussions are far from innocuous events. There is a brain underneath that helmet! That brain is not designed for the abuse that can come with a hockey game. After a hit to the head, a player may temporarily lose consciousness. The aftereffects of a concussion can last for months or years. Memory loss, headaches, attention problems, dizziness, depression, anxiety, and other neurological deficits can occur. Concussions are not unique to hockey. Football players also frequently suffer concussions. Soccer players get concussions. Scientists are learning that sports-related concussions are more common than previously thought and can lead to serious and long-lasting health problems. Even just one concussion can result in measurable brain volume loss visible on an MRI scan one year later (Grush, 2013; Zhou et al., 2013).

Two National Hockey League players have recently made public their battles with depression and anxiety after serious concussions. Chris Pronger has been a great hockey player. In 2007, Pronger led the Anaheim Ducks to a championship. Pronger also has two Olympic gold medals. However, this Philadelphia Flyers player recently revealed his struggle with depression and other neurological symptoms from serious concussions. Indeed, Pronger has not played since November 2011 due to postconcussion complications from three separate hits. A similar story was told by Steve Montador, a defenseman for the Chicago Blackhawks (Figure 13-1). Like Pronger, Montador has had a long and successful NHL career. Also similar to Pronger, Montador suffered a serious concussion and has being experiencing depression, anxiety, and

Figure 13-1
Steve Montador is a National Hockey League defenseman who recently discussed how he experienced depression and anxiety following a serious concussion.

other neurological symptoms ever since (Brough, 2013). A concussion is not the only source of the development of depression or anxiety. However, when a mood or anxiety disorder develops, patients have options. Psychotherapeutic drugs can be incredibly helpful for patients experiencing symptoms of depression, regardless of the underlying cause.

> *"The first time I ever heard the word depression . . . there's some stigma around it. What I've learned from my condition (is that) actual neural transmitters are being prevented from connecting and being used in the brain, so it's an actual physical issue."*
> Steve Montador, NHL Chicago Blackhawks Defenseman, *NBC Sports* (March 8, 2013)

LEARNING OBJECTIVES

Learning objectives can help organize your studying. Before we begin the topic of antidepressant, mood-stabilizing, and antianxiety drugs, keep in mind that by the end of this chapter, you should be able to . . .

1. Describe the various mood and anxiety disorders and the prevalence of these mental disorders.
2. Describe the various antidepressant, antianxiety, and mood-stabilizing drugs.
3. Explain the brief history of antidepressant, antianxiety, and mood-stabilizing drugs, including how long they have been available.
4. Explain the acute effects of antidepressant, antianxiety, and mood-stabilizing drugs, including how they act in the central nervous system.
5. Explain the chronic effects of psychotherapeutic drug use for mood and anxiety disorders.
6. Describe how mood and anxiety disorders are typically treated.

Mood and Anxiety Disorders

It is normal sometimes to feel depressed or anxious. Such is the nature of being human. Life has its ups and downs, and our mood states vary accordingly. However, chronic feelings of depression and anxiety can interfere with one's ability to function in life. Though the distinction between normal and abnormal emotions can be unclear, there often comes a point when a person realizes that he or she is not coping and needs some help. While each case is unique, clinicians rely on diagnostic criteria to determine if symptoms of anxiety or mood dysregulation warrant diagnosis and treatment. A **mental disorder** is a clinically significant behavioral or psychological syndrome with key features including distress, disability or impaired functioning, violation of social norms, and dysfunction. This chapter focuses on treatment of disorders with mood regulation or anxiety as key symptoms. **Psychotherapeutic drugs** can be extremely helpful to patients, since these drugs decrease symptoms of depression, stabilize mood, or decrease anxiety.

Mood Disorders

Mood disorders are disturbances in emotion that affect well-being and functioning. An individual may alternatively feel extremely sad and down or extremely ecstatic and irritable. Mood disorders vary considerably, but most clinicians attempt to clarify whether the depression does or does not include manic episodes. **Major depressive disorder** is a mental condition with symptoms including persistent sadness, loss of pleasure, decreased energy, feeling worthless, experiencing guilt, or withdrawal from others. An individual suffering from a major depressive disorder may report disturbed sleep or appetite. Sleep and appetite disruptions can include too little or too much of either. The person may be unable to fall asleep or stay asleep. Waking up at 3 a.m. every morning (assuming that is not normal behavior) may be a symptom of a major depressive disorder. Alternatively, the individual may sleep 10 hours or more each night and still constantly feel exhausted. An individual may also be extremely hungry or have no appetite at all. Body weight may increase or decrease as a result of changes in appetite. Thoughts and behaviors may be slowed, though some individuals may experience agitation. Complaints about memory problems and an inability to concentrate are common. Increased sensitivity to physical aches and pains may also occur. All of these symptoms of depression can impair one's ability to take care of everyday responsibilities. A diagnosis of major depressive disorder is made when symptoms persist for at least 2 weeks (Figure 13-2). Symptoms must include depressed mood and loss of interest or pleasure (APA, 2000; Kring et al., 2012).

Depression can vary considerably, ranging from mild to severe. In mild cases, patients may have difficulty with work or social activities, though they may still be functioning. For mild cases, psychotherapeutic drug treatment may or may not be indicated. In severe cases, patients may have to be briefly hospitalized if the sufferer is unable to continue with normal life activities. Hospitalization may also help if a patient has become suicidal. The likelihood of developing depression and the severity of the depressive episode depend on a variety of factors. Genes play a role, and the environment is also important. Psychosocial stressors, such as poverty or serving in active duty in the military (especially in combat zones), are examples of chronic stress that increase the likelihood that depression emerges and/or is more severe (Gadermann et al., 2012). Moderate to severe cases of depression are not merely unpleasant for the sufferer; such cases can also result in fatalities. Worldwide, almost 1 million lives are lost every year to suicide. Shockingly, for every person who completes a suicide, 20 more attempt to end their lives. Thus, while depression is incredibly common, it can also be a serious or even life-threatening condition (APA, 2000; Kring et al., 2012; WHO, 2012).

While far less common than major depressive disorder, **bipolar disorder** is a mental disorder with symptoms including both depression and mania. In bipolar disorder, mood is not stable but instead swings from one extreme to the other (hence the label "bipolar"). The patient has periods in which they experience depression. Bipolar disorder is also characterized by manic episodes, which are periods of significantly elevated mood and increased energy. Significant activity levels, fast speech, decreased need for sleep, increased anxiety, and increased tension may be present. During a manic episode, the individual will act or think in atypical ways. For example, individuals may exhibit self-confidence and stay up all night in an effort to solve a world problem. They may also overuse a credit card and not think about how those bills will get paid. Depressive and manic episodes may be separated by periods in which mood is essentially normal. Similar to major depressive disorder, risk of suicide is a serious problem for patients with bipolar disorder (APA, 2000; Kring et al., 2012; WHO, 2012).

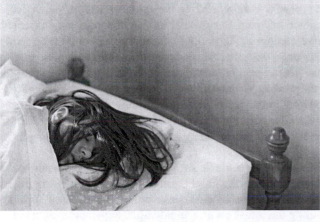

©Shannon Fagan/Stone/Getty Images

Figure 13-2
Symptoms of depression can include trouble falling asleep or staying asleep. Other individuals may experience pronounced increases in duration of sleep yet still feel exhausted.

There are several subtype diagnoses that clinicians make for depressive and bipolar conditions. For example, in the Seasonal Pattern subtype of Major Depressive Disorder, the depressive episodes seem to occur during times of reduced environmental daylight (during the winter). The individual may report feeling fine for most of the year and then predictably slip into depression during the winter months. Light levels are important, and the patient often responds well to treatment involving exposure to bright light. Bipolar Disorder has separate diagnoses related to the severity of the manic episodes. However, the key factor in planning psychotherapeutic drug treatment is whether mood is persistently low or unstable. Antidepressants are typically used for Major Depressive Disorder, while mood stabilizers are used for Bipolar Disorder (Kring et al., 2012).

Anxiety Disorders

Anxiety disorders arise when anxiety has become debilitating. Anxiety is a normal aspect of the human experience, so clarification is required to distinguish normal from abnormal anxiety. It is normal to feel shaky, sweat, have an upset stomach, have difficulty sleeping, and feel anxious before a big presentation or competition in a sporting event. Heightened arousal, if not excessive, may help you be more attentive and do a better presentation, or alternatively arousal may help you run a faster race. However, when signs of anxiety (muscle tension, sympathetic nervous system activity, apprehension, and increased vigilance) are experienced chronically and in unexpected contexts, an anxiety disorder may be present (APA, 2000). In **generalized anxiety disorder**, anxiety and worry persist across all contexts. These worries are excessive and long-lasting. The person may wake up worried, spend most of the day worried, and have difficulty falling asleep because of worry. The worries may be about relationships, health, finances, or daily hassles. Of course, constant worry is exhausting.

Other anxiety disorders are specific to particular situations or stimuli. **Phobias** are disproportionate fears of an object or situation. The person is often aware that their fear is irrational but nevertheless goes to great lengths to avoid the phobic object or situation (Kring et al., 2012). For example, I used to volunteer in a long-term care facility as part of a pet therapy program. One of the nurses who worked in the facility had a significant fear of cats. When the animals came to visit the residents, the nurse would leave her work station and go to a separate part of the building in order to avoid encountering the cat in the pet therapy program. This particular cat was cuddly and very old. It would happily sit on the lap or bed of any elderly person who wanted to pet it. Given that this cat had been in close proximity to hundreds of frail elderly people, the nurse's fear was completely irrational. However, her behavior of avoiding the cat any time it came to the facility ensured that her phobia would persist. Phobias can occur for all kinds of objects, including snakes, spiders, mice, blood, needles, heights, and enclosed spaces.

There are also anxiety disorders specific to certain situations. In **social anxiety disorder**, an individual fears unfamiliar people or social scrutiny. While we can all relate to the anxiety of starting at a new school, an individual suffering from social anxiety disorder may experience anxiety about a wide variety of social situations (Figure 13-3). Similar to a phobia, an individual suffering from social anxiety disorder may avoid situations where interactions with new people or potential social scrutiny might occur. Unfortunately for the person suffering from social anxiety disorder, modern life is filled with these types of interactions. A college student must speak up in classes or meetings, meet new people, and talk to professors. Many classes require public speaking. Note that social anxiety disorder is not just about being shy. An individual with this disorder might even avoid using public restrooms or eating in public for fear of judgment from others (Kring et al., 2012).

When individuals are exposed to severe or chronic stress, **posttraumatic stress disorder (PTSD)** may arise. Examples of traumatic events that might lead to PTSD include being a victim of a crime, exposure to a natural disaster (such as an earthquake or hurricane), being in war, or being in an automobile accident. During the actual event, the individual experiences extreme fear

©Carlo Allegri/Getty Images

Figure 13-3
Barbara Streisand is a famous singer and actor. Her experience with social anxiety was intense and prevented her from performing in public for 27 years. With the help of antianxiety medication and therapy, she has been able to perform.

and helplessness. After the event is over, the individual experiences flashbacks (strong and vivid memories of the event) and nightmares. Difficulty sleeping, irritability, persistent hyperarousal, and a feeling of numbness are often reported. With advances in brain imaging, we've learned that smaller amygdala and hippocampal volumes are associated with PTSD. This loss of brain matter might reflect damage resulting from the disorder or a preexisting vulnerability leading to PTSD after a traumatic event (Morey et al., 2012). Regardless of the cause of brain matter loss from PTSD, the symptoms of this disorder may be debilitating and lead to suicide. Among U.S. combat veterans who served in either Iraq or Afghanistan, PTSD is a primary mental health diagnoses seen by Veterans Affairs (Jakupcak et al., 2013).

Finally, **panic disorder** is an anxiety disorder not tied to a particular object or situation. Panic disorder is characterized by frequent **panic attacks**, which are sudden feelings of doom, apprehension, and terror. Many individuals experience physical symptoms during the attack that resemble the symptoms of a heart attack. Heart palpitations, rapid breathing, chest pain, nausea, dizziness, lightheadedness, chills, sweating, and trembling are reported. The person may feel that he or she is losing control or dying. Symptom onset is rapid, peaks in intensity within 10 minutes, and then diminishes in intensity shortly thereafter. Panic attacks occur without warning. For this reason, the individual may experience constant worry about experiencing another panic attack. The experience of a panic attack is so intense and frightening that many of those experiencing a panic attack seek medical care (Figure 13-4). Cardiologists are left to determine if the attack is a mild heart attack or a panic attack.

Anxiety disorders are categorized by whether the anxiety is experienced constantly or intermittently. Anxiety may be triggered by a specific object or situation. Anxiety can also persist across situations and be experienced almost continuously. Anxiety disorders are not only unpleasant, but they also seem to increase the likelihood of various health risks. One study found that men who experienced phobic symptoms were three times more likely to develop coronary heart disease (Kawachi et al., 1994). Thus, people experiencing panic attacks that feel like a heart attack may actually also really have a real heart attack (myocardial infarction). Fortunately, there are a variety of treatment options to decrease anxiety and help the individual return to a relatively normal level of functioning. These treatment options include antianxiety medications, among others.

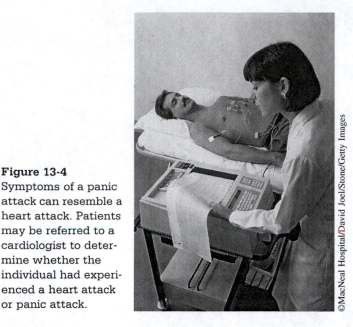

Figure 13-4
Symptoms of a panic attack can resemble a heart attack. Patients may be referred to a cardiologist to determine whether the individual had experienced a heart attack or panic attack.

Mood Disorders and Anxiety Disorders: Together or Separate?

Depression and anxiety are separate symptoms that can lead to different diagnoses. However, there is substantial overlap between depression and anxiety in clinical symptoms and neurophysiological causes. The comorbidity (overlap) of depression and anxiety is in fact more common than either disorder alone. Indeed, the comorbidity between mood and anxiety disorders occurs at much higher rates than expected by chance alone. One U.S. study reported that 58% of individuals with depression also suffer from an anxiety disorder (Baldwin, Evans, Hirschfeld, & Kasper, 2002). Another study reported that 60% of individuals suffering from some kind of anxiety disorder also met the diagnostic criteria for major depression (Brown, Campbell, Lehman, Grisham, & Mancill, 2001). Depression and anxiety are so closely related that some scientists suggest the disorders are different phenotypic expressions having a common neurobiological origin. A **phenotype** refers to the exhibited physical or behavioral trait that is a product of interactions between genetics and the environment. While the neurobiological origins of depression and anxiety are still under investigation, dysregulation of serotonin and norepinephrine activity in the brain is implicated in both (Baldwin et al., 2002). Given that a patient is likely to describe both symptoms of anxiety and mood problems, this chapter will discuss antidepressants, mood stabilizers, and antianxiety medications together. In many cases, a patient might require the use of more than one class of these common psychotherapeutic medications, at least until the disorder is under control. It should also be noted that mood and anxiety disorders also overlap with substance abuse disorders. Before seeking help, patients often attempt to self-medicate with readily available drugs like alcohol. Comorbidity between substance abuse disorders and mood and/or anxiety disorders is common (Jakupcak et al., 2013).

Antidepressant, Mood-Stabilizing, and Antianxiety Drugs

Antidepressant Drugs

Antidepressant drugs are psychotherapeutic drugs that reduce symptoms of depression. Persistent sadness, loss of pleasure, and decreased energy are symptoms of depression that abate with antidepressant drug treatment. Given that approximately 1 in 5 individuals will experience a major depressive episode in their lifetime, it is unsurprising that antidepressant drugs are widely used (Bromet et al., 2011). Depression seems to be associated with deficient levels of monoamine neurotransmitters. Antidepressant drugs elevate the activity of these monoamine neurotransmitters in the brain. However, the return to a relatively normal level of functioning tends to be frustratingly slow, with most patients not experiencing symptom relief until after a month of treatment. There are four major categories of antidepressant drugs (Table 13-1). The four major categories are differentiated based on their mechanism of action. Tricyclic antidepressants, monoamine oxidase inhibitors (MAOIs), selective serotonin reuptake inhibitors (SSRIs)/selective serotonin norepinephrine reuptake inhibitors (SNRIs), and atypical antidepressants will all improve the symptoms of major depressive disorder. The tricyclic antidepressants, such as imipramine, have been available for decades. Currently, the SSRIs/SNRIs (such as Celexa®, Lexapro®, or Prozac®) are the dominant medications for treatment of depressive disorders, and those same medicines are also widely used to treat severe anxiety disorders. The tricyclics, MAOIs, and SSRIs all increase levels of serotonin and norepinephrine in the brain, with some drugs mainly acting to elevate activity of one type of neurotransmitter and other drugs acting on both. The atypical antidepressants (such as Wellbutrin®) are mild psychostimulants that elevate activity of norepinephrine and dopamine. The atypical antidepressants are effective in treating major depression but have also been widely used to help individuals quit smoking. Interestingly, the use of antidepressant drugs by healthy individuals not suffering from depression results in no discernible psychoactive effects. These drugs only elevate mood in individuals suffering from depression (Baldessarini, 2001).

Mood Stabilizers

Mood stabilizers are psychotherapeutic drugs that reduce the depression and mania that are symptoms of bipolar disorder. Mood stabilizers bring wide swings in mood under better control and back into a normalized range. Similar to antidepressant drugs, patients will find that improvements in symptoms are frustratingly slow with these medications. Improvement may only be evident after a month of treatment. The drug options for bipolar disorder are markedly smaller than the range of psychotherapeutic drugs available to treat major depression. For several decades, the use of lithium carbonate or citrate has been the standard of care for patients with bipolar disorder. Limitations and side effects of lithium salts have become better known over time. Thus, efforts to find new drugs to treat bipolar disorder have intensified, but unfortunately there has been little success thus far. Partly this is due to the mechanism of action of lithium and other similar drugs being unclear. Some cellular actions have been identified, however. Similar to antidepressant drugs, mood stabilizers result in no discernible psychoactive effects in individuals not suffering from a mood disorder. The mood stabilizers only alter mood in individuals who are suffering from bipolar disorder (Baldessarini & Tarazi, 2001).

Antianxiety Drugs

Most sedative drugs, including alcohol and opiates, decrease anxiety. However, treatment of anxiety disorders with potentially addictive drugs is not advisable given that anxiety disorders are often chronic. **Antianxiety drugs** (also referred to as anxiolytics) refer to those psychotherapeutic drugs that reduce anxiety and may also be useful in treating symptoms of anxiety disorders. These drugs may also be used for brief episodes of anxiety, such as the anxiety accompanying surgical procedures. The most common antianxiety drugs are **benzodiazepines** (such as Xanax®, Ativan®, or Valium®). These psychotherapeutic drugs produce an immediate calming effect, usually a few hours or less after the drug is administered. Benzodiazepines produce a calming effect by increasing the activity of the inhibitory neurotransmitter, GABA, in the brain. Benzodiazepines are clearly effective in decreasing anxiety, with the most favorable responses observed in patients who experience acute anxiety. However, there are also serious considerations associated with benzodiazepines. First, consistent use can lead to tolerance and dependence. Second,

Table 13.1 Examples of psychotherapeutic drugs used to treat mood and anxiety disorders.

Mental Disorder	Drug Category	Trade Name	Generic Name
Major depression	Tricyclic antidepressants	Tofranil®	Imipramine
		Elavil®	Amitriptyline
	Monoamine oxidase inhibitors (MAOIs)	Eldepryl®	Selegiline
		Nardil®	Parnate
		Parnate®	Tranylcypromine
	Selective serotonin reuptake inhibitors (SSRIs)	Celexa®	Citalopram
		Lexapro®	Escitalopram
		Luvox®	Fluvoxamine
		Paxil®	Paroxetine
		Prozac®	Fluoxetine
		Zoloft®	Sertraline
	Selective serotonin norepinephrine reuptake inhibitors (SNRIs)	Effexor®	Venlafaxine
		Cymbalta®	Duloxetine
	Atypical antidepressants	Wellbutrin®	Buproprion
Bipolar depression	Mood stabilizers	Lithium®	Lithium carbonate
		Depakote®	Valproic acid
Anxiety disorders	Benzodiazepines	Ativan®	Lorazepam
		Halcion®	Triazolam
		Klonopin®	Clonazepam
		Serax®	Oxazepam
		Valium®	Diazepam
		Versed®	Midazolam
		Xanax®	Alprazolam
	Atypical antianxiety drugs	Ambien®	Zolpidem
		BuSpar®	Buspirone
	Antihistamines	Atarax®	Hydroxyzine

benzodiazepines lead to sedating effects that interfere with cognitive and motor skills, including driving. Obviously, patients need to be careful with benzodiazepines for this reason. One further risk of benzodiazepines is that high doses can suppress respiration, leading to fatalities. Most commonly, accidental overdoses or suicides occur when patients combine benzodiazepines with alcohol or opiate pain medications. Given these risks, physicians try to limit use of benzodiazepines; anxiety disorders are thus often treated with antidepressants such as the SSRIs (Baldessarini, 2001).

Sometimes anxiety can be transient, such as the anxiety experienced before giving a big presentation or taking exams. **Antihistamines** are allergy medications that decrease itching but in addition can decrease short-term anxiety. Several other drugs can also decrease anxiety and induce sleep. Ambien CR® (zolpidem) is similar to the benzodiazepines in acting as an agonist of GABA receptors. However, zolpidem is more effective than benzodiazepines at inducing sleep, and it is now one of the most widely used treatments for insomnia (Rush & Griffiths, 1996). There are other nonbenzodiazepine drugs used to treat anxiety. Unlike the benzodiazepine drugs, BuSpar® (buspirone) does not increase GABA activity. Instead, BuSpar® alters serotonin activity. Due to its different underlying mechanism of action, BuSpar® is less likely to induce sedation or motor impairment. However, weeks of treatment tend to be necessary for BuSpar® to induce antianxiety effects, while most benzodiazepines are effective with the first dose (Rush & Griffiths, 1997). In the past, the depressant drugs **barbiturates** (commonly known as sleeping pills) were used to treat anxiety. However, use of barbiturates declined considerably after concerns arose about their use. While low doses of barbiturates decrease anxiety, higher doses of barbiturates can lead to general anesthesia, coma, and death. The risks from barbiturates are similar to those associated with other sedative drugs like alcohol and opiates. In the past, overdose cases from barbiturate use were far too common. Overdoses were especially common when a patient mixed a barbiturate with alcohol. Repeated use of barbiturates can also lead to rapid tolerance development and dependence. As a result, barbiturates are not ideal for the treatment of chronic anxiety. However, barbiturates are still used for anesthesia and to treat epilepsy (Baldessarini, 2001).

Brief History of Antidepressant, Antianxiety, and Mood-Stabilizing Drugs

In the previous chapter, the pre-chlorpromazine era (before the 1950s) of mental illness treatment was described in some detail (see Chapter 12). Recall that individuals were either considered possessed by evil spirits or inhumanely locked up in asylums. For the most part, individuals suffering from mood or anxiety disorders probably escaped such dire fates. Persistent sadness or anxiety, while unpleasant, was not so disruptive that affected individuals would need to be removed from society. Self-medicating with alcohol or other psychoactive drugs was common. Physicians tried amphetamines and opiates to treat mood and anxiety disorders, but addiction problems prevented widespread adoption of those drugs. The 1950s represented a turning point in psychotherapeutic drug treatment of mental illness. The initial discoveries were drugs, having other medical uses, which were found also to be therapeutically useful for treating mental illness. The discovery of chlorpromazine's ability to reduce psychotic symptoms was a groundbreaking event in psychopharmacology. Available for prescription in 1952, physicians quickly adopted its use and viewed chlorpromazine as a miracle drug. Patients could be released from asylums as a result of no longer hearing voices and experiencing delusions (Ban, 2007). Just before the introduction of chlorpromazine, another important discovery was made, though not with such a big initial impact. In 1949, lithium salts were first reported to be useful in the treatment of mania or psychotic excitement. Dr. John Cade, an Australian psychiatrist, published an account documenting the effectiveness of lithium. His observations stemmed from his research on guinea pigs, in which he observed that lithium made guinea pigs sedated. Lithium is an alkaline metal found in nature, and its sedative action seemed well suited to counteract manic symptoms. The discovery of its benefits for humans should have resulted in quick adoption of lithium, given that the only treatment alternatives for bipolar disorder were either electroconvulsive shock therapy or lobotomy surgery. However, concerns about toxicity resulted in slow adoption of lithium by the medical community, unlike the quick embrace that occurred with chlorpromazine (Baldessarini, 2001; Baldessarini & Tarazi, 2001; Cade, 1949).

Other psychiatric medications to treat mood and anxiety problems were also discovered in the 1950s. In 1954, the discovery of the first antianxiety drug was reported. Meprobamate was used as a muscle relaxer, and it was discovered that meprobamate also reduced anxiety (Berger, 1954). Additional sedative drugs to treat anxiety followed from the discovery of meprobamate. The first benzodiazepine, chlordiazepoxide, was reported to reduce anxiety in 1957. A drug that had been used to treat tuberculosis, iproniazid, was reported in 1958 also to be an effective antidepressant. Iproniazid was the first monoamine oxidase inhibitor (Kline, 1958). Also in 1958, imipramine was discovered to be useful as an antidepressant, even though it had originally been investigated as an antipsychotic. Imipramine was the first tricyclic antidepressant (Kuhn, 1958). These discoveries in the 1950s revolutionized the treatment of mental disorders, including the treatment of mood and anxiety disorders. In the 1960s, research expanded upon these initial discoveries, with many new theories advanced about how these drugs worked. Moreover, the clinical efficacy of all of these drugs had been firmly established by the end of the 1960s. These drugs worked to help patients with mood and anxiety disorders, and many of these drugs are still in use today.

The use of barbiturates (also known as sleeping pills) to treat anxiety was popular in the 1950s and 1960s. The 1967 American film *Valley of the Dolls* (based on the novel by Jacqueline Susann) portrayed the appeal of barbiturates to Hollywood actresses and others to treat anxiety. "Dolls" in the title referred to dolophine, a barbiturate, with the term later used to refer to all barbiturates. As mentioned, barbiturates do reduce anxiety. Barbiturates have some similarity to alcohol in the intoxication that results as the dose increases. At higher doses of barbiturates, unconsciousness, coma, and death can occur. Addiction and overdose deaths were part of the fictional story portrayed in the novel and film. Addiction and overdose deaths also occurred in real life, and many deaths that were either accidental or intentional resulted from use of barbiturates. Famous actresses and singers like Marilyn Monroe (d. 1962) and Judy Garland (d. 1969) experienced tragic early deaths as a result of barbiturates. Ironically, Judy Garland was supposed to be the star of Valley of the Dolls, but she was fired when she showed up to work intoxicated. Garland's overdose death was the culmination of several years of abuse of alcohol and barbiturates (Clark, 2001). By the 1970s, barbiturates were no longer used to treat anxiety, after it became clear that they were addictive and resulted in accidental overdose deaths.

The development of new psychotherapeutic drugs to treat mood and anxiety disorders followed from the discovery of how these mental disorders arose and why these drugs worked. It came to be understood that depression resulted from a brain deficiency in the level of monoamines (serotonin, norepinephrine, and less so dopamine). The tricyclic antidepressants, such as imipramine, blocked monoamine reuptake sites. This action increased the levels of monoamine neurotransmitters in the brain, which resulted in mood improvements. Evidence to support this theory of depression came from the observation that the drug reserpine led to a depressed state in either an animal or human. Reserpine decreases the level of norepinephrine in the brain. Similarly, it was shown that depleted levels of serotonin also induced a depressed state. Using this new knowledge, more specialized medications were developed targeting serotonin and/or norepinephrine in the brain. The first selective serotonin reuptake inhibitor (SSRI) was fluoxetine, which became available in 1988. The SSRIs were found to lead to symptom relief for depressed patients, with the additional benefit of reduced side effects. Antidepressants, mood stabilizers, and antianxiety medications are all now widely used (Baldessarini, 2001; Baldessarini & Tarazi, 2001).

Epidemiology of Mood and Anxiety Disorders

Depression is so widespread that it is sometimes referred to as the common cold of mental illness. While studies differ slightly in lifetime prevalence estimates for major depression, most estimate that approximately 20% of Americans will experience at least one episode of depression in their lifetimes (Bromet et al., 2011; Kessler, Petukhova, Sampson, Zaslavsky, & Wittchen, 2012).

While depression is common, it can nevertheless be a very serious concern. It leads to disability when people are unable to work or attend school. Depression can also lead to suicide. Depression is one of the leading causes of disease worldwide. One way to determine prevalence of depression worldwide has been through the World Health Organization's (WHO) World Health Surveys. In these surveys, adults are asked about all aspects of health and disease using the diagnostic criteria found in the ICD system (see Chapter 1 for details about this system). Participants from 60 countries around the world are assessed. One year prevalence rates of depression are approximately 3% to 5% worldwide, depending on the year of the survey. As a result, researchers estimate that depression affects 350 million people worldwide every year. Gender is important to the epidemiology of depression, since females are 50% more likely to experience depression than men. This gender difference is observed in both the United States and also around the world. Individuals who suffer from a chronic disease (angina, arthritis, asthma, or diabetes) are also more likely to experience depression. The overlap between depression and chronic physical disease is pronounced, with up to 23% of individuals suffering from chronic physical disease also suffering from depression (Marcus, Yasamy, van Ommeren, Chisolm, & Saxena, 2012; Moussavi et al., 2007).

While depression is the most common mental disorder around the world, there are some interesting differences by country that may seem counterintuitive (Table 13-2). While direct data on prevalence rates for depression are not available for every country, the available data suggests that lower- to middle-income countries have lower rates of depression than high-income countries. One study reported that the lifetime prevalence of depression was approximately 15% for high-income countries versus 11% for low- to middle-income countries. These differences are not a function of better diagnoses of depression in high-income countries. Researchers coordinating these studies ask about symptoms in face-to-face interviews with respondents. These findings seem to suggest that the social conditions of a country may influence prevalence of depression. It seems perplexing that some of the wealthiest countries actually have the highest depression rates. Scientists are unsure why this is the case. Some have suggested that income inequality, which is more visible in relatively affluent countries, might contribute to depression. In developing countries, such as India and China, the majority of citizens may be relatively poor. The United States has great affluence and also great poverty. The poor in the United States may be faced with more frequent reminders of the reality of their situation. It may also be that expectations about happiness differ across societies (Bromet et al., 2011). Another possibility is that social support differs dramatically in more and less affluent countries. Individuals living in more affluent countries may have more money, but they are less likely to have family members living in their household that can provide daily social support. There are many other possible explanations for this counterintuitive finding. Can you think of some others?

Recent data suggests that mood disorders are slightly more common than anxiety disorders, although comorbidity (overlap) between these two mental disorders is considerable. One study examined the prevalence of mood and anxiety disorders based on U.S. epidemiological surveys among individuals 13 and older. In this study, highest lifetime prevalence rates for specific mood or anxiety disorders were estimated to be approximately 17% for major depressive disorder, 16% for a specific phobia, and 11% for social phobia (Kessler et al., 2012). Clearly, mood and anxiety disorders are extremely common. As is the case with mood disorders, anxiety disorders are more likely in women than men. Mood and anxiety disorders make up the majority of diagnosed cases of mental illness. About one in every four adults in the United States experiences some form of mental disorder in any given year, with mood and anxiety disorders being the most common form of mental disorder. This translates to approximately 60 million adults in the United States suffering from some form of mental illness. Note that only about a quarter of the people with mental illness experience significantly disrupted day-to-day functioning. The rest are at work and at school while experiencing symptoms. The top three mental illness categories are mood disorders, anxiety disorders, and substance abuse. Researchers estimate that half of the cases of mild mental illness go away with time and probably do not

Table 13.2   **High-income and low-to-middle income countries differ in lifetime prevalence rates for major depression.**

Economic Status	Country	Lifetime Prevalence (%)
High-Income Country	Belgium	14
	France	21
	Germany	10
	Israel	10
	Italy	10
	Japan	7
	Netherlands	18
	New Zealand	18
	Spain	11
	United States	19
Average for High-Income Countries	**15**	
Low- to Middle-Income Country	Brazil	18
	Colombia	13
	India	9
	Lebanon	11
	Mexico	8
	China	7
	South Africa	10
	Ukraine	15
Average for Low- to Middle-Income Countries	**11**	

Note: Table adapted from Table 2 of Bromet et al. (2011). Prevalence rates only include data from survey respondents ages 18 and older.

require treatment. For the rest, whether their illness is mild yet persistent, moderate, or severe, the symptoms are treatable with therapy and/or psychotherapeutic drugs. Despite good treatment options being available, only about half of individuals who need treatment will access it (Wang et al., 2005a,b).

Acute and Chronic Effects of Antidepressants

A depressed patient may receive a prescription for an antidepressant drug. Can this patient expect to start feeling better immediately? No. Antidepressant drugs are notoriously and frustratingly slow to take effect. Many physicians warn their patients that any appreciable improvement in symptoms will probably not occur for several weeks. A month or more is quite a long time for a patient experiencing depression to wait to feel better. For this reason, the acute effects of antidepressants are dominated by side effects rather than desired treatment effects. When treatment is initiated, patients may experience various negative side effects within the first few days. Dry mouth, drowsiness, constipation, difficulties with urination, blurred vision, dizziness, tachycardia, weight gain, and/or sexual dysfunctions have been reported for all antidepressants.

The MAOIs are also known to induce low blood pressure, especially when a person changes position (such as getting up from a chair). Early in treatment, patients taking MAOIs must also adapt to dietary restrictions. Foods that contain tyramine (found in most cheeses and some alcoholic beverages) can cause severe hypertension in users of MAOIs (Baldessarini, 2001).

For a patient already depressed, experiencing side effects without beneficial treatment effects can be distressing. Some patients may find the side effects so problematic that they discontinue treatment before the drug has had a chance to demonstrate a benefit. However, patients who persist through the side effects may notice an improvement in symptoms of depression after several weeks. The change is typically not dramatic, but rather the individual reports gradual improvement over weeks. Sleep gets better, and the patient does not feel so consistently down throughout the day. Appetite may gradually return to normal and feelings of worthlessness may diminish. For many, antidepressant medication can assist in becoming more proactive about life's problems, a good outcome if life problems contributed to the depression. If the patient is in therapy, improvements in mood may help the patient engage more with the therapist. If the patient is feeling lonely, antidepressants may help the patient be more proactive about calling friends. If the patient is depressed about a job loss, improvements in mood may help the individual be more proactive about their job search. For many individuals suffering from depression, antidepressant drugs are incredibly helpful. Moreover, side effects tend to diminish over time. For patients also suffering from a comorbid anxiety disorder, the symptoms of anxiety may diminish somewhat as well. In these cases, the patient may also reduce their reliance on antianxiety medications (Baldessarini, 2001).

The above describes an ideal outcome. The patient may be frustrated by the slow progress, but after several weeks the patient will notice that depression has started to lift. However, each person's individual response to any particular antidepressant drug can vary considerably. Clinical trials have demonstrated that 50% to 70% of patients suffering from a depressive disorder will experience major improvements in symptoms following antidepressant treatment (Nemeroff & Schatzberg, 1998). However, these clinical trials tend to include relatively simple cases. Recall that a large proportion of patients experiencing depression may also be suffering from anxiety. Comorbidity of major depression with other psychiatric disorders is also relatively common. One large study, the STAR-D study, examined the effectiveness of antidepressants in 3,671 patients whose conditions were more like complex, real-world cases. All patients were started on Celexa® (citalopram), a popular SSRI antidepressant. As part of the study design, patients who did not respond favorably to Celexa® were given the option to add another medication to Celexa® or stop using Celexa® and switch to a different antidepressant medication. The prescribing physicians had the option to try different medications, in order to mirror what happens in the real world. The results of this study indicated that only 30% of the patients achieved full symptom relief from the Celexa® alone (Trivedi et al., 2006). There were further improvements in some of the patients given a second medication or switched to a different medication. Even with all of the treatment options, only 43% of patients were considered recovered by the end of the study (Nelson, 2006). Therefore, this study suggests that less than half of depressed patients are going to get better with antidepressant treatment, even when the physician is trying new drugs to adapt to lack of progress. While antidepressant drugs can be incredibly helpful for some individuals, they are far from universally effective for all cases of major depression.

Scientists and clinicians have been perplexed by the length of time required for antidepressants to take effect. If these drugs are increasing the levels of serotonin and norepinephrine in the brain, why doesn't the patient immediately feel better? Why does it take many weeks for a patient to feel an improvement in mood? The answer seems to be tied to the action that antidepressants have on **neurogenesis** (the birth of new neurons in the brain). Depression, anxiety, and exposure to chronic stress can cause damage to the brain. Both human and animal studies have demonstrated that a chronic depressed state is associated with both neuronal atrophy and neuronal death in the brain. Neurons are shrinking and dying when a person is depressed, with these changes particularly pronounced in the hippocampus. The **hippocampus** is found in the center of the brain, and it is a structure that is important for memory formation and spatial navigation. Given that neurons are dying in the hippocampus, it is perhaps not surprising that depressed patients often report memory difficulties. Treatment with antidepressant drugs seems to reverse some of this depression-induced damage. With treatment, new cells in the hippocampus are formed and the neurons that already exist tend to grow. Neurogenesis in the hippocampus is not an immediate change; it requires several weeks of antidepressant drug treatment (Boldrini et al., 2012; Mateus-Pinheiro et al., 2013). The timeline for neurogenesis seems to coincide with patient reports that it takes several weeks before depression symptoms abate (Harmer & Cowen, 2013).

Treatment with antidepressants over the long term also seems to alter functioning in other regions of the brain. For example, the **amygdala** is a structure in the center of the brain important for the regulation of strong emotions. Patients experiencing depression exhibit hyperactivity in the amygdala, especially in response to negative stimuli such as sad faces. With antidepressant treatment, amygdala hyperactivity tends to normalize (Fu et al., 2004; Sheline et al., 2001).

One counterintuitive observation about antidepressant drug treatment is that some antidepressants, especially SSRIs, are associated with an increased risk of suicide. This risk is more pronounced in children and adolescents when compared with adults. One would imagine that as depression symptoms decrease, an individual should be less likely, not more likely, to commit suicide. While the exact mechanism underlying this association is unknown, several theories have been advanced. First, it has been suggested that severely depressed patients are too lethargic and exhibiting too many cognitive deficits to complete a suicide. As depression starts to lift, the suicidal patient may develop a plan of suicide and be able to follow through with it. Children and adolescents suffering from depression may be more likely to attempt suicide for the following reason: less life experience may prevent them from understanding that time will pass and things will get better. Given the association between suicide risk in children and SSRIs, the U.S. Food and Drug Association (FDA) placed a black box warning on 10 brands of antidepressants in 2004. The warning informs that patients, especially children, using SSRI antidepressants may become suicidal and should be monitored closely. Subsequent research has confirmed that suicide and self-harm episodes are associated with antidepressant treatment in patients under the age of 18. Further, the older tricyclic drugs (such as imipramine) are similar to the newer SSRIs in this risk (Schneeweiss et al., 2010). Physicians often closely monitor prescriptions of both antidepressant and antianxiety drugs, given the risk of suicide for depressed patients. If a patient is suicidal, they make take many available pills at once. High doses of antidepressants or antianxiety medications can cause serious health concerns or even death. Overdoses of SSRIs can induce cardiac problems, coma, and death. MAOIs are slightly safer, with overdoses somewhat less common. However, MAOIs have been found to be slightly less effective than SSRIs, and MAOIs tend to be used in cases where depression has not responded to SSRI treatment (Baldessarini, 2001).

More about the Science:

Norbury et al. (2009). Short-term antidepressant treatment modulates amygdala response to happy faces. *Psychopharmacology*, *206*, 197–204.

A patient experiencing depression may begin a course of antidepressant drug treatment and experience no near-term symptom improvement. However, after several weeks of treatment, mood lifts and depression symptoms subside. Researchers have wondered if there is a way to determine if antidepressant drug treatment is altering brain processing early in the treatment regimen, before the behavioral benefits of the drug are observed. To answer this question, researchers in this study relied on functional magnetic resonance imaging to investigate if the brain is responding to the drug treatment. Healthy subjects (who had no mental disorder) were recruited for this study and were randomly assigned to either a drug or a placebo condition. Subjects assigned to the drug condition were treated with the antidepressant drug, citalopram, in a dose similar to what would be prescribed for patients suffering from depression. Brain imaging occurred approximately 7–10 days after treatment was initiated. Subjects were exposed to pictures of positive (smiling) and negative (fearful) faces while their brains were imaged. The researchers focused on activity in the amygdala, the region of the brain that is important for the regulation of strong emotions. The researchers observed that the citalopram treatment was associated with increased amygdala activation with happy faces and decreased amygdala activation with fearful faces. No change in mood state was reported by the citalopram-treated or control subjects. The researchers concluded that the antidepressant drug might act by reversing the negative bias seen in depression and anxiety. This change may occur early in drug treatment, before the overall emotional state has been altered in patients.

More about the Science Thought Questions:

1. In this study, healthy volunteers were administered antidepressant drugs. No change in mood state was reported with this treatment. Would this have been an expected outcome for these individuals?

2. The researchers concluded that antidepressant drug treatment may reverse the negative bias seen in depression. Is this assertion justified by the findings of this study?

More about the Science Thought Question Answers:

1. Yes, this outcome would have been expected. Antidepressant drug treatment seems to have no discernible effect on mood in individuals not suffering from depression. Even with a longer duration of treatment, mood is not altered by psychotherapeutic drugs for individuals not experiencing depression.

2. This assertion may be somewhat premature given that patients with depression were not included in this study. The participants in this study were healthy and thus not exhibiting any abnormal negative bias in processing emotional states. While the short-term treatment with the antidepressant did seem to alter amygdala activation in a manner that seemed to favor happy faces, this finding would need replication with a depressed patient population.

Tolerance and Withdrawal for Antidepressants

Antidepressants are psychotherapeutic drugs administered in a chronic fashion to produce symptom improvements in depressed patients. Patients may take antidepressants for months or years, depending on the nature of their mood disorder. To prevent recurrence, physicians typically recommend continuous treatment with antidepressants for patients who have experienced multiple depressive episodes. Given the long duration of treatment, concerns about tolerance emerge. Some tolerance generally develops to the early side effects experienced in treatment. Patients who initially report side effect symptoms such as sedation, dizziness, or tachycardia may find that these symptoms decline in intensity or even dissipate with repeated drug exposure. By contrast, tolerance does not appear to develop to the effectiveness of the antidepressant in reducing depressive symptoms, even with a year of treatment. The newer SSRI and SNRI antidepressants appear to retain greater effectiveness over time than the older tricyclic antidepressants (Baldessarini, 2001; Cohen & Baldessarini, 1985). However, some evidence suggests that patients using antidepressants for long periods (years rather than months) do develop some tolerance to them

(Fava & Offidani, 2011). Although tolerance develops slowly with antidepressants, the mechanism of tolerance development seems to be the same as with all psychoactive drugs. Continued drug treatment recruits processes in the body that oppose the initial effect of the therapeutic drug. Over time, these opponent processes counteract the drug effect in an effort to return the body to homeostasis. As this is occurring, the physician will need to escalate the dose or switch to a different antidepressant. If drug treatment has been discontinued, the patient may actually experience a worse depressive episode than would have been experienced without any treatment. There is little doubt that antidepressant drugs are incredibly helpful in treating mood disorders. Thus, tolerance development should not dissuade patients from using them if needed (Fava, 2003; Kaymaz, van Os, Loonen, & Nolen, 2008).

Abrupt cessation of treatment with antidepressants is not recommended due to the possibility that withdrawal symptoms may emerge. Withdrawal symptoms may vary somewhat depending on the specific antidepressant that had been taken, but most clinicians refer to evidence of withdrawal as **discontinuation syndrome**. Discontinuation syndrome can occur for all types of antidepressants, but it is more common with MAOIs. The most commonly reported symptoms include dizziness, nausea, vomiting, fatigue, chills, flu-like illness, sensory abnormalities, and sleep disturbances. The individual may experience crying spells, anxiety, irritability, and agitation. Many of these symptoms resemble depression itself, which can lead both the patient and physician to suspect that a relapse may be occurring. Therefore, patients should be forewarned that these symptoms may emerge, but they are generally mild and last only a short time. Moreover, discontinuation syndrome can be avoided by very slowly titrating the dose down over time until the patient finally stops taking the drug. Slowly tapering off the drug tends to be the most effective approach for avoiding discontinuation syndrome (Haddad, 1997; Lejoyeux & Ades, 1997; Rosenbaum & Zajecka, 1997).

Myth Busters: Women Who Are Pregnant or Breastfeeding Can't Take Psychotherapeutic Drugs

Mood and anxiety disorders do not go away when a woman becomes pregnant. Indeed, postpartum depression and anxiety arising in the new mother shortly after giving birth is the most common complication of pregnancy (Figure 13-5). While all new mothers may experience some alteration in mood state, up to 19% of women who give birth will develop a mood and/or anxiety disorder, with dramatic hormonal changes being partly responsible for this development (Bener, Gerber, & Sheikh, 2012; Paul, Downs, Schaefer,

Figure 13-5
Mood and anxiety disorders are common in new mothers.

Beiler, & Weisman, 2013; Toohey, 2012). Many people perceive that pregnant or breastfeeding women should not take any drugs, including psychotherapeutic drugs. Many physicians and pharmacists also hold this position. The Food and Drug Administration (FDA) does have warnings on most psychotherapeutic drugs about limiting use by pregnant and breastfeeding women, except in cases where absolutely necessary. However, it is a myth that women who are pregnant or breastfeeding cannot be treated with psychotherapeutic drugs. In fact, the failure to treat mood or anxiety disorders can be risky for both the mother and infant. The worst-case scenario obviously involves a pregnant woman or new mother who is suicidal. However, even a more moderate depression or anxiety disorder can be problematic. A depressed pregnant woman may not eat properly or may use alcohol or other drugs to self-medicate. While an antidepressant may present a small risk to the developing fetus, alcohol is a devastating teratogen that can cause substantial birth defects (see Chapter 8). After birth, breastfeeding provides nutrition and antibodies to a newborn infant. However, breastfeeding is a learned skill for both a mother and infant. A mother who is sleep-deprived, anxious, and continuously crying will not only have difficulty bonding with her new baby but will also have difficulty feeding her baby. The feeding difficulties and lack of bonding will increase anxiety, potentially leading to a more serious mood and/or anxiety disorder. If depression and anxiety persist, the baby may fail to gain weight or otherwise thrive. While new mothers may worry about the impact of antidepressant drugs on their baby, the literature has revealed that most of the newer SSRI antidepressants produce very low to undetectable plasma concentrations in infants being nursed. However, some antidepressants are slightly better than others in this regard. Mothers taking fluoxetine, citalopram, or venlafaxine may be switched to a different SSRI or SNRI that is less likely to be transmissible in breast milk (Berle & Spigset, 2011; Toohey, 2012). The main concern for an infant who is exposed to antidepressants in utero or through breast milk is discontinuation syndrome, which occurs when the infant is no longer exposed to the drug. Symptoms of discontinuation syndrome in an infant include inconsolable crying, low body temperature, nursing difficulties, and sleeping difficulties. One study examined symptoms of discontinuation syndrome in infants born to mothers who used antidepressants during pregnancy and/or while breastfeeding. The data suggested that symptoms were more likely in infants who were exposed to antidepressants in utero. Up to 17% of infants exhibited at least one symptom of discontinuation syndrome, with inconsolable crying being the most frequently reported symptom (Hale, Kendall-Tackett, Cong, Votta, & McCurdy, 2010). Health care providers agree that limiting exposure to psychotherapeutic drugs in pregnancy or while breastfeeding is ideal to minimize risks of exposure to the baby. Talk therapy is useful in helping new mothers manage stress, anxiety, and depression. However, mood and anxiety disorders do occur in pregnant and breastfeeding women. Helping a mother get a mood or anxiety disorder under control is important to the well-being of both the mother and her baby. Cautious and careful use of antidepressants can be helpful in many of these cases.

Pharmacology of Antidepressants

Sites of Action

Antidepressant drugs act by elevating levels of the brain's monoamine neurotransmitters, which are thought to be deficient in depression. Serotonin, norepinephrine, and dopamine are all monoamine neurotransmitters. Antidepressant drugs directly increase serotonin and/or norepinephrine activity, while exhibiting little direct action on dopamine. There are four major

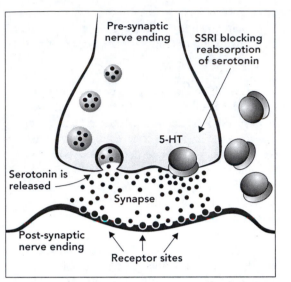

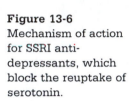

Figure 13-6
Mechanism of action for SSRI anti-depressants, which block the reuptake of serotonin.

categories of antidepressant drugs: tricyclic antidepressants, monoamine oxidase inhibitors (MAOIs), selective serotonin reuptake inhibitors (SSRIs)/serotonin norepinephrine reuptake inhibitors (SNRIs), and atypical antidepressants. Each category of antidepressant drug acts slightly differently in restoring monoamine neurotransmitter activity, and there can also be subtle differences among drugs found in the same category. However, general statements can be made about how these drugs act at their sites of action. The tricyclic antidepressants (such as imipramine) block reuptake (recycling) of both norepinephrine and serotonin, with the action on norepinephrine being more pronounced. When reuptake is blocked, increased levels of the neurotransmitter are left in the synaptic gap. Thus, more neurotransmitter is likely to bind with the postsynaptic neuron, and this action is fairly rapid. As mentioned earlier in this chapter, the slow onset of therapeutic effectiveness of antidepressants is due to these immediate actions later leading to longer-term changes such as neuronal growth and neurogenesis in various regions of the brain. The selective serotonin reuptake inhibitors (SSRIs) are more specific in their action (Figure 13-6); they block serotonin reuptake sites. The serotonin norepinephrine reuptake inhibitors (SNRIs) block both serotonin and norepinephrine reuptake sites, making them similar to the older tricyclic antidepressants. The older tricyclic drugs tend to have a more pronounced action on norepinephrine reuptake sites (Baldessarini, 2001).

The monoamine oxidase inhibitors act by blocking the normal enzyme breakdown of monoamine neurotransmitters. Monoamine oxidase is the enzyme involved in the metabolic breakdown of norepinephrine and serotonin. Monoamine oxidase inhibitors block the action of monoamine oxidase. When the normal breakdown of serotonin and norepinephrine is prevented, a larger amount of these neurotransmitters is available to bind to postsynaptic neurons.

The mechanism of action for atypical antidepressants is somewhat less well understood since these are the newest drugs. An atypical antidepressant, such as Wellbutrin®, seems to act by blocking the reuptake of dopamine and norepinephrine. This increases the levels of dopamine and norepinephrine in the brain. Given that increased dopamine activity is not the primary result observed with other antidepressant drugs, the atypical antidepressants act more like mild psychostimulants, similar to amphetamines (discussed in Chapter 7). Therapeutically, the atypical antidepressants may be most helpful to patients experiencing strong fatigue and sleepiness as part of their depression. Interestingly, amphetamines had been tried back in the 1930s as a treatment for depression. As discussed in Chapter 7, there are problems with the repeated use of amphetamines, such as risk of psychosis, rendering these drugs problematic for the long-term treatment of depression (Rasmussen, 2008). However, it is interesting that the newest antidepressant drugs act in ways that somewhat draw from the oldest approaches in treating depression.

Pharmacokinetics

Given their long duration of action, antidepressants are typically orally administered once daily. Absorption is relatively rapid, although some antidepressants may cause gastrointestinal upset or slow gastric emptying. These gastric complications typically arise early in use, and they can result in slow or slightly erratic drug absorption. However, most drug doses are typically absorbed without major issues, and peak blood levels are achieved within a few hours. Antidepressants are widely distributed throughout the body via the bloodstream. Antidepressants readily cross the blood–brain barrier and thus easily reach the site of action. These drugs are metabolized and eliminated from the body over several days. Most tricyclic antidepressants are completely eliminated from the body in approximately 10 days. The SSRI antidepressants are eliminated from the body more rapidly, with most being eliminated in about 3 days. The MAOIs are long acting and require 14 days to be eliminated from the body. Antidepressants can be used across the lifespan. In children, antidepressants may be metabolized more rapidly. Patients ages 60 and older typically have slower metabolization rates. Doses and timing of doses may need to be adjusted for these specific populations (Baldessarini, 2001).

Focus on Careers: Science Journalist

Do you enjoy reading and writing about science? Why not build a career from this interest? The general public seems to have an increasing thirst for scientific information. This is particularly true for topics related to psychopharmacology. On any given day, you can search the website of any major news network and find at least one, if not many, new stories about one of the drugs talked about in this book. Journalists write often about new research on psychotherapeutic drugs, in part because readers can relate to problems like mood and anxiety disorders. Journalism is a broad field with a wide variety of career paths. While a career writing for television or a newspaper may easily come to mind, there are also journalists that work for magazines, content producers for Internet websites, and copyeditors. Some technical writers work directly for pharmaceutical companies developing marketing materials. Many journalists have formal training. Journalism graduate programs are a means to get this formal training, with some programs specializing in science writing. Typically, these programs last 2 years, and an M.A. degree is obtained upon completion. Similar to any graduate program, the application process involves submitting Graduate Record Examination (GRE) scores, letters of recommendation, and writing samples. While graduate training in journalism may open doors, many journalists do not have this training. Many started their journalism careers at the student newspaper at their college. Science journalists in particular may or may not have formal training in journalism. Regardless of how one is trained, the business is competitive. One must be a superb writer and be able to work very quickly. The stress of deadlines is greatest for the news media, while a bit less intense for magazines and technical writing. Budding journalists want to tell stories, and the best science journalists have the ability to make complicated science accessible to a wide audience. As a scientist who has worked with many journalists, I am appreciative of their efforts in bringing science to the general public. They reach so many more people than I ever could with my scientific writing alone.

Some websites to explore:

Society for Professional Journalists
http://www.spj.org/careeradvice.asp
Council for the Advancement of Science Writing
http://casw.org/casw/guide-careers-science-writing

QUICK QUIZ 13-1

1. Worldwide, what is the approximate one-year prevalence rate for depression?
   a. 1% to 2%
   b. 3% to 5%
   c. 6% to 9%
   d. 10% to 19%
   e. 20% to 25%

2. The first psychotherapeutic medications used to treat mood and anxiety disorders were discovered in the
   a. 1850s
   b. 1900s
   c. 1950s
   d. 1970s

3. Jordan is a combat veteran who served a tour of duty in Afghanistan. Since returning, he has experienced flashbacks of being in combat, nightmares, hyperarousal, and difficulty sleeping. Which diagnosis is most likely?
   a. Phobia
   b. Major depression
   c. Bipolar depression
   d. Generalized anxiety disorder
   e. Posttraumatic stress disorder

4. Angelina is suffering from comorbid depression and anxiety. Her physician started her on an antidepressant drug, which she has taken as prescribed for about 7 days. At this point, Angelina would probably be experiencing:
   a. Reduction in her depression symptoms
   b. Reduction in her anxiety symptoms

   c. Side effects such as dry mouth and constipation
   d. a and b
   e. All of the above

5. Tolerance to the therapeutic effectiveness of antidepressants is typically observed with use that has occurred over _____.
   a. hours
   b. days
   c. weeks
   d. months
   e. years

6. The atypical antidepressants, such as Wellbutrin®, have a mechanism of action that is similar to the action of _____.
   a. alcohol
   b. amphetamines
   c. marijuana
   d. nicotine
   e. opiates

7. Barbiturates are no longer used to treat anxiety disorders. When and why was use of barbiturates discontinued?

8. What is the relationship between a country's socioeconomic status and its rate of depression? Why might this relationship be observed?

9. Explain the relationship between antidepressant drug treatment and neurogenesis.

ANSWERS TO QUICK QUIZ 13-1:

1. b – 3% to 5%
2. c – 1950s
3. e – posttraumatic stress disorder
4. c – side effects such as dry mouth and constipation
5. e – years
6. b – amphetamines
7. Barbiturates stopped being used to treat anxiety by the 1970s. Though popular in the 1950s and 1960s, these drugs were addictive and also led to too many accidental and intentional overdose deaths.
8. Lower- to middle-income countries tend to have lower rates of depression than high-income countries. This counterintuitive relationship may be observed because for people living in developing countries, such as India and China, many individuals are poor. In the United States, there is great affluence and also great poverty. The poor in the United States may face the stark reality of their situation more often. It could also be that expectations about how happy one should be differ across societies.
9. Depression, anxiety, and chronic stress can induce brain damage, as evidenced by neuronal death observed in structures of the brain such as the hippocampus. Antidepressant drug treatment induces neurogenesis in the hippocampus. With several weeks of drug treatment, new neurons will form in this region of the brain. The timing of neurogenesis coincides with the long time that antidepressants must be taken before the patient reports beneficial symptom relief.

Acute and Chronic Effects of Mood Stabilizers

The extreme mood states associated with bipolar disorder can be controlled with mood-stabilizing drugs such as lithium. These drugs control the symptoms of both mania and depression. However, lithium is notoriously slow in its therapeutic onset of action, like all antidepressant drugs. It may take weeks to see improvement in stabilizing mood. When a patient is experiencing mania, the patient may be agitated and can even be psychotic. Given that mood symptoms are so slow to respond to treatment, the patient may need a brief hospital stay until symptoms come under control (Figure 13-7) (Serjean & Dobuzinskis, 2011). Antipsychotic drugs may also be used initially to control manic symptoms, especially until lithium has had a chance to take effect. As with antidepressants, there are several side effects that may emerge early in treatment before symptoms come under control. Gastrointestinal upset, tremors, dry mouth, and frequent urination may all emerge as initial side effects that typically decrease after a

©Jeff Vespa/Getty Images

Figure 13-7
In 2011, actress Catherine Zeta-Jones's publicist announced that she was admitted to a mental health facility for a brief stay to treat her bipolar disorder.

few weeks of treatment. However, once mood has stabilized, the patient can return home, and good results may subsequently be achieved with mood-stabilizing medication alone. Interestingly, lithium is the only psychotherapeutic drug which is considered to be an effective **prophylactic drug** (because it prevents a mental illness). Patients with bipolar disorder are typically treated with lithium long-term, to prevent recurrence of extreme mood states. Patients with bipolar disorder are far less likely to relapse or attempt suicide if maintained long-term with lithium drug treatment. If a patient wishes to discontinue treatment, a very gradual decrease in the dose of the drug is recommended, to carefully assess if symptoms of bipolar disorder reemerge (Baldessarini & Tarazi, 2001; Calkin & Alda, 2012).

There are several medical concerns that might make lithium treatment inappropriate for a patient. Lithium can lead to cardiac complications, and it would therefore be inappropriate for a patient with heart problems. Also, lithium is primarily excreted from the body in urine through the action of the kidneys. Thus, any patient with renal problems would also not be suited to lithium treatment. Some anticonvulsant drugs, such as valproate and carbamazepine, have been used successfully to treat mania, either as an adjunct or instead of lithium. Lithium may also lead to weight gain, which can result in other health problems requiring medical treatment (Baldessarini & Tarazi, 2001; Calkin & Alda, 2012).

Tolerance and Withdrawal for Mood Stabilizers

Tolerance and withdrawal concerns are similar for mood stabilizers and antidepressants. Physicians typically recommend continuous treatment with mood stabilizers, just like the antidepressant drugs, to prevent relapses. Patients suffering from bipolar disorder are particularly prone to relapses if not continuously maintained on lithium. Given this long duration approach to treatment, one may wonder if tolerance will be a concern. Tolerance does develop to the early side effects experienced in treatment. Patients who initially report side effects such as gastrointestinal upset, tremors, and dry mouth may find that these symptoms decline in intensity or dissipate within a few weeks of drug treatment. Importantly, tolerance does not appear to develop for the effectiveness of the lithium to control mood states, even after years of treatment for many patients (Calkin & Alda, 2012). However, some patients do develop treatment resistance to lithium and then start to reexperience symptoms. The physician can deal with this concern by carefully increasing the dose or adding an antipsychotic drug to help manage manic episodes. Given that there are few available drugs to treat bipolar depression, tolerance development can be problematic in condition management (Post, 2012).

Abrupt cessation of treatment with mood stabilizers is not recommended because withdrawal symptoms may emerge. Similar to rapid withdrawal of antidepressants, symptoms of illness may also appear with cessation of mood stabilizers. Reemergence of depression and mania is more likely with a rapid discontinuation of lithium drug treatment. It is recommended that patients very slowly come off these medications, over a period of weeks or even months, to avoid these concerns (Baldessarini, Tondo, Ghiani, & Lepri, 2010).

Pharmacology of Mood Stabilizers

Sites of Action

In bipolar depression, it is thought that the depression and mania arise from insufficient and excess levels of monoamine neurotransmitters, respectively. However, the mechanism by which lithium regulates these extreme mood states is poorly understood. Lithium may partly function by inhibiting the release of norepinephrine and dopamine. This action would plausibly decrease mania. Lithium may also enhance the release of serotonin, especially in the limbic system, which would account for the antidepressant action. Lithium may also alter some hormonal responses that contribute to mood state (Baldessarini & Tarazi, 2001; Hafeman, Chang, Garret, Sanders, & Phillips, 2012).

Pharmacokinetics

Mood stabilizers like lithium are typically administered orally in pill form. Absorption in the bloodstream occurs through the walls of the small intestine. Peak concentration of lithium in the blood occurs 2 to 4 hours after an oral dose. Complete absorption throughout the body occurs within about 8 hours. Lithium can be administered several times per day, or it can be administered once a day in a slow-release form. Once in the bloodstream, lithium crosses the blood–brain barrier, albeit somewhat more slowly than other psychoactive drugs. Lithium is metabolized once it has reached the site of action, and excretion occurs mainly by the kidneys. Up to 95% of lithium is eliminated through urine, with up to two-thirds of an acute dose being eliminated within 12 hours, and the rest being slowly excreted over about 2 weeks (Baldessarini & Tarazi, 2001).

For patients likely to experience manic episodes, it is important that physicians closely monitor drug treatment. Lithium has a small safety ratio, meaning that the effective dose that controls symptoms is not that much smaller than the lethal dose. Moreover, there is some variability in patients' pharmacokinetic response to the drug. As such, physicians must be vigilant about the possibility of an overdose, especially early in treatment. Vomiting, profuse diarrhea, drowsiness, ataxia (poor control over motor movements), cardiac problems, confusion, blurred vision, seizures, and/or coma are all possible symptoms of an overdose of lithium (Baldessarini & Tarazi, 2001).

Acute and Chronic Effects of Antianxiety Drugs

Antianxiety drugs (such as benzodiazepines) act immediately, in contrast to the antidepressants and mood stabilizers that often require weeks of treatment before a patient notices an effect. After only one dose of an antianxiety drug, the patient may already report decreased anxiety. The antianxiety effects of benzodiazepines are also readily observable in animal models. When a rat or mouse is placed in a novel (unfamiliar) open-field environment, the animal will exhibit **thigmotaxis**, in which the animal remains close to the walls while it explores its new location (Figure 13-8). Thigmotaxic behavior is thought to be an index of anxiety. One dose of a

©Tetra Images/Alamy

Figure 13-8
An open-field test can be used to measure the antianxiety properties of benzodiazepines. Thigmotaxis (staying near the walls) is thought to be a measure of anxiety in rodents such as mice and rats. Benzodiazepine treatment tends to result in less thigmotaxic behavior in mice.

benzodiazepine drug will decrease the amount of thigmotaxic behavior observed during an open-field test, as the animal will increase the amount of time spent in the center of the open field (Simon, Dupuis, & Costentin, 1994).

Anxiety disorders can result in transient or persistent states of anxiety. As a result, the choice of antianxiety drug for a patient depends on the nature of the particular anxiety being treated. An individual with a fear of flying may simply take an antianxiety drug, such as a benzodiazepine, prior to boarding an airplane. This individual may find use of the benzodiazepine limited to the situation that induces anxiety and feelings of panic. Ideally, the benzodiazepine should have a short duration of action, so that the effect of the drug wears off by the time the individual is ready to exit the airplane. By contrast, someone with generalized anxiety disorder may experience anxiety from the time he or she wakes up until going to sleep for the night. A longer-acting benzodiazepine would be more appropriate for treating generalized anxiety disorder. The half-lives for commonly used benzodiazepines such as triazolam, alprazolam, and diazepam, are 4, 15, and 50 hours, respectively. Depending on the nature of the anxiety symptoms, there are several choices of benzodiazepine drug that can fit with those needs. Most benzodiazepines are administered orally, and patients typically report some reduction in anxiety symptoms within 15 minutes to an hour after oral administration. Faster onset of action also occurs when there is no food in the stomach. For chronic anxiety, such as generalized anxiety disorder, several days of treatment may be necessary before the patient reports improvement in symptoms (Charney, Mihic, & Harris, 2001).

Once a benzodiazepine has taken effect, patients may not only feel less anxiety, but their muscles may feel less tense and more relaxed. The individual may also report feeling tired. If the dose is high, pronounced sedation, hypnosis, and anterograde amnesia may result. Patients experiencing anxiety-induced insomnia may have more restful sleep with benzodiazepines. However, benzodiazepines do decrease the rapid eye movement (REM) portion of sleep, which is when dreaming occurs. Given that REM is important for the consolidation of memories, individuals using benzodiazepines may report concerns about memory problems. Decreased duration of REM sleep may also result in so-called "hangover" effects the next day, in which an individual feels groggy and not rested, despite having had a deep sleep. Some antianxiety medications marketed as sleeping aids, such as Ambien CR® (zolpidem), do counteract anxiety and insomnia, but they are also less likely to result in hangover effects. Benzodiazepines are also prescribed for various medical conditions in addition to anxiety disorders. Benzodiazepines decrease the likelihood of seizures, and they are often used by patients withdrawing from alcohol for this purpose (Charney et al., 2001).

There are several concerns associated with both the acute and chronic use of benzodiazepines. First, benzodiazepines may interfere with various cognitive abilities and induce sedation. Therefore, it is recommended that benzodiazepines not be taken by a patient that needs to drive. Reaction time is negatively affected, as is psychomotor coordination. Use of benzodiazepines may also interfere with the ability to perform well at work or school, although the effects on cognitive performance are less problematic than the effects on motor performance. Benzodiazepines also should not be mixed with alcohol, opiates, or other sedative drugs (Figure 13-9). Each of these sedative drugs has a similar mechanism of action for inducing sedation. Benzodiazepines alone are considered to be quite safe, and they cannot independently induce respiratory depression. However, the combined effects of various sedative drugs can suppress respiration and heart rate, which may lead to coma or death. A final, lesser concern with benzodiazepine use is the emergence of various side effects. Headaches, weakness, blurred vision, dizziness, gastrointestinal upset, chest pains, and incontinence are the most frequently reported side effects (Charney et al., 2001; Julien, 2005).

Antianxiety medications are infrequently abused, in part because they do not produce feelings of being high or other subjective responses that lead to abuse. However, chronic use may cause some patients to become overly reliant on benzodiazepines. This potential circumstance should be monitored closely by the prescribing physician. However, benzodiazepines are infrequently diverted prescription medications that do not typically end up on the street. For individuals having

©Everett Collection

Figure 13-9
An autopsy report revealed that actor Heath Ledger died after consuming benzodiazepines, prescription opiates, and sleeping pills (Barron, 2008). While benzodiazepines alone are considered safe, they should always be taken as directed and never mixed with alcohol or opiate drugs.

problems abusing other drugs, psychotherapeutic drugs may be employed to manage the negative effects of drug use, including withdrawal symptoms from other drugs. There is one potent benzodiazepine that seems to be frequently abused as a street drug. **Rohypnol**® (flunitrazepam) is marketed as a sleeping pill in Europe and Latin America, although it is not used in the United States. Users refer to this drug as "roofies." Rohypnol® acts like other benzodiazepines, albeit with more pronounced effects. Its use can lead to memory loss and blackouts, similar to high doses of alcohol. "Roofies" have become widely known as a date rape drug, in part because it can be slipped into an alcoholic drink and the consumer, typically a woman, may not realize this has occurred given that Rohypnol® has no appreciable taste or smell. The crime of sexual assault thus may evade detection if the victim is unable to remember anything about the crime. Moreover, this drug combination can accidentally lead to death, because alcohol and the Rohypnol® in combination can suppress respiration (Charney et al., 2001).

Tolerance and Withdrawal for Antianxiety Drugs

Chronic use of benzodiazepines is more likely to result in tolerance than chronic use of antidepressant or mood-stabilizing drugs. However, relatively high doses of benzodiazepines are typically needed before appreciable tolerance develops. Thus, clinicians still consider antianxiety medications to be relatively safe, at least where tolerance development is concerned. When tolerance does seem to develop, the repeated use of benzodiazepines can result in diminished control over anxiety symptoms over time. The physician may then need to increase the dose or switch the patient to a different medication. Current best practices suggest that daily use of benzodiazepines should be limited to a month or less. For patients having chronic anxiety that persists longer than a month, antidepressants are typically prescribed, which can help keep the needed dose of antianxiety drug lower or even limit its use altogether (Julien, 2005).

If benzodiazepines are used chronically, an abrupt cessation of use might induce withdrawal symptoms. Among patients maintained on high doses, withdrawal symptoms may occur in as many as one-third of patients. Typical withdrawal symptoms include anxiety, tremors, sweating, and insomnia. In extreme cases, seizures may result. These withdrawal symptoms can remain problematic for several weeks. Interestingly, these withdrawal symptoms may not emerge immediately upon cessation of use of the drug, but instead they may arise after several days (Miller & Greenblatt, 1996). One concern with stopping use of antianxiety drugs is that a significant withdrawal symptom is actually anxiety, which is obviously the primary symptom of an anxiety disorder. Therefore, when physicians are taking a patient off an antianxiety medication, for whatever reason, the dose should be reduced very slowly. Moreover, the patient needs to be warned that reemergence of anxiety can be a symptom of withdrawal and may not necessarily reflect a relapse of the anxiety disorder.

Pharmacology of Antianxiety Drugs

Sites of Action

Benzodiazepines act by enhancing the activity of GABA, an inhibitory neurotransmitter. GABA decreases neural communication between cells, which leads to a calming effect on the brain. Benzodiazepines bind to modulatory sites on a subset of GABA$_A$ receptors, which are known as **benzodiazepine receptors**. This action enhances the effect of GABA by increasing the overall conductance of these GABA$_A$ channels. Antianxiety drugs thus decrease overall neural communication in the brain. Barbiturates (sleeping pills) and alcohol also bind to benzodiazepine receptors, which explains the similarity of these drugs to benzodiazepines in decreasing anxiety and inducing sedation (Santhakumar, Wallner, & Otis, 2007; Sigel & Steinmann, 2012). Other nonbenzodiazepine drugs that are used to treat anxiety, such as buspirone, do not increase GABA activity but instead increase serotonin activity (Rush & Griffiths, 1997).

Pharmacokinetics

Antianxiety drugs are typically administered orally, although other routes of administration, such as injection, are also used. When orally administered, benzodiazepines are readily absorbed from the gastrointestinal tract through the small intestine. Consumption of food slows absorption. The various benzodiazepines have similar mechanisms of action, but they can differ considerably in the speed of onset and duration of action. The benzodiazepines that have greater lipid solubility more readily pass through the blood–brain barrier, which results in a faster onset of drug action. On average, peak drug effects occur about one hour after drug administration, although different effects may be observed depending on the particular benzodiazepine in question. The duration of drug action can also vary considerably, from an hour up to two days. Short duration of action benzodiazepines tend to be quickly metabolized into inactive metabolites that no longer exert effects on GABA receptors and are excreted from the body. By contrast, the long duration of action benzodiazepines tend to undergo metabolic changes once in the body, leading to various metabolites that remain active and continue to bind to GABA receptors. Longer-acting benzodiazepines tend to be inappropriate for elderly patients, who have a reduced ability to metabolize these benzodiazepines and their associated metabolites. Even when shorter-acting benzodiazepines are used in the elderly, the dose typically needs to be reduced because of a lower capacity to metabolize this type of drug (Charney et al., 2001; Julien, 2005).

Among all patients, speed of onset and duration of drug action should be considered when selecting an appropriate antianxiety medication. These considerations will be impacted by the nature of the anxiety disorder. For example, a patient needing treatment for anxiety before a medical procedure would potentially benefit from a fast onset yet short duration of action benzodiazepine. A patient experiencing generalized anxiety disorder may instead need a long duration of action benzodiazepine, given the persistent and chronic nature of their anxiety. Once benzodiazepines have had their effect, excretion of benzodiazepine metabolites occurs primarily through urine (Charney et al., 2001; Julien, 2005).

Treatment of Mood and Anxiety Disorders

Mood and anxiety disorders can develop at any age. Even after a depressive episode ends, the disorder can later recur. Given the risk of recurrence, depression can reduce people's functioning over a lifetime if not properly managed. The World Health Organization states that depression is the leading cause of disability worldwide, based on examining total years lost because of disability (WHO, 2012). That statement is remarkable since many people, when considering disabilities that may prevent one from working, might not immediately think of depression. Therefore, effective treatment for mood and anxiety disorders is critical for long-term well-being and general health in society.

There are a variety of approaches for dealing with a mental disorder. One common approach is to do nothing and wait for the symptoms to go away. For many individuals, this is the chosen route. The individual may experience symptoms for weeks or months, and they may hope that the symptoms will decline in intensity over time. In the majority of cases, symptom dissipation does occur. However, there are cases where the mental disorder persists, and the individual's inability to function becomes evident. At that point, treatment is necessary, with several available approaches to treatment. One approach involves relying on psychological treatments such as talk therapy to overcome the disorder. The individual suffering from the mood or anxiety disorder may seek a mental health care specialist, such as a psychologist, psychiatrist, or social worker for therapy. Behavior therapies are highly effective in treating anxiety disorders, which frequently have a learned component. For example, a fear of cats can be unlearned by exposing the individual to cats in a therapeutic setting. This is appropriately known as exposure therapy. Stress that contributes to mood and anxiety disorders can often be better managed with the help of a therapist. Cognitive behavioral therapy is one approach the therapist might employ in dealing with the negative thoughts and ruminations that accompany major depression (Kring et al., 2012).

While talk therapy can be incredibly helpful for individuals suffering from a mood or anxiety disorder, the most common current approach to treating mood and anxiety disorders is to begin treatment with a psychotherapeutic drug. The diagnosis and treatment of mood and anxiety disorders typically occurs in primary care settings. Referral to a specialist (psychiatrist, psychologist, or neurologist) typically only occurs for more difficult cases. Most psychotherapeutic drugs for mood and anxiety disorders are prescribed by a general care physician. Though brief duration psychological talk therapy would help in many of these cases, the reality is that though health insurance companies will cover prescription medications, they may not cover a visit to a psychologist or other mental health care specialist. Various psychotherapies have been demonstrated to be effective in the treatment of depression, including brief duration cognitive behavior therapy. While most clinicians concur that medication may be unnecessary in mild or subclinical cases, medication is often used in these cases anyway. Lack of social support and lack of easy access to talk therapy contribute to the unnecessary overuse of psychotherapeutic drugs (Kring et al., 2012; WHO, 2012).

While psychotherapeutic drugs are helpful for many depressed and anxious patients, there are also cases where patients do not respond to drug treatment. For persistent anxiety disorders, long-term use of benzodiazepines is inadvisable given concerns such as tolerance development. The prescribing physician may change the treatment from antianxiety medication to antidepressant medication, even when anxiety is the primary concern. Recall from earlier in this chapter that mood and anxiety disorders tend to be highly comorbid. Many patients may be using more than one type of medication to manage their symptoms. For cases where the patient is suicidal or in an uncontrolled manic state, a brief duration hospitalization may be warranted. The manic patient may require close monitoring and antipsychotic drug treatment until the appropriate dose of mood stabilizer has become effective. The use of electroconvulsive shock therapy (ECT) is risky, but it can be effective for severe cases of depression. Exposing a patient's brain to electricity may seem barbaric, yet it does appear to reset the brain. With even a few sessions of ECT, a severely depressed and suicidal patient may suddenly seem to have returned to normal. The transition can be remarkable. However, there are risks to ECT, such as permanent memory impairment. Thus, ECT is only used for extreme cases that aren't easily addressed by other techniques (Kring et al., 2012).

The significant burden of mood and anxiety disorders is a major public health challenge worldwide. Interventions such as psychotherapeutic drug treatment and brief psychotherapy can significantly reduce these problems. Even though treatment is effective, the majority of people, both in the United States and worldwide, never receive it. Individuals are either hoping their problem goes away with time or they do not have access to the needed care, usually due to economic considerations. Globally, it is estimated that only about 50% of individuals with depression who need treatment are receiving it. In some countries, only about 10% of individuals who need treatment for depression are receiving it (WHO, 2012).

Given the prevalence of mood and anxiety disorders, a brief mention about prevention is warranted. Are there ways to prevent the onset of these disorders? The answer is yes. Strengthening protective factors and reducing risk factors can both reduce the likelihood that individuals will develop these common mental disorders. Children and adolescents represent ideal populations on which to focus prevention programs. School-based programs can help children and adolescents improve their social and problem-solving skills; indeed, these programs have been demonstrated to be effective. Among adults, stress can contribute to anxiety and depression in employees. Many workplaces offer stress management workshops and other employee wellness initiatives in an effort to limit the development of common mental disorders. Even simple interventions such as implementation of exercise programs for the elderly can limit depression among this demographic group. In all of these cases, the costs associated with prevention are far less than the costs associated with treating a mood or anxiety disorder, including lost wages and productivity (Kring et al., 2012; WHO, 2012).

In the News:

Gray, K. (2013, March 16). Are we over-diagnosing mental illness? *CNN*.

In this news story, the journalist introduces Kelli Montgomery, a recently pregnant woman who has unfortunately suffered a stillbirth. She is devastated and feeling depressed, so her physicians immediately suggest antidepressants and sleeping aids. However, Kelli chose not to take the drugs. Her view, similar to that of a small but growing number of mental health practitioners, is that it is appropriate to feel depressed when life presents a tough challenge.

Montgomery had experienced something extremely traumatic. Her baby had died, which was terribly upsetting. While she was amenable to therapy to discuss her feelings, she felt that her depressed state was appropriate, not abnormal and requiring drug treatment. The journalist further provides evidence from a variety of psychologists and psychiatrists suggesting that far too many people are prescribed psychotherapeutic drugs without needing them. For example, the frequency of diagnosis of bipolar disorder in children has jumped 40-fold in the last two decades, states Dr. Bernard Carroll, formerly the chairman of Duke University's psychiatry department. In Dr. Carroll's view, there are far too many children given mood stabilizers or antipsychotic drugs who have yet to exhibit a clear manic episode, the hallmark indicating that bipolar disorder is present. Diagnoses for other mood and anxiety disorders have also increased. Not surprisingly, prescriptions for antidepressant, mood-stabilizing, and antianxiety medications have also increased over the last few decades.

Use this news article to test and apply your knowledge:

1. This article suggests that physicians view mood and anxiety disorders as common and requiring treatment. Does epidemiological data agree with the views of prescribing physicians?
2. Dr. Carroll is concerned about the use of mood-stabilizing medications and other psychotherapeutic drugs in children. Why might the doctor be concerned?

Answers:

1. Epidemiological studies suggest that 1 in 4 individuals may suffer from a mental disorder in any given year. Although half of these individuals may only have a mild illness, requiring no treatment, the other half may need treatment. The three most common mental disorder categories are mood disorders, anxiety disorders, and substance abuse disorders.
2. All psychotherapeutic drugs, even when used as directed, can result in side effects. Problems like weight gain, sexual dysfunction, and other concerns arise from treatment with antidepressants, mood stabilizers, or antianxiety medications. Moreover, the brain is still developing in children and adolescents. Given that these drugs alter neurotransmitter activity, the long-term implications of drug treatment are a concern.

What do you think about this news story?

Kelli Montgomery experienced a traumatic event. She felt that a drug to help her overcome her grief was inappropriate. Do you think that we as a society are uncomfortable with unhappiness, even when it is appropriate given the circumstances? Do you think that psychotherapeutic drugs are overused to treat depression and anxiety? What might be the best approach to prevent overuse of these drugs, while still helping the individuals who really need these drugs?

QUICK QUIZ 13-2

1. Which psychotherapeutic drug is used prophylactically?
   a. Chlorpromazine
   b. Lithium
   c. Imipramine
   d. All of the above
   e. None of the above

2. Repeated use of which type of psychotherapeutic drug is most likely to result in tolerance development to its intended therapeutic effects?
   a. Tricyclic antidepressants
   b. SSRI antidepressants
   c. MAOIs
   d. Mood stabilizers
   e. Benzodiazepines

3. One concern with prescribing lithium is that _____.
   a. the safety ratio is small.
   b. the safety ratio is large.
   c. the therapeutic effectiveness is low.
   d. the therapeutic effectiveness is variable.
   e. None of the above

4. A patient experiencing a manic episode is admitted to hospital. The patient is started on lithium but has been slow to respond. What other drug might also be used while the patient's condition is difficult to manage (until the manic episode subsides)?
   a. Antianxiety drug
   b. Antipsychotic drug
   c. SSRI antidepressant
   d. MAOI antidepressant
   e. Tricyclic antidepressant

5. Benzodiazepines enhance the activity of which neurotransmitter?
   a. Dopamine
   b. Serotonin
   c. Norepinephrine
   d. GABA
   e. Adenosine

6. Focusing on the risk of overdose, which drug is the least safe?
   a. SSRI antidepressant
   b. MAOI antidepressant
   c. Benzodiazepine
   d. Barbiturate

7. Mildred is 70 years old and has recently developed symptoms of generalized anxiety disorder. What medication would her physician likely prescribe for her? Be specific about ideal duration of action and dose when explaining your answer.

8. Every time you go to a party with your friend Stella, she tends to stay near the edge of the room and appears hesitant to join the group. What term describes this behavior, and what might this behavior reflect? What type of drug discussed in this chapter might change her behavior?

9. Elton has a prescription for a benzodiazepine. He also smokes, drinks alcohol, and sometimes snorts cocaine. Which recreational drug is most risky when combined with the benzodiazepine, and why?

ANSWERS TO QUICK QUIZ 13-2:

1. b – lithium
2. e – benzodiazepines
3. a – the safety ratio is small
4. b – antipsychotic drug
5. d – GABA
6. d – barbiturate
7. Given Mildred's age, her physician would likely prescribe a short-acting benzodiazepine, but at a dose that would be less than would be prescribed for a younger patient. This choice would reflect the reduced metabolism capacity in elderly patients, especially for benzodiazepines. Moreover, if her symptoms persist for more than 4 weeks, her physician may try an antidepressant medication, given concerns about tolerance developing to daily use of benzodiazepines.

8. Stella's behavior is called thigmotaxis and might indicate anxiety. She may be experiencing some social anxiety. A benzodiazepine might change her behavior, making her more likely to leave the wall and interact with others.

9. Alcohol is the most risky drug to combine with the benzodiazepine because both are sedatives. When combined, they could suppress respiration, which could lead to a coma or even death.

CHAPTER SUMMARY

Mood disorders reflect disturbances in emotion that affect well-being and functioning. Clinicians distinguish between mood disorders wherein depression either does or does not include manic episodes. Anxiety disorders reflect conditions whereby anxiety has become debilitating. Anxiety disorders can be specific to certain situations or stimuli or anxiety can be generalized. Mood and anxiety disorders are highly comorbid. Interestingly, mood disorders are more common in high-income countries than low- to middle-income countries. Various psychotherapeutic drugs can be used to treat mood and anxiety disorders. Antidepressant drugs are used to reduce symptoms of depression. The four major categories of antidepressant drugs (tricyclic, MAOI, SSRI/SNRI, or atypical) are differentiated based on mechanism of action. Antidepressants act in various ways to elevate brain levels of the monoamine neurotransmitters serotonin and/or norepinephrine. Mood stabilizers such as lithium are used to treat bipolar disorder, although the mechanism of action of lithium is not well understood. Antianxiety drugs such as benzodiazepines are used to reduce symptoms of anxiety. Benzodiazepines decrease anxiety by enhancing the action of the neurotransmitter GABA. Antidepressants, mood stabilizers, and antianxiety medications have been available since the 1950s, with newer versions becoming available all the time. Antidepressants and mood stabilizers are typically slow to act, with patients often requiring weeks of treatment before appreciable symptom improvements occur. By contrast, antianxiety medications may be effective within an hour of the first dose. Antidepressants are typically used for months until the patient recovers. Mood stabilizers may be used for a lifetime. Lithium is considered the only prophylactic drug available to prevent the recurrence of a mental disorder. Physicians usually limit the duration of daily use of anti-anxiety medications to about a month, given concerns about tolerance and withdrawal. If a patient requires longer duration treatment for an anxiety disorder, an antidepressant medication is typically another option. The treatment of mood and anxiety disorders would ideally include both medication and psychological therapy. However, medication is relied upon more heavily in practice. Many patients who would benefit from brief duration treatment with a therapist may never receive it for a variety of reasons.

14 STEROIDS AND SMART DRUGS

Introduction

Major League Baseball has been on a mission to clean up its image. In the 1980s and 1990s, there was a surge in home runs by players like Mark McGwire, Sammy Sosa, and Barry Bonds. Records were broken. Also broken was the expectation of avoiding use of performance-enhancing drugs. Major League Baseball dealt with a storm of allegations that it had turned a blind eye to players using anabolic steroids to facilitate historic accomplishments (Figure 14-1). The league acknowledges that the loss of goodwill from steroid use injured its reputation, hurting the relationship the league had with its fans. To regain trust, the league, in coordination with the players' union, has intensified its drug-testing programs and made penalties harsher for those who cheat. Despite progress, a story recently broke of a clinic in Florida that was supplying at least a dozen players with steroids (Sutton & Botelho, 2013). The drive to enhance performance, both mental and physical, is part of what makes us human. We love to watch athletes accomplish historic feats. Psychoactive drugs can provide an edge to users in accomplishing great things either in the intellectual or physical domain. An elderly person may legitimately need a cognitive-enhancing drug to counteract progressive mental decline from dementia. Nevertheless, most would probably agree that reliance on performance-enhancing drugs to improve athletic prowess constitutes cheating. As with all psychoactive drugs, there are benefits and costs to the use of steroids. As some Major League Baseball players have discovered, the costs are not limited to health concerns or legal issues from getting caught. An association with steroid use can mar a player's legacy permanently. While Mark McGwire's accomplishments arguably qualify him for

Figure 14-1
Major League Baseball dealt with a storm of allegations that it had turned a blind eye to players using anabolic steroids.

©Sporting News Archive/Getty Images

induction to the Hall of Fame, his awkward confessions of cheating have left him far short of the votes required for that honor. Indeed, on January 9, 2013, Baseball Hall of Fame's vote was clear about how it perceives suspected steroid use in players. Along with McGwire, Barry Bonds, Roger Clemens, and Sammy Sosa were also denied entry, despite their seeming worthiness based on significant career accomplishments (Ginnetti, 2013)

LEARNING OBJECTIVES

Learning objectives can help organize your studying. Before we begin the topic of steroids and smart drugs, keep in mind that by the end of this chapter, you should be able to . . .

1. Describe how various psychoactive drugs can improve physical and mental performance.
2. Explain the brief history of anabolic steroids and smart drugs, including how long they have been available for use.
3. Describe how widespread steroid use is in athletics and how prevalent dementia is in society.
4. Describe the acute and chronic effects of steroids and smart drugs.
5. Explain how tolerance and withdrawal play a role in the action of steroids and smart drugs.
6. Describe the pharmacology of steroids and smart drugs.

Enhancing Physical and Mental Performance

Enhancement of physical and mental performance can occur with effort. Want to run a faster race? You need to spend hours training. Want to raise your grades? You need to spend hours studying. We all understand the relationship between effort and performance. However, some psychoactive drugs can enhance physical and mental performance by providing a bit of an additional edge beyond effort alone (Figure 14-2). In most cases, the motive for using steroids is not recreational. The user does not choose the drug to feel high or experience an altered mental state. Instead, the user is looking to improve an outcome. There are several legitimate purposes for these drugs. When the brain starts to deteriorate, such as occurs with dementia in the elderly, the use of cognitive-enhancing drugs can help the patient tremendously. Various medications are available for treatment of memory impairments in the elderly. Improving (or maintaining) intellectual performance can help these individuals maintain their lifestyle and avoid institutionalized care. For patients and their caregivers, drugs that enhance mental performance, such as the cholinesterase inhibitors that will be described later in this chapter, are often miracle drugs. By contrast, other cases of enhanced physical and mental performance are viewed by many in society as clearly unethical. The use of anabolic steroids to enhance athletic performance is often viewed as cheating. While we all love to watch professional athletes demonstrate athletic prowess, many of us discount their accomplishments when we learn that their achievements may have been enhanced by drugs.

Judgment is often harsh for athletes who cheat by enhancing "physical" performance via drugs. Enhancement of mental performance also occurs, with many viewing "mental" cheating somewhat less harshly. In Chapter 7, we discussed the increasing diversion of prescription stimulant medications intended for attention deficit/hyperactivity disorder (ADHD). High school and college students use these drugs to enhance grades (although some diversion also occurs by individuals using the drug recreationally to get high). Recent survey data indicates that full-time college students (ages 18 to 22) are twice as likely as their non-college-attending peers to have used the prescription stimulant, Adderall®, nonmedically in the past year (6.4% versus 3.0%) (SAMHSA, 2009). Improved focus and longer study sessions can potentially lead to increased

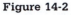

Figure 14-2
Some psychoactive drugs can enhance physical and mental performance by providing a bit of an additional edge beyond effort alone.

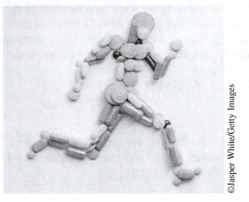

©Jasper White/Getty Images

test scores and improved grades. Unfortunately, illicit use of prescription medication can also lead to abuse of amphetamines, especially when individuals feel high with an increased dose. Moreover, significant health risks are associated with nontherapeutic use of amphetamines, including heart attacks and strokes (Arria, O'Grady, Caldeira, Vincent, & Wish, 2008; Schwartz, 2012). The dangers of diverted prescription stimulant medications are also present for drugs that enhance physical performance. Improvements in outcomes may occur with performance-enhancing drugs, but the costs must also be considered. In this final chapter, we will focus on the steroids and smart drugs that can enhance physical and mental performance.

More about the Science:

Dodge et al. (2012). Judging cheaters: Is substance misuse viewed similarly in the athletic and academic domains? *Psychology of Addictive Behaviors*, 26, 678–682.

As a society, we view as unethical the use of steroids to get an edge in athletic competition. We also view as unethical the use of prescription stimulant medications to improve one's grades (see Chapter 7 for more on how prescription stimulants might enhance cognitive performance). The researchers in this study asked college men whether using performance-enhancing drugs for sports or school represented the same kind of cheating. In this research, 1,200 college freshmen (only males) were presented with a questionnaire presenting two scenarios. One scenario described "Bill," a college sprinter who uses steroids to perform better in a race, because he does not have enough time to train. The second scenario described "Jeff," a college student who uses the prescription stimulant Adderall® to perform better on midterm exams, because he does not have enough time to study. Both Bill and Jeff perform better than expected because of the drug. After the participants in the study read each description, they were asked to determine if Bill and Jeff are cheaters. The participants rated Bill, who used steroids to enhance athletic performance, as more of a cheater than Jeff, who used Adderall® to improve his grades.

More about the Science Thought Questions:

1. What is one issue with the generalizability of the study's findings, given the sample recruited?
2. The statistics on the misuse of steroids and prescription stimulants indicates that the two occur at very different rates among college students. In this study, less than 1% of the sample reported having ever used anabolic steroids. By contrast, about 8% of the sample reported having misused a prescription stimulant (use without having a prescription) in the past year. How might the use patterns of the sample influence the results?

More about the Science Thought Question Answers:

1. The sample was exclusively male college students. It is not known if female college students or non-college-attending adults would have the same perspective.

2. Individuals who have misused a drug for performance enhancement themselves may view such behavior with less ethical concern. Since steroid use was less common in this sample, it is perhaps not surprising the misuse of steroids would be viewed as more unethical than the misuse of prescription stimulants.

What Are the Implications of This Research?

Both drug-enhanced athletic and intellectual performance are arguably unethical. However, we seem not to view them as the same. Why do you think this is the case? Do you think the general public has a more negative perception about steroids than diverted prescription stimulant medications? Do people view drugs as less influential on intelligence than athletic ability? What other reasons might explain these results?

Anabolic Steroids

Anabolic steroids are synthetic hormones related to the naturally occurring male hormone testosterone. Anabolic steroids have muscle-building (**anabolic**) and masculinizing (**androgenic**) effects. **Testosterone** is a naturally occurring male steroid hormone that is synthesized in the human body from cholesterol. Testosterone serves a variety of roles throughout development. In the developing embryo, testosterone plays a role in the emergence of male characteristics. At puberty, testosterone is responsible for the emergence of secondary sexual characteristics that accompany male development, including increased body hair and deepened voice. In the adult male, testosterone regulates many physiological processes, including sexual functioning and muscle protein metabolism. Anabolic steroids are drugs modified to enhance the anabolic actions of testosterone, such as promotion of protein synthesis and muscle growth. By increasing the available protein in muscle cells, more muscle growth occurs. Athletes, body builders, and others may abuse anabolic steroids to improve athletic performance, muscle strength, and appearance. Anabolic steroids also have legitimate medical uses (Figure 14-3). They can be used to induce puberty in males whose puberty is delayed or whose testicles have been removed because of a tumor or injury. After major surgery, anabolic steroids can help inhibit the loss of protein and aid muscle regeneration in patients. Steroids are also used to treat chronic wasting associated with cancer or AIDS. However, anabolic steroids are also misused to enhance athletic performance, among other reasons. Misuse is most common in athletes who seek greater muscle mass for their sport, such as football, baseball, and bodybuilding. The most frequently abused anabolic steroids in the United States include testosterone, nandrolone, stanozolol, methandienone, and boldenone. Testosterone precursors, such as androstenedione, also enhance muscle mass. Anabolic steroids can be administered as tablets, capsules, gels, creams, transdermal patches, and injectable solutions. The route of administration depends on the steroid in question. Anabolic steroids are included in the group of drugs that enhance athletic performance and are more generally referred to as **performance-enhancing drugs (PEDs)** (DEA, 2013d; Hildebrandt, Langenbucher, Carr, & Sanjuan, 2007; Julien, 2005; Saudan et al., 2006). For example, caffeine and amphetamines are stimulant drugs that can enhance athletic performance. Both caffeine and amphetamines are considered PEDs (see Chapters 4 and 7).

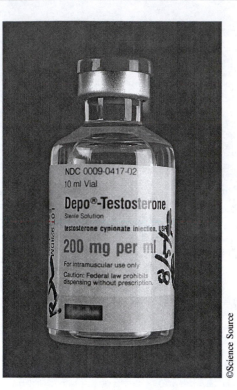

Figure 14-3
Anabolic steroids.

Brief History of Steroid Drugs

Enhancing athletic performance has a long history, as humans have always been looking for ways to improve their ability with drugs. The word *doping* is thought to be derived from the Dutch word *dop*, which is the name of an alcoholic drink consumed by Zulu warriors to enhance performance in battle. Ancient Greek athletes consumed various stimulating potions to improve performance. Going back to the 1800s, endurance athletes were reported to have used caffeine, cocaine, and alcohol to improve performance in cycling and similar activities. Doping was most associated with professional cycling in this early era, with some cyclist deaths possibly due to use of strong stimulant drugs. Doping was not historically limited to humans; racehorses were also drugged in the early 1900s to allow them to run faster. By the 1920s, it was becoming clear that restrictions on drug use in sports were necessary, though the techniques to detect drug use were not yet available (WADA, 2013a,b).

Testosterone was first isolated in 1935. When taken orally, testosterone is inactive and leads to no changes in the user. However, the discovery of testosterone set the stage for its chemical modification to produce anabolic steroids. In the 1930s, anabolic steroids were developed in Nazi Germany. The original Nazi intention for their use was to create an army of supermen (Marshall, 1988). Though the army of supermen never materialized, the discovery of anabolic steroids did change the nature of doping in sports. Previously, athletes had used stimulants (amphetamine, cocaine, strychnine, or ephedrine) just prior to an event to enhance athletic performance temporarily. Anabolic steroids were not used during the actual athletic event itself, but rather as a drug to enhance training. Anabolic steroid users could train more intensely and efficiently. The anabolic steroid user would discontinue the drug as the time for competition approached. Once anabolic steroids were made available, athletes were quick to notice the effectiveness of these drugs. The use of anabolic steroids to enhance physical performance became of increasing concern in the 1950s. Russian weightlifters were forthcoming about steroid use. However, there was no scientific method available to detect steroid use, even though it was clear that they were being used in strength events such as javelin throwing and weightlifting. Concerns about doping in sports escalated in 1960, when a Danish cyclist died during the Olympic Games. In 1974, a reliable test for anabolic steroids became available, and the International Olympic Committee added anabolic steroids to its list of prohibited substances in 1976. The large-scale urine drug testing of athletes for anabolic steroids began at the 1976 Olympic Games. During those games, eight athletes tested positive for anabolic steroids (Caitlin, Fitch, & Ljungqvist, 2008; Saudan et al., 2006).

Concern about steroid use in sports increased in the 1980s, and such concern has remained significant ever since. One famous case involved the Canadian sprinter, Ben Johnson, the 100-meter champion at the 1988 Olympic Games. He ran the 100 meters in 9.79 seconds, a time that not only won him the gold medal but also broke the world record. Three days later, his gold medal was stripped when the devastating news broke that steroid use contributed to his achievement. Johnson's urine drug test had been positive for stanozolol, an anabolic steroid. Johnson was disgraced, and he lost his world record in addition to his gold medal. Johnson's defense of himself was that all top athletes were doping, so he had to use performance-enhancing drugs to keep up with the competition. His assertions were probably not far from the truth, because many sprinters and other top athletes later tested positive for steroids or admitted to using them during training. Since the 1988 Olympic Games, vigilance has increased for the detection of stimulants, steroids, and other drugs in athletes. Today, athletes at all levels are frequently required to provide urine samples to test for banned substances. With increased interest in fighting performance-enhancing drugs, it became clear that an international agency was needed to systemically combat doping. After all, high-level athletes train in countries with legal systems having different laws about drugs. As a result, the **World Anti-Doping Agency (WADA)** was formed in 1999 and charged with combating doping in sports (Figure 14-4). WADA is funded by both the International Olympic Committee and participating governments. WADA provides accreditation to drug-testing laboratories such as those used by the International Olympic Committee, an important consideration given that drug testing must be seen to be trustworthy. Moreover, drug testing of athletes tends to be comprehensive, as athletes must be tested both "in-competition" and "out-of-competition." Just like it sounds, "in-competition" testing occurs around the time of the athletic event itself, and it usually detects drugs used to enhance performance during the event, such as stimulants. By contrast, "out-of-competition" testing is random and intended to detect drugs used to enhance training, such as anabolic steroids. WADA has a World Anti-Doping Code that is strict. The athlete must provide his or her location at all times to allow contact for unannounced "out-of-competition" testing at any time. So much for privacy and spontaneity! Failure to comply with these requests is considered an anti-doping rule violation and renders an athlete ineligible for competition (Caitlin et al., 2008; Fitch, 2012; Saudan et al., 2006; WADA, 2013b).

In recent years, the fight against doping has not only focused on the use of performance-enhancing drugs, but also biological methods to enhance performance. WADA has a lengthy prohibited list of both drugs and methods considered doping. For example, blood doping has become an increasingly common concern, although the practice has been around since the 1970s. **Blood doping** refers to the removal and then replacement of an athlete's blood to increase the blood level of oxygen-carrying hemoglobin. Blood doping allows more oxygen to reach muscles, which decreases fatigue and provides the athlete an edge in competition. Other drugs such as erythropoietin (EPO) also increase hemoglobin levels. EPO and blood doping are both banned because they enhance endurance in sports like cycling. Several other drugs are banned as well. Beta-blockers are prohibited because they are beneficial in archery and skeet shooting. Diuretics are banned because they assist athletes in achieving a particular weight. Given that both drugs and methods of doping are often difficult to detect, the drug detection approach has recently shifted to the maintenance of a **biological passport**. A biological passport is essentially the complete record of urine and blood test results for an athlete. For most individuals, biological parameters stay relatively steady across time. Abrupt changes in parameters typically only occur with disease

©POOL/Reuters/Corbis

Figure 14-4
The World Anti-Doping Agency (WADA) provides accreditation for laboratories that will test urine and blood samples from athletes for doping.

or doping. For example, testosterone is a naturally occurring hormone. Some banned dietary supplements are **prohormones** (which are precursors of hormones) that are converted by the body into naturally occurring testosterone. A spike in naturally occurring testosterone may be sufficient to open disciplinary proceedings against an athlete, even though no "drug" was ever detected on a test. The biological passport also protects those athletes who require particular banned substances for the maintenance of health. There is a Therapeutic Use Exemption that can be approved when a drug is needed for a genuine medical condition, with this need documented in the biological passport. For example, beta-blockers are used in the treatment of cardiac arrhythmias (Caitlin et al., 2008; Fitch, 2012; Saudan et al., 2006; WADA, 2013a).

Anabolic steroids are currently listed as Schedule III drugs under the Controlled Substances Act (see Chapter 1). The use of steroids in human or veterinary medicine is fairly limited, restricted to cases of testosterone deficiency, delayed puberty, wasting from cancer or AIDS, and a few other medical conditions. Congress passed the Anabolic Steroid Control Acts of 1990 and 2004. These acts placed a total of 59 anabolic steroids in Schedule III. Most anabolic steroids sold illegally in the United States come from abroad, although there is also some domestic diversion from otherwise legitimate medical use of steroids. Clandestine laboratories are continuously developing designer steroids that can avoid detection by standard urine drug testing. The Drug Enforcement Administration has discovered low doses of some of these designer steroids in various dietary supplements sold commercially. Even with improvements in drug detection, concerns about the illicit use of anabolic steroids will not be dissipating any time soon (DEA, 2013d).

Table 14-1 World Anti-Doping Agency (WADA) criteria of a substance or method that is on the "Prohibited List" for athletes and examples of prohibited substances and methods (WADA, 2013b).

A substance or method that meets at least 2 out of 3 of the following:

1. The substance or method can be performance-enhancing.
2. The use of the substance or method can endanger the athlete's health.
3. The use of the substance or method is against the spirit of sport.

Examples of prohibited substances and methods:

	Category	Examples
Substances and Methods Prohibited at all Times (In- and Out-of-Competition) (exogenous)	Anabolic Androgenic Steroids	Boldenone Methandienone Nandrolone Stanozolol
	Anabolic Androgenic Steroids (endogenous)	Androstenediol Dihydrotestosterone Testosterone
	Peptide Hormones and Growth Factors	Erythropoietin (EPO) Corticotrophins Growth hormone (GH)
	Beta-2 agonists	Albuterol
	Diuretics	Furosemide
	Manipulation of blood and blood components	Artificially enhancing the uptake, transport or delivery of oxygen by physical or chemical means
Substances and Methods Prohibited In-Competition	Stimulants	Adrenaline Cocaine Ephedrine Methamphetamine Methylphenidate Strychnine
	Narcotics	Buprenorphine Diamorphine (heroin) Fentanyl Methandone Morphine Oxycodone
	Cannabinoids	Natural (marijuana, hashish) Synthetic (THC)
	Glucocorticosteroids	Prednisone
	Alcohol (in some sports such as archery and karate)	Alcohol
	Beta-blockers (in some sports such as archery, golf, and skeet shooting)	Acebutolol

Adapted from Caitlin et al. (2008). See WADA's website for the full 2013 Prohibited List http://www.wada-ama.org/

Epidemiology of Steroid Use

According to 2004 statistics from the World Anti-Doping Agency (WADA), in testing high-level athletes, about 36% of failed drug tests involve steroids (Table 14-1). Among the positive cases, the most commonly used substances are testosterone and nandrolone (Saudan et al., 2006). While it may seem that anabolic steroids would be mainly abused by professional athletes and bodybuilders, the data

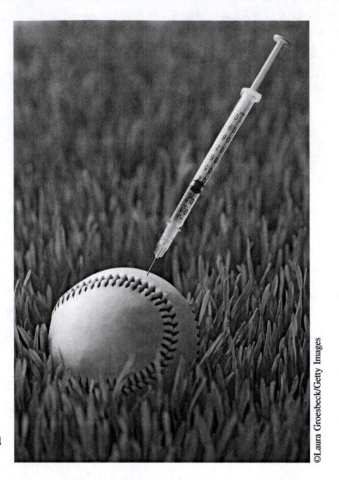

©Laura Groesbeck/Getty Images

Figure 14-5
Steroids are misused by professional, amateur, and recreational athletes.

suggests that many individuals outside these groups also use anabolic steroids. Amateur and recreational athletes use steroids (Figure 14-5). Adolescents and young adults abuse steroids to achieve muscle growth or enhance appearance. Up to 2% of high school seniors report having used steroids at least once. Males are far more likely than females to use anabolic steroids. Data from the 2011 *Monitoring the Future* survey (see Chapter 1 for methodology) indicated that 1.8% of 12th grade boys reported having used steroids at least once in the past year. By contrast, only 0.5% of 12th grade girls reported use of steroids at least once in the past year (Hoffman et al., 2008; Johnston et al., 2012).

Acute and Chronic Effects of Steroids

Most anabolic steroids are synthetic versions of testosterone; not surprisingly, anabolic steroids act like testosterone in the body. One dose of a steroid drug may not lead to appreciable physiological changes. It is with repeated use of anabolic steroids that dramatic physical changes occur. Knowledge about typical use of anabolic steroids in bodybuilders and other athletes is limited. However, it appears that use follows a typical pattern referred to as "stacking." The user administers several oral and injectable anabolic steroids during cycles lasting anywhere from 4 to 12 weeks. Doses range from 250 mg to 3500 mg per week. Such doses are up to 100 times the therapeutically recommended dose in medical settings. Users will typically take two (or more) anabolic steroids, switching back and forth between drugs. Cycling is believed by illicit users to improve effectiveness while also minimizing adverse side effects (DEA, 2013d).

With chronic steroid use, athletes report that fatigue is reduced and training can occur more frequently. A mild euphoria or feeling of being high may be reported. The time needed between training sessions can be reduced, since recovery of muscles occurs more quickly. With the steroid and intense training, growth of skeletal and cardiac muscle occurs. Increased red blood cells and bone growth may also occur (DEA, 2013d; Saudan et al., 2006).

Among behavioral changes, increased aggressiveness and increased sexual desire may develop. Some athletes view increased aggressiveness as an advantage in their training. However, increased aggressiveness may also coincide with greater irritability and hostility. The individual may become difficult to get along with and easily provoked. Even a slightly negative comment may be all that is needed to elicit an aggressive, or even violent, reaction from the steroid user. Outside of the gym, this can lead to violence, sometimes referred to colloquially as "roid rage." Such behavioral changes are more likely in individuals who already had higher levels of aggressiveness and hostility before starting steroids. However, even animal studies have demonstrated that chronic administration of anabolic steroids increases aggression and dominance behavior, particularly in provoking situations (Breuer, McGinnis, Lumia, & Possidente, 2001; Wood et al., 2013). In humans, increased anxiety, paranoia, confusion, and hallucinations can also occur with chronic use of steroids (DEA, 2013d; Saudan et al., 2006).

Problems from chronic steroid use vary depending on whether the user is male or female and also whether the user is fully developed or still in puberty. In adolescent boys, anabolic steroids can stunt final height attained because steroids cause premature bone fusion. Early sexual development and extreme acne can also occur in boys. In adolescent girls and women who chronically use steroids, permanent physical changes, similar to male traits, may occur. These changes include deepening of the voice, increased facial and body hair, menstrual cycle irregularities, male pattern baldness, and lengthening of the clitoris. For men who use steroids, the testicles may shrink, sperm counts may become reduced, and male breast tissue may enlarge. In adult males, some of these changes may be reversible when steroid use ceases. Steroid use in men is also associated with an increased risk of sterility or prostate cancer (DEA, 2013d; Saudan et al., 2006).

For both men and women, steroid use will result in increased sebum production resulting in oily skin and hair. The development of acne is a concern for all users of steroids. With heavy use, the skin and eyes may appear yellowish. The yellow color is due to the development of jaundice, which is reversible with abstinence from steroids. However, if steroid use continues, permanent liver damage can occur. Chronic steroid use can increase the risk of coronary artery disease, stroke, and heart attack. This risk is thought to be attributable to high cholesterol levels that develop with use of steroids. The use of injectable steroids brings additional concerns. If injection techniques are not sterile, various viral and bacterial infections may be contracted. Abusers may contract HIV/AIDS or hepatitis by sharing dirty needles. Moreover, steroid drugs may be prepared in nonsterile environments. Note, however, one concern that does not arise with anabolic steroids is the risk of a fatal overdose. Anabolic steroids do not influence breathing and heart rate and thus cannot directly lead to death (DEA, 2013d).

Tolerance and Withdrawal for Steroids

Given that steroids are used clandestinely to enhance athletic performance, there is little good objective research examining if appreciable tolerance to steroids develops with repeated use. The consensus seems to be that some tolerance may develop, although such changes appear to be relatively modest. However, chronic use of anabolic steroids can result in some dependence on the drug. Abrupt cessation of steroid use can lead to withdrawal symptoms. Most commonly, users will report feeling very depressed. Suicidal ideation and actual suicides may occur during withdrawal. Other symptoms such as fatigue, insomnia, loss of appetite, restlessness, and loss of sex drive may also occur. Withdrawal symptoms seem to arise in approximately one-third of users (Julien, 2005; Kanayama et al., 2009).

Pharmacology of Steroids

Sites of Action

The male sex hormone occurring naturally in the body is testosterone. Use of anabolic steroids involves modification of the delicate homeostatic balance of testosterone. Testosterone is synthesized in the testes. The hypothalamus in the brain and the pituitary gland provide feedback that keeps testosterone levels in the appropriate range for an adult male. If testosterone levels fall too low, the hypothalamus detects the deficiency and begins producing gonadotropin-releasing factor (GRF). GRF is released in the blood and reaches the pituitary gland. Next, the pituitary gland releases two hormones, follicle-stimulating hormone (FSH) and luteinizing hormone (LH). Both FSH and LH will result in the production of sperm in the testes and synthesis and release of testosterone. When testosterone levels rise too high, the process reverses, and the hypothalamus decreases production of GRF. Not surprisingly, administration of anabolic steroids dramatically alters this delicately balanced system. Moreover, altering the balance of testosterone in the body also results in changes to other naturally occurring steroids, such as cortisol (the hormone released during stress) and estrogen and progesterone (in women) (Julien, 2005).

Anabolic steroids lead to both anabolic and androgenic effects. **Anabolic** effects of steroids include growth of muscle and red blood cells. When either an anabolic steroid or testosterone is in the bloodstream, it passes through cell walls to target tissues. The steroid attaches to steroid androgen receptors on cells, which leads to the production of new proteins. These new proteins allow muscles to grow. With time and training (such as weight lifting), this muscle growth can lead to appreciable changes in muscle size. Training is important in producing these changes. Muscles will not grow and strengthen in an individual who takes steroids but does not use his or her muscles. Steroids also have a second action. Steroids block natural cortisol, the steroid in the body that increases energy in times of stress and training. In normal circumstances, cortisol breaks down proteins into amino acids, allowing energy to become available for use. If this is excessive, muscles break down. Since the action of natural cortisol is greatly diminished when steroids are used, muscle mass increases. Thus, anabolic steroids may cause two important changes: building muscle and preventing muscle breakdown (Julien, 2005; Snyder, 2001).

Anabolic steroids also result in **androgenic** effects related to male secondary sexual characteristics. These effects are very pronounced in women who take anabolic steroids. Masculinizing effects, such as developing facial hair and a deeper voice, occur. Cessation of the menstrual cycle can occur. In males, the body detects the exogenous presence of testosterone from anabolic steroids and over time shuts down the process that normally regulates testosterone. Reproductive system effects that are maintained by testosterone tend to diminish with decreased testosterone production. The testes atrophy and less sperm are produced. Male sex drive diminishes. Infertility and enlargement of the breasts may both occur, although these changes may be reversible a few months after steroid use stops. However, women who use steroids tend to experience more pronounced changes, and infertility in women can be permanent (Julien, 2005).

Repeated use of anabolic steroids may also have effects on brain structures involved in aggression. One study with rats revealed that chronic administration of anabolic steroids resulted in decreased activity in the caudate-putamen. This area of the brain is important for motor control and inhibition of impulses. Thus, changes in the caudate-putamen may underlie the increased aggression seen in chronic users of anabolic steroids (Wood et al., 2013).

Pharmacokinetics

Anabolic steroids are most often administered orally or by injection (although transdermal administration using a cream is possible). The onset of drug action occurs over hours, and users may not notice appreciable changes except with repeated daily use over several weeks. Anabolic steroids differ in how the liver degrades the drug. If testosterone is administered orally, no physiological effects occur. Orally administered testosterone is absorbed from the intestine, where it is transported to the liver via the bloodstream. In the liver, testosterone is immediately metabolized, such that almost none of the testosterone reaches intended sites of action. Since the intended sites of action for steroid abusers are muscles around the body, the steroid needs to be circulated throughout the body to lead to physiological changes. Anabolic steroids are modifications of the chemical testosterone. These modifications allow the drug to bypass the immediate liver metabolism process that normally occurs for testosterone, which results in the drug staying in the body longer and reaching sites of action via the bloodstream. Once steroids have acted in the body, they are excreted through urine. Steroids can be detected in urine up to 14 days after the most recent use. One exception to this is nandrolone, which might be detectable in positive urine drug tests up to a year after the last use (Julien, 2005; Marshall, 1988; Snyder, 2001).

Myth Busters: Claims for Dietary Supplements Are Backed by Strong Science

Dietary supplements are found in health food stores, grocery stores, pharmacies, and on the Internet. These supplements contain vitamins, mineral, botanicals, and other ingredients. They are marketed as providing several benefits, including improved physical health and treatment of various medical conditions. Want to build more muscle at the gym? There are an endless variety of pills and powders that you can buy in the supplement aisle to help you to achieve that goal. Want to improve your memory or decrease your depression? There are supplements for those too. Many people believe that these dietary supplement claims are backed by strong science. However, this is a myth. In fact, relatively little science is required to make marketing claims on these products, which makes them different from other drugs. The U.S. Food and Drug Administration (FDA) regulates dietary supplement products and dietary ingredients. However, there is a big difference between how the FDA regulates pharmaceutical drugs and supplements. Manufacturers of supplements do not need to register their products with the FDA or obtain FDA approval before producing or selling these products. An example might make the distinction clear. A pharmaceutical company may have a drug that seems to increase muscle mass. The company follows the FDA approval process (see Chapter 12). If all stages of clinical trials conclusively demonstrate that users of the drug develop more muscle mass (without problematic side effects), the FDA may approve the drug. By contrast, the science is unsystematic and sometimes sketchy for supplements. A supplement maker need only give gym users a paper survey that inquires whether a supplement led to improvements in muscle composition. If the users of the supplement responded that their muscles seemed to get bigger, that would constitute sufficient evidence to market the supplement. Thus, the science required to back marketing claims tends to be significantly less rigorous for dietary supplements than for pharmaceutical drugs. Supplement makers contend that their products have known effects, and they also argue that it is difficult to conduct expensive clinical trials demonstrating effectiveness (especially when the supplement is a plant product that cannot be patented). This may be true. However, the lax regulation of supplements has led to some instances where dietary supplements sold over the Internet actually contained illegal ingredients, including anabolic steroids (Baker, 2008). Additionally, there are probably many supplements that have no active ingredients, and consumers using them are just wasting their money (Figure 14-6). Therefore, the next time you have a chance to visit the supplement aisle in your local grocery story, take a look at some of the bottles. There should be wording that says, *"This statement has not been evaluated by the Food and Drug Administration. This product is not intended to diagnose, treat, cure, or prevent any disease."* This wording does not guarantee that the supplement won't work as advertised. What it does indicate is that there has been no formal scientific evaluation of the claim on the product (FDA, 2013a). As far as supplements are concerned, the buyer should always beware.

For more information, visit this website:

http://www.fda.gov/Food/DietarySupplements/default.htm

©Camilo Morales/Glowimages/Corbis

Figure 14-6
Consumers should be wary about what is contained in various health supplements.

QUICK QUIZ 14-1

1. Anabolic steroids are Schedule _____ drugs according to the Controlled Substances Act.
   a. I
   b. II
   c. III
   d. IV
   e. V

2. Which of the following are considered performance-enhancing drugs?
   a. Anabolic steroids
   b. Amphetamines
   c. Methylphenidate
   d. a and b only
   e. All of the above

3. Anabolic steroids are synthetic drugs that act similarly to _____.
   a. testosterone
   b. estrogen
   c. progesterone
   d. cortisol

4. Anabolic steroid use results in _____ effects such as building muscle and _____ effects such as increasing the amount of body hair or deepening the voice.
   a. androgenic, anabolic
   b. anabolic, androgenic
   c. dopaminergic, serotonergic

   d. serotonergic, dopaminergic
   e. None of the above

5. The use of several different anabolic steroids over a course of about 12 weeks is called _____.
   a. blood doping
   b. performance enhancement
   c. stacking
   d. in-competition steroid use

6. Which of the following might indicate that a female body-builder is using anabolic steroids?
   a. Baldness
   b. Deepening of the voice
   c. Facial hair
   d. Acne
   e. All of the above

7. Drug testing of athletes includes in-competition and out-of-competition testing. Which type of testing is most likely to detect stimulants, and which is most likely to detect anabolic steroids?

8. Sarah is training for the upcoming Olympics. The Olympic trials are about a month away. At the last minute, she decides with several friends to go away for spring break to Mexico. They are gone for a week. While Sarah was gone, WADA left several phone messages for her. What was the likely purpose of their calls? What are some possible repercussions of her having missed the calls?

9. What are two ways that anabolic steroids act in the body?

ANSWERS TO QUICK QUIZ 14-1:

1. c – III
2. e – all of the above
3. a – testosterone
4. b – anabolic, androgenic
5. c – stacking
6. e – all of the above
7. In-competition testing is most likely to detect stimulants taken at the time of the athletic event to improve performance. By contrast, out-of-competition testing is more likely to detect anabolic steroids taken during training to improve the intensity and efficiency of training.
8. WADA conducts random and unannounced drug testing of athletes. They were probably contacting her for an "out-of-competition" drug test. Given that WADA could not reach her, she violated the World Anti-Doping Code. She may be deemed ineligible for competition and may miss the Olympic trials due to her carelessness.
9. Anabolic steroids help build muscle and prevent muscle breakdown.

Smart Drugs

Just as physical performance can be enhanced by various psychoactive drugs, mental performance can also be improved. **Smart drugs** are a category of pharmaceutical drugs, supplements, nutraceuticals, and functional foods that enhance cognitive performance. Smart drugs are also referred to as nootropics, although that term is not widely used. There is a range of possibilities by which cognition can be enhanced by various smart drugs, which makes this a broad category. Earlier in this book, we discussed the role of amphetamines in enhancing cognitive performance in treating attention deficit hyperactivity disorder (see Chapter 7). While many psychopharmacologists may not categorize amphetamines as typical smart drugs, there is no doubt that amphetamine medications improve attention span and motivation to work. Amphetamines are also diverted by individuals to get high or focus for long periods on effortful tasks such as writing papers or studying for exams. Thus, the enhancement of cognitive performance by psychoactive drugs can occur either in individuals experiencing symptoms of a disorder or healthy individuals looking for an edge. In fact, most stimulants (cocaine, amphetamines, nicotine, and caffeine) enhance mental performance to varying degrees. However, stimulant drugs are not the only way to enhance cognitive performance. The ability to think depends on a wide variety of cognitive skills, including attention, memory, language, and problem solving. Stimulants seem to have the most pronounced effects on attention. However, stimulants have more modest (or even deleterious effects) on other aspects of cognition. Are there other psychoactive drugs that can improve memory or problem solving? The answer is yes.

Smart drugs can help slow the inevitable decline that occurs with dementia. Our population is aging, and a large number of elderly individuals have developed some form of dementia. **Dementia** is a significant loss of global cognitive ability that appears inconsistent with the individual's prior level of intelligence and is unexpected in the context of the normal aging process. Dementia in most cases is degenerative in nature, meaning that the disease process is progressive and cannot be cured. A mental decline over time is unfortunately inevitable. Initially, a patient may exhibit a little forgetfulness. Assessment by a neuropsychologist or neurologist may reveal difficulties with simple cognitive tasks, such as drawing a clock (Blair, Kertesz, McMonagle, Davidson, & Bodi, 2006; Feldman et al., 2008). With time (usually over years), the patient will slowly need more help until eventually assistance is needed with all activities of daily living, such as eating or bathing. For the most part, smart drugs are used to treat the worsening cognitive and behavioral impairments that accompany dementia. While it is common for people to think that dementia is synonymous with memory impairment, smart drugs may also help with the development of language deficits or problem-solving difficulties that result from dementia. Regardless of the profile of cognitive deficits seen in patients with dementia, dementia is devastating to quality of life (Figure 14-7). A patient who repeatedly forgets to turn off the stove because of memory impairments cannot live alone and may require institutionalized care.

Figure 14-7
Dementia is devastating to quality of life.

A patient who is having difficulty making decisions may be unable to manage his or her own finances. Fortunately for both patients and their caregivers, several smart drug psychotherapeutic medications can improve cognitive performance and also quality of life (Kertesz, 2006).

The most consistent and widely conducted research on smart drugs has focused on the treatment of memory impairments in Alzheimer's disease, a common form of dementia. **Alzheimer's disease** involves a progressive atrophy of cortical and hippocampal brain tissue that leads to symptoms such as memory impairment and intellectual decline. Alzheimer's disease typically has an age of onset of approximately 60 years when the first symptoms appear. As the disease progresses, various other symptoms may emerge, including psychosis. The definitive diagnosis for most dementias, including Alzheimer's disease, can only be made with an autopsy after death. However, many cases are so clear by the symptoms that appropriate drug treatment can be initiated. There are currently five FDA-approved pharmaceutical drugs that have demonstrated efficacy in treating memory problems. Four of the drugs are **acetylcholinesterase inhibitors** (also referred to as cholinesterase inhibitors or more generally as cholinergic drugs). Acetylcholinesterase inhibitors improve memory by increasing the brain's available acetylcholine, the neurotransmitter important in memory. FDA-approved acetylcholinesterase inhibitors used to treat Alzheimer's disease include Aricept® (donepezil), Razadyne® (galantamine), Exelon® (rivastigmine), and Cognex® (tacrine). The other pharmaceutical approach to treating memory impairments in dementia involves an **NMDA receptor antagonist drug**. The one currently available drug that is an NMDA receptor antagonist is Memantine® (namenda). Memantine® acts by antagonizing the action of the neurotransmitter glutamate in the brain. It is believed that excess glutamate damages neurons, so Memantine® is thought to prevent some destruction of neurons that contributes to cognitive problems (Feldman et al., 2008; Julien, 2005).

Brief History of Smart Drugs

Humans have a long history of trying to enhance intelligence through drugs. Many plants have long been thought to enhance memory or other cognitive functions. References to the use of *cannabis sativa* (the marijuana plant) by Chinese Emperor Shen Nung are dated to 2737 BCE. In the emperor's writings, cannabis tea was recommended for many ailments, including poor memory (see Chapter 10). However, the history of pharmacological approaches to treating the intellectual decline that comes from dementia is actually rather short. In 1911, German physician Dr. Alois Alzheimer reported that intellectual decline from aging is not a function of age, but rather is due to a specific disease process. One of his patients had severe memory problems and confusion that was inconsistent with normal aging. After this patient died, Dr. Alzheimer performed an autopsy and observed pathology in the brain. There were dense deposits around neurons (neurotic plaques) and twisted bands of fibers inside neurons (neurofibrillary tangles). Plaques and tangles characterize a case of Alzheimer's disease, which even today is a suspicion based on clinical criteria that can only be definitively confirmed with an autopsy after death. While Alzheimer's disease is the most common form of dementia, the idea that brain pathology underlies dementia was first advanced somewhat prior to Alzheimer's discovery. A less common form of dementia, **frontotemporal dementia**, was identified by a Czech physician, Dr. Arnold Pick, in a series of papers beginning in 1892. He described a new disease that developed with age and whose features included language loss and bizarre behavior (such as poor impulse control). Dr. Pick performed autopsies on patients experiencing these symptoms and noted focal atrophy in the frontal and/or temporal lobes. He also observed abnormal round inclusions in the brain (named Pick bodies) in some, but not all, patients. Over time, focal atrophy came to define a case of frontotemporal dementia, and the label of Pick's disease was reserved for the subset of cases where Pick bodies were observed on autopsy (Kertesz, 1998, 2006). Unfortunately for patients experiencing any kind of dementia, until recently there was very little available medical help. Interestingly, the problem of dementia in the elderly is really a function of overall improvement in medicine throughout history. In the past, it was rare that an individual would live long enough to reach an age where dementia is prevalent. Today, of course, the human lifespan is indeed long enough that many will reach an age where dementia is common. Medicine has become so successful at curing cancer, treating cardiovascular disease, or limiting the lethality of other medical conditions that people are now living historically long lives.

Before the 1990s arrival of new specific drugs to treat Alzheimer's disease, patients were treated with antidepressants, antianxiety drugs, or antipsychotic drugs to help manage symptoms. These other classes of drugs have been available since the 1950s (see Chapters 12 and 13). Currently, there are only five FDA-approved drugs available for the treatment of Alzheimer's disease. That number is low considering the number of people who suffer from Alzheimer's disease globally and how devastating the condition is. The first acetylcholinesterase drug approved by the FDA was Cognex® (tacrine) in 1993. Several similar drugs were approved later in the 1990s. The most recent FDA approval to treat Alzheimer's disease was Memantine® (namenda) in 2003. As an NMDA receptor antagonist, Memantine® acts differently than the other four acetylcholinesterase inhibitors, and Memantine® is also thought to be more effective in severe cases of Alzheimer's disease (Annweiler & Beauchet, 2012). Unfortunately, no drug has been demonstrated effective in clinical trials to treat frontotemporal dementia, which is very frustrating to patients, caregivers, and physicians (Boxer et al., 2013; Hodges, 2013; Wang, Shen, & Chen, 2013). All cases of dementia are degenerative, meaning that they worsen until death occurs. There is no cure for any form of dementia. Smart drugs used to treat dementia only help manage symptoms and slow the cognitive decline. The need for more research is great.

Epidemiology of Dementia

Cognitive impairment or dementia is present in approximately 20% of individuals age 65 and older (Feldman et al., 2008). Approximately 50% of dementia cases are thought to be due to Alzheimer's disease. The rest may be attributable to vascular dementia (a stroke caused the dementia), frontotemporal dementia (the brain atrophy is isolated to the frontal and/or temporal cortices of the brain), or Parkinson's disease. In the United States, approximately 5 million Americans suffer from Alzheimer's disease, and another 5 million suffer from various other kinds of dementia (Brookmeyer et al., 2011). Worldwide, there are approximately 35 million cases of Alzheimer's disease and another 35 million cases of other types of dementia. Prevalence rates for dementia in individuals ages 60 and older occur in a relatively narrow range of 5% to 7% of individuals in most regions of the world. Slightly higher prevalence rates occur in Latin America (9%), and lower rates are observed in sub-Saharan Africa (3%), where access to adequate health care is more of an issue resulting in shorter lifespans (Prince et al., 2013; Selkoe, 2012). The global estimated worldwide cost of all dementia cases in 2010 was approximately $600 billion and 70% of those costs were incurred in North America and Western Europe (Wimo et al., 2013).

The global prevalence rates of Alzheimer's disease (and other dementias) rise with age. Only about 1% of individuals age 65 to 69 have been diagnosed with Alzheimer's disease. By the time individuals reach age 95, up to 50% are diagnosed with Alzheimer's disease. Prevalence of Alzheimer's disease approximately doubles every five years after age 65 (Grossberg, 2003; Julien, 2005). The number of cases of Alzheimer's disease alone is projected to grow dramatically as the population ages. The projected growth is expected to result in a doubling of cases every 20 years, with approximately 66 million cases predicted in 2030 and 115 million cases predicted in 2050. The rate of growth is predicted to be even greater in the developing world, where population growth and better medical care are both increasing steadily (Selkoe, 2012; Prince et al., 2013; Wimo & Prince, 2010).

Acute and Chronic Effects of Smart Drugs

There are various reasons why an older individual may be experiencing cognitive impairment. When dementia is suspected, the appropriate diagnosis is based on clinical criteria (physical exam including patient history, neuroimaging, and neuropsychological testing). The goal is to identify a logical cause of the cognitive impairment and also treat comorbid conditions making the dementia more pronounced. Not all elderly patients experiencing cognitive impairments need treatment with smart drugs such as acetylcholinesterase inhibitors or NMDA receptor antagonists. For example, a patient experiencing depression, especially an older patient, may exhibit pronounced cognitive deficits. However, once the depression has been treated with antidepressant medication and/or psychological therapy, improved cognition may indicate that any prior cognitive impairment was not caused by dementia. In other cases, dementia leads to symptoms of cognitive impairment. Clinical criteria may help the physician determine which drug treatment is appropriate. For suspected Alzheimer's disease, smart drugs are appropriate. For frontotemporal dementia, treatment with smart drugs has not been shown to be efficacious, so symptoms can only be treated with antidepressants, antianxiety drugs, or antipsychotic drugs. Intellectual decline over years is inevitable with dementia, as there is no cure. In Alzheimer's disease, if the patient is not treated with a smart drug, the time between the onset of symptoms and eventual death is approximately 10 years (Grossberg, 2003). Therefore, the goal in using acetylcholinesterase inhibitors or NMDA receptor antagonists is to slow the inevitable decline and lengthen the patient's life.

Early identification of dementia is important so that patients can begin drug treatment. Treatment occurs over years. After one dose of drug, no appreciable changes will be observed, although initial side effects may emerge. Unfortunately, similar to other psychotherapeutic drugs, the most pronounced changes early in treatment with acetylcholinesterase inhibitors are side effects. Gastrointestinal symptoms such as nausea, abdominal cramps, vomiting, and loss of appetite may occur, especially in older adults who are already frail. For some patients, the gastrointestinal symptoms can result in severe weight loss and necessitate stopping treatment for a period. Careful management of dosing in older patients is necessary. Most patients are started on a very low dose of any smart drug, with the dose very slowly increased over time. A smaller number of patients may also become more aggressive after being treated with smart drugs, which is a concern for a patient already agitated. In the brain, some of the early benefits of drug treatment may take months to occur. Even after six months of treatment, patients and caregivers may still not notice any improvement in cognitive symptoms. Brain-imaging studies measuring cerebral blood flow have shown that patients being treated with Aricept® (donepezil) have significant increases in blood flow in various regions of the cortex and the cerebellum after several months of treatment (Kanaya et al., 2012). Thus, it is only with the chronic administration of smart drugs (such as a year or longer) that clear benefits start to become evident. For example, the long-term use of both acetylcholinesterase inhibitors and NMDA receptor antagonists prevent some of the mental decline and brain atrophy observed with Alzheimer's disease. Brain atrophy tends to correlate strongly with cognitive functioning. Thus, acetylcholinesterase inhibitors or NMDA receptor antagonists seem to be protecting against neuronal loss. While these neurological outcomes are very important, the practical result is that the patient has a better quality of life. Patients who remain relatively high-functioning with medication can stay in their own home, even if they might require intermittent support. Relatives or visiting nurses may check in on patients to ensure that they are remembering to take their medication and otherwise caring for themselves. Though smart drugs themselves are fairly costly, delaying the inevitable need for a long-term care facility can save a tremendous amount of money (Wilkinson et al., 2012).

There are a few concerns about continuing use of smart drugs for years. Patients may have difficulty tolerating them because of significant side effects. Gastrointestinal symptoms can persist, while some patients experience irritability and agitation. Concerns such as headaches and dizziness can emerge (Kanaya et al., 2012). Some drugs, particularly Cognex® (tacrine), can result in liver toxicity. Fortunately, liver toxicity is reversible. Even if problematic side effects are fairly minimal, the drugs used to treat dementia are effective only after 6 to 12 months of treatment and only about half of patients who take them experience benefits. Evidence from clinical trials indicates that many of the drugs used to treat Alzheimer's disease seem to be most effective when initiated early in the disease process (Selkoe, 2012). If diagnosis is delayed, patients exhibiting more symptoms will benefit less from treatment with smart drugs. Patients with severe Alzheimer's disease have acetylcholine activity that is less than half the level present in a healthy individual of the same age. The disease process results in a selective and devastating loss of cholinergic neurons, which are necessary for cognitive functioning. Once these neurons die, there is little that can be done to increase acetylcholine levels in the brain. Memantine® (namenda) is often reserved for treatment of moderate to severe Alzheimer's disease, after the acetylcholinesterase inhibitors seem to lose effectiveness (Giacobini, 2003).

In the News:

Kolata, G. (2013, March 13). F.D.A. plans looser rules on approving Alzheimer's drugs.
The New York Times.

In the past, the U.S. Food and Drug Administration (FDA) approved a new drug to treat Alzheimer's disease only if evidence from clinical trials indicated that the drug improved memory and everyday functioning such as feeding, dressing, or bathing. However, the FDA recently announced plans to change the approval process for new drugs to treat Alzheimer's disease. If a drug could result in subtle improvement in memory or reasoning tests alone, the drug can now qualify for approval. Cognitive tests might include remembering a list of words or following instructions to change symbols into letters. Scientists interviewed for this article favored the change and suggested there may be greater motivation to conduct research on medicines for Alzheimer's disease with this new standard for approval (Figure 14-8).

©Jose Luis Pelaez, Inc./Blend Images/Corbis

Figure 14-8
There is a great need for more research on medicines for Alzheimer's disease.

Use this news article to test and apply your knowledge:

1. Why might scientists be in favor of this change, given what is known about the response to smart drug treatment during the course of Alzheimer's disease?
2. Considering currently available drug treatments for Alzheimer's disease, is it correct to assert that this change might result in greater interest in researching new drugs?

Answers:

1. Acetylcholinesterase inhibitors are most effective early in the course of Alzheimer's disease, before too many cholinergic neurons have died. Drug treatment might be even more effective in slowing the progression of the disease if it can be started even earlier, before clear behavioral problems appear.
2. There are presently only five FDA-approved drugs to treat Alzheimer's disease. More research on new medications is clearly needed. Alzheimer's disease is the most common form of dementia among older people. Worldwide, there are approximately 35 million cases of Alzheimer's disease. Expanding treatment of such an enormous group of patients would be beneficial to the patients themselves and their families and communities. Patients early in the disease process are typically able to care for themselves. Keeping patients self-sufficient for a longer period will help avoid cost and lessen the burden placed on family members and supportive health care facilities such as nursing homes.

What do you think about this news story?

College and high school students currently use, illegally and inappropriately, diverted amphetamine ADHD medications to help them study (see Chapter 7). Enhancement of cognitive performance is obviously appealing to young people. If a larger number of older adults begin using Alzheimer's drugs to address memory problems, even before significant symptoms emerge, do you think that a problem of drug diversion will emerge? If these drugs improve memory and reasoning abilities, would all healthy people in society want a "smart drug" that would allow them to experience cognitive enhancement? Interestingly, studies with animals have demonstrated that acetylcholinesterase inhibitors may be beneficial in treating cocaine and morphine addiction. Enhancement of acetylcholine activity in the brain may thus have wide benefits beyond treating Alzheimer's disease (Hikida, Kitabatake, Pastan, & Nakanishi, 2003). Do you think that society would embrace the wider use of smart drugs or consider this another form of cheating, just like the steroid use discussed earlier in this chapter?

Tolerance and Withdrawal for Smart Drugs

Patients with Alzheimer's disease are typically treated for years with smart drugs such as acetylcholinesterase inhibitors or NMDA receptor antagonists. Given that long-term use of these drugs is normal, tolerance is a potential concern. Do these drugs lose effectiveness with long-term use? Fortunately, the answer is no. Tolerance development for the cognitive enhancement effects does not appear to be a major concern with a long duration of use of these drugs. Over years of treatment, the dose of drug may need to be increased. However, this is likely not a function of tolerance development, but rather the progression of the inevitable disease process that is continuously damaging more of the brain. With respect to tolerance to side effects, there appears to be some tolerance development for symptoms such as gastrointestinal distress. The nausea or loss of appetite that occurs early in treatment is a problem that may go away with time. However, some patients still experience side effects with treatment, even when use is long term. If the patient experiences too many side effects, the physician may switch the patient to another drug. Given that little appreciable tolerance develops to smart drugs, it is unsurprising that withdrawal is also not a major concern with these drugs. When drug treatment ceases, there are very few withdrawal symptoms. The most common development when drug treatment is stopped is cognitive deterioration. In some dementia syndromes where hallucinations are a symptom, hallucinations decrease while on the drug, reemerge if drug treatment ceases, and then decline again when drug treatment restarts. Therefore, abrupt discontinuation is not recommended. The concern with discontinuation is not withdrawal but rather the underlying dementia. The underlying dementia can very quickly become a concern when the drug is no longer in the body (Julien, 2005; Minett et al., 2003).

Pharmacology of Smart Drugs

Sites of Action

Acetylcholinesterase inhibitors improve memory by increasing the availability in the brain of acetylcholine, which is the neurotransmitter that is important in memory. In various dementias, including Alzheimer's disease, the level of acetylcholine is thought to be deficient. This deficiency impairs memory and also can lead to death of neurons. By increasing the amount of acetylcholine available in the brain, the inevitable decline that occurs with Alzheimer's disease can be substantially slowed. Acetylcholinesterase inhibitors act by inhibiting the action of the acetylcholine enzyme, which normally metabolizes acetylcholine in the synapse. Inhibiting the action of this enzyme increases the amount of acetylcholine in the synapse so that more is available for binding with the postsynaptic receptors. Similar to other psychotherapeutic drugs (antidepressants and antipsychotics), altering the acetylcholine level in the brain does not seem to result in symptom improvement for a significant period of time. Many months may pass before patients and caregivers notice benefits. It should also be noted that while acetylcholine is found both in the central and peripheral nervous system, acetylcholinesterase inhibitors selectively increase acetylcholine in the brain, rather than the periphery (Anand & Singh, 2013; Julien, 2005).

NMDA receptor antagonist drugs improve cognitive functioning by antagonizing (blocking) the action of the neurotransmitter glutamate in the brain. Glutamate is thought to be important to learning and memory, and excess glutamate is thought to damage neurons. In normal brain activity, the binding of glutamate with a NMDA receptor site allows calcium to freely flow into the cell. If this process happens too much, chronic overexposure to calcium becomes harmful and can speed up cell damage. NMDA receptor antagonist drugs block NMDA receptor sites and thus prevent some destruction of neurons that results in cognitive problems. Memantine® (namenda) is described as a weak NMDA receptor antagonist, putting it in a similar class as the hallucinogenic drug, ketamine, which is a strong affinity NMDA receptor antagonist (see Chapter 11). If Memantine® were administered at very high doses, like ketamine it would induce amnesia. However, the dose of Memantine® in treatment is low, which actually preserves memory. Similar to the acetylcholinesterase inhibitors, many months will pass before any beneficial effects are observed with Memantine® (Anand & Singh, 2013; Annweiler & Beauchet, 2012; Julien, 2005).

Pharmacokinetics

Both acetylcholinesterase inhibitors and NMDA receptor antagonists act slowly and have long half-lives when administered as oral medications. Once daily dosing is common. After oral administration, peak plasma concentration for Aricept® (donepezil) occurs at about 4 hours. The drug accumulates in the plasma, and a steady level is achieved within 15 days of daily use. The drug readily crosses the blood–brain barrier resulting in a strong correlation between plasma concentrations of the drug and the inhibiting action on the acetylcholine enzyme in the brain. Once the drug has produced its effect, the kidneys metabolize the drug. The rate of clearance from the body is independent of the dose administered. Approximately 80% of the drug is cleared from the body in the urine, with the rest exiting the body in feces (Rogers & Friedhoff, 1998).

Focus on Careers: Heath Care Administrator

The combined effects of better medical care lengthening lifespans and an aging population mean that a greater number of people will need some long-term care or nursing home care in their lives. These facilities need administrators and managers to plan, direct, and coordinate health services for individuals needing long-term care. Facilities are constantly being built to address an ever-increasing demand. A patient with Alzheimer's disease or other form of dementia has many needs. Moreover, dementia is not a static condition, but unfortunately worsens over time. Thus, the patient with dementia will progress through different types of care over time. Nursing care may be largely supportive early in the illness and very intensive as the disease progresses. Social workers help families find care options for their loved ones. Care may initially occur at home but later may need to transition to other facilities including a nursing home or hospital. The role of a health care administrator is to coordinate all of the efforts of the professional staff in best serving a patient. The demand for individuals who can fill the role of a health care administrator is high, and it is expected to grow by 22% from 2010 to 2020 (a rate much higher than the average for all occupations). In 2010, the median pay was $84,000 for individuals in this career. To enter this field, some individuals have a bachelor's degree, but most have a master's degree in health care administration. The role demands many skills. Knowledge about medicine must be combined with interpersonal skills. Managing budgets is essential to being an administrator. In addition, families can often be stressed and upset as an elderly relative declines in health. An individual well suited for this profession must be compassionate but also quickly able to solve problems. Administrators must keep apprised of new laws and ensure that facilities are following current regulations. Communication is central to managing a large number of employees, who range from physicians to the kitchen staff preparing meals for residents. The role is demanding, yet also very rewarding. In many cases, the administrator plays a significant role in making the last part of a person's life as positive as possible.

Some websites to explore:

Bureau of Labor Statistics—Medical and Health Services Managers
    http://www.bls.gov/ooh/Management/Medical-and-health-services-managers.htm
Health Care Administration
    http://www.healthcareadministration.com
In addition, many universities offer master's degrees in health care administration, long-
    term care administration, or public health. Look for programs that offer coursework
    such as hospital organization and management, accounting and budgeting, human
    resources administration, strategic planning, and health information systems.

Preventing Dementia

Dementia is devastating for patients and families. For patients, there is the slow yet inevitable loss of independence. The cognitive decline in patients is often more frustrating for family members. It is heartbreaking to have loved a family member so much only to have that person no longer recognize you because of dementia. The burden of dementia on society is also a great concern. It is extremely expensive to care for patients with dementia. When a patient is no longer able to dress, bathe, or feed himself or herself, care must be provided 24 hours a day. An experience with any form of dementia leads to an important question, is there anything that can be done to prevent it? While research on this topic is incomplete, there are some findings suggesting that environmental factors can reduce the risk for developing Alzheimer's disease. Even though the risk for Alzheimer's disease has a genetic component, there appear to be lifestyle factors that can reduce the risk or at least delay the emergence of disease symptoms. Lifestyle factors important in reducing the risk of dementia include physical exercise, diet, cognitive activity, and educational attainment. For exercise, it appears that cardiovascular fitness directly benefits blood vessels in the brain (cerebrovascular health). Exercise also controls stress, which is known to result in neuronal death, particularly when stress levels are extreme. A diet rich in fruits and vegetables is beneficial to the brain. Lifelong intellectual activity and higher educational levels also decrease the risk of dementia or delay the onset of dementia. Getting a college degree not only benefits your future career, but it also helps protect your brain against dementia. Once you graduate, it is important to maintain your curiosity and find intellectual enrichment in your life. This effect is clear from research with animals. Mice provided with environmental enrichment (toys, running wheels, and new foods) were less likely to develop the neurological markers of Alzheimer's disease than animals not provided with this enrichment. Finally, strong social structures and lack of isolation are known to lower the risk of dementia, and they also slow the progression of the disease in individuals exhibiting symptoms. Most importantly, research suggests that lifestyle factors, while somewhat beneficial, make a smaller impact when they occur closer to the onset of the disease. Lifestyle factors should be in place years or decades before the illness emerges to provide the greatest reduction in risk (Selkoe, 2012). Therefore, protecting your brain should be a lifelong endeavor.

QUICK QUIZ 14-2

1. How many FDA-approved pharmaceutical drugs are available to treat memory impairments?
   a. 1
   b. 5
   c. 25
   d. 50
   e. 500

2. The types of drugs that can be used to treat memory impairments include which of the following?
   a. Acetylcholinesterase inhibitors
   b. NMDA receptor antagonists
   c. Anabolic steroids
   d. a and b
   e. All of the above

3. How long have acetylcholinesterase inhibitors been available for use?
   a. 100 years
   b. 50 years
   c. 20 years
   d. 10 years
   e. 5 years

4. What role do acetylcholinesterase inhibitors and NMDA receptor antagonists play in the treatment of Alzheimer's disease?
   a. These drugs cure the disease.
   b. These drugs slow the inevitable intellectual decline seen with this disease.
   c. These drugs treat the emotional symptoms that accompany the disease.
   d. These drugs repair lost brain matter.

5. By the time individuals reach 95 years of age, what proportion will likely be diagnosed with Alzheimer's disease?
   a. 1%
   b. 5%
   c. 10%
   d. 25%
   e. 50%

6. Which neurotransmitter is thought to be deficient in Alzheimer's disease?
   a. Dopamine
   b. Serotonin
   c. Norepinephrine
   d. Acetylcholine
   e. GABA

7. Mrs. Jones and Mrs. Hernandez are both 70 years old and both have developed memory problems such as forgetfulness. Mrs. Jones also has some difficulty dressing and undressing herself. A neurologist determines that both probably have Alzheimer's disease, with Mrs. Jones's case being more severe than Mrs. Hernandez's case. If both start treatment with an acetylcholinesterase inhibitor, what is the predicted prognosis for each of them? Why?

8. Mr. Stevens has been diagnosed with frontotemporal dementia. Would Mr. Stevens's physician begin treatment with an acetylcholinesterase inhibitor or NMDA antagonist? Explain your answer.

9. Explain the difference between how acetylcholinesterase inhibitors and NMDA receptor antagonists act in the brain to help patients with Alzheimer's disease.

ANSWERS TO QUICK QUIZ 14-2:

1. b – 5
2. d – a and b
3. c – 20 years
4. b – These drugs slow the inevitable intellectual decline seen with this disease.
5. e – 50%
6. d – acetylcholine
7. Both ladies should benefit from the drug treatment slowing the inevitable progression of the disease. However, Mrs. Hernandez should benefit slightly more from the drug treatment since she appears to be earlier in the disease process. Her brain is likely not to have had as much neuronal death as the brain of Mrs. Jones (who is already experiencing symptoms such as deficits in self-care).

8. Mr. Stevens would not be given an acetylcholinesterase inhibitor or NMDA antagonist, because these drugs have not been demonstrated to be efficacious in frontotemporal dementia.

9. Acetylcholinesterase inhibitors act by inhibiting the action of the acetylcholine enzyme, which normally metabolizes acetylcholine in the synapse. Inhibiting the action of this enzyme increases the amount of acetylcholine in the brain. This improves cognitive functioning, as acetylcholine is important for memory and acetylcholine levels are deficient in patients with Alzheimer's disease. NMDA receptor antagonists block the NMDA glutamate receptor. Excess glutamate is thought to damage neurons. NMDA receptor antagonists limit glutamate activity and thus prevent some of the overexposure of calcium that freely flows into neurons and causes damage. NMDA receptor antagonists prevent some of the destruction of neurons that contributes to cognitive problems.

CHAPTER SUMMARY

Some psychoactive drugs, including anabolic steroids and smart drugs, can enhance physical and mental performance. Anabolic steroids are synthetic hormones related to naturally occurring testosterone. Anabolic steroids have been available since the 1930s. Their use enhances muscle mass, and they are classified as Schedule III drugs under the Controlled Substances Act. Anabolic steroids can improve athletic performance when used during training, and the illicit use of anabolic steroids has been a consistent concern in sports. The World Anti-Doping Agency was formed in 1999 to combat doping of all kinds in sports, including steroid use. Anabolic steroids have both anabolic (muscle growth) and androgenic (masculinizing) effects. Use of anabolic steroids can cause various health concerns, ranging from behavior problems such as increased aggression to psychological concerns such as psychotic symptoms. With chronic use of steroids, males may grow breasts or experience shrinkage of the testicles, whereas women may grow facial hair and develop a deepening voice. In both men and women, use of steroids can increase the risk of heart attack and stroke.

Smart drugs are psychotherapeutic drugs used to enhance mental performance. Their primary use is the treatment of dementias such as Alzheimer's disease. Acetylcholinesterase inhibitors and NMDA receptor antagonist drugs are used to delay the inevitable decline in memory and other cognitive functions that occur with Alzheimer's disease. Acetylcholinesterase inhibitors act to increase the amount of acetylcholine in the brain, thus improving memory and other cognitive functioning. NMDA receptor antagonists act by blocking NMDA glutamate receptors. Excess glutamate is thought to damage neurons. Thus, NMDA receptor antagonists prevent some of the destruction of neurons that contributes to cognitive problems. Both types of drugs (acetylcholinesterase inhibitors and NMDA receptor antagonists) have only been available since the 1990s. Currently, there are approximately 5 million people in the United States suffering from Alzheimer's disease and another 5 million who suffer from another form of dementia. Smart drugs slow the inevitable decline of Alzheimer's disease, but their use does not result in any appreciable change until months of treatment have passed. These drugs are typically used for years, and over this time period, the benefits of these drugs are clear. Treatment for Alzheimer's disease is most effective when begun early in the disease process. Improvements in medical care and an aging population mean that cases of Alzheimer's disease and other dementias are projected to grow substantially over time, with a doubling of cases expected every 20 years. Worldwide, 66 million cases of Alzheimer's disease are predicted by the year 2030. Given that there are only five FDA-approved medications currently used to treat Alzheimer's disease, the need for more research is urgent.

Glossary

Absorption – the processes and mechanisms by which a drug moves from outside the body into the bloodstream

Abstinence syndrome – dysphoria and drug craving for opiates that can last up to 6 months after drug use stops

Acamprosate (Campral®) – drug used to treat alcohol dependence; reduces alcohol craving by antagonizing glutamate and GABA receptors

Acetaldehyde – product of alcohol metabolism that does not result in intoxication but that can cause hangover symptoms

Acetylcholine – neurotransmitter important for memory, attention, and sensory processing

Acetylcholinesterase inhibitors – drugs that increase the availability of acetylcholine in the brain, thus improving memory function; used to treat patients suffering from dementia

Action Potential – the electrical signal that is sent along the axon when a neuron fires

Acute tolerance – functional tolerance that has developed within the course of a single drug dose

Addiction – compulsive drug use; present when one is strongly involved with using a drug, getting an adequate supply of it, and having a strong tendency to resume use of it after stopping for a time period

Adenosine – an inhibitory neurotransmitter thought to play a role in promoting sleep and suppressing arousal

Adulterant – a chemical substance that should not be contained within another substance; also called a cutting agent when mixed with an illicit drug

Agonist drug – chemical that occupies a neural receptor and activates it just as a naturally occurring neurotransmitter would

Alcohol – a central nervous system sedative drug

Alcohol dehydrogenase – enzyme that breaks down alcohol into acetaldehyde

Alcohol Prohibition – following the passage of the Eighteenth Amendment to the Constitution of the United States, the production, sale, transportation, and importation of alcohol was prohibited; this amendment was repealed 13 years later

Alcohol without liquid (AWOL) – process of inhaling vaporized alcohol

Alcoholics Anonymous (AA) – largest self-help group in the world that embraces abstinence to treat alcohol dependence; the only requirement for membership is a desire to stop drinking

Alkaloid – a nitrogen-containing organic metabolite produced by a plant; alkaloids such as nicotine, caffeine, morphine, and cocaine taste extremely bitter and are sometimes toxic

Alzheimer's disease – degenerative dementia that involves a progressive atrophy of cortical brain tissue; symptoms include memory impairment and intellectual decline

Amotivational syndrome – lack of motivation to achieve conventional goals that may be associated with chronic marijuana use

Amphetamines – group of psychoactive stimulant drugs that are used and abused as recreational drugs and also are legitimate psychotherapeutic drugs used to treat various medical conditions such as attention deficit/hyperactivity disorder (ADHD) and narcolepsy

Amygdala – forebrain structure involved in the regulation of strong emotions

Anabolic effect – effect of steroid use resulting in growth of muscle and red blood cells

Anabolic steroid – synthetic hormone that is related to testosterone; can be misused to enhance athletic performance, enhance muscle mass, or improve physical appearance

Analgesia – the ability to block pain without loss of consciousness

Anandamide – an inhibitory lipid neurotransmitter thought to play a role in appetite, sleep, and pain perception

Androgenic effect – effect of steroid use resulting in the development of male secondary sexual characteristics

Anorexia – absence of appetite

Antagonist drug – a drug that occupies a neural receptor and blocks normal synaptic transmission

Antianxiety drugs – psychotherapeutic drugs that reduce anxiety and may be used to treat symptoms of anxiety disorders or used to treat anxiety that accompanies medical procedures

Anticholinergic hallucinogen – a psychoactive drug that can induce hallucinations; act as acetylcholine receptor antagonist

Antidepressant drugs – psychotherapeutic drugs the reduce symptoms of depression

Antihistamines – allergy medications that decrease itching; will also decrease short-term anxiety

Antipsychotic drugs – psychoactive drugs that reduce psychotic symptoms; long-term side effects of antipsychotic drugs can resemble symptoms of neurological disease

Apoptosis – an internal signal received by neurons to "commit suicide"

Asian flushing response – physical reaction in individuals of Asian descent consisting of cutaneous flushing and other symptoms due to a buildup of acetaldehyde when drinking alcohol

Asylum – a hospital where people with mental illness are confined and cared for

Attention deficit/hyperactivity disorder (ADHD) – disorder characterized by symptoms of inattention, difficulty concentrating, overactivity, restlessness, and impulsivity

Autism spectrum disorder – disorder beginning in childhood that includes deficits in social communication and social interactions, repetitive and restricted behaviors, and speech deficits, which sometimes can be severe

Autonomic nervous system (ANS) – division of the peripheral nervous system that controls the sensory and motor nerves over which we normally have no conscious control (such as the heart and intestines)

Axon – long ropelike extension coming out of the cell body of a neuron; used to send a message on to the next cell

Bad trip – adverse reaction to a hallucinogen; symptoms include frightening hallucinations, confusion, paranoia, disorientation, agitation, panic, and feelings of terror

Barbiturates – depressant drugs (referred to in the past as sleeping pills) that are no longer used to treat anxiety because of concerns about tolerance and dependence

Bath salts – designer synthetic cathinone drugs that have amphetamine-like effects

Behavioral tolerance – an adjustment of behavior through experience in using a drug to compensate for its effects

Benzodiazepine receptors – subset of $GABA_A$ receptors to which antianxiety benzodiazepine drugs bind, thus enhancing GABA activity in the brain

Benzodiazepines – antianxiety medications that induce a calming effect; they increase the activity of the inhibitory neurotransmitter, GABA

Between-subjects research design – research where individuals are randomly assigned to two groups, one of which would receive the active drug (such as caffeine) and the other would be given the placebo and then the outcome is compared

Binge – the continuous use of a drug, lasting hours to days, terminating when supplies of the drug are exhausted

Bioavailability – the portion of the original drug dose that reaches its intended site of action

Biological passport – the complete set of records of urine and blood test results for an athlete; abrupt changes in biological parameters may indicate doping since most parameters will stay relatively steady across time

Biphasic drug – the effect of a drug may go in one direction, but then the response changes direction as the dose continues to be increased

Biphasic – in a dose-response curve, the response to the drug goes in one direction with the dose, but then the response changes direction as the dose continues to increase

Bipolar disorder – mental disorder with symptoms including both depression and mania

Blackout – alcohol-induced amnesia; a failure to recall a period of time during drinking even though there was no loss of consciousness

Blood alcohol concentration (BAC) – the amount of alcohol that is circulating in the bloodstream

Blood doping – the removal and then replacement of an athlete's blood to increase the level of oxygen-carrying hemoglobin in the blood

Blood–brain barrier – a filtering system for the blood before it can enter the brain, thus protecting the brain from toxic compounds

Blunt – marijuana in a hollowed-out cigar, which is smoked

Brain – the most complex organ in the body that regulates all basic body functions, enables you to interpret and respond to everything you experience and shapes thoughts, emotions, and behaviors

Bruxism – teeth grinding; an acute effect of MDMA (ecstasy)

Cachexia – when a patient who "wastes away" from weight loss, often due to cancer or AIDS

Caffeine – a mild stimulant drug that is found in a variety of beverages and foods, including coffee, tea, soft drinks, energy drinks, and chocolate

Caffeinism – caffeine intoxication that occurs when caffeine is administered at high doses with symptoms similar to generalized anxiety

Cannabinoids – chemicals that bind to cannabinoid receptors in the brain; cannabinoids can be endocannabinoids (produced by the body), phytocannabinoids (found in the cannabis plant), or synthetic cannabinoids (produced chemically by humans)

Capgras delusion – delusion where one thinks that a friend or family member has been replaced by an identical imposter

Cathinones – chemicals related to amphetamines; referred to as bath salts when synthetic (made in the lab), but can be ingested as khat since cathinones occur in a plant native to East Africa and southern Arabia

Cell body – contains the nucleus with the genetic material for the neuron and other processes involved in metabolic activities; the command center of a neuron

Central nervous system (CNS) – nervous tissue in the brain and spinal cord

Cerebellum – region of the brain in the brain stem area that looks like a cauliflower; responsible for balance and motor coordination

Cerebral cortex – region at the top of the brain that is divided into different areas that control specific functions, such as processing information from our senses (seeing, feeling, hearing, and tasting)

Chlorpromazine – the first antipsychotic drug discovered in 1950

Club drug – a psychoactive drug popular at night clubs and raves

Coca paste – the crude extract from coca leaves containing cocaine

Cocaethylene – a novel chemical produced when cocaine is biotransformed by the liver in the presence of alcohol; cocaethylene intensifies cocaine's euphoric effects but is also more lethal than cocaine alone

Cocaine – a powerful central nervous system stimulant drug

Cocaine hydrochloride – most common form of pure cocaine

Combat Methamphetamine Epidemic Act – federal legislation passed in 2006 that restricted access to chemicals used to make methamphetamine by monitoring purchases of these preparation chemicals, and that increased penalties for the possession of chemicals and/or equipment used to make methamphetamine; all pseudoephedrine products were moved behind the counter in pharmacies and tracked

Comprehensive Methamphetamine Control Act – federal legislation passed in 1996 that aimed to prevent the illegal manufacture and use of methamphetamine

Computerized axial tomography (CAT) – brain-imaging technique that uses X-rays to produce a three-dimensional image of the brain

Conduct disorder – disorder diagnosed in children in adolescents when a pattern of extreme disobedience, including theft, vandalism, lying, and early drug use, is observed

Controlled Substances Act – federal legislation passed in 1970 that serves as the current U.S. federal drug policy regulating the manufacture, importation, possession, use, and distribution of certain substances; most psychoactive drugs (except alcohol, nicotine, and caffeine) are classified into one of the five schedules according to their medical use, their potential abuse, and their likelihood for producing dependence

Crack – street name for cocaine that has been chemically processed to make a rock crystal; when heated, the crystal produces vapors that are smoked by the user

Crack lung – scarred and damaged lung tissue from chronic crack cocaine use; symptoms include chronic cough, difficulty breathing, severe chest pain, and/or fever

Crank bugs – tactile hallucination whereby stimulant user feels like bugs are crawling underneath the skin; also see formication

Craving – the strong or intense desire to use a drug

Cross-tolerance – tolerance that has developed to one drug crosses over to another similar drug

Delirium tremens – hallucinations, delusions, and tremors; symptoms that may emerge with withdrawal from alcohol

Delusion – thought that is inconsistent with reality; false belief about what is taking place or who one is; a symptom of stimulant psychosis or schizophrenia

Dementia – serious loss of global cognitive ability that appears inconsistent with the individual's prior level of intelligence and is unexpected in the context of the normal aging process

Dendrites – branch-like structures that extend from a neuron; dendrites have many receptor sites, which are important for neural transmission

Detoxification – withdrawal from alcohol; the first step in treating alcohol dependence

Dextromethorphan – a cough-suppressing ingredient found in over-the-counter cough and cold medications; induces dissociative anesthetic effects at high doses

Diagnosis – a name given to a cluster of symptoms

Diamorphine – heroin used for medical use; diamorphine is used in palliative care in other countries around the world, but not the United States

Discontinuation syndrome – withdrawal syndrome that emerges upon abrupt cessation of antidepressant drug treatment; symptoms include dizziness, nausea, vomiting, fatigue, chills, flulike illness, sensory abnormalities, sleep disturbances, crying spells, anxiety, irritability, and agitation

Dispositional tolerance – an increase in the metabolism rate of a drug due to regular drug use

Dissociative anesthetic – drug that produces feelings of detachment (dissociation) from the environment and self and induces distortions of visual and auditory perceptions

Distillation – process of heating a fermented beverage to increase the alcohol content

Distribution – the processes by which the drug is dispersed throughout the body by the circulating blood and passing through various barriers to reach its site of action – the receptors

Disulfiram (Antabuse®) – drug used to treat alcohol dependence; induces violent vomiting when a user also consumes alcohol

Dopamine – neurotransmitter involved in the regulation of movement, emotion, cognition, motivation, and feelings of pleasure; drugs of abuse upregulate the dopamine system, resulting in the feeling of euphoria

Dopamine hypothesis of schizophrenia – posits that excess dopamine release and/or excess sensitivity of dopamine neurons causes psychotic symptoms (also called positive symptoms) in schizophrenia

Dopamine transporter – membrane-spanning protein that pumps dopamine out of the synapse and back into the presynaptic neuron for storage and later release; also called dopamine active transporter (DAT)

Dose-response curve – a graphical representation of the responses to a drug across a range of doses

Drug – any chemical entity or mixture of entities, other than those required for the maintenance of normal health (like food), the administration of which alters biological function and possibly structure

Drug discrimination study – study protocol using drugs as discriminative stimuli to indicate how reinforcers are obtained

Drug diversion – any case where a legitimately prescribed medication is used for illicit recreational use

Drug dose – a measure of the quantity of the drug administered

Drug holidays – a period of time when an individual does not take a therapeutic drug

Drug testing – various methods used to determine if someone has used a psychoactive drug

Effective dose (ED) – the dose of drug at which a given percentage of individuals experience a particular effect

Electroencephalography (EEG) – technique that measures the brain's electrical activity through the scalp

Emesis – vomiting

En bloc blackout – instance of full and permanent memory loss for intoxicated events

Endorphins – peptides that function as neurotransmitters and act like endogenous morphine by blocking pain

Energy drink – a beverage like a soft drink that contains a combination of caffeine and other plant-based stimulants and amino acids; energy drinks are often carbonated and contain sugar or sweeteners like soft drinks

Enzyme breakdown – process of neurotransmitters being broken into an inactive form by enzymes

Ephedrine – an alkaloid from plants of the genus *Ephedra* that has a similar structure to amphetamines and methamphetamine

Excitatory receptors – receptors where if a neurotransmitter binds, it is likely to result in an action potential

Excretion – the process of how a drug, or its metabolite, leaves the body

Exorcism – ritualistic casting out of evil spirits thought to render the body uninhabitable by the devil

Family Smoking Prevention and Tobacco Control Act – federal legislation passed in 2009 that authorized the Food and Drug Administration (FDA) to regulate tobacco products, including the manufacture, marketing, and sale of these products; includes a strong focus on stopping young people from smoking

Fermentation – process by which yeast eats sugar in the presence of water and air; the byproducts of yeast metabolism are alcohol and carbon dioxide

Fetal alcohol syndrome (FAS) – diagnosis given to a child that was prenatally exposed to alcohol; characteristics of FAS include craniofacial abnormalities, central nervous system dysfunction, and pre- and/or postnatal growth deficiencies

Fight-or-flight response – in response to stress and danger, the sympathetic nervous system is activated to prepare the body for a sudden expenditure of energy

Flashback – a recurrence of the drug experience even though no drug has been actually taken

Forebrain – largest part of the brain located above the midbrain; includes structures that serve a variety of purposes from regulating body temperature to cognitive functioning

Formication syndrome – tactile hallucination of feeling like bugs are crawling underneath or on the skin; also see crank bugs

Fragmentary blackout – instance of incomplete memory loss for intoxicated events where the poor memories can be aided by the provision of cues to help reconstruct events to "fill in the blanks"

Frontal cortex – the thinking center of the brain involved in planning, solving problems, and making decisions

Frontotemporal dementia – degenerative dementia that involves a progressive atrophy of the frontal and/or temporal lobes of the brain; symptoms include bizarre behavior and/or language loss

Functional magnetic resonance imaging (fMRI) – imaging technique that views brain activity across time using MRI technology

Functional selectivity – when a drug has a stabilizing action on receptors; the drug may exert different effects through a single receptor, such as acting as a full agonist in one pathway in the brain and an antagonist in a second pathway

Functional tolerance – the decreased behavioral effects of a drug as a result of its regular use; can be acute or chronic

Gamma amino-butyric acid (GABA) – very common inhibitory neurotransmitter important for sedation

Gateway drug theory – idea that marijuana needed to be controlled because it would eventually lead users to other highly addictive drugs such as heroin

Generalized anxiety disorder – mental disorder with symptoms of anxiety and worry that persistent across most contexts

Generic drug – a cheaper version of a drug that can be sold after a certain length of time by companies that did not pay for the original drug development and FDA approval process

Glaucoma – medical disorder that results in increased pressure in the eye and can lead to blindness

Glutamate – common excitatory neurotransmitter important for learning and memory

Green tobacco sickness – nicotine poisoning that occurs when farm workers touch wet tobacco leaves and water-soluble nicotine goes through their skin

Half-life – the amount of time that is required for the dose of drug in the body to be reduced by half

Hallucination – a false perception that is inconsistent with reality; when a symptom of stimulant psychosis, hallucinations are often auditory or tactile

Hallucinogen – a psychoactive drug that alters one's perceptions, mood, and thoughts

Hallucinogen-induced persisting perceptual disorder (HPPD) – mental disorder with symptoms of persistent flashbacks; HPPD causes significant distress and impairs social and occupational functioning

Hangover – minor alcohol withdrawal symptoms following excessive use of alcohol; symptoms include feeling ill, such as upset stomach, fatigue, headache, thirst, depression, and anxiety

Harrison Narcotics Tax Act – federal law passed in 1914 that strictly regulated the legal supply of certain psychoactive drugs, including opiates

Hashish – psychoactive drug produced from resin found on the flowers of the hemp plant, *Cannabis sativa*; has stronger effects than marijuana

Hepatic encephalopathy – neurological disease that emerges in chronic alcoholics whose liver cells are damaged, allowing toxic amounts of ammonia and manganese to enter the brain and damage brain cells; in very serious cases, the patient may slip into a coma, which can be fatal

Heroin – purified version of morphine that is highly addictive; there are currently no acceptable medical uses for it in the United States

Hindbrain – region of the brain closest to the spinal cord; includes medulla, pons, and cerebellum; controls functions such as heart rate, breathing, sleeping, and motor movements

Hippocampus – forebrain structure that is important for memory formation and spatial navigation

Homeostasis – the stable environment in the body; processes are in place in the body to regulate its internal environment, thus maintaining a relatively constant set of conditions

Hospice care – medical care for the terminally ill patient that focuses on comforting measures like pain control rather than trying to achieve a cure

Hypothalamus – forebrain structure that regulates motivated behavior, including eating, drinking, control of body temperature, aggression, and sexual behavior

Ibogaine – hallucinogenic drug found in the shrub *Tabernathe iboga*, which grows in West Africa; researchers have been examining if ibogaine may be useful in treating addiction

In vivo microdialysis – technique whereby a tiny probe is placed in the brain so that extracellular fluid can be collected and analyzed for the presence of various neurotransmitters

Incidence – the number of new cases in a population in a given time

Inhalation – a route of drug administration involving inhaling the drug, with drug absorption occurring through the lung's membranes; fast and effective method of drug administration, particularly when the drug can be changed into a gaseous state

Inhibitory control – control over one's behavior; self-control

Inhibitory receptors – receptors where if a neurotransmitter binds, it is less likely to result in an action potential

Injection – route of drug administration requiring a needle and syringe

Interdisciplinary research – research that combines two or more traditionally defined academic disciplines

Intramuscular injection – route of drug administration whereby a needle is inserted into a muscle to inject a drug

Intranasal – a route of drug administration through the nose; fast and effective method of drug administration

Intraperitoneal (i.p.) injection – route of drug administration mainly used in animals whereby a needle is inserted into the peritoneum (abdominal cavity) to inject a drug

Intravenous injection – route of drug administration whereby a needle is inserted directly into a vein to inject a drug

Investigational New Drug (IND) – label given by the FDA for a new drug that seems promising after preclinical studies (animal studies) have been completed and before clinical trials with humans can begin

Joint – marijuana in a rolled cigarette, which is smoked

Kappa opiate hallucinogens – drugs that act as kappa opiate agonists and produce hallucinogenic effects; salvia is a kappa opiate hallucinogen

Khat – stimulant drug acquired from the *Catha edulis* shrub that is native to East Africa and southern Arabia

Lethal dose (LD) – the dose of drug at which a given percentage of individuals die within a specific time period

Limbic system – regions of the brain that contains the reward circuitry, controlling and regulating our ability to feel pleasure; region is also responsible for our perception of emotions

Lobbyist – someone who is employed to persuade legislators to vote for legislation favored by the lobbyist's employer

Loquaciousness – talkativeness

Lysergic acid diethylamide (LSD) – synthetic serotonergic hallucinogen that induces vivid visual hallucinations; sometimes referred to as acid

Magnetic resonance imaging (MRI) – brain imaging technique that uses strong magnetic fields to create a detailed three-dimensional image of the brain

Mainlining – slang term referring to an intravenous injection

Major depressive disorder – mental disorder with symptoms including persistent sadness, loss of pleasure, feelings of worthlessness, guilt, withdrawal from others, and loss of pleasure

Marijuana – psychoactive sedative drug made from the dried crushed leaves from the hemp plant, *Cannabis sativa*; it is typically smoked, but it can also be orally ingested

Marijuana Tax Act – federal legislation passed in 1930 that required authorized producers, manufacturers, importers, and dispensers of marijuana to register and pay an annual license fee

MDMA (ecstasy) – a methylated amphetamine drug that induces both mildly hallucinogenic and stimulant effects

Medulla – the lowest hindbrain structure, important in the regulation of breathing, heart rate, swallowing, and blood pressure; vomiting will result if toxins reach high levels in the medulla

Mental disorder – clinically significant behavioral or psychological syndrome or patterns; key features include distress, disability or impaired functioning, violation of social norms, and dysfunction

Mescaline – natural serotonergic hallucinogen that comes from the peyote cactus

Mesolimbic dopaminergic pathway – the pleasure center in the brain; release of the neurotransmitter dopamine in this pathway is rewarding; nicotine leads to the release of dopamine in this pathway, which explains the rewarding properties of nicotine

Metabolism – the biochemical modification of a drug typically via enzyme systems

Meth mouth – dental condition that develops with chronic methamphetamine use; symptoms include severe tooth decay (dental caries), enamel erosion, and loss of teeth

Methamphetamine – amphetamine-type drug with a high potential for abuse; referred to as crank, crystal, crystal meth, ice, and speed

Methylated amphetamines – psychoactive drugs that are chemically similar to amphetamines but induce hallucinations

Midbrain – relatively small region of the brain located above the hindbrain and below the forebrain; important relay center for visual and auditory information; includes the substantia nigra, which produces dopamine and is important for motivation and reward

Mimicry – process whereby the chemical structure of the drug resembles the natural neurotransmitter

Monoamines – family of neurotransmitters including dopamine, norepinephrine, and serotonin

Mood stabilizers – psychotherapeutic drugs that reduce the depression and mania, which are symptoms of bipolar disorder

Morphine – the principal alkaloid found in opium; widely used in medicine to treat severe pain

Motor nerve – used to send a message from the brain to a muscle

Multiple sclerosis (MS) – an autoimmune disease that damages myelin in the central nervous system, thus slowing neural transmission

Myelin – a layer of fatty tissue wrapped around the axon that speeds communication; composed of glial cells

Myocardial infarction – commonly called a heart attack, which can result in sudden death; when blood flow is completely obstructed in a coronary artery, death of an area of heart tissue from the lack of blood supply results

Nalmefene – an opiate antagonist drug used to treat an opiate overdose

Naloxone – an opiate antagonist drug used to treat an opiate overdose

Naltrexone (ReVia® or Vivitrol®) – drug used to treat alcohol dependence; reduces craving for alcohol by blocking endorphin activity (opiate antagonist)

Narcolepsy – a chronic sleep disorder characterized by excessive sleepiness and falling asleep at inappropriate times

Narcotic – a psychoactive drug that induces stupor, coma, or insensibility to pain; the term usually refers to opiates or opioids (narcotic analgesics) although the term is often used imprecisely to refer to all illicit drugs

Nerve – an enclosed cable-like bundle of axons found in the peripheral nervous system

Nesbitt's paradox – the perplexing observation that smokers report that smoking relaxes them and helps deal with stress, even though experimental studies have actually found that smoking increases arousal and stress

Neurogenesis – the birth of new neurons in the brain

Neuroleptic drug – antipsychotic drug; term is used more frequently in Europe

Neuromuscular junction – a space similar to a synapse where a neuron meets muscle; when acetylcholine is released by a neuron into the neuromuscular junction, the muscle contracts

Neuron – unique type of cell that can receive and transmit information electrochemically

Neurotransmitter – chemical used by neurons for communication; neurotransmitters are stored in the axon terminal until an action potential arrives and the neurotransmitters are released into the synapse; neurotransmitters influence the activity of postsynaptic neurons

Nicotine – an alkaloid stimulant drug that comes from tobacco; nicotine is highly addictive

Nicotine poisoning – an illness that results from a nicotine overdose with symptoms that include nausea, vomiting, dizziness, weakness, diarrhea, fluctuations in blood pressure and heart rate, and increased perspiration

NMDA receptor – type of glutamate receptor thought to be involved in tolerance to opiates

NMDA receptor antagonist drug – drug that antagonizes the action of glutamate in the brain, thus protecting neurons from damage

Nociception – the ability to perceive pain

Nonpharmacological factor – anything not related to a drug's pharmacological action, which contributes to a drug experience; includes things like personality characteristics or the setting in which the drug is used

Norepinephrine – neurotransmitter that plays an important role in emotional arousal, regulation of hunger, and alertness

Opiate-induced hyperalgesia – when the patient being treated with opiates becomes increasingly sensitive to pain over time

Opiate – powerful psychoactive sedative drug that blocks pain and induces euphoria; when abused, opiates can result in severe dependence

Opiophobia – an irrational fear of using opiate drugs in medicine because they might lead to addiction

Opium – the dried milky white sap that is present inside the seed pod of the poppy plant, *Papaver somniferum*

Oral drug administration – route of administration whereby the drug is swallowed

OxyContin® – controlled-release form of the oxycodone prescription medication; referred to as oxy or hillbilly heroin by abusers

Pain – an unpleasant sensory and emotional experience associated with actual or potential tissue damage

Panic attack – sudden attack of feeling of doom, apprehension, and terror; physical symptoms resemble a heart attack

Panic disorder – mental disorder characterized by frequent panic attacks and worry about having more panic attacks

Parasympathetic nervous system – dominant division of the autonomic nervous system, which keeps the internal functioning of the body operating smoothly; balances the actions of the sympathetic branch by decreasing heart rate, blood pressure, and respiration

Peak drug effect – the dose level at which the response is the greatest

Performance-enhancing drug (PED) – any drug used to enhance athletic performance; includes anabolic steroids and some other similar drugs

Peripheral nervous system (PNS) – all nervous tissue outside of the CNS

Pharmacodynamics – the interactions of a drug with its receptor or how the drug produces its effects

Pharmacokinetics – the area of pharmacology that examines absorption, distribution, biotransformation, and excretion of drugs

Pharmacological factor – anything related to a drug's biochemical and/or physiological action, including chemical structure, route of administration, and drug dose

Phenotype – the physical or behavioral trait exhibited by individual that is a product of interactions between genetics and the environment

Phobia – disproportionate fear of an object or situation; common phobias include snakes, spiders, mice, blood, injections, heights, and enclosed spaces

Physical dependence – a state in which the use of the drug is required just so the person can function normally

Placebo – a chemically inactive substance

Polydrug use – when an individual uses two or more psychoactive drugs at once to achieve a certain effect

Pons – hindbrain region that controls sleep and wakefulness

Positron emission tomography (PET) – a brain imaging technique used to measure brain activity that involves injecting weak radioisotopes so that activity of certain types of receptors in selected brain regions can be assessed

Posttraumatic stress disorder (PTSD) – anxiety disorder that develops after exposure to a severe and sometimes chronic traumatic event

Prefrontal cortex – region of the frontal cortex that is involved in the ability to plan, control impulses, and consider the long-term consequences of actions

Prevalence – the total number of cases in the population at a given time

Prohormone – precursor to a hormone

Proof – proportion of alcohol by volume, or twice the percentage of alcohol

Prophylactic drug – a drug that is used to prevent the occurrence of a disease; lithium is used prophylactically to treat bipolar depression

Protracted tolerance – functional tolerance that has developed over the course of two or more drug administrations

Psilocybin – natural serotonergic hallucinogen that comes from some mushrooms

Psychoactive drug – a drug that alters mood, cognition, and behavior

Psychological dependence – the compulsive use of a drug for its pleasurable effects; craving for a drug without the presence of physical withdrawal symptoms

Psychopharmacology – the scientific study of the effects of drugs on behavior

Psychosis – a loss of contact with reality, which can include delusions and hallucinations

Psychotherapeutic drug – psychoactive drug used to improve mood state and mental functioning

Psychotomimetic – drug that mimics the functional psychosis characteristic of the serious mental disorder of schizophrenia

Psychotropic drug – see psychotherapeutic drug

Pure Food and Drug Act – federal law passed in 1906 emphasizing that the truth must be stated on the label; the law highlighted opiates (opium, morphine, heroin), but it also mandated the accurate labeling of products containing alcohol, cocaine, and marijuana

Racemic mixture – drug mixture of equal proportions of stereoisomers

Rave – large gathering of people who party and dance to electronic music; casual sex and use of hallucinogenic drugs including MDMA (ecstasy) and LSD may be common

Receptor sites – structures on neurons into which neurotransmitters can fit

Reinforcer – a stimulus that is rewarding that increases the probability of a behavior being repeated

Reticular activating system – brain pathway that runs through the medulla and pons; regulates alertness and arousal

Reuptake – process of neurotransmitters being taken back up into the presynaptic neuron's axon, thus inactivating the neurotransmitter

Rohypnol® (flunitrazepam) – potent benzodiazepine that is not legal in the United States that can lead to memory loss and blackouts; users refer to this drug as "roofies"; also known as a date rape drug

Route of administration – how the drug enters the body

Safety ratio – therapeutic index for psychoactive drugs; calculated as LD_{50}/ED_{50}

San Francisco Ordinance – an 1875 local drug law that banned opium dens (locations where people smoked opium) in San Francisco

Schizophrenia – very serious mental disorder characterized by disturbances in thought, emotion, and behavior; patients experience psychotic symptoms like delusions (false beliefs) and hallucinations (false perceptions)

Second-generation (atypical) antipsychotic drug – drug (such as risperidone) similar to a traditional antipsychotic drug except that the dopamine-blocking agent is less potent and is balanced by other actions on serotonin receptors

Sedative drug – a drug that decreases alertness, heightens fatigue, and slows cognitive processing

Sensitization – reverse tolerance whereby repeated administration of a drug results in greater sensitivity to the effects of a drug

Sensorimotor gating – neurological processes filter out redundant or unnecessary stimuli

Sensory nerve – used to send a message from a sense organ (such as the eye or ear) to the brain

Serotonergic hallucinogens – psychoactive drugs that powerfully alter perception, mood, and cognitive processing by increasing the action of serotonin in the brain; vivid visual hallucinations are likely with prototypical drugs like LSD, mescaline, or psilocybin

Serotonin – neurotransmitter that plays an important role in the regulation of sleep, mood, and appetite

Skin-popping – slang term referring to a subcutaneous injection

Smart drugs – category of pharmaceutical drugs, supplements, nutra-ceuticals, and functional foods that enhance cognitive performance; nootropics are smart drugs

Social anxiety disorder – mental disorder with symptom of excessive fears about unfamiliar people or social scrutiny

Soft drink – a beverage that contains water (often carbonated), a sweetener, and a flavoring agent; caffeine is found in many soft drinks

Somatic nervous system – division of the peripheral nervous system that is made up of all the sensory and motor neurons that function under conscious awareness

Speedball – injection of heroin mixed with cocaine; this drug combination is likely to result in drug overdoses since the aversive side effects of each drug are masked by the other drug

Standard drink – a beverage containing 14 grams of pure alcohol, which is typically found in 12 fluid ounces of beer, 5 fluid ounces of wine, or 1.5 fluid ounces 80 proof liquor (such as vodka, bourbon, or rum)

Stereoisomers – molecules with the same molecular formula and sequence of bonded atoms but differing in the three-dimensional orientation of the atoms in space

Stimulant drug – a drug that increases alertness, decreases fatigue, and heightens mood

Stimulant psychosis – syndrome that appears when high doses of amphetamines or cocaine are ingested; the user may experience paranoia, delusions, or hallucinations and may become paranoid, hostile, and violent

Subcutaneous injection – route of drug administration whereby a needle is inserted into the fatty tissue just beneath the skin to inject a drug

Sublingual – route of administration whereby the drug is placed under the tongue and dissolves in saliva

Substantia nigra – midbrain structure that produces dopamine

Sympathetic nervous system – the portion of the autonomic nervous system that is activated during emotional arousal and is responsible for the physiological changes that occur during a "fight-or-flight" response; sympathetic activity increases heart rate, blood pressure, respiration, sweating, and moves blood away from the internal organs and to the brain and large muscle groups

Synapse – the space in between two neurons into which neuro-transmitters are released

Synaptogenesis – a developmental period in a fetus that is considered a critical time period when synaptic connections are made

Synesthesia – acute effect of hallucinogens whereby senses meld and the user may report seeing music or hearing colors

Synthetic Drug Abuse Prevention Act – federal legislation passed in 2012 that was designed to address the threat of synthetic drugs by banning various synthetic compounds

Tardive dyskinesia – syndrome that includes involuntary movements of the mouth, tongue, trunk, arms, and legs; syndrome can result from the chronic use of antipsychotic drugs

Teratogen – any agent or influence that causes developmental defects in an embryo; alcohol is a teratogen

Testosterone – steroid hormone that is synthesized in the human body from cholesterol; in the adult male, testosterone regulates many physiological processes, including sexual functioning and muscle protein metabolism

Thalamus – forebrain structure that relays incoming sensory input to relevant locations throughout the brain

THC – delta-9-tetrahydrocannabinol is the psychoactive chemical found in marijuana and is also a synthetically produced medicine

Therapeutic index – measure of how safe a drug is; calculated as LD_{50}/ED_{50}

Thigmotaxis – tendency to remain close to the walls in an open-field test; an index of anxiety in mice and rats

Third-generation antipsychotic drug – drug (such as aripiprazole) that decreases psychotic symptoms by exerting a stabilizing action on dopamine receptors

Tolerance – the need for increased amounts of the drug to achieve intoxication or the diminished effect with continued use of the same amount of the drug

Tourette syndrome – syndrome with symptoms such as uncontrolled movements (motor tics) or vocal outbursts (vocal tics)

Tract – a bundle of axons found in the central nervous system

Traditional (typical) antipsychotic drug – drug (such as chlorprom-azine) that decreases psychotic symptoms by blocking dopamine receptors; some undesirable side effects emerge associated with decreased dopamine activity

Transdermal – route of administration whereby the drug is absorbed by placing it on the skin using a patch

Translational research – research that attempts to translate basic research findings into practice

Trip – the experience of being under the influence of a hallucinogenic drug

Vesicles – tiny bubbles that store neurotransmitters; located in axon terminals

Wernicke–Korsakoff syndrome – neurological syndrome consisting of two related diseases that arise in chronic alcoholics who experience thiamine deficiency; Wernicke's encephalopathy is a short-lived and severe condition that includes symptoms such as mental confusion, paralysis of the nerves that control the eyes, and muscle incoordination; Korsakoff's syndrome is a long-lasting and debilitating condition characterized by learning and memory problems

Withdrawal – the characteristic syndrome that occurs when the use of a drug is stopped or decreased

Withdrawal reversal hypothesis – hypothesis that caffeine use is maintained because individuals wish to avoid or terminate head-aches or other withdrawal symptoms that are aversive

Within-subjects research design – research that involves the same person or animal receiving the active drug (such as caffeine) and the placebo on different occasions and comparing outcomes

World Anti-Doping Agency (WADA) – agency that combats athletic doping in a collaboration between sports and governments

Xanthine – a purine base found in the body tissues and fluids of many organisms, including humans; derivatives of xanthines include caffeine, theophylline, and theobromine

REFERENCES

Aaron, P., & Musto, D. (1981). Temperance and prohibition in America: A historical overview. In M. H. Moore & D. R. Gerstein (Eds.), *Alcohol and public policy* (pp. 127–181). Washington, DC: Academy Press.

Abbey, A. (2011). Alcohol's role in sexual violence perpetration: Theoretical explanations, existing evidence and future directions. *Drug and Alcohol Review, 30*, 481–489.

Abel, E. L. (1980). *Marihuana: The first twelve thousand years.* New York: Plenum Press.

Abel, E. L. (1999). Was the fetal alcohol syndrome recognized by the Greeks and Romans? *Alcohol and Alcoholism, 34*, 868–872.

Abikoff, H., Gallagher, R., Wells, K. C., Murray, D. W., Huang, L., Lu, F., & Petkova, E. (2013). Remediating organizational functioning in children with ADHD: Immediate and long-term effects from a randomized controlled trial. *Journal of Consulting and Clinical Psychology, 81*, 113–128.

Abramson, J. (2008). *Overdo$ed America.* New York: HarperCollins.

Abreau, R. V., Silva-Oliveira, E. M., Moraes, M. F., Pereira, G. S., & Moraes-Santos, T. (2011). Chronic coffee and caffeine ingestion effects on the cognitive function and antioxidant system of rat brains. *Pharmacology, Biochemistry and Behavior, 99*, 659–664.

Aggarwal, S. K., Carter, G. T., Sullivan, M. D., ZumBrunnen, C., Morrill, R., & Mayer, J. D. (2009). Medicinal use of cannabis in the United States: Historical perspectives, current trends, and future directions. *Journal of Opioid Management, 5*, 153–168.

Aigner, T. G., & Balster, R. L. (1978). Choice behavior in rhesus monkeys: Cocaine versus food. *Science, 201*, 534–535.

Albarelli, H. P., Jr. (2009). *A terrible mistake: The murder of Frank Olson and the CIA's secret Cold War experiments.* Walterville, OR: Trine Day.

Aldrich, M. R. (1977). Tantric cannabis use in India. *Journal of Psychoactive Drugs, 9*, 227–233.

Alkan, I., Koprulu, O., & Alkan, B. (2009). Latest advances in world tea production and trade, Turkey's aspect. *World Journal of Agricultural Sciences, 5*(3), 345–349.

Alper, K. R., Lotsof, H. S., & Kaplan, C. D. (2008). The ibogaine medical subculture. *Journal of Ethnopharmacology, 115*, 9–24.

Ambre, J. J., Belknap, S. M., Nelson, J., Ruo, T. I., Shin, S. G., & Atkinson, A. J. Jr. (1988). Acute tolerance to cocaine in humans. *Clinical Pharmacology Therapy, 44*, 1–8.

Ameri, A., Wilhelm, A., & Simmet, T. (1999). Effects of the endogenous cannabinoid, anandamide, on neuronal activity in rat hippocampal slices. *British Journal of Pharmacology, 126*, 1831–1839.

American Association of Poison Control Centers. (2012). Calls to poison control centers for human exposure to bath salts, 2010 to January 2012. Author. Retrieved from http://www.aapcc.org/alerts/bath-salts/

American Beverage Association. (2011). Soft drinks and diet soft drinks: History. Retrieved from http://www.ameribev.org/minisites/products/

American Beverage Association. (2011, November 22). Beverage industry responds to DAWN report on energy drinks. Press release retrieved from http://www.ameribev.org/newsmedia/news-releases--statements/more/257/

American Psychiatric Association (APA). (1994). *Diagnostic and statistical manual of mental disorders: DSM-IV.* Washington, DC: Author.

American Psychiatric Association (APA). (2000). *Diagnostic and statistical manual of mental disorders: DSM-IV-TR.* Washington, DC: Author.

Anand, P., & Singh, B. (2013). A review on cholinesterase inhibitors for Alzheimer's disease. *Archives for Pharmacological Research, 36*, 375–399.

Anand, P., Whiteside, G., Fowlder, C. J., & Hohmann, A. G. (2009). Targeting CB2 receptors and the endocannabinoid system for the treatment of pain. *Brain Research Review, 60*, 255–266.

Anderson, B. M., Stevens, M. C., Meda, S., Jordan, K., Calhoun, V. D., & Pearlson, G. D. (2011). Functional imaging of cognitive control during acute alcohol intoxication. *Alcoholism: Clinical and Experimental Research, 35*, 156–165.

Anderson, D. M. (2010). Does information matter? The effect of the Meth Project on meth use among youths. *Journal of Health Economics, 29*, 732–742.

Andreuccetti, G., Carvalho, H. B., Cherpitel, C. J., Ye, Y., Ponce, J. C., Kahn, T., & Leyton, V. (2011). Reducing the legal blood alcohol concentration limit for driving in developing countries: A time for change? Results and implications derived from a time-series analysis (2001–10) conducted in Brazil. *Addiction, 106*, 2124–2131.

Annweiler, C., & Beauchet, O. (2012). Possibility of a new anti-Alzheimer's disease pharmaceutical composition combining memantine and vitamin D. *Drugs and Aging, 29*, 81–91.

Aragon-Poce, F., Martinez-Fernandez, E., Marquez-Espinos, C., Perez, A., Mora, R., & Torres, L. M. (2002). History of opium. *International Congress Series, 1242*, 19–21.

Arena, J. M., & Drew, R. H. (1986). *Poisoning: Toxicology, symptoms, treatments* (5th ed.). Springfield, IL: Thomas.

Arnaud, M. J. (1993). Metabolism of caffeine and other components of coffee. In S. Garattini (Ed.), *Caffeine, coffee and health.* New York: Raven Press.

Arnsten, A. F. (2006). Stimulants: Therapeutic actions in ADHD. *Neuropsychopharmacology, 31*, 2376–2383.

Arria, A. M., O'Grady, K. E., Caldeira, K. M., Vincent, K. B., & Wish, E. D. (2008). Nonmedical use of prescription stimulants and analgesics: Associations with social and academic behaviors among college students. *Journal of Drug Issues, 38*, 1045–1060.

Ashton, H., & Watson, D. W. (1970). Puffing frequency and nicotine intake in cigarette smokers. *British Medical Journal, 3*, 679–681.

Ashton, R. (2002). *This is heroin.* London: Sanctuary.

Auret, K., & Schug, S. A. (2005). Underutilisation of opioids in elderly patients with chronic pain: Approaches to correcting the problem. *Drugs and Aging, 22,* 641–654.

Baker, M. (2008, May 3). DEA identifies 22 dietary supplements containing anabolic steroids. *Bleacher Report.* Retrieved from http://bleacherreport.com/articles/21320-dea-identifies-22-dietary-supplements-containing-anabolic-steroids

Bakker, R., Steegers, E. A. P., Obradov, A., Raat, H., Hofman, A., & Jaddoe, V. W. V. (2010). Maternal caffeine intake from coffee and tea, fetal growth, and the risks of adverse birth outcomes: The Generation R Study. *American Journal of Clinical Nutrition, 91,* 1691–1698.

Baldessarini, R. J. (2001). Drugs and the treatment of psychiatric disorders: Depression and anxiety disorders. In J. G. Hardman, L. E. Limbird, & A. G. Gilman (Eds.), *The pharmacological basis of therapeutics* (10th ed.) (pp. 447–483). New York: McGraw-Hill.

Baldessarini, R. J., & Tarazi, F. I. (2001). Drugs and the treatment of psychiatric disorders: Psychosis and mania. In J. G. Hardman, L. E. Limbird, & A. G. Gilman (Eds.), *The pharmacological basis of therapeutics* (10th ed.) (pp. 485–520). New York: McGraw-Hill.

Baldessarini, R. J., Tondo, L., Ghiani, C., & Lepri, B. (2010). Illness risk following rapid versus gradual discontinuation of antidepressants. *American Journal of Psychiatry, 167,* 934–941.

Baldwin, D. S., Evans, D. L., Hirschfeld, R. M., & Kasper, S. (2002). Can we distinguish anxiety from depression? *Psychopharmacology Bulletin, 36* Suppl 2, 158–165.

Ban, T. A. (2007). Fifty years chlorpromazine: A historical perspective. *Neuropsychiatric Disease and Treatment, 3,* 495–500.

Barbor, T. F., Higgins-Biddle, J. C., Saunders, J.B., & Monteiro, M. G. (2001). *AUDIT: The Alcohol Use Disorders Identification Test* (2nd ed.). WHO/MSD/MSB/01.6a. Geneva, Switzerland: World Health Organization, Department of Mental Health and Substance Dependence.

Barbor, T. F., Meyer, R. E., Mirin, S. M., McNamee, H. B., & Davies, M. (1976). Behavioral and social effects of heroin self-administration and withdrawal. *Archives of General Psychiatry, 33,* 363–367.

Bardgett, M. E., Franks-Henry, J. M., Colemire, K. R., Juneau, K. R., Stevens, R. M., Marczinski, C. A., & Griffith, M. S. (2013). Adult rats treated with risperidone during development are hyperactive. *Experimental and Clinical Psychopharmacology, 21,* 259–267.

Bari, M., Battista, N., Pirazzi, V., & Maccarrone, M. (2011). The manifold actions of endocannabinoids on female and male reproductive events. *Frontiers in Bioscience, 16,* 498–516.

Barkley, R. A., Fischer, M., Smallish, L., & Fletcher, K. (2003). Does the treatment of attention-deficit/hyperactivity disorder with stimulants contribute to drug use/abuse? A 13-year prospective study. *Pediatrics, 111,* 97–109.

Barnwell, S. S., Earleywine, M., & Wilcox, R. (2006). Cannabis, motivation, and life satisfaction in an internet sample. *Substance Abuse Treatment, Prevention, and Policy, 1,* 2.

Barone, J. J., & Roberts, H. R. (1996). Caffeine consumption. *Food and Chemical Toxicology, 34,* 119–129.

Barron, A. B., Maleszka, R., Helliwell, P. G., & Robinson, G. E. (2009). Effects of cocaine on honey bee dance behaviour. *Journal of Experimental Biology, 212,* 163–168.

Barron, J. (2008). Medical examiner rules Ledger's death accidental. *New York Times.* Retrieved from http://www.nytimes.com/2008/02/07/nyregion/07ledger.html?_r=0

Battig, K., Buzzi, R., Martin, J. R., & Feierabend, J. M. (1984). The effects of caffeine on physiological functions and mental performance. *Experientia, 40,* 1218–1223.

Baumann, M. H., Ayestas, M. A., Jr., Partilla, J. S., Sink, J. R., Shulgin, A. T., Daley, P. F., Brandt, S. D., Rothman, R. B., Ruoho, A. E., & Cozzi, N. V. (2012). The designer methcathinone analogs, mephedrone and methylone, are substrates for monoamine transporters in brain tissue. *Neuropsychopharmacology, 37,* 1192–1203.

Becker, D. E. (2007). Drug therapy in dental practice: General principles. *Anesthesia Progress, 54,* 19–24.

Beers, M. H. (2003). *The Merck Manual of medical information* (2nd ed.). Rahway, NJ: Merck.

Beirness, D. J. (1987). Self-estimates of blood alcohol concentration in drinking-driving context. *Drug and Alcohol Dependence, 19,* 79–90.

Belluzzi, J. D., Lee, A. G., Oliff, H. S., & Leslie, F. M. (2004). Age-dependent effects of nicotine on locomotor activity and conditioned place preference in rats. *Psychopharmacology, 174,* 389–395.

Belluzzi, J. D., Wang, R., & Leslie, F. M. (2005). Acetaldehyde enhances acquisition of nicotine self-administration in adolescent rats. *Neuropsychopharmacology, 30,* 705–712.

Bener, A., Gerber, L. M., & Sheikh, J. (2012). Prevalence of psychiatric disorders and associated risk factors in women during their postpartum period: A major public health problem and global comparison. *International Journal of Women's Health, 4,* 191–200.

Benet, L. Z., Mitchell, J. R., & Sheiner, L. B. (1990). Pharmacokinetics: The dynamics of drug absorption, distribution and elimination. In A. G. Gilman, T. W. Rall, A. S. Nies, & P. Taylor (Eds.), *Goodman and Gilman's the pharmacological basis of therapeutics* (8th ed., p. 3032). New York: Pergamon.

Benjamin, G. A., Darling, E. J., & Sales, B. (1990). The prevalence of depression, alcohol abuse, and cocaine abuse among United States lawyers. *International Journal of Law and Psychiatry, 13,* 233–246.

Bennett, R. H., Cherek, D. R., & Spiga, R. (1993). Acute and chronic alcohol tolerance in humans: Effects of dose and consecutive days of exposure. *Alcoholism: Clinical and Experimental Research, 17,* 740–745.

Berger, F. M. (1954). The pharmacological properties of 2-methyl-2-n-propyl-1,3 propanediol dicarbamate (miltown), a new interneuronal blocking agent. *Journal of Pharmacology and Experimental Therapeutics, 112,* 413–423.

Berle, J. O., & Spigset, O. (2011). Antidepressant use during breast-feeding. *Current Women's Health Review, 7,* 28–34.

Bernhoft, I. M., & Behrensdorff, I. (2003). Effect of lowering the alcohol limit in Denmark. *Accident Analysis and Prevention, 35,* 515–525.

Berridge, C. W., & Devilbiss, D. M. (2011). Psychostimulants as cognitive enhancers: The prefrontal cortex, catecholamines, and attention-deficit/hyperactivity disorder. *Biological Psychiatry, 69,* e101–e111.

Berridge, M. S., Apana, S. M., Nagano, K. K., Berridge, C. E., Leisure, G. P., & Boswell, M. V. (2010). Smoking produces rapid rise of [11C] nicotine in human brain. *Psychopharmacology, 209,* 383–394.

Birkley, E. L., Giancola, P. R., & Lance, C. E. (2013). Psychopathy and the prediction of alcohol-related physical aggression: The roles of impulsive antisociality and fearless dominance. *Drug and Alcohol Dependence, 128,* 58–63.

Bjartveit, K., Tverdal, A. (2005). Health consequences of smoking 1–4 cigarettes per day. *Tobacco Control, 14,* 315–320.

Blader, J. C. (2011). Acute inpatient care for psychiatric disorders in the United States, 1996 through 2007. *Archives of General Psychiatry, 68,* 1276–1283.

Blair, M., Kertesz, A., McMonagle, P., Davidson, W., & Bodi, N. (2006). Quantitative and qualitative analyses of clock drawing in fronto-temporal dementia and Alzheimer's disease. *Journal of the International Neuropsychological Society, 12*, 159–165.

Blakeslee, S. (2004, July 20). This is your brain on meth: A "forest fire" of damage. *The New York Times*.

Blanchard, J., & Sawers, S. J. (1983). The absolute bioavailability of caffeine in man. *European Journal of Clinical Pharmacology, 24*, 93–98.

Bloomquist, E. R. (1971). *Marijuana: The second trip*. Beverly Hills, CA: Glencoe.

Blum, K. (1984). *Handbook of abusable drugs*. New York: Gardner Press.

Boecker, H., Sprenger, T., Spilker, M. E., Henriksen, G., Koppenhoefer, M., Wagner, K. J., et al. (2008). The runner's high: Opioidergic mechanisms in the human brain. *Cerebral Cortex, 18*, 2523–2531.

Boldrini, M., Hen, R., Underwood, M. D., Rosoklifa, G. B., Dwork, A. J., Mann, J. J., & Arango, V. (2012). Hippocampal angiogenesis and progenitor cell proliferation are increased with antidepressant use in major depression. *Biological Psychiatry, 72*, 562–571.

Bolla, K. I., Eldreth, D. A., Matochik, J. A., & Cadet, J. L. (2005). Neural substrates of faulty decision-making in abstinent marijuana users. *Neuroimage, 26*, 480–492.

Booth, M. (1996). *Opium: A history*. New York: St. Martin's Press.

Borders, A., & Giancola, P. R. (2011). Trait and state hostile rumination facilitate alcohol-related aggression. *Journal of Studies on Alcohol and Drugs, 72*, 545–554.

Borio, G. (2011). *The tobacco timeline*. Retrieved from http://www.tobacco.org/History/Tobacco_History.html

Borne, J., Riascos, R., Cuellar, H., Vargas, D., & Rojas, R. (2005). Neuroimaging in drug and substance use part II: Opioids and solvents. *Topics in Magnetic Resonance Imaging, 16*, 239–245.

Bostwick, J. M. (2012). Blurred boundaries: The therapeutics and politics of medical marijuana. *Mayo Clinic Proceedings, 87*, 172–186.

Bovett, R. (2006). Meth epidemic solutions. *North Dakota Law Review, 82*, 1195–1215.

Bowles, D. W., O'Bryant, C. L., Camidge, D. R., & Jimeno, A. (2012). The intersection between cannabis and cancer in the United States. *Critical Reviews in Oncology/Hematology, 83*, 1–10.

Boxer, A. L., Knopman, D. S., Kaufer, D. I., Grossman, M., Onyike, C., Graf-Radford, N., et al. (2013). Memantine in patients with frontotemporal lobar degeneration: A multicentre, randomised, double-blind, placebo-controlled trial. *Lancet Neurology, 12*, 149–156.

Boyle, N. T., & Connor, T. J. (2010). Methylenedioxymethamphetamine ("ecstasy")-induced immunosuppression: A cause for concern? *British Journal of Pharmacology, 161*, 17–32.

Braff, D. L., & Geyer, M. A. (1990). Sensorimotor gating and schizophrenia: Human and animal model studies. *Archives of General Psychiatry, 47*, 181–188.

Braiden, R. W., Fellingham, G. W., & Conlee, R. K. (1994). Effects of cocaine on glycogen metabolism and endurance during high intensity exercise. *Medicine and Science in Sports and Exercise, 26*, 695–700.

Brecher, E. J. (2012, May 30). MacArthur causeway attack victim Ronald Poppo was a high school achiever. *The Miami Herald*. Retrieved from http://www.miamiherald.com/2012/05/30/2824786/face-eating-victim-ronald-poppo.html

Brecher, E. M. (1972). *Licit and illicit drugs*. Boston: Little, Brown.

Brecher, E. M. (1986). Drug laws and drug law enforcement: A review and evaluation based on 111 years of experience. *Drugs and Society, 1*, 1–27.

Breiter, H. C., Gollub, R. L., Weisskoff, R. M., Kennedy, D. N., Makris, N., Berke, J. D., et al. (1997). Acute effects of cocaine on human brain activity and emotion. *Neuron, 19*, 591–611.

Breslau, N., & Peterson, E. L. (1996). Smoking cessation in young adults: Age at initiation of cigarette smoking and other suspected influences. *American Journal of Public Health, 86*, 214–220.

Breuer, M. E., McGinnis, M. Y., Lumia, A. R., & Possidente, B. P. (2001). Aggression in male rats receiving anabolic androgenic steroids: Effects of social and environmental provocation. *Hormones and Behavior, 40*, 409–418.

Bridge, J. (2010). Route transition interventions: Potential public health gains from reducing or preventing injecting. *International Journal of Drug Policy, 21*, 125–128.

Brodie, L. (2013, February 27). Cramer smells opportunity in biopharma. *CNBC*. Retrieved from http://www.cnbc.com/id/100503375

Bromet, E., Andrade, L. H., Hwang, I., Sampson, N. A., Alonso, J., de Girolamo, G., et al. (2011). Cross-national epidemiology of DSM-IV major depressive episode. *BMC Medicine, 9*, 90.

Brookmeyer, R., Evans, D. A., Hebert, L., Langa, K. M., Heeringa, S. G., Plassman, B. L., & Kukull, W. A. (2011). National estimates of the prevalence of Alzheimer's disease in the United States. *Alzheimers and Dementia, 7*, 61–73.

Brough, J. (2013, March 8). "Anxiety and depression" came with Montador's concussion. *NBC Sports*. Retrieved from http://prohockeytalk.nbcsports.com/2013/03/08/anxiety-and-depression-came-with-montadors-concussion/

Brown, H. L., & Graves, C. R. (2013). Smoking and marijuana use in pregnancy. *Clinical Obstetrics and Gynecology, 56*, 107–113.

Brown, R. L., Saunders, L. A., Bobula, J. A., Mundt, M. P., & Koch, P. E. (2007). Randomized-controlled trial of a telephone and mail intervention for alcohol use disorders: Three-month drinking outcomes. *Alcoholism: Clinical and Experimental Research, 31*, 1372–1379.

Brown, T. A., Campbell, L. A., Lehman, C. L., Grisham, J. R., & Mancill, R. B. (2001). Current and lifetime comorbidity of the DM-IV anxiety and mood disorders in a large clinical sample. *Journal of Abnormal Psychology, 110*, 585–599.

Bruce, M., & Lader, M. (1986). Caffeine: Clinical and experimental effects in humans. *Human Psychopharmacology, 1*, 63–82.

Brunye, T. T., Mahoney, C. R., Rapp, D. N., Ditman, T., & Taylor, H. A. (2012). Caffeine enhances real-world language processing: Evidence from a proofreading task. *Journal of Experimental Psychology: Applied, 18*, 95–108.

Buckholtz, N. S., Freedman, D. X., & Middaugh, L. D. (1985). Daily LSD administration selectively decreases serotonin$_2$ receptor binding in rat brain. *European Journal of Pharmacology, 109*, 421–425.

Buckholtz, N. S., Zhou, D. F., Freedman, D. X., & Potter, W. Z. (1990). Lysergic acid diethylamide (LSD) administration selectively down-regulates serotonin$_2$ receptors in rat brain. *Neuropharmacology, 3*, 137–148.

Buckley, N. A., Dawson, A. H., Whyte, I. M., & O'Connell, D. L. (1995). Relative toxicity of benzodiazepines in overdose. *British Medical Journal, 310*, 219–221.

Bush, G., Spencer, T. J., Holmes, J., Shin, L. M., Valera, E. M., Seidman, L. J., Makris, N., Surman, C., Aleardi, M., Mick, E., & Biederman, J. (2008). Functional magnetic resonance imaging of methylphenidate and placebo in attention-deficit/hyperactivity disorder during the multi-source interference task. *Archives of General Psychiatry, 65,* 102–114.

Bushman, B. J., Giancola, P. R., Parrott, D. J., & Roth, R. M. (2012). Failure to consider future consequences increases the effects of alcohol on aggression. *Journal of Experimental Social Psychology, 48,* 591–595.

Busse, G. D., & Riley, A. L. (2003). Effects of alcohol on cocaine lethality in rats: Acute and chronic assessments. *Neurotoxicology and Teratology, 25,* 361–364.

Butler, T. R., & Prendergast, M. A. (2012). Neuroadaptations in adenosine receptor signaling following long-term ethanol exposure and withdrawal. *Alcoholism: Clinical and Experimental Research, 36,* 4–13.

Buttner, A., Mall, G., Penning, R., & Weis, S. (2000). The neuropathology of heroin abuse. *Forensic Science International, 113,* 435–442.

Byck, R. (1974). *Cocaine papers: Sigmund Freud.* New York: Stonehill.

Cade, J. F. J. (1949). Lithium salts in the treatment of psychotic excitement. *Medical Journal of Australia, 2,* 349–352.

Cadet, J. L., Krasnova, I. N., Jayanthi, S., & Lyles, J. (2007). Neurotoxicity of substituted amphetamines: Molecular and cellular mechanisms. *Neurotoxicity Research, 11,* 183–202.

Caitlin, D. H., Fitch, K. D., & Ljungqvist, A. (2008). Medicine and science in the fight against doping in sport. *Journal of Internal Medicine, 264,* 99–114.

Calhoun, F., & Warren, K. (2007). Fetal alcohol syndrome: Historical perspectives. *Neuroscience and Biobehavioral Reviews, 31,* 168–171.

Calkin, C., & Alda, M. (2012). Beyond the guidelines for bipolar disorder: Practical issues in long-term treatment with lithium. *Canadian Journal of Psychiatry, 57,* 437–445.

Cami, J., Guerra, D., Ugena, B., Segura, J., & de la Torre, R. (1991). Effect of subject expectancy on the THC intoxication and disposition from smoked hashish cigarettes. *Pharmacology, Biochemistry and Behavior, 40,* 115–119.

Carey, B. (2012, November 19). A 'party drug' may help the brain cope with trauma. *The New York Times.* Retrieved from http://www.nytimes.com/2012/11/20/health/ecstasy-treatment-for-post-traumatic-stress-shows-promise.html?pagewanted=all&_r=0

Carey, K. B., Scott-Sheldon, L. A., Carey, M. P., & DeMartini, K. S. (2007). Individual-level interventions to reduce college student drinking: A meta-analytic review. *Addictive Behaviors, 32,* 2469–2494.

Carlo, W. A. (2007). *Fetal alcohol syndrome.* In R. M. Kliegman, R. E. Behrman, H. B. Jenson, & B. F. Stanton (Eds.), *Nelson textbook of pediatrics* (18th ed.). Philadelphia: Saunders Elsevier.

Carlson, N. R. (2008). *Foundations of physiological psychology* (7th ed.). Boston: Pearson.

Carvey, P. M. (1988). *Drug action in the central nervous system.* Oxford: Oxford University Press.

Casey, B. J., & Jones, R. M. (2010). Neurobiology of the adolescent brain and behavior: Implications for substance use disorders. *Journal of the American Academy of Child and Adolescent Psychiatry, 49,* 1189–1201.

Casselman, I., & Heinrich, M. (2011). Novel use patterns of *Salvia divinorum*: Unobtrusive observation using YouTube. *Journal of Ethnopharmacology, 128,* 662–667.

Centers for Substance Abuse Treatment. (2005). Medication-assisted treatment for opioid addiction in opioid treatment programs. Treatment improvement protocol (TIP) series, No. 43. Rockville, MD: Substance Abuse and Mental Health Services Administration.

Centers for Disease Control and Prevention (CDC). (2012). Community-based opioid overdose prevention programs providing naloxone—United States, 2010. *MMWR Morbidity and Mortality Weekly Report, 61,* 101–105.

Centers for Disease Control and Prevention (CDC). (2011a). Current cigarette smoking prevalence among working adults—United States, 2004–2010. *MMWR Morbidity and Mortality Weekly Report, 60,* 1305–1309.

Centers for Disease Control and Prevention (CDC). (2011b). State Highlights: Kentucky. *Tobacco Control State Highlights 2010.* Retrieved from http://www.cdc.gov/tobacco/data_statistics/state_data/state_highlights/2010/states/kentucky

Centers for Disease Control and Prevention (CDC). (2011c). Vital signs: Current cigarette smoking among adults aged ≥ 18 years—United States, 2005–2010. *MMWR Morbidity and Mortality Weekly Report, 60,* 1207–1212.

Centers for Disease Control and Prevention (CDC). (2011d). Vital signs: Overdoses of prescription opioid pain relievers—United States, 1999–2008. *Morbidity and Mortality Weekly, 60,* 1487–1492.

Centers for Disease Control and Prevention (CDC). (1995). Jimson weed poisoning—Texas, New York, and California, 1994. *Morbidity and Mortality Weekly Report, 44,* 41–44.

Centers for Disease Control and Prevention (CDC). (2009). Prevalence of autism spectrum disorders—autism and developmental disabilities monitoring network, 2006. *Morbidity and Mortality Weekly Report, 58,* 1–20.

Centers for Disease Control and Prevention (CDC). (2010a). Jimsonweed poisoning associated with a homemade stew—Maryland, 2008. *Morbidity and Mortality Weekly Report, 59,* 102–104.

Centers for Disease Control and Prevention (CDC). (2010b). Smoking & tobacco use. State Tobacco Activities Tracking and Evaluation (STATE) System. Retrieved from http://apps.nccd.cdc.gov/statesystem/ComparisonReport/ComparisonReports.aspx

Chai, G., Governale, L., McMahon, A. W., Trinidad, J. P., Staffa, J., & Murphy, D. (2012). Trends of outpatient prescription drug utilization in U.S. children, 2002–2010. *Pediatrics, 130,* 23–31.

Chakos, M. H., Mayerhoff, D. I., Loebel, A. D., Alvir, J. M., & Lieberman, J. A. (1992). Incidence and correlates of acute extrapyramidal symptoms in first episode of schizophrenia. *Psychopharmacology Bulletin, 28,* 81–86.

Charles, B. G., Townsend, S. R., Steer, P. A., Flenady, V. J., Gray, P. H., & Shearman, A. (2008). Caffeine citrate treatment for extremely premature infants with apnea: Population pharmacokinetics, absolute bioavailability and implications for therapeutic drug monitoring. *Therapeutic Drug Monitoring, 30,* 709–716.

Charney, D. S., Mihic, S. J., & Harris, R. A. (2001). Hypnotics and sedatives. In J. G. Hardman, L. E. Limbird, & A. G. Gilman (Eds.), *The pharmacological basis of therapeutics* (10th ed.) (pp. 399–427). New York: McGraw-Hill.

Charuvastra, A., Friedmann, P. D., & Stein, M. D. (2005). Physician attitudes regarding the prescription of medical marijuana. *Journal of Addictive Diseases, 24,* 87–93.

Chau, D. L., Walker, V., Pai, L., & Cho, L. M. (2008). Opiates and elderly: Use and side effects. *Clinical Interventions in Aging, 3,* 273–278.

Chen, C., Kostakis, C., Harpas, P., Felgate, P. D., Irvine, R. J., & White, J. M. (2011). Marked decline in 3,4-methylenedioxymethamphetamine (MDMA) based on wastewater analysis. *Journal of Studies on Alcohol and Drugs, 72*, 737–740.

Chen, W. J., Fu, T. C., Ting, T. T., Huang, W. L., Tang, G. M., Hsiao, C. K., & Chen, C. Y. (2009). Use of ecstasy and other psychoactive substances among school-attending adolescents in Taiwan: National surveys 2004–2006. *BMC Public Health, 9*, 27.

Cherpitel, C. J., & Ye, Y. (2012). Trends in alcohol- and drug-related emergency department and primary care visits: Data from four U.S. national surveys (1995–2010). *Journal of Studies on Alcohol and Drugs, 73*, 454–458.

Chilcoat, H. D., & Schutz, C. G. (1996). Age-specific patterns of hallucinogen use in the U.S. population: An analysis of generalized additive models. *Drug and Alcohol Dependence, 43*, 143–153.

Childress, A. C., & Berry, S. A. (2010). The single-dose pharmacokinetics of NWP06, a novel extended-release methylphenidate oral suspension. *Postgraduate Medicine, 122*, 35–41.

Childs, E., & de Wit, H. (2006). Subjective, behavioral, and physiological effects of acute caffeine in light, nondependent caffeine users. *Psychopharmacology, 185*, 514–523.

Childs, E., & de Wit, H. (2008). Enhanced mood and psychomotor performance by a caffeine-containing energy capsule in fatigued individuals. *Experimental and Clinical Psychopharmacology, 16*, 13–21.

Chin, J. M., Merves, M. L., Goldberger, B. A., Sampson-Cone, A., & Cone, E. J. (2008). Caffeine content of brewed teas. *Journal of Analytical Toxicology, 32*(8), 702–704.

Ciccarone, D. (2011). Stimulant abuse: Pharmacology, cocaine, methamphetamine, treatment, attempts at pharmacotherapy. *Primary Care, 38*, 41–58.

Cicero, T. J. (1980). Alcohol self-administration, tolerance, and withdrawal in humans and animals: Theoretical and methodological issues. In H. Rigter & J. Crabbe, Jr. (Eds.), *Alcohol tolerance and dependence* (pp. 1–50). Amsterdam: Elsevier/North-Holland Biomedical Press.

Clarke, G. (2001). *Get happy: The life of Judy Garland.* New York: Dell.

Clements, J. A., Nimo, W. S., & Grant, I. S. (1982). Bioavailability, pharmacokinetics and analgesic activity of ketamine in humans. *Journal of Pharmaceutical Sciences, 71*, 539–542.

CNN. (2012, May 29). *Reports: Miami "zombie" attacker may have been using "bath salts."* Retrieved from http://news.blogs.cnn.com/2012/05/29/reports-miami-zombie-attacker-may-have-been-using-bath-salts/?iref=allsearch

Cochrane, C., Malcolm, R., & Brewerton, T. (1998). The role of weight control as a motivation for cocaine abuse. *Addictive Behaviors, 23*, 201–207.

Coelho-Santos, V., Goncalves, J., Fontes-Ribeiro, C., & Silva, A. P. (2012). Prevention of methamphetamine-induced microglial cell death by TNF-α and IL-6 through activation of the JAK-STAT pathway. *Journal of Neuroinflammation, 9*, 103.

Cohen, B. M., & Baldessarini, R. J. (1985). Tolerance to therapeutic effects of antidepressants. *American Journal of Psychiatry, 142*, 489–490.

Cole, C., Jones, L., McVeigh, J., Kicman, A., Syed, Q., & Bellis, M. (2011). Adulterants in illicit drugs: A review of empirical evidence. *Drug Testing and Analysis, 3*, 89–96.

Coleman, L. G., Jr., He, J., Lee, J., Styner, M., & Crews, F. T. (2011). Adolescent binge drinking alters adult brain neurotransmitter gene expression, behavior, brain regional volumes, and neurochemistry in mice. *Alcoholism: Clinical and Experimental Research, 35*, 671–688.

Collins, M. A., & Neafsey, E. J. (2012). Neuroinflammatory pathways in binge alcohol-induced neuronal degeneration: Oxidative stress cascade involving aquaporin, brain edema, and phospholipase A2 activation. *Neurotoxicity Research, 21*, 70–78.

Compton, P., Canamar, C. P., Hillhouse, M., & Ling, W. (2012). Hyperalgesia in heroin dependent patients and the effects of opioid substitution therapy. *Journal of Pain, 13*, 401–409.

Conason, A., Teixeira, J., Hsu, C. H., Puma, L., Knafo, D., & Geliebter, A. (2013). Substance use following bariatric weight loss surgery. *Archives of Surgery, 148*, 145–150.

Cooper, E., & Vernon, J. (2013). The effectiveness of pharmacological approaches in the treatment of alcohol withdrawal syndrome (AWS): A literature review. *Journal of Psychiatric and Mental Health Nursing, 20*, 601–612.

Cooper, Z. D., & Haney, M. (2009). Comparison of subjective, pharmacokinetic, and physiological effects of marijuana smoked as joints and blunts. *Drug and Alcohol Dependence, 103*, 107–113.

Cooper, Z. D., Sullivan, M. A., Vosburg, S. K., Manubay, J. M., Haney, M., Foltin, R. W., et al. (2012). Effects of repeated oxycodone administration on its analgesic and subjective effects in normal, healthy volunteers. *Behavioral Pharmacology, 23*, 271–279.

Corfee, F. A. (2011). Alcohol withdrawal in the critical care unit. *Austrian Critical Care, 24*, 110–116.

Correll, C. U., Manu, P., Olshanskiy, V., Napolitano, B., Kane, J. M., & Malhotra, A. K. (2009). Cardiometabolic risk of second-generation antipsychotic medications during first-time use in children and adolescents. *JAMA: Journal of the American Medical Association, 302*, 1765–1773.

Cousijn, J., Wiers, R. W., Ridderinkhof, K. R., can den Brink, W., Veltman, D. J., Porrino, L. J., & Goudriaan, A. E. (2012). Individual differences in decision making and reward processing predict changes in cannabis use: A prospective functional magnetic resonance imaging study. *Addiction Biology*, article in press.

Cowell, A. J., Brown, J. M., Mills, M. J., Bender, R. H., & Wedehase, B. J. (2012). Cost-effectiveness analysis of motivational interviewing with feedback to reduce drinking among a sample of college students. *Journal of Studies on Alcohol and Drugs, 73*, 226–237.

Cox, D. J., Davis, M., Mikami, A. Y., Singh, H., Merkel, R. L., & Burket, R. (2012). Long-acting methylphenidate reduces collision rates of young adult drivers with attention-deficit/hyperactivity disorder. *Journal of Clinical Psychopharmacology, 32*, 225–230.

Crandall, J., Matragoon, S., Khalifa, Y. M., Borlongan, C., Tsai, N. T., Caldwell, R. B., & Liou, G. I. (2007). Neuroprotective and intraocular pressure-lowering effects of (–)delta9-tetrahydrocannabinol in a rat model of glaucoma. *Ophthalmic Research, 39*, 69–75.

Crean, R. D., Crane, N. A., & Mason, B. J. (2011). An evidence based review of acute and long-term effects of cannabis use on executive cognitive functions. *Journal of Addiction Medicine, 5*, 1–8.

Crews, F. T. (2000). Neurotoxicity of alcohol: Excitotoxicity, oxidative stress, neurotrophic factors, apoptosis, and cell adhesion molecules. In A. Noronha, M. J. Eckardt, & K. Warren (Eds.), *Review of NIAAA's neuroscience and behavioral research portfolio* (pp. 189–206). National Institute on Alcohol Abuse and Alcoholism (NIAAA) Research Monograph No. 34. Bethesda, MD: NIAAA.

Crews, F. T., & Nixon, K. (2009). Mechanisms of neurodegeneration and regeneration in alcoholism. *Alcohol and Alcoholism, 44*, 115–127.

Crews, F. T., Braun, C. J., Hoplight, B., Switzer, R. C. 3rd, & Knapp, D. J. (2000). Binge ethanol consumption causes differential brain damage in young adolescent rats compared with adult rats. *Alcoholism: Clinical and Experimental Research, 24,* 1712–1723.

Cruickshank, C. C., & Dyer, K. R. (2009). A review of the clinical pharmacology of methamphetamine. *Addiction, 104,* 1085–1099.

Cunningham, C. E., & Boyle, M. H. (2002). Preschoolers at risk for attention-deficit hyperactivity disorder and oppositional defiant disorder: Family, parenting, and behavioral correlates. *Journal of Abnormal Child Psychology, 30,* 555–569.

Cunningham, C. W., Rothman, R. B., & Prisinzano, T. E. (2011). Neuropharmacology of the naturally occurring kappa-opioid hallucinogen salvinorin A. *Pharmacology Review, 63,* 316–347.

Cunningham, F. G., Leveno, K. J., Bloom, S. L., Hauth, J. C., Rouse, D., & Spong, C. Y. (2010). Teratology and medications that affect the fetus (pp. 312–333). In F. G. Cunningham, K. J. Leveno, S. L. Bloom, J. C. Hauth, D. Rouse, & C. Y. Spong (Eds.), *Williams obstetrics* (23rd ed.). New York: McGraw-Hill.

Cuomo, V., Cagiano, R., Coen, E., Mocchetti, I., Cattabeni, F., & Racagni, G. (1981). Enduring behavioural and biochemical effects in the adult rat after prolonged postnatal administration of haloperidol. *Psychopharmacology, 74,* 166–169.

Cuomo, V., Cagiano, R., Mocchetti, I., Coen, E., Cattabeni, F., & Racagni, G. (1983). Behavioural and biochemical effects in the adult rat after prolonged postnatal administration of clozapine. *Psychopharmacology, 81,* 239–243.

Currie, C. L. (2013). Epidemiology of adolescent *Salvia divinorum* use in Canada. *Drug and Alcohol Dependence, 128,* 166–170.

Curtis, L. H., Masselink, L. E., Ostbye, T., Hutchison, S., Dans, P. E., Wright, A., et al. (2005). Prevalence of antipsychotic drug use among commercially insured youths in the United States. *Archives of Pediatric & Adolescent Medicine, 159,* 362–366.

Danaceau, J. P., Deering, C. E., Day, J. E., Smeal, S. J., Johnson-Davis, K. L., Fleckenstein, A. E., & Wilkins, D. G. (2007). Persistence of tolerance to methamphetamine-induced monoamine deficits. *European Journal of Pharmacology, 559,* 46–54.

Danaei, G., Ding, E. L., Mozaffarian, D., Taylor, B., Rehm, J., Murray, C. J., & Ezzati, M. (2009). The preventable causes of death in the United States: A comparative risk assessment of dietary, lifestyle, and metabolic risk factors. *PLoS Medicine, 6,* e1000058.

Dar, R., & Frenk, H. (2007). Reevaluating the nicotine delivery kinetics hypothesis. *Psychopharmacology, 192,* 1–7.

Davidson, M. G. (2011). Herbal-caffeinated chewing gum, but not bubble gum, improves aspects of memory. *Appetite, 57,* 303–307.

Davis, W. R., Johnson, B. D., Randolph, D., & Liberty, H. J. (2006). Risks for HIV infection among users and sellers of crack, powder cocaine and heroin in central Harlem. Implications for interventions. *AIDS Care, 18,* 158–165.

Day, N. L., & Richardson, G. A. (1991). Prenatal marijuana use: Epidemiology, methodologic issues, and infant outcome. *Clinical Perinatology, 18,* 77–91.

de Almeida, R. M., Rowlett, J. K., Cook, J. M., Yin, W., & Miczek, K. A. (2004). GABAA/alpha1 receptor agonists and antagonists: Effects on species-typical and heightened aggressive behavior after alcohol self-administration in mice. *Psychopharmacology, 172,* 255–263.

De Giovanni, N., & Marchetti, D. (2012). Cocaine and its metabolites in the placenta: A systematic review of the literature. *Reproductive Toxicology, 33,* 1–14.

de la Torre, R., Farre, M., Ortuno, J., Mas, M., Brenneisen, R., Roset, P. N., Segura, J., & Cami, J. (2000). Non-linear pharmacokinetics of MDMA ("ecstasy") in humans. *British Journal of Clinical Pharmacology, 49,* 104–109.

de Saint Phalle, A. (1969, April 23). . . . When old is said in one and maker mates with made. *The Harvard Crimson.* Retrieved from http://www.thecrimson.com/article/1969/4/23/-when-old-is-said-in/

de Wit, H., & Zacny, J. (1995). Abuse potential of nicotine replacement therapies. *CNS Drugs, 4,* 456–468.

DeFrates, L. J., Hoehns, J. D., Sakornbut, E. L., Glascock, D. G., & Tew, A. R. (2005). Antimuscarinic intoxication resulting from the ingestion of moonflower seeds. *The Annals of Pharmacotherapy, 39,* 173–176.

Degenhardt, L., & Hall, W. (2012). Extent of illicit drug use and dependence, and their contribution to the global burden of disease. *Lancet, 379* (9810), 55–70.

Degenhardt, L., Bruno, R., & Topp, L. (2010a). Is ecstasy a drug of dependence? *Drug and Alcohol Dependence, 107,* 1–10.

Degenhardt, L., Bucello, C., Calabria, B., Nelson, P., Roberts, A., Hall, W., et al. (2011). What data are available on the extent of illicit drug use and dependence globally? Results of four systematic reviews. *Drug and Alcohol Dependence, 117,* 85–101.

Degenhardt, L., Bucello, C., Mathers, B., Briegleb, C., Ali, H., Hickman, M., & McLaren, J. (2010b). Mortality among regular or dependent users of heroin and other opioids: A systematic review and meta-analysis of cohort studies. *Addiction, 106,* 32–51.

Degenhardt, L., Chiu, W. T., Sampson, N., Kessler, R. C., Anthony, J. C., Angermeyer, M., et al. (2008). Toward a global view of alcohol, tobacco, cannabis, and cocaine use: Findings from the WHO world mental health surveys. *PLoS Medicine, 5,* e141. doi:10.1371/journal.pmed.0050141

Degenhardt, L., Day, C., Hall, W., Conroy, E., & Gilmour, S. (2005). Was an increase in cocaine use among injecting drug users in New South Wales, Australia, accompanied by an increase in violent crime? *BMC Public Health, 5,* 40.

Del Seppia, C., Ghione, S., Luschi, P., Ossenkopp, K.-P., Choleris, E., & Kavaliers, M. (2007). Pain perception and electromagnetic fields. *Neuroscience and Biobehavioral Reviews, 31,* 619–642.

Denissenko, M. F., Pao, A., Tang, M., & Pfeiffer, G. P. (1996). Preferential formation of benzo[a]pyrene adducts at lung cancer mutational hotspots in *P53. Science, 274,* 430–432.

DeNoon, D. J. (March 12, 2009). Kentucky is top state for smoking. *WebMD Health News.* Retrieved from http://webmd.com/smoking-cessation/news/20090312/states-with-most-smokers-ky-tops-list

Des Jarlais, D. C., Arasteh, K., Perlis, T., Hagan, H., Heckathorn, D. D., McKnight, C., Bramson, H., & Friedman, S. R. (2007). The transition from injection to non-injection drug use: Long-term outcomes among heroin and cocaine users in New York City. *Addiction, 102,* 778–785.

Desai, R. I., Thakur, G. A., Vemuri, K., Bajaj, S., Makriyannis, A., & Bergman, J. (2013). Analysis of tolerance and behavioral/physical dependence during chronic CB1 agonist treatment: Effects of CB1 agonists, antagonists, and non-cannabinoid drugs. *Journal of Pharmacology and Experimental Therapeutics, 344,* 319–328.

Deutsch, A. Y., & Roth, R. H. (2009). Neurochemical systems in the central nervous system. In D. S. Charney & E. J. Nestler (Eds.), *Neurobiology of mental illness* (3rd ed.). New York: Oxford University Press.

Devane, W. A., Hanus, L., Breuer, A., Pertwee, R. G., Stevenson, L. A., Griffin, G., Gibson, D., Mandelbaum, A., Etinger, A., & Mechoulam, R.

(1992). Isolation and structure of a brain constituent that binds to the cannabinoid receptor. *Science, 258*, 1946–1949.

Devilbiss, D. M., & Berridge, C. W. (2008). Cognition-enhancing doses of methylphenidate preferentially increase prefrontal cortex neuronal responsiveness. *Biological Psychiatry, 64*, 626–635.

Dewall, C. N., Bushman, B. J., Giancola, P. R., & Webster, G. D. (2010). The big, the bad, and the booze-up: Weight moderates the effect of alcohol on aggression. *Journal of Experimental Social Psychology, 46*, 619–623.

Di Maio, V. J., & Garriott, J. C. (1978). Four deaths due to intravenous injection of cocaine. *Forensic Science International, 12*, 119–125.

Dias, A. C., Araujo, M. R., Dunn, J., Sesso, R. C., de Castro, V., & Laranjeira, R. (2011). Mortality rate among crack/cocaine-dependent patients: A 12-year prospective cohort study conducted in Brazil. *Journal of Substance Abuse Treatment, 41*, 273–278.

Diazgranados, N., Ibrahim, L., Brutsche, N. E., Newberg, A., Kronstein, P., Khalife, S., et al. (2010). A randomized add-on trial of N-methyl-D-aspartate antagonist in treatment-resistant bipolar depression. *Archives of General Psychiatry, 67*, 793–802.

Difranza, J. R., Ursprung, W. W., & Biller, L. (2012a). The developmental sequence of tobacco withdrawal symptoms of wanting, craving and needing. *Pharmacology, Biochemistry and Behavior, 100*, 494–497.

Difranza, J. R., Wellman, R. J., & Savageau, J. A. (2012b). Does progression through the stages of physical addiction indicate increasing overall addiction to tobacco? *Psychopharmacology, 219*, 815–822.

Dinis-Oliveira, R. J., Carvalho, F., Duarte, J. A., Proenca, J. B., Santos, A., & Magalhaes, T. (2012). Clinical and forensic signs related to cocaine abuse. *Current Drug Abuse Reviews, 5*, 64–83.

Dodge, T., Williams, K. J., Marzell, M., & Turrisi, R. (2012). Judging cheaters: Is substance misuse viewed similarly in the athletic and academic domains? *Psychology of Addictive Behaviors, 26*, 678–682.

Dolak, K., & Murphy, E. (March 23, 2012). Whitney Houston cause of death: How cocaine contributes to heart disease. *ABC News.* Retrieved from http://abcnews.go.com/Health/whitney-houston-death-cocaine-contributed-heart-disease/story?id=15984196

Domino, M. E., & Swartz, M. S. (2008). Who are the new users of antipsychotic medications? *Psychiatric Services, 59*, 507–514.

Donny, E. C., Caggiula, A. R., Weaver, M. T., Levin, M. E., & Sved, A. F. (2011). The reinforcement-enhancing effects of nicotine: Implications for the relationship between smoking, eating and weight. *Physiology & Behavior, 104*, 143–148.

Doucet, S., Jones, I., Letourneau, N., Dennis, C. L., & Blackmore, E. R. (2011). Interventions for the prevention and treatment of postpartum psychosis: A systematic review. *Archives of Women's Mental Health, 14*, 89–98.

Dove, D., Warren, Z., McPheeters, M. L., Taylor, J. L., Sathe, N. A., & Veenstra-VanderWeele, J. (2012). Medications for adolescents and young adults with autism spectrum disorders: A systematic review. *Pediatrics, 130*, 717–726.

Dowdall, G. W. (2009). *College drinking: Reframing a social problem.* Westport, CT: Praeger.

Drdla-Schutting, R., Benrath, J., Wunderbaldinger, G., & Sandkuhler, J. (2012). Erasure of a spinal memory trace of pain by a brief, high-dose opioid administration. *Science, 335*, 235–238.

Drug Enforcement Administration (DEA). (2011). *The DEA position on marijuana.* Author. Retrieved from http://www.justice.gov/dea/docs/marijuana_position_2011.pdf

Drug Enforcement Administration (DEA). (2012a). *Controlled substances.* Author. Retrieved from http://www.deadiversion.usdoj.gov/schedules/orangebook/c_cs_alpha.pdf

Drug Enforcement Administration (DEA). (2012b). *Drug fact sheet: Bath salts or designer cathinones (synthetic stimulants).* Author. Retrieved from http://www.justice.gov/dea/druginfo/drug_data_sheets/Bath_Salts.pdf

Drug Enforcement Administration (DEA). (2012c). *Drug fact sheet: Narcotics.* Author. Retrieved from http://www.justice.gov/dea/druginfo/drug_data_sheets/Narcotics.pdf

Drug Enforcement Administration (DEA). (2012d). *Drug fact sheet: Oxycodone.* Author. Retrieved from http://www.justice.gov/dea/druginfo/drug_data_sheets/Oxycodone.pdf

Drug Enforcement Administration (DEA). (2013a). *Drug fact sheet: Hallucinogens.* Author. Retrieved from http://www.justice.gov/dea/druginfo/drug_data_sheets/Hallucinogens.pdf

Drug Enforcement Administration (DEA). (2013b). *Drug fact sheet: LSD.* Author. Retrieved from http://www.justice.gov/dea/druginfo/drug_data_sheets/LSD.pdf

Drug Enforcement Administration (DEA). (2013c). *Drug fact sheet: Peyote and mescaline.* Retrieved from http://www.justice.gov/dea/druginfo/drug_data_sheets/Peyote_Mescaline.pdf

Drug Enforcement Administration (DEA). (2013d). *Drug fact sheet: Steroids.* Author. Retrieved from http://www.justice.gov/dea/druginfo/drug_data_sheets/Steroids.pdf

Drug Enforcement Administration (DEA) & Office of Diversion Control. (2012a). *3,4-methylenedioxymethamphetamine.* Retrieved from http://www.deadiversion.usdoj.gov/drugs_concern/

Drug Enforcement Administration (DEA) & Office of Diversion Control. (2012b). *Jimson weed (Datura stramonium).* Retrieved from http://www.deadiversion.usdoj.gov/drugs_concern/

Drug Enforcement Administration (DEA) & Office of Diversion Control. (2012c). *Phencyclidine.* Retrieved from http://www.deadiversion.usdoj.gov/drugs_concern/

Drug Enforcement Administration (DEA) & Office of Diversion Control. (2012d). *Salvia Divinorum and Salvinorin A.* Retrieved from http://www.deadiversion.usdoj.gov/drugs_concern/

Dudish-Poulsen, S., & Hatsukami, D. K. (2000). Acute abstinence effects following smoked cocaine administration in humans. *Experimental and Clinical Psychopharmacology, 8*, 472–482.

Duke, A. (March 23, 2012). Cocaine, heart disease contributed to Houston's drowning, coroner says. *CNN.* Retrieved from http://www.cnn.com/2012/03/22/showbiz/whitney-houston-autopsy/index.html

Duke, A. A., Giancola, P. R., Morris, D. H., Holt, J. C., & Gunn, R. L. (2011). Alcohol dose and aggression: Another reason why drinking more is a bad idea. *Journal of Studies on Alcohol and Drugs, 72*, 34–43.

Dumas, A. (1844, reprinted 2005). *The Count of Monte Cristo.* New York: Signet Classics.

Earleywine, M. (2002). *Understanding marijuana: A new look at the scientific evidence.* New York: Oxford University Press.

Earleywine, M. (2007). *Pot politics: Marijuana and the costs of prohibition.* New York: Oxford University Press.

Eaton, W. W., & McLeod, J. (1984). Consumption of coffee or tea and symptoms of anxiety. *American Journal of Public Health, 74*, 66–68.

Eaves, C. S. (2004). Heroin use among female adolescents: The role of partner influence in path of initiation and route of administration. *American Journal of Drug and Alcohol Abuse, 30*, 21–38.

Edney, A. (2013, March 1). Otsuka, Lundbeck win approval for monthly Abilify shot. *Bloomberg*. Retrieved from http://www.bloomberg.com/news/2013-02-28/otsuka-lundbeck-win-approval-for-monthly-abilify-shot.html?cmpid=yhoo

Edwards, D. D. (1986). Nicotine: A drug of choice? *Science News, 129*, 44–45.

Ehrenfeld, R. (2009). Stop the Afghan drug trade, stop terrorism. *Forbes Magazine*. Retrieved from http://www.forbes.com/2009/02/26/drug-trade-afghanistan-opinions-contributors_terrorism_mycoherbicides.html

Eichler, O. (1976). Zentrale wirkung. In O. Eichler (ed.), *Kaffee und Coffein* (pp. 65–102). Berlin: Springer-Verlag.

Einstein, S. (1989). *Drug and alcohol use: Issues and factors*. New York: Plenum Press.

Ellenhorn, M. J., & Barceloux, D. G. (1988). *Medical toxicology, diagnosis and treatment of human poisoning* (pp. 508–514). New York: Elsevier.

Engeli, S. (2012). Central and peripheral cannabinoid receptors as therapeutic targets in the control of food intake and body weight. *Handbook of Experimental Pharmacology, 209*, 357–381.

Ersche, K. D., Jones, P. S., Williams, G. B., Turton, A. J., Robbins, T. W., & Bullmore, E. T. (2012). Abnormal brain structure implicated in stimulant drug addiction. *Science, 335*, 601–604.

Escobar-Chavez, J. J., Dominguez-Delgado, C. L., & Rodrigeuz-Cruz, I. M. (2011). Targeting nicotine addiction: The possibility of a therapeutic vaccine. *Drug Design, Development and Therapy, 5*, 211–224.

Eskelinen, M. H., Ngandu, T., Tuomilehto, J., Soininen, H., & Kivipelto, M. (2009). Midlife coffee and tea drinking and the risk of late-life dementia: A population-based CAIDE study. *Journal of Alzheimer's Disease, 16*, 85–91.

Eyer, F., Schuster, T., Felgenhauer, N., Pfab, R., Strubel, T., Saugel, B., & Zilker, T. (2011). Risk assessment of moderate to severe alcohol withdrawal—predictors for seizures and delirium tremens in the course of withdrawal. *Alcohol and Alcoholism, 46*, 427–433.

Falck, R. S., Wang, J., Siegal, H. A., & Carlson, R. G. (2003). Current physical health problems and their predictors among a community sample of crack-cocaine smokers in Ohio. *Journal of Psychoactive Drugs, 35*, 471–478.

Farahmandfar, M., Naghdi, N., Karimian, S. M., Kadivar, M., & Zarrindast, M. R. (2012). Amnesia induced by morphine in spatial memory retrieval inhibited in morphine-sensitized rats. *European Journal of Pharmacology, 683*, 132–139.

Farber, N. B., & Olney, J. W. (2003). Drugs of abuse that cause developing neurons to commit suicide. *Brain Research: Developmental Brain Research, 147*, 37–45.

Fareed, A., Casarella, J., Amar, R., Vayalapalli, S., & Drexler, K. (2010). Methadone maintenance dosing guideline for opioid dependence, a literature review. *Journal of Addictive Diseases, 29*, 1–14.

Farquhar-Smith, W. P., & Rice, A. S. C. (2003). A novel neuroimmune mechanism in cannabinoid-mediated attenuation of nerve growth factor-induced hyperalgesia. *Anesthesiology, 99*, 1391–1401.

Fava, G. A. (2003). Can long-term treatment with antidepressant drugs worsen the course of depression? *Journal of Clinical Psychiatry, 64*, 123–133.

Fava, G. A., & Offidani, E. (2011). The mechanisms of tolerance in antidepressant action. *Progress in Neuropsychopharmacology and Biological Psychiatry, 35*, 1593–1602.

Feeney, G. F., & Connor, J. P. (2011). Acamprosate reduces risk of return to drinking after detoxification, but is similarly effective to naltrexone. *Evidence-Based Mental Health, 14*, 22.

Feldman, H. H., Jacova, C., Robillard, A., Garcia, A., Chow, T., Borrie, M., et al. (2008). Diagnosis and treatment of dementia: 2. Diagnosis. *Canadian Medical Association Journal, 178*, 825–536.

Fell, J. C., & Voas, R. B. (2006). The effectiveness of reducing illegal blood alcohol concentration (BAC) limits for driving: Evidence for lowering the limit to. 05 BAC. *Journal of Safety Research, 37*, 233–243.

Fell, J. C., Fisher, D. A., Voas, R. B., Blackman, K., & Tippetts, A. S. (2009). The impact of underage drinking laws on alcohol-related fatal crashes of young drivers. *Alcoholism: Clinical and Experimental Research, 33*, 1208–1219.

Femenia, T., Garcia-Cutierrez, M. S., & Manzanares, J. (2010). CB1 receptor blockade decreases ethanol intake and associated neurochemical changes in fawn-hooded rats. *Alcoholism: Clinical and Experimental Research, 34*, 131–141.

Feng, Y., He, X., Yang, Y., Chao, D., Lazarus, L. H., & Xia, Y. (2012). Current research on opioid receptor function. *Current Drug Targets, 13*, 230–246.

Ferrari, F., & Giuliani, D. (1997). Involvement of dopamine D2 receptors in the effect of cocaine on sexual behaviour and stretching-yawning of male rats. *Neuropharmacology, 36*, 769–777.

Ferre, S. (2008). An update in the psychostimulant effects of caffeine. *Journal of Neurochemistry, 105*, 1067–1079.

Fettes, D. L., & Aarons, G. A. (2011). Smoking behavior of U.S. youths: A comparison between child welfare system and community populations. *American Journal of Public Health, 101*, 2342–2348.

ffytche, D. H., Howard, R. J., Brammer, M. J., David, A., Woodruff, P., & Williams, S. (1998). The anatomy of conscious vision: An fMRI study of visual hallucinations. *Nature Neuroscience, 1*, 738–742.

Fiks, A. G., Mayne, S., Hughes, C. C., Debartolo, E., Behrens, C., Guevara, J. P., & Power, T. (2012). Development of an instrument to measure parents' preferences and goals for the treatment of attention deficit-hyperactivity disorder. *Academic Pediatrics, 12*, 445–455.

Fillmore, M. T. (2003). Drug abuse as a problem of impaired control: Current approaches and findings. *Behavioral and Cognitive Neuroscience Reviews, 2*, 179–197.

Fillmore, M. T., Carscadden, J. L., & Vogel-Sprott, M. (1998). Alcohol, cognitive impairment and expectancies. *Journal of Studies on Alcohol, 59*, 174–179.

Fillmore, M. T., Rush, C. R., & Hays, L. (2002). Acute effects of oral cocaine on inhibitory control of behavior in humans. *Drug and Alcohol Dependence, 67*, 157–167.

Fillmore, M. T., Rush, C. R., & Hays, L. (2006). Acute effects of cocaine in two models of inhibitory control: Implications of non-linear dose effects. *Addiction, 101*, 1323–1332.

Fillmore, M. T., Rush, C. R., & Marczinski, C. A. (2003). Effects of *d*-amphetamine on behavioral control in stimulant abusers: The role of prepotent response tendencies. *Drug and Alcohol Dependence, 71*, 143–152.

Finnegan, L. P. (1982). Outcome of children born to women dependent on narcotics. *Advances in Alcohol and Substance Abuse, 1*, 55–101.

Fischer, B. D., Miller, L. L., Henry, F. E., Picker, M. J., & Dykstra, L. A. (2008). Increased efficacy of microopioid induced antinociception by metabotropic glutamate receptor antagonists in C57BL/6 mice:

Comparison with 6-phosphonomethyl-deca-hydroisoquinoline-3-carboxylic acid (LY235959). *Psychopharmacology, 198*, 271–278.

Fishbein, D. H., Krupitsky, E., Flannery, B. A., Langevin, D. J., Bobashev, G., Verbitskaya, E., et al. (2007). Neurocognitive characterizations of Russian heroin addicts without a significant history of other drug use. *Drug and Alcohol Dependence, 90*, 25–38.

Fisher, D. J., Daniels, R., Jaworska, N., Knobelsdorf, A., & Knott, V. J. (2012). Effects of acute nicotine administration on resting EEG in nonsmokers. *Experimental and Clinical Psychopharmacology, 20*, 71–75.

Fitch, K. (2012). Proscribed drugs at the Olympic Games: Permitted use and misuse (doping) by athletes. *Clinical Medicine, 12*, 257–260.

Flanagan, R. J., & Ives, R. J. (1994). Volatile substance abuse. *Bulletin on Narcotics, 46*, 49–78.

Fleming, M., Mihic, S. J., & Harris, R. A. (2001). *Ethanol*. In J. G. Hardman, L. E. Limbird, & A. G. Gilman (Eds.), *The pharmacological basis of therapeutics* (10th ed.) (pp. 429–445). New York: McGraw-Hill.

Foltin, R. W., & Haney, M. (2004). Intranasal cocaine in humans: Acute tolerance, cardiovascular and subjective effects. *Pharmacology, Biochemistry & Behavior, 78*, 93–101.

Foltin, R. W., Fischman, M. W., & Levin, F. R. (1995). Cardiovascular effects of cocaine in humans: Laboratory studies. *Drug and Alcohol Dependence, 37*, 193–210.

Fonsi Elbreder, M., de Souza e Silva, R., Pillon, S. C., & Laranjeira, R. (2011). Alcohol dependence: Analysis of factors associated with retention of patients in outpatient treatment. *Alcohol and Alcoholism, 46*, 74–76.

Food and Drug Administration (FDA). (1980). Caffeine: Deletion of GRAS status, proposed declaration that no prior sanction exists, and use on an interim basis pending additional study. Federal Register 69817-69838.

Food and Drug Administration (FDA). (2003). Substances generally recognized as safe. Code of Federal Regulations. Title 21, Volume 3, Sec. 182.1180.

Food and Drug Administration (FDA). (2013a). *Dietary supplements*. Retrieved from http://www.fda.gov/Food/DietarySupplements/default.htm

Food and Drug Administration (FDA). (2013b). *Facts about generic drugs*. Retrieved from http://www.fda.gov/Drugs/ResourcesForYou/Consumers/BuyingUsingMedicineSafely/UnderstandingGenericDrugs/ucm167991.htm

Food and Drug Administration (FDA). (2013c). *Overview of the family smoking prevention and Tobacco Control Act: Consumer fact sheet.* Retrieved from http://www.fda.gov/tobaccoproducts/guidancecompliancergulatoryinformation/ucm246129.htm

Foran, H. M., & O'Leary, K. D. (2008). Alcohol and intimate partner violence: A meta-analytic review. *Clinical Psychology Review, 28*, 1222–1234.

Foroud, T., & Phillips, T. J. (2012). Assessing the genetic risk for alcohol use disorders. *Alcohol Research & Health, 34*, 266–272.

Forrester, M. B. (2012). Synthetic cathinone exposures reported to Texas poison centers. *American Journal of Drug and Alcohol Abuse, 38*, 609–615.

Franzen, J. D., & Wilson, T. W. (2012). Amphetamines modulate prefrontal y oscillations during attention processing. *Neuroreport, 23*, 731–735.

Frary, C. D., Johnson, R. K., & Wang, M. Q. (2005). Food sources and intakes of caffeine in the diets of persons in the United States. *Journal of the American Dietetic Association, 105*, 110–113.

Fredholm, B. B., Battig, K., Holmen, J., Nehlig, A., & Zvartau, E. E. (1999). Actions of caffeine in the brain with special reference to factors that contribute to its widespread use. *Pharmacology Reviews, 51*, 83–133.

Freedman, K. S., Nelson, N. M., & Feldman, L. L. (2012). Smoking initiation among young adults in the United States and Canada, 1998–2010: A systematic review. *Prevention of Chronic Diseases, 9*, E05.

Freudenreich, O., Weiss, A. P., & Goff, D. C. (2008). Psychosis and schizophrenia. In T. A. Stern, J. F. Rosenbaum, M. Fava, J. Biederman, & S. L. Rauch (Eds.), *Massachusetts General Hospital comprehensive clinical psychiatry* (1st ed.). Philadelphia: Mosby Elsevier.

Friedman, R. A. (2012, September 24). A call for caution on antipsychotic drugs. *The New York Times*. Retrieved from http://www.nytimes.com/2012/09/25/health/a-call-for-caution-in-the-use-of-antipsychotic-drugs.html?_r=0

Frum, D. (2013, January 7). Marijuana use is too risky a choice. *CNN*. Retrieved from http://www.cnn.com/2013/01/07/opinion/frum-marijuana-risk/index.html

Fu, C. H., Williams, S. C., Cleare, A. J., Brammer, M. J., Walsh, N. D., Kim, J., et al. (2004). Attenuation of the neural response to sad faces in major depression by antidepressant treatment: A prospective, event-related functional magnetic resonance imaging study. *Archives of General Psychiatry, 61*, 877–889.

Fullilove, M. T., Golden, E., Fullilove, R. E., 3rd, Lennon, R., Porterfield, D., Schwarcz, S., & Bolan, G. (1993). Crack cocaine use and high-risk behaviors among sexually active black adolescents. *Journal of Adolescent Health, 14*, 295–300.

Gable, R. S. (2004). Comparison of acute lethal toxicity of commonly abuse psychoactive substances. *Addiction, 99*, 686–696.

Gable, R. S. (2006). Acute toxicity of drugs versus regulatory status. In J. M. Fish (Ed.), *Drugs and society: U.S. public policy* (pp. 149–162). Lanham, MD: Rowman & Littlefield Publishers.

Gadermann, A. M., Engel, C. C., Naifeh, J. A., Nock, M. K., Petukhova, M., Santiago, P. N., et al. (2012). Prevalence of DSM-IV major depression among U.S. military personnel: Meta-analysis and simulation. *Military Medicine, 177*, 47–59.

Garcia, A. (2012, April 15). Heroin vaccine won't "cure" what ails addicts. *Los Angeles Times*. Retrieved from http://articles.latimes.com/2012/apr/15/opinion/la-e-garcia-anti-addiction-vaccine-20120415

Garrett, B. E., & Griffiths, R. R. (1997). The role of dopamine in the behavioral effects of caffeine in animals and man. *Pharmacology, Biochemistry and Behavior, 57*, 533–541.

Gatch, M. B. (2009). Ethanol withdrawal and hyperalgesia. *Current Drug Abuse Reviews, 2*, 41–50.

Gately, I. (2008). *Drink: A cultural history of alcohol*. New York: Penguin.

Gawin, F. H., & Kleber, H. D. (1985). Abstinence symptomatology and psychiatry diagnosis in cocaine abusers: Clinical observations. *Archives of General Psychiatry, 43*, 107–113.

Gentry, R. T., Baraona, E., Amir, I., Roine, R., Chayes, Z. W., Sharma, R., & Lieber, C. S. (1999). Mechanism of the aspirin-induced rise in blood alcohol levels. *Life Sciences, 65*, 2505–2512.

Giacobini, E. (2003). Cholinergic function and Alzheimer's disease. *International Journal of Geriatric Psychiatry, 18*, S1–S5.

Giancola, P. R., Godlaski, A. J., & Roth, R. M. (2012). Identifying component-processes of executive functioning that serve as risk factors for the alcohol-aggression relation. *Psychology of Addictive Behaviors*, *26*, 201–211.

Gill, K. E., Pierre, P. J., Daunais, J., Bennett, A. J., Martelle, S., Gage, H. D., Swanson, J. M., Nader, M. A., & Porrino, L. J. (2012). Chronic treatment with extended release methylphenidate does not alter dopamine systems or increase vulnerability for cocaine self-administration: A study in nonhuman primates. *Neuropsychopharmacology*, *37*, 2555–2565.

Gilman, J. M. Ramchandani, V. A., Crouss, T., & Hommer, D. W. (2012). Subjective and neural responses to intravenous alcohol in young adults with light and heavy drinking patterns. *Neuropsychopharmacology*, *37*, 467–477.

Ginnetti, T. (2013, January 9). Hall of Fame says "no" to Bonds, Clemens, Sosa. *Chicago Sun Times*. Retrieved from http://www.suntimes.com/17478624-761/hall-of-fame-says-no-to-bonds-clemens-sosa.html

Glade, M. J. (2010). Caffeine—not just a stimulant. *Nutrition*, *26*, 932–938.

Glare, P. (2011). Choice of opioids and the WHO Ladder. *Journal of Pediatric Hematology and Oncology*, *33* Suppl 1, S6–S11.

Gleason, K. A., Birnbaum, S. G., Shukla, A., & Ghose, S. (2012). Susceptibility of the adolescent brain to cannabinoids: Long-term hippocampal effects and relevance to schizophrenia. *Translational Psychiatry*, *2*, e199.

Gold, M. S., Kobeissy, F. H., Wang, K. K., Merlo, L. J., Bruijnzeel, A. W., Krasnova, I. N., & Cadet, J. L. (2009). Methamphetamine- and trauma-induced brain injuries: Comparative cellular and molecular neurobiological substrates. *Biological Psychiatry*, *66*, 118–127.

Goldstein, A. (2001). *Addiction: From biology to social policy* (2nd ed.). New York: Oxford University Press.

Gorelick, D. A., Goodwin, R. S., Schwilke, E., Schwope, D. M., Darwin, W. D., Kelly, D. L., et al. (2012). Tolerance to effects of high-dose oral {delta}9-tetrahydrocannabinol and plasma cannabinoid concentrations in male daily cannabis smokers. *Journal of Analytical Toxicology*, *37*, 11–16.

Gosselin, R. E., Smith, R. P., & Hodge, H. C. (1984). *Clinical toxicology of commercial products* (5th ed.). Baltimore: Williams & Wilkins.

Gouin, K., Murphy, K., Shah, P. S., & Knowledge Synthesis Group on Determinants of Low Birth Weight and Preterm Births. (2011). Effects of cocaine use during pregnancy on low birthweight and preterm birth: Systematic review and meta-analyses. *American Journal of Obstetrics and Gynecology*, *204*, 340.e1–e12.

Gould E. (2007). How widespread is adult neurogenesis in mammals? *Nature Reviews Neuroscience*, *8*, 481–488.

Gould E., Reeves, A. J., Graziano, M. S., & Gross, C. G. (1999). Neurogenesis in the neocortex of adult primates. *Science*, *286*, 548–552.

Gould, R. W., Gage, H. D., & Nader, M. A. (2012). Effects of chronic cocaine self-administration on cognition and cerebral glucose utilization in rhesus monkeys. *Biological Psychiatry*, *72*, 856–863.

Gourlay, D. L., Heit, H. A., & Almahrezi, A. (2005). Universal precautions in pain medicine: A rational approach to the treatment of chronic pain. *Pain Medicine*, *6*, 107–112.

Graber, C. (2008, July 28). Fact or fiction? Animals *like* to get drunk. *Scientific American*. Retrieved from http://www.scientificamerican.com/article.cfm?id=animals-like-to-get-drunk

Graham, D. M. (1978). Caffeine—its identity, dietary sources, intake and biological effects. *Nutrition Review*, *36*, 97–102.

Granderson, L. Z. (2012, December 11). Drunken driving is not about the NFL. *CNN*. Retrieved from http://www.cnn.com/2012/12/11/opinion/granderson-football-drunken-driving/index.html

Gray, K. (2013, March 16). Are we over-diagnosing mental illness? *CNN*. Retrieved from http://www.cnn.com/2013/03/16/health/mental-illness-overdiagnosis/index.html

Greden, J. F. (1974). Anxiety or caffeinism: A diagnostic dilemma. *American Journal of Psychiatry*, *131*, 1089–1092.

Greenfield, B. L., & Tonigan, J. S. (2012). The general Alcoholics Anonymous tools of recovery: The adoption of 12-step practices and beliefs. *Psychology of Addictive Behaviors*, article in press.

Grey-Wilson, C. (2002). *Poppies: A guide to the poppy family in the wild and in cultivation (revised)*. Portland, OR: Timber.

Griffiths, R. R., & Vernotica, E. M. (2000). Is caffeine a flavoring agent in cola soft drinks? *Archives of Family Medicine*, *9*, 727–734.

Griffiths, R. R., Evans, S. M., Heishman, S. J., Preston, K. L., Sannerud, C. A., Wolf, B., & Woodson, P. P. (1990). Low-dose caffeine discrimination in humans. *Journal of Pharmacology Experimental Therapeutics*, *252*, 970–978.

Grinspoon, L., & Bakalar, J. B. (1976). *Cocaine: A drug and its social evolution*. New York: Harper Books.

Grossberg, G. T. (2003). Diagnosis and treatment of Alzheimer's disease. *Journal of Clinical Psychiatry*, *64* Suppl 9, 3–6.

Grotenhermen, F. (2003). Pharmacokinetics and pharmacodynamics of cannabinoids. *Clinical Pharmacokinetics*, *42*, 327–360.

Grotenhermen, F. (2007). The toxicology of cannabis and cannabis prohibition. *Chemistry & Biodiversity*, *4*, 1744–1769.

Grush, L. (2013, March 12). Single concussion can cause lasting damage to the brain, study finds. *Fox News*. Retrieved from http://www.foxnews.com/health/2013/03/12/single-concussion-can-cause-lasting-damage-to-brain-study-finds/

Gudelsky, G. A., & Yamamoto, B. K. (2008). Actions of 3,4-methylenedioxymethamphetamine (MDMA) on cerebral dopaminergic, serotonergic and cholinergic neurons. *Pharmacology, Biochemistry and Behavior*, *90*, 198–207.

Gudjonsson, G. H., Sigurdsson, J. F., Sigfusdottir, I. D., & Young, S. (2012). An epidemiological study of ADHD symptoms among young persons and the relationship with cigarette smoking, alcohol consumption and illicit drug use. *Journal of Child Psychology and Psychiatry*, *53*, 304–312.

Guerri, C., & Pascual, M. (2010). Mechanisms involved in the neurotoxic, cognitive, and neurobehavioral effects of alcohol consumption during adolescence. *Alcohol*, *44*, 15–26.

Gunderson, E. W., Haughey, H. M., Ait-Daoud, N., Joshi, A. S., & Hart, C. L. (2012). "Spice" and "K2" herbal highs: A case series and systematic review of the clinical effects of biopsychosocial implications of synthetic cannabinoid use in humans. *American Journal of Addiction*, *21*, 320–326.

Gutstein, H. B., & Akil, H. (2001). Opioid analgesics. In J. G. Hardman, L. E. Limbird, & A. G. Gilman (Eds.), *The pharmacological basis of therapeutics* (10th ed.) (pp. 569–619). New York: McGraw-Hill.

Haddad, P. (1997). Newer antidepressants and the discontinuation syndrome. *Journal of Clinical Psychiatry*, *58* Suppl 7, 17–21.

Hafeman, D. M., Chang, K. D., Garrett, A. S., Sanders, E. M., & Phillips, M. L. (2012). Effects of medication on neuroimaging findings in bipolar disorder: An updated review. *Bipolar Disorders*, *14*, 375–410.

Hale, T. W., Kendall-Tackett, K., Cong, Z., Votta, R., & McCurdy, F. (2010). Discontinuation syndrome in newborns whose mothers took antidepressants while pregnant or breastfeeding. *Breastfeeding Medicine, 5*, 283–288.

Hall, R. C., Popkin, M. K., & McHenry, L. E. (1977). Angel's trumpet psychosis: A central nervous system anticholinergic syndrome. *American Journal of Psychiatry, 134*, 312–314.

Halpern, J. H., Sherwood, A. R., Hudson, J. I., Yurgelun-Todd, D., & Pope, H. G., Jr. (2005). Psychological and cognitive effects of long-term peyote use among Native Americans. *Biological Psychiatry, 58*, 624–631.

Hamamoto, D. T., & Rhodus, N. L. (2009). Methamphetamine abuse and dentistry. *Oral Diseases, 15*, 27–37.

Hamilton, G. R., & Baskett, T. F. (2000). In the arms of Morpheus the development of morphine for postoperative pain relief. *Canadian Journal of Anaesthesiology, 47*, 367–374.

Harmer, C. J., & Cowen, P. J. (2013). "It's the way that you look at it"—a cognitive neuropsychological account of SSRI action in depression. *Philosophical Transactions of the Royal Society of London B Biological Sciences, 368*, 1471–2970.

Harrell, P. T., Mancha, B. E., Petras, H., Trenz, R. C., & Latimer, W. W. (2012). Latent classes of heroin and cocaine users predict unique HIV/HCV risk factors. *Drug and Alcohol Dependence, 122*, 220–227.

Harris, D. S., Everhart, E. T., Mendelson, J., & Jones, R. T. (2003). The pharmacology of cocaethylene in humans following cocaine and ethanol administration. *Drug and Alcohol Dependence, 72*, 169–182.

Hart, C. L., Ward, A. S., Haney, M., Comer, S. D., Foltin, R. W., & Fischman, M. W. (2002). Comparison of smoked marijuana and oral delta(9)-tetrahydrocannabinol in humans. *Psychopharmacology, 164*, 407–415.

Hartzler, B., & Fromme, K. (2003). Fragmentary and en bloc blackouts: Similarity and distinction among episodes of alcohol-induced memory loss. *Journal of Studies on Alcohol, 64*, 547–550.

Hatzidimitriou, G., McCann, U. D., & Ricaurte, G. A. (1999). Altered serotonin innervations patterns in the forebrain of monkeys treated with (+/−)3,4-Methylenedioxymethamphetamine seven years previously: Factors influencing abnormal recovery. *The Journal of Neuroscience, 19*, 5096–5107.

Haughey, H. M., Marshall, E., Schacht, J. P., Louis, A., & Hutchison, K. E. (2008). Marijuana withdrawal and craving: Influence of the cannabinoid receptor I (CNRI) and fatty acid amide hydrolase (FAAH) genes. *Addiction, 103*, 1678–1686.

Hawks, R. L., & Chiang, C. N. (1986). *Urine testing for drugs of abuse.* Research Monograph 73. Washington, DC: National Institute on Drug Abuse.

Heath, A. C., Bucholz, K. K., Madden, P. A., Dinwiddie, S. H., Slutske, W. S., Bierut, L. J., et al. (1997). Genetic and environmental contributions to alcohol dependence risk in a national twin sample: Consistency of findings in women and men. *Psychological Medicine, 27*, 1381–1396.

Heatley, M. K., & Crane, J. (1990). The blood alcohol concentration at post-mortem in 175 fatal cases of alcohol intoxication. *Medical Science and the Law, 30*, 101–105.

Heckman, M. A., Weil, J., & Gonzalez de Mejia, E. (2010). Caffeine (1, 3, 7-trimethylxanthine) in foods: A comprehensive review on consumption, functionality, safety, and regulatory matters. *Journal of Food Science, 75*, R77–R87.

Heilig, M., Egli, M., Crabbe, J. C., & Becker, H. C. (2010). Acute withdrawal, protracted abstinence and negative affect in alcoholism: Are they linked? *Addiction Biology, 15*, 169–184.

Heinz, A. J., Beck, A., Meyer-Lindenberg, A., Sterzer, P., & Heinz, A. (2011). Cognitive and neurobiological mechanisms of alcohol-related aggression. *Nature Reviews Neuroscience, 12*, 400–413.

Heishman, S. J. (1999). Behavioral and cognitive effects of smoking: Relationship to nicotine addiction. *Nicotine and Tobacco Research, 1* Suppl 2, S143–S1247.

Heishman, S. J., Kleykamp, B. A., & Singleton, E. G. (2010). Meta-analysis of the acute effects of nicotine and smoking on human performance. *Psychopharmacology, 210*, 453–469.

Henningfield, J. E., London, E. D., & Pogun, S. (2009). *Handbook of experimental pharmacology: Nicotine pharmacology.* Heidelberg, Germany: Springer-Verlag.

Henningfield, J. E., Lucas, S. E., & Bigelow, G. E. (1986). Human studies of drugs as reinforcers. In S. R. Goldberg & I. P. Stollerman (Eds.), *Behavioral analysis of drug dependence* (pp. 69–122). Orlando, FL: Academic Press.

Henningfield, J. E., Miyasato, K., & Jasinski, D. R. (1985). Abuse liability and pharmacodynamic characteristics of intravenous and inhaled nicotine. *Journal of Pharmacology and Experimental Therapeutics, 234*, 1–12.

Herbst, E. D., Harris, D. W., Everhart, E. T., Mendelson, J., Jacob, P., & Jones, R. T. (2011). Cocaethylene formation following ethanol and cocaine administration by different routes. *Experimental and Clinical Psychopharmacology, 19*, 95–104.

Hester, R., Nestor, L., & Garavan, H. (2009). Impaired error awareness and anterior cingulate cortex hypoactivity in chronic cannabis users. *Neuropsychopharmacology, 34*, 2450–2458.

Higdon, J. V., & Frei, B. (2006). Coffee and health: A review of recent human research. *Critical Reviews in Food Science and Nutrition, 46*, 101–123.

Higginson, I. J., & Gao, W. (2012). Opioid prescribing for cancer pain during the last 3 months of life: Associated factors and 9-year trends in a nationwide United Kingdom cohort study. *Journal of Clinical Oncology, 30*, 4373–4379.

Hikida, T., Kitabatake, Y., Pastan, I., & Nakanishi, S. (2003). Acetylcholine enhancement in the nucleus accumbens prevents addictive behaviors of cocaine and morphine. *Proceedings of the National Academy of Sciences USA, 100*, 6169–6173.

Hildebrandt, T., Langenbucher, J. W., Carr, S. J., & Sanjuan, P. (2007). Modeling population heterogeneity in appearance- and performance-enhancing drug (APED) use: Application of mixture modeling in 400 APED users. *Journal of Abnormal Psychology, 116*, 717–733.

Hill, A. J., Williams, C. M., Whalley, B. J., & Stephens, G. J. (2012). Phytocannabinoids as novel therapeutic agents in CNS disorders. *Pharmacology & Therapeutics, 133*, 79–97.

Hipwell, A. E., White, H. R., Loeber, R., Stouthamer-Loeber, M., Chung, T., & Sembower, M. A. (2005). Young girls' expectancies about the effects of alcohol, future intentions and patterns of use. *Journal of Studies on Alcohol, 66*, 630–639.

Hirvoven, J., Goodwin, R. S., Li, C. T., Terry, G. E., Zoghbi, S. S., Morse, C., et al. (2012). Reversible and regionally selective down-regulation of brain cannabinoid CB(1) receptors in chronic daily cannabis smokers. *Molecular Psychiatry, 17*, 642–649.

Hodges, J. R. (2013). Hope abandoned: Memantine therapy in frontotemporal dementia. *Lancet Neurology, 12*, 121–123.

Hoffman, A. (2009). *LSD: My problem child.* Saline, MI: McNaughton & Gunn.

Hoffman, B. B. (2001). Catecholamines, sympathomimetic drugs, and adrenergic receptor antagonists. In J. G. Hardman, L. E. Limbird, & A. G. Gilman (Eds.), *The pharmacological basis of therapeutics* (10th ed.) (pp. 621–642). New York: McGraw-Hill.

Hoffman, J. R., Faigenbaum, A. D., Ratamess, N. A., Ross, R., Kang, J., & Tenenbaum, G. (2008). Nutritional supplementation and anabolic steroid use in adolescents. *Medicine & Science in Sport & Exercise, 40,* 15–24.

Holland, J. (2001). The history of MDMA. In J. Holland (Ed.), *Ecstasy: The complete guide.* Rochester, VT: Park Street.

Holmes, A. D., Copland, D. A., Silburn, P. A., & Chenery, H. J. (2011). Nicotine effects on general semantic priming in Parkinson's disease. *Experimental and Clinical Psychopharmacology, 19,* 215–223.

Horne, J. A., & Reyner, L. A. (1996). Counteracting driver sleepiness: Effects of napping, caffeine, and placebo. *Psychophysiology, 33,* 306–309.

Howard, M. A., & Marczinski, C. A. (2010). Acute effects of a glucose energy drink on behavioral control. *Experimental and Clinical Psychopharmacology, 18,* 553–561.

Howell, L. L., Votaw, J. R., Goodman, M. M., & Lindsey, K. P. (2010). Cortical activation during cocaine use and extinction in rhesus monkeys. *Psychopharmacology, 208,* 191–199.

Hoza, B., Gerdes, A. C., Mrug, S., Hingshaw, S. P., Bukowski, W. M., Gold, J. A., et al. (2005a). Peer-assessed outcomes in the multimodal treatment study of children with attention deficit hyperactivity disorder. *Journal of Clinical Child and Adolescent Psychology, 34,* 74–86.

Hoza, B., Mrug, S., Gerdes, A. C., Hinshaw, S. P., Bukowski, W. M., Gold, J. A., et al. (2005b). What aspects of peer relationships are impaired in children with attention-deficit/hyperactivity disorder? *Journal of Consulting and Clinical Psychology, 73,* 411–423.

Hser, Y.-I., Hoffman, V., Grella, C. E., & Anglin, M. D. (2001). A 33-year follow-up of narcotics addicts. *Archives of General Psychiatry, 58,* 503–508.

Huffer, S., Clark, M. E., Ning, J. C., Blanch, H. W., & Clark, D. S. (2011). Role of alcohols in growth, lipid composition, and membrane fluidity of yeasts, bacteria, and archaea. *Applied and Environmental Microbiology, 77,* 6400–6408.

Hughes, J. R. (1986). Genetics of smoking: A review. *Behavior Therapy, 17,* 335–345.

Hurtado-Gumucio, J. (2000). Coca leaf chewing as therapy for cocaine maintenance. *Annales de Medicine (Paris), 151* Suppl B, B44–B48.

Ibrahim, L., Diazgranados, N., Luckenbaugh, D. A., Machado-Vieira, R., Baumann, J., Mallinger, A. G., & Zarate, C. A., Jr. (2011). Rapid decrease in depressive symptoms with an N-methyl-D-aspartate antagonist in ECT-resistant major depression. *Progress in Neuro-Psychopharmacology & Biological Psychiatry, 35,* 1155–1159.

Idova, G. V., Alperina, E. L., & Cheido, M. A. (2012). Contribution of brain dopamine, serotonin and opioid receptors in the mechanisms of neuroimmunomodulation: Evidence from pharmacological analysis. *International Immunopharmacology, 12,* 618–625.

Indriati, E., & Buikstra, J. E. (2001). Coca chewing in prehistoric coastal Peru: Dental evidence. *American Journal of Physical Anthropology, 114,* 242–257.

International Olympic Committee (IOC). (2012). *Factsheet: The fight against doping and promotion of athletes' health, update – July 2012.* Retrieved from http://www.olympic.org/Documents/Reference_documents_Factsheets/Fight_against_doping.pdf

Issac, P. F., & Rand, M. J. (1972). Cigarette smoking and plasma levels of nicotine. *Nature, 236,* 308–310.

Iversen, L. L. (2008). *The science of marijuana* (2nd ed.). New York: Oxford University Press.

Iversen, L. L., Iversen, S. D., Bloom, F. E., & Roth, R. H. (2009). *Introduction to Neuropsychopharmacology.* New York: Oxford University Press.

Jakupcak, M., Hoerster, K. D., Blais, R. K., Malte, C. A., Hunt, S., & Seal, K. (2013). Readiness for change predicts VA mental healthcare utilization among Iraq and Afghanistan war veterans. *Journal of Traumatic Stress, 26,* 165–168.

James, J. E. (1991). *Caffeine and health.* London: Academic Press.

Janes, A. C., Frederick, B., Richardt, S., Burbridge, C., Merlo-Pich, E., Renshaw, P. F., Evins, A. E., Fava, M., & Kaufman, M. J. (2009). Brain fMRI reactivity to smoking-related images before and during extended smoking abstinence. *Experimental and Clinical Psychopharmacology, 17,* 365–373.

Jarbe, T. U. (1993). Repeated testing within drug discrimination learning: Time course studies with cocaine, amphetamine, and 3-PPP. *Pharmacology, Biochemistry & Behavior, 44,* 481–486.

Jatoi, A., Qi, Y., Wampfler, J. A., Busta, A. J., Yang, P., & Mandrekar, S. (2011). The purported effects of alcohol on appetite and weight in lung cancer patients. *Nutrition and Cancer, 63,* 1251–1255.

Javid, J. I., Musa, M. N., Fischman, M., Schuster, C. R., & Davis, J. M. (1983). Kinetics of cocaine in humans after intravenous and intranasal administration. *Biopharmaceutics and Drug Disposition, 4,* 9–18.

Jayaram, M., Rattehalli, R. D., & Adams, C. E. (2012). Where does evidence from new trials for schizophrenia fit with the existing evidence: A case of the emperor's new clothes? *Schizophrenia Research Treatment, 6255738.*

Joe Laidler, K. A. (2005). The rise of club drugs in a heroin society: The case of Hong Kong. *Substance Use and Misuse, 40,* 1257–1278.

Johnson, G. (2012, December 6). A history of pot, from George Washington to legalizing ganja. *NBC News.* Retrieved from http://usnews.nbcnews.com/_news/2012/12/06/15726635-a-history-of-pot-from-george-washington-to-legalizing-ganja?lite

Johnson, M. W., MacLean, K. A., Reissig, C. J., Prisinzano, T. E., & Griffiths, R. R. (2011). Human psychopharmacology and dose-effects of salvinorin A, a kappa opioid agonist hallucinogen present in the plant *Salvia divinorum. Drug and Alcohol Dependence, 115,* 150–155.

Johnston, L. D., O'Malley, P. M., Bachman, J. G., & Schulenberg, J. E. (2012). *Monitoring the future national results on adolescent drug use: Overview of key findings, 2011.* Ann Arbor, MI: Institute for Social Research, The University of Michigan.

Johnstone, E., Humphreys, M., Lang, F., Lawrie, S., & Sandler, R. (1999). *Schizophrenia: Concepts and clinical management.* Cambridge, UK: Cambridge University Press.

Jones, A. W., & Holmgren, A. (2009). Concentration distributions of the drugs most frequently identified in post-mortem femoral blood representing all causes of death. *Medical Science and the Law, 49,* 257–273.

Jones, K. L., & Smith, D. W. (1973). Recognition of the fetal alcohol syndrome in early infancy. *Lancet, 2,* 999–1001.

Jones, K. L., Smith, D. W., Ulleland, C. N., & Streissguth, A. P. (1973). Pattern of malformation in offspring of chronic alcoholic mothers. *Lancet, 1,* 1267–1271.

Jones, R. T. (1987). Tobacco dependence. In H. Y. Meltzer (Ed.), *Psychopharmacology: The third generation of progress* (pp. 1589–1595). New York: Raven.

Joutsa, J., Johansson, J., Niemela, S., Ollikainen, A., Hirvonen, M. M., Piepponen, P., et al. (2012). Mesolimbic dopamine release is linked to symptom severity in pathological gambling. *Neuroimage, 60,* 1992–1999.

Julien, R. M. (2005). *A primer of drug action* (10th ed.). New York: Worth.

Jutkiewicz, E. M. (2006). The antidepressant-like effects of delta-opioid receptor agonists. *Molecular Interventions, 6,* 162–169.

Kadota, K., Takeshima, F., Inoue, K., Takamori, K., Yoshioka, S., Nakayama, S., Abe, K., Mizuta, Y., Kohno, S., & Ozono, Y. (2010). Effects of smoking cessation on gastric emptying in smokers. *Journal of Clinical Gastroenterology, 44,* e71–e75.

Kalapatapu, R. K., Bedi, G., Haney, M., Evans, S. M., Rubin, E., & Foltin, R. W. (2012). The subjective effects of cocaine: Relationship to years of cocaine use and current age. *American Journal of Drug and Alcohol Abuse, 38,* 530–534.

Kalix, P. (1981). Cathinone, an alkaloid from khat leaves with an amphetamine-like releasing effect. *Psychopharmacology, 74,* 269–270.

Kalman, D., & Smith, S. S. (2005). Does nicotine do what we think it does? A meta-analytic review of the subjective effects of nicotine in nasal spray and intravenous studies with smokers and nonsmokers. *Nicotine Tobacco Research, 7,* 317–333.

Kameda, S. R., Fukushiro, D. F., Trombin, T. F., Procopio-Souza, R., Patti, C. L., Hollais, A. W., et al. (2011). Adolescent mice are more vulnerable than adults to single injection-induced behavioral sensitization to amphetamine. *Pharmacology, Biochemistry & Behavior, 98,* 320–324.

Kampman, K. M. (2010). What's news in the treatment of cocaine addiction? *Current Psychiatry Reports, 12,* 441–447.

Kanaya, K., Abe, S., Sakai, M., Fujii, H., Koizumi, K., & Iwamoto, T. (2012). Efficacy of a high dosage of donepezil for Alzheimer's disease as examined by single-photon emission computed tomography imaging. *Psychogeriatrics, 12,* 172–178.

Kanayama, G., Hudson, J. I., & Pope, H. G. (2009). Features of men with anabolic-androgenic steroid dependence: A comparison with nondependent AAS users and with AAS nonusers. *Drug and Alcohol Dependence, 102,* 130–137.

Kaplan. G. B., Greenblatt, D. J., Ehrenberg, B. L., Goddard, J. E., Cotreau, M. M., Harmatz, J. S., & Shader, R. I. (1997). Dose-dependent pharmacokinetics and psychomotor effects of caffeine in humans. *Journal of Clinical Psychopharmacology, 37,* 693–703.

Kavaliers, M., & Ossenkopp, K.-P. (1993). Repeated naloxone treatments and exposure to weak 60-Hz magnetic fields have "analgesic" effects in snails. *Brain Research, 620,* 159–162.

Kavaliers, M., & Perrot-Sinal, T. S. (1996). Pronociceptive effects of the neuropeptide, nociceptin, in the land snail, *Cepaea nemoralis. Peptides, 17,* 763–768.

Kawachi, I., Colditz, G. A., Ascherio, A., Rimm, E. B., Giovannucci, E., Stampfer, M. J., & Willett, W. C. (1994). Prospective study of phobic anxiety and risk of coronary heart disease in men. *Circulation, 89,* 1992–1997.

Kawachi, I., Colditz, G. A., Speizer, F. E., Manson, J. E., Stampfer, M. J., Willett, W. C. et al. (1997). A prospective study of passive smoking and coronary heart disease. *Circulation, 95,* 2374–2379.

Kawachi, I., Troisi, R. J., Rotnitzky, A. G., Coakley, E. H., & Colditz, G. A. (1996). Can physical activity minimize weight gain in women after smoking cessation? *American Journal of Public Health, 86,* 999–1004.

Kaymaz, N., van Os, J., Loonen, A. J., & Nolen, W. A. (2008). Evidence that patients with single versus recurrent depressive episodes are differentially sensitive to treatment discontinuation: A meta-analysis of placebo-controlled randomized trials. *Journal of Clinical Psychiatry, 69,* 1423–1436.

Keast, R. S., & Riddell, L. J. (2007). Caffeine as a flavor additive in softdrinks. *Appetite, 49,* 255–259.

Kedzior, K. K., & Martin-Iverson, M. T. (2007). Attention-dependent reduction in prepulse inhibition of the startle reflex in cannabis users and schizophrenia patients—A pilot study. *European Journal of Pharmacology, 560,* 176–182.

Kelly, E., Darke, S., & Ross, J. (2004). A review of drug use and driving: Epidemiology, impairment, risk factors and risk perceptions. *Drug and Alcohol Review, 23,* 319–344.

Kelly, J. P. (2011). Cathinone derivatives: A review of their chemistry, pharmacology and toxicology. *Drug Testing and Analysis, 3,* 439–453.

Kelly, T. H., Foltin, R. W., & Fischman, M. W. (1993). Effects of smoked marijuana on heart rate, drug ratings and task performance by humans. *Behavioural Pharmacology, 4,* 167–178.

Kelly, T. H., Foltin, R. W., Emurian, C. S., & Fischman, M. W. (1990). Multidimensional behavioral effects of marijuana. *Progress in Neuropsychopharmacology & Biological Psychiatry, 14,* 885–902.

Kenny, M., & Darragh, A. (1985). Central effects of caffeine in man. In S. D. Iversen (Ed.), *Psychopharmacology: Recent advances and future prospects* (pp. 278–288). Oxford: Oxford University Press.

Kertesz, A. (1998). Pick's disease and Pick complex: Introductory nosology. In A. Kertesz and D. G. Munoz (Eds.), *Pick's disease and Pick complex.* New York: Wiley-Liss.

Kertesz, A. (2006). *The banana lady and other stories of curious behaviour and speech.* Victoria, Canada: Trafford.

Kerwin, D., & Claus, T. H. (2011). Severe Alzheimer's disease: Treatment effects on function and care requirements. *Journal of the American Medical Director's Association, 12,* 99–104.

Kessler, R. C., Petukhova, M., Sampson, N. A., Zaslavsky, A. M., & Wittchen, H. U. (2012). Twelve-month and lifetime prevalence and lifetime morbid risk of anxiety and mood disorders in the United States. *International Journal of Methods in Psychiatric Research, 21,* 169–184.

Khademi, H., Malekzadeh, R., Pourshams, A., Jafari, E., Salahi, R., Semnani, S., et al. (2012). Opium use and mortality in Golestan cohort study: Prospective cohort study of 50,000 adults in Iran. *British Medical Journal, 344,* e2502.

Kidorf, M., King, V. L., Gandotra, N., Kolodner, K., & Brooner, R. K. (2012). Improvement treatment enrollment and re-enrollment rates of syringe exchangers: 12-month outcomes. *Drug and Alcohol Dependence, 124,* 162–166.

Kieffer, B. L. (1999). Opioids: First lessons from knockout mice. *Trends in Pharmacological Sciences, 20,* 19–26.

Killinger, B. A., Peet, M. M., & Baker, L. E. (2010). Salvinorin A fails to substitute for the discriminative stimulus effects of LSD or ketamine in Sprague-Dawley rats. *Pharmacology, Biochemistry and Behavior, 96,* 260–265.

King, W. C., Chen, J. Y., Mitchell, J. E., Kalarchian, M. A., Steffen, K. J., Engel, S. G., Courcoulas, A. P., Pories, W. J., & Yanovski, S. Z. (2012). Prevalence of alcohol use disorders before and after bariatric surgery. *JAMA, 307,* 2156–2525.

Kirkey, S. (2012, October 22). Stroke cures man of cocaine addiction, researchers report. *Vancouver Sun.* Retrieved from http://www.vancouversun.com/health/Stroke+cures+cocaine+addiction+researchers+report/7426976/story.html

Kirkpatrick, M. G., Gunderson, E. W., Johanson, C. E., Levin, F. R., Foltin, R. W., & Hart, C. L. (2012a). Comparison of intranasal methamphetamine and *d*-amphetamine self-administration by humans. *Addiction*, *107*, 783–791.

Kirkpatrick, M. G., Gunderson, E. W., Levin, F. R., Foltin, R. W., & Hart, C. L. (2012b). Acute and residual interactive effects of repeated administrations of oral methamphetamine and alcohol in humans. *Psychopharmacology*, *219*, 191–204.

Kitano, H. H. L. (1989). Alcohol and the Asian American. In T. D. Watts & R. Wright, Jr. (Eds), *Alcoholism in minority populations* (pp. 143–158). Springfield, IL: Charles C Thomas.

Kittirattanapaiboon, P., Mahatnirunkul, S., Booncharoen, H., Thummawomg, P., Dumrongchai, U., & Chutha, W. (2010). Long-term outcomes in methamphetamine psychosis patients after first hospitalisation. *Drug and Alcohol Review*, *29*, 456–461.

Kitty, J. E., Lorang, D., & Amara, S. G. (1991). Cloning and expression of a cocaine-sensitive rat dopamine transporter. *Science*, *254*, 578–579.

Klepstad, P., Kaasa, S., Cherny, N., Hanks, G., de Conno, F., & Research Steering Committee of the EAPC. (2005). Pain and pain treatments in European palliative care units. A cross sectional survey from the European Association for Palliative Care Research Network. *Palliative Medicine*, *19*, 477–484.

Kline, N. S. (1958). Clinical experience with iproniazid (Marsilid). *Journal of Clinical and Experimental Psychopathology*, *19*(supplement), 72–78.

Kolata, G. (2013, March 13). F.D.A. plans looser rules on approving Alzheimer's drugs. *The New York Times*. Retrieved from http://www.nytimes.com/2013/03/14/health/fda-to-ease-alzheimers-drug-approval-rules.html?pagewanted=all

Kollins, S. H., & Rush, C. R. (2002). Sensitization to the cardiovascular but not subject-rated effects of oral cocaine in humans. *Biological Psychiatry*, *51*, 143–150.

Konrad, E., & Reid, A. (2013). Colorado family physicians' attitudes toward medical marijuana. *Journal of the American Board of Family Medicine*, *26*, 52–60.

Koob, G. F., & Le Moal, M. (2006). *Neurobiology of addiction*. London: Academic Press.

Koranek, A. M., Smith, T. L., Mican, L. M., & Rascati, K. L. (2012). Impact of the CATIE trial on antipsychotic prescribing patterns at a state psychiatric facility. *Schizophrenia Research*, *137*, 137–140.

Kozlowski, L. T., & Henningfield, J. E. (1995). Thinking the unthinkable: The prospect of regulation of nicotine in cigarettes by the United States government. *Addiction*, *90*, 165–167.

Kring, A. M., Johnson, S. L., Davison, G. C., & Neale, J. M. (2012). *Abnormal psychology* (12th ed.). Hoboken, NJ: John Wiley & Sons.

Kruhoffer, P. W. (1983). Handling of inspired vaporized ethanol in the airways and lungs (with comments on forensic aspects). *Forensic Science International*, *21*, 1–17.

Kuehn, B. M. (2009). FDA panel OKs 3 antipsychotic drugs for pediatric use, cautions against overuse. *JAMA: Journal of the American Medical Association*, *302*, 833–834.

Kuehn, D., Aros, S., Cassorla, F., Avaria, M., Unanue, N., Henriquez, C., et al. (2012). A prospective cohort study of the prevalence of growth, facial, and central nervous system abnormalities in children with heavy prenatal alcohol exposure. *Alcoholism: Clinical and Experimental Research*, *36*, 1811–1819.

Kuhn, C., Swartzwelder, S., & Wilson, W. (2008). *Buzzed: The straight facts about the most used and abused drugs from alcohol to ecstasy* (3rd ed.). New York: W. W. Norton.

Kuhn, R. (1958). The treatment of depressive states with G22355 (imipramine hydrochloride). *American Journal of Psychiatry*, *115*, 459–464.

Kumar, S., Porcu, P., Werner, D. F., Matthews, D. B., Diaz-Granados, J. L., Helfand, R. S., & Morrow, A. L. (2009). The role of GABA$_{(A)}$ receptors in the acute and chronic effects of ethanol: A decade of progress. *Psychopharmacology*, *205*, 529–564.

Kuo, M., Adlaf, E. M., Lee, H., Gliksman, L., Demers, A., & Wechsler, H. (2002). More Canadian students drink but American students drink more: Comparing college alcohol use in two countries. *Addiction*, *97*, 1583–1592.

Laaksonen, E., Koski-Jannes, A., Salaspuro, M., Ahtinen, H., & Alho, H. (2008). A randomized, multicentre, open-label, comparative trial of disulfiram, naltrexone and acamprosate in the treatment of alcohol dependence. *Alcohol and Alcoholism*, *43*, 53–61.

LaGasse, L. L., Derauf, C., Smith, L. M., Newman, E., Shah, R., Neal, C., et al. (2012). Prenatal methamphetamine exposure and childhood behavior problems at 3 and 5 years of age. *Pediatrics*, *129*, 681–688.

Landry, M. J. (1992). An overview of cocaethylene, an alcohol-derived, psychoactive, cocaine metabolite. *Journal of Psychoactive Drugs*, *24*, 273–276.

Larney, S., Randall, D., Gibson, A., & Degenhardt, L. (2013). The contributions of viral hepatitis and alcohol to liver-related deaths in opioid-dependent people. *Drug and Alcohol Dependence*, *131*, 252–257.

Lattin, D. (2011). *The Harvard psychedelic club*. New York: HarperCollins.

Laumon, B., Gadegbeku, B., Martin, J. L., Biecheler, M. B., & the SAM Group. (2005). Cannabis intoxication and fatal road crashes in France: Population based case-control study. *British Medical Journal*, *331*, 1371.

Laviolette, S. R., & van der Kooy, D. (2004). The neurobiology of nicotine addiction: Bridging the gap from molecules to behaviour. *Nature Reviews Neuroscience*, *5*, 55–65.

Lawrence, D., Mitrou, F., & Zubrick, S. R. (2009). Smoking and mental illness: Results from population surveys in Australia and the United States. *BMC Public Health*, *9*, 285.

Lazarus, M., Shen, H. Y., Cherasse, Y., Qu, W. M., Huang, Z. L., Bass, C. E., Winsky-Sommerer, R., Semba, K., Fredholm, B. B., Boison, D., Hayaishi, O., Urade, Y., & Chen, J. F. (2011). Arousal effect of caffeine depends on adenosine A2A receptors in the shell of the nucleus accumbens. *Journal of Neuroscience*, *31*, 10067–10075.

Le Houezec, J. (2003). Role of nicotine pharmacokinetics in nicotine addiction and nicotine replacement therapy: A review. *International Journal of Tuberculosis and Lung Diseases*, *7*, 811–819.

Le Houezec, J., Halliday, R., Benowitz, N. L., Callaway, E., Naylor, H., & Herzig, K. (1994). A low dose of subcutaneous nicotine improves information processing in non-smokers. *Psychopharmacology*, *114*, 628–634.

Lea, A. G. H., & Piggott, J. R. (2003). *Fermented beverage production* (2nd ed.). New York: Kluwer Academic/Plenum Publishers.

Leamon, M. H., Gibson, D. R., Canning, R. D., & Benjamin, L. (2002). Hospitalization of patients with cocaine and amphetamine use disorders from a psychiatric emergency service. *Psychiatric Services*, *53*, 1461–1466.

Leatherdale, S. T., & Burkhalter, R. (2012). The substance use profile of Canadian youth: Exploring the prevalence of alcohol, drug and tobacco use by gender and grade. *Addictive Behaviors*, *37*, 318–322.

Lee, L. O., Young-Wolff, K. C., Kendler, K. S., & Prescott, C. A. (2012). The effects of age of onset and stressful life events on alcohol use in adulthood: A replication and extension using a population-based twin sample. *Alcoholism: Clinical and Experimental Research, 36*, 693–704.

Lee, M. C., Ploner, M., Wiech, K., Bingel, U., Wanigasekera, V., Brooks, J., et al. (2013). Amygdala activity contributes to the dissociative effect of cannabis on pain perception. *Pain, 154*, 124–134.

Lejoyeux, M., & Ades, J. (1997). Antidepressant discontinuation: A review of the literature. *Journal of Clinical Psychiatry, 58* Suppl 7, 11–15.

Lemoine, P., Harousseau, H., Borteyru, J. P., & Menuet, J. C. (1968). Les enfants des parents alcooliques: Anomolies observes a propos de 127 cas (The children of alcoholic parents: Anomalies observed in 127 cases). *Quest Medical, 25*, 476–482.

Lender, M. E., & Martin, J. K. (1982). *Drinking in America.* New York: Free Press.

Lendler, I. (2005). *Alcoholica esoterica.* New York: Penguin.

Levin, E. D. (1992). Nicotinic systems and cognitive function. *Psychopharmacology, 108*, 417–431.

Levin, E. D., Bushnell, P. J., & Rezvani, A. H. (2011). Attention-modulating effects of cognitive enhancers. *Pharmacology, Biochemistry and Behavior, 99*, 146–154.

Levine, B., & Smialek, J. E. (2000). Status of alcohol absorption in drinking drivers killed in traffic accidents. *Journal of Forensic Science, 45*, 3–6.

Lev-Ran, S., Imtiaz, S., & Le Foll, B. (2012). Self-reported psychotic disorders among individuals with substance use disorders: Findings from the national epidemiologic survey on alcohol and related conditions. *American Journal of Addiction, 21*, 531–535.

Li, Q., Hsia, J., & Yang, G. (2011). Prevalence of smoking in China in 2010. *New England Journal of Medicine, 364*, 2469–2470.

Lichlyter, B., Purdon, S., & Tibbo, P. (2011). Predictors of psychosis severity in individuals with primary stimulant addictions. *Addictive Behaviors, 36*, 137–139.

Liguori, A., Gatto, C. P., & Robinson, J. H. (1998). Effects of marijuana on equilibrium, psychomotor performance, and simulated driving. *Behavioural Pharmacology, 9*, 599–609.

Lim, K. B., Kim, Y. S., & Kim, J. A. (2012). Sonographically guided alcohol injection in painful stump neuroma. *Annals of Rehabilitation Medicine, 36*, 404–408.

Ling, W., Rawson, R. A., & Compton, M. A. (1994). Substitution pharmacotherapies for opioid addiction: From methadone to LAAM and buprenorphine. *Journal of Psychoactive Drugs, 26*, 119–128.

Lisdahl, K. M., Thayer, R., Squeglia, L. M., McQueeny, T. M., & Tapert, S. F. (2013). Recent binge drinking predicts smaller cerebellar volumes in adolescents. *Psychiatry Research, 211*, 17–23.

Lloyd-Smith, E., Wood, E., Zhang, R., Tyndall, M. W., Montaner, J. S., & Kerr, T. (2008). Risk factors for developing a cutaneous injection-related infection among injection drug users: A cohort study. *BMC Public Health, 8*, 405.

Lodge, D. J., & Grace, A. A. (2011). Hippocampal dysregulation of dopamine system function and the pathophysiology of schizophrenia. *Trends in Pharmacological Sciences, 32*, 507–513.

Lucas, P. (2012). Cannabis as an adjunct to or substitute for opiates in the treatment of chronic pain. *Journal of Psychoactive Drugs, 44*, 125–133.

Lynskey, M., & Hall, W. (2000). The effects of adolescent cannabis use on educational attainment: A review. *Addiction, 95*, 1621–1630.

Maclean, K. A., Johnson, M. W., Reissig, C. J., Prisinzano, T. E., & Griffiths, R. R. (2013). Dose-related effects of salvinorin A in humans: Dissociative, hallucinogenic, and memory effects. *Psychopharmacology, 226*, 381–392.

Macleod, J., Oakes, R., Copello, A., Crome, I., Egger, M., Hickman, M., et al. (2004). Psychological and social sequelae of cannabis and other illicit drug use by young people: A systematic review of longitudinal, general population studies. *Lancet, 363*, 1579–1588.

Magura, S., McKeen, J., Kosten, S., & Tonigan, J. S. (2013). A novel application of propensity score matching to estimate Alcoholics Anonymous' effect on drinking outcomes. *Drug and Alcohol Dependence, 129*, 54–59.

Mahoney, J. J. 3rd, Hawkins, R. Y., De La Garza, R. 2nd, Kalechstein, A. D., & Newton, T. F. (2010). Relationship between gender and psychotic symptoms in cocaine-dependent and methamphetamine-dependent participants. *Gender Medicine, 7*, 414–421.

Mahoney, J. J. 3rd, Kalechstein, A. D., De La Garza, R. 2nd, & Newton, T. F. (2008). Presence and persistence of psychotic symptoms in cocaine- versus methamphetamine-dependent participants. *American Journal of Addiction, 17*, 83–98.

Mailman, R. B., & Murthy, V. (2010). Third generation antipsychotic drugs: Partial agonism or receptor functional selectivity? *Current Pharmaceutical Design, 16*, 488–501.

Malaiyandi, V., Lerman, C., Benowitz, N. L., Jepson, C., Patterson, F., & Tyndale, R. F. (2006). Impact of CYP2A6 genotype on pretreatment smoking behaviour and nicotine levels from and usage of nicotine replacement therapy. *Molecular Psychiatry, 11*, 400–409.

Mancall, P. C. (1997). *Deadly medicine: Indians and alcohol in early America.* Ithaca, NY: Cornell University Press.

Manchikanti, L., Helm, S. 2nd, Fellows, B., Janata, J. W., Pampati, V., Grider, J. S., & Boswell, M. V. (2012). Opioid epidemic in the United States. *Pain Physician, 15*(3 Suppl), ES9–ES38.

Manghi, R. A., Broers, B., Khan, R., Benguettat, D., Khazaal, Y., & Zullino, D. F. (2009). Khat use: Lifestyle or addiction? *Journal of Psychoactive Drugs, 41*, 1–10.

Marcus, M., Yasamy, M. T., van Ommeren, M., Chisolm, D., & Saxena, S. (2012). *Depression: A global public health concern.* Geneva, Switzerland: WHO Department of Mental Health and Substance Abuse. Retrieved from http://www.who.int/mental_health/management/depression/who_paper_depression_wfmh_2012.pdf

Marczinski, C. A., & Fillmore, M. T. (2003). Dissociative antagonistic effects of caffeine on alcohol-induced impairment of behavioral control. *Experimental and Clinical Psychopharmacology, 11*, 228–236.

Marczinski, C. A., & Fillmore, M. T. (2006). Clubgoers and their trendy cocktails: Implications of mixing caffeine into alcohol on information processing and subjective reports of intoxication. *Experimental and Clinical Psychopharmacology, 14*, 450–458.

Marczinski, C. A., & Fillmore, M. T. (2009). Acute alcohol tolerance on subjective intoxication and simulated driving performance in binge drinkers. *Psychology of Addictive Behaviors, 23*, 238–247.

Marczinski, C. A., & Stamates, A. L. (2013). Artificial sweeteners versus regular mixers increase breath alcohol concentrations in male and female social drinkers. *Alcoholism: Clinical and Experimental Research, 37*, 696–702.

Marczinski, C. A., Fillmore, M. T., Bardgett, M. E., & Howard, M. A. (2011). Effects of energy drinks mixed with alcohol on behavioral control: Risks for college students consuming trendy cocktails. *Alcoholism: Clinical and Experimental Research, 35*, 1282–1292.

Marczinski, C. A., Fillmore, M. T., Henges, A. L., Ramsey, M. A., & Young, C. R. (2012). Effects of energy drinks mixed with alcohol on information processing, motor coordination and subjective reports of intoxication. *Experimental and Clinical Psychopharmacology, 20,* 129–138.

Marczinski, C. A., Grant, E. C., & Grant, V. J. (2009). *Binge drinking in adolescents and college students.* Hauppauge, NY: Nova Science.

Marczinski, C. A., Harrison, E. L. R., & Fillmore, M. T. (2008). Effects of alcohol on simulated driving and perceived driving impairment in binge drinkers. *Alcoholism: Clinical and Experimental Research, 32,* 1329–1337.

Markway, E. C., & Baker, S. N. (2011). A review of the methods, interpretation, and limitations of the urine drug screen. *Orthopedics, 34,* 877–881.

Marlatt, G. A., & Gordon, J. R. (Eds.). (1985). *Relapse prevention: Maintenance strategies in the treatment of addictive behaviors.* New York: Guilford.

Marshall, E. (1988). The drug of champions. *Science, 242,* 183–184.

Marshall, J. F., & O'Dell, S. J. (2012). Methamphetamine influences on brain and behavior: Unsafe at any speed? *Trends in Neuroscience, 35,* 536–545.

Martin, C. S., Earleywine, M., Musty, R. E., Perrine, M. W., & Swift, R. M. (1993). Development and validation of the Biphasic Alcohol Effects Scale. *Alcoholism: Clinical and Experimental Research, 17,* 140–146.

Martinez-Raga, J., Gonzalez-Saiz, F., Onate, J., Oyaguez, I., Sabater, E., & Casado, M. A. (2012). Budgetary impact analysis of buprenorphine-naloxone combination (Suboxone®) in Spain. *Health Economics Review, 2,* 3.

Mateus-Pinheiro, A., Pinto, L., Bessa, J. M., Morais, M., Alves, N. D., Monteiro, S., et al. (2013). Sustained remission from depressive-like behavior depends on hippocampal neurogenesis. *Translational Psychiatry, 3,* e210.

Mathurin, P., Moreno, C., Samuel, D., Dumortier, J., Salleron, J., Durand, F., et al. (2011). Early liver transplantation for severe alcoholic hepatitis. *New England Journal of Medicine, 36,* 1790–1800.

Maugh, T. H., II (2002, October 18). "Sobering" state report calls autism an epidemic. *Los Angeles Times, A1,* A25.

Maxwell, J. C., & Brecht, M.-L. (2011). Methamphetamine: Here we go again? *Addictive Behaviors, 36,* 1168–1173.

May, C. D. (1988, July 1). How Coca-Cola obtains its coca. *The New York Times.* Retrieved from http://www.nytimes.com/1988/07/01/business/how-coca-cola-obtains-its-coca.html

McBride, J. S., Altman, D. G., Klein, M., & White, W. (1998). Green tobacco sickness. *Tobacco Control, 7,* 294–298.

McCance-Katz, E. F., Price, L. H., McDougle, C. J., Kosten, T. R., Black, J. E., & Jatlow, P. I. (1993). Concurrent cocaine-ethanol ingestion in humans: Pharmacology, physiology, behavior, and the role of cocaethylene. *Psychopharmacology, 111,* 39–46.

McCann, U. D., Edwards, R. R., Smith, M. T., Kelly, K., Wilson, M., Sgambati, F., & Ricaurte, G. (2011). Altered pain responses in abstinent (+/–)3,4-methylenedioxymethamphetamine (MDMA, "ecstasy") users. *Psychopharmacology, 217,* 475–484.

McClure, E. A., Saulsgiver, K. A., & Wynne, C. D. (2009). Effects of acute and chronic *d*-amphetamine on two variations of a temporal discrimination procedure. *Behavioral Pharmacology, 20,* 668–672.

McCusker, R. R., Goldberger, B. A., & Cone, E. J. (2003). Caffeine content of specialty coffees. *Journal of Analytical Toxicology, 27,* 520–522.

McCusker, R. R., Goldberger, B. A., & Cone, E. J. (2006). Caffeine content of energy drinks, carbonated sodas, and other beverages. *Journal of Analytical Toxicology, 30,* 112–114.

McDonald, A. J. 3rd, Wang, B., & Camargo, C. A. Jr. (2004). U.S. emergency department visits for alcohol-related diseases and injuries between 1992 and 2000. *Archives of Internal Medicine, 164,* 531–537.

McNally, B. (2013, January 2). Redskins' Cedric Griffin embarrassed by drug suspension. *The Washington Examiner.* Retrieved from http://washingtonexaminer.com/redskins-cedric-griffin-embarrassed-by-drug-suspension/article/2517441

McQueeny, T., Schweinsburg, B. C., Schweinsburg, A. D., Jacobus, J., Bava, S., Frank, L. R., & Tapert, S. F. (2009). Altered white matter integrity in adolescent binge drinkers. *Alcoholism: Clinical and Experimental Research, 33,* 1278–1285.

Meehan, S. M., & Schechter, M. D. (1995). Cocaethylene-induced lethality in mice is potentiated by alcohol. *Alcohol, 12,* 383–385.

Mehta, M., Adem, A., Kahlon, M. S., & Sabbagh, M. N. (2012). The nicotinic acetylcholine receptor: Smoking and Alzheimer's disease revisited. *Frontiers in Bioscience, 4,* 169–180.

Meier, B. (2003). *Pain killer: A "wonder" drug's trail of addiction and death.* Emmaus, PA: Rodale.

Meier, B. (2012, April 8). Tightening the lid on pain prescriptions. *The New York Times.* Retrieved from http://www.nytimes.com/2012/04/09/health/opioid-painkiller-prescriptions-pose-danger-without-oversight.html?ref=barrymeier&_r=0

Meier, M. H., Caspi, A., Ambler, A., Harrington, H., Houts, R., Keefe, R. S. E., et al. (2012). Persistent cannabis users show neuropsychological decline from childhood to midlife. *Proceedings of the National Academy of Sciences of the United States of America, 109,* E2657–E2664.

Mendelson, J. H., & Mellow, N. K. (1985). *Alcohol: Use and abuse in America.* Boston: Little, Brown.

Merikangas, K. R., He, J.-P., Brody, D., Fisher, P. W., Bourdon, K., & Koretz, D. S. (2010). Prevalence and treatment of mental disorders among U.S. children in the 2001–2004 NHANES. *Pediatrics, 125,* 75–81.

Merskey, D. M. (1983). Classification of chronic pain. *Pain Supplement, 3,* S217.

Mets, M. A. J., Ketzer, S., Blom, C., van Gerven, M. H., van Willigenburg, G. M., Olivier, B., & Verster, J. C. (2011). Positive effects of Red Bull energy drink on driving performance during prolonged driving. *Psychopharmacology, 214,* 737–745.

Michel, R. H., McGovern, P. E., & Badler, V. R. (1993). The first wine & beer: Chemical detection of ancient fermented beverages. *Analytical Chemistry, 65,* 408–413.

Milan, N. F., Kacsoh, B. Z., & Schlenke, T. A. (2012). Alcohol consumption as self-medication against blood-borne parasites in the fruit fly. *Current Biology, 22,* 488–493.

Miller, G. (2003, January 4). "Go" pills for F-16 pilots get close look: Amphetamines prescribed for mission that killed Canadians. *San Francisco Chronicle.* Retrieved from http://www.sfgate.com/news/article/Go-pills-for-F-16-pilots-get-close-look-2687644.php

Miller, H. W., Naimi, T. S., Brewer, R. D., & Jones, S. E. (2007). Binge drinking and associated health risk behaviors among high school students. *Pediatrics, 119,* 76–85.

Miller, L. G., & Greenblatt, D. J. (1996). Benzodiazepine discontinuation syndromes: Clinical and experimental aspects. In C. R. Schuster & M. J. Kuhar (Eds.), *Pharmacological aspects of drug dependence: Toward an integrated neurobehavioral approach* (pp. 53–82). Berlin: Springer-Verlag.

Miller, N. S. (1991). *The pharmacology of alcohol and drugs of abuse/ addiction*. New York: Springer-Verlag.

Miller, P. M., Book, S. W., & Stewart, S. H. (2011). Medical treatment of alcohol dependence: A systematic review. *International Journal of Psychiatry Medicine, 42*, 227–266.

Minett, T. S., Thomas, A., Wilkinson, L. M., Daniel, S. L., Sanders, J., Richardson, J., et al. (2003). What happens when donepezil is suddenly withdrawn? An open label trial in dementia with Lewy bodies and Parkinson's disease with dementia. *International Journal of Geriatric Psychiatry, 18*, 988–993.

Minor, R. L., Jr., Scott, B. D., Brown, D. D., & Winniford, M. D. (1991). Cocaine-induced myocardial infarction in patients with normal coronary arteries. *Annals of Internal Medicine, 115*, 797–806.

Mitchell, J. M., O'Neil, J. P., Janabi, M., Marks, S. M., Jagust, W. J., & Fields, H. L. (2012). Alcohol consumption induces endogenous opioid release in the human orbitofrontal cortex and nucleus accumbens. *Science Translational Medicine, 4*, 116ra6.

Mittleman, R. E., & Wetli, C. V. (1984). Death caused by recreational cocaine use. An update. *Journal of the American Medical Association, 252*, 1889–1893.

Moeller, S. J., Maloney, T., Parvaz, M. A., Alia-Klein, N., Woicik, P. A., Telang, F., Wang, G.-J., Volkow, N. D., & Goldstein, R. Z. (2010). Impaired insight in cocaine addiction: Laboratory evidence and effects on cocaine-seeking behavior. *Brain, 133*, 1484–1493.

Mogey, G. A. (1953). Centenary of hypodermic injection. *British Medical Journal, 2*, 1180–1185.

Moore, S. C., Shepherd, J. P., Eden, S., & Sivarajasingam, V. (2007). The effect of rugby match outcome on spectator aggression and intention to drink alcohol. *Criminal Behavior and Mental Health, 17*, 118–127.

Moran-Gates, T., Grady, C., Shik Park, Y., Baldessarini, R. J., & Tarazi, F. I. (2007). Effects of risperidone on dopamine receptor subtypes in developing rat brain. *European Neuropsychopharmacology, 17*, 448–455.

Morean, M. E., Corbin, W. R., & Fromme, K. (2012). Age of first use and delay to first intoxication in relation to trajectories of heavy drinking and alcohol related problems during emerging adulthood. *Alcoholism: Clinical and Experimental Research, 36*, 1991–1999.

Moreno, M. A., Christakis, D. A., Egan, K. G., Brockman, L. N., & Becker, T. (2012). Associations between displayed alcohol references on Facebook and problem drinking among college students. *Archives of Pediatrics and Adolescent Medicine, 166*(2), 157–163.

Morey, R. A., Gold, A. L., LaBar, K. S., Beall, S. K., Brown, V. M., Haswell, C. C., et al. (2012). Amygdala volume changes in post-traumatic stress disorder in a large case-controlled veterans group. *Archives of General Psychiatry, 69*, 1169–1178.

Morgan, K. J., Stults, V. J., Zabik, M. E. (1982). Amount and dietary sources of caffeine and saccharin intake by individuals ages 5 to 18 years. *Regulatory Toxicology and Pharmacology, 2*(4), 296–307.

Motov, S. M., & Khan, A. N. (2008). Problems and barriers of pain management in the emergency department: Are we ever going to get better? *Journal of Pain Research, 2*, 5–11.

Moussavi, S., Chatterji, S., Verdes, E., Tandon, A., Patel, V., & Ustun, B. (2007). Depression, chronic disease, and decrements in health: Results from the World Health Surveys. *The Lancet, 370*, 851–858.

Muller, J. L. (1998). Love potions and the ointment of witches: Historical aspects of the nightshade alkaloids. *Journal of Toxicology Clinical Toxicology, 36*, 617–627.

Mundel, T., & Jones, D. A. (2006). Effect of transdermal nicotine administration on exercise endurance in men. *Experimental Physiology, 91*, 705–713.

Nakama, H., Chang, L., Fein, G., Shimotsu, R., Jiang, C. S., & Ernst, T. (2011). Methamphetamine users show greater than normal age-related cortical gray matter loss. *Addiction, 106*, 1474–1483.

Nam, H. W., McIver, S. R., Hinton, D. J., Thakkar, M. M., Sari, Y., Parkison, F. E., Haydon, P. G., & Choi, D. S. (2012). Adenosine and glutamate signaling in neuron-glial interactions: Implications in alcoholism and sleep disorders. *Alcoholism: Clinical and Experimental Research, 36*, 1117–1125.

Nash, R. A., & Takarangi, M. K. (2011). Reconstructing alcohol-induced memory blackouts. *Memory, 19*, 566–573.

National Highway Traffic Safety Administration (NHTSA). (2001). *Development of a standardized field sobriety test*. DOT HS 809 400. Washington, DC: Author. Retrieved from http://www.nhtsa.gov /people/injury/alcohol/sfst/contents.htm

National Highway Traffic Safety Administration (NHTSA). (2012). *Traffic safety facts: 2010 data*. DOT HS 811 606. Washington, DC: Author. Retrieved from http://www-nrd.nhtsa.dot.gov/Pubs /811606.pdf

National Institute on Alcohol Abuse and Alcoholism (NIAAA). (2004). Alcohol's damaging effects on the brain. *Alcohol Alert, 64*. Rockville, MD: Author. Retrieved from http://pubs.niaaa.nih.gov/publications /aa63/aa63.pdf

National Institute on Alcohol Abuse and Alcoholism (NIAAA). (2008). *Research findings on college drinking and the minimum drinking age*. Bethesda, MD: Author. Retrieved from http://pubs.niaaa.nih.gov /publications/CollegeDrinkingMLDA.pdf

National Institute on Alcohol Abuse and Alcoholism (NIAAA). (2012a). The genetics of alcoholism. *Alcohol Alert*, 84. Rockville, MD: Retrieved from http://www.niaaa.nih.gov

National Institute on Alcohol Abuse and Alcoholism (NIAAA). (2012b). *What is a standard drink?* Author. Retrieved from http://pubs.niaaa .nih.gov/publications/Practitioner/pocketguide/pocket_guide2.htm

National Institute on Alcohol Abuse and Alcoholism (NIAAA). (2002). *A call to action: Changing the culture of drinking at U.S. colleges*. Washington, DC: U.S. Department of Health and Human Services. Retrieved from http://www.collegedrinkingprevention.gov/media /TaskForceReport.pdf

National Institute on Drug Abuse (NIDA). (1993). *Acute cocaine intoxication: Current methods of treatment*. NIH Publication 93-3498. National Institutes of Health, U.S. Department of Health & Human Services. Retrieved from http://archives.drugabuse.gov/pdf/monographs /123.pdf

National Institute on Drug Abuse (NIDA). (2001). *Hallucinogens and dissociative drugs including LSD, PCP, ketamine, dextromethorphan (NIH Publication 01-4209)*. National Institutes of Health, U.S. Department of Health & Human Services. Retrieved from http://www .drugabuse.gov/sites/default/files/rrhalluc.pdf

National Institute on Drug Abuse (NIDA). (2009). *NIDA InfoFacts hallucinogens: LSD, peyote, psilocybin, and PCP*. National Institutes of Health, U.S. Department of Health & Human Services. Retrieved from http://www.drugabuse.gov/sites/default/files/hallucinogens09.pdf

National Institute on Drug Abuse (NIDA). (2010a). *Cocaine: Abuse and addiction*. NIH Publication 10-4166. National Institutes of Health, U.S. Department of Health & Human Services. Retrieved from http:// www.drugabuse.gov/sites/default/files/rrcocaine.pdf

National Institute on Drug Abuse (NIDA). (2010b). *NIDA info facts: Cocaine*. National Institutes of Health, U.S. Department of Health & Human Services. Retrieved from http://www.drugabuse.gov/sites /default/files/cocaine10.pdf

National Institute on Drug Abuse (NIDA). (2012a). *NIDA drugfacts: Is marijuana medicine?* National Institutes of Health, U.S. Department of Health & Human Services. Retrieved from http://www.drugabuse.gov/sites/default/files/drugfactsmedicalmarijuana.pdf

National Institute on Drug Abuse (NIDA). (2012b). *NIDA drugfacts: Marijuana.* National Institutes of Health, U.S. Department of Health & Human Services. Retrieved from http://www.drugabuse.gov/sites/default/files/marijuana_0.pdf

National Institute on Drug Abuse (NIDA). (2012c). *NIDA drugfacts: Spice (synthetic marijuana).* National Institutes of Health, U.S. Department of Health & Human Services. Retrieved from http://www.drugabuse.gov/sites/default/files/spice_1.pdf

National Institute on Drug Abuse (NIDA). (December 2011a). *Tobacco addiction: A research update from the National Institute on Drug Abuse.* Retrieved from http://www.drugabuse.gov/tib/tobacco.html

National Institute on Drug Abuse (NIDA). (2010c). *Drugs, brains, and behavior: The science of addiction.* National Institutes of Health, U.S. Department of Health and Human Services. NIH Publication No. 10-5605. Author. Retrieved from http://www.drugabuse.gov/publications/science-addiction

National Institute on Drug Abuse (NIDA). (2006). *Methamphetamine: Abuse and addiction.* National Institutes of Health, U.S. Department of Health and Human Services. NIH Publication No. 06-4210. Author. Retrieved from http://www.drugabuse.gov/sites/default/files/rrmetham.pdf

National Institute on Drug Abuse (NIDA). (2009). *Stimulant ADHD medications: Methylphenidate and amphetamines.* National Institutes of Health, U.S. Department of Health and Human Services. Author. Retrieved from http://www.drugabuse.gov/sites/default/files/adhd09.pdf

National Institute on Drug Abuse (NIDA). (2010d). *Methamphetamine.* National Institutes of Health, U.S. Department of Health and Human Services. Author. Retrieved from http://www.drugabuse.gov/sites/default/files/methamphetamine10.pdf

National Institute on Drug Abuse (NIDA). (2011b). *Khat.* National Institutes of Health, U.S. Department of Health and Human Services. Author. Retrieved from http://www.drugabuse.gov/sites/default/files/khat.pdf

Nehlig, A. (1999). Are we dependent upon coffee and caffeine? A review on human and animal data. *Neuroscience and Biobehavioral Reviews, 23,* 563–576.

Nelson, J. C. (2006). The STAR*D study: A four-course meal that leaves us wanting more. *American Journal of Psychiatry, 163,* 1864–1866.

Nelson, R.A., Boyd, S. J., Ziegelstein, R. C., Herning, R., Cadet, J. L., Henningfield, J. E., Schuster, C. R., Contoreggi, C., & Gorelick, D. A. (2006). Effect of rate of administration on subjective and physiological effects of intravenous cocaine in humans. *Drug and Alcohol Dependence, 82,* 19–24.

Nemeroff, C. B., & Schatzberg, A. F. (1998). Pharmacological treatment in unipolar depression. In P. E. Nathan & J. M. Gorman (Eds.), *A guide to treatments that work* (pp. 212–225). New York: Oxford University Press.

Nencini, P., & Ahmed, A. M. (1989). Khat consumption: A pharmacological review. *Drug and Alcohol Dependence, 23,* 19–29.

Nestler, E. J. (2009). Cellular and molecular mechanisms of drug addiction. In D. S. Charney & E. J. Nestler (Eds.), *Neurobiology of mental illness* (3rd ed.). New York: Oxford University Press.

Neumeister, A., Normandin, M. D., Murrough, J. W., Henry, S., Bailey, C. R., Luckenbaugh, D. A., et al. (2012). Positron emission tomography shows elevated cannabinoid CB1 receptor binding in men with alcohol dependence. *Alcoholism: Clinical and Experimental Research, 36,* 2104–2109.

Newton, T. F., De La Garza, R., Kalechstein, A. D., & Nestor, L. (2005). Cocaine and methamphetamine produce different patterns of subjective and cardiovascular effects. *Pharmacology, Biochemistry & Behavior, 82,* 90–97.

Nichols, D. E. (2004). Hallucinogens. *Pharmacology & Therapeutics, 101,* 131–181.

Norbury, R., Taylor, M. J., Selvaraj, S., Murphy, S. E., Harmer, C. J., & Cowen, P. J. (2009). Short-term antidepressant treatment modulates amygdala response to happy faces. *Psychopharmacology, 206,* 197–204.

Novak, S. P., & Kral, A. H. (2011). Comparing injection and non-injection routes of administration for heroin, methamphetamine, and cocaine users in the United States. *Journal of Addictive Diseases, 30,* 248–257.

Nunberg, H., Kilmer, B., Pacula, R. L., & Burgdorf, J. R. (2011). An analysis of applicants presenting to a medical marijuana specialty practice in California. *Journal of Drug Policy Analysis, 4,* 1–16.

Nutt, D., King, L. A., Saulsbury, W., & Blakemore, C. (2007). Development of a rational scale to assess the harm of drugs and potential misuse. *The Lancet, 369,* 1047–1053.

Nuutinen, H., Lindros, K., Hekali, P., & Salaspuro, M. (1985). Elevated blood acetate as indicator of fast ethanol elimination in chronic alcoholics. *Alcohol, 2,* 623–626.

O'Brien, C. P. (2001). Drug addiction and drug abuse. In J. G. Hardman, L. E. Limbird, & A. G. Gilman (Eds.), *The pharmacological basis of therapeutics* (10th ed.) (pp. 621–642). New York: McGraw-Hill.

O'Brien, M. C., McCoy, T. P., Rhodes, S. D., Wagoner, A., & Wolfson, M. (2008). Caffeinated cocktails: Energy drink consumption, high-risk drinking, and alcohol-related consequences among college students. *Academic Emergency Medicine, 15,* 453–460.

O'Neill, J. (April 28, 2012). Hospital seeing more babies born exposed to prescription drugs. *CNN.* Retrieved from http://www.cnn.com/2012/04/28/health/drug-babies/index.html

Office of National Drug Control Policy. (2012). *Methamphetamine.* Author. Retrieved from http://www.whitehouse.gov/ondcp/meth-intro

Ogawa, H., & Ueki, N. (2007). Clinical importance of caffeine dependence and abuse. *Psychiatry and Clinical Neuroscience, 61,* 263–268.

Ogborne, A. C. (1989). Some limitations of Alcoholics Anonymous. *Recent Developments in Alcoholism, 7,* 55–65.

Olds, J., & Milner, P. (1954). Positive reinforcement produced by electrical stimulation of septal area and other regions of rat brains. *Journal of Comparative and Physiological Psychology, 47,* 419–427.

Oliveto, A. H., McCance-Katz, E., Singha, A., Hameedi, F., & Kosten, T. R. (1998). Effects of d-amphetamine and caffeine in humans under a cocaine discrimination procedure. *Behavioral Pharmacology, 9,* 207–217.

Oreja-Guevara, C. (2012). Clinical efficacy and effectiveness of Sativex, a combined cannabinoid medicine, in multiple sclerosis-related spasticity. *Expert Review of Neurotherapeutics, 12* (4 Suppl), 3–8.

Oscar-Berman, M., & Schendan, H. E. (2000). Asymmetries of brain function in alcoholism: Relationship to aging. In L. T. Connor & L. K. Obler (Eds.), *Neurobehavior of language and cognition: Studies of normal aging and brain damage* (pp. 213–240). New York: Kluwer Academic.

Osler, M. (2012, November 13). U.S. should honor states' new pot laws. *CNN.* Retrieved from http://www.cnn.com/2012/11/13/opinion/osler-marijuana-federal-law/index.html

Parada, M., Corral, M., Mota, N., Crego, A., Rodrigeuz Holguin, S., & Cadaveira, F. (2012). Executive functioning and alcohol binge drinking in university students. *Addictive Behaviors, 37*, 167–172.

Parri, H. R., Hernandez, C. M., & Dineley, K. T. (2011). Research update: Alpha7 nicotinic acetylcholine receptor mechanisms in Alzheimer's disease. *Biochemistry and Pharmacology, 82*, 931–942.

Parrott, A. C. (2012). MDMA and temperature: A review of the thermal effects of "ecstasy" in humans. *Drug and Alcohol Dependence, 121*, 1–9.

Parsons, A. C., Shraim, M., Inglis, J., Aveyard, P., & Hajek, P. (2009). Interventions for preventing weight gain after smoking cessation. *Cochrane Database of Systematic Reviews, 21*, CD006219.

Paul, I. M., Downs, D. S., Schaefer, E. W., Beiler, J. S., & Weisman, C. S. (2013). Postpartum anxiety and maternal-infant health outcomes. *Pediatrics, 131*, e1218–e1224.

Paule, M. G., Allen, R. R., Bailey, J. R., Scallet, A. C., Ali, S. F., Brown, R. M., & Slikker, W., Jr. (1992). Chronic marijuana smoke exposure in the rhesus monkey. II: Effects on progressive ratio and conditioned position responding. *Journal of Pharmacology and Experimental Therapeutics, 260*, 210–222.

Pava, M. J., & Woodward, J. J. (2012). A review of the interactions between alcohol and the endocannabinoid system: Implications for alcohol dependence and future directions for research. *Alcohol, 46*, 185–204.

Pells, E., Dunbar, G., Logothetis, P., & Raia, J. (2012, August 24). Lance Armstrong banned for life, career vacated. *Sports Illustrated*. Retrieved from http://sportsillustrated.cnn.com/2012/cycling/wires/08/24/2080 .ap.cyc.armstrong.doping.9th.ld.writethru.2279/index.html

Pendergrast, M. (1999). *Uncommon grounds: The history of coffee and how it transformed our world*. New York: Basic Books.

Pendergrast, M. (2000). *For god, country and Coca-Cola* (2nd ed.). New York: Perseus.

Pennay, A. E., & Lee, N. K. (2011). Putting the call out for more research: The poor evidence base for treating methamphetamine withdrawal. *Drug and Alcohol Review, 30*, 216–222.

Penning, R., McKinney, A., & Verster, J. C. (2012). Alcohol hangover symptoms and their contribution to the overall hangover severity. *Alcohol and Alcoholism, 47*, 248–252.

PepsiCo Inc. (1981). The physical or technical effect of caffeine in cola beverages, vol. III. Appendix XII of comments of the National Soft Drink Association submitted to the Department of Health and Human Services Food and Drug Administration in response to the proposal to delete caffeine in cola-type beverages from the list of substances generally recognized as safe and to issue an interim food additive regulation governing its future use. July 29, FDA docket No. 80N-0418.

Perkins, K. A., Gerlach, D., Broge, M., Fonte, C., & Wilson, A. (2001). Reinforcing effects of nicotine as a function of smoking status. *Experimental and Clinical Psychopharmacology, 9*, 243–250.

Perkins, K. A., Jetton, C., & Keenan, J. (2003). Common factors across acute subjective effects of nicotine. *Nicotine Tobacco Research, 5*, 869–875.

Persad, L. A. B. (2011). Energy drinks and the neurophysiological impact of caffeine. *Frontiers in Neuroscience, 5*, 1–8.

Pert, C. B. (1997). *Molecules of emotion: The science behind mind-body medicine*. New York: Touchstone.

Pert, C. B., & Snyder, S. H. (1973). Opiate receptor: Demonstration in nervous tissue. *Science, 179*, 1011–1014.

Pertwee, R. G. (2005). Pharmacological actions of cannabinoids. *Handbook of Experimental Pharmacology, 168*, 1–51.

Pertwee, R. G. (2012). Targeting the endocannabinoid system with cannabinoid receptor agonists: Pharmacological strategies and therapeutic possibilities. *Philosophical Transactions of the Royal Society of London*. Series B, *Biological Sciences, 367*, 3353–3363.

Petry, N. M., Peirce, J. M., Stitzer, M. L., Blaine, J., Roll, J. M., Cohen, A., et al. (2005). Effect of prize-based incentives on outcomes in stimulant abusers in outpatient psychosocial treatment programs: A national drug abuse treatment clinical trials network study. *Archives of General Psychiatry, 62*, 1148–1156.

Pettit, M. L., & DeBarr, K. A. (2011). Perceived stress, energy drink consumption, and academic performance among college students. *Journal of American College Health, 59*(5), 335–341.

Pfefferbaum, A., Sullivan, E. V., Mathalon, D. H., & Lim, K. O. (1997). Frontal lobe volume loss observed with magnetic resonance imaging in older chronic alcoholics. *Alcoholism: Clinical and Experimental Research, 21*, 521–529.

Pfefferbaum, A., Zahr, N. M., Mayer, D., Vinco, S., Orduna, J., Rohlfing, T., & Sullivan, E. V. (2008). Ventricular expansion of wild-type Wistar rats after alcohol exposure by vapor chamber. *Alcoholism: Clinical and Experimental Research, 32*, 1459–1467.

Phillips, D. P., & Brewer, K. M. (2011). The relationship between serious injury and blood alcohol concentration (BAC) in fatal motor vehicle accidents: BAC = 0.01% is associated with significantly more dangerous accidents than BAC = 0.00%. *Addiction, 106*, 1614–1622.

Pikaar, N. A., Wedel, M., & Hermus, R. J. (1988). Influence of several factors on blood alcohol concentrations after drinking alcohol. *Alcohol and Alcoholism, 23*, 289–297.

Piper, T. M., Rudenstine, S., Stancliff, S., Sherman, S., Nandi, V., Clear, A., & Galea, S. (2007). Overdose prevention for injection drug users: Lessons learned from naloxone training and distribution programs in New York City. *Harm Reduction Journal, 4*, 3.

Pliszka, S. R., Matthews, T. L., Braslow, K. J., & Watson, M. A. (2006). Comparative effects of methylphenidate and mixed salts amphetamine on height and weight in children with attention-deficit/hyperactivity disorder. *Journal of American Academy of Child and Adolescent Psychiatry, 45*, 520–526.

Pollanen, M. S., Chiasson, D. A., Cairns, J. T., & Young, J. G. (1998). Unexpected death related to restraint for excited delirium: A retrospective study of deaths in police custody and in the community. *Canadian Medical Association Journal, 158*, 1603–1607.

Polston, J. E., Cunningham, C. S., Rodvelt, K. R., & Miller, K. D. (2006). Lobeline augments and inhibits cocaine-induced hyperactivity in rats. *Life Sciences, 79*, 981–990.

Pomara, C., Cassano, T., D'Errico, S., Bello, S., Romano, A. D., Altomare, E., & Serviddio, G. (2012). Data available on the extent of cocaine use and dependence: Biochemistry, pharmacologic effects and global burden of disease of cocaine abusers. *Current Medicinal Chemistry, 19*, 5647–5657.

Porath, A. J., & Fried, P. A. (2005). Effects of prenatal cigarette and marijuana exposure on drug use among offspring. *Neurotoxicology and Teratology, 27*, 267–277.

Porter, R. S. (2011). *The Merck manual* (19th ed.). Rahway, NJ: Merck, Sharp & Dohme.

Post, R. M. (2012). Acquired lithium resistance revisited: Discontinuation-induced refractoriness versus tolerance. *Journal of Affective Disorders, 140*, 6–13.

Poulos, C. X., & Cappell, H. (1991). Homeostatic theory of drug tolerance: A general model of physiological adaptation. *Psychological Review, 98*, 390–408.

Powers, R. L., Marks, D. J., Miller, C. J., Newcorn, J. H., & Halperin, J. M. (2008). Stimulant treatment in children with attention-deficit/hyperactivity disorder moderates adolescent academic outcome. *Journal of Child and Adolescent Psychopharmacology, 18,* 449–459.

Prapavessis, H., Cameron, L., Baldi, J. C., Robinson, S., Borrie, K., Harper, T., & Grove, J. R. (2007). The effects of exercise and nicotine replacement therapy on smoking rates in women. *Addictive Behaviors, 32,* 1416–1432.

Preller, K. H., Ingold, N., Hulka, L. M., Vonmoos, M., Jenni, D., Baumgartner, M. R., Vollenweider, F. X., & Quednow, B. B. (2013). Increased sensorimotor gating in recreational and dependent cocaine users is modulated by craving and attention-deficit/hyperactivity disorder symptoms. *Biological Psychiatry, 73,* 225–234.

Prendergrast, M. (1999). *Uncommon grounds: The history of coffee and how it transformed our world.* New York: Basic Books.

Prendergrast, M. (2009). Coffee: Second to oil. *Tea & Coffee Trade Journal, 181*(4), 38–41.

Prince, M., Bryce, R., Albanese, E., Wimo, A., Robeiro, W., & Ferri, C. P. (2013). The global prevalence of dementia: A systematic review and meta-analysis. *Alzheimers and Dementia, 9,* 63–75.

Pristach, C. A., Smith, C. M., & Whitney, R. B. (1983). Alcohol withdrawal syndromes—prediction from detailed medical and drinking histories. *Drug and Alcohol Dependence, 11,* 177–199.

Pryce, G., & Baker, D. (2012). Potential control of multiple sclerosis by cannabis and the endocannabinoid system. *CNS Neurological Disorders and Drug Targets, 11,* 624–641.

Purves, D., Augustine, G. J., Fitzpatrick, D., & Hall, W. C. (2011). *Neuroscience* (5th ed.). Sunderland, MA: Sinauer.

Ramaekers, J. G., Berghaus, G., van Laar, M., & Drummer, O. H. (2004). Dose related risk of motor vehicle crashes after cannabis use. *Drug and Alcohol Dependence, 73,* 109–119.

Ranganathan, M., Carbuto, M., Braley, G., Elander, J., Perry, E., Pittman, B., et al. (2012). Naltrexone does not attenuate the effects of intravenous delta9-tetrahydrocannabinol in health humans. *International Journal of Neuropsychopharmacology, 15,* 1251–1264.

Rasmussen, N. (2008). *On speed: The many lives of amphetamine.* New York: New York University Press.

Rau, T. F., Kothiwal, A. S., Rova, A. R., Brooks, D. M., & Poulsen, D. J. (2012). Treatment with low-dose methamphetamine improves behavioral and cognitive function after severe traumatic brain injury. *Journal of Trauma and Acute Care Surgery, 73,* S165–S172.

Rawson, R. A., Marinelli-Casey, P., Anglin, M. D., Dickow, A., Frazier, Y., Gallagher, C. et al. (2003). A multi-site comparison of psychosocial approaches for the treatment of methamphetamine dependence. *Addiction, 99,* 708–717.

Regan, A. K., Dube, S. R., & Arrazola, R. (2012). Smokeless and flavored tobacco products in the U.S. 2009 styles survey results. *American Journal of Preventative Medicine, 42,* 29–36.

Reid, M. S., Flammino, F., Howard, B., Nilsen, D., & Prichep, L. S. (2006). Topographic imaging of quantitative EEG in response to smoked cocaine self-administration in humans. *Neuropsychopharmacology, 31,* 872–884.

Reiff, J., & Jost, W. H. (2011). Drug-induced impulse control disorders in Parkinson's disease. *Journal of Neurology, 258*(Suppl 2), S323–S327.

Reinarman, C., Nunberg, H., Lanthier, F., & Heddleston T. (2011). Who are medical marijuana patients? Population characteristics from nine California assessment clinics. *Journal of Psychoactive Drugs, 43,* 128–135.

Reissig, C. J., Strain, E. C., & Griffiths, R. R. (2009). Caffeinated energy drinks—A growing problem. *Drug and Alcohol Dependence, 99,* 1–10.

Renner, U. D., Oertel, R., & Kirch, W. (2005). Pharmacokinetics and pharmacodynamics in clinical use of scopolamine. *Therapeutic Drug Monitoring, 27,* 655–665.

Rezkalla, S. H., & Kloner, R. A. (2007). Cocaine-induced myocardial infarction. *Clinical Medicine & Research, 5,* 172–176.

Rhodes, T., Briggs, D., Kimber, J., Jones, S., & Holloway, G. (2007). Crack-heroin speedball injection and its implications for vein care: Qualitative study. *Addiction, 102,* 1782–1790.

Rigotti, N. A., Lee, J. E., & Wechsler, H. (2000). U.S. college students' use of tobacco products: Results of a national survey. *Journal of the American Medical Association, 284,* 699–705.

Rinaldi, R. C., Steindler, E. M., Wilford, B. B., & Goodwin, D. (1988). Clarification and standardization of substance abuse terminology. *Journal of the American Medical Association, 259,* 555–557.

Ringmets, I., Tuusov, J., Lang, K., Vali, M., Parna, K., Tonisson, M., Helander, A., McKee, M., & Leon, D. A. (2012). Alcohol and premature death in Estonian men: A study of forensic autopsies using novel biomarkers and proxy informants. *BMC Public Health, 12,* 146.

Riper, H., van Straten, A., Keuken, M., Smit, F., Schippers, G., & Cuijpers, P. (2009). Curbing problem drinking with personalized-feedback interventions: A meta-analysis. *American Journal of Preventative Medicine, 36,* 247–255.

Risinger, F. O., & Brown, M. M. (1996). Genetic differences in nicotine-induced conditioned taste aversion. *Life Sciences, 58,* 223–229.

Rivera, M. A., Aufderheide, A. C., Cartmell, L. W., Torres, C. M., & Langsjoen, E. (2005). Antiquity of coca-leaf chewing in the south central Andes: A 3,000 year archeological record of coca-leaf chewing from northern Chile. *Journal of Psychoactive Drugs, 37,* 455–458.

Roberts, M. T., & Henderson, R. S. (1981). Pituitary fossa injection with alcohol for widespread cancer pain. *New Zealand Medical Journal, 93,* 1–3.

Robins, L. N. (1974). *The Vietnam drug user returns.* Special Action Office from Drug Abuse Prevention Monograph, Series A, No. 2, Contract No. HSM-42-72-75. Washington, DC: Special Action Office from Drug Abuse Prevention. Retrieved from http://prhome.defense.gov/RFM/READINESS/DDRP/docs/35%20Final%20Report.%20The%20Vietnam%20drug%20user%20returns.pdf

Robinson, T. E., & Berridge, K. C. (1993). The neural basis of drug craving: An incentive-sensitization theory of addiction. *Brain Research Reviews, 18,* 247–291.

Robinson, T. E., & Berridge, K. C. (2003). Addiction. *Annual Review of Psychology, 54,* 25–53.

Rodgman, A., & Perfetti, T. A. (2009). *The chemical components of tobacco and tobacco smoke.* Boca Raton, FL: CRC Press.

Rog, D. J., Nurmikko, T. J., Friede, T., & Young, C. A. (2005). Randomized, controlled trial of cannabis-based medicine in central pain in multiple sclerosis. *Neurology, 65,* 812–819.

Rogers, S. L., & Friedhoff, L. T. (1998). Pharmacokinetic and pharmacodynamics profile of donepezil HCl following single oral doses. *British Journal of Pharmacology, 46*(S1), 1–6.

Rose, J. E. (1991). Transdermal nicotine and nasal nicotine administration as smoking cessation treatments. In J. A. Cocores (Ed.), *The clinical management of nicotine dependence.* New York: Springer-Verlag.

Rose, M. E., & Grant, J. E. (2010). Alcohol-induced blackout. Phenomenology, biological basis, and gender differences. *Journal of Addictive Medicine, 4,* 61–73.

Rosenbaum, J. F., & Zajecka, J. (1997). Clinical management of antidepressant discontinuation. *Journal of Clinical Psychiatry, 58* Suppl 7, 37–40.

Rosenheck, R. A., Leslie, D. L., Sindelar, J., Miller, E. A., Lin, H., Stroup, T. S., et al. (2006). Cost-effectiveness of second generation antipsychotics and perphenazine in a randomized trial of treatment for chronic schizophrenia. *American Journal of Psychiatry, 163,* 2080–2089.

Ross, E. M., & Kenakin, T. P. (2001). Pharmacodynamics: Mechanisms of drug action and the relationship between drug concentration and effect. In L. S. Goodman, J. G. Hardman, L. L. Limbird, & A. G. Gilman (Eds.), *Goodman and Gilman's The pharmacological basis of therapeutics* (10th ed., pp. 3–30). New York: McGraw-Hill.

Ross, M. W., Hwang, L. Y., Zack, C., Bull, L., & Williams, M. L. (2002). Sexual risk behaviours and STIs in drug abuse treatment populations whose drug of choice is crack cocaine. *International Journal of STD AIDS, 13,* 769–774.

Rubin, A. J. (2012, November 20). Opium cultivation rose this year in Afghanistan, U.N. survey shows. *The New York Times.* Retrieved from http://www.nytimes.com/2012/11/21/world/asia/afghan-opium-cultivation-rose-in-2012-un-says.html?_r=0

Rubin, A. J., & Rosenberg, M. (2012, May 26). U.S. efforts fail to curtail trade in Afghan opium. *The New York Times.* Retrieved from http://www.nytimes.com/2012/05/27/world/asia/drug-traffic-remains-as-us-nears-afghanistan-exit.html?pagewanted=all

Rubio, K., Halari, R., Mohammad, A. M., Taylor, E., & Brammer, M. (2011). Methylphenidate normalizes frontocingulate underactivation during error processing in attention-deficit/hyperactivity disorder. *Biological Psychiatry, 70,* 255–262.

Rush, C. R., & Griffiths, R. R. (1996). Zolpidem, triazolam, and temazepam: Behavioral and subject-rated effects in normal volunteers. *Journal of Clinical Psychopharmacology, 16,* 146–157.

Rush, C. R., & Griffiths, R. R. (1997). Acute participant-rated and behavioral effects of alprazolam and buspirone, alone and in combination with ethanol in normal volunteers. *Experimental and Clinical Psychopharmacology, 5,* 28–38.

Rush, C. R., & Stoops, W. W. (2012). Agonist replacement therapy for cocaine dependence: A translational review. *Future Medicinal Chemistry, 4,* 245–265.

Rush, C. R., Essman, W. D., Simpson, C. A., & Baker, R. W. (2001). Reinforcing and subject-rated effects of methylphenidate and d-amphetamine in non-drug-abusing humans. *Journal of Clinical Psychopharmacology, 21,* 273–286.

Ryder, D., Walker, N., & Salmon, A. (2006). *Drug use and drug-related harm: A delicate balance* (2nd ed.). East Hawthorn, Australia: IP Communications.

Sacks, O. (2012). *Hallucinations.* New York: Alfred A. Knopf.

Sagvolden, T., & Xu, T. (2008). l-amphetamine improves poor sustained attention while d-amphetamine reduces overactivity and impulsiveness as well as improves sustained attention in an animal model of attention-deficit/hyperactivity disorder (ADHD). *Behavioral and Brain Functions, 4,*3.

Saks, E. R. (2007). *The center cannot hold: My journey through madness.* New York: Hyperion.

Saks, E. R. (2013, January 25). Successful and schizophrenic. *The New York Times.* Retrieved from http://www.nytimes.com/2013/01/27/opinion/sunday/schizophrenic-not-stupid.html

Sakurai, H., Bies, R. R., Stroup, S. T., Keefe, R. S., Rajji, T. K., Suzuki, T., et al. (2013). Dopamine D_2 receptor occupancy and cognition in schizophrenia: Analysis of the CATIE data. *Schizophrenia Bulletin, 39,* 564–574.

Salgado, M. V., Perez-Stable, E. J., Primack, B. A., Kaplan, C. P., Mejia, R. M., Gregorich, S. E., & Alderete, E. (2012). Association of media literacy with cigarette smoking among youth in Jujuy, Argentina. *Nicotine Tobacco Research, 14,* 516–521.

Salter, J. (2012, October 11). Mexican cartels fill demand for meth in USA. *USA Today.* Retrieved from http://www.usatoday.com/story/news/nation/2012/10/11/mexico-cartels-meth/1626383/#

Samaha, A. N., & Robinson, T. E. (2002). The rate of intravenous cocaine administration determines susceptibility to sensitization. *Journal of Neuroscience, 22,* 3244–3250.

Samaha, A. N., & Robinson, T. E. (2005). Why does the rapid delivery of drugs to the brain promote addiction? *Trends in Pharmacological Science, 26,* 82–87.

Samuel, H. (2010, March 11). French bread spiked with LSD in CIA experiment. *The London Telegraph.* Retrieved from http://www.telegraph.co.uk/news/worldnews/europe/france/7415082/French-bread-spiked-with-LSD-in-CIA-experiment.html

Sanders, L. (2013, February 23). No new meds. *Science News, 183*(4), 26.

Santhakumar, V., Wallner, M., & Otis, T. S. (2007). Ethanol acts directly on extrasynaptic subtypes of $GABA_A$ receptors to increase tonic inhibition. *Alcohol, 41,* 211–221.

Santoro, D., Bellinghieri, G., & Savica, V. (2011). Development of the concept of pain in history. *Journal of Nephrology, 24* Suppl 17, S133–S136.

Saudan, C., Baume, B., Robinson, N., Avois, L., Mangin, P., & Saugy, M. (2006). Testosterone and doping control. *British Journal of Sports Medicine, 40,* i21–i24.

Sawyer, D. A., Julia, H. L., & Turin, A. C. (1982). Caffeine and human behavior: Arousal, anxiety, and performance effects. *Journal of Behavioral Medicine, 5,* 415–439.

Scalzo, F. M., & Spear, L. P. (1985). Chronic haloperidol during development attenuates dopamine autoreceptor function in striatal and mesolimbic brain regions of young and older adult rats. *Psychopharmacology, 85,* 271–276.

Schachar, R., & Tannock, R. (1993). Childhood hyperactivity and psychostimulants: A review of extended treatment studies. *Journal of Child and Adolescent Psychopharmacology, 3,* 81–97.

Schachter, S. (1973). Nesbitt's paradox. In W. L. Dunn (Ed.), *Smoking behavior: Motives and incentives* (pp. 147–155). Washington, DC: Winston.

Schechter, M. D. (1989). Temporal parameters of cathinone, amphetamine and cocaine. *Pharmacology, Biochemistry & Behavior, 34,* 289–292.

Schmidt, H. D., & Pierce, R. C. (2010). Cocaine-induced neuroadaptations in glutamate transmission: Potential therapeutic targets for craving and addiction. *Annals of the New York Academy of Sciences, 1187,* 35–75.

Schneeweiss, S., Patrick, A. R., Solomon, D. H., Dormuth, C. R., Miller, M., Mehta, J., Lee, J. C., & Wang, P. S. (2010). Comparative safety of antidepressant agents for children and adolescents regarding suicidal acts. *Pediatrics, 125,* 876–888.

Schreiber, S., Rigai, T., Katz, Y., & Pick, C. G. (2002). The antinociceptive effect of mitrazapine in mice is mediated through serotonergic, noradrenergic and opioid mechanisms. *Brain Research Bulletin, 58,* 601–605.

Schwartz, A. (2012, June 9). Risky rise of the good-grade pill. *The New York Times.* Retrieved from http://www.nytimes.com/2012/06/10

/education/seeking-academic-edge-teenagers-abuse-stimulants.html?pagewanted=all&_r=0

Schwartz, R. H., & Beveridge, R. A. (1994). Marijuana as an antiemetic drug: How useful is it today? Opinions from clinical oncologists. *Journal of Addictive Disorders, 13*, 53–65.

Schwartz, R. H., Estroff, T., Fairbanks, D. N., & Hoffmann, N. G. (1989). Nasal symptoms associated with cocaine abuse during adolescence. *Archives of Otolaryngology Head and Neck Surgery, 115*, 63–64.

Schwartz, R. H., Voth, E. A., & Sheridan, M. J. (1997). Marijuana to prevent nausea and vomiting in cancer patients: A survey of clinical oncologists. *Southern Medical Journal, 90*, 167–172.

Scott, I. (1998). Heroin: A hundred-year habit. *History Today, 48*(6).

Scott-Sheldon, L. A., Terry, D. L., Carey, K. B., Garey, L., & Carey, M. P. (2012). Efficacy of expectancy challenge interventions to reduce college student drinking: A meta-analytic review. *Psychology of Addictive Behaviors, 26*, 393–405.

Seeman, P., Schwarz, J., Chen, J. F., Szechtman, H., Perreault, M., McKnight, G. S., et al. (2006). Psychosis pathways converge via D2high dopamine receptors. *Synapse, 60*, 319–346.

Seifert, S. M., Schaechter, J. L., Hershorin, E. R., & Lipshultz, S. E. (2011). Health effects of energy drinks on children, adolescents, and young adults. *Pediatrics, 127*(3), 511–528. doi:10.1542/peds.2009-3592

Selkoe, D. J. (2012). Preventing Alzheimer's disease. *Science Magazine, 337*, 1488–1492.

Sellings, L. H., Baharnouri, G., McQuade, L. E., & Clarke, P. B. (2008). Rewarding and aversive effects of nicotine are segregated within the nucleus accumbens. *European Journal of Neuroscience, 28*, 342–352.

Selvaraj, S., Hoshi, R., Bhagwagar, Z., Murthy, N. V., Vinz, R., Cowen, P., Curran, H. V., & Grasby, P. (2009). Brain serotonin transporter binding in former users of MDMA (ecstasy). *British Journal of Psychiatry, 194*, 355–359.

Semple, S., Apsley, A., Galea, K. S., MacCalman, L., Friel, B., & Snelgrove, V. (2012). Secondhand smoke in cars: Assessing children's potential exposure during typical journey conditions. *Tobacco Control, 21*, 578–583.

Serjeant, J., & Dobuzinskis, A. (2011, April 13). Catherine Zeta-Jones treated for bipolar disorder. *Reuters*. Retrieved from http://www.reuters.com/article/2011/04/13/us-zetajones-idUSTRE73C6BI20110413.

Shaheen, P. E., Walsh, D., Lasheen, W., Davis, M. P., & Lagman, R. L. (2009). Opioid equianalgesic tables: Are they all equally dangerous? *Journal of Pain and Symptom Management, 38*, 409–417.

Shalaby, I. A., & Spear, L. P. (1980). Chronic administration of haloperidol during development: Later psychopharmacological responses to apomorphine and arecoline. *Pharmacology, Biochemistry, & Behavior, 13*, 685–690.

Sharma, A., & Shaw, S. R. (2012). Efficacy of risperidone in managing maladaptive behaviors for children with autism spectrum disorder: A meta-analysis. *Journal of Pediatric Health Care, 26*, 291–299.

Sheline, Y. I., Barch, D. M., Donnelly, J. M., Ollinger, J. M., Snyder, A. Z., & Mintun, M. A. (2001). Increased amygdala response to masked emotional faces in depressed subjects resolves with antidepressant treatment: An fMRI study. *Biological Psychiatry, 50*, 651–658.

Shen, X. Y., Kosten, T. A., Lopez, A. Y., Kinsey, B. M., Kosten, T. R., & Orson, F. M. (2013). A vaccine against methamphetamine attenuates its behavioral effects in mice. *Drug and Alcohol Dependence, 129*, 41–48.

Sherwood, N. (1995). Effects of cigarette smoking on performance in a simulated driving task. *Neuropsychobiology, 32*, 161–165.

Shimada, A., Yamaguchi, K., & Yanagita, T. (1996). Neurochemical analysis of the psychotoxicity of methamphetamine and cocaine by microdialysis in the rat brain. *Annals of the New York Academy of Sciences, 801*, 361–370.

Siegal, H. A., Falck, R. S., Wang, J., Carlson, R. G., & Massimino, K. P. (2006). Emergency department utilization by crack-cocaine smokers in Dayton, Ohio. *American Journal of Drug and Alcohol Abuse, 32*, 55–68.

Siegel, S. (1988). State dependent learning and morphine tolerance. *Behavioral Neuroscience, 102*, 228–232.

Siegel, S., Baptista, M. A., Kim, J. A., McDonald, R. V., & Weise-Kelly, L. (2000). Pavlovian psychopharmacology: The associative basis of tolerance. *Experimental and Clinical Psychopharmacology, 8*, 276–293.

Siegel, S., Hinson, R. E., & Krank, M. D. (1978). The role of predrug signals in morphine analgesic tolerance: Support for a Pavlovian conditioning model of tolerance. *Journal of Experimental Psychology: Animal Behavior Processes, 4*, 188–196.

Siegel, S., Hinson, R. E., Krank, M. D., & McCully, J. (1982). Heroin "overdose" death: Contribution of drug-associated environmental cues. *Science, 216*, 436–437.

Sigel, E., & Steinmann, M. E. (2012). Structure, function, and modulation of GABA$_{(A)}$ receptors. *Journal of Biological Chemistry, 287*, 40224–40231.

Silagy, C., Mant, D., Fowler, G., & Lodge, M. (1994). Meta-analysis of efficacy of nicotine replacement therapies in smoking cessation. *Lancet, 343*, 139–142.

Simmler, L. D., Buser, T. A., Donzelli, M., Schramm, Y., Dieu, L. H., Huwyler, J., Chaboz, S., Hoener, M. C., & Liechti, M. E. (2013). Pharmacological characterization of designer cathinones in vitro. *British Journal of Pharmacology, 168*, 458–470.

Simon, P., Dupuis, R., & Costentin, J. (1994). Thigmotaxis as an index of anxiety in mice: Influence of dopaminergic transmissions. *Behavioral Brain Research, 61*, 59–64.

Simon, M., & Mosher, J. (2007). *Alcohol, energy drinks, and youth: A dangerous mix*. San Rafael, CA: Marin Institute.

Simons-Morton, B., Pickett, W., Boyce, W., ter Bogt, T. F., & Vollebergh, W. (2010). Cross-national comparison of adolescent drinking and cannabis use in the United States, Canada, and the Netherlands. *International Journal of Drug Policy, 21*, 64–69.

Singer, L. T., Garber, R., & Kliegman, R. (1991). Neurobehavioral sequelae of fetal cocaine exposure. *Journal of Pediatrics, 119*, 667–672.

Smith, H. W. 3rd, Liberman, H. A., Brody, S. L., Battey, L. L., Donohue, B. C., & Morris, D. C. (1987). Acute myocardial infarction temporally related to cocaine use. Clinical, angiographic, and pathophysiologic observations. *Annals of Internal Medicine, 107*, 13–18.

Smith, M., Garner, D., & Niemann, J. T. (1991). Pharmacologic interventions after an LD50 cocaine insult in a chronically instrumented rat model: Are beta-blockers contraindicated? *Annals of Emergency Medicine, 20*, 768–771.

Snyder, P. J. (2001). Androgens. In J. G. Hardman, L. E. Limbird, & A. G. Gilman (Eds.), *The pharmacological basis of therapeutics* (10th ed.) (pp. 1635–1648). New York: McGraw-Hill.

Snyder, S. H. (1989). *Brainstorming: The science and politics of opiates research*. Cambridge, MA: Harvard University Press.

Soar, K., Mason, C., Potton, A., & Dawkins, L. (2012). Neuropsychological effects associated with recreational cocaine use. *Psychopharmacology, 222*, 633–634.

Sobell, L. C., & Sobell, M. B. (1993). *Problem drinkers: Guided self-change treatment.* New York: Guilford.

Sobell, L. C., & Sobell, M. B. (1996). *Timeline followback user's guide: A calendar method for assessing alcohol and drug use.* Toronto, CA: Addiction Research Foundation.

Sobell, L. C., Sobell, M. B., & Agrawal, S. (2009). Randomized controlled trial of a cognitive-behavioral motivational intervention in a group versus individual format for substance use disorders. *Psychology of Addictive Behaviors, 23,* 672–683.

Solinas, M., Panlilio, L. V., Justinova, Z., Yasar, S., & Goldberg, S. R. (2006). Using drug-discrimination techniques to study the abuse-related effects of psychoactive drugs in rats. *Nature Protocols, 1,* 1194–1206.

Solowij, N. (1998). *Cannabis and cognitive functioning.* Cambridge, UK: Cambridge University Press.

Soria, R., Stapleton, J. M., Gilson, S. F., Sampson-Cone, A., Henningfield, J. E., & London, E. D. (1996). Subjective and cardiovascular effects of intravenous nicotine in smokers and non-smokers. *Psychopharmacology, 128,* 221–226.

Soroko, S., Chang, J., & Barrett-Connor, E. (1996). Reasons for changing caffeinated coffee consumption: The Rancho Bernardo Study. *Journal of American College of Nutrition, 15,* 97–101.

Spencer, T. J., Faraone, S. V., Biederman, J., Lerner, M., Cooper, K. M., Zimmerman, B., & Concerta Study Group. (2006). Does prolonged therapy with a long-acting stimulant suppress growth in children with ADHD? *Journal of the American Academy of Child and Adolescent Psychiatry, 45,* 527–537.

Spiller, G. A. (1998). *Caffeine.* Boca Raton, FL: CRC Press.

Stolberg, V. B. (2011). The use of coca: Prehistory, history, and ethnography. *Journal of Ethnicity in Substance Abuse, 10,* 126–146.

Stoops, W. W., Poole, M. M., Vansickel, A. R., & Rush, C. R. (2011). Influence of escalating alternative reinforce values on cigarette choice. *Behavior Processes, 87,* 302–305.

Stough, C., Downey, L. A., King, R., Papafotiou, K., Swann, P., & Ogden, E. (2012). The acute effects of 3,4-methlenedioxymethamphetamine and methamphetamine on driving: A simulator study. *Accident Analysis and Prevention, 45,* 493–497.

Straus, R., & Bacon, S. D. (1953). *Drinking in college.* New Haven, CT: Yale University Press.

Streatfeild, D. (2001). *Cocaine: An unauthorized biography.* New York: St. Martin's Press.

Streather, A., & Hinson, R. E. (1985). Neurochemical and behavioral factors in the development of tolerance to anorectics. *Behavioral Neuroscience, 99,* 842–852.

Stroup, A. L., & Manderscheid, R. W. (1988). The development of the state mental hospital system in the United States, 1840–1980. *Journal of the Washington Academy of Sciences, 78,* 59–68.

Stroup, T. S., Lieberman, J. A., McEvoy, J. P., Swartz, M. S., Davis, S. M., Capuano, G. A., et al. (2007). Effectiveness of olanzapine, quetiapine, and risperidone in patients with chronic schizophrenia after discontinuing perphenazine: A CATIE study. *American Journal of Psychiatry, 164,* 415–427.

Strubelt, S., & Maas, U. (2008). The near-death experience: A cerebellar method to protect body and soul—lessons from the Iboga healing ceremony in Gabon. *Alternative Therapies in Health and Medicine, 14,* 30–34.

Stuster, J. (2006). Validation of the standardized field sobriety test battery at 0.08% blood alcohol concentration. *Human Factors, 48,* 608–614.

Substance Abuse and Mental Health Services Administration (SAMHSA), U.S. Department of Health and Human Services.

(2011a). *Results from the 2010 National Survey on Drug Use and Health: National findings.* NSDUH Series H-41, HHS Publication No. (SMA) 11-4658. Rockville, MD: SAMHSA Office of Applied Studies. Retrieved from http://www.samhsa.gov/data/NSDUH /2k10NSDUH/2k10Results.htm

Substance Abuse and Mental Health Services Administration (SAMHSA), Center for Behavioral Health Statistics and Quality. (November 22, 2011b). Emergency department visits involving energy drinks. *The DAWN Report.* Retrieved from http://oas.samhsa.gov or http:// www.samhsa.gov/data/2k11/WEB_DAWN_089/WEB_DAWN_089_ HTML.pdf

Substance Abuse and Mental Health Services Administration (SAMHSA), Office of Applied Studies. (2009, April 7). *The NSDUH Report: Nonmedical use of Adderall®among full-time college students.* Author. Rockville, MD.

Sulzer, D., Sonders, M. S., Poulsen, N. W., & Galli, A. (2005). Mechanisms of neurotransmitter release by amphetamines: A review. *Progress in Neurobiology, 75,* 406–433.

Sutton, J., & Botelho, G. (2013, March 23). MLB sues Florida clinic linked to supplying players with PEDs. *CNN.* Retrieved from http:// www.cnn.com/2013/03/22/us/florida-mlb-sues-clinic/

Swanson, J. W., Van Dorn, R. A., Swartz, M. S., Smith, A., Elbogen, E. B., & Monahan, J. (2008). Alternative pathways to violence in persons with schizophrenia: The role of childhood antisocial behavior problems. *Law and Human Behavior, 32,* 228–240.

Swartz, M. S., Perkins, D. P., Stroup, T. S., Davis, S. M., Capuano, G., Rosenheck, R. A., et al. (2007). Effects of antipsychotic medications on psychosocial functioning in patients with chronic schizophrenia: Findings from the NIMH CATIE study. *American Journal of Psychiatry, 164,* 428–436.

Szklo, A. S., de Almeida, L. M., Figueiredo, V. C., Autran, M., Malta, D., Caixeta, R., & Szklo, M. (2012). A snapshot of the striking decrease in cigarette smoking prevalence in Brazil between 1989 and 2008. *Preventative Medicine, 54,* 162–167.

Szpunar, K. K., McDermott, K. B., & Roediger, H. L. (2008). Testing during study insulates against the buildup of proactive interference. *Journal of Experimental Psychology, 34,* 1392–1399.

Talbert, J., Blumenschein, K., Burke, A., Stromberg, A., & Freeman, P. (2012). Pseudoephedrine sales and seizures of clandestine methamphetamine laboratories in Kentucky. *JAMA, 308,* 1524–1526.

Talbott, J. A. (2004). Lessons learned about the chronic mentally ill since 1955. *Psychiatric Services, 55,* 1152–1159.

Thomas, K. V., Bijlsma, L., Castiglioni, S., Covaci, A., Emke, E., Grabic, R., et al. (2012). Comparing illicit drug use in 19 European cities through sewage analysis. *Science of the Total Environment, 432,* 432–439.

Thomasius, R., Zapletalova, P., Petersen, K., Buchert, R., Andresen, B., Wartberg, L., Nebeling, B., & Schmoldt, A. (2006). Mood, cognition and serotonin transporter availability in current and former ecstasy (MDMA) users: The longitudinal perspective. *Journal of Psychopharmacology, 20,* 211–225.

Thombs, D. L., O'Mara, R. J., Tsukamoto, M., Rossheim, M. E., Weiler, R. M., Merves, M. L., & Goldberger, B. A. (2010). Event-level analyses of energy drink consumption and alcohol intoxication in bar patrons. *Addictive Behaviors, 35,* 325–330.

Thompson, P. M., Hayashi, K. M., Simon, S. L., Geaga, J. A., Hong, M. S., Sui, Y., et al. (2004). Structural abnormalities in the brains of human subjects who use methamphetamine. *The Journal of Neuroscience, 24,* 6028–6036.

Toledano, A., Alvarez, M. I., & Toledano-Diaz, A. (2010). Diversity and variability of nicotine on different cortical regions of the brain— therapeutic and toxicological implications. *Central Nervous Systems Agents Medical Chemistry*, 10, 180–206.

Toohey, J. (2012). Depression during pregnancy and postpartum. *Clinical Obstetrics and Gynecology*, 55, 788–797.

Tortora, G. J., & Derrickson, B. (2012). *Principles of anatomy & physiology* (13 ed.). Hoboken, NJ: John Wiley & Sons.

Tosato, S., Lasalvia, A., Bonetto, C., Mazzoncini, R., Cristofalo, D., De Santi, K., et al. (2013). The impact of cannabis use on age of onset and clinical characteristics in first-episode psychotic patients. Data from the Psychosis Incident Cohort Outcome Study (PICOS). *Journal of Psychiatry Research*, 47, 438–444.

Treno, A. J., Gruenewald, P. J., Remer, L. G., Johnson, F., & Lascala, E. A. (2008). Examining multi-level relationships between bars, hostility and aggression: Social selection and social influence. *Addiction*, 103, 66–77.

Trezza, V., Damsteegt, R., Achterberg, E. J., & Vanderschuren, L. J. (2011). Nucleus accumbens μ-opioid receptors mediate social reward. *Journal of Neuroscience*, 31, 6362–6370.

Trivedi, M. H., Rush, A. J., Wisniewski, S. R., Nierenberg, A. A., Warden, D., Ritz, L., et al. (2006). Evaluation of outcomes with citalopram for depression using measurement-based care in STAR*D: Implications for clinical practice. *American Journal of Psychiatry*, 163, 28–40.

Turillazzi, E., Riezzo, I., Neri, M., Bello, S., & Fineschi, V. (2010). MDMA toxicity and pathological consequences: A review about experimental data and autopsy findings. *Current Pharmaceutical Biotechnology*, 11, 500–509.

Uchtenhagen, A. A. (2011). Heroin maintenance treatment: From idea to research to practice. *Drug and Alcohol Review*, 30, 130–137.

Ujike, H., & Sato, M. (2004). Clinical features of sensitization to methamphetamine observed in patients with methamphetamine dependence and psychosis. *Annals of the New York Academy of Sciences*, 1025, 279–287.

U.S. Department of Health and Human Services (USDHHS). (2010). *How tobacco smoke causes disease: The biology and behavioral basis for smoking-attributable disease: A report of the surgeon general*. Atlanta, GA: Author. Retrieved from http://ww.cdc.gov/tobacco

U.S. Drug Enforcement Administration (DEA). (2012). *DEA history book, 1975–1980*. Retrieved from http://www.justice.gov/dea/about /history/1975-1980.pdf

Vaccarino, A. L., & Couret, L. C. Jr. (1993). Formalin-induced pain antagonizes the development of opioid dependence in the rat. *Neuroscience Letters*, 161, 195–198.

Vaccarino, A. L., Marek, P., Kest, B., Ben-Eliyahu, S., Couret, L.C. Jr., Kao, B., & Liebeskind, J. C. (1993). Morphine fails to produce tolerance when administered in the presence of formalin pain in rats. *Brain Research*, 627, 287–290.

Vale, A. (2007). Methanol. *Medicine*, 35, 633–634.

Valenstein, E. S. (2005). *The war of the soups and the sparks: The discovery of neurotransmitters and the dispute over how nerves communicate*. New York: Columbia University Press.

Valenzuela, C. F. (1997). Alcohol and neurotransmitter interactions. *Alcohol Health & Research World*, 21, 144–148.

Valverde, O., & Torrens, M. (2012). CB1 receptor-deficient mice as a model for depression. *Neuroscience*, 204, 193–206.

Valverde, O., Karsak, M., & Zimmer, A. (2005). Analysis of the endocannabinoid system by using CB1 cannabinoid receptor knockout mice. *Handbook of Experimental Pharmacology*, 168, 117–145.

Vander Velde, J. (2012, October 14). As Florida bath salts deaths rise, drug enforcers stymied. *Tampa Bay Times*. Retrieved from http://www.tampabay.com/news/publicsafety/article1256057.ece

Vansickel, A. R., Weaver, M. F., & Eissenberg, T. (2012). Clinical laboratory assessment of the abuse liability of an electronic cigarette. *Addiction*, 107, 1493–1500.

Varner, J. M. (2012). Safe and effective pain management in elders. *The Alabama Nurse*, 39, 11–13.

Vega, W. A., Aguilar-Gaxiola, S., Andrade, L., Bijl, R., Borges, G., Caraveo-Anduaga, J. J., et al. (2002). Prevalence and age of onset for drug use in seven international sites: Results from the international consortium of psychiatric epidemiology. *Drug and Alcohol Dependence*, 68, 285–297.

Verster, J. C., Pandi-Perumal, S. R., Ramaekers, J. G., & de Gier, J. J. (2009). *Drugs, driving and traffic safety*. Basel, Switzerland: Birhauser Verlag.

Verstraete, A. G. (2004). Detection times of drugs of abuse in blood, urine, and oral fluid. *Therapeutic Drug Monitoring*, 26, 200–205.

Vetreno, R. P., & Crews, F. T. (2012). Adolescent binge drinking increases expression of the danger signal receptor agonist HMGB1 and toll-like receptors in the adult prefrontal cortex. *Neuroscience*, 226, 475–488.

Villaneuva, C. M., Cantor, K. P., King, W. D., Jaakkola, J. J., Cordier, S., Lynch, C. F., Porru, S., & Kogevinas, M. (2006). Total and specific fluid consumption as determinants of bladder cancer risk. *Internal Journal of Cancer*, 118(8), 2040–2047.

Vinod, K. Y., Yalamanchili, R., Thanos, P. K., Vadasz, C., Cooper, T. B., Volkow, N. D., & Hungund, B. L. (2008). Genetic and pharmacological manipulations of the CB(1) receptor alter ethanol preference and dependence in ethanol preferring and nonpreferring mice. *Synapse*, 62, 574–581.

Voas, R. B., Tippetts, A. S., & Fell, J. C. (2003). Assessing the effectiveness of minimum legal drinking age and zero tolerance laws in the United States. *Accident Analysis and Prevention*, 35, 579–587.

Voas, R. B., Tippetts, A. S., & Taylor, E. P. (2002). The Illinois .08 law. An evaluation. *Journal of Safety Research*, 33, 73–80.

Vogel-Sprott, M. (1992). *Alcohol tolerance and social drinking: Learning the consequences*. New York: Guilford.

Volkow, N. D., Chang, L., Wang, G. J., Fowler, J. S., Jeonido-Yee, M., Franceschi, D., et al. (2001). Association of dopamine transporter reduction with psychomotor impairment in methamphetamine abusers. *American Journal of Psychiatry*, 158, 377–382.

Volkow, N.D., Wang, G.-J., Fowler, J.S., & Telang, F. (2008). Overlapping neuronal circuits in addiction and obesity: Evidence of systems pathology. *Philosophical Transactions of the Royal Society B*, 363, 3191–3200. doi:10.1098/rstb.2008.0107

Voon, V., Fernagut, P. O., Wickens, J., Baunez, C., Rodriguez, M., Pavon, N., et al. (2009). Chronic dopaminergic stimulation in Parkinson's disease: From dyskinesias to impulse control disorders. *Lancet Neurology*, 8, 1140–1149.

Wachtel, S. R., ElSohly, M. A., Ross, S. A., Ambre, J., & de Wit, H. (2002). Comparison of the subjective effects of delta(9)-tetrahydrocannabinol and marijuana in humans. *Psychopharmacology*, 161, 331–339.

Wagenaar, A. C., Maldonado-Molina, M. M., Ma, L., Tobler, A. L., & Komro, K. A. (2007). Effects of legal BAC limits on fatal crash involvement: Analyses of 28 states from 1976 through 2002. *Journal of Safety Research*, 38, 493–499.

Wagner, K. D., Valente, T. W., Casanova, M., Partovi, S. M., Mendenhall, B. M., Hundley, J. H., Gonzalez, M., & Unger, J. B. (2010).

Evaluation of an overdose prevention and response training programme for injection drug users in the Skid Row area of Los Angeles, CA. *The International Journal of Drug Policy*, *21*, 186–193.

Walberg, M., & St. Clair, S. (2012, December 18). 22 NIU frat members charged in freshman's hazing death. *The Chicago Tribune*. Retrieved from http://www.chicagotribune.com/news/local/suburbs/palatine/chi-charges-filed-in-niu-hazing-death-20121217,0,7298099.story

Wallace, T. L., & Porter, R. H. P. (2011). Targeting the nicotinic alpha7 acetylcholine receptor to enhance cognition in disease. *Biochemical Pharmacology*, *82*, 891–903.

Walsh, S. L., Stoops, W. W., Moody, D. E., Lin, S.-N., & Bigelow, G. E. (2009). Repeated dosing with oral cocaine in humans: Assessment of direct effects, withdrawal, and pharmacokinetics. *Experimental and Clinical Psychopharmacology*, *17*, 205–216.

Walters, P. G. (1992). FDA's new drug evaluation process: A general overview. *Journal of Public Health and Dentistry*, *52*, 333–337.

Walwyn, W. M., Miotto, K. A., & Evans, C. J. (2010). Opioid pharmaceuticals and addiction: The issues, and research directions seeking solutions. *Drug and Alcohol Dependence*, *108*, 156–165.

Wang, P. S., Berglund, P., Olfson, M., Pincus, H. A., Wells, K. B., & Kessler, R. C. (2005a). Failure and delay in initial treatment contact after first onset of mental disorders in the national comorbidity survey replication. *Archives of General Psychiatry*, *62*, 603–613.

Wang, P. S., Lane, M., Olfson, M., Pincus, H. A., Wells, K. B., & Kessler, R. C. (2005b). Twelve-month use of mental health services in the United States. *Archives of General Psychiatry*, *62*, 629–640.

Wang, X., Shen, Y., Chen, W. (2013). Progress in frontotemporal dementia research. *American Journal of Alzheimer's Disease and Other Dementias*, *28*, 15–23.

Ward, R. J., Lallemand, F., & de Witte, P. (2009). Biochemical and neurotransmitter changes implicated in alcohol-induced brain damage in chronic or "binge drinking" alcohol abuse. *Alcohol and Alcoholism*, *44*, 128–135.

Warner, C. H., Bobo, W., Warner, C., Reid, S., & Rachal, J. (2006). Antidepressant discontinuation syndrome. *American Family Physician*, *74*, 449–456.

Watson, P. E., Watson, I. D., & Bat, R. D. (1981). Prediction of blood alcohol concentrations in human subjects: Updating the Widmark equation. *Journal of Studies on Alcohol*, *42*, 547–556.

Weaver, M. T., Dallery, J., & Branch, M. N. (2010). Response topography in behavioral tolerance to cocaine with rats. *Behavioral Pharmacology*, *21*, 660–667.

Wechsler, H., & Wuethrich, B. (2002). *Dying to drink: Confronting binge drinking on college campuses*. Emmaus, PA: Rodale.

Wechsler, H., Davenport, A., Dowdall, G. W., Moeykens, B., & Castillo, S. (1994). Health and behavioral consequences of binge-drinking in college: A national survey of students at 140 campuses. *Journal of the American Medical Association*, *272*, 1672–1677.

Wechsler, H., Dowdall, G. W., Davenport, A., & Castillo, S. (1995). Correlates of college student binge drinking. *American Journal of Public Health*, *85*, 921–926.

Wechsler, H., Lee, J. E., Kuo, M., Seibring, M., Nelson, T. F., & Lee, H. P. (2002). Trends in college binge drinking during a period of increased prevention efforts: Findings from four Harvard School of Public Health study surveys, 1993–2001. *Journal of American College Health*, *50*, 203–217.

Weidner, G., & Istvan, J. (1985). Dietary sources of caffeine. *New England Journal of Medicine*, *313*, 1421.

Weinberg, B. A., & Bealer, B. K. (2001). *The world of caffeine: The science and culture of the world's most popular drug*. New York: Routledge.

Weiss, F., & Porrino, L. J. (2002). Behavioral neurobiology of alcohol addiction: Recent advances and challenges. *Journal of Neuroscience*, *22*, 3332–3337.

Weissman, B. A., & Raveh, L. (2008). Therapy against organophosphate poisoning: The importance of anticholinergic drugs with antiglutamatergic properties. *Toxicology and Applied Pharmacology*, *232*, 351–358.

Wells, L., Opacka-Juffry, J., Fisher, D., Ledent, C., Hourani, S., & Kitchen, I. (2012). In vivo dopaminergic and behavioral responses to acute cocaine are altered in adenosine A(2A) receptor knockout mice. *Synapse*, *66*, 383–390.

West, R. (1993). Beneficial effects of nicotine: Fact or fiction. *Addiction*, *88*, 589–590.

West, R. J., & Russell, M. A. H. (1985). Nicotine pharmacology and smoking dependence. In S. D. Iverson (Ed.), *Psychopharmacology: Recent advances and future prospects* (pp. 303–314). Oxford, UK: Oxford University Press.

Westman, E. C., Levin, E. D., & Rose, J. E. (1995). Nicotine as a therapeutic drug. *North Carolina Medical Journal*, *56*, 48–51.

Wetli, C. V., & Wright, R. K. (1979). Death caused by recreational cocaine use. *Journal of the American Medical Association*, *241*, 2519–2522.

Whistler, J. L. (2012). Examining the role of mu opioid receptor endocytosis in the beneficial and side-effects of prolonged opioid use: From a symposium on new concepts of *mu*-opioid pharmacology. *Drug and Alcohol Dependence*, *121*, 189–204.

White, A. M., Jamieson-Drake, D. W., & Swartzwelder, H. S. (2002). Prevalence and correlates of alcohol-induced blackouts among college students: Results of an e-mail survey. *Journal of American College Health*, *51*, 117–131.

White, S. J., Laurenzana, E. M., Gentry, W. B., Hendrickson, H. P., Williams, D. K., Ward, K. W., & Owens, S. M. (2009). Vulnerability to (+)-methamphetamine effects and the relationship to drug disposition in pregnant rats during chronic infusion. *Toxicological Sciences*, *111*, 27–36.

Whoriskey, P. (2012, December 30). Rising painkiller addiction shows damage from drugmakers' role in shaping medical opinion. *The Washington Post*. Retrieved from http://articles.washingtonpost.com/2012-12-30/business/36071087_1_opioids-painkiller-addiction-chronic-pain

Wiebe, T. H., Sigurdson, E. S., & Katz, L. Y. (2008). Angel's trumpet (Datura stramonium) poisoning and delirium in adolescents in Winnipeg, Manitoba: Summer 2006. *Paediatric Child Health*, *13*, 193–196.

Wiens, F., Zitzmann, A., Lachance, M. A., Yegles, M., Pragst, F., Wurst, F. M., von Holst, D., Guan, S. L., & Spanagel, R. (2008). Chronic intake of fermented floral nectar by wild treeshrews. *Proceedings of the National Academy of Sciences*, *105*, 10426–10431.

Wignall, N. D., & de Wit, H. (2011). Effects of nicotine on attention and inhibitory control in healthy nonsmokers. *Experimental and Clinical Psychopharmacology*, *19*, 183–191.

Wilens, T. E., Faraone, S. V., Biederman, J., & Gunawardene, S. (2003). Does stimulant therapy of attention-deficit/hyperactivity disorder beget later substance abuse? A meta-analytic review of the literature. *Pediatrics*, *111*, 179–185.

Wilkinson, D., Fox, N. C., Barkhof, F., Phul, R., Lemming, O., & Scheltens, P. (2012). Memantine and brain atrophy in Alzheimer's disease: A 1-year randomized controlled trial. *Journal of Alzheimer's Disease*, *29*, 459–469.

Wilkinson, G. R. (2001). Pharmacokinetics: The dynamics of drug absorption, distribution and elimination. In L.S. Goodman, J. G. Hardman, L. L. Limbird, & A. G. Gilman (Eds.), *Goodman and Gilman's the pharmacological basis of therapeutics* (10th ed., pp. 3–30). New York: McGraw-Hill.

Williams, N. (1996). How the ancient Egyptians brewed beer. *Science*, *273*, 432.

Williamson, E. M., & Evans, F. J. (2000). Cannabinoids in clinical practice. *Drugs*, *60*, 13030–1314.

Wilsey, B., Marcotte, T., Deutsch, R., Gouaux, B., Sakai, S., & Donaghe, H. (2013). Low-dose vaporized cannabis significantly improved neuropathic pain. *Journal of Pain*, *14*, 136–148.

Wimo, A., & Prince, M. (2010). *World Alzheimer Report 2010; The global impact of dementia*. London: Alzheimer's Disease International.

Wimo, A., Jonsson, L., Bond, J., Prince, M., Winblad, B., & Alzheimer Disease International (2013). The worldwide economic impact of dementia 2010. *Alzheimers and Dementia*, *9*, 1–11.

Winstock, A. R., & Barratt, M. J. (2013). Synthetic cannabis: A comparison of patterns of use and effect profile with natural cannabis in a large global sample. *Drug and Alcohol Dependence*, *131*, 106–111.

Winterer, G. (2010). Why do patients with schizophrenia smoke? *Current Opinions in Psychiatry*, *23*, 112–119.

Wong, D. L., Hockenberry-Eaton, M., Wilson, D., Winkelstein, M. L., & Schwartz, P. (2001). *Wong's essentials of pediatric nursing*, 6th ed. St. Louis, MO: Mosby.

Wong, C. G., & Stevens, M. C. (2012). The effects of stimulant medication on working memory functional connectivity in attention-deficit/hyperactivity disorder. *Biological Psychiatry*, *71*, 458–466.

Wong, D. L., & Baker, C. M. (1988). Pain in children: Comparison of assessment scales. *Pediatric Nursing*, *14*, 9–17.

Woo, T. M., & Hanley, J. R. (2013). "How high do they look?": Identification and treatment of common ingestions in adolescents. *Journal of Pediatric Health Care*, *27*, 135–144.

Wood, R. I., Armstrong, A., Fridkin, V., Shah, V., Najafi, A., & Jakowec, M. (2013). Roid rage in rats? Testosterone effects on aggressive motivation, impulsivity and tyrosine hydroxylase. *Physiology and Behavior*, *110–111*, 6–12.

World Anti-Doping Agency (WADA). (2013a). A brief history of anti-doping. Author. Retrieved from http://www.wada-ama.org/en/About-WADA/History/A-Brief-History-of-Anti-Doping/

World Anti-Doping Agency (WADA). (2013b). *The 2013 prohibited list: International standard*. Author. Retrieved from http://www.wada-ama.org/Documents/World_Anti-Doping_Program/WADP-Prohibited-list/2013/WADA-Prohibited-List-2013-EN.pdf

World Health Organization (WHO). (2011a). Global status report on alcohol and health. Geneva, Switzerland: Author. Retrieved from http://www.who.int/substance_abuse/publications/global_alcohol_report/en/index.html

World Health Organization (WHO). (1990). *International statistical classification of diseases and related health problems 10th Revision*. Geneva, Switzerland: Author. Retrieved from http://www.who.int/classificaton/icd/en/

World Health Organization (WHO). (1992). *International statistical classification of diseases and related health problems 10th Revision*. Geneva, Switzerland: Author. Retrieved from http://www.who.int/classificaton/icd/en/

World Health Organization (WHO). (2012). *Lexicon of alcohol and drug terms*. Retrieved from http://www.who.int/substance_abuse/terminology/who_lexicon/en/

World Health Organization (WHO). (1981). Nomenclature and classification of drugs and alcohol-related problems: A WHO memorandum. *Bulletin of the World Health Organization*, *59*, 225–242.

World Health Organization (WHO). (1996). *The tobacco epidemic: A global public health emergency* (Fact sheet N118). Geneva, Switzerland: Author.

World Health Organization (WHO). (2011b). *WHO report on the global tobacco epidemic, 2011: Warning about the dangers of tobacco*. Geneva, Switzerland: Author. Retrieved from http://whqlibdoc.who.int/hq/2011/WHO_NMH_TFI_11.3_eng.pdf

Wright, S. W., & Slovis, C. M. (1996). Drinking on campus: Undergraduate intoxication requiring emergency care. *Archives of Pediatric and Adolescent Medicine*, *150*, 699–702.

Wright, S. W., Norton, V. C., Dake, A. D., Pinkston, J. R., & Slovis, C. M. (1998). Alcohol on campus: Alcohol-related emergencies in undergraduate college students. *Southern Medical Journal*, *91*, 909–913.

Wu, J. M., & Hsieh, T. C. (2011). Resveratrol: A cardioprotective substance. *Annals of the New York Academy of Sciences*, *1215*, 16–21.

Wu, J. M., Wang, Z. R., Hsieh, T. C., Bruder, J. L., Zou, J. G., & Huang, Y. Z. (2001). Mechanism of cardioprotection by resveratrol, a phenolic antioxidant present in red wine. *International Journal of Molecular Medicine*, *8*, 3–17.

Wu, K. L., Chaikomin, R., Doran, S., Jones, K. L., Horowitz, M., & Rayner, C. K. (2006). Artificially sweetened versus regular mixers increase gastric emptying and alcohol absorption. *American Journal of Medicine*, *119*, 802–804.

Wynder, E. L., & Muscat, J. E. (1995). The changing epidemiology of smoking and lung cancer histology. *Environmental Health Perspectives*, *103* Suppl 8, 143–148.

Yalachkov, Y., Kaiser, J., & Naumer, M. J. (2012). Functional neuroimaging studies in addiction: Multisensory drug stimuli and neural cue reactivity. *Neuroscience and Biobehavioral Reviews*, *36*, 825–835.

Yang, P. B., Atkins, K. D., & Dafny, N. (2011). Behavioral sensitization and cross-sensitization between methylphenidate, amphetamine, and 3,4-methylenedioxymethamphetamine (MDMA) in female SD rats. *European Journal of Pharmacology*, *661*, 72–85.

Young, A. M., Havens, J. R., & Leukefeld, C. G. (2012). A comparison of rural and urban nonmedical prescription opioid users' lifetime and recent drug use. *American Journal of Drug and Alcohol Abuse*, *38*, 220–227.

Zacny, J., Bigelow, G., Compton, P., Foley, K., Iguchi, M., & Sannerud, C. (2003). College on Problems of Drug Dependence taskforce on prescription opioid non-medical use and abuse: Position statement. *Drug and Alcohol Dependence*, *69*, 215–232.

Zajicek, J. P., Hobart, J. C., Slade, A. Barnes, D., Mattison, P. G., & MUSEC Research Group (2012). Multiple sclerosis and extract of cannabis: Results of the MUSEC trial. *Journal of Neurology, Neurosurgery, and Psychiatry*, *83*, 1125–1132.

Zenz, M., & Willweber-Strumpf, A. (1993). Opiophobia and cancer pain in Europe. *Lancet*, *341*, 1075–1076.

Zhou, Y., Kierans, A., Kenul, D., Ge, Y., Rath, J., Reaume, J., Grossman, R. I., & Lui, Y. W. (2013). Mild traumatic brain injury: Longitudinal regional brain volume changes. *Radiology*, *267*, 880–890.

Zorick, T., Nestor, L., Miotto, K., Sugar, C., Hellemann, G., Scanlon, G., Rawson, R., & London, E. D. (2010). Withdrawal symptoms in abstinent methamphetamine-dependent subjects. *Addiction*, *105*, 1809–1818.

Zuckerman, B., Frank, D. A., & Mayes, L. (2002). Cocaine-exposed infants and developmental outcomes: "crack kids" revisited. *Journal of the American Medical Association*, *287*, 1990–1991.

INDEX

CPSIA information can be obtained at www.ICGtesting.com
Printed in the USA
BVOW05n0401271213

340047BV00021B/33/P